P9-CFY-843

EXECUTIVE SUCCESS
MAKING IT IN MANAGEMENT

HARVARD BUSINESS REVIEW EXECUTIVE BOOK SERIES

Executive Success: Making It in Management

Survival Strategies for American Industry

Managing Effectively in the World Marketplace

Catching up with the Computer Revolution

Strategic Management

Financial Management

Marketing Management

Using Logical Techniques for Making Better Decisions

EXECUTIVE SUCCESS
MAKING IT IN MANAGEMENT

ELIZA G. C. COLLINS
Editor

JOHN WILEY & SONS, INC.
New York • Chichester • Brisbane • Toronto • Singapore

This publication is designed to provide accurate and authoritative information in regard to the subject matter covered. It is sold with the understanding that the publisher is not engaged in rendering legal, accounting, or other professional service. If legal advice or other expert assistance is required, the services of a competent professional person should be sought. *From a Declaration of Principles jointly adopted by a Committee of the American Bar Association and a Committee of Publishers.*

Library of Congress Cataloging in Publication Data:

Main entry under title:

Executive success.

(Harvard business review executive book series)
Includes index.
1. Executive ability—Addresses, essays, lectures.
2. Success—Addresses, essays, lectures. I. Collins, Eliza G. C. II. Series.

HF5500.2.E986 1982 658.4'09 82-11037
ISBN 0-471-87595-3

10 9 8 7 6 5 4 3 2 1

Foreword

For sixty years, the *Harvard Business Review* has been the farthest reaching executive program of the Harvard Business School. It is devoted to the continuing education of executives and aspiring managers primarily in business organizations, but also in not-for-profit institutions, in government, and in the professions. Through its publishing partners, reprints, and translation programs, it finds an audience in many languages in most countries in the world, occasionally penetrating even the barrier between East and West.

The *Harvard Business Review* draws on the talents of the most creative people in modern business and in management education. About half its content comes from practicing managers, the rest from professional people and university researchers. Everything *HBR* publishes has something to do with the skills, attitudes, and knowledge essential to the competent and ethical practice of management.

This book consists of 32 articles dealing with what is required of executive leadership and the opportunities for its effective exercise. Neither abstruse nor superficial, the articles chosen for this volume are intended to be usefully analytical, challenging, and carefully prescriptive. Every well-informed business person can follow the exposition in its path away from the obvious and into the territory of independent thought. I hope that readers can adapt these ideas to their own unique situations and thus make their professional careers more productive.

Kenneth R. Andrews, Editor
Harvard Business Review

Contents

Part Three Understanding Organizational Power

Part Four The Skills of an Effective Executive

EXECUTIVE SUCCESS

MAKING IT IN MANAGEMENT

Introduction

ELIZA G. C. COLLINS

In his book *The Right Stuff*, Tom Wolfe describes what it took for the early military test pilots to succeed in the awesome career they chose:

> A career in flying was like climbing one of those ancient Babylonian pyramids made up of a dizzy progression of steps and ledges, a ziggurat, a pyramid extraordinarily high and steep; and the idea was to prove at every foot of the way up that pyramid that you were one of the elected and anointed ones who had *the right stuff* and could move higher and higher and even—ultimately, God willing, one day—that you might be able to join that special few at the very top, that elite who had the capacity to bring tears to men's eyes, the very Brotherhood of the Right Stuff itself.

For the test pilots, the right stuff turns out to be an ineffable combination of bravery, bravado, elan, and maybe more important than these, a sense that you are very special and above the rest of mankind because you can daily face death, with zest.

Although success as a business executive definitely does not include feeling superior or facing death with glee, it does require that a person have a special set of qualities and skills with which to exercise good judgment, make wise decisions, get along with and lead others. Some of the skills—especially functional ones like marketing, finance, or production—can be learned in a didactic process. Others have to be acquired through less rational means; these are the skills of being an effective human being. Like flying skills for test pilots, functional skills can take managers far in an organization, but what determines their success at the highest levels is their completeness as people. The undesirable parts of ourselves don't get left at home when we set out for work in the morning or in the parking lot where we leave our cars. People with stunted characters who have not achieved a level of integration, a sense of being comfortable in their own skins, are going to take their unfinished selves with them to the job.

Without personal skills, awareness of one's own limitations, a capacity to grow and withstand stress, and the ability to integrate one's own conflicting emotions, an executive will sometimes act out of his or her own personal needs and thereby seem inconsistent to others in the organization. As Paul Brouwer defines it in *The Power to See Ourselves,* "effective consistent behavior is integrated behavior, while unintegrated behavior is the behavior of conflict." Being seen as inconsistent, a person cannot lead.

Leadership, the top of the ziggurat in an executive job, demands personal authenticity. The requirements of leadership—gaining the cooperation and the allegiance of others and altering the ways they think about things—cannot be filled by people who, lacking a personal vision, cannot form an organizational one, or who, lacking a personal coherence, cannot integrate the disparate parts of an organization into a functioning whole. In this view, using power to achieve organizational goals rather than personal ends depends on a person's having grown into an integrated human being. Power that is not tempered by maturity is the power Lord Acton spoke of as corrupting.

Also, to perform the executive job, to maintain control of the diverse aspects of an organization and at the same time allow people the flexibility to be creative and productive, a person must have the capacity to tolerate ambiguity as well as possess the fortitude to be tough when necessary and not give in to others' ideas of what is right.

The articles in this collection explore from different viewpoints what it takes, what "the right stuff" is for the executive job. I've divided the collection into four sections. The first looks at personal growth, which is the basis for success. The second contains articles that show how the nature of the individual determines his or her success as a leader. The third section features articles on power that illustrate how executives' understanding of the dynamics of power will help them realize their organizational vision. The fourth contains articles that describe aspects of that executive job that require an ability to be consistent and flexible at the same time. As Richard Pascale says in his article "Zen and The Art of Management," "the real organization you are working for is the organization called yourself. The problems and challenges of the organization that you are working for 'out there' and the one 'in here' are not two separate things. They grow toward excellence together."

The Power to See Yourself

How can an executive become a more integrated person? By doing the devilishly hard work of changing how he or she sees himself or herself. The bedrocks of our personalities are our self-concepts. As children, we see ourselves often in terms of whether we're good at sports or whether we please our parents, and as we get older, whether we're attractive to people in our dancing school class. Despite these outward signs of our acceptance by the world, we hold inner convictions about the kinds of people we *really* are, whether we thought we had to cheat at sports to get on the team, lie to our parents to please them, or adopt faddish ways to attract our dancing partners—or whether we are acceptable just the way we are.

Most of us have portions of ourselves that we regard highly, things we do without having to fool anyone to please. But each of us has chunks of self-doubt about our basic worth that we learn to cover up in ways that seem acceptable to others. We adopt machismo ways to appear strong when we're afraid, or we adopt weak and helpless ways when we believe that's the only way we can attract. These ways of adapting to our misconceptions about ourselves (by definition, neurotic self-doubts are based on myths) worked at certain times in our lives and with certain people. But as boys and girls grow older and assume positions of managerial responsibility, these adaptions can sabotage them. In acting out our old self-concepts, we alienate others and stay divided from ourselves.

To grow, then, an executive first must change his or her self-concept, which is neither easy nor painless. Growth in self-concept means acquiring a realistic view of what one is, but it also entails facing what one thought one was. It means freeing oneself of outmoded misconceptions of how one has to act and behave in the world, but it means abandoning familiar authority figures. It means looking to oneself rather than to others for final approval, but it can also mean being alone.

Clearly, growing isn't as easy as it was when we were children, when it was merely a matter of inches. It's not something we do in our spare time or in our sleep. Why is it so difficult for us to continue what once came naturally? For one thing, cultural norms encourage us to remain as we were. So we continue to believe that men don't cry and that women go soft during certain periods of the month. Business norms are just as static. It's easy for us to accept the common belief that success in business means we have to be tough and independent, so we maintain the false toughness of the fearful, the false independence of the dependent.

But there are other reasons change is difficult. People who are afraid of a change often see it as an absolute. One executive might fear that if she expresses her needs, she will always be needy, and another, if he expresses tenderness, his toughness will not be there when he needs it. Also many of the emotions that we experience in exploring our self-concepts are feelings we learned we shouldn't have. If the taboos are strong enough, growth stops.

Assuming the desire to grow and change overpowers the resistance, how does an executive begin? How do we separate the myths of ourselves from reality? One way is to explore how other people perceive us and how we affect them, perhaps through direct and open conversations with a boss or a spouse, though these are the people whose responses we are likely to fear the most. (When we test the myth that we have to be self-sufficient, however, we often find that a spouse can love us even more for needing their help.)

Another way is to observe other executives and people outside of work who act in an integrated way. Much literature discusses the importance of mentors for executive learning in an organization. But mentors also play an important role by providing a model of behavior of how one can achieve the desired end in a nonabrasive way. And in dealing openly with their mentors, young executives can learn it is possible to disagree and still be of value, which may challenge their old self-concepts. But while others can play a role, self-examinaion is ultimately the route to change.

Growth, changing one's self-concept, takes time, and it's understandable that many people resist or, having undertaken the process, give up. They might very well ask, What are the payoffs of all this hard work? Does it really make a difference? Yes, it does, and here's why.

People who cannot accept their own feelings characteristically have difficulty in their relationships with their families. Driven to achieve self-esteem through their work, they deny themselves the enormous resources of comfort that await them at home. Rather than turning to mates and children for support, they see these relationships as more demands. With growth, however, with themselves as the source of their self-esteem, they can more freely turn to the imperfect world of their families for gratification.

Great dividends await them at work as well. Again quoting Paul Brouwer, "Growth in self-concept is at the heart of a real manager development effort." A broader perception of self is crucial to perceiving the broader perspectives characteristic of a general manager's point of view. Specifically, an enlarged sense of self helps us better deal with conflict, tolerate ambiguity, relate openly and consistently to others, and handle the burdens of top executive positions.

At best, conflicts are difficult to resolve. Two subordinates come to you with different and conflicting demands. Each has a good argument as to why you should decide in favor of his position. If you do not see subordinates as sources of basic approval, you are free to solve the conflict according to what you think is right without fear of losing that approval.

Resolving conflicts can take time, and executives who can accept the subtle ambivalences in their own natures can better tolerate the ambiguities that inhere in all times of organizational change (as well as in every emotional relationship). Executives who don't feel the need to push events to premature conclusions are free to experiment.

Of all the problems that bewilder executives perhaps the most perplexing is how to achieve open and constructive communication with others at work. Candid conversation is crucial to making good judgments. The executive who hears contrary opinions as challenges to his or her authority will not hear what a subordinate or a peer has to say and could lose valuable information. Executives who measure their own worth by the words of others are going to find even simple interactions a constant source of pain that daily challenges their good manners and tolerances.

The responsibilities that go with top executive jobs, the burdens of making difficult decisions are such that no one can perform the job without some support or help. At times top executives need to talk openly about their concerns and to have supportive contact not only to hear other people's opinions but also, and more important, to get relief from the loneliness and stress of the job. Executives who can accept their own limitations and needs have the confidence to ask for help, which can help them withstand the pressure inherent in any top position.

Because changing in the way I've described is such a personal task, executives who undertake it will succeed only if they do so out of a drive to grow for growth's sake. For people who undergo this process, the means of their lives become the ends. And the ends are not merely personal. The qualities that characterize executives who test their self-concepts against reality and who see, however painfully, where change must occur are the same qualities that characterize leaders who see where organizational change is necessary and set their organizations in motion to achieve a goal. First comes the recognition of the present, and then the vision of future possibilities.

Communicating the Vision

When we look at the things leaders do, we find they group neatly into three main tasks: envisioning the future, gaining the cooperation of others, and altering the way others think about things. What these tasks entail and how leaders carry them out are the questions the authors of the articles in this section address. In dealing with them, the authors pick up the major theme from the first section—that personal growth is a precondition for effective leadership.

The first task of a leader, perhaps the essence of leadership, is forming an organizational vision and making a commitment to it. To form a vision, a person has to be free of his or her personal past. If an executive's energies are tied up in resolving old conflicts, harboring old feuds, and nourishing old self-concepts, that person will not be able to perceive other possibilities. Such an executive may do well in managing stable industries in a stable economy but will have trouble in times of change.

To perceive the future possibilities, an executive must also see the present for what it is. Obviously it is impossible for any person to have a completely clean perceptual slate. As numerous psychological tests have shown, all of us perceive things according to our own needs. But leaders better than most of us can distinguish their own needs and know when gratifying those needs is inappropriate. As much as possible leaders ground their actions in objective reality.

Forming a vision also calls on the capacity to take risks, to, literally, suffer change. In a sense, forming a commitment to a vision means giving up the present for a limbo state, somewhere between what is and what will be. This limbo can be a shifty, treacherous place. For one thing it is chaotic—in fact, it is the epitome of the ambiguous. As a number of authors in this book assert, bureaucracies love order and hate chaos. In disturbing a company to take it through a period of change a leader not only has to be able to tolerate the inevitable resistance organization members will exert but also he or she must, in the name of the vision, be able to hold to the uncertain course.

The second major task of leaders is gaining the cooperation and allegiance of others. To move an organization, leaders must convince the individuals in the organization that the new way is worth the struggle. In explaining how leaders do this, many fall back on the notion of charisma, the mystery that surrounds some people and makes others want to follow them. Charisma certainly helps gain that allegiance, but it's not the whole story. Nor is it enough to say that effective leaders merely employ management techniques more faithfully than others. In the hands of a good manager, good management techniques, motivation systems, and compensation policies will keep an organization functioning smoothly with people working for individual reward the same way they do in the hands of a leader. But working for a leader, people receive another reward as well, one that is almost transcendent. The leader appeals to the need in all of us to strive for a higher goal, and in attaining it, to almost mystically become part of something bigger than ourselves.

Everyone who has ever sung in a chorus has experienced that transcendent moment when their own voice is lost in the full glorious sound the chorus makes, when absorption in the whole is gained. One can explain in various ways what makes this pehnomenon. Psychologists, for instance, might say that people want to lose their separateness. Whatever, the leader makes an appeal to this basic human need to join up, to contribute, to be part of something bigger than ourselves. What leaders do, to continue the metaphor, is make singing the music for its own sake—not theirs—worth doing.

Before a leader can garner the allegiance of individuals for the group effort, however, he or she ensures that people's need to be recognized as valuable, diverse individuals have been met. Pouring oil on troubled waters may preserve order, but it also stifles the opportunity for diversity and individual creativity as well as the chance to appeal to a higher integrating principle. The leader's task is, as Abram Collier says in "Business Leadership and a Creative Society," "to create an environment in which there can flourish not only individual genius but, more important, the collective capacities of other people in the organization." When individual goals are concommitant with a shared goal, subordinacy is bearable.

The final major task of the leader is altering the way people think about things. In inspiring people to reach for higher goals, the leader is requesting them to share his or her values. To most people, whether they like it or not, the job defines their lives. It marks the beginning and the end of their days, they have to schedule vacations around it, and they may spend more time with their co-workers and bosses than with members of their families. Regardless of the material rewards they receive from work, people more than ever are looking to work for meaning, for something of value. As O.A. Ohmann says in "Skyhooks," "Workers have a fine sensitivity to spiritual qualities and want to work for a boss who believes in something and in whom they can believe."

A boss in whom people can believe is, by definition, credible, that is, trustworthy, in the sense that people see him or her as consistent. Leaders don't make capricious decisions, vacillating with political expediencies from their stated directions. Maintaining their courses and integrating conflicting organizational demands, leaders show their subordinates that the world is not always defined by win–lose situations. Leaders educate by example through consistently embodying their own values in shaping their organizations over time. As they work on their own personal growth, leaders transmit to their organizations a faith in individual growth as well as a recognition that working to enlarge one's own self-concept is a condition for the exercise of power.

Understanding Organizational Power

A university professor somewhere is supposed to have quipped that university life would be OK if it weren't for the students. One can imagine executives in organizations buffeted by conflict and tension harboring the same kind of sentiment—that organizations would be OK places to work if it weren't for all the people. Organizations of all kinds—not-for-profit, for profit, public, family-owned, small, large, or somewhere in between—share one constant reality: people. And people are, by definition, different from one another. The creative juices of an organization might flow from the diversity among its people but, if unstrained, can clog the works. The sad result can be power struggles that can impede a manager from implementing his or her vision.

Power is such a complex concept that I find it helpful to look at power problems from the point of view of how they present themselves. With this in mind, we can see power problems as structural, motivational, or ideological. None of these categories is discrete, of course; some problems drift with ease from one class to another.

Let's look first at the structural problems. As we have seen, executives need information and resources to affect their organizations. Without them, they are powerless, lose their capacity to act, and resort to the manipulative and Machiavellian ways that give power such a bad name. People who act in these ways are seen as power hungry, and because they are in such powerless positions they are precisely that. Rosabeth Moss Kanter describes this phenomenon in "Power Failures in Management Circuits" well when she says "Powerlessness . . . tends to breed bossiness rather than true leadership. In large organizations at least, it is powerlessness that often creates ineffective, desultory management and petty, dictatorial, rules-minded managerial styles."

The power problems that arise from people being in powerless positions are not going to be solved by sending the inhabitants of those positions to sensitivity training. The solutions have to be structural. An executive who recognizes this kind of power problem should try to devise ways to distribute power to the positions that need it. This can be done by making sure that people have the information and resources needed to perform well, by not isolating them in dead-end jobs, and by supporting their efforts.

But we can't rely on rational organizational procedures, promotion and compensation policies, organizational charts and structures to solve all the power problems that will arise and to keep people's creative juices flowing freely. As the authors of the articles in the previous sections indicate, one of the realities of organizational life is conflict between the legitimate power-based needs of its members. Abraham Zaleznik states in "Power and Politics in Organizational Life," "Power problems are the effects of personality on structure." In this view, power problems cannot be eradicated from an organization by structural solutions alone any more than good medicine can eradicate all the health problems of the human body. For their own reasons people don't always take the medicine.

Executives who do have power can also present problems. When we start talking about the problems of executives having, as opposed to not having, power we're really talking about the use of power—whether wisely for organizational betterment or for personal aggrandizement. When we look at it in this way, power becomes an issue of motivation of both executives and their subordinates.

Effective executives use power for productive purposes to further their organizational goals. It is here that the importance of executives having attained a personal maturity becomes especially important.

Executives who need neither the approval of others in the organization nor the trappings of power to heighten their own self-esteem try to influence their subordinates to perform for the organization's—not their own—sake. In action the true authoritarian makes subordinates feel weak; the influencer makes them feel strong. Recognizing that they are dependent on their subordinates to accomplish their ends, effective executives share power with subordinates rather than hoard it. An executive who has a need to influence rather than dominate may anger and frustrate people in the short run, but in the long run he or she creates a consistent pattern of behavior that will make subordinates feel more secure and, ultimately, more productive.

When subordinates perceive that an executive's actions are grounded in reality and that he or she is not motivated by personal needs, they confer effective power on that person. In a sense, in permitting them to lead, subordinates give an executive power.

The power problems that arise from subordinates' motivations present executives with a different set of conflicts altogether. For one thing, as we've seen, people are never completely free of their old self-concepts, one of the most prevalent of which is the need to be dependent. Because of this dependency, even the most mature of us will see our bosses through a filter of our own emotional needs. In doing so, we objectify our bosses and lose sight of them as individual people acting out their own self-concepts. Instead we see them as if their motivation is to satisfy or not satisfy our needs.

Executives who don't realize the power of the objectifying process will be baffled by the sometime unrealistic expectations subordinates have as well as by their attachments and attempts to gain recognition, which often appear as power moves. Because changing a person's personality requires such extensive psychological work, as Abraham Zeleznik points out, executives are often forced to find political solutions to many of the conflicts that arise. In making political moves, however, it is imperative that an executive already have created an atmosphere where trust prevails so that subordinates see these moves as an effort to integrate organizational conflicts and not as divisive.

In changing organizational structures, executives run into the third kind of power problem, the ideological ones. Organizations are living systems with their own histories, backgrounds, and ways of doing things. Roger Harrison says in "Understanding Your Organization's Character," "Much of the conflict that surrounds organizational change is really ideological struggle."

Like people, organizations need to be approached in nonthreatening ways. For instance, in trying to change behavior in a company where the members are very competitive and keep information and resources to themselves, an executive could exemplify the desired new behavior by openly requesting information from another division. But he or she must do it in ways that do not appear weak to division members. Ultimately, the executive who behaves consistently out of one set of motivations—the organization's best interest—will appear strong and trustworthy. In this light, the key to having effective organizational power turns out to be having understood the dynamics of the organization and perceiving what might be the best way to introduce new behavior.

When confronted with a power problem, executives first need to sort out what kind of a problem it is: structural, motivational, or ideological. The key to an accurate perception of the problem is having done the hard work to gain a strong, consistent sense of self.

The Skills of the Effective Executive

The concepts I've been discussing so far—tolerating ambiguity, having values, and being integrated—are fairly abstract. Many executives might agree it's all well and good to understand these things but wonder what they have to do with actually getting the job done. That's an important question. I believe that these processes underlie what executives actually accomplish. Content may define executive jobs, but the processes executives use will determine how well they perform them.

Let's look at the content of the executive job. Managers attend meetings, settle disputes among employees, negotiate with union leaders, decide on compensation policies, give speeches, decide where to spend money, begin new projects and stop old ones, praise subordinates when they've done well and instruct them when they've performed poorly—I could take pages describing all the different possible combinations of managerial activities. It's helpful then to look at what managers do in terms of the roles they play, as Henry Mintzberg does in "The Manager's Job: Folklore and Fact," where he divides the manager's job into three roles: interpersonal, informational, and decisional.

How do the processes I've described affect how managers play these roles?

In the interpersonal roles the manager leads his or her employees and has to give them feedback on their performance. Understanding that subordinates become threatened when confronted with negative criticism, managers skilled in the use of ambiguity can convey the message that improvement is required without putting the subordinate in a position where he or she has to defend the action to preserve self-esteem. In an artful way, by not having to be "right" at the expense of subordinates managers let subordinates save face. As Richard Pascale says in "Zen and the Art of Management," "Clearing the air can be more helpful to the clearer than to others who are starkly revealed." As George Clements, a past CEO of the Jewel Companies, said talking about giving Donald Perkins, who later became CEO, a chance to take a big risk, "What was more important, Don's learning or my being right?"

In the informational role, the manager relays to subordinates information that they need to act. But much of the information managers receive comes second-hand from computer printouts, written reports, financial sheets, and so forth. To keep truly well-informed, managers need to trust the information that is most useful to them, that which their subordinates and others in the organization pass on. And we know that executives are often isolated from what really happens in their companies, partly because their subordinates filter information, reporting only what they think the executive wants to hear.

Executives who have demonstrated to their subordinates that the interests of the organization are more important to them than their own personal needs establish an atmosphere where subordinates feel free to report the truth.

In the decisional role, the executive has to be able to objectively weigh the conditions in a given situation. When making tough decisions it is tempting to give in to magical thinking, irrationally arriving at connections between events. But for an executive to make good decisions, his or her vision must be unclouded by past conditions and habitual patterns of thought. To stare reality in the face, executives need to have made peace with their own needs to have things be otherwise, which is the root of magical thinking. (Perhaps we can trace some of the problems with the Kennedy administration to Kennedy's inability to give up Camelot for the realities of Cuba.)

In making decisions, too, executives have to suspend the need to be liked. A decision that has to suit an executive's need to be accepted will most likely not suit the needs of the situation. As Peter Drucker says in "The Effective Decision," "It is a waste of time to worry about what will be acceptable and what the decisionmaker should or should not say so as not to evoke resistance."

Whatever managers do—raise ethical issues, make policy decisions, or simply attend a meeting—they bring with them their own concepts of who they are. In working to understand and enlarge their self-perceptions, executives develop into more effective human beings and can then bring to their jobs "the right stuff" for success.

PART ONE
THE POWER TO SEE YOURSELF

AN OVERVIEW

The articles in this section celebrate growth. They urge executives to develop their self-concepts because it is worth it.

In "The Power to See Ourselves," Paul J. Brouwer emphasizes that growth in one's self-concept is essential to executive growth simply because the change brings with it a new depth of motivation and a sharper sense of direction. Brouwer describes how the conflicts in executives' self-concepts affect their performance at work, and then shows how executives can take steps to achieve maturity through self-examination and a shift in their expectations. Because this work is difficult, Brouwer cautions that "real executive development is impossible unless the executive seeks it."

One of the dividends of an enlarged self-concept is, ironically, a loss of feeling self-important. The executive who has successfully resolved his or her own conflicts and is "shielded from fears and anxieties about his (or her) personal life" acquires a "self-expendable attitude," which is one of the "Clues for Success in the President's Job" that Joseph C. Bailey describes. In studying successful presidents, Bailey found that they characteristically manage their own stress well and concentrate on the task at hand, partly because their own self-esteem is not at stake.

The "self-expendable attitude" that Bailey describes underlies the gateways that Carl R. Rogers and F.J. Roethlisberger write about in "Barriers and Gateways to Communication." The major hinderance to communication is the tendency people have to evaluate what others say from their own points of view. This barrier distorts information and makes it impossible for people to understand the context that another person speaks from. By lowering their defenses, by adopting a self-expendable attitude, executives find that others' defensive barriers drop away and they can achieve a truthful mutual communication.

To change oneself is not simply a question of altering goals and expectations and of acquiring communication skills, it also involves a change in one's emotional life, in one's capacity to recognize a need for love, tenderness, and interdependence. In "Executives as Human Beings," Fernando Bartolomé describes interviews he conducted with 40 male executives who revealed how difficult it is for them to express their feelings. In being so cut off, executives not only lose the affection they could derive at home but also approach relationships with people at work in an unfeeling way. Being able to express one's feelings is "functional for any man and essential to an executive who has constant contact with other individuals."

Carrying on the theme that a rich emotional life is important to work, in "Must Success Cost So Much?" Fernando Bartolomé and Paul A. Lee Evans explore some of the pitfalls that can occur in that life because of work.

Many executives carry the stresses of the job home with them and suffer from an "emotional spillover" that can damage their home lives. Some executives, however, are able to integrate the two well. Their success lies in that they can cope with a new job, take the right jobs, and handle career disappointments. Aside from external rewards and organizational pressures, one of the reasons executives take the wrong jobs is their inability to say "no" or, put another way, their lack of "self-knowledge and the ability to assess themselves accurately." They also need to perceive reality clearly to deal with the disappointments that can occur in any career path.

The last two selections in this section are interviews with successful executives who display some of the qualities in practice that I've been discussing. In "Everyone Who Makes It Has a Mentor," Franklin Lunding, George Clements, and Donald Perkins talk about how a personal relationship with a mentor is crucial to the younger executive's development. Also, to develop younger people, it is important that a superior have a "self-expendable" attitude.

Finally, John H. Johnson reveals, in "Failure Is a Word I Don't Accept," that achieving a goal requires not letting anger and frustration, products of an incomplete self-concept, get in the way.

1 The Power to See Ourselves

PAUL J. BROUWER

Many articles describe what the ideal executive is and the qualities that go into making him or her effective. Most of these articles concentrate on the skills executives need to do their jobs well. The author of this article, however, isn't concerned with what the executive does at work to be effective, rather his concern is what the executive can do to become a more effective human being. Starting with the notion that an effective human being is one who has been able to integrate his or her own internal conflicts, the author goes on to describe how people can achieve that maturity. First, executives have to explore what they are and what their expectations are of themselves. Once they can perceive their current realities, executives can begin the process of changing their self-concepts. Because "real executive development is impossible unless the executive seeks it," this process of change must be self-directed. The result of all this effort is an enlarged perception of self that can lead executives to a broader view of themselves in relation to their organizations.

A psychological fact is that manager development means change in the manager's self-concept. Each of us, whether we realize it or not, has a self-image. We see ourselves in some way—smart, slow, kindly, well-intentioned, lazy, misunderstood, meticulous, or shrewd; we all can pick adjectives that describe ourselves. This is the "I" behind the face in the mirror, the "I" that thinks, dreams, talks, feels, and believes, the "I" that no one knows fully. In this article we will explore the meaning of the self-image, particularly in relation to changing behavior in the growing manager, and how changes in self-concept come about.

One reason this self-concept is crucial is that it has a great deal to do

Author's Note. This article is drawn from material that appeared as a chapter in *Managers for Tomorrow,* published in 1965 by The New American Library of World Literature, Inc., New York.

with manager development—with being a growing person and eventually realizing one's self-potential. Note the term *manager* development rather than *management* development; the purpose of such development is to help individual managers to grow. After all, they have to do most of the job themselves. As a member of a firm of consulting psychologists to management, I can report that fact from experience—and add the further observation that no one can tell a manager exactly how to grow. Rather, the most one can do is to help the manager understand the present situation, and then trust the manager to find the best direction in the situation.

Filters for Reality

In the first place, the self-concept is important because everything we do or say, everything we hear, feel, or otherwise perceive, is influenced by how we see ourselves. For example:

☐ A businessman, who had traveled in many parts of the world, was incorrigibly curious about the customs, speech, local places of interest, history, and traditions of any place he visited. However, on a one-week visit to London—his first—on a delicate mission for his company, he might just as well have been in Indianapolis for all he learned of English ways of life. Being on a business trip, he saw himself as a businessman, and actually perceived little of what was around him. But as a vacationer in London he would have seen England in depth, because he would have seen himself coming to London for that purpose.

Photographers often slip a reddish filter over the lens when snapping pictures of clouds on black and white film. The filter prevents some of the light rays from reaching the film, so that the final picture shows much darker skies and more sharply whitened clouds. The self-concept is like a filter that screens out what we do not want to hear and see and passes through what we do want to see and hear. In the reverse direction, it gives an idiosyncratic flavor to our behavior. Who among us doesn't usually pick his or her name out of a jumble of words on a page? Or hear his or her name announced at an airport amidst all of the other announcements? This is called selective listening, and it is a function of our self-concept. Thus, how we see ourselves determines generally what we react to, what we perceive, and, in broad terms, how we behave in general.

And this shows up in business situations too. Imagine two executives, A and B, in identical situations. Each calls in a subordinate and delegates an assignment. The italicized words below give partial indications of their self-concepts. Executive A says:

Tom, I'm *concerned* about our relations with the XYZ Company. Its *purchases* from us have fallen off lately and *rather abruptly*. You know

> our history with it. *Will* you *investigate* and find out the cause of the reduced volume? *Let me know* if you run into anything you don't understand.

Executive A is confident of his ability to handle the situation. He sees himself as unthreatened, able to cope with whatever Tom's investigation discloses, and willing to delay action until the facts are gathered and studied.

Executive B, on the other hand, says:

> George, the XYZ Company has cut back its purchases from us for the third month in a row. *We've got to get on this and quick.* Now, you go visit it. *I wish I could but I'm tied down here.* Talk to the purchasing agent—uh, what's his name again? Uh . . . (shuffling papers) . . . here it is . . . Bailey. *See* Bailey. Oh . . . and you'd better see the chief engineer, a nice guy . . . named . . . uh . . . his name slips me *for the moment* . . . you can get it from Bailey. But don't go near Sam Awful—he'll cover up whatever's happening anyway, and might use your visit as a sign we're scared of old XYZ. *I've got to have some answers on this one, George.* The boss is on my neck but good. So. . . .

Executive B is obviously less confident. She feels threatened by the situation. She doesn't trust George to use his own common sense—as indicated by her explicit "do"s and "don't"s—probably because she herself lacks confidence.

Continuing Changes

Although the self-concept is important in understanding human behavior *generally,* it becomes critically so in understanding *manager development,* where changes in behavior are the objective. As a matter of cold, hard, psychological fact, a change in behavior on the job, for better or worse, means a change in self-concept. Thus, we are dealing with an immensely and immediately practical consideration.

Human beings constantly change their behavior, as we see if we examine ourselves (and others) critically enough. It is a superficial observation to say that so-and-so is the same person of five years ago. Technically, so-and-so isn't exactly the same today as even yesterday. For one thing, he or she is one day older and has learned something new, however negligible, that becomes incorporated in an apperceptive mass. As a result, the perception of today's events is different, however slightly and undetectably, from what it was yesterday. Nothing "significant" may have happened—no promotion, no accident, no soul-searching upset—but so-and-so will be different, even though only a person with Solomon's wisdom would know it. Change in behavior is constant.

The difficulties managers have in thinking about changes in behavior come from their inability to detect change, and from fuzzy thinking behind such comforting, though fallacious, notions as, "You can't teach an old dog new tricks," "She was born that way," or "He's been like that ever since I've known him."

On the other hand, sometimes superficial behavior changes are erroneously thought to be basic. For example, consider the simplest level of change in behavior, which is brought about by increased knowledge or skill:

☐ The newly appointed foreman learns his new duties, dons a white shirt, delegates jobs he used to do himself, and learns to participate in his superintendent's meetings. His company provides him with instruction through manuals, books, conferences, sessions with his boss, and management training courses. He joins the National Foremen's Association, attends lectures, and may even be sent to a two-week seminar at the local university. He learns much and becomes suitably skillful in discharging his new functions. This new way of life changes the foreman's behavior, of course; but only peripherally, just as living in a new house does not basically alter the marriage relation. He knows more, sees more, has more and better skills.

If companies do want such "simple-level" changes, and only these, then management training is called for. Some learn to type; some learn how to sell; the new zone manager learns the policy manual; and the new vice president of manufacturing learns how the company's controller figures costs. These specific learnings are the objectives of training, and can become changes in behavior produced by training.

Keystone for Growth

If, however, a company wants growth in the *deeper* sense, then something more subtle and basic in its impact is called for in the manager development effort. Such deeper growth is, of course, a change in self-concept. The manager whose judgment was once unreliable or who lacked drive *grows* toward reliability in judgment or toward stronger drive. Growth in this sense brings observable changes in outward behavior, because each person is now inwardly different—different, for example, in perception of self, in attitude toward job and company as both relate to the person's own life or feeling of responsibility for others.

But experience shows that such growth is as difficult to achieve as it is desirable. It demands the full-fledged participation of the manager. Actually the trite expression, "Management development is self-development," is psychologically sound. The growing manager changes because he or she wants to and has to in response to new insights and understandings gained on the job. This manager does not change because of orders or exhortation, nor for change to a popular technique.

Such growth implies changes in the person—in how knowledge is used, in the ends to which skills are applied, and, in short, in the person's self-image. The point is clear that the growing person is self-examining; and as this is done there emerge new depths of motivation, a sharper sense of direction, and a more vital awareness of how life on the job should be.

Growth in this sense is personalized and vital. And such growth in self-concept is at the heart of a real manager development effort.

But growth in self-concept is not always simple and clear.

Conflicts in Self-Concept

Each human being is several selves, living comfortably in the role of parent, spouse, business executive, president, golfer, bridge player, the life of the party, and so on. But if there are conflicts among any of these roles, then discomfort arises. And such conflict brings with it such dynamics as tension, guilt feelings, and compensation. Let us illustrate with a familiar example:

> ☐ A man sees himself both as a good father and as a good businessman. As a father, he spends time with his children; but as a businessman, he finds the demands on his time overwhelming. Now what does he do? He obviously cannot be home most evenings with his family and also be out of town on necessary business trips. He cannot realize both self-concepts simultaneously. So what happens? He compromises by giving his business his time Monday through Friday, and his family the weekend.

This seems like an easy resolution. What, then, is the problem? The man in our example has had to modify both self-concepts and may feel deeply dissatisfied with such a necessity. So his dissatisfaction, his psychological discomfort, his basic conflict in self-concepts, may show in his behavior. He may be unduly critical of business associates (or subordinates) who will not follow his example and give up their family life during the week. Or he may resent his children, who blithely go about their own activities on the weekend, ignoring him. And if by chance his teen-age son develops any emotional problems which are ascribed to "parental neglect," our man really hits the ceiling! "Neglect? How can that be? Haven't I given my boy every weekend?" he asks.

In the deeper sense, conflicts lie behind many self-concepts, but it is beyond our scope to explore them. In an individual case, this is a matter for professional study and expert handling. By definition, effective, consistent behavior is integrated behavior, while unintegrated behavior is the behavior of conflict.

Unrealism in Self-Concept

In addition to conflicts between self-concepts as a cause of ineffective behavior, there is the crucial matter of disparity between "how I see myself" and "how others see me." Unrealistic self-appraisal has cost many managers their jobs. Think of people you know who have been fired, eased out, or moved laterally because they no longer "seemed up to the job." Has there not been in many such cases the subtle flavor of unadaptability, of a rigid inability in these managers to adjust their sights to new roles as times have changed?

Most familiar are the unnecessarily tragic cases of people who cannot grow old gracefully. Next are those uncounted misfits who fail through lack of realistic insight into their true worth. For example, take the good vice president who flunks as president because she never realized her inability to endure the rigors of being on top. There are endless instances of failures owing to a disparity between "who I am" and "who I think I am."

Unfortunately, not only outright failure may come from disparities in self-concept; more insidious is the effect of partial or fuzzy self-appraisal. In fact, if the proposition is right that realism in the individual's view of self has a one-to-one relationship with effectiveness on the job, then it surely follows that all of us can improve our effectiveness by the simple expedient of developing a more realistic, more accurate self-concept!

In short, the more realistic one's view of self, the more guaranteed is personal effectiveness. Here is an example that underscores this point:

☐ George H., the vice president of sales for a $50-million company with a staff of 250 in sales and service, was in serious organizational trouble. The group had increased in size so rapidly that it had long since outgrown its organizational pattern. There were constant complaints such as: "Whom do I work for?" "Nobody knows whether I'm doing well or poorly." "We haven't any system to follow in service to customers." The executives under George tried to do twice and three times as much as they had always done. The situation was, frankly, a mess.

George as a person was well liked and respected. He was democratic, attentive to others, soft-spoken, unlikely to "order," always likely to "suggest," and unsure of himself as an administrator. In general he saw himself as a stimulator and coordinator of his people, an excellent personal salesman, but not a supervisor. Somehow he had completely missed sensing that his people waited for directions from him. He felt that a sensible district sales manager should know what to do. His own perception of himself and his people's perception of him as vice president of sales were poles apart.

The impasse was breached when an outsider on whom George relied heavily (and who also had the confidence of the top people in the department) finally told him bluntly, "George, your people are waiting for you to clear the air. They'll follow any organizational plan you want them to. This step only you can take. They respect you and want your leadership. They value you. Don't ask them; tell them, for goodness' sake, how you're going to organize their activities."

George tried to integrate this new dimension into his self-concept. At first, he swung to one extreme and "got tough." He made explicit, directive demands; he swore; he told everybody, in effect, "I want

> what I want when I want it—and that's right now!" But soon he abandoned his pretense and absorbed into his self-concept the new "take-charge" aspect of his functioning. He defined an organizational plan, set up policies and procedures which sorted out sales and service duties, discussed them fully with all involved, and said, in effect, "This is it. Let's go."

This example is, of course, an oversimplification; it highlights the fact that disparity in perception can reduce managerial effectiveness. What George saw himself to be in the office of vice president of sales precluded his seeing the needs of his people. And this blind spot nearly cost him prolonged chaos, if not the loss of his job.

Finally, it is manifestly clear that change in self-concept as a function of executive growth has a payoff. Recall situations where a critical appointment has to be made. Who gets the nod? Usually it is the individual who *as a person* is thought to have potential and who is able through style of life on the job to make a contribution to the "mix" of key executives. Consequently, many companies, in selecting their handpicked future executives, feed in "trainees" with liberal arts degrees. They are looking for the *person*, not the person's knowledge or special skills. By the same token, as the young person grows, it is self-concept that will change and come more into line with what the person is becoming in relation to potential. It is on the basis of self-concept that he or she emerges as a top executive. To twist an old adage, it isn't what you know that finally counts; it's who you *are*.

Natural Resistance

But there is still one big question to answer. If changes in the self-concept of the executive are desirable, just what brings them about? In fact, are changes in self-concept possible? Of course changes are possible, but there is one obvious block to growth.

Even when executives want to change, the lurking suspicion that such effort is futile tends to vitiate the process of change. Faint mutterings of self-discontent tend to get quashed by the notion that "an old dog can't learn new tricks." And the basic comfort of the status quo seems to outweigh the value of the new mode of behavior.

One reason for such feelings of resistance is that, psychologically, the mature person resists change. By definition, the self-concept is an organization or patterning of attitudes, habits, knowledge, drives, and the like. And also, by definition, the fact of organization means a cementing together of all these complex components.

For example, the person who for many years has been highly and aggressively competitive cannot, except with difficulty, either suddenly or gradually become insightfully cooperative; he or she will still tend to perceive the need to surpass someone else. The individual retains the old pattern, consistency, and basic characteristics and in this sense resists change. Indeed, this is a good thing, or we still would all be in the throes of "finding ourselves" as we were as adolescents.

When the mature person changes, therefore, it is done against a natural resistance; but it is a moot question whether this resistance is a deeply stabilizing influence that helps to retain basic direction and character or whether it is a cocoon that makes the mature person unreachable. Resistance, though built in, may thus be either a roadblock or a gyroscope.

We have noted that changes in the self-concept of the executive are "gut-level," not peripheral. They are changes in perception and attitude and understanding, not changes in knowledge or experience or skills. So our exploration of how change occurs must include those factors which seem to operate more deeply within the individual and which polarize new directions and behaviors. We are looking for those basic, vital factors which, as they operate, really change the person beyond the power of dissimulation or pretense. This is change in the fundamental makeup of the person, not change in apparel. When such changes occur, the person is different.

Steps to Maturity

Let us be clear about one point. Growth does not proceed in clear-cut, discrete, logical steps. Sometimes it occurs in inexplicable spurts; at other times, with agonizing slowness. There are cases where real learning is so deeply unconscious that no overt behavioral change shows up for a long time. Even regressions will occur, as when an adolescent, perhaps troubled by the day's activities, will sleep with a stuffed animal as he did at age six. The process of growth is a nebulous, multifactored, fluid, dynamic process, often astounding, and usually only partially controllable.

But for the sake of discussion, and understanding, we can postulate a sequence of steps.

Self-Examination

If we were to attempt a systematic analysis of what happens when growth in a manager occurs, we would need to begin with self-examination. For here the individual first knows he or she *doesn't know* or first gets an inkling that it is desirable for a particular behavior to be different in some respect. The manager is forced, either by circumstance or design, to become introspective. This is what happens when golfers see movies of their swings, or when a mother scolds her child by saying, "Just look at yourself—all dirty." Or when the supervisor's thinly veiled anger over a subordinate's sloppy work finally becomes known. Every man sees himself each time he shaves, but does he really examine what he sees? Doe he appraise and evaluate and study what manner of man he is?

The function of self-examination is to lay the groundwork for insight, without which no growth can occur. Insight is the "oh, I see now" feeling which must, consciously or unconsciously, precede change in behavior.

Insights—real, genuine glimpses of ourselves as we really are— are reached only with difficulty and sometimes with real psychic pain. But they are the building blocks of growth. Thus self-examination is a preparation for insight, a groundbreaking for the seeds of self-understanding which gradually bloom into changed behavior.

Self-Expectation

As individuals raise their sights for themselves, as they get an insight into the direction in which they want to grow, as they "see" themselves in a particular respect that they do not like, then they are changing their self-expectations. (This is the next step.) New demands on themselves are set up, not by anyone else, just by themselves. This is another way of saying what the theologians insist on, namely, that a conviction of sin precedes salvation. Or, as the psychologists put it, first accept the fact that *you* have the problem—not anyone else—and then you are ready to find a solution. Here are two cases that illustrate the importance of self-expectation through insight:

☐ John P. was a chronic complainer. Nothing was ever his fault. He frequently and self-pityingly inveighed against his boss, his subordinates, his peers, and the competition. He was capable, knowledgeable, a hard worker, critical. And never once, when he sang the old refrain, "Why does this always happen to me?" did an inner voice whisper back, "It's no different for you, old boy, than for anyone else. It's just the way you take it."

Efforts by his boss and his friends to develop some insight in John seem wasted. Logical explanations, patiently made, were of course futile. Anger toward him only proved to him he was picked on. Gentle tolerance only gave him a bigger pool to wallow in.

One day in a meeting of executives to find answers to a particular crisis that had hit everyone (an unexpected price slash by a major competitor), he held forth at length on the uselessness of market research, on the futility of keeping a "pipeline" on the competitor's situation, on how his department (sales) couldn't be blamed for not anticipating the vagaries of the competition's pricing policy, and so on. He finally stopped. And, as though by prearrangement, the whole group, perhaps in complete disgust at his immaturity and irrelevance, sat in stony silence.

At length the silence became so oppressive that it suddenly dawned on the complainer that he was just that—an immature complainer. He recalled the words of his colleagues and his own dim awareness that he did complain a lot. Insight finally occurred.

At long last he was ready to begin to grow out of his immaturity. He saw (and disliked) himself at this point. Now his growth could become self-directed; he could easily find many opportunities to quash feelings of self-pity and to face reality in a more statesmanlike fashion, because now he expected more statesmanlike attitudes of himself.

□ Pete B., age 58, was vice president of engineering of a company that made fine-quality capital goods equipment. He had been with his company 35 years. He was a good engineer, who knew the product inside out; and through the years he had learned to know the customers, too. He felt proud of and personally involved in each installation of the product. It was not unusual to see him on an evening, coatless and with his tie loose, perched on a stool before a drafting board, surrounded by young engineers, digging at a tough installation problem. While some thought Pete did too much himself, others felt that with him on the job the customer would be satisfied.

About four years ago, however, the president, whose family owned the company, sold it to a large corporation, and the company became a wholly owned subsidiary. One allied product line was acquired, then another. Finally Pete's department was asked to do the engineering work for several subsidiaries that were not set up to do their own.

Now Pete's job had changed, subtly but surely, and trouble began to brew for Pete because he couldn't seem to change with the situation.

Psychologically, Pete saw himself as a one-man department (with assistants as trainees) who personally engineered the product for the customer, his friend. He resisted the impersonality of working on engineering problems of "sister companies" whose customers and products he barely knew and cared less about. The newfangled system of a "home office" engineering vice president who was "staff" seemed to him just another unnecessary complication. Nothing worked the way it used to. He saw himself bypassed by progress and change.

So, unconsciously, he began to resist and to fight. His yearning for the "good old days" subconsciously forced him to run faster and faster in order to know more customers and more product lines; to work more evenings; to press new systems into the form of old procedures. And, of course, he began to slip, and badly. Gradually, Pete was viewed by his superiors as "good old Pete, but let's not get him in on this matter or he'll have to take it over himself and we'll get bogged down," and by his subordinates as a fine fellow, but stodgy and old-fashioned.

Fortunately, before the situation compelled a major organizational shift, Pete took stock of his situation, and really saw himself as he was. He got the insight that his self-image of a kind of personal engineer was no longer applicable to the corporation's greatly expanded needs. And right then, with this new glimpse of himself (and the courage and self-honesty to face it), he began to change. He started by focusing on how his years of experience could be applied to the coaching of his subordinates. He put himself in the shoes of the staff vice president and could then see how to mesh gears better. Then he stopped resisting the newfangled data processing and automation procedures. His growth began with a new self-expectation.

Change in Self-Expectation

How does one get a new self-demand, a new self-expectation? How does one find out that the present self-concept is inadequate? How does one know that difference is not only possible but desirable as well? Unfortunately for those who like recipes or formulas, such questions are perennially bothersome because there is no one best way.

What can be done to stimulate change in self-expectation besides honest, realistic, self-appraising introspection? In the business context, the constructive pointing up of an executive's needs for growth by a superior is a tremendous source of insight. The emphasis, of course, is on the word *constructive,* which means helpful, insightful ideas from the superior and not, as so often happens, a ceremonial judgmental, "I'll tell you what I think about you" appraisal.

Perceptive spouses are a further source of insight. They have unique ways of letting one another know when their self-images become distorted.

In fact, anything which enables people to get a new perception—reading, observing, studying, going to conferences, attending meetings, and participating in clubs—can provide insight. *Out of insight comes change in self-expectation.*

And, of course, life situations which are kaleidoscopic always enable perceptive people to see themselves in a new light. Here is another example:

☐ Paul W. was acutely self-critical, often to the point where his fear of failure immobilized him. He delayed decisions, fussed endlessly with details, and generally strained to be perfect. In time his relation with the psychologist, who genuinely accepted him without criticism, praise, blame, or hostility, enabled him to "see" how his self-critical attitudes really stemmed from his self-pride. He felt he had to be perfect because it was "safer" to be free from criticism and failure. But he finally "rejoined the human race" and demanded of himself only that he do his best. The insight that he was human after all freed him to change his self-expectations.

Self-Direction

People are masters of their own destiny in the sense that they take charge of their own development if they want to grow. Nothing can be done to them to make them grow; they grow only as they want to and as their own insights enable them to.

The change in self-concept that executives undergo must continue primarily through self-direction. It is clear that many development programs miss their mark badly at this point. They make the naive assumption that exposure to experiences or people or books or courses is enough to produce growth. Not so. They effect change in participants only as they reach out and appropriate something—a bit of wisdom, a new idea, or a new concept—that stretches them, and gives them answers to their own self-generated problems.

Put another way, we might say that, just as learning is impossible without motivation, so real executive development is impossible unless executives seek it. Furthermore, the strength of their desire is infinitely stronger if they seek development because they want to develop than if they are merely trying to please their bosses or do what is expected of them. As any teacher knows, the pupils who listen and learn merely in order to pass the course are far poorer learners than those who want to learn.

Fundamentally, this is the age-old problem of motivation, of keeping steam up in the boiler. The maintenance of a growing edge, as executives emerge from insight to insight to realize their potential, is a consequence of intrinsic motivation. They are driven toward unrealized objectives, perhaps toward unrealizable goals; this is what keeps executives honing their growing edges.

After developing insight into themselves *in relation to what they want to be,* the power that keeps them growing is the veritable necessity of doing something that to them is intrinsically, basically, and lastingly worthwhile. Growing executives are so because they derive their strength and desire and drive from inner, unachieved goals and their satisfactions from self-realization. This is intrinsic motivation as it relates to self-concept.

Broadened Perceptions

The dynamics of this factor of growth are very clear: people must see themselves in relation to their environment, both personal and impersonal, and must develop their images of themselves partly in response to their surroundings. So if they see a very small world (as a child does), their concepts of themselves must necessarily be narrow; if they see themselves as citizens of the world (as world travelers might), their self-concepts embrace the world. This is the difference between real provincials and true sophisticates.

A most common complaint of superiors is that subordinates are too narrow in their outlooks. For example, the sales manager promoted to vice president of sales irritates his peers in manufacturing or research by having "only a salesman's point of view." The former production supervisor, now a vice president, is derided by the people in sales for her attitude of "We'll make it at low cost; it's up to you to sell it, and don't bother me with special runs for special customers or model changes—sell 'em." Both people suffer from constraint of the self-concept: they perceive their jobs (and themselves) too narrowly. For instance:

☐ A vice president of sales was brought in from outside the company to gear up the effort of merchandising a new line of products. He did a magnificent job, old pro that he was, of shaping up and vitalizing a sales force. Volume of sales picked up excellently, and he was the hero of the hour.

But after a year, when he felt on top of his job, some of his attitudes and habits reasserted themselves, annoying others and stalling progress. For instance, he persisted in making frequent references to his former (and larger) company. He climbed on manufacturing for delivery delays, and on research and engineering for perfectionism before releasing the specifications for what he felt were needed product changes. The time it took to explain to him, pacify him, and argue with him was ill-spent and futile. He was rapidly becoming a block in the path of progress.

One day the president approached him directly. "George," said the president, "what's your title?"

"Why," said George, puzzled, "vice president of sales."

"Right. And what does vice president mean to you?"

George paused. What was the president getting at? "Well," he said, "it means lots of things, I guess. Responsibility for sales, building a. . . ."

"Stop right there," interrupted the president. "Responsibility for sales, you say. True in a way. But the sales manager also has this responsibility, doesn't he?"

"Well, yes."

"Then what does the word *vice president* mean in your title?"

"Oh, I see. . . . Well, I guess it means seeing or having responsibility for the sales function of the company from the point of view of the company . . . that part of your office."

"You got my point before I mentioned it, George," said the president. "A vice president speaks from the company point of view, not just that of his department. He tries to keep the overall good of the company in mind."

George thought this conversation over. He got the point. He realized the narrowness of his own view. He had been thinking of himself as "on loan" from his former employer to straighten things out here. As he pondered the president's comments, he broadened his perception of his job—and of himself. And sometime later he began to act as an officer of the total company.

Self-Realization Power

It is not enough, however, just to see ourselves as we are now. Such understanding is a necessary starting point, or basis on which to build. But we must also see what our real selves *could* be, and grow into that.

The strong people of history have had one psychological characteristic in common; they seem always to have been themselves as persons:

- ☐ Michelangelo, fighting against odds for a chance to sculpt;
- ☐ Beethoven, continuing to compose after he became deaf;
- ☐ Milton, who didn't allow blindness to interfere with his writing.

Such people have given meaning to the phrase "fulfilling one's destiny."

In less dramatic form, strong executives fulfill themselves as they live lives that are unfoldings of their potentials. They must be themselves. In this sense, the self-concept of strong executives is a constantly evolving, changing thing as they continuously realize themselves. This is, indeed, genuine growth and the kind that continues until senescence sets in.

Can all people aspire to be this strong—to accomplish such self-realization? Of course not. But growing people (by definition) have unrealized power if their self-concept, self-expectation, self-direction, and constantly broadening perceptions (wisdom) allow them to find it. The difference between strong people and weak people may not be a difference in ability, for many clerks have keen intelligence; or in drive, for many ambitious people get nowhere; or in opportunity, for somehow, strong people *make* opportunity. No, the difference lies in self-concept. How much do I value my life? What do I want to do with it? What must I do to be myself? Strong people have emerged with clear-cut answers to such questions; weak people equivocate and temporize and never dare.

Thus growth, finally, is the evolvement of personal goals and the sense of venture in pursuing them. This is the meaning of the dedicated person. Personal goals, company goals, and job goals have coincidence to a great extent; and personal power is directed single-mindedly toward seeing the self in relation to the fulfillment of executive potential.

2

Clues for Success in the President's Job

JOSEPH C. BAILEY

At every level in an organization but one, managers can look around them and see their peers tackling the same sort of problems they do, and probably coming up with the same kind of solutions. The person at the top of the organization, however, has no peers and by the very nature of the position is confronted with a set of problems that no one else in the organization can resolve. In studying company presidents, the author of this article finds that those who are successful in the president's job have several characteristics in common. The common problem they have to resolve is the conflicts in codes that occur in every organization. The common qualities they share are their abilities to handle the stress that conflict causes, their sense that they themselves are less important than resolving of the conflicts, their ability to concentrate all of their energies on performing the task at hand, and finally their capacities to have learned first-hand from a mentor (either a positive or a negative one) how to deal with complex organizational problems. Although successful presidents, of course, have individual characteristics, for the most part they share traits that researchers have found describe creative and innovative people.

Is it the role of a company president to do what other members of the organization do not do, cannot do, or should not do? Does the president have a special function, or are the things to do merely *more* of the same things others do—on a far bigger and broader scale? Is there a common denominator among those who successfully handle the "toughest problems" of their organizations that cuts across industries, companies, types of or-

---

Author's Note. This article is based on an investigation supported by the Division of Research, Harvard Business School. For the data on which it rests, I am gratefully indebted to the many executives who so freely made their experiences available. I owe much also to help given from time to time by Professors Bertrand Fox, F. J. Roethlisberger, and Renato Tagiuri of the Harvard Business School; the late Abraham H. Maslow of Brandeis University; and Professor Warren G. Bennis then of Massachusetts Institute of Technology.

ganizations, and even cultures? Must the ability to find solutions to such problems be a requirement of the president's job, inevitable to the role? Is there some largely concealed aspect of the job that is worthy of a serious research undertaking?

The answers to these questions, based on my current sample of company presidents (see appendix), are decidedly in the affirmative. Yes, there does seem to be a common denominator. There do seem to be clear reasons why the organization's toughest problems demand—and *must* receive—the president's exclusive attention. Moreover, there seem to be utterly understandable reasons why these problems often remain shrouded in silence and secrecy. And finally, there seems to me clearly to be a challenge for a major research effort of a most difficult and sophisticated character.

The single-common-denominator clue which I have elected to pursue in my current inquiry is one that was alluded to in the "conflict of codes" concept presented by Chester I. Barnard in *The Functions of the Executive*.[1] Essentially, this concept claims that in every formally organized cooperative human activity there will arise from time to time inevitable and inescapable conflict between the codes that control the conduct of different individuals and the groups who are contributing to the overall cooperative purpose.

At the very apex of the executive responsibility, Barnard puts the burden of resolving the recurring conflict of codes that will inevitably arise in every formal organization. He sees this task as the key to successful leadership, and acutely so for the role of the president. He further contends that the solution to such problems has to be the "creation of a higher moral code"—one that will encompass and reconcile at a higher and more embracing level the interests and values that come into unanticipated, yet still legitimate, conflict as the organization pursues its ever-evolving goals.

Clues for Success

This view of the importance and the difficulties of the creative art and skills required in successfully handling serious conflict of codes is offered here because my long experience with such problems, as well as my current inquiry, seems to confirm it.

Should it stand confirmed, then it follows that the hidden key to success in the president's role of final and ultimate decision maker for the organization may rest more on the president's capabilities in this limited area than in any other single segment of the total presidential task. And should that prove to be the case, then it further follows that this is a less urgent inquiry than the one inevitably linked with it, to wit: What kinds of behavior, and what attitudes, values, skills, and training are characteristic of those chief executives who do relatively better than their peers in handling "conflict" issues? Can any uniformities be discerned among them, or among their problem-handling attributes, that may provide provisional clues for their relatively greater success?

There do seem to be some. In fact, I feel rather certain that there are even though the ones I shall present in this article may turn out to be merely a first approximation of those that are truly indispensable. It is much too soon at this juncture, and my present sample of top executives is much too limited, to be confident that anything more than clues for further exploration have made an appearance.

Yet the frequent recurrence of some uncommon patterns of behavior, accompanied and supported by some key values and attitudes the presidents hold toward their jobs and themselves, stand out in sharp contrast to those of a large number of their peers. In my experience, the latter generally have greater difficulties with their toughest problems, are less self-confident of a healing solution, and are clearly more inclined both to minimize the seriousness of and to postpone, ignore, or evade (rather than deliberately and consciously confront) their problems.

It must be kept in mind, then, that the uniformities discussed here are drawn from a random sample of presidents who have learned somehow, somewhere, to do relatively better than their peers with the toughest problems that beset their jobs.

Management of Stress

Of all the individual uniformities common to chief executives, the most immediately self-evident is their ability to cope with stress. They all have learned to live—and for most of the time alone—with heavy stress. They have learned how to control it, contain it, channel it, offset it, or simply "lock the door" on it, while they rest and refresh themselves to resume their quest for an alternative that will acceptably resolve the conflict of codes.

The practices, devices, habits, and mental and emotional points of view that are utilized in coping with heavy stress are seemingly infinite in their variety and ingenuity. They are strongly influenced by the temperament, the background, and the idiosyncrasies of each individual executive. Yet behind all this seeming diversity is an implicit—and frequently quite explicit—acknowledgment that unless heavy stress is "managed"—that is, held within some tolerable limit—it can quickly become unmanageable, inducing panic and collapse of promising remedies.

To cope with stress, some top executives deliberately turn to a strikingly different kind of problem and immerse themselves thoroughly in it for a few hours. Or they sometimes return to their offices at unconventional hours—late at night or early in the morning—when the building is deserted and they can isolate themselves and think. Often they carefully compose a memorandum to themselves stating the problem as bluntly and concisely as possible and indicating what an adequate solution will require. This practice has a dual purpose:

1 It forces out the plainest possible statement of the problem and its desired solution. This, when well done, enables them to "forget"

the problem or, more accurately, to force it down to the level of their subconscious for attention there.

2 It forces them to do all they can with the problem at the intellectual level and to signify this to their nervous systems by drafting the most up-to-date résumé of the situation that they can then prepare.

In either case they rid themselves of a persistent nagging from their minds and nerves and win a respite that they can use to renew themselves before resuming the search and struggle.

Further along on the spectrum above, or on one like it, some of these executives occasionally seem to find the means to tap serendipity. After prolonged and intensive struggle with the issues at conflict, suddenly they take off for a distant region and a sport or pleasure (perhaps taking a Greek island cruise or skiing high in the Alps) that is a keen joy in life to them. After two or three weeks out of all old ruts and routines, removed physically and emotionally as far as they can get, they sometimes discover—perhaps on the journey home—that the answer comes to them. They know that this practice is not surefire; but when they are "at wit's end," there is little to lose and, maybe, an inspiration to gain.

One president I talked with secured such a gain on the morning of the day I saw him. Over his wife's demur, he rose at four o'clock, took a long horseback ride in the mountain foothills near his home, and returned jubilantly with the reconciling solution to a problem that had vexed him for months. It was a deep-seated and unyielding conflict of codes that had nearly brought open warfare among members of his board, various groups of stockholders, and a large number of civic leaders whose communities' welfare seemed to them to be involved. He made that story the subject of his toughest-problem narrative.

Self-Expendable Attitude

Another recurring uniformity of belief and behavior among these executives is their readiness to view themselves as "expendable." Because this attitude is so clearly the ultimate device employed in standing—and in *withstanding*—stress, it could have been placed under the success clue just discussed. Yet, because of its decisive importance, I have chosen to present it separately.

The readiness to put their jobs on the line over an issue they deem fundamental to their organization's long-range welfare is perhaps the simplest touchstone by which the more successful company presidents are distinguishable.

Sometimes it is utilized directly, virtually in the form of an ultimatum: "If continued, our labor relations policy will incur liquidation or bankruptcy in less than five years. It must be revised and reformulated radically, even at the risk of an immediate strike. Either our current policy goes, or I go."

Far more often, the readiness of presidents to put their jobs on the line is merely latent in crisis situations. Nonetheless, it is clearly present and perceived by those who deal with them on these peak decisions. And it *is* present because when the top executives do their utmost in working out a resolution to the conflict issues, they are the ones prepared to undertake its implementation and abide by the consequences. No one can do more than shoulder that decisive responsibility—and the moment sometimes comes when a vote of confidence is called for.

People less sure of themselves—those lacking the opportunity to practice and achieve some preliminary successes with such problems or those unable to face with equanimity the loss or surrender of their job with its power, prominence, and inward gratification—are generally tempted to rationalize away the importance of making such an ultimate decision and to minimize the hazards that they hope to be able to postpone or evade. They find it uncomfortable to view themselves as expendable and to contemplate the disquieting prospect of having to renew their careers in other environments where they might not regain such organizational eminence.

Psychological forces, deeply hidden yet very powerful, are so obviously involved in this ability to view oneself as expendable in the role of president that it is only necessary to call attention to the uniformity with which I find it present among my interviewees. (I leave its further explanation to those better equipped to interpret its psychic importance.) Organizationally, however, its value to presidents when they are confronted alone with heavy stress is unmistakable. For them it is the ultimate safety valve, and I think it enables them to labor at their critical decision making well shielded from fears and anxieties about their personal fate. That bridge they have crossed beforehand.

That most of these top executives recognize the value of this ability to view themselves as expendable usually comes out when I ask them whom they look to for approval, approbation, or understanding once a serious crisis has been satisfactorily surmounted. Reference groups frequently mentioned include: members of the board, the business community (watching from the sidelines), members of their own executive organization, the investment community (frequently privy to the severity and seriousness of some of these crises), and their whole organization as a total system cognizant in some degree of what has been afoot.

Surprisingly, a near majority of the presidents in my sample—after some quiet reflection on my query—named none of the reference groups above. The answer simply was something like this: "Me. I must satisfy myself, above all, that I have done the best I can do. When I can do that, anything else or anyone's approval is pleasant, but superfluous."

When I questioned the chief executives who named other groups first about the importance of self-approval, it was instantly accepted as being so self-evident that each had taken for granted that I understood its priority and its indispensability to his view of his role in the organization.

Capacity to Concentrate

Another factor, closely related to the one just given, appears with sufficient frequency that I believe it to be a uniformity also. Sometimes it is mentioned early in the interviews, when the presidents feel that a brief résumé of the assignments given them as they rose through the ranks is relevant. Sometimes it is supplied later, when I request a recapitulation of their advancement by rank and increasing responsibility.

Beginning usually with their very first task after entering the organization, they reveal a capacity to immerse themselves with so much zest and with such an uncommon self-forgetfulness in the job assigned that it is completed ahead of schedule—and completed so well that another and a more demanding one is promptly supplied. Not only are these assignments expected, but so are the rewards: more work and more responsibility!

These top executives seem to have risen faster than their peers (and faster than is customary) principally because of a demonstrated capacity or appetite for exacting assignments into which they plunge *for the sake of the challenge* rather than for an opportunity to get ahead of their competitors. None are naive about organizational politics; yet it is displaced—both as a major preoccupation in their minds and as a diversion to their energies—by their preference to get a job well done ahead of anything else. This trait of deep absorption in the task at hand creates, in a manner of speaking, a pull upward in the nature of assignments to ever-increasing responsibilities.

From listening carefully to these executives' stories, by studying the details written down later, and by occasionally hearing about some of them from other people who know them personally, I have formed the opinion that not many of these top executives invest much of their time or thought in the race of "getting to the top." They get there, but rather as an afterthought, as it were, or as something secondary and extrinsic to doing well the job at hand. (With several of the men interviewed, I gained the impression that their job as president had come as something of a surprise at the time.)

This ability of the more successful people to concentrate deeply on each day's work not only serves to conserve time and energy that other contenders invest in clique activities, power plays, empire-building pursuits, and so on, but it leaves them largely free of the leftover resentments from old feuds and battle scars that handicap those unsuccessful candidates when the president's position becomes vacant at a time all are ready for consideration. In some cases it may tip the scales in their favor because they are less beholden to others for their advancement; in other cases, the deciding factor may be that they are more acceptable to more of their future subordinates than are their "rivals" who have made numerous enemies on *their* way up.

Influence of "Model"

In my early interviews with top executives, it often happened that a leading second executive was soon brought into the conversation and reappeared repeatedly as the discussions unfolded. Although seldom involved directly in the specific cases being presented, he was pictured as being of dominant importance in the president's organization career.

He usually was about 30 years older than the speaker, and most often their acquaintance began soon after the younger one first entered the company and was assigned to the older man's organizational unit. Typically, the rank of the elder man at the time of first meeting was general manager or division vice president. Again, typically, the older man went on to become president, then chairman, and only recently retired or died.

Positive Pattern. I now have come to expect this "model" background figure to appear in my interviews, and in nearly every case such a person does so.

He frequently threatens to run away with the "case" at hand because the narrator's enthusiasm about him is so evident, as is his admiration and gratitude. It is common to hear a president say, "You should have known *him;* he was the best executive I've ever known." Or, "He brought me up; he taught me the ropes." Or, "He gave me the chance to show what I could do." Or, "He really made this company." The speaker sometimes has difficulty in returning to the thread of the narrative he is relating and does so with regret and visible reluctance because he plainly feels we are dropping a more engrossing topic—namely, the personality and behavior of the man who "taught me all I know about this job I've got."

A father figure? Probably, as far as that tired phrase can carry us toward any agreed-on significance. At another level of discourse, however, the part this older individual has played in helping his young associate to form, to work out, and to *practice* his own patterns of organizational behavior is unmistakable. Aside from their expressions of admiration, 90% of the material my narrators supply about their older sponsor (tutor? coach? mentor?) consists of concrete illustrations of *his* organizational behavior that was exceptionally skillful as to morale-building, performance-producing, conflict-reducing, and so forth. And his were the patterns on which the younger executive consciously chose to model developing organizational behavior. Whatever else the older man may be, he is clearly a model the young associate eagerly copies and to whom he renders tribute and gives predominant credit for most of his or her accomplishments.

Negative Figure. The very few presidents who fail to immediately introduce their model invariably later bring into their stories a similar background figure who seems to serve the same need in a reverse manner. For want of a better phrase, I have come to see this older man in the same way many presidents do—as an anti-model.

He is usually introduced not only later on in these discourses, but in a different fashion, such as: "Do you know anything about So-and-so, an earlier predecessor of mine? I ask because he was quite well known in his day.'' From this opening, they then characterize So-and-so as the chief executive who ''brought this organization to the brink of ruin'' because ''he made *all* the decisions.'' Or, ''He trusted no one but himself; he just couldn't delegate.'' Or, ''You couldn't talk to him because he wouldn't listen.'' Or, he was ''arbitrary,'' ''insensitive,'' ''ruthless,'' ''vindictive,'' ''obstinate,'' ''vain.''

The refrain about the anti-model is unvarying: ''I watched every move he made because I couldn't believe what I saw. I asked myself, doesn't he know what damaging and costly results that move he is making (illustrated with a concrete example of the predecessor's behavior) will have on the people in this organization, or doesn't he care? How could a man be so stupid about organizational matters and ever get to be president?'' (In one of these cases, the individual in question had bought control of the company with an enormous fortune made in stock market operations; in another, he had been ensconced through a famous family's influence.)

The lessons these presidents draw from their anti-models are vivid and explicit: ''I made up my mind that should I ever be a president, I would do exactly the opposite of X, and I could not lose!'' Or, ''I could hardly wait for a chance to replace him and try to undo the damage he had done.'' Or, ''I wanted to try and see if we could ever catch up with all the opportunities he let slip by.''

Again, whether anti-father figure or not, his every move was followed with minute vigilance by his anti-acolytes; his policies and managerial practices were daily scrutinized, analyzed, and criticized by an intent observer who was driven to declare—at least mutely or to a confidant from time to time—what he or she would do differently as the top executive, and in what specific ways the organization would be better, and why. Such resistance to, and disapproval of, the organizational behavior of Mr. Anti produced for these presidents nearly the same first-hand knowledge-in-detail about administration-in-detail that was acquired by their counterparts under more agreeable (but scarcely more instructive) circumstances.

Other Attributes

Beyond these four uniformities, there seem to be some others, perhaps of equal or greater relevance. One of these might be the value the presidents clearly attach to having a temperamental opposite—some person available and near their level in the organization—who is a formidable and constructive critic or skeptic on whom they can test out their schemes for innovation. Such loyal opposition is encouraged and rewarded because ''he's saved us from some God-awful blunders''; or because ''if he can punch holes in it that I can't overcome, I usually drop it.''

Most of the other attributes I have discerned, in addition to those I have given as examples, do not recur as frequently or have not been articulated as unmistakably. They must wait for the collection of more data from more top executives, although I am inclined now to believe that, fully pursued, enough separate individual uniformities will disclose themselves to reappear as linked indissolubly together in patterns of mutually reinforcing uniformities common to top executives of the caliber I have had the good fortune to listen to.

Innate or Acquired?

The age-old issue of nature versus nurture presents itself at this point. How do executives such as these get to be what they are? What aspects of their organizational behavior is learned behavior? What portion rests on natural endowments? How much of it stems from, let us say, a quarter-century of career training opportunities *before* taking over the top job? How much of it is role-induced *after* assuming the presidential task? How much of their fitness for that role was actually present well before they even entered their organizations? Does the constant daily testing on the various jobs they hold tend to sift out and to favor those with some inherent aptitude for the top organizational job?

Literature Inconclusive

Definitive answers to this long-standing issue still elude us. Since even a little light thereon is better than no light at all, readers who share my involvement in this pursuit may welcome a few further comments from the literature now accumulating rapidly on creativity and creative people. I, myself, ventured into this area some time past to see what others have found pertinent to the question of how these executives "get that way." To what extent can the relatively better performance of some presidents be traced to their career training? To what extent must it be ascribed to a fortuitous combination of factors, some of them genetic and hence beyond our present ability to duplicate and transmit to others? Specifically, I wanted to find out what the chances are that a sizable segment of top executives could have been—and *now* can be—better equipped by experience, training, or any kind of help to deal more constructively and creatively with the conflict of codes inherited with their office.

The views of writers on this topic range the spectrum from a few who hold that "they are born that way" to a larger number who feel that creativity is present as a variable in all healthy humans and can be strongly developed through the efforts of others if such "training" is understood to be the total influence exerted 24 hours a day by all other individuals on the subject in question. This view, of course, identifies education as an individual's total life experience and, for our purposes, begs the issue. In the center of this spectrum of views as to training are found the majority—those who are in doubt or decline to offer an opinion.

My present view is that since the question is currently beyond our reach to settle with certainty, we should follow the lead given us by those who hold that more creativity is available if we seek it. Not *all* creativity. And maybe not creativity for *all*. But more creativity for most of us *if* we take a culture-wide view of what an individual's total life experience actually does—and does not—"teach" us. This view has been strongly reinforced by my sample of some of the better top executives, all of whom insist on pounding home the value and indispensability of (a) the training they received over 25 or 30 years of managing and (b) having a model figure to emulate—or to repudiate—in terms of specific day-in, day-out episodes of organizational behavior.

Training for "Comers"

If additional data support my present surmise that the attributes I find are indeed uniformities in common, then it seems to me that it should be possible to devise tests or screening procedures to locate more quickly and more accurately individuals who possess, or are busy developing, the traits most often associated with the behavior of the more successful presidents. If the improvement in selectivity were to be no more than 5% to 10%, the larger yield would still be an enormous benefit. The most direct beneficiaries, naturally, would be the individuals possessing or acquiring the cluster of special talents required for the president's role.

Of course, other individuals intensely pursuing the job, but plainly lacking some of the essential traits, would also gain by having their drives redirected away from reasonably certain frustration and defeat toward goals more compatible with their capabilities. Their organizations would so palpably gain from better placement of executives for tasks to which their behavior patterns point that the savings from futility, frayed nerves, loss of forward movement, and so on, would simply be monumental. And the general society, in which these corporations' activities occupy an ever-increasing importance, would be the gainer by finding its affairs more often in the most competent hands.

The opportunities to improve, enlarge, and hasten the better training of more promising candidates would multiply the same benefits indicated above. Consider, for example, the manifold ways in which any total organization would flourish if the potential presidential timber within its ranks could be tentatively identified and placed under the skillful and nurturing supervision of some excelling "model" such as most of my sample presidents have had the supreme good fortune to attract! At the very least, another 5% to 10% improvement over our current trial-and-error methods would be another huge source of gain at trifling cost.

Aid for Incumbents

Returning to the present, I feel an obligation to call attention to the crushing character of the burdens—whose weight is often grossly underestimated or airily dismissed as being overcompensated—the more successful presidents assume on behalf of the whole organization and indirectly on behalf of society-at-large. It does not reduce the seriousness of the point I am making to reply that many of these presidents actually relish opportunities to wrestle with seemingly insoluble problems. I know they do. I am glad they do. But I seriously want to see a far greater number of their peers feel the same way, and this brings me to the very point I most wish to make.

These top executives face their most stressful, most important organizational problems alone—too much alone with respect to their own health and/or optimum task performance. And, in my opinion, needlessly too much alone.

They need, most of all, the vast relief of someone to talk with. They need to share, at least in part, the stress—to explore and clarify it, and to speed up the process of identifying the key issues from the more clamorous ones. In short, they need someone to aid them in expediting their search for the jugular.

They do not need a prop, a substitute problem-solver, or a pinch hitter. They do not need an expert or other specialist in some given area for a problem that embraces a conflict of codes issue; there are no specialists in an area where each problem seldom has an applicable precedent. They do not need either a yes-man or a no-man. Preferably, they need most a non-involved alter ego who can share their diagnostic search for the core problem—one who can stimulate the seeking for creative alternatives, but who resolutely leaves the ultimate decision to the top executive for the simple and all-sufficient reason that the alter ego can never share the costs and risks of implementation.

The top executives most in need of the kind of help so roughly outlined are not the relatively more successful presidents that I know. (Being what they are, these successful men would probably be the first to use such expediting assistance!) Rather, the chief executives most in need of assistance are those whose batting averages are currently at the midpoint. Aid just a few times at critical junctures could possibly tip the scales favorably and put them—and their self-confidence—on a more equal footing with the fortunate sample of company presidents I have come to know.

Conclusion

Where have we gotten to? How can this limited first step of inquiry be summed up? I shall attempt to do this by enumerating the four essential things that I feel I have learned from this preliminary reconnaissance.

1. *Presidents do have to face problems for their organizations that other executives do not—and cannot—handle.* This is a matter of necessity, not of choice. It comes affixed to their role of final decision maker and cannot be evaded. Nor can it be delegated, at least as a totality, although portions—especially some of the technical and financial aspects—can be assigned for study and analysis.

On this part of my query, I feel reasonably confident that further research will confirm and not significantly modify the position stated.

2. *Problems that presidents must handle force their way upward because their resolution demands an ultimate "yes" or "no."* They demand the attention of the person whose authority is the widest and whose responsibility is the broadest in acting for the organization as a whole. These problems demand not only the ultimate in authority, but also the ultimate in overall ability because they are the most fraught with risks to the system. They compel admission to where "the buck stops."

Beyond their potential threat, these problems generally are also confusing in their complexity—cutting across all formal organization structures and frequently being intertwined with unheard-of nonorganizational elements of decisive importance. They are obscure as well as complex; one or more facets that are only dimly glimpsed, or even hidden, may conceal the core issue or contain the king pin to releasing the whole log jam.

Complicated, obscure, freighted with risk, attended by a welter of strong contradictory individual feelings of anger, frustration, anxiety, and fear, it is small wonder that these problems get passed rapidly upward ("Let the president solve *this* one! Isn't that the president's job?").

This part of my quest seems rather clearly established too; namely, that the toughest, most unprecedented, most embracing, and touchiest problems in all organizations unfailingly make their way to the presidential desk. And they rightly are the chief executive's problems because that *is* the president's job—to handle the problems that no one else is sufficiently empowered to cope with and to handle these alone, somehow, or see the chief executive's influence slowly dwindle.

3. *Conflict of codes—and the necessity of reconciling it through the creation of a higher, more embracing code—is inevitably present in every formal organization.* Since this is the interpretation and judgment of only one person, its merit must remain indeterminate pending the accumulation of a much broader sample, but more especially its verification by other investigators and methods.

4. *The patterns of organizational behavior disclosed by the data secured thus far strike me strongly with numerous parallels to the behavior of creative people encountered in the literature.* For those who may wish to look at some of the parallels involved, I suggest for a starter, Abraham H. Maslow's unconventional book, *Eupsychian Management*.[2] His long-pursued interest in those whom he labels "superior people" leads him to identify many of their traits and characteristics as the necessary attributes to make such people outstanding candidates for leadership and management. There is, in fact, a close fit between the uniformities I find common to my subjects and those he ascribes to the superior people. I offer this reference to Maslow's work chiefly to promote—and perhaps to provoke—relevant speculation as to where and how we can increase our supply of such people or, more exactly, the creative behavior they display.

Appendix

The provisional clues for success discussed here are drawn from a sample skewed by accident of selection toward a group of two dozen company presidents. I say "accident of selection" advisedly. When I began my current inquiry two years ago, I sent out a large number of letters to those I knew to be involved in or close to the president's problems. I told them I would appreciate an opportunity to hear from the president some personal examples of what were the toughest problems, what made them so, and how they were handled. I received far more responses than I could reply to, let alone interview. From the most accessible, I selected randomly a dozen presidents whose companies varied in size from quite small to exceedingly large and from close family ownerships to multinational corporate ventures. Another dozen presidents were chosen as they were made available by introduction from friends.

In all instances, I sought appointments with top executives who gave the most unqualified, unhesitant assent. I did so, frankly, because that promised to economize my time; but—as it worked out later—I discovered I had unwittingly selected a sample of the presidents who were more self-confident and more successful in coping with their toughest problems.

My findings from this limited sample reaffirm, and never stand at variance with, a far larger number of confidential disclosures (many unsought, but gladly accepted) that I have received during four and a half decades of teaching as well as management experiences of my own. These voluntary disclosures have totaled a hundred that I can easily identify and perhaps an equal number of others I cannot identify so positively.

Notes

1. Chester I. Barnard, *The Functions of the Executive* (Cambridge, Mass., Harvard University Press, 1938), Chapter 17.

2. Abraham H. Maslow, *Eupsychian Management* (Homewood, Ill., Richard D. Irwin and Dorsey Press, 1965).

3

Barriers and Gateways to Communication

CARL R. ROGERS and F. J. ROETHLISBERGER

Communication among human beings has always been a problem. But it is only fairly recently that management and management advisers have become so concerned about it and the way it works or does not work in industry. Now, as the result of endless discussion, speculation, and plans of action, a whole cloud of catchwords and catchthoughts has sprung up and surrounded it.

The following two descriptions of barriers and gateways to communication are presented in the thought that they may help to bring the problem down to earth and show what it means in terms of simple fundamentals. First Carl R. Rogers analyzes it from the standpoint of human behavior generally (Part I); then F. J. Roethlisberger illustrates it in an industrial context (Part II).

PART I

It may seem curious that a person like myself, whose whole professional effort is devoted to psychotherapy, should be interested in problems of communication. What relationship is there between obstacles to communication and providing therapeutic help to individuals with emotional maladjustments?

Actually the relationship is very close indeed. The whole task of psychotherapy is the task of dealing with a failure in communication. The emotionally maladjusted person, the "neurotic," is in difficulty, first, because communication within the self has broken down and, second, because as a result of this communication with others has been damaged. To put it another way, in the "neurotic" individual parts of the self which have been termed

---

Editors' Note. Mr. Rogers' and Mr. Roethlisberger's observations are based on their contributions to a panel discussion at the Centennial Conference on Communications, Northwestern University, October 1951. A complete report of this conference may be secured by writing to the Publications Office, Northwestern University, Evanston, Illinois.

unconscious, or repressed, or denied to awareness, become blocked off so that they no longer communicate themselves to the conscious or managing part of the self; as long as this is true, there are distortions in the way the individual communicates the self to others, and so the individual suffers both within the self and in interpersonal relations.

The task of psychotherapy is to help the person achieve, through a special relationship with a therapist, good communication within the self. Once this is achieved, the person can communicate more freely and more effectively with others. We may say then that psychotherapy is good communication, within and between people. We may also turn that statement around and it will still be true. Good communication, free communication, within or between people, is always therapeutic.

It is, then, from a background of experience with communication in counseling and psychotherapy that I want to present two ideas: (1) I wish to state what I believe is one of the major factors in blocking or impeding communication, and then (2) I wish to present what in our experience has proved to be a very important way of improving or facilitating communication.

Barrier: The Tendency to Evaluate

I should like to propose, as a hypothesis for consideration, that the major barrier to mutual interpersonal communication is our very natural tendency to judge, to evaluate, to approve (or disapprove) the statement of the other person or the other group. Let me illustrate my meaning with some very simple examples. Suppose someone, commenting on this discussion, makes the statement, "I didn't like what that man said." What will you respond? Almost invariably your reply will be either approval or disapproval of the attitude expressed. Either you respond, "I didn't either; I thought it was terrible," or else you tend to reply, "Oh, I thought it was really good." In other words, your primary reaction is to evaluate it from *your* point of view your own frame of reference.

Or take another example. Suppose I say with some feeling, "I think the Republicans are behaving in ways that show a lot of good sound sense these days." What is the response that arises in your mind? The overwhelming likelihood is that it will be evaluative. In other words, you will find yourself agreeing, or disagreeing, or making some judgment about me such as "He must be a conservative," or "He seems solid in his thinking." Or let us take an illustration from the international scene. Russia says vehemently, "The treaty with Japan is a war plot on the part of the United States." We rise as one person to say, "That's a lie!"

This last illustration brings in another element connected with my hypothesis. Although the tendency to make evaluations is common in almost all interchange of language, it is very much heightened in those situations where feelings and emotions are deeply involved. So the stronger our feelings, the more likely it is that there will be no mutual element in the communication. There will be just two ideas, two feelings, two judgments, missing each other in psychological space.

I am sure you recognize this from your own experience. When you have not been emotionally involved yourself and have listened to a heated discussion, you often go away thinking, "Well, they actually weren't talking about the same thing." And they were not. Each was making a judgment, an evaluation, from a personal frame of reference. There was really nothing which could be called communication in any genuine sense. This tendency to react to any emotionally meaningful statement by forming an evaluation of it from our own point of view is, I repeat, the major barrier to interpersonal communication.

Gateway: Listening with Understanding

Is there any way of solving this problem, of avoiding this barrier? I feel that we are making exciting progress toward this goal, and I should like to present it as simply as I can. Real communication occurs, and this evaluative tendency is avoided, when we listen with understanding. What does that mean? It means seeing the expressed idea and attitude from the other person's point of view, sensing how it feels to the other person, achieving his or her frame of reference in regard to the thing being talked about.

Stated so briefly, this may sound absurdly simple, but it is not. It is an approach which we have found extremely potent in the field of psychotherapy. It is the most effective agent we know for altering the basic personality structure of an individual and for improving relationships and communications with others. If I can listen to what you can tell me, if I can understand how it seems to you, if I can see its personal meaning for you, if I can sense the emotional flavor which it has for you, then I will be releasing potent forces of change in you.

Again, if I can really understand how you hate your father, or hate the company, or hate Communists—if I can catch the flavor of your fear of insanity, or your fear of atom bombs, or of Russia—it will be of the greatest help to you in altering those hatreds and fears and in establishing realistic and harmonious relationships with the very people and situations toward which you have felt hatred and fear. We know from our research that such empathic understanding—understanding *with* you, not *about* you—is such an effective approach that it can bring about major changes in personality.

Some of you may be feeling that you listen well to people and yet you have never seen such results. The chances are great indeed that your listening has not been of the type I have described. Fortunately, I can suggest a little laboratory experiment which you can try to test the quality of your understanding. The next time you get into an argument with your wife, or your friend, or with a small group of friends, just stop the discussion for a moment and, for an experiment, institute this rule: "Each person can air a view only *after* first restating the ideas and feelings of the previous speaker accurately and to that speaker's satisfaction."

You see what this would mean. It would simply mean that before presenting your own point of view, it would be necessary for you to achieve the other speaker's frame of reference—to understand the other person's thoughts and feelings so well that you could summarize them for that person. Sounds simple, doesn't it? But if you try it, you will discover that it is one of the most difficult things you have ever tried to do. However, once you have been able to see the other's point of view, your own comments will have to be drastically revised. You will also find the emotion going out of the discussion, the differences being reduced, and those differences which remain being of a rational and understandable sort.

Can you imagine what this kind of an approach would mean if it were projected into larger areas? What would happen to a labor-management dispute if it were conducted in such a way that labor, without necessarily agreeing, could accurately state management's point of view in a way that management could accept; and management, without approving labor's stand, could state labor's case in a way that labor agreed was accurate? It would mean that real communication was established, and one could practically guarantee that some reasonable solution would be reached.

If, then, this way of approach is an effective avenue to good communication and good relationships, as I am quite sure you will agree if you try the experiment I have mentioned, why is it not more widely tried and used? I will try to list the difficulties which keep it from being utilized.

Need for Courage

In the first place it takes courage, a quality which is not too widespread. I am indebted to Dr. S. I. Hayakawa, the semanticist, for pointing out that to carry on psychotherapy in this fashion is to take a very real risk, and that courage is required. If I really understand you in this way, if I am willing to enter your private world and see the way life appears to you, without any attempt to make evaluative judgments, I run the risk of being changed myself. I might see it your way; I might find myself influenced in my attitudes or my personality.

This risk of being changed is one of the most frightening prospects many of us can face. If I enter, as fully as I am able, into the private world of a neurotic or psychotic individual, isn't there a risk that I might become lost in that world? Most of us are afraid to take that risk. Or if we were listening to a Russian Communist, or Senator Joe McCarthy, how many of us would dare to try to see the world from each of their points of view? The great majority of us could not *listen;* we would find ouselves compelled to *evaluate,* because listening would seem too dangerous. So the first requirement is courage, and we do not always have it.

Heightened Emotions

But there is a second obstacle. It is just when emotions are strongest that it is most difficult to achieve the frame of reference of the other person or group. Yet it is then that the attitude is most needed if communication is to be established. We have not found this to be an insuperable obstacle in our experience in psychotherapy. A third party, who is able to lay aside personal feelings and evaluations, can assist greatly by listening with understanding to each person or group and clarifying the views and attitudes each holds.

We have found this effective in small groups in which contradictory or antagonistic attitudes exist. When the parties to a dispute realize that they are being understood, that someone sees how the situation seems to them, the statements grow less exaggerated and less defensive, and it is no longer necessary to maintain the attitude, "I am 100% right and you are 100% wrong." The influence of such an understanding catalyst in the group permits the members to come closer and closer to the objective truth involved in the relationship. In this way mutual communication is established, and some type of agreement becomes much more possible.

So we may say that though heightened emotions make it much more difficult to understand *with* an opponent, our experience makes it clear that a neutral, understanding, catalyst type of leader or therapist can overcome this obstacle in a small group.

Size of Group

That last phrase, however, suggests another obstacle to utilizing the approach I have described. Thus far all our experience has been with small face-to-face groups—groups exhibiting industrial tensions, religious tensions, racial tensions, and therapy groups in which many personal tensions are present. In these small groups our experience, confirmed by a limited amount of research, shows that this basic approach leads to improved communication, to greater acceptance of others and by others, and to attitudes which are more positive and more problem-solving in nature. There is a decrease in defensiveness, in exaggerated statements, in evaluative and critical behavior.

But these findings are from small groups. What about trying to achieve understanding between larger groups that are geographically remote, or between face-to-face groups that are not speaking for themselves but simply as representatives of others, like the delegates at Kaesong? Frankly we do not know the answers to these questions. I believe the situation might be put this way: As social scientists we have a tentative test-tube solution of the problem of breakdown in communication. But to confirm the validity of this test-tube solution and to adapt it to the enormous problems of communication breakdown between classes, groups, and nations would involve additional funds, much more research, and creative thinking of a high order.

Yet with our present limited knowledge we can see some steps which might be taken even in large groups to increase the amount of listening *with* and decrease the amount of evaluation *about*. To be imaginative for a moment, let us suppose that a therapeutically oriented international group went to the Russian leaders and said, "We want to achieve a genuine understanding of your views and, even more important, of your attitudes and feelings toward the United States. We will summarize and resummarize these views and feelings if necessary, until you agree that our description represents the situation as it seems to you."

Then suppose they did the same thing with the leaders in our own country. If they then gave the widest possible distribution to these two views, with the feelings clearly described but not expressed in name-calling, might not the effect be very great? It would not guarantee the type of understanding I have been describing, but it would make it much more possible. We can understand the feelings of a person who hates us much more readily when that person's attitudes are accurately described to us by a neutral third party than we can when the person is shaking a fist at us.

Faith in Social Sciences

But even to describe such a first step is to suggest another obstacle to this approach of understanding. Our civilization does not yet have enough faith in the social sciences to utilize their findings. The opposite is true of the physical sciences. During the war when a test-tube solution was found to the problem of synthetic rubber, millions of dollars and an army of talent were turned loose on the problem of using that finding. If synthetic rubber could be made in milligrams, it could and would be made in the thousands of tons. And it was. But in the social science realm, if a way is found of facilitating communication and mutual understanding in small groups, there is no guarantee that the finding will be utilized. It may be a generation or more before the money and the brains will be turned loose to exploit that finding.

Summary

In closing, I should like to summarize this small-scale solution to the problem of barriers in communication, and to point out certain of its characteristics.

I have said that our research and experience to date would make it appear that breakdowns in communication, and the evaluative tendency which is the major barrier to communication, can be avoided. The solution is provided by creating a situation in which each of the different parties comes to understand the other from the *other's* point of view. This has been achieved, in practice, even when feelings run high, by the influence of a person who is willing to understand each point of view empathically, and who thus acts as a catalyst to precipitate further understanding.

This procedure has important characteristics. It can be initiated by one party, without waiting for the other to be ready. It can even be initiated by a neutral third person, provided a minimum of cooperation from one of the parties can be gained.

This procedure can deal with the insincerities, the defensive exaggerations, the lies, the "false fronts" which characterize almost every failure in communication. These defensive distortions drop away with astonishing speed as people find that the only intent is to understand, not to judge.

This approach leads steadily and rapidly toward the discovery of the truth, toward a realistic appraisal of the objective barriers to communication. The dropping of some defensiveness by one party leads to further dropping of defensiveness by the other party, and truth is thus approached.

This procedure gradually achieves mutual communication. Mutual communication tends to be pointed toward solving a problem rather than toward attacking a person or group. It leads to a situation in which I see how the problem appears to you as well as to me, and you see how it appears to me as well as to you. Thus accurately and realistically defined, the problem is almost certain to yield to intelligent attack; or if it is in part insoluble, it will be comfortably accepted as such.

This then appears to be a test-tube solution to the breakdown of communication as it occurs in small groups. Can we take this small-scale answer, investigate it further, refine it, develop it, and apply it to the tragic and well-nigh fatal failures of communication which threaten the very existence of our modern world? It seems to me that this is a possibility and a challenge which we should explore.

PART II

In thinking about the many barriers to personal communication, particularly those that are due to differences of background, experience, and motivation, it seems to me extraordinary that any two persons can ever understand each other. Such reflections provoke the question of how communication is possible when people do not see and assume the same things and share the same values.

On this question there are two schools of thought. One school assumes that communication between A and B, for example, has failed when B does not accept what A has to say as being fact, true, or valid; and that the goal of communication is to get B to agree with A's opinions, ideas, facts, or information.

The position of the other school of thought is quite different. It assumes that communication has failed when B does not feel free to express his feelings to A because B fears they will not be accepted by A. Communication is facilitated when on the part of A or B or both there is a willingness to express and accept differences.

Author's Note. For the concepts I use to present my material I am greatly indebted to some very interesting conversations I have had with my friend, Irving Lee.—*F. J. R.*

As these are quite divergent conceptions, let us explore them further with an example. Bill, an employee, is talking with his boss in the boss's office. The boss says, "I think, Bill, that this is the best way to do your job." Bill says, "Oh yeah!" According to the first school of thought, this reply would be a sign of poor communication. Bill does not understand the best way of doing his work. To improve communication, therefore, it is up to the boss to explain to Bill why his way is the best.

From the point of view of the second school of thought, Bill's reply is a sign neither of good nor of bad communication. Bill's response is indeterminate. But the boss has an opportunity to find out what Bill means if he so desires. Let us assume that this is what he chooses to do, that is, find out what Bill means. So this boss tries to get Bill to talk more about his job while he (the boss) listens.

For purposes of simplification, I shall call the boss representing the first school of thought *"Smith"* and the boss representing the second school of thought *"Jones."* In the presence of the so-called same stimulus each behaves differently. Smith chooses to *explain;* Jones chooses to *listen*. In my experience Jones's response works better than Smith's. It works better because Jones is making a more proper evaluation of what is taking place between him and Bill than Smith is. Let us test this hypothesis by continuing with our example.

What Smith Assumes, Sees, and Feels

Smith assumes that he understands what Bill means when Bill says, "Oh yeah!" so there is no need to find out. Smith is sure that Bill does not understand why this is the best way to do his job, so Smith has to tell him. In this process let us assume Smith is logical, lucid, and clear. He presents his facts and evidence well. But, alas, Bill remains unconvinced. What does Smith do? Operating under the assumption that what is taking place between him and Bill is something essentially logical, Smith can draw only one of two conclusions: either (1) he has not been clear enough, or (2) Bill is too damned stupid to understand. So he either has to "spell out" his case in words of fewer and fewer syllables or give up. Smith is reluctant to do the latter, so he continues to explain. What happens?

If Bill still does not accept Smith's explanation of why this is the best way for him to do his job, a pattern of interacting feelings is produced of which Smith is often unaware. The more Smith cannot get Bill to understand him, the more frustrated Smith becomes and the more Bill becomes a threat to his logical capacity. Since Smith sees himself as a fairly reasonable and logical chap, this is a difficult feeling to accept. It is much easier for him to perceive Bill as uncooperative or stupid. This perception, however, will affect what Smith says and does. Under these pressures Bill comes to be evaluated more and more in terms of Smith's values. By this process Smith tends to treat Bill's values as unimportant. He tends to deny Bill's uniqueness and difference. He treats Bill as if he had little capacity for self-direction.

Let us be clear. Smith does not see that he is doing these things. When he is feverishly scratching hieroglyphics on the back of an envelope, trying to explain to Bill why this is the best way to do his job, Smith is trying to be helpful. He is a man of goodwill, and he wants to set Bill straight. This is the way Smith sees himself and his behavior. But it is for this very reason that Bill's "Oh yeah!" is getting under Smith's skin.

"How dumb can a guy be?" is Smith's attitude, and unfortunately Bill will hear that more than Smith's good intentions. Bill will feel misunderstood. He will not see Smith as a man of goodwill trying to be helpful. Rather he will perceive him as a threat to his self-esteem and personal integrity. Against this threat Bill will feel the need to defend himself at all cost. Not being so logically articulate as Smith, Bill expresses this need, again, by saying, "Oh yeah!"

What Jones Assumes, Sees, and Feels

Let us leave this sad scene between Smith and Bill, which I fear is going to terminate by Bill's either leaving in a huff or being kicked out of Smith's office. Let us turn for a moment to Jones and see what he is assuming, seeing, hearing, feeling, doing, and saying when he interacts with Bill.

Jones, it will be remembered, does not assume that he knows what Bill means when he says, "Oh yeah!" so he has to find out. Moreover, he assumes that when Bill said this, he had not exhausted his vocabulary or his feelings. Bill may not necessarily mean one thing; he may mean several different things. So Jones decides to listen.

In this process Jones is not under any illusion that what will take place will be eventually logical. Rather he is assuming that what will take place will be primarily an interaction of feelings. Therefore, he cannot ignore the feelings of Bill, the effect of Bill's feelings on him, or the effect of his feelings on Bill. In other words, he cannot ignore his relationship to Bill; he cannot assume that it will make no difference to what Bill will hear or accept.

Therefore, Jones will be paying strict attention to all of the things Smith has ignored. He will be addressing himself to Bill's feelings, his own, and the interactions between them.

Jones will therefore realize that he has ruffled Bill's feelings with his comment, "I think, Bill, this is the best way to do your job." So instead of trying to get Bill to understand him, he decides to try to understand Bill. He does this by encouraging Bill to speak. Instead of telling Bill how he should feel or think, he asks Bill such questions as, "Is this what you feel?" "Is this what you see?" "Is this what you assume?" Instead of ignoring Bill's evaluations as irrelevant, not valid, inconsequential, or false, he tries to understand Bill's reality as he feels it, perceives it, and assumes it to be. As Bill begins to open up, Jones's curiosity is piqued by this process.

"Bill isn't so dumb; he's quite an interesting guy" becomes Jones's attitude. And that is what Bill hears. Therefore Bill feels understood and accepted as a person. He becomes less defensive. He is in a better frame of mind to explore and re-examine his own perceptions, feelings, and assumptions. In this process he perceives Jones as a source of help. Bill feels free to express his differences. He feels that Jones has some respect for his capacity for self-direction. These positive feelings toward Jones make Bill more inclined to say, "Well, Jones, I don't quite agree with you that this is the best way to do my job, but I'll tell you what I'll do. I'll try to do it that way for a few days, and then I'll tell you what I think."

Conclusion

I grant that my two orientations do not work themselves out in practice in quite so simple or neat a fashion as I have been able to work them out on paper. There are many other ways in which Bill could have responded to Smith in the first place. He might even have said, "O.K., boss, I agree that your way of doing my job is better." But Smith still would not have known how Bill felt when he made this statement or whether Bill was actually going to do his job differently. Likewise, Bill could have responded to Jones in a way different from my example. In spite of Jones's attitude, Bill might still be reluctant to express himself freely to his boss.

The purpose of my examples has not been to demonstrate the right or wrong way of communicating. My purpose has been simply to provide something concrete to point to when I make the following generalizations:

1. Smith represents to me a very common pattern of misunderstanding. The misunderstanding does not arise because Smith is not clear enough in expressing himself. It arises because of Smith's misevaluation of what is taking place when two people are talking together.

2. Smith's misevaluation of the process of personal communication consists of certain very common assumptions, for example, (a) that what is taking place is something essentially logical; (b) that words in themselves apart from the people involved mean something; and (c) that the purpose of the interaction is to get Bill to see things from Smith's point of view.

3. Because of these assumptions, a chain reaction of perceptions and negative feelings is engendered which blocks communication. By ignoring Bill's feelings and by rationalizing his own, Smith ignores his relationship to Bill as one of the most important determinants of the communication. As a result, Bill hears Smith's attitude more clearly than the logical content of Smith's words. Bill feels that his individual uniqueness is being denied. His personal integrity being at stake, he becomes defensive and belligerent. As a result, Smith feels frustrated. He perceives Bill as stupid. So he says and does things which only provoke more defensiveness on the part of Bill.

4. In the case of Jones, I have tried to show what might possibly happen if we made a different evaluation of what is taking place when two people are talking together. Jones makes a different set of assumptions. He assumes (a) that what is taking place between him and Bill is an interaction of sentiments; (b) that Bill—not his words in themselves—means something; (c) that the object of the interaction is to give Bill an opportunity to express freely his differences.

5. Because of these assumptions, a psychological chain reaction of reinforcing feelings and perceptions is set up which facilitates communication between Bill and him. When Jones addresses himself to Bill's feelings and perceptions from Bill's point of view, Bill feels understood and accepted as a person; he feels free to express his differences. Bill sees Jones as a source of help; Jones sees Bill as an interesting person. Bill in turn becomes more cooperative.

6. If I have identified correctly these very common patterns of personal communication, then some interesting hypotheses can be stated:

(a) Jones's method works better than Smith's, not because of any magic, but because Jones has a better map than Smith of the process of personal communication.

(b) The practice of Jones's method, however, is not merely an intellectual exercise. It depends on Jones's capacity and willingness to see and accept points of view different from his own, and to practice this orientation in a face-to-face relationship. This practice involves an emotional as well as an intellectual achievement. It depends in part on Jones's awareness of himself, in part on the practice of a skill.

(c) Although our colleges and universities try to get students to appreciate intellectually points of view different from their own, very little is done to help them to implement this general intellectual appreciation in a simple face-to-face relationship—at the level of a skill. Most educational institutions train their students to be logical, lucid, and clear. Very little is done to help them to listen more skillfully. As a result, our educated world contains too many Smiths and too few Joneses.

(d) The biggest block to personal communication is one person's inability to listen intelligently, understandingly, and skillfully to another person. This deficiency in the modern world is widespread and appalling. In our universities as well as elsewhere, too little is being done about it.

7. In conclusion, let me apologize for acting toward you the way Smith did. But who am I to violate a long-standing academic tradition!

4

Executives as Human Beings

FERNANDO BARTOLOMÉ

Like most men, business executives have difficulty in showing tenderness toward the persons they love and in acknowledging any need for others. "It's difficult for me to express dependence," one businessman told the author of this article. "Feelings of dependence are identified with weakness or 'untoughness,' and our culture doesn't accept these things in men." The author's revealing interviews of 40 mid-career corporate officers and their wives throw light on the effects of masculine reticence and aloofness on their home life. He shows how cultural values (including the notion that the toughest men are the most successful), fear of losing others' respect, and the work environment inhibit men from openly expressing warmth or love toward others. Being able to deal with one's emotions is important to an executive who is in constant contact with people, the author says, and it is essential to becoming a more alive human being.

Since a human being's only possession is life, or rather living, the most fundamental question is, "How will I do my living?" So the search for a meaningful way of being alive should be a central aspect of life.

People should be free from stereotypes, self-imposed or otherwise, and rigid role definitions that limit their existence. The American male business executive is, in my opinion, a man caught in a stereotype. He is limited by a role definition obliging him to be super-masculine, super-tough, super-self-sufficient, and super-strong. It allows him very little freedom to be that mixture of strength and weakness, independence and dependence, toughness and tenderness which a human being is.

When one thinks of the executive's situation, several questions come to mind:

☐ How does he relate to himself, to others, and to the world?

☐ Does he conceive of different ways of living his life, different ways of relating to himself, to others, and to the world?

☐ Does he want to live his life differently? Is he tired of being the strong and reliable one, the one who is always on top of things?

The executive, I suspect, has great difficulty conceiving of alternative lifestyles in realistic terms. But only when he understands and is "tuned in" to these alternatives can he be in a position to choose his own lifestyle.

Not long ago I conducted a study dealing with these questions. At great length I interviewed 40 younger executives and their wives. The executives' average age was 37 and they had been married an average of 13 years. Nearly half (19) were employed by large or medium-sized companies, 5 by small companies; 7 were entrepreneurs, and 9 were managers of organizations other than business.

I tried to learn how the executive relates to himself, to others, and to the world; and I tried to understand why he lives the way he does. In this article I shall discuss what I learned and say what I think it means in terms of alternatives open to the executive.

In the study I tried to discover to what extent executives acknowledge to themselves their own feelings of dependence and tenderness and reveal those feelings at home. And I tried to establish connections between their behavior or "styles" at the office and at home. In general, I tried to discover the factors that influenced the degree to which these executives acknowledged to themselves their own feelings and disclosed or expressed them at home.

Under the label "feelings of dependence" I grouped a complex set of feelings. All of them relate to the experiencing of a temporary or permanent inability or insufficient capacity to cope alone with a situation or event, and the feeling (conscious or unconscious) of a need for outside help to deal with the phenomenon. When somebody fills that need—with love, money, cooperation, sympathy, companionship, or whatever—the one in need experiences a feeling of dependence on that person.

By "feelings of tenderness" I mean feelings of caring for, being moved by, loving, taking care of, or being involved with another human being. In other words, I mean all those emotions aroused when people allow themselves to be deeply touched by another person and, being touched, feels warmth toward the other.

Relevance to Executives

A human being should have the courage and the skill to become aware of feelings, to keep trying to learn how to deal with them, and to become free to choose how and when to express them. It would be good for the executive to increase this awareness, to develop those skills, and to gain that freedom.

Will this sensitivity and this skill improve his performance on the job? The executive's personal growth will improve his functioning in any area of human relations. Moreover, many organizational problems arise from people's inability to cope openly with emotions aroused in performance of their jobs. So, as the executive develops his capacity in private life to relate to his feelings and deal with them constructively, the greater is his capacity to deal with them in performing his executive functions.

If, however, the cultural environment is very rigid in its established behavioral patterns and highly resistant to change, not much individual self-exploration will take place. There are signs that the rigid cultural environment in the United States is breaking down. (More on this later.)

At any rate, the home milieu, because of its small size and private nature, is more flexible than the work milieu. So it is a more suitable place for a man to start exploring himself and trying new behavioral styles.

The failure of methods to improve the executive's performance in the area of relating to others at work is partly due to the erroneous assumption that we should focus our attention on his tasks and behavioral demands at work. In other words, try to improve the executive, not the man. This false dichotomy, executive/man, is the basis for many mistakes. When we do not directly address the man, we fail; and everything that we provide "the executive" so he can manage people better is a gimmick and will not last.

Therefore, I have chosen to relate to the executive as a man and to care about his growth as a human being. This growth will have a positive effect when the person is engaged in managerial functions.

Expression of Feeling

In the interviews I conducted, nearly all the men (36) described themselves as seldom experiencing feelings of dependence. While unable to confirm it, I believe they experienced these feelings more often than they acknowledged to themselves. Also, the great majority (32) admitted great reluctance to reveal to their wives their feelings of dependence when they experienced them.

"It's difficult for me to express dependence," said one executive. "Feelings of dependence are identified with weakness or 'untoughness' and our culture doesn't accept these things in men."

With respect to feelings of tenderness, the executives (with one or two exceptions) acknowledged having them often. Nevertheless, they recognized some difficulty in expressing them and great difficulty in fully experiencing and sharing these feelings.

Most of the men acknowledged that their expressions of tenderness were usually limited to members of their families, especially young children. And even displays of tenderness to their children, particularly boys, were inhibited by fear of "smothering" them or making them too dependent on their parents. "Doing things is more important than people," said one executive during an interview. "I want my children to learn to ski well. In skiing one only needs man and hill; nobody else is needed."

With few exceptions, the women I interviewed shared their husbands' reticence in expressing feelings and desire to encourage childrens' independence. The wife of the executive I just quoted said, "I'm trying to make my children stand on their own feet. I wouldn't express openly my affection for them because I don't want to smother them. I'm quite cold."

During the course of many hours of interviewing and many purely social occasions, I observed little physical contact between couples and their children, although the parents seemed to love them a lot.

To my surprise, I heard very few complaints on the part of husband or wife about the other's inability to express tenderness, even in those cases where I perceived displays of affection to be rather meager and not very rich in form.

Expression of tenderness to outsiders, including friends—especially a man's display of affection or even regard for a male friend—was very difficult for the men. One of them said, "I consider myself a sentimentalist and I think I am quite able to express my feelings. But the other day my wife described a friend of mine to some people as being my best friend and I felt embarrassed when I heard her say it."

On thinking about what these men and women had told me, I emerged with some ideas about the factors that seem to influence their expression of feelings of dependence and tenderness. They are cultural beliefs, fear of repercussions, and job characteristics. I shall discuss each in turn in the sections that follow.

Cultural Beliefs

All the persons I interviewed mentioned that the Anglo-Saxon culture discourages open and rich expression of emotion—any kind of emotion. Only the four couples of Irish extraction described themselves as experiencing less difficulty in expressing their feelings.

The men interviewed considered character traits such as strength, self-reliance, and "keeping a stiff upper lip" as both masculine and conducive to success. The picture of an executive one gets from one couple's remarks was typical.

Wife. *My husband is very self-reliant, secure, self-sufficient. He never expresses his needs.*

Husband. *At work one gets accustomed not to express dependence and one does the same at home. As a matter of fact, at work I never think in terms of asking for help or expressing my needs but rather in terms of making good use of the available human resources. When I get home, I don't want to talk about any big problem; I just want to rest.*

In contrast, the executives considered such characteristics as dependency, a need to be cared for, enjoyment of passive things, and tenderness as unmasculine and leading to failure—except for persons such as artists and "people of that kind." One gets a flavor of this point of view from what one executive said:

> I group my friends in two ways, those who have made it and don't complain and those who haven't made it. And only the latter spend time talking to their wives about their problems and how bad their boss is and all that. The ones who concentrate more on communicating with their wives and families are those who have realized that they aren't going to make it and therefore they have changed their focus of attention.
>
> The top executive really enjoys himself; he has the company plane and a lot of staff and has it easy. The ones who get the ulcers are those who are trying to get up there.

In some cases the men seemed to agree fully with the cultural beliefs and were intent on inculcating them and developing those culturally desirable characteristics in their children. In other cases, however, I saw indications that these men and women were becoming aware of the relative value of those cultural norms, and I got the impression that they had started to explore the worth of different value systems.

But even in those cases where the process of reevaluation had started on an intellectual level, the executives still appeared to be willing to conform to societal values even if they opposed them. Their conformity influenced what feelings they revealed to their wives and others.

The values of strength and self-reliance remained unquestioned, while the values of toughness and controlled expressiveness were starting to be reconsidered. Often I heard these couples criticize the excessive competitiveness of the American elementary and high school systems, while at the same time they indicated they valued highly the development of the child's strength by facing life without returning to ask for shelter. They wanted to make their children more sensitive but also strong and with equally big needs for high achievement.

With respect to themselves, they were quite conscious of the difficulty of abiding by the values they had adopted. But at the same time they seemed unable to move in another direction. An example of what I mean is their relationship with friends. Their restraint is typified by one executive's remark: "A very good friend of mine, a school roommate, came to visit and grabbed and hugged me. I felt very uncomfortable and awkward."

Many of the men acknowledged that they felt more affection, and with more intensity, than they were able to show, and they would like to express affection more fully. Yet none of them manifested any intention of exploring ways of establishing new and more open forms of relating to their friends and expressing their feelings to them.

Either/or Proposition

Some of the executives believed strongly that, in the conduct of life, you must be either dependent or independent, expressive or restrained in expression. As one of them put it:

> You can't express dependence when you feel it, because it's a kind of absolute. If you are loyal 90% of the time and disloyal 10%, would you be considered to be loyal? Well, the same happens with dependence: you are either dependent or independent; you can't be both.

They were educated to believe that you cannot develop "contradictory" traits at the same time—you cannot, for example, develop both artistic self-expression and manly self-restraint. This sounds very logical. Furthermore, this dichotomic educational philosophy attaches judgmental labels to character traits, considering some to be "good" and some to be "bad."

So it is no surprise that, having been educated in a system filled with either/or choices and having learned that in developing a character trait you have to do it at the expense of something else, most of these executives believe in the impossibility of being two things at once and having "conflicting" characteristics. Therefore they try to eliminate the "bad" tendencies in themselves—if they admit to them at all—and encourage their children to do the same.

Effects of Fear

Carl R. Rogers describes how "as experiences occur in the life of the individual they are either (a) symbolized, perceived, and organized into some relation to the self, (b) ignored, because there is no perceived relationship to the self-structure, (c) denied symbolization, or given a distorted symbolization, because the experience is inconsistent with the structure of the self."[1]

The desire to avoid or ignore experience which people unconsciously perceive as damaging to their concept of themselves appeared to be quite strong in the group of men I interviewed. They had difficulty in admitting or even thinking about the possibility that "opposing" feelings or characteristics could exist within them at the same time.

The "either/or" value system made it hard to accept as belonging to them those "bad" character traits that the culture condemns. According to Rogers' theory, when the organism encounters information about an experience that threatens the organism's need to view itself as consistent, it automatically sets up defense mechanisms to repress or distort the disturbing information.

Such a reaction could also be construed as a result of a person's natural inclination to adapt to the environment in order to avoid being hurt by it. One executive expressed this reaction in saying, "I know I'm inhibited, but when one has felt dependent many times in his life and has been rebuffed, he finally learns and becomes independent for reasons of security."

This statement implies that the process is conscious, but it actually seldom is. The person fears to acknowledge even to himself the existence of culturally defined negative characteristics that if recognized could trigger punitive action from his social environment.

Personal Relationships

Fear of injury in personal relationships appeared to be a significant factor in inhibiting the executives from fuller and more open expression of their feelings.

Most important was the fear of rejection—that is, if you let your defenses down and let somebody know the depth of your needs, he will not only fail to satisfy your needs but will also lose respect for you. As a consequence, you learn to "play it cool," as evidenced by this executive's remark: "You act out certain games or rituals to provoke the desired reaction in the other and have your needs satisfied without having to ask for anything."

The fear of rejection is closely related to the man's belief that it is his manliness that makes him attractive to his wife and motivates her to give him what he needs. The traits which the culture calls masculine are toughness, strength, self-sufficiency, and ability to succeed. Therefore, a man avoids expressing his needs, disclosing his dependence, or showing tenderness lest his wife think him a weakling and be "turned off" by him.

When a man thinks this way, it becomes easy for him to rationalize his reluctance to "open up" in any way to his wife. "I try to solve my problems by myself before asking for help," one executive asserted. "Anyway, what's the use of troubling my wife about my job problems when there's nothing she can do about them?"

When the husband expresses dependency, he is for the moment giving up any pretension of superiority or ability to control and determine the relationship. The husband who is engaged in a power struggle with his wife perceives such a temporary abdication as very risky. Here are the comments of one couple.

Husband. *If I express tenderness to my wife or let her get away with it in front of my friends, they give me hell. Besides, if you express tenderness and don't get it back, that's also a problem. And it's also a problem because you're always trying to have some authority at home and there is often competition with the wife about who wears the pants, and you can't afford to show dependence or tenderness when these other things are going on.*

Wife. *We compete all the time, for our friends' affection, for the children's affection, for authority at home, for everything!*

When such a power struggle is going on, a man's expression of dependence or tenderness to his wife is conditioned on her previous submission to him. She must already have abdicated her power some time ago.

Today women are reexamining the male-female relationship and trying to reclaim equal dignity and equal rights within the relationship. As they do, the issues of power and domination will become central; men, who have previously had the upper hand, will find themselves put increasingly on the defensive. In a defensive position men will tend to disclose less of their feelings of dependence and tenderness than they do now.

Eventually, new ground rules will be established, and, one hopes, women will be less constrained by a definition of what they should be and what their role in the marital relationship should be. In other words, they will gain for themselves the right and the freedom to become more fully themselves.

At the same time, men will be deprived of the unjust privileges that they have enjoyed until today at the expense of women. But they also will be liberated to some extent from the limitations that have been imposed on them by a narrow definition of the masculine role. This deprives them of their freedom to acknowledge their feelings to themselves and to enjoy and express them.

Harming the Child. Still another inhibiting factor for the executives was fear of hurting others, particularly their children.

Most of the parents considered themselves free to express physically and in other ways their feelings of tenderness to their children. Only a few recognized having difficulty doing it. However, my impression was that they were far from free in this regard; they seemed quite restrained in showing affection to their children. Their children also seemed to need affection shown to them more openly and frequently and more physically than they were getting it.

The parents' rationale was, as I mentioned earlier, their fear of smothering them, making them overdependent and weak, or violating their right to be independent.

The fear of harming the child by giving him "too much" affection is a wrong interpretation of the basic educational principle of respecting the child as an individual. Giving him love provides him with the confidence and strength to accept his own limitations and the fact of interdependence with other human beings. Acceptance of dependence as well as achievement of self-sufficiency is essential to the development of the mature person.

Job Characteristics

Most of the executives seemed quite satisfied with their work, though they complained that their jobs left too little time for family and other activities. Some of them were indeed putting in a lot of hours.

The consequences can be inhibiting for both husband and wife, as illustrated by the candid remarks of one couple.

> **Husband.** *A lot of executives are seduced by their jobs. They become fanatical about their jobs because they like the work and because their companies reward their fanaticism. But as a result they have very little time to be at home and talk about their feelings. When they come back home, there are a thousand things to do or take care of before they have time for themselves.*
>
> **Wife.** *When he goes away because of his job, I'm left alone and I have to take care of things. When he comes back, I resent him for abandoning me and it takes some time to unwind, to relax, and be able to feel and express tenderness.*

Those who seemed to be most involved in their work described how it took not only most of their time, but also nearly all of their energy. So when they returned home, they felt "drained" and able to communicate very little with their wives and children.

The competitive atmosphere, the premium placed on success, and the great value given to self-reliance on the job obviously affect the way an executive feels about himself when he leaves the office for home. And his attitude toward his performance affects his ability, once at home, to "unwind," let his needs be known, and accept affection from his family. As one wife put it:

> When they don't achieve what they think they should, they don't like themselves. And when they don't like themselves, how can they let others know them, how can they believe that others love them?

Restive Achievers

Most of the men I talked with seemed to have abandoned any romantic views they once had of their marriages. They had seen their marital relationships turn from being in love to loving each other. They had come to realize how marriages change, mature, and lose their original charm and intensity to become partnerships in living. The observation of one man reflected this pragmatic realization:

> It's much riskier to express tenderness and dependence when you're married because you can't interrupt the relationship. Therefore, if your needs are not satisfied or your tenderness is rejected—if the other person doesn't accept what you have to give, or doesn't fulfill your needs, or doesn't understand you and rejects you—there is very little you can do about it. You are rejected and yet you can't abandon the boat you share with the other person.

These men, being very competent and doing interesting work, I felt had learned to examine their jobs for rewards as important as those they received at home—for a sense of work accomplished, objectives achieved, and something built. In their jobs these men sought and often found their creativity, a limited transcendence, and sometimes a way of spending their lives without being aware of too much pain.

Why do they devote so much of their lives to their work and so little, comparatively speaking, to achieving awareness in living and experiencing their feelings? It seems to me there are two reasons:

1. While we train men to become "doers," to succeed in the world of action, we do not train them to explore the world of emotions. As the testimony of executives and their wives in this article has shown, feelings are to be controlled, channeled, repressed, or forced into acceptable molds. Not only are men told how they should express their feelings—big boys don't cry—they are also told what and how to feel.

In the world of business, feelings are considered a nuisance that must be coped with or a possible threat to the effective functioning of the organization. The research of Chris Argyris has amply demonstrated the practice in organizations of denial of feelings and the maneuvers of people in those organizations to avoid situations where emotions might come into play and to smooth over situations where deep emotions have been expressed.[2]

The result is a vicious circle: the less we recognize our feelings and learn to relate to them, the less chance we have of developing skills to deal with them—our own and others'. And the less skillful we are, the more threatening feelings seem, and the more vehemently we deny them or avoid dealing with them.

Men's lack of skill in relating to their feelings exists not only in the business milieu but also in the home environment and in their personal relationships. If you are skeptical of this, stop and think for a minute about the means that you have available to express your tenderness or your needs or your joy to your wife, children, and close friends. Then reflect on your ability to express richly these feelings to people who are close to you.

2. One always falls frustratingly short of gaining complete satisfaction of one's needs. In our personal relationships we often search, in vain, for somebody who will fulfill us completely, give us all we need.

On the other hand, at work we can complete something—reach our goal. (The goal being usually modest, achieving it may give us a sense of being let down—and perhaps we will feel the shadow of death that is present whenever anything ends.) For an instant we touched our work and it gave us a good feeling because we had created it.

So, men seem to learn to enjoy their achievements as they have learned to give up the search for "everything" in a relationship. Their more or less meaningful world of companionship and work is enough for them.

It should be kept in mind that executives are people with high achievement needs, and one of their characteristics is the desire to measure accurately and unambiguously the extent of their achievement. This is not difficult in the world of action, but indications of achievement in the unstable world of feelings and personal relationships are hard to perceive and measure.

It Begins at Home

As long as the man perceives the culture as standing ready to condemn him if he acts or feels in a manner counter to its norms and expectations, it is unlikely that he will explore new forms of behavior. So in trying to modify behavior we have to be concerned not only with the "unfreezing" and rearranging of the individual's value system and the development of courage and skills to implement his new values, but also with the unfreezing of his environment.

The environment at home, it seems to me, is already ripe for change. The younger generation insists on the validity of the emotions and wants to become "together" (a great cliché expressing the idea of a better balance of action and feeling, reason and sentiment, objectivity and fantasy). The home is the best place today for a member of the older generation to try exploring the world of feeling actively.

The next time you return home from work and see your son, stop for a second and try to get in touch with what you feel at that moment on seeing him. The feeling may be intense or weak, positive or negative, familiar or unfamiliar, painful or joyful—or to your surprise, you may seem to feel very little. Take it easy and try to stay with your feeling and experience it as fully as you can. Keep exploring your feelings at home and start trying new behavior there.

The executive is *a man relating to the world*. When he walks into his place of work, he is still himself. He should remain true to himself not only by doing but also by opening up his feelings as he lives.

Tomorrow, when you walk into your office and meet those you work with, take a minute to establish contact with your feelings or lack of feelings toward them. Try to become aware of how alive (or how numb) you are. If you discover that you have strong positive or negative feelings toward the men and women you work with, then ask yourself the simple questions that follow:

☐ What am I doing with these feelings?

☐ What do I want to do with them?

☐ How do they affect my living as a man and therefore as a man/executive?

In suggesting this, I am not talking to you as an executive, a manager, or a businessman. I am talking to you as a man—a man who can become a fuller, more alive human being.

The development of an ability to get in touch with and deal with one's own feelings and those of others, and to express one's feelings as richly as one wishes, is functional for any man and essential to an executive who has constant contact with other individuals.

But being able to get more closely in contact with our own feelings and engaging more deeply in experiencing and expressing them is not something that we can make happen overnight. It requires the development of difficult skills—skills to contact our feelings without being overwhelmed or scared by them, skills to cope with the feelings once we get in touch with them, skills to express our feelings when we want to, and skills to experience and express those feelings richly and confidently.

I have no method to offer for proceeding down this road, but I have found some of the suggestions of the Gestalt therapists very helpful in the process of owning more of one's self.[3]

The principal purpose of this article is not to offer solutions but to present the landscape of an exciting territory to explore: the land of our own feelings. I could try to incite you to explore this territory by saying that, when you know it better, you will have become a better administrator or a better father and husband. But nobody can guarantee you that.

All I can tell you is that in the process of getting more in touch with our own feelings, we become more fully ourselves and we live more fully the only thing we have, our own lives.

Notes

1. Carl R. Rogers, *Client-Centered Therapy* (Boston, Houghton Mifflin, 1951), p. 503.

2. See, for example, Chris Argyris, "Interpersonal Barriers to Decision Making," *HBR*, March–April 1966, p. 84.

3. Try the exercises suggested by Frederick Perls, Ralph F. Hefferline, and Paul Goodman in *Gestalt Therapy* (New York, Dell, 1951).

5
Must Success Cost So Much?

FERNANDO BARTOLOMÉ and PAUL A. LEE EVANS

Undeniably, many people who reach executive levels in organizations do so at the expense of their personal lives. They spend long hours at difficult and tension-filled jobs and retreat to their homes not for comfort and sustenance but for a place to hide or to vent feelings left over from a bad day at the office. Yet other executives who endure the same long hours and tension-filled jobs come home full of energy and excited by the day. What distinguishes the two groups of people? After studying more than 2,000 executives and interviewing many husbands and wives, these authors have found that, psychological differences aside, the executives who successfully cross the line from job to private life are able to do three things better than the other executives. They adapt well to change in jobs, they find the right jobs for them, and they handle career disappointments well. The authors discuss these sources of potential negative emotional spillover; then they investigate how organizations might minimize obstacles to coordinating one's private and professional lives.

A good number of executives accept the cliché that success always demands a price and that the price is usually deterioration of private life. This cliché does not always reflect reality, however—some executives seem to be exempt. What distinguishes the executives who pay a heavy personal price for their success from those who are able to maintain and develop fulfilling private lives?

Authors' Note. The ideas described in this article are the result of many hours of conversation with executives and their wives. Both of us are conducting research on the relationship between the professional and private lives of male executives; our extensive questionnaire has been completed by 700 international managers. The quotations are taken directly from interviews conducted with 44 executive couples in the United Kingdom and France and from exchanges with more than 2,000 executives of many different nationalities who attended executive development courses and seminars at the European Institute of Business Administration over a period of five years.

In studying the private and professional lives of more than 2,000 male managers for nearly five years, we've seen that some very successful executives have meaningful private lives. One thing that does *not* distinguish these executives is professional commitment. (To succeed, individuals have to give their jobs a high priority in their lives.) Nor is it easier for these executives to develop a private life. For everyone, it is difficult.

What *does* distinguish the two groups is this: The executives whose private lives deteriorate are subject to the negative effects of what we call emotional spillover; work consistently produces negative feelings that overflow into private life. In contrast, the other group of executives have learned to manage their work and careers so that negative emotional spillover is minimized, and thus they achieve a balance between their professional and private lives.

After countless exchanges with managers and their wives and after careful analysis of research data, we concluded that the major determinant of work's impact on private life is whether negative emotional feelings aroused at work spill over into family and leisure time. When an executive experiences worry, tension, fear, doubt, or stress intensely, he is not able to shake these feelings when he goes home, and they render him psychologically unavailable for a rich private life. The manager who is unhappy in his work has a limited chance of being happy at home—no matter how little time is spent traveling, how much time is spent at home, or frequency of vacations.

When individuals feel competent and satisfied in their work—not simply contented, but challenged in the right measure by what they are doing—negative spillover does not exist. During these periods executives are open to involvement in private life; they experience positive spillover. When work goes well, it can have the same effect as healthy physical exercise—instead of leading to fatigue, it is invigorating.

If things go right at work, a feeling of well-being places people in the right mood to relate to others. They open up, they are available, they may search for contact. That, of course, does not guarantee that such contact will be successful. A person may not be skillful at it, or there may be deep conflicts from the past that make contact difficult. But when the executive feels good at work, contact at home is at least possible.

We can summarize our findings this way: for an ambitious person, a well-functioning professional life is a necessary though not sufficient condition for a well-functioning private one.

For the time being, our study has focused on male managers only. We have not yet studied female executives, but our exchanges with some women and our reading of the literature on women managers lead us to believe strongly that the ideas we present apply to them as well.

The dilemmas and conflicts women face in trying to manage the relationship between their professional and private lives may be even more difficult than those faced by men. While in many cultures it is acceptable for men to specialize in their professional roles and delegate the main responsibility for private life to their wives, our impression is that even in the more liberal and advanced cultures the married woman who chooses to pursue a career is still expected to be responsible for the quality of the couple's private life.

Women are under more pressure to manage skillfully the boundaries between professional and private life. They are probably more aware of what causes the conflicts than many men. As increasing numbers of women join the work force, these issues are being more openly considered at work.

The Price Some Managers Pay

Even though we recognize that positive spillover exists, for the most part in this article we're going to be concerned with the negative emotions that spill over from work into executives' private lives. What are its sources? How can individuals manage it, and what can companies do to minimize the likelihood that people will suffer from it?

The experience of this 36-year-old manager typifies the spillover phenomenon: "When I started working for my boss four years ago, that affected my family life. He was very different from my previous boss. He was a bit of a tyrant. From working with someone who was terribly easygoing to someone who's an absolute dynamo—that certainly had an influence on my family life. It made me slightly—how can I put it? Well, I'd come home to my wife talking about him, about decisions he had reversed on a certain proposal I'd made. I'd talk it over with my wife, but I couldn't get it out of my mind, because it was such a different way of operating from my previous boss."

All of us have experienced spillover at one time or another in our careers. The problem is that some executives lead lifestyles that pave the way for never-ending spillover. Such an executive's wife is likely to react with this sort of comment: "What annoys me is when he comes home tense and exhausted. He flops into a chair and turns on the TV. Or else he worries, and it drives me up the wall."

Work spills over into private life in two ways: through fatigue and through emotional tension, like worry. Fatigue is the natural consequence of a hectic day at the office. But curiously enough, a hectic day—if it has gone well—can make us feel less worn out, often almost energetic. On the other hand, a boring day at the office, when the executive feels he has not accomplished anything, is exhausting. He comes home tired. Home is not a place for private life; it simply becomes a haven—a place to rest, relax, and recharge batteries to survive the next day.

Worrying, the other symptom of negative emotional spillover, is caused by frustration, self-doubt, and unfinished business. One wife puts it this way:

"Yes, his mind is often on other things. Yes, he often worries and it *does* disturb the family life. When he is like that he can't stand the noise of the children. . . . He can't stand the fact that the children are tired. In general we have dinner together so that he can be with them. And obviously they chatter, they spill things, they tease each other—and he blows his top. He is tense and uptight—it's disturbing; I can't stand it. I have to try to mediate between them and cool things down. The only thing is to finish everything as soon as possible and get everyone quickly off to bed."

The feelings that spill over from work are acted out at home. Sometimes they are expressed through psychological absence, sometimes through acts of aggression. One loses one's temper with the children. One explodes in fury if one's wife makes a minor mistake. Such aggression is visible and painful, but withdrawal is equally damaging to family relationships. As one wife said:

"My husband is not one of those men who vents all his frustrations on the family. One cannot reproach him for being aggressive or for beating his wife. Instead he closes up like a shell. Total closure. The time he thinks he spends here isn't spent here."

Because psychological withdrawal can make a person blind to what is going on at home, it can have very serious consequences. A 40-year-old executive described the most painful period of his marriage this way:

> It was just after the birth of the third child, eight years ago. The birth coincided with a move to another part of the country and with a complete change in job. And there I have to admit that I was completely unaware of the consequences that all this had for my wife. She was overloaded with work and worries. It went on for some time, and I just wasn't aware of what was happening. Finally she fell ill and had to be hospitalized. It was only then that it began to dawn on me. I was quite unconscious of everything I was doing.
>
> *You were overloaded in your work?*
>
> Yes. Well, not really overloaded. I was worried about my work. I didn't feel very sure of myself and so was very worried. . . . It was the time of a merger between two companies and a period of great uncertainty. That had led to my new job and the move. And I just couldn't get my work out of my mind. I think back even today—the uncertainties of the time were real. It was normal, but anyway I couldn't get the work out of my mind. Today I'm much more sure of myself. I find it a lot easier to switch off.

When negative emotions spill over, managers often express dissatisfaction with their lifestyles and complain of wanting more time for private life. But because their minds are numbed by tension, these people cannot use even their available time in a fulfilling way. Some report needing a double martini just to summon the energy to switch on the television. Many read the newspaper, not because they're interested in world events, but to escape into personal privacy. Some mooch around in the basement or the garden as a way of just getting through the day.

Again and again, the wives of these executives express the same idea: "I don't really mind the amount of work he has to do. That is, if he is happy in his work. What I resent is the unhappiness that he brings home."

Or sometimes they agree with this 42-year-old wife: "The very best moment in our marriage is, without any doubt, right now. We have never before had such a complete life together. The children are interesting to my husband and he is very happy with his work. On the other hand, the most difficult moments have been when he wasn't happy with what he was doing."

Managing Spillover

To have a healthy private life, one must manage the negative emotions that arise at work. When we began our investigation into the work lives and private lives of managers five years ago, we held the biased belief that these two sides of life are in fundamental conflict with each other. During these five years we have gathered more and more evidence suggesting that, among managers at least, individual and organizational interests can be in harmony. Moreover, a healthy professional life is a precondition for a healthy private one.

Job and home can be in harmony and mutually reinforce each other if—and only if—one avoids various pitfalls in the management of self and career and one copes satisfactorily with the emotions that arise at work. Conversely, executives who fail to manage the emotional side of work achieve professional success at the expense of private life.

Let's look now at what the executive can do to manage the emotional side of work better. We single out three major causes of negative emotional spillover: the problems of adapting to a new job, the lack of fit between a person and the job, and career disappointments.

Coping With a New Job

Without doubt, the most common trigger of spillover tension is the process of settling into a new job following promotion, reorganization, or a move to another company. Since all of us change jobs from time to time, we all experience spillover caused by the problems of adaptation. Having to familiarize ourselves with a new task, learn to work with new people, settle in a different town and environment, and establish new relationships with superiors, subordinates, and peers—all at the same time—overloads our emotional systems.

That work dominates the emotional life of a person adapting to a new job is natural and necessary. It allows him to master major changes. Once that is done, the spillover effects begin to fade away.

What is vital is that the individual assess and recognize how important the job change is to both the individual and the individual's family. The more new skills the job requires and the more radical the change in environment, the longer the adaptation period is likely to be and the longer the negative spillover is likely to last. To deny this reality in an attempt to persuade a reluctant family that the job change will also be good for them is risky.

Top managers often fail to assess correctly the magnitude of the changes and adaptations they ask of executives and their families. Often individual executives, driven by their own ambition, also fail to assess accurately the difficulty of tasks they accept. Only a realistic evaluation of the degree of change executives and their families will face allows them to come through the process of adaptation relatively unscathed.

In talking to executive couples, we have found too often the case of the ambitious executive who accepted an exciting job in a developing country that sounded like a wonderful opportunity and a major career step. His wife was unhappy about it, but there was no heart-to-heart discussion about the decision. The wife felt that her husband's mind was made up and was reluctant to hold him back. Her fears were half-assuaged by his assurances that the move would be challenging and exciting and that he would be there to help out. They moved.

What executives do not realize is that the change to a new and important job, to a new locale, and to a new culture will create massive amounts of tension. The negative spillover into private life will be immense. For a year or more, they will have minimal psychological availability for private life. If their wives expect and need that availability, its absence will aggravate the adaptation problems that they are undergoing themselves. Far too often, the story ends catastrophically for all concerned.

And yet it doesn't need to happen this way. We have heard executives describe enthusiastically how similar moves brought their families together and how dealing with the difficulties of adaptation as a family was a most positive experience.

What accounts for the difference in experiences? These latter executives analyzed the change carefully with their families before the move, negotiated the decision with them, openly expressed the problems they would all confront, and did not promise what they could not deliver.

Most wives will understand and accept that for some time their husbands will be preoccupied with the job and won't be readily available. If they recognize this in advance and as long as they know that emotional spillover will fade away, they may even support him at this difficult time. But sometimes spillover does not fade away. The new job turns out to be beyond the person's talents or capacities.

If after a reasonable period of time—say, one year—negative spillover is increasing rather than fading away, a misfit situation (where the only way of mastering the job is through sheer brute energy rather than skill) could be in the making. Because wives experience the spillover consequences directly, they are good judges as to whether it is increasing or decreasing. If it's increasing, the time has come to negotiate a move out.

Taking the Right Job

The lack of fit between an individual and a job is the second most common source of negative spillover. Judgments on the "shape" of people and jobs are difficult to make; square pegs are often put in round holes. Top managers may overemphasize skills and experience while ignoring the very important factors of personality and individual goals. Consider the experiences of Jack and Melinda:

Three years ago, Jack was a computer company's research manager, content in his job and very ambitious. Top management offered him a promotion to a job as manager of administrative services. While at first Jack didn't like the position offered him, management persuaded him to accept it by arguing that it would be an important step in his career development. Since Jack's ambition was to become research director, the argument seemed logical. The new job would give him administrative experience that would help qualify him for the post he wanted. Jack accepted the job.

Jack has already spent three years in this job, yet spillover tension is not on the wane. On the contrary, during the past three years it has increased steadily and is now an almost inextricable part of his life. But while he is hurting, his wife Melinda and his two children are hurting even more.

Melinda talks of how Jack has brought nothing but sadness and tension into the family's life since he undertook his new job. Since then, she says, "He hasn't even been interested in talking about our problems." In fact, she has often considered divorce.

For his part, Jack finds it difficult to say anything positive about his job. "You meet interesting people and a wide variety of situations," he says, "but one part of the work consists of acting as the office boy to deal with everyone's banal problems." The other part consists of negotiating with trade union officials on grievances, a duty that Jack finds tiring and frustrating. "You have no authority over anyone," he says, "and what I didn't realize at the beginning is that one doesn't have any real contact with the people in research."

The tension and doubt that Jack feels—and which his wife experiences even more strongly—are growing. At the end of a two-hour interview, he spoke of the feeling of being trapped: "I'm not really content in this job, but if I do well it will help me in my next job in research. It's a thankless task, being at everybody's beck and call. The trouble is that it's getting to me. I can't take the strain much longer. I went to my boss last month and told him that I want to move back to research. He told me that they would take care of that in due time, that I was doing a grand job now, and that they needed me here.

"The trouble is—did he really mean it that I was doing a grand job? I feel that things can only go downhill from here. And I'm drifting further and further away from research."

Lack of Fit

Jack is a misfit. However valid or invalid his reasons for accepting his present job, the work does not suit his personality. It makes him permanently tense without satisfying him. Yet because he took the job as a "stepping stone," he *must* perform.

Lacking deep interest and natural skill for the work, the misfit can only compensate with an overinvestment of energy. This investment may lead to success—but at the price of enormous internal tension, reinforced fear of failure, and the suspension of an investment in private life.

Tension and deep fear of failure are the natural consequences of going against one's grain. People who take jobs for which they are ill-fitted are often afraid that their weaknesses will show, that they will be found out. These inner doubts can be so intense that no amount of external recognition or acknowledgment of success can eliminate them.

For misfits the ultimate irony is that, instead of decreasing with each new success, fear of failure increases. Outward success does not reassure them. Instead, their successes trap them in jobs they do not enjoy. With their bridges burned behind them, they feel snared in situations that create permanent and increasing tension.

Let us define what we mean by the fit between individual and job. A perfect fit occurs when you experience three positive feelings at the same time: you feel competent, you enjoy the work, and you feel that your work and your moral values coincide. To express this in another way, a job should fit not only with skills and abilities but also with motives and values.

A misfit situation occurs whenever one of these three conditions is absent. In the case of the *total misfit,* none of the conditions is fulfilled: he is not particularly competent at what he does, he enjoys few aspects of his work, and he feels ashamed doing things that go against his values or ideals. Jack, the manager we just described, is an example.

Absence of Skill. The *competence misfit* enjoys his work and is proud of what he does. He works hard enough to keep his job, but he is not sure of his ability to really master the work. For example, a manager in a line position may find it difficult to make decisions, or someone taking a personnel administrator's job hoping to broaden his skills may not work well with people. For the time being, those executives may manage well, but they live with the persistent fear that things will get out of hand. This sense of insecurity tends to diminish their enjoyment of the job and spills over into their private lives.

This "competence misfit" most typically happens to people in the early stages of their careers, when they haven't yet found out what they are good at doing. It is the type of misfit that organizations are most sensitive to, which they try hardest to avoid. But two other kinds of misfit, which most organizations fail to recognize, are equally important. We call them the "enjoyment misfit" and the "moral misfit."

Dislike for the Job. An *enjoyment misfit* occurs when an individual is competent at his job and proud of doing it but does not like it. One executive had the necessary qualities to be a manager and was promoted to a managerial job even though he would have rather remained in a technical position. Despite his preference for individual challenge over the laborious process of working through other people, he succumbed to a sense of duty and to unanimous pressure and accepted the job. He is unhappy in his new job and consequently suffers from negative spillover.

The most frequent cause of "enjoyment misfit" is intrinsic dislike of various work characteristics, but other causes are common as well. Staying in a job for too long can transform enjoyment into boredom; persons can be competent but see what they do as predictable variations of a humdrum theme. Having too much work to do can also destroy enjoyment: some people, finding it very difficult to say no to challenges and tasks they enjoy doing, agree to do too much. The consequent stress gradually erodes the intrinsic pleasure of the tasks.

Different Values. The last type of misfit, *moral misfit,* results when individuals enjoy their work and are competent but do not feel proud of what they do, when they feel they compromise their values. A sales manager we met, for example, was good at his job, but he did not believe in the merits of the product he was selling. He would not have bought it himself and could not wholeheartedly recommend it to others. He used to reassure himself by saying that "as long as there is a market for it, it must be O.K." After a successful and important sale, rather than feeling proud of himself he would come out feeling "thank goodness that's over."

The negative spillover created by going along with unethical business practices (such as bribing foreign officials) has two additional painful twists to it. The person fears potential legal consequences, and he cannot vent his feelings by expressing them to others because the position dictates secrecy.

Each of these ways of not fitting a job is dangerous. If individuals accept tasks for which they lack the competence, they risk feeling continual self-doubt. If they accept jobs for which they are skilled but which they do not like doing, they will be bored. If they accept jobs in which they do not feel pride, they will not feel at peace with themselves.

The incompetent misfit may be the only type of misfit the organization is able to spot; whatever the cause of the misfit, however, the individuals and their families will suffer. For an individual in top management to avoid putting the wrong person in the wrong job, it is essential to understand what causes some of the mistakes.

Why People Take the Wrong Job

We find four main reasons why people are in the wrong jobs: the strong attraction of external rewards, organizational pressure, inability to say no, and lack of self-knowledge or self-assessment. Let's examine each one of these issues in turn.

External Rewards. We all like and need money and have some healthy needs for status and recognition as well. But because in our Western society having these things implies that one is a "good" person, we sometimes put too much value on them. As a result, many people end up doing what will bring rewards rather than what fits them. They are seen as good members of society but don't feel good about themselves.

Executives we spoke with often justified accepting jobs they didn't really want on the ground that the material rewards the jobs provided were essential to realizing a fulfilling private life. They fail to realize (except in hindsight) that no matter how much they earn, no matter how much status is attached to the position, their private lives will suffer through emotional spillover if the job doesn't fit them.

Organizational Pressures. When management approaches an individual in the organization or outside it to offer a job, in most cases it does so after carefully analyzing available candidates. The person chosen is usually the one management deems most competent for the job.

But management pays little if any attention to the two other dimensions of fit—the person's enjoyment of and pride in the job. If it assesses these dimensions at all, management will often dismiss any problem as an individual or personal concern. A person's capacity to do the job well is all that counts. Some managers assume that if the person believes there is no self-enjoyment or pride in the job, then the person will say no; some also assume that if the person doesn't say no, the personal issues don't exist.

But here is the problem. When management reaches its final decision and offers the person the promotion or the new job, the applicant is no longer simply a candidate for that job. Management has made a statement that it has found the best person available. To refuse is to deny management what it wants. Of course, the person is free to say no on emotional grounds, but the pressures to accept are considerable, blunting that freedom.

Management often adopts a selling attitude that manifests itself in a variety of ways. The rewards and incentives are expressively described, the fact that this is a "unique opportunity" is stressed, and the argument that "this will be good for your career" is emphasized. If the individual points out a personal lack of some of the necessary skills for the job, management is likely to say that this is "an exceptional opportunity to develop such skills," expressing vague doubts about the future otherwise. At the end of the process, management often brings the ultimate pressure to bear. It makes it clear that a decision has to be reached quickly, that an answer is expected "let's say, in 72 hours."

By this time many executives will have succumbed to the appeal of external rewards or to the fear of saying no or of showing hesitation. Nevertheless, the best of them will indeed insist on enough time to analyze as thoroughly as possible the intrinsic characteristics of the job and the extent to which it fits them.

These people are deeply aware that their decisions will influence not only every working hour in the years ahead but also every hour of their private lives. And these are the people most likely to avoid becoming misfits and suffering from massive spillover. In most cases, their attitudes are reinforced by a real concern for their families and a deep understanding of the impact that changing jobs may have on them.

Above all, such executives realize that they hold the main responsibility for managing their careers and are unwilling to transfer that responsibility to anybody else.

The Ability to Say No. If learning to ask for sufficient time to think over accepting a job is difficult, learning to say no is even more difficult, particularly in times of economic crisis.

Learning to say no requires, first of all, the ability to estimate realistically the consequences of refusal. Many people assume fearsome consequences that they often are too afraid to test. But one also has to estimate realistically the negative effects of acceptance. Executives we spoke to mentioned they had sometimes made the decision easier by minimizing the difficulties they would face.

Ability to assess consequences realistically is one of the characteristics of highly successful people. They can do this because they have the final and most important quality of people who want to avoid spillover—namely, self-knowledge and the ability to assess themselves accurately.

Self-Assessment. Much of our behavior is rooted in unconscious motives, and it is difficult to know that part of ourselves. Also, as we age we are continually changing and acquiring new experiences. So, even under the best of circumstances, to assess whether one will fit with a new job is difficult.

Self-assessment implies that one can accurately recognize one's competences—acknowledging limitations as well as strengths, identifying what brings pleasure or pain, and knowing what elicits pride or guilt in different work situations. It requires admitting to feelings rather than masking them.

The raw data for self-assessment are past experiences. Because of limited experiences, the task is especially difficult for the younger manager. During one's 20s and early 30s, the only way to assess oneself is to take different jobs in different companies to find out what kind of work one does best, enjoys most, and finds most meaningful. Our research indicates that foreclosing this phase of exploration too quickly may have negative consequences later in one's career.[1]

This exploration, however, does not need to be a blind process. Under ideal circumstances, a mentor successfully guides the younger person in the trial and error stages of his career. The mentor—an older, experienced, and trusted guide (often a boss with whom one enjoys an open and special relationship)—does more than simply provide new challenges and experiences. This mentor also helps the younger manager learn from those experiences what his skills, needs, and values are, and thus speeds up the process of self-assessment.

No matter how well this process of starting one's own career and finding one's professional identity goes, the individual will suffer from considerable tension and stress. Managers at this stage in life are predominantly oriented toward launching their careers, and emotional spillover often pervades private life.

After such a period of exploration and with better knowledge of themselves, some individuals in their mid-30s eventually find jobs or positions that fit them in the three dimensions outlined earlier. The young person assessing a job asks above all "Can I do it?" But the more mature person asks two other questions as well: "Will I enjoy doing it?" and "Is it worth doing?" The mature person is likely to accept the job only if all three answers are positive.

People at this stage in their careers turn more toward their private lives. They are no longer content simply with the competence fit. They aim for total fit that ensures minimal spillover and full availability for private life. They can achieve this if they have developed sufficient self-knowledge to guide their careers. This knowledge will also allow them, after having benefited from a mentor in their early careers, to become mentors themselves.[2]

For some people, self-knowledge grows with experience, and consequently they are able to manage their careers and avoid spillover. Others, however, fail to learn from experience and as a result are likely to suffer from the third main cause of spillover—namely, career disappointment.

Learning From Disappointments

Prevention is better than cure. Individuals skilled at self-assessment run a smaller risk not only of finding themselves in the wrong job but also of suffering serious disappointments. But all of us face disappointment at one time or another in our careers. It can have immense psychological impact, especially if work is an important part of our lives.

The most frequent type of disappointment that we have found in our research is experienced by the older manager whose career flattens out below the level the manager expected to reach. This recognition of having plateaued comes more or less consciously. Individual signals of the end—a turned-down promotion, a merit raise refused, a bad appraisal, or a shuffling aside in a reorganization—are bitter blows.

When deeply hurt, most of us will automatically react in a defensive way. While some individuals can eventually react healthily and learn from a painful experience, many become disillusioned and turn into bitter, plateaued performers. Often such executives disengage from activity. Abraham Zaleznik suggests that two things are necessary to cope well with disappointment: the ability "to become intimately acquainted with one's own emotional reactions" and the capacity to "face the disappointment squarely." And, he adds, "The temptation and the psychology of individual response to disappointment is to avoid the pain of self-examination. If an avoidance pattern sets in, the individual will pay dearly for it later."[3] In all cases, the danger is distortion of reality.

In our contacts with executives, we have found ample confirmation of Zaleznik's observations. It is indeed difficult for people to face disappointment squarely. The experience often triggers in them strong feelings of loss that they turn into anger against themselves, which sometimes manifests itself as depression or withdrawal. But people cope with such situations in diverse ways. After a short period of mourning their losses, some bounce back (having learned something) and adapt successfully; others get permanently stuck in bitter and self-destructive positions.

Those who do not recover from severe disappointment often find themselves stuck in no-exit jobs that they do not enjoy and are not particularly proud of. They find it difficult to accept that their careers have plateaued in this way. They feel cheated. The emotional tension of an unenjoyable job, now aggravated by bitterness, often spills over into their home lives, where everyone else also pays for their sense of failure. Private life, as well as professional life, becomes hollow and empty. The injury to self-esteem they received in the professional world seems to color their whole experience of life.

Other plateaued managers recover their enthusiasm for their professional and private lives in a constructive way. They may compensate for their disappointment by enriching their present jobs—for example, adopting a role as mentor.

Often this positive compensation comes through developing leisure activities. These activities have, however, a professional quality to them rather than being mere relaxation. One man transformed his hobby of riding into a weekend riding school. Another got involved in community activities. A third broadened his home redecorating pastime into buying, redoing, and selling old houses. In these examples, work became more meaningful in that it helped to finance an active leisure interest; family life benefited since the man recovered his sense of self-esteem.

We can add a nuance to Freud's idea that the main sources of self-esteem and pleasure in an individual's life are work and love. Failure at work cannot be fully compensated by success in love. Failure at work has to be compensated by success in worklike activities. Only when work and love coexist in parallel and appropriate proportions do we achieve happiness and fulfillment.

What Organizations Can Do

We have suggested that the main responsibility for managing a career, reducing negative spillover, and achieving a good balance between professional and private life lies with the individual executive. It makes more sense for individuals to feel responsible for managing their own professional lives (taking care that career does not destroy private life) than to expect the organization to do this for them. Management in organizations, however, bears the responsibility for practices and policies that may make it unnecessarily difficult for the individual executive to manage the relationship between his professional and private lives. We see four things top managers can do to reduce the work pressures.

Broaden Organizational Values

Our first recommendation to managers is likely to be the most heretical. Managers can help their people by encouraging them not to be devoted solely to career success. Many managers attach too high a value to effort, drive, dedication, dynamism, and energy. Managers often take long hours at work and apparent single-minded dedication to professional success as indicators of drive and ambition. Attachment to private life and efforts to protect it by working "only" 45 hours a week are interpreted as signs of weakness in today's middle aged; in younger managers, this pattern signifies an erosion of the work ethic, a symptom of what is wrong with the younger generation.

We find little evidence in our research, however, of an erosion of the work ethic among younger managers. Their professional commitment is strong, but it represents a commitment to what interests them rather than a blind commitment to their companies. They resist simply doing what has to be done and conforming to organizational practices, even if they are compensated by incentives. They are aware that a lot of office time is wasted by engaging in ritualistic, nonproductive "work" and that few people make a real success of activities that fail to excite and interest them. Above all they appreciate that the quality of an individual's work life has an enormous impact, positive or negative, on his private life.

Paradoxically, organizations do not necessarily work better when they are full of highly ambitious, career-centered individuals striving to get to the top. As a matter of fact, these "jungle fighters" are often ostracized by their colleagues and superiors because they have too much ambition and too little ability to work with others. What organizations ideally need are a few ambitious and talented high achievers (who fit with their jobs) and a majority of balanced, less ambitious but conscientious people more interested in doing a good job that they enjoy and are adequately rewarded for than in climbing the organizational pyramid.

Organizational practices that overvalue effort and climbing and undervalue pride in one's job and good performance are counterproductive. Economic recessions in years to come will make this even more apparent.

As the growth rates of organizations stabilize, the possibilities for advancement and promotion will diminish. People will be productive only if they enjoy the intrinsic value of what they are doing and if they draw their satisfaction simultaneously from two sources—work and private life—instead of one.

Create Multiple Reward and Career Ladders

Since external rewards often pressure people into accepting jobs they don't fit, our second recommendation concerns the reward policies and ladders of organizations.

The reward ladder of most organizations is a very simple, one-dimensional hierarchy; the higher, the more "managerial" one is, the more one is rewarded. People come to equate success with the managerial ladder, which would be appropriate if skilled managerial people were the only skilled people we need. But this is far from the case. Most organizations have relatively few general managerial positions and, while these are important posts, the life blood of the company is provided by people who fit with their jobs in other ways. To encourage these people, reward ladders need to be far more differentiated than they are at present.

Edgar H. Schein shows how managers fit with their work and careers in at least five different ways that he calls "career anchors."[4] While some people indeed have managerial anchors (i.e., they aspire to positions in general management), others are oriented toward expertise in a technical or functional area. A desire to be creative is the central motive in the careers of a third group. (And do we not need more entrepreneurs in our large organizations today?) The fourth and fifth groups are anchored in needs for security and autonomy, respectively.

The obvious implication is that organizations must create multiple career and reward ladders to develop the different types of people required for their operations. Some high technology companies that rely heavily on technical innovation have indeed experimented with offering both managerial and technical reward ladders. In the future, we will probably see the development of reward ladders that reinforce creativity and entrepreneurship as well.

The problem with the simple structures of many organizations is that they channel ambition and talent in only one direction, creating unnecessary conflict for the many individuals who are ambitious or talented but do not walk the single prescribed path. We can warn individuals against being blinded by ambition to the emotional aspects of fit; yet we must also warn organizations, not against fostering ambition, but against channeling it into a single career path.

Give Realistic Performance Appraisals

Our third recommendation is that managers help individuals in their own self-assessment, thus reducing the chances that they will either move into positions that do not fit them or be promoted to their "Peter Principle" level of incompetence. To do this, managers need to pay greater attention to their subordinates' performances and also to be honest in discussions of the subordinates' strengths and weaknesses. Managers should also encourage self-assessment. Contrary to standard assessment practices that only emphasize skills and competence, self-assessment should focus as well on the extent to which the individual enjoys his job—both as a whole and in its component parts.

Many researchers have called for accurate and realistic feedback in performance appraisal.[5] We also ask that managers be as concerned and realistic about enjoyment and value as about competence.

Of all managerial omissions, lack of candor about a subordinate's chances for promotion can be most destructive. At one time or another, to one degree or another, most managers have agonized over trying to motivate individuals with the lure of promotion while knowing that these individuals do not have much of a chance. Candor may result in employees' short-term unhappiness and even in their leaving the company, but we suggest that the long-run effects of dissembling are far worse. Eventually truth will out, and the negative effects of disappointment are likely to harm not only the individuals' performance at work but also, through the spillover effect, their private lives—at a time when perhaps it's too late for them to change jobs.

Reduce Organizational Uncertainty

Uncertainty is an increasingly frequent fixture of today's world. Sudden, unpredictable events—like an oil shortage or the taking of hostages in Iran—can have massive impact on the lives of managers in Dallas, Paris, or Bogotá. Economic recession lurks in the background, and no one feels entirely safe. The jobless executive next door makes many a manager aware that "it could also happen to me." Reorganization and restructuring of companies have become almost annual events; and sudden policy changes have vast repercussions on people's lives that create worries and preoccupations and lead to emotional spillover.

Managers can help reduce unnecessary stress and uncertainty by protecting their subordinates from worry about events over which they have no control. A good example of this is the young manager of a foreign exchange department in a large bank. It is difficult to imagine a more uncertain, hectic, anxiety-ridden job. When we asked him how he managed, he answered: "I protect my subordinates and I trust them. When my superiors drop by to tell us how stupid what we did yesterday was and ask who did it, I tell them that it's none of their business. I offer them my job if they want it. That shuts them up quite fast."

We asked him how he could trust his subordinates in a department that could lose millions in a day. He answered: "I trust them because I have to. And I have learned to show them that I trust them by leaving them alone to do their jobs and helping them only when they ask for help."

Here we have a "shock-absorbing" manager. However, the price for his courage is enormous. He absorbs a lot of the anxiety around him, acting as a buffer against many pressures. He has an ulcer and no nails, but his subordinates love him.

Top managers cannot expect to have many people like this in their ranks. But they clearly need people who can absorb as many shocks for others as possible. And they owe it to such people to relieve them from positions where uncertainty is too high by systematically rotating these jobs after a certain time. People can protect others from uncertainty and anxiety (to some extent this is part of a manager's job), but only for so long.

Whose Life Is It Anyway?

In managerial circles, there's something almost sacred about the separation between private and professional life. The respect for an individual's privacy is one of our fundamental values. However, no one can deny that work has a powerful effect on private life. The issue is where does responsible behavior stop and where does interference begin?

The individual executive adheres to the principle that his private life is none of the organization's business. But today he does expect the organization asking him to accept a big new job in Latin America to consider as legitimate his concerns about, say, his three children and his wife with her own career. In the interest of his future performance, the corporation is well advised to listen and respond to his concerns.

We do not need to invoke altruism to recommend that organizations make sure their people are in jobs that fit them, that they can cope with the changes the organization may ask of them, and that they have the tools for realistic self-assessment. Doing this is essential to the morale and productivity of the organization.

Responsible behavior on the part of the organization is simply behavior that is in its own best interest. This means recognizing the emotional aspects of work and career. A person's capacity to enjoy doing a job is as important a consideration as potential competence.

Even if organizations choose not to deal with these issues, the changing values and lifestyles of younger managers—especially those in dual-career marriages—may eventually force top management to face the impact work has on private life.

Notes

1. See Fernando Bartolomé and Paul A. Lee Evans, "Professional Lives Versus Private Lives—Shifting Patterns of Managerial Commitment," *Organizational Dynamics*, Spring 1979, p. 2.

2. Ibid.

3. Abraham Zaleznik, ''Management of Disappointment,'' *HBR*, November–December 1967, p. 59.

4. Edgar H. Schein, *Career Dynamics* (Reading, Mass., Addison-Wesley, 1978).

5. See, for example, Harry Levinson, ''Emotional Health in the World of Work'' in *Management by Guilt* (New York, Harper & Row, 1964), pp. 267–291.

6

Everyone Who Makes It Has a Mentor

Interviews with F. J. LUNDING, G. L. CLEMENTS, and D. S. PERKINS

In 1931 John Hancock, chairman of Jewel Tea Company, hired a young lawyer, Franklin J. Lunding, to negotiate the acquisition of some food stores in Chicago. By 1942, Lunding was president of Jewel Tea Co. Inc. He was only 36 years old. Like Hancock, Lunding also needed help running the food stores, so he appointed the young office manager, George L. Clements, to be assistant to the president. By 1951, Clements was president, and he was 41 years old. In 1953, in an effort to bring new blood into the organization, Lunding hired Donald S. Perkins as a trainee. With the far-sighted guidance of both Lunding and Clements, Perkins became president of the Jewel Companies in 1965, when he was 37 years old. Perkins is now chairman and chief executive officer. That simple fact epitomizes what is now a Jewel tradition; young people shall be given their heads, to challenge the organization to grow. These young people will also have an older person in the organization to look after them in their early years to ensure that their careers get off to a good start. Out of these relationships it is hoped that young people learn to take risks, accept a philosophical commitment to sharing, and learn to relate to people in an intuitive, empathetic way. In Abraham Zaleznik's terms (see *HBR*, July–August, 1977) these mentor relationships develop leaders. In the interviews that follow, we discussed some of these issues with Messrs. Lunding, Clements, and Perkins to discover how these men affected each other's lives, and ultimately how the imprints of their personalities and relationships can be seen in the strategies and policies of the Jewel Companies.

These interviews were conducted and edited by Eliza G. C. Collins, senior editor, and Patricia Scott, manuscript editor, *HBR*.

Franklin J. Lunding

Was there anyone in your background who gave you the idea that to give young people responsibility early is the way to help them grow in a business?

For instance, did John Hancock (chairman of Jewel Tea, 1924–1954) do anything for you when you were a young man?

Yes he did. He recommended me as general counsel of this company in 1931 when I was only 25 years old. I came out here to Chicago, and the first thing I had to do was buy a group of food stores. I handled that negotiation, the contract, and the whole works myself.

How did Hancock know you?

I knew Hancock because his daughter was in my class at the University of North Dakota. He was always interested in young people. Maybe that's one of the reasons I developed somewhat the same interest. Although we were very different people, we got along fine. He stayed on in the business, as chairman of the board. That was fine with me; I was still running it.

Did you feel that you got a sense of confidence from Hancock's choosing you?

No, I never thought about it. I didn't have any feeling that I couldn't do things. I was brought up in the country, in North Dakota, where my father was a farm implement dealer. My parents were both immigrants, one from Norway, one from Sweden. My four sisters and I, immigrants' children, all got through college and some professional schools. But we did it on our own.

Between my freshman and sophomore years, that would be 1924, I went as an immigrant with a bicycle and about three dollars in my pocket to Mossbank, Saskatchewan to sell books to farmers. I started riding on my bike from farm to farm on those country roads selling books—"12 courses on agriculture, 11,200 simple practical ideas all indexed." You get used to doing things for yourself.

So by the time you got to Jewel Tea with Hancock and Maurice Karker (president 1924–1942), you had nothing to lose by accepting the challenge and running the business?

No, in fact I liked it. By 1934 I was assistant to the president, Karker, and then in 1937, merchandise manager, in effect running things in our Food Stores.

Did Hancock leave you alone or was there a lot of coaching in your relationship?

I did things my way. Of course, that might have been his way for all I knew. I would call him up and tell him I was going to do something, and he'd usually say, "That's fine."

You felt you could challenge Hancock and Karker's judgment and experience?

There was no need. I was responsible for the business. I used my own judgment and they understood that. For instance, in 1938 the Food Stores were failing and the meat markets were really losing money. I had an experienced meat man, but every time I'd reduce prices to get more sales, he'd go out and reduce the quality. You can't run markets like that, so I said to him, "As a company we aren't going to be here much longer if things go on this way," and he said, "You're just going to have an awful time without me." I said, "Do you mean we'd lose money?" He said, "Yes." So I said, "How much are we making now? I'm going to lose it my way."

So, you had a sense of your own responsibility; you weren't saying, "Oh well, Karker's the president, and if the stores go bust, it's in his lap."

No, I was desperate because I was responsible for running those stores. And, eventually, I offered to quit because of them. Karker had said I could have only eight new meat markets, when I knew meat markets were the key to survival. So I said, "If I'm going to fail, I'll fail based on my own judgment. I'm not going to risk my reputation on someone else's judgment. I'll take my lumps on my own, but not on someone else's if I think they're wrong." Karker approved an unlimited number of markets.

Say a subordinate of yours felt exactly the same way about a decision you'd made.

If someone felt that way, I'd be glad to have him come and tell me I was wrong. This is connected to the idea I was interested in more than any other, and that is to have a philosophy people can believe in and that will last. The way you hear Perkins talking these days, I guess it's lasted. And that's what I called the first assistant philosophy.

What was the philosophy?

Simply that executive responsibility involves assisting the people down the line to be successful. The boss in any department is the first assistant to those who report to him. You've got to live your life in a worthwhile way. This is a worthwhile philosophy. It doesn't hurt people, it helps them; and after it helps them, it helps the business.

But it was unique for the time. People weren't used to thinking in terms of an upside down organization in those days. The typical executive was more like a king, saying, "I make all the decisions, and all you little gnomes do my bidding, or else."

In any event, in the 1950s, I finally got my thoughts down on paper and put out a little book called *Sharing a Business,* which tells how I felt about whose responsibility was what.[1]

Would you say that Hancock had any direct influence on the philosophy that you thought up for Jewel Tea?

No, that was all my own thinking. It's a much harder job to be a first assistant to people working for you than to tell them what to do. It makes doing your job the same thing as trying to bring people along. If you *can't* do it, and they don't fit, then first try to help them, but if that doesn't work get them out . . . don't let them be dead on the job.

Did you choose George Clements the way Hancock chose you?

George was already in the company. He started out in the Expense Section as a very young kid. When I became president of the company, in 1942, there was a war on and there were a lot of problems. Previously I was running the Food Stores, but then I had to go look out for all of the business.

George was the office manager and did some accounting work. But it seemed to me that he had an administrative ability and some talents that the two older, more experienced people there didn't have, so I just pulled him out and made him vice president. I had to have someone good to get some of these things done.

Did you feel like his first assistant?

Yes. George needed help. But he sure could take it, and run with it.

Could he have done it without your sponsorship?

I guess not, but . . . I couldn't have done it without him either; remember, I needed him more than he needed me. What I loved was that all you had to do was give him a go. I just worked hell out of him. He's one of the great operating doers.

When you picked George Clements out over the heads of these other two fellows, were you consciously choosing him to be a successor to yourself?

No, I just wanted to make sure someone was looking after the Food Stores. But I had a feeling he had it.

Isn't it true that you actually brought Donald Perkins to Jewel?

Yes. In 1951 he married a girl whose name was Phyllis Babb, and her father was with Lever Brothers, where I was chairman of the Executive Committee. I was able to get a good look at Don.

What was it about Donald Perkins that made you think he was someone who ought to be in your company?

Well, his school record was very good. He was a poor kid, and had a widowed mother. Somewhat accidently he happened to end up at Yale; he hadn't thought about it, in fact, until someone came along with a scholarship. When he was graduated, his mother came down on a bus to New Haven and they went home to St. Louis on a bus together. That's pretty good.

Did you plan that Perkins would advance in the company?

Consider what this business looked like in those days. We didn't have a very high social standing. Mothers would rather have their boys and girls be bankers or lawyers. When you're in the chain store business, people kind of assume that you have a weak mind and a strong back. So we had to figure out ways of getting brains into the business. That's another way the first assistant philosophy helps the business; it attracts the smart ones.

Most young people fear that they'll get out someplace and no one will notice them. So you ask, how did I get Don Perkins? Well, I think he was willing to believe me. I said to him, "If you have it, you'll make it, and if you don't, you won't. And you can make it early. Look at my record—I'm not going to deny anyone the same chance."

Did you spend a considerable amount of your time handpicking people?

I'm looking for them all the time. Still am. Can't stop. Perkins wasn't as hard to get as Walter Elisha, who is president of our Jewel Food Stores. He took me a few years and three martinis.

Once, I wrote to the secretary of the Alumni Association at the University of North Dakota, Lloyd Stone, whom I knew, and said, "Lloyd, if you see a really unique, unusual person, send him to me, but don't bother me with anyone else." He only sent me one, Wes Christopherson, who's now president of Jewel Companies, of course.

What is it you look for?

I think anyone who can get through college with a good record must have some brains. Don Perkins was a Baker Scholar. We didn't insist that all be Phi Beta Kappas or MBAs or anything like that, but you have a much better chance with people with brains than with dimwits. There aren't many people like the ones I'm talking about. There aren't many like Christopherson, Perkins, or Clements . . . you have to locate them.

Did you actively encourage George Clements to look out for the young Don Perkins?

No, Clements' job was to take care of everyone in the business. He did a first-class job of it, too. However, I think there was a direct mentor relationship between George and Don. But Don wasn't the fair-haired boy; he earned everything he got. I wouldn't have pushed for him to be what he is if he didn't have it, in my judgment. I knew what he was doing, but I wasn't paying any unusual attention to Perkins, any more than to anyone else.

It seems as if you think that the way to encourage young people to produce is to let them alone on a day-to-day level.

Sure, and you put them into a program. We sent Don out to California for several months to travel door-to-door for our Routes Department, in which we sell directly to the homemaker.

So you actually manage their careers?

Of course, and the Routes is a great way to find out a lot about the public. You can't sell in 35 or 40 kitchens a day for months and not find out about what goes on in the kitchens of America. Young people hate it while they do it, but they all say afterward that it is great. You see, you're face to face with the customer and the hard business of selling. In top management, you can get too sophisticated, whereas the Routes put you up against people of all kinds. It's the greatest training ground there is.

Like you riding your bicycle in Canada, going door to door?

That's right, I learned a lot. The guy who is going to go out and knock on cold doors is a pretty strong individual.

George L. Clements

Do you feel that mentor relationships have played a strong part in shaping Jewel leadership?

Absolutely. The first thing that was important for Jewel in forming mentor relationships, which I never thought of before, is that John Hancock, who was president of Jewel right after World War I, brought in Franklin Lunding. Hancock placed the young Lunding in Jewel. To my knowledge that began the sponsorship of young people, and Lunding followed that by bringing in young men. I don't know what Lunding would say to this, but I think that's what started it.

Another important thing that happened, and he may not be conscious of this, is that along the way Lunding went to the Harvard Business School for one of those Advanced Management courses, and he came back with an increased awareness that business has a social responsibility—that it isn't just there to make money and sell people, take a profit and use people, but it has to give people something. This, I think, was important to what happened.

The next important thing is that Lunding gave me my first leg-up in the business.

How did you feel when he did that?

I was more than a little floored. I was the office manager at the time and the youngest of the lot. He had men who knew merchandising and operating a hell of a lot better than I did. I remember saying to him, "I don't know. You jumped me over these guys. I don't know how I'm going to make it and I don't know what to do." He said, "Well, why don't you go to work for them?" That was all I needed.

So I got the fellows in, heads of parts of the business, and said, "Look, I'm it . . . he made me the executive vice president. But, here's the business, and these are your responsibilities. Now my job, as I look at it, is to work for you, not you for me. I'm going to keep you off each other's throats; I'm going to pull you together when I have to. There may be times when there's a difference of opinion, and I'll have to make a decision. But, fundamentally, I'm going to work for you."

Did you feel that Lunding was working for you?

Lunding was a leader. Lunding was the one that gave me, gave the others, the philosophy by which to live. In other words, he gave us that first assistant philosophy—that's what he did.

We were visiting one day and he said, "George, your aim in life is to make Jewel a better place to trade, a better place to work." I don't think he realized what he said, but I took it and ran with it. And all the way through our relationship it was like that. He'd say it and I'd run with it.

Would you say that your relationship with him changed you?

Oh yes, oh yes. I would say he gave me a direction, a personal philosophy, I'd been missing. When he brought up the idea that to run a business is to share it, I could convert that immediately to care and share, and I could take that out and sell it to the organization—the more you care, the more you share.

If something was not going the way you thought it ought to, did you feel that you could challenge him openly?

You've got to understand Lunding. There are ways, if you think somebody's wrong, to manage the situation so that egos are not hurt or punctured and, sometimes, you can get around it. Sure there were times when I could give him the hard sell, and he'd take it. He was great; he'd give me something to work with and leave me alone.

Lunding left the Food Stores office early and moved his office down to the Loop, and sat there all by himself. He was that kind of a man. He could work from that office with a secretary all alone; I could never do that. He would read things, then telephone, make suggestions, ask questions, or go to conventions and make speeches. Me, I had to be involved in the organization, be involved with people, involved in the problems. I'm the type of guy that somebody always had to put something in my head and heart for me to really go.

How would you describe your relationship with Perkins?

Perkins was brought in by Lunding, around 1953. Don Booz was the first MBA; Perkins was the second or third. But he hadn't been here too long before I knew he was my successor. He had such tremendous ability; with numbers and with people, his peers, bosses, and subordinates. In fact, I remember one job he was on; the person who ran the department said, "You know, he's really good. This is the first time I've ever had someone working for me that I know I'm eventually going to work for."

What do you think most characterized him?

He was very mature. Like myself and Lunding he had a background of hard work, and he could work with people. If he had a question about somebody, he'd keep it to himself. He wouldn't run that person down; he'd just forget it and work around it. When I realized that he had it—and that was early in his career—he was still in his twenties—I never said anything, never told him, never told anybody. But I felt it was my job to give him experience around the organization, to do it carefully, and try to teach him patience and take some of the Harvard influence out of him.

What was particularly bothersome?

I don't know that Don agrees with me—but I think that the case study method teaches people that there is *a* problem and there is *an* answer. And once you find that answer, then you're all through. Business life isn't like that . . . it's not all black and white; it's gray. It's not simple; it's very grand. Sometimes problems are never solved. You have to keep going with them. You struggle with them; you work with them and it takes time, years sometimes. Don had to learn to be patient and not say, "I did that; what do you have for me now."

How did you help him do that?

I just sat on him. I'd let him make a mistake, and he'd never make the same mistake twice. For instance, after he'd been on his first real assignment as merchandising manager of the Routes for a while, he felt he'd been there long enough. So I said to him, "Do you have a replacement?" He said, "Oh, sure, so and so . . . ." Well, I didn't think the person was qualified, but as far as Don was concerned, he was, enough for Don to be able to move to another job, which was uppermost in his mind.

What happened?

The man wasn't right for the job.

And guessing the person wasn't right you were able to sit back and let Perkins do this?

Oh sure, sure. Maybe I was wrong about the man. I've been wrong many times, and young people absolutely have to have the freedom to make mistakes. Just so they aren't too big. What was more important, me being right or Don learning?

With that kind of incident, would the two of you discuss it afterward?

I mentioned it and he admitted he was wrong, but he didn't want to talk about it. If you're trying to develop a person, you don't hammer into him again and again that he made a mistake, He knows he made a mistake. The question then is—what are you going to do about it?

Would it have been difficult for you if Perkins had challenged you?

Not really, though it's very difficult for some executives to give young people their heads and accept their challenges, and there were a lot of young people who had no sound basis for what they were saying, but Perkins wasn't one of them. Another important thing in developing young people is to let them know what is going on so that they can challenge you.

How did you do that?

Way early in the game, I heard that a pretty smart young guy had said, "I wonder what the secret six are up to now." That was me and my Food Stores staff. Very obviously we weren't communicating what went on in our meetings. I decided we had to let people know what we were doing. They needed that. Any young person needs that. And out of this came, we gave it a fancy name, the Management Development Council.

When was this?

It was after 1960 when we started annual recruiting of MBAs. That council is still operating because I talked to them this year. It was an attempt to bring together young people with potential from every part of the business to communicate what was going on in their parts of the business.

The council also brings in a Perkins, a Clements, a Dick Cline of Osco, or a Jim Hensen of Star Markets, and the young people ask them point-blank questions. They are really encouraged to challenge top management as to what it is doing. The Osco person on the Council might not ask Dick Cline a touchy question, but some Food Stores person might.

Were you consciously trying to develop Perkins?

Oh, sure, but it wasn't hard, he was so ambitious. The only other thing I had to do besides give him experience was to get him—you know "the bright boy right out of the Harvard Business School"—accepted in the organization. I knew he had to have a success. So the idea was to expose him to many parts of the business—first, so that he knew the business; and second, so people like the one I mentioned earlier who said, "I never had somebody work for me whom I'm going to work for," would know him.

The best place to put him at one point early on was in Jewel Food Stores, so we made him chief of staff, Store Operating. That was the best way to slip him in there. And it wasn't long before his tremendous talent showed itself: he was always writing speeches for the boss, working out all sorts of problems. He became, very obviously, a guy that people respected. Those that didn't probably weren't worth a damn anyway.

Was that enough of a success for him?

No, he needed a real tough baby. So after he was in charge of growth planning, and development, I made him vice president of the Routes department. And he squealed. He really didn't want to go there, but it wasn't going to be easy. We were starting to franchise the Routes, and if he could help make that work, he'd have a success in store operating, merchandising, and management.

Would his chances to advance have been affected if he'd failed?

It would have been too bad. But it never came to my mind that it was a make-or-break thing because it never occurred to me that he couldn't do it. I just knew he had to have a success, and was confident he would.

Is an ingredient of success the superior's confidence?

Absolutely. A boss has to have every bit of confidence in a person. The minute the boss loses confidence, the person will feel it, and he's going to go downhill. But remember, I don't think that there was a real personal relationship with Perkins before he was executive vice president. He was just working for the company. He was one individual. After all, I was trying to do the same thing with a lot of individuals. I tried to see what I could put into them rather than what they could do for me.

Did Lunding share your feelings about Perkins, as early on as you did?

Lunding felt strongly about Perkins. He certainly pushed him at me.

He pushed him at you?

Perkins had an ear with Lunding. Well, there were times that I suspected he did, though I'm not sure. I didn't raise the question. I don't give a damn. But there were times when it seemed to me that something would come from Lunding that would indicate that Perkins had said something. But I can't ever remember a situation where Lunding said, "Now, look, Perkins talked to me about this and don't you think you ought to do something?" I can't ever remember a situation like that.

If Perkins had run around me all the time, he wouldn't have been the man I thought he was.

What was your relationship like when he was executive vice president and you were president?

It was a much closer relationship then because he and I were running the company. He could take the ball, or I could take the ball. I wouldn't worry about who had the ball or who was doing what. I'd support what he did. He'd support what I did. When there were disagreements, if I felt strongly about it, we did it, and if he felt strongly about it, I let him do it. Well . . . sometimes I'd let him think about it for awhile. You know, if your relationship is right as it was with us, you can work that out. It's not a problem.

Do you feel Perkins is a leader in the same way Franklin Lunding was?

Not the same. No. And of course, he isn't quite as stubborn as Lunding. But I think Perkins is both a leader and a manager.

How did you feel when you saw him come along and you said to yourself, "OK, there's my successor?" You're talking as if you had great delight in bringing this person along.

I did. It was a joy to me to work with someone like that. I could use his brains, his ability, strengths, and youthfulness. Our relationship was a great pleasure for me; our personalities matched so well.

You never felt threatened by his success?

John Hancock told me something once I'll never forget. He said, "There's always enough credit to go around." Perkins's success meant that I was doing my job.

Sometimes with close mentor relationships there comes a point where there's a split, where a younger person has made it and needs the older person to let go. Did you feel that way about Lunding?

No. I was too indebted to Lunding to take that attitude. With Perkins I was very anxious to get off his back if that was necessary. It's hard to lose the daily involvement, but when you realize that someone else can do it better, it's time to go.

What were the things you were most concerned to pass on to Perkins?

Social consciousness, first assistant philosophy, willingness to dare to do things. These were strengths we had in this business. Oh gosh, the years I spent with Perkins, you know, starting out together when he was executive vice president ending with him as chairman of the board, those were some of the best times of my life.

Donald S. Perkins

We'd like to discuss whether your relationships with Mr. Clements and Mr. Lunding helped you develop leadership qualities and what you feel each contributed.

I came to work for Jewel because Frank Lunding heard about me from my mother-in-law and invited me to come in for an interview. I was very impressed with the fact that the chairman would spend time with me; you won't be surprised that I try to do that today with prospective MBAs.

Frank found out that I drank tea instead of coffee, and when I got back to Wright Patterson Air Force Base in Ohio where I was stationed, a package of Jewel tea and one of these old-fashioned teapots that Jewel had been giving away in the Routes business for years arrived in the mail with a note saying, "Thought you ought to have some good tea," or something like that. It's pretty hard not to be impressed with someone that thoughtful.

What about George Clements?

I did not meet George Clements until I came back from my Routes training, and he debriefed me to find out what I'd learned. At that time I began to realize that the real challenge for someone like me at Jewel was to prove myself to George Clements. By the nature of what Frank thought the business needed, I felt I was more or less acceptable early, but in terms of what George felt might be needed, I had to do a lot of proving. I said to myself early in the game that I would succeed at Jewel when I got George Clements's acceptance and support.

What was it about Clements that you recognized was different?

I can be more comfortable about saying this now, because at a recent retirement dinner for Frank Lunding, the subject of Abraham Zaleznik's article, "Leaders and Managers: Are They Different?" came up.[2] Frank and George agreed that Frank was the leader and George was the manager. If that discussion had not been held, I couldn't be this candid. George is a tough-minded excellent manager and, as such, believes you aren't worth anything just because you have a good education, did well in school, or for any other reason, except that you get things done through people and do them well and honorably and are successful.

Were you aware at the beginning that you were, in a sense, chosen?

I never felt as though I was chosen within Jewel. I grew up in St. Louis, was raised by a working mother, and knew that the way out of a less-than-affluent neighborhood was through education. After a couple of academic experiences that were reasonably successful, I did have some confidence in myself as you would, I think, expect me to have. So if you ask me what was most important in terms of my attitude in my first few years at Jewel—my self-confidence was significantly more important than any thought that I had a special relationship with anybody in the business, because I didn't.

When would you say you were first aware of Clements taking an interest in you?

For the first five or six years at Jewel, I was always aware that George was very hepful in a management sense—always asking about the problems in the business, and how we might solve them. When I'd been in the business six years or so, I had a major change from being the merchandise manager of the Routes to being the assistant to the operating head of the Food Stores. That's when I realized that George was taking more than a general interest in me.

When you came to Jewel, were you aware of wanting a mentor or of needing something, or that there was something lacking?

Absolutely. I knew I needed to be developed. In typical business school fashion, I wanted to join a company that met certain criteria. First, it had to be in the consumer goods business, because that's what I consider to be fun. Second, it had to be a well-managed business because I didn't think that I'd learned how to actually manage anything at the Harvard Business School. Third, it had to be a company that was financially strong. Jewel met all of those very well.

I didn't use the word "mentor," but since one of my important yardsticks was to work for a well-managed business, I knew I needed to learn.

Did Clements and Lunding spend time with you in your early years?

My relationship with Frank Lunding and George Clements wasn't so close then that I could really discuss how the business was working or why they didn't do things the way I would. But I could discuss things with Don Booz, who's now running his own consulting firm. He was the personnel manager at the time I was hired. I had known him at the Business School and then, of course, knew him while he was at Jewel.

Don Booz was a great help in the early years. We lived near each other and commuted together. I seldom saw him in the personnel department, but we had a lot of conversations driving in an automobile. Young people in our business sometimes blush when I say to them, "Well, have you reorganized the business recently?" but I am just remembering those conversations we had driving to and from work.

But once I began to have enough success in the business to make it reasonable for me to have more contact with them, the mentor relationships with Clements and Lunding became very real.

One of the things that often characterizes successful mentor relationships is a strong emotional interchange between the younger and older person, where the younger person feels encouraged to challenge directly the older person's ideas, and the older person has enough confidence in himself to take it. Did that characterize your relationship with Clements later on?

Very much so with George. I think the best way to characterize the relationship that developed was that though in many ways we had different backgrounds, George and I admired each other so much and came at problems from different angles so that when we agreed on something, we stopped worrying about it and went ahead and did it.

But if you thought he was wrong, did you feel even though you were considerably younger—19 years difference—you could say, "I don't think you're right"?

Yes, we had a relationship like that. It didn't start the first time I came in to tell him about my experience on the Routes, I'll assure you of that. Exactly when it started, I'm not sure. Who knows where close human relationships start? I don't.

It was all a very businesslike relationship at first, but from the time I moved to the office next to him and he asked me to be responsible for growth planning and development, he had time to talk about anything that I thought was important. But I never had to say, "I think you're wrong." Anything that I thought was worth talking about, he thought was worth listening to. Needless to say, anything that he thought was worth talking about, I thought was worth listening to.

We had respect for each other's contributions. He knew the business needed to be changed, and I think that the role I played for him was as a suggester of possible changes. He could tap whatever creativity I had and bounce it off of his experience; that made a pretty good working relationship.

Did he ever have to override your decisions or pull rank on you?

No, we never had a conversation that ever came close to his saying, "I'm the chairman."

You may not know this but Clements said he knew you were his successor from the beginning.

I didn't know that. He has a very kind memory. In a way I'm sure George saw me as one potential successor. George was enough of a manager and enough of an outstanding developer of people that I believe he must have known that had he made that very obvious to me, whenever it was, it would have done me and our relationship more harm than good. So there were times early in my career when I wasn't sure that anybody was looking at me or was particularly interested in me.

Did your early experiences at Jewel affect you personally?

The greatest change, I think, came from learning how to relate to people, how to make sure that everyone knows that you want to get something done, without applying pressure or demanding something be done. When I was the number two person in the advertising department in the Routes, I was picked to be the successor to the general merchandise manager. I'd never been a buyer and all the key people in that department were buyers.

So I sat down with each person and said, "You know, I don't know anything about the buying business, so why don't you tell me what you'd do if you had my job?" They suggested more things than I had time to do. I suppose that's an illustration of being a first assistant, particularly when you aren't sure about what you're supposed to do.

What do you think was the most important thing you learned from the Routes?

First I learned the business. When I was running a Route, it was a lonesome job. I remember one night at 6 o'clock it was raining, I had a number of back calls to make to customers who hadn't been home earlier. I looked up in the truck mirror and said, "What am I doing here?"

But when I came back and talked to the people in the office who were responsible for making decisions for the Routes business, I realized that even with that brief experience, I had an up-to-date knowledge about what was really going on in the field. That didn't hurt my confidence about suggesting what might be done differently.

Were you aware that when Clements sent you back to the Routes after you were in the Food Stores that he was presenting you with a challenge so that you would be accepted by the rest of the company?

No, I didn't think of it that way . . . I thought he was giving me a job I didn't want. I was having fun working on the future of the business, and he was sending me to its past. But he did that because that's George Clements the manager. As much as he was a supporter, he was still going to find out at each level what I could do. That was 1961. I'd been with Jewel for eight years.

The first six years, other than a brief training relationship with the Food Stores, were spent in the Routes business, I'd just got away for a year or a year and a half, had great fun doing what I was doing . . . and he wanted me to go back. I tried my best to talk him out of it.

You've said your early experiences at Jewel influenced your ways of relating to people. Mentors often help people develop other leadership qualities as well, such as their philosophic attitudes and their ability to take risks. Would you say this was true for you?

I had had enough of a struggle before coming to Jewel that I wasn't sure that the world was full of people who were out to help me. Phyllis, my wife, began to change my thinking when I first met her. Then I had a chance to observe Frank Lunding and George Clements, and to realize that success at Jewel was based on human concern.

At Jewel, I saw it not only acceptable but necessary to be yourself, to be honest and straightforward, ideals that are fundamental to the idea of sharing. To observe such a pattern, and then to feel comfortable in being able to develop your own business style against that framework—that was really important.

Have these concepts had a real influence in the company?

Yes. The changes Jewel had gone through in the 1960s were significant. That was when I asked George, Frank, and a wonderful man named Robert

Updegraff, a Jewel director for 25 years, to agree to come to try to put on paper the concepts and influences that have been important to our business.

Instead of rewriting Frank's book *Sharing a Business,* we wrote *The Jewel Concepts*. I'm delighted to find that these concepts of the book are referred to throughout the business by, in many cases, relatively new people and often in speeches made by the officers of our operating companies. It's a way of thinking that is comfortable and appropriate for Jewel. Even a summer MBA finds out what a first assistant is.

In your daily working with Clements, were you aware of his taking risks with you, of him letting you go ahead down a path?

Absolutely. When I was in the Routes department, most of the action was in the Stores. We had a Routes catalog, very much like the one that we still have today, and I persuaded George to let us put some catalog desks in stores to sell merchandise. I remember that we lost $50,000 on the venture, but I suppose that isn't as expensive as a training cost. But, yes, George let me spend the $50,000 on an idea, and never said, "I told you so." He said, "OK, what do we do next?"

Did you find that the relationship you had with Clements and Lunding affected strategy decisions you might make?

I can't imagine a major decision could be made at Jewel that wouldn't consider the people involved. Formalizing the concept of autonomous companies in 1966 was a good example. Decentralization was natural to the Routes business even though the Food Stores were highly centralized.

In this matter of autonomy I give George Clements great credit. I remember a conversation that we had when we were talking about how to organize the business as we were acquiring Star Markets and Osco Drugs. He remembered that when he was operating the Food Stores in Chicago, an attractive location would become available and he could analyze it and approve it while another company was waiting to hear from corporate headquarters. He understood the value of being independent and being on the spot when he was in the leadership position at Jewel, and he didn't want to lose that as the business got more complicated. That thinking dictated our approach to the development of autonomous operating companies.

We understand that at Jewel each MBA trainee is assigned an officer as a sponsor to act as a mentor. Is that true?

Yes, just as Don Booz was a sponsor for me. I remember writing him letters about the rigors of operating Routes, and I would receive both sympathetic and unsympathetic replies, but at least feel good about the communication.

How did this program start?

Our MBA recruiting program started in answer to a request from George in the late 1950s or early 1960s to add some more talented people to our business. And I said, "Develop a recruiting program that offers them what you offered me," which meant a chance to find out what happens in our business for a period of time before settling down in a more typical regular job. Then we merchandized that idea and the idea of a sponsorship so that the trainee would have someone to relate to during the training period.

How far do you expect the sponsors to be responsible for these people?

If the individual trainee does a poor job, and if no one else will tell him or her about it, the sponsor should do it. If the trainee is doing a good job, I would expect the sponsor to tell him or her that. I would expect the sponsor to know enough about that trainee to have discussions during the training period, to be very influential in deciding where and what kind of more permanent job that trainee takes. A sponsor should know more about his or her trainee than anyone else in Jewel.

And he or she actually helps the trainee plan his career and talks to other people about him?

Exactly, but then we cut the apron strings, because the individual typically goes to work for somebody else. However, the friendships that have developed during that sponsorship period probably never end. You can cut the apron strings, but you don't cut the friendship. One of the wonderful things that happens to a trainee as he or she touches base with all parts of Jewel, is getting to know people throughout the company. Walter Elisha, president of the Jewel Food Stores, who went through this kind of training program, is delighted to have as his top operating officer a man who was the manager of a store in which he trained.

So the sponsor is usually somebody who does not become the person's direct boss?

Only rarely would it turn out that he would be. It's not ruled out, but it isn't likely to happen. Also I don't think it's fair to overemphasize the sponsor relationship to MBA recruiting. We try to give every person that comes into this business—MBA or high school student—sponsorship. Sometimes we do this well and sometimes we do it poorly. But we do try to encourage all of our people to empathize with the new employee's concerns.

Is this part of the first assistant philosophy?

It's consistent with it. Let's put it another way. There are a lot of people at Jewel who understand systems and know how to operate a group of stores. The people that Wes Christopherson and I look for to become key management people in the business have these abilities, but they also are able to recruit, develop, and motivate outstanding people.

Do you expect the vice presidents who act as sponsors to get emotionally involved with these people if they have to? To get to know them well . . . to become to them what Clements was to you?

If you are asking me if you can work with people without love, the answer is no. On the other hand, if you are asking if it is possible to help people grow by expressing love only in terms of permissiveness, by never hurting them and never being candid with them, the answer is also no. So sponsorship is somewhat like parenthood.

I think George and I had a relationship that we would have been proud to have had we been father and son, but one we could not likely have had if we *had* been father and son. So many of the good elements were there without other complicating problems such as the son having to prove his independence of the father.

Over the years have you noticed a qualitative difference between managers who were brought up with the sponsor approach and those who were not?

I don't know that anyone has ever succeeded in any business without having some unselfish sponsorship or mentorship, whatever it might have been called. Everyone who succeeds has had a mentor or mentors. We've all been helped. For some the help comes with more warmth than for others, and with some it's done with more forethought, but most people who succeed in a business will remember fondly individuals who helped them in their early days.

Do you see a real difference at Jewel, for instance?

No, but I see great difference in the ability of people to be sponsors.

When you became CEO in 1970, five of your division presidents were under 45, so that those five today would still be under 55. How do you make room for motivated, trained MBAs?

Room is made in two ways. One is through the attrition of those who are not the most outstanding.

But second, and probably more important numerically, our retirement program supports and perhaps even encourages early retirement. This retirement program is not only important to the retiree but is important in terms of opening up new opportunities. We have 170 or so operating company officers. I believe that right now only two of those are over 60.

Are the top men and women able to accept this rush of young, talented people? Doesn't that create tension for some of them?

Beginning with Frank Lunding's presidency at the age of 36 and his successful stewardship of the business at that time, there's been a degree of pride and expectation in the business that Jewel would have youthful leaders.

When Wes Christopherson became assistant sales manager in the Routes, Ed Johnson, an absolutely marvelous person now retired, and I agreed that in working with Christopherson, Johnson was probably developing his boss.

This training probably wouldn't exist in organizations that you acquire such as Turnstyle or Star Markets. How do you change the thinking of people who are already there?

With tender, loving care, and over time. When we've acquired businesses, we've always thought that we were acquiring good management. If we were to help those managers continue to be successful, they would need to continue to do things in their own way. That's part of the idea of decentralization; it's also part of being the first assistant to the group of managers that we may have or acquire. We don't demand that they do many things in one certain fashion. Some things they adopt and adapt, and some they don't like.

One of the other risks often associated with mentor relationships is that the younger person at some point might become overly dependent on the older person. Did you feel at any time that if you didn't have these strong people around, you might not be able to make it?

Was I as cocky and confident when I became president as when I was a trainee? Absolutely not. But I don't think that this was a matter of being dependent. Rather I had matured enough to understand realistically what the problems might be, that there was no easy answer to many of the questions of the business, and that many goals can't be reached in a year. If I'd understood what the problems turned out to be, I'd have been even less confident.

Clearly, Clements and Lunding were confident you could do it.

Frank Lunding gave up the job of chairman at, I believe, the age of 58, because he and George had decided I was ready to be president. And George Clements made basically the same decision at the age of 61 because he decided Wes Christopherson was ready to be president.

These decisions were based on when people were ready, rather than on chronology. For that reason I said in 1970 that the right tenure for the CEO of Jewel should be 10 years. And my 10 years will be up soon. If we want to have a vibrant questioning management that's looking out for changing customers' wants today, we should operate in a way that ensures top management change from time to time.

Do you feel now that being a mentor is part of your responsibility?

Yes, I'm proud to be a sponsor. Yes, I'm proud when I find myself able to be a good first assistant. Wes Christopherson and I try to know the young talent in Jewel. But the organization is not going to let someone succeed just because either of us takes an interest in that person. We must have thousands of sponsors. Every manager must be a sponsor.

Some people think that the main values to mentor relationships occur after they've ended. Have you been aware since your day-to-day contact with Clements and Lunding has broken that there is something that reveals itself that you weren't aware of before?

I've developed a frame of reference over the years that I use as I consider the problems of the business—I mentally ask myself in dealing with a tough problem how I might explain our action to Frank, or George, or Phyllis, or my children—Betsy, Jerry, and Susan—in such a way that they'd say, "Yes, that makes sense. You're not just being a hard-driving, thoughtless businessman who's forgotten the human lessons that were there in Jewel to be learned."

Notes

1. Franklin J. Lunding, *Sharing a Business* (Chicago, Updegraff Press, 1954).

2. Abraham Zaleznik, "Leaders and Managers: Are They Different?" *HBR*, May–June 1977, p. 67.

7

"Failure Is a Word I Don't Accept"

AN INTERVIEW WITH JOHN H. JOHNSON

According to John H. Johnson, success in business requires many things, but above all "a burning commitment to succeed." To make it, a manager has to get the best out of his or her people, for employees are the stuff of which success is made. Getting the best entails teaching, leading, and caring. In this interview, Mr. Johnson discusses his own philosophy of success and illustrates how he has translated it into a management style. He also discusses how the need for successful models is as important for all young blacks as it is for his own employees.

The interview with Mr. Johnson was conducted and edited by Eliza G. C. Collins, senior editor, and Wanda A. Lankenner, editorial assistant, at the Harvard Business Review.

Mr. Johnson, an admirer of yours quotes you as saying, "Success in business is a time-honored process involving hard work, risk-taking, money, a good product, maybe a little bit of luck, and most of all a burning commitment to succeed." We'd like to talk about most of these, but we'd like to start with the last one. What do you mean by a burning commitment to succeed?

I don't see, never did see, failure as an option. When *Life* went out of business, the guys who made the decision to discontinue it knew that it was not going to disturb their lives. As a matter of fact, Time, Inc.'s stock went up that day. But if *Ebony* didn't succeed, it was going to destroy my life. So I had total commitment; my whole life depended on *Ebony*. I had no options. So I had to learn the rules of the game to win.

What kind of rules do you mean?

If you're drowning, and two guys are standing above you, one with a long stick and one with a short stick, and the one with the short stick tosses it to you, you can say, "Oh, no, I want the longer stick." But if there's only one stick there, you're going to take it, whatever it is.

For instance, once I was trying to get a second-class permit for *Tan,* which had some suggestive stories in it. When I went to the post office, the man said he didn't like *Tan,* he couldn't approve it. I tried all kinds of ways to get him to approve it, including saying, "Well, gee, you must be prejudiced because I'm black, and you've okayed similar magazines, like *True Story, True Confessions,* and so on. Why do you want to do this to me?" But the man just kept rejecting my application. So finally I went down to see him again, and I said, "Mr. So-and-So, I've got to have this second-class permit. I can't survive without it. You're in charge, and I've concluded that the only thing I can do is to do what you want. Will you please tell me what you want me to do?" He said, "Now you're talking, Johnson." And then, really, he told me to do what I was doing right then, namely, being persistent but not hostile. I learned the rules of the game. It wasn't always easy, but I learned them.

Are you aware of any sacrifices or personal compromises you've had to make?

I don't think I've had to compromise any integrity along the way. I can't recall any instance when I knowingly did it. I think I have stooped to conquer. I saw I wasn't going to get anywhere by burning things down. So I tried not to let anger and emotions interfere with logical decisions.

How do you deal with the anger?

If I'm mad at somebody, I just go in a room, close the door, and cuss him or her out where nobody can hear me. Sometimes I write a letter that I don't mail. I've done a lot of that. I think we have to let the steam off, but I can't recall when I've openly expressed anger in front of anyone or to anyone for a very long time. You just lose. You really do. Fussing and arguing just don't work, so I try to avoid them.

Have you ever wanted to lash out rather than figure a way around a problem?

Yes, all the time. All of us would like to lash out sometimes. I think you always have to keep in mind what your goal is, though; and lashing out will not achieve it. You see, one disadvantage blacks have with anger and dealing with it is not knowing how to behave in a business situation. Most don't know, so they may respond inappropriately and get very frustrated. I was lucky; at a very early age—18—when I graduated from high school and went to work at Supreme Life Insurance Company as an office boy, I was a kind of flunky to Harry H. Pace, who was the president of the company. He took great pride in developing young people, and he regarded me as one of his discoveries. So he spent a lot of time with me, telling me about business, and why certain decisions had been made. I learned a lot by just being with him and listening to him.

One valuable lesson I learned was that you have to work with people you don't like, and you have to be willing to forgive and forget if what you've objected to has been corrected.

Do you apply that lesson to the way you manage?

I sure do. Just yesterday I was talking to one of our vice presidents. He had fired a certain guy in anger, and this person was the best we had for the particular job he was in. So I said to the vice president, "Now, let's bring the guy to Chicago. Let's sit down and talk to him together. Let's give him another chance, and if he apologizes, and if he has learned his lesson, let's go with him again." I think many people would be inclined to say, "Well, that guy's no good; he insulted me, and I'm never going to deal with him again." I think we have to be prepared to deal with anybody and anything if the circumstances change. And we have to be prepared to go with what we've got. I always remind myself that my employees are the best people I have, and they're the only people I have. So I have to work with them.

It sounds as if you're translating your own success or philosophy of success into a management style. Would that be a fair statement?

Yes, it would. Back in 1954, I made up a list of 25 or 30 people that I thought I needed to run the magazines. I have a secret office in the heart of my company in which I keep those names before me at all times. I try to think of all the things that I can do to make those people happy and well-satisfied with their work here. This often involves more than salary. It involves an upgrading in title, maybe occasional trips, recognition of something well-done, like a little note thanking them for it, calling attention to an outstanding job. It may involve my asking some private club to invite them to be a member, if that's what they want. I think you have to understand the people that work for you, find out what they want, and try to respond to it, because these are the people you need to succeed.

Traditionally, the entrepreneur is the person who wants to do it all on his own. It seems you recognized early on that you couldn't do it all yourself.

I want to be big and I want to be bigger, and I can't do it all by myself. So I try to do only those things that I can't get anybody else to do. In other words, I don't really have a job at Johnson Publishing Company. Everything here is supposed to be done by somebody else. My job is to see that they do it, or to show them how.

So you see part of your function as teaching people?

Teaching, training, leading, and demonstrating. I try hard to save people now, much harder than I did in my younger years. Most of the people we employ, less now than before, are people who were previously in something else. We have had to convert them. For example, most of our ad salesmen had never sold ads for anybody else. They were Urban League secretaries, school teachers, and post office workers. We had to mold these people, and train and direct them into becoming marketing experts and advertising salespeople.

Is training one of the responsibilities of all your managers?

A key responsibility; the best manager is a good teacher. To give you an example, three years ago we started a cosmetic company called Fashion Fair, which is now very successful.

Now, there were no black people trained in that area. Before then, black people had not worked at high levels in the cosmetic industry. We looked around, and there were no black salesmen working for Revlon or Estée Lauder. They were not going to send black people in to sell Marshall Field and Bonwit Teller, so there was no company we could really raid.

What did you do?

We made our own experts. For instance, Mr. J. Lance Clarke, who is our vice president of sales of cosmetics, had never worked in this field before. He didn't know how to go into a store like Marshall Field or Bonwit Teller. So I took him with me, and he and I together opened accounts in about 20 stores. He listened to what I said, he watched when I backed off, he watched when I went forward. And he learned. It isn't really that I'm a better salesman than he is; it's that there was and still is more mystique connected with me. I'm the head of the business. So I can sometimes get more done simply because of who I am. For this reason, there are still certain store accounts I have to open myself, but by and large, Mr. Clarke's doing it himself. And he's doing it because he watched me, and he learned.

Do you get personally involved in the selection of employees?

Yes, yes. If I told you, you wouldn't believe it. Along with the personnel manager, I interview every person that we employ for our Chicago building. I don't do it for the New York office or for other offices, but for this building, yes. I don't say that it guarantees you'll like everybody. There're still a lot of people I don't particularly like for one reason or another. But because I'm interested, I think my interviewing guarantees that I'm getting the best people I can get. It also lets me learn enough about them so that I can get as much out of them as I know how.

Do you think it difficult to manage when you know everybody personally?

Yes. But it has its advantages and disadvantages. The advantage is that we don't have a union. The disadvantages are that you genuinely have to work and help people. You just can't say you're going to do it. You've got to do it. Their concerns have to be your concerns. For example, if I know someone has died in an employee's family, and he's got to travel some distance and might be short of cash, I've got to offer to help.

How do you deal with the people who can't make it?

As a matter of fact, I only fuss with the people I love. Of course, some people say I shouldn't love them so much. I try to push and fuss and cajole and do whatever I can to get the most out of them. But after we fuss and fight and argue, if nothing changes, we fire them. There's nothing else to do. If you do all that you can do—you warn people, you set goals, you tell them what the issues are, you tell them what's expected—and if they fail over and over again, then you have to get rid of them. We have no other choice. We reward success, and we punish failure. It's a known policy; it's not a secret. If people do well, we're going to find some way to reward them. If they do badly consistently, then we have to dismiss them. And it works.

How do you recognize a good man or woman?

By observing. I look for dedication and commitment, and willingness to learn. I think it's more the last than it is anything else, because an intelligent person can be taught almost anything that's not purely technical. So we look primarily for a desire to learn and a dedication to the job. If they have these, we can teach them the rest.

How do you teach judgment, which takes time to acquire?

I work with my people day in and day out. When I was young, I would see an employee doing something wrong and I'd let it go by instead of stopping it. Eventually, the employee would get to the point where I would have to dismiss him. Now that's a waste. I learned early in the game that if you dismiss the people you have, then the new people you hire are sometimes worse than the ones you dismissed. Very often, just the shock of having the kind of conversation we had with the guy we brought to Chicago to talk to will turn a man around. Another way to have turned him around, of course, would have been to challenge him on every little defection. We try to teach the regular corrective process to our managers so that they don't rush out and do something that we'll be sorry for.

Doesn't your persistence sometimes frighten people?

If I've been really, really hard on a person, then I'll back off and let a few things go by. Very often, the people will correct themselves. If you've really been riding somebody, say, about coming to work on time, sometimes when they try real hard, they'll be late just from trying so hard. Then it's better to step back and let things ride for a few days rather than to sit in the lobby every day to see whether or not they come on time. Not long ago I wrote a memo giving everybody hell for coming to work late. I haven't even been in the lobby since I did that. But next week I'm going to be there.

Being visible is important, then?

Well, as a matter of fact, when people visit the building, they're shocked to see me walking around the floors or riding on the elevator. If I want to see someone, I don't order him up to my office. I go down and see him. I'm all over the building all the time. It's not a thing I plan; it's just a thing I do. I know my people, I socialize with them, and we're friends.

There isn't any tension between your roles as friend and as employer?

I don't think I've lost anything by being friendly with the people on the staff. If they get out of line, I challenge them. I say, we're friends, but this is the way it has to be. I don't find it to be a problem, but I guess there's always some tension. We don't have Christmas parties anymore because people would very often have too much to drink and say things either to me or to some manager that they shouldn't have said. We've lost several people through Christmas parties.

In effect, you're making it difficult for people to get out on a limb?

That's right. If somebody challenges you out in the open, you've got to do something about it. You can be visible and available and friendly, but not too social with most of the people. You're never quite sure that your position will be respected. I don't want to be exposed to something that I'll have to take recognition of, and yet I think it's a risk I have to run.

How do you handle that tension in making business decisions?

When we have staff meetings, I will listen very patiently to everyone's opinions. If I feel really strongly about something, the chances are I will try to put my own ideas over. But I cannot ever recall doing anything that everybody was against. If all of the people in whom I have confidence were against something, I would not go forward with it no matter how much I wanted to do it. I'd think that if all these people were against it, there must be something wrong with it.

Do you ever simply lay down the law?

Not really, but if there's a tie, or a division of opinion, then I'll do as I feel. Or if I feel so strongly about something that I know that it's absolutely the right thing to do, then I don't call a meeting at all. I just say we're going to do it. I used to call employees together if there was a big dispute to see if I could mediate it. I didn't want one to think that I said anything that the others didn't know about. But that's a mistake, because all they did was scream and holler at each other. You're much better off to meet with each employee privately, and try to get each one to commit himself to a change of attitude without bringing them together for a confrontation.

From sitting on the boards of companies and universities, do you have a sense of how other people manage their businesses in ways distinct from the ways you do?

I think our management is more personal and more direct. In most large corporations, the board and the management are so far removed that they'll have maybe only three people reporting to them. That's all the chief executive officer's exposed to. In my case, I have the heads of every department reporting directly to me. Not only that, but I talk directly to people, if I want to. As a matter of fact, if something is really wrong, anybody can petition to see me, if he or she really feels he or she has been mistreated. In any event, my theory is that even though you have a lot of people who could see you, you really have to deal only with those who have a problem.

You are chief executive officer at Supreme Life Insurance Company. Are things the same there? In one article about you, your business methods at Supreme were described as "arrogant and ruthless."

Before I became CEO at Supreme, no matter what you did there, you couldn't get fired. Management just kept transferring people from one job to another. (I understand that they did that at the *Saturday Evening Post* too, which is probably why they folded.) When I went to Supreme, I made one statement: no one could be transferred. You had to succeed in your job; you were going to be given an adequate opportunity, but if you didn't succeed in that job, you were going to be dismissed, no matter how many years you had been there. Now, that was called arrogant. Maybe it was, but it turned the company around.

You didn't bring in your own management staff?

No, we didn't change the people; we changed the method of operation. For instance, Supreme's executives and supervisors were supposed to go to work at 9:00, and the lowly employees were supposed to go to work at 8:30. Well, the executives really came in around 10:00. So we changed that; everybody had to come to work at 9:00. The guy who said I was arrogant was probably one of the people who had to start coming to work at the same time all the other employees did.

Do you find that you now can manage both companies the same way?

Yes, because we have a very good president at Supreme now. I think the two companies' problems are basically the same. You've got to look after the interest of the employee and then insist that the employee looks after the interest of the company. In other words, in both organizations we paid the employees more money, we gave them more liberal benefits, and then we insisted that they do their work. I used to tell a joke about my New York manager. We gave him a big office. We paid him a big salary. We gave him a beautiful secretary. And then we threatened to take it all away from him. You'd be surprised how much we got out of him.

Do you think, using your own or other black companies as examples, that black organizations operate differently from white organizations?

Generally, black organizations are more sentimental, more emotional, and less businesslike than white organizations, I think. We work with people we like a little bit more than we should.

Why is it more than you should?

Well, when you dismiss people, it gives you a bad reputation in the black community, which is small. For example, in the early days I was known as someone who was ruthless in terms of dismissing people. That's partly why I got the reputation, which I often said was well-earned. If people didn't do their work, they were dismissed, period.

Do you think that black companies ought to try to stay separate from large white organizations?

Well, you have to understand that I don't believe in black capitalism. Black people ought to have the right to become capitalists, but black capitalism presupposes that you're only going to sell to black people. If I sold only to black people, I wouldn't have a very successful company. Most of my subscriptions and newsstand sales are made to blacks, but 90% of my advertising is made to whites. So I don't believe that we ought to limit our sales to the black community. I think a black businessman ought to strive to be a businessman and to sell to any customers who will buy from him. If Kentucky Fried Chicken can sell chicken to blacks, we ought to be able to sell something to whites.

You have been quoted as saying, "I do not believe that the overriding desire to succeed has reached the desired intensity in minority business." Why do you think that's so?

I said that because I meet so many men who want to go into business, and they can't because the SBA won't give them a loan. Now, if you truly want to go into business and you try all the banks and they say no, and you try all the SBAs and governmental agencies and they say no, then you have to talk individual people into buying stock and making investments.

It sounds as if what's missing is the motivation to go out there and succeed.

That's the whole point. If blacks had the motivation, we would do some of these things. We would not give up our dream of going into business simply because a particular agency would not let us have the money to do it. I think the culture is such that we are taught to believe that everything good has happened, that all the new businesses have been started, that this is the age of big business, and that without friends and influence one cannot succeed.

Do you think that's the system's message?

Yes, and I think that's bad. Most people don't believe success is possible. So they get discouraged before they start. They think that all the cards are stacked against them; and many blacks think the white man's not going to let him succeed. I was interviewed on television not long ago, and the interviewer was telling me that Chicago's a terrible town, that Mayor Daley's doing this and Mayor Daley's doing that. I said, Mayor Daley's not keeping anybody from succeeding. Mayor Daley's not keeping anyone from going to school; he's not keeping anybody from getting a job. Many of these things are within our own power to do, and so we can't blame the system for everything. Anger and fear of failure get in the way.

And the lack of successful models?

Yes, you do need visible successful models. I think it's very important for a black person to see another black person, someone like himself, who is doing the thing that he wants to do. It lets him know, particularly in a country like ours, where you read so much about racial barriers and difficulties, that in spite of all those difficulties, it is still possible to make it. That's very important for black people to know.

And that is what Ebony *is all about.*

Absolutely. That's why we always play a positive role. It is why we are telling people what they can do rather than what they cannot do. Enough people are out there giving examples of what you can't do. Whenever there is a black person doing a successful job in a unique situation, there is an *Ebony* story. We want to show our readers, "Look, he's doing it in transportation, he's doing it in this, he's doing it in that. And if he can do it, you can do it."

There is a nice dualism in the role that Ebony *plays in the black world. It is a symbol of black success, it is a success, and it has success as its main product. One could look at you in the same way. Do you see yourself as in a sense your own best product?*

Well, I think that might be overly immodest. But I would say that I see myself as representing what I'm trying to sell in *Ebony*, yes. Yes, I do. I'm one of the models. There are a lot of them now, but I'm one of them. I'm one of the people who says you can succeed against the odds. I'm not saying the odds aren't there. Many people assume that *Ebony* is saying everything is just great. But we're not saying that. We're saying we have to deal with the world as we find it. And within the context of what we find, these are the ways we think you can succeed within the system.

So in a sense you're creating a whole new cultural ideal or concept?

Well, we're trying to apply the American culture to the black experience, to bring them together. If we learned anything during the 1960s, it was that perhaps we can make the system a little more responsive. We really can't change it, even if we wanted to. And the only way to succeed in the system is to learn the rules, and to try as nearly as possible to play by those rules.

What about the young blacks who are in large corporations? How would you advise them to stay with the system, to be active rather than angry?

I think they have to find ways to get their bosses to help them without admitting guilt, without feeling uncomfortable. The boss is not going to promote you if in the process he has to admit that he was wrong all the years that he didn't move you up. He's got to somehow feel that you did something that came to his attention and that justifies the promotion in the present.

You've got to let everybody save face.

Yes, that's right. Face-saving is important. But also, I think young people can be uniquely qualified. The important thing for all of us to have, particularly blacks, is some kind of power. And power comes in many forms. It comes in knowledge, it comes in experience, it comes in being beautiful. Some women have power by being beautiful; they can use their beauty, and that's power. It comes with sex. They can use sex, and that's power. It comes from being better at your job than anybody else, and that's power. For example, somebody here who can do a better job than anybody else has got a whole lot of power with me. They have what it takes to command a lot from me.

What if the corporation or system doesn't recognize power, or allow it? What can young blacks do then?

I think they are obligated to try to make each system work, and to try to persuade the people who could make the system more responsive. Failing that, if they still want to work for a large company, then I think they need to try another one. I don't think we ought to say that all big business is bad simply because a particular company has not treated somebody fairly.

What can large white corporations do to keep young blacks motivated to stay?

Well, I think they can do this by trying to promote them according to their abilities. I'm not sure that some of the large corporations are yet ready to do that for blacks. In many instances, the policy is straight at the top; management enunciates an equal opportunity policy, and I believe that many of the people on the board and in top management believe in it. But the policy is interpreted and operated on at a lower level, and here the prejudices of local supervisors can completely negate what top management would genuinely like to do.

Do you think then that white managers should deal with black subordinates differently from the way they do whites?

No, I just think they should deal with them equally.

How can top management be sure this happens?

Well, let me put it this way. I think that large white corporations ought to have an equal opportunity auditing committee. I never really thought about that before, but since you've asked me, I'll expand. Just as we have Arthur Andersen and Peat, Marwick come in and look over our business records to determine if the people lower down are doing what in fact they tell us they are doing, an equal opportunity auditing committee ought to examine the qualifications of the various people in the company and determine whether the blacks, based on their experience and qualifications, are in fact being given equal opportunity according to the policies announced. An audit would make the guys who are making the promotions and who are looking into the situation think more seriously about it.

Do you finance black enterprises on your own?

No, no. I never invest in any business that I don't control. And I just don't believe that it's my obligation to finance every guy who wants to go into business. I believe it's my obligation to try to be a successful model, to build businesses, to contribute to the community in other ways, but I don't believe it's my obligation to invest every time some guy believes he's got a good idea.

When you encourage young blacks to start their own businesses, what new markets do you see? These are tight times!

They are. To tell you the truth, if I were starting out, I would go into some phase of the franchise food business. Fortunes are being made every day because people have to eat. Look at McDonald's and Kentucky Fried Chicken. Some blacks should move in quickly. Not only have whites taken over fried chicken, which black people cook better, but they've also now taken over ribs, which we cook better too. I say, when they take ribs, they're going too far! So if I didn't have any other business, I'd start a chain of chicken shacks. Or I'd start an insurance agency, selling insurance on a brokerage basis. These are things that you wouldn't need capital for.

How would you feel about someone taking over the lead in your field?

I would consider it a personal failure if someone took over. I wouldn't feel bad if someone started a new, good magazine, but if someone could move past me in circulation and in advertising, I would consider that a personal failure. And failure is a word I don't accept. I don't really think anybody could do it though. I have a circulation of a million three. . .what would I be doing while somebody else was getting a million three?

I have a little niece who's always saying, "There's a big bully in our school." She says, "When I grow up, I'm going to punch him in the nose, and hit him in the mouth." I always say to her, "When you grow up, he's going to be bigger." You know, she keeps thinking that she's going to grow up, and he's going to stay where he is. If somebody came in the field, while he was getting successful, what would I be doing? I'd be working like hell to maintain my lead. As a matter of fact, I'm not too sure some good competition wouldn't be a good thing.

From what you say, your position seems secure. Do you have specific anxieties or fears connected with the future?

I'm afraid I cannot maintain my position. Life is very like a merry-go-round—you can't slow it down, and you don't want to get off. There are times when I feel that I would rather not be working as hard as I am. I'm actually working harder now than I did when I started, and that's because I want to maintain my leadership position. The responsibility of trying to be a leader and of trying to maintain that leadership is heavy. But I see my success here as something that I can't walk away from. And I can't slow it down.

Do you ever experience doubts?

Yes, there are doubts and fears. Each time I started a new magazine, I had a certain amount of fear about it. I wondered, Well, will it succeed? Is this the right time? Am I making a mistake? I think all of us have fears. But in the end, it's what you come out with that makes the difference; it's what finally emerges as your decision. And my decision has always been to go forward.

Risk-taking is part of your formula for success.

It's true. You have to dare to be things that you're afraid of. As a matter of fact, my editors often identify a hot story, one that will sell in *Ebony*, as one that I'm afraid to publish. Some of our best articles have been ones that I had a certain amount of fear about publishing. For example, I was fearful of the one called "Was Abraham Lincoln a Segregationist?" But it succeeded. Then we devoted a whole issue to the "white problem" in America; I was afraid of that. But in each case, after thinking about it and weighing all the circumstances, I'd say, "I've got to go forward with this."

Were the fears in those instances that you'd lose some of your advertisers?

Right. I thought it was going too far and that advertisers would reject it. And *Ebony* has to have advertising. Yes, I was fearful of that. As a matter of fact, I remember the night before we went to press, one of the editors, it was a woman, said, "Boss, do you know what you're doing?" And I said, "No, I really don't, but I'm going to do it anyway."

So there is a fear that the system could suddenly turn on you?

Oh yes, I always have that fear now. Don't get me wrong. I'm not saying that I'm going around strongly confident. I live in fear all the time. I run scared all the time. I think you have to in order to make it in business. I really don't think you can ever get the knots out of your stomach. It's never going to get better than it is now. You've just got to keep trying; when it's easy, you're dead.

Does this fear get in your way?

I don't tell others what I'm telling you. I walk around here with great confidence. I issue edicts and statements and policy as though it were the final word, and I'd gotten it from on high. But I'm trembling in my boots. I think that's what a good manager has to do. Once I decide I'm really going to do something, I psych myself up and convince myself that I'm going to do it. And in effect I gain confidence from expressing confidence.

So living with fear can be an asset?

I think it's very important to live with fear. One of the things that fear tells you is that you care about what you are doing.

PART TWO

COMMUNICATING THE VISION

AN OVERVIEW

At some time in their careers, people who later become leaders appear like everyone else. Generally, they don't join an organization with any special fanfare or undertake special rites of passage that mark them for a future high position. That is on the surface. If we could look closer, however, Abraham Zaleznik maintains in "Managers and Leaders: Are They Different?," we would see that managers and leaders are basically different types of people. And, in a sense, leaders have undergone a psychological rite of passage, a development through personal mastery, that managers do not. Leaders are what William James called the "twice-born," people whose lives have been "marked by continual struggle to attain some sense of order." They are people who conduct life as a pilgrimage for its own sake. Zaleznik stresses that one of the conditions crucial to leaders' reaching their potential is an intense one-on-one relationship with a mentor.

But what distinguishes leaders from other people in practice is not their personal histories but what they do. The essence of leadership, W.C.H. Prentice writes in "Understanding Leadership," is "the accomplishment of a goal through the direction of human assistants." To achieve this, whether the leader is popular, displays power, or is remarkable in his or her methods is of little significance. What matters is how much the leader understands the people who work for him or her and how their individual needs relate to the organizational goal he or she set. Understanding the needs of subordinates, however, does not mean that a leader should create a loose organization where everyone can "do his or her thing." Rather leaders see that people feel more secure in a well-ordered system that allows them to chose the means to fulfill their potential within bounds.

How to balance order and chaos is a tricky business. It's not always evident just how democratic or directive a leader ought to be in a given situation. In "How to Choose a Leadership Pattern," Robert Tannenbaum and Warren H. Schmidt offer a range of styles that leaders can adopt. "The successful leader is one who is keenly aware of those forces which are most relevant to his (or her) behavior at any given time. He (or she) accurately understands himself (or herself), the individuals and group he (or she) is dealing with, and the company and broader social environment in which he (or she) operates."

In the next article in this section, "Business Leadership and a Creative Society," Abram T. Collier looks at what leaders need to do from a different perspective. Leaders muster the creative energies of their people for a common good not just because of the kind of people they are but because creativity and innovation are the ultimate ends of business and of a company's members. In Collier's view "business, particularly in these days, affords the principal and the only means whereby individuals may gain the satisfaction of accomplishing something more than merely sustaining their own lives." It is the obligation of leaders, therefore, to provide an environment in which people can exploit their talents and join together in being creative.

Leaders, then, have an obligation to provide an opportunity for members of their organizations to be creative. O.A. Ohmann takes this idea a step further and implores leaders to provide not only a place where organizational members can fulfill themselves but also a place where they can find something to believe in. In Ohmann's perspective people need to believe that their leader has values and that what he or she does every day is related to those values. He writes that "people's real values have a subtle but inevitable way of being communicated and they affect the significance of everything they do." The vague values, the "skyhooks" of the title of Ohmann's article, provide a structure that give the experience of everyday meaning and give people something to work for besides material rewards.

Thomas J. Peters in "Leadership: Sad Facts and Silver Linings," also emphasizes the need for leaders to impart their values to the organization. They do so, he says, through persistently embodying them in how they deal with the myriad, ad hoc isolated events of every day. Because it is practically impossible for leaders to accomplish their ends directly, it is their capacities to shape values and educate by example that ultimately move the organization. Leaders communicate their vision by living it before it is a reality to anyone but themselves.

As Peters' article makes clear, the business of leadership is not straightforward. Nor is it for leaders themselves. As Abraham Zaleznik describes in "The Human Dilemmas of Leadership," leaders are isolated from both people in the organization with whom they used to be friends and former mentors. Because of this isolation it is important that they give themselves a sense of approval.

Also, because they may not be able to accomplish everything they want to, leaders are prone to suffer dissappointments. If they can see these setbacks not as permanent derailments but as opportunities for further growth, as Zaleznik urges in "Management of Disappointment," they can progress to even further heights. The key to this growth lies in the leader's capacity to use the present situation as a time to resolve still unsettled old conflicts from the past. The rewards of the present will "remain obscure so long as the individual is intent in his (or her) quest for restitutive rewards to make up for felt losses of the past." Only when they relinquish the past can leaders truly strive for a future.

8

Managers and Leaders:
Are They Different?

ABRAHAM ZALEZNIK

Most societies, and that includes business organizations, are caught between two conflicting needs: one for managers to maintain the balance of operations, and one for leaders to create new approaches and imagine new areas to explore. One might well ask why there is a conflict. Cannot both managers and leaders exist in the same society, or even better, cannot one person be both a manager and a leader? The author of this article does not say this is impossible but suggests that because leaders and managers are basically different types of people, the conditions favorable to the growth of one may be inimical to the other. Exploring the world views of managers and leaders, the author illustrates, using Alfred P. Sloan and Edwin Land among others as examples, that managers and leaders have different attitudes toward their goals, careers, relations with others, and themselves. And tracing their different lines of development, the author shows how leaders are of a psychological type different from managers; their development depends on their forming a one-to-one relationship with a mentor.

What is the ideal way to develop leadership? Every society provides its own answer to this question, and each, in groping for answers, defines its deepest concerns about the purposes, distributions, and uses of power. Business has contributed its answer to the leadership question by evolving a new breed called the manager. Simultaneously, business has established a new power ethic that favors collective over individual leadership, the cult of the group over that of personality. While ensuring the competence, control, and balance of power relations among groups with the potential for rivalry, managerial leadership unfortunately does not necessarily ensure imagination, creativity, or ethical behavior in guiding the destinies of corporate enterprises.

Leadership inevitably requires using power to influence the thoughts and actions of other people. Power in the hands of an individual entails human risks: first, the risk of equating power with the ability to get immediate results; second, the risk of ignoring the many different ways people can legitimately accumulate power; and third, the risk of losing self-control in the desire for power. The need to hedge these risks accounts in part for the development of collective leadership and the managerial ethic. Consequently, an inherent conservatism dominates the culture of large organizations. In *The Second American Revolution*, John D. Rockefeller, 3rd, describes the conservatism of organizations:

> An organization is a system, with a logic of its own, and all the weight of tradition and inertia. The deck is stacked in favor of the tried and proven way of doing things and against the taking of risks and striking out in new directions.[1]

Out of this conservatism and inertia organizations provide succession to power through the development of managers rather than individual leaders. And the irony of the managerial ethic is that it fosters a bureaucratic culture in business, supposedly the last bastion protecting us from the encroachments and controls of bureaucracy in government and education. Perhaps the risks associated with power in the hands of an individual may be necessary ones for business to take if organizations are to break free of their inertia and bureaucratic conservatism.

Manager vs. Leader Personality

Theodore Levitt has described the essential features of a managerial culture with its emphasis on rationality and control:

> Management consists of the rational assessment of a situation and the systematic selection of goals and purposes (what is to be done?); the systematic development of strategies to achieve these goals; the marshalling of the required resources; the rational design, organization, direction, and control of the activities required to attain the selected purposes; and, finally, the motivating and rewarding of people to do the work.[2]

In other words, whether his or her energies are directed toward goals, resources, organization structures, or people, a manager is a problem solver. The manager asks himself, "What problems have to be solved, and what are the best ways to achieve results so that people will continue to contribute to this organization?" In this conception, leadership is a practical effort to direct affairs; and to fulfill the task, a manager requires that many people operate at different levels of status and responsibility. Our democratic society is, in fact, unique in having solved the problem of providing well-trained managers for business. The same solution stands ready to be applied to government, education, health care, and other institutions. It takes neither genius nor heroism to be a manager, but rather persistence, tough-mindedness, hard work, intelligence, analytical ability, and, perhaps most important, tolerance and good will.

Another conception, however, attaches almost mystical beliefs to what leadership is and assumes that only great people are worthy of the drama of power and politics. Here, leadership is a psychodrama in which, as a precondition for control of a political structure, a lonely person must gain control of himself or herself. Such an expectation of leadership contrasts sharply with the mundane, practical, and yet important conception that leadership is really managing work of other people.

Two questions come to mind. Is this mystique of leadership merely a holdover from our collective childhood of dependency and our longing for good and heroic parents? Or is there a basic truth lurking behind the need for leaders that no matter how competent managers are, their leadership stagnates because of their limitations in visualizing purposes and generating value in work? Without this imaginative capacity and the ability to communicate, managers, driven by their narrow purposes, perpetuate group conflicts instead of reforming them into broader desires and goals.

If indeed problems demand greatness, then, judging by past performance, the selection and development of leaders leave a great deal to chance. There are no known ways to train "great" leaders. Furthermore, beyond what we leave to chance, there is a deeper issue in the relationship between the need for competent managers and the longing for great leaders.

What it takes to ensure the supply of people who will assume practical responsibility may inhibit the development of great leaders. Conversely, the presence of great leaders may undermine the development of managers who become very anxious in the relative disorder that leaders seem to generate. The antagonism in aim (to have many competent managers as well as great leaders) often remains obscure in stable and well-developed societies. But the antagonism surfaces during periods of stress and change, as it did in the Western countries during both the Great Depression and World War II. The tension also appears in the struggle for power between theorists and professional managers in revolutionary societies.

It is easy enough to dismiss the dilemma I pose (of training managers while we may need new leaders, or leaders at the expense of managers) by saying that the need is for people who can be *both* managers and leaders. The truth of the matter as I see it, however, is that just as a managerial culture is different from the entrepreneurial culture that develops when leaders appear in organizations, managers and leaders are very different kinds of people. They differ in motivation, personal history, and in how they think and act.

A technologically oriented and economically successful society tends to depreciate the need for great leaders. Such societies hold a deep and abiding faith in rational methods of solving problems, including problems of value, economics, and justice. Once rational methods of solving problems are broken down into elements, organized, and taught as skills, then society's faith in technique over personal qualities in leadership remains the guiding conception for a democratic society contemplating its leadership requirements. But there are times when tinkering and trial and error prove inadequate to the emerging problems of selecting goals, allocating resources, and distributing wealth and opportunity. During such times, the democratic society needs to find leaders who use themselves as the instruments of learning and acting, instead of managers who use their accumulation of collective experience to get where they are going.

The most impressive spokesman, as well as exemplar of the managerial viewpoint, was Alfred P. Sloan, Jr. who, along with Pierre du Pont, designed the modern corporate structure. Reflecting on what makes one management structure successful while another fails, Sloan suggested that "good management rests on a reconciliation of centralization and decentralization, or 'decentralization with coordinated control.' "[3]

Sloan's conception of management, as well as his practice, developed by trial and error, and by the accumulation of experience. Sloan wrote:

> There is no hard and fast rule for sorting out the various responsibilities and the best way to assign them. The balance which is struck. . .varies according to what is being decided, the circumstances of the time, past experience, and the temperaments and skills of the executive involved.[4]

In other words, in much the same way that the inventors of the late nineteenth century tried, failed, and fitted until they hit on a product or method, managers who innovate in developing organizations are "tinkerers." They do not have a grand design or experience the intuitive flash of insight that, borrowing from modern science, we have come to call the "breakthrough."

Managers and leaders differ fundamentally in their world views. The dimensions for assessing these differences include managers' and leaders' orientations toward their goals, their work, their human relations, and their selves.

Attitudes Toward Goals

Managers tend to adopt impersonal, if not passive, attitudes toward goals. Managerial goals arise out of necessities rather than desires, and therefore are deeply embedded in the history and culture of the organization.

Frederic G. Donner, chairman and chief executive officer of General Motors from 1958 to 1967, expressed this impersonal and passive attitude toward goals in defining GM's position on product development:

> To meet the challenge of the marketplace, we must recognize changes in customer needs and desires far enough ahead to have the right products in the right places at the right time and in the right quantity.

> We must balance trends in preference against the many compromises that are necessary to make a final product that is both reliable and good looking, that performs well and that sells at a competitive price in the necessary volume. We must design, not just the cars we would like to build, but more importantly, the cars that our customers want to buy.[5]

Nowhere in this formulation of how a product comes into being is there a notion that consumer tastes and preferences arise in part as a result of what manufacturers do. In reality, through product design, advertising, and promotion, consumers learn to like what they then say they need. Few would argue that people who enjoy taking snapshots *need* a camera that also develops pictures. But in response to novelty, convenience, a shorter interval between acting (taking the snap) and gaining pleasure (seeing the shot), the Polaroid camera succeeded in the marketplace. But it is inconceivable that Edwin Land responded to impressions of consumer need. Instead, he translated a technology (polarization of light) into a product, which proliferated and stimulated consumers' desires.

The example of Polaroid and Land suggests how leaders think about goals. They are active instead of reactive, shaping ideas instead of responding to them. Leaders adopt a personal and active attitude toward goals. The influence a leader exerts in altering moods, evoking images and expectations, and in establishing specific desires and objectives determines the direction a business takes. The net result of this influence is to change the way people think about what is desirable, possible, and necessary.

Conceptions of Work

What do managers and leaders do? What is the nature of their respective work? Leaders and managers differ in their conceptions.Managers tend to view work as an enabling process involving some combination of people and ideas interacting to establish strategies and make decisions. Managers help the process along by a range of skills, including calculating the interests in opposition, staging and timing the surfacing of controversial issues, and reducing tensions. In this enabling process, managers appear flexible in the use of tactics: they negotiate and bargain, on the one hand, and use rewards and punishments, and other forms of coercion, on the other. Machiavelli wrote for managers and not necessarily for leaders.

Alfred Sloan illustrated how this enabling process works in situations of conflict. The time was the early 1920s when the Ford Motor Co. still dominated the automobile industry using, as did General Motors, the conventional water-cooled engine. With the full backing of Pierre du Pont, Charles Kettering dedicated himself to the design of an air-cooled engine, which, if successful, would have been a great technical and market coup for GM. Kettering believed in his product, but the manufacturing division heads at GM remained skeptical and later opposed the new design on two grounds: first, that it was technically unreliable, and second, that the corporation was putting all its eggs in one basket by investing in a new product instead of attending to the current marketing situation.

In the summer of 1923 after a series of false starts and after its decision to recall the copper-cooled Chevrolets from dealers and customers, GM management reorganized and finally scrapped the project. When it finally dawned on Kettering that the company had rejected the engine, he was deeply discouraged and wrote to Sloan that without the "organized resistance" against the project it would succeed and that unless the project were saved, he would leave the company.

Alfred Sloan was all too aware of the fact that Kettering was unhappy and indeed intended to leave General Motors. Sloan was also aware of the fact that, while the manufacturing divisions strongly opposed the new engine, Pierre du Pont supported Kettering. Furthermore, Sloan had himself gone on record in a letter to Kettering less than two years earlier expressing full confidence in him. The problem Sloan now had was to make his decision stick, keep Kettering in the organization (he was much too valuable to lose), avoid alienating du Pont, and encourage the division heads to move speedily in developing product lines using conventional water-cooled engines.

The actions that Sloan took in the face of this conflict reveal much about how managers work. First, he tried to reassure Kettering by presenting the problem in a very ambiguous fashion, suggesting that he and the Executive Committee sided with Kettering, but that it would not be practical to force the divisions to do what they were opposed to. He presented the problem as being a question of the people, not the product. Second, he proposed to reorganize around the problem by consolidating all functions in a new division that would be responsible for the design, production, and marketing of the new car. This solution, however, appeared as ambiguous as his efforts to placate and keep Kettering in General Motors. Sloan wrote: "My plan was to create an independent pilot operation under the sole jurisdiction of Mr. Kettering, a kind of copper-cooled-car division. Mr. Kettering would designate his own chief engineer and his production staff to solve the technical problems of manufacture."[6]

While Sloan did not discuss the practical value of this solution, which included saddling an inventor with management responsibility, he in effect used this plan to limit his conflict with Pierre du Pont.

In effect, the managerial solution that Sloan arranged and pressed for adoption limited the options available to others. The structural solution narrowed choices, even limiting emotional reactions to the point where the key people could do nothing but go along, and even allowed Sloan to say in his memorandum to du Pont, "We have discussed the matter with Mr. Kettering at some length this morning and he agrees with us absolutely on every point we made. He appears to receive the suggestion enthusiastically and has every confidence that it can be put across along these lines."[7]

Having placated people who opposed his views by developing a structural solution that appeared to give something but in reality only limited options, Sloan could then authorize the car division's general manager, with whom he basically agreed, to move quickly in designing water-cooled cars for the immediate market demand.

Years later Sloan wrote, evidently with tongue in cheek, "The copper-cooled car never came up again in a big way. It just died out, I don't know why."[8]

In order to get people to accept solutions to problems, managers need to coordinate and balance continually. Interestingly enough, this managerial work has much in common with what diplomats and mediators do, with Henry Kissinger apparently an outstanding practitioner. The manager aims at shifting balances of power toward solutions acceptable as a compromise among conflicting values.

What about leaders, what do they do? Where managers act to limit choices, leaders work in the opposite direction, to develop fresh approaches to long-standing problems and to open issues for new options. Stanley and Inge Hoffmann, the political scientists, liken the leader's work to that of the artist. But unlike most artists, the leader himself is an integral part of the aesthetic product. One cannot look at a leader's art without looking at the artist. On Charles de Gaulle as a political artist, they wrote: "And each of his major political acts, however tortuous the means or the details, has been whole, indivisible and unmistakably his own, like an artistic act."[9]

The closest one can get to a product apart from the artist is the ideas that occupy, indeed at times obsess, the leader's mental life. To be effective, however, the leader needs to project ideas into images that excite people, and only then develop choices that give the projected images substance. Consequently, leaders create excitement in work.

John F. Kennedy's brief Presidency shows both the strengths and weaknesses connected with the excitement leaders generate in their work. In his inaugural address he said, "Let every nation know, whether it wishes us well or ill, that we shall pay any price, bear any burden, meet any hardship, support any friend, oppose any foe, in order to assure the survival and the success of liberty."

This much-quoted statement forced people to react beyond immediate concerns and to identify with Kennedy and with important shared ideals. But upon closer scrutiny the statement must be seen as absurd because it promises a position which if in fact adopted, as in the Viet Nam War, could produce disastrous results. Yet unless expectations are aroused and mobilized, with all the dangers of frustration inherent in heightened desire, new thinking and new choice can never come to light.

Leaders work from high-risk positions, indeed often are temperamentally disposed to seek out risk and danger, especially where opportunity and reward appear high. From my observations, why one individual seeks risks while another approaches problems conservatively depends more on personality and less on conscious choice. For some, especially those who become managers, the instinct for survival dominates their need for risk, and their ability to tolerate mundane, practical work assists their survival. The same cannot be said for leaders who sometimes react to mundane work as to an affliction.

Relations With Others

Managers prefer to work with people; they avoid solitary activity because it makes them anxious. Several years ago, I directed studies on the psychological aspects of career. The need to seek out others with whom to work and collaborate seemed to stand out as important characteristics of managers. When asked, for example, to write imaginative stories in response to a picture showing a single figure (a boy contemplating a violin, or a man silhouetted in a state of reflection), managers populated their stories with people. The following is an example of a manager's imaginative story about the young boy contemplating a violin:

> Mom and Dad insisted that junior take music lessons so that someday he can become a concert musician. His instrument was ordered and had just arrived. Junior is weighing the alternatives of playing football with the other kids or playing with the squeak box. He can't understand how his parents could think a violin is better than a touchdown.
>
> After four months of practicing the violin, junior has had more than enough, Daddy is going out of his mind, and Mommy is willing to give in reluctantly to the men's wishes. Football season is now over, but a good third baseman will take the field next spring.[10]

This story illustrates two themes that clarify managerial attitudes toward human relations. The first, as I have suggested, is to seek out activity with other people (e.g., the football team), and the second is to maintain a low level of emotional involvement in these relationships. The low emotional involvement appears in the writer's use of conventional metaphors, even clichés, and in the depiction of the ready transformation of potential conflict into harmonious decisions. In this case, Junior, Mommy, and Daddy agree to give up the violin for sports.

These two themes may seem paradoxical, but their coexistence supports what a manager does, including reconciling differences, seeking compromises, and establishing a balance of power. A further idea demonstrated by how the manager wrote the story is that managers may lack empathy, or the capacity to sense intuitively the thoughts and feelings of others. To illustrate attempts to be empathic, here is another story written to the same stimulus picture by someone considered by peers to be a leader:

> This little boy has the appearance of being a sincere artist, one who is deeply affected by the violin, and has an intense desire to master the instrument.

> He seems to have just completed his normal practice session and appears to be somewhat crestfallen at his inability to produce the sounds which he is sure lie within the violin.
>
> He appears to be in the process of making a vow to himself to expend the necessary time and effort to play this instrument until he satisfies himself that he is able to bring forth the qualities of music which he feels within himself.
>
> With this type of determination and carry through, this boy became one of the great violinists of his day.[11]

Empathy is not simply a matter of paying attention to other people. It is also the capacity to take in emotional signals and to make them mean something in a relationship with an individual. People who describe another person as "deeply affected" with "intense desire," as capable of feeling "crestfallen" and as one who can "vow to himself," would seem to have an inner perceptiveness that they can use in their relationships with others.

Managers relate to people according to the role they play in a sequence of events or in a decision-making *process*, while leaders, who are concerned with ideas, relate in more intuitive and empathetic ways. The manager's orientation to people, as actors in a sequence of events, deflects his or her attention away from the substance of people's concerns and toward their roles in a process. The distinction is simply between a manager's attention to *how* things get done and a leader's to *what* the events and decisions mean to participants.

In recent years, managers have taken from game theory the notion that decision-making events can be one of two types: the win-lose situation (or zero-sum game) or the win-win situation in which everybody in the action comes out ahead. As part of the process of reconciling differences among people and maintaining balances of power, managers strive to convert win-lose into win-win situations.

As an illustration, take the decision of how to allocate capital resources among operating divisions in a large, decentralized organization. On the face of it, the dollars available for distribution are limited at any given time. Presumably, therefore, the more one division gets, the less is available for other divisions.

Managers tend to view this situation (as it affects human relations) as a conversion issue: how to make what seems like a win-lose problem into a win-win problem. Several solutions to this situation come to mind. First, the manager focuses others' attention on procedure and not on substance. Here the actors become engrossed in the bigger problem of *how* to make decisions, not *what* decisions to make. Once committed to the bigger problem, the actors have to support the outcome since they were involved in formulating decision rules. Because the actors believe in the rules they formulated, they will accept present losses in the expectation that next time they will win.

Second, the manager communicates to subordinates indirectly, using "signals" instead of "messages." A signal has a number of possible implicit positions in it while a message clearly states a position. Signals are inconclusive and subject to reinterpretation should people become upset and angry, while messages involve the direct consequence that some people will indeed not like what they hear. The nature of messages heightens emotional response, and, as I have indicated, emotionally makes managers anxious. With signals, the question of who wins and who loses often becomes obscured.

Third, the manager plays for time. Managers seem to recognize that with the passage of time and the delay of major decisions, compromises emerge that take the sting out of win-lose situations; and the original "game" will be superseded by additional ones. Therefore, compromises may mean that one wins and loses simultaneously, depending on which of the games one evaluates.

There are undoubtedly many other tactical moves managers use to change human situations from win-lose to win-win. But the point to be made is that such tactics focus on the decision-making process itself and interest managers rather than leaders. The interest in tactics involves costs as well as benefits, including making organizations fatter in bureaucratic and political intrigue and leaner in direct, hard activity and warm human relationships. Consequently, one often hears subordinates characterize managers as inscrutable, detached, and manipulative. These adjectives arise from the subordinates' perception that they are linked together in a process whose purpose, beyond simply making decisions, is to maintain a controlled as well as rational and equitable structure. These adjectives suggest that managers need order in the face of the potential chaos that many fear in human relationships.

In contrast, one often hears leaders referred to in adjectives rich in emotional content. Leaders attract strong feelings of identity and difference, or of love and hate. Human relations in leader-dominated structures often appear turbulent, intense, and at times even disorganized. Such an atmosphere intensifies individual motivation and often produces unanticipated outcomes. Does this intense motivation lead to innovation and high performance, or does it represent wasted energy?

Senses of Self

In *The Varieties of Religious Experience*, William James describes two basic personality types, "once-born" and "twice-born."[12] People of the former personality type are those for whom adjustments to life have been straightforward and whose lives have been more or less a peaceful flow from the moment of their births. The twice-borns, on the other hand, have not had an easy time of it. Their lives are marked by a continual struggle to attain some sense of order. Unlike the once-borns they cannot take things for granted. According to James, these personalities have equally different world views. For a once-born personality, the sense of self, as a guide to conduct and attitude, derives from a feeling of being at home and in harmony with one's environment. For a twice-born, the sense of self derives from a feeling of profound separateness.

A sense of belonging or of being separate has a practical significance for the kinds of investments managers and leaders make in their careers. Managers see themselves as conservators and regulators of an existing order of affairs with which they personally identify and from which they gain rewards. Perpetuating and strengthening existing institutions enhances a manager's sense of self-worth: He or she is performing in a role that harmonizes with the ideals of duty and responsibility. William James had this harmony in mind—this sense of self as flowing easily to and from the outer world—in defining a once-born personality. If one feels oneself as a member of institutions, contributing to their well-being, then one fulfills a mission in life and feels rewarded for having measured up to ideals. This reward transcends material gains and answers the more fundamental desire for personal integrity which is achieved by identifying with existing institutions.

Leaders tend to be twice-born personalities, people who feel separate from their environment, including other people. They may work in organizations, but they never belong to them. Their sense of who they are does not depend upon memberships, work roles, or other social indicators of identity. What seems to follow from this idea about separateness is some theoretical basis for explaining why certain individuals search out opportunities for change. The methods to bring about change may be technological, political, or ideological, but the object is the same: to profoundly alter human, economic, and political relationships.

Sociologists refer to the preparation individuals undergo to perform in roles as the socialization process. Where individuals experience themselves as an integral part of the social structure (their self-esteem gains strength through participation and conformity), social standards exert powerful effects in maintaining the individual's personal sense of continuity, even beyond the early years in the family. The line of development from the family to schools, then to career is cumulative and reinforcing. When the line of development is not reinforcing because of significant disruptions in relationships or other problems experienced in the family or other social institutions, the individual turns inward and struggles to establish self-esteem, identity, and order. Here the psychological dynamics center on the experience with loss and the efforts at recovery.

In considering the development of leadership, we have to examine two different courses of life history: (1) development through socialization, which prepares the individual to guide institutions and to maintain the existing balance of social relations; and (2) development through personal mastery, which impels an individual to struggle for psychological and social change. Society produces its managerial talent through the first line of development, while through the second leaders emerge.

Development of Leadership

The development of every person begins in the family. Each person experiences the traumas associated with separating from parents, as well as the pain that follows such frustration. In the same vein, all individuals face the difficulties of achieving self-regulation and self-control. But for some, perhaps a majority, the fortunes of childhood provide adequate gratifications and sufficient opportunities to find substitutes for rewards no longer available. Such individuals, the "once-borns," make moderate identifications with parents and find a harmony between what they expect and what they are able to realize from life.

But suppose the pains of separation are amplified by a combination of parental demands and the individual's needs to the degree that a sense of isolation, of being special, and of wariness disrupts the bonds that attach children to parents and other authority figures? Under such conditions, and given a special aptitude, the origins of which remain mysterious, the person becomes deeply involved in the inner world at the expense of interest in the outer world. For such a person, self-esteem no longer depends solely upon positive attachments and real rewards. A form of self-reliance takes hold along with expectations of performance and achievement, and perhaps even the desire to do great works.

Such self-perceptions can come to nothing if the individual's talents are negligible. Even with strong talents, there are no guarantees that achievement will follow, let alone that the end result will be for good rather than evil. Other factors enter into development. For one thing, leaders are like artists and other gifted people who often struggle with neuroses; their ability to function varies considerably even over the short run, and some potential leaders may lose the struggle altogether. Also, beyond early childhood, the patterns of development that affect managers and leaders involve the selective influence of particular people. Just as they appear flexible and evenly distributed in the types of talents available for development, managers form moderate and widely distributed attachments. Leaders, on the other hand, establish, and also break off, intensive one-to-one relationships.

It is a common observation that people with great talents are often only indifferent students. No one, for example, could have predicted Einstein's great achievements on the basis of his mediocre record in school. The reason for mediocrity is obviously not the absence of ability. It may result, instead, from self-absorption and the inability to pay attention to the ordinary tasks at hand. The only sure way an individual can interrupt reverie-like preoccupation and self-absorption is to form a deep attachment to a great teacher or other benevolent person who understands and has the ability to communicate with the gifted individual.

Whether gifted individuals find what they need in one-to-one relationships depends on the availability of sensitive and intuitive mentors who have a vocation in cultivating talent. Fortunately, when the generations do meet and the self-selections occur, we learn more about how to develop leaders and how talented people of different generations influence each other.

While apparently destined for a mediocre career, people who form important one-to-one relationships are able to accelerate and intensify their development through an apprenticeship. The background for such apprenticeships, or the psychological readiness of an individual to benefit from an intensive relationship, depends upon some experience in life that forces the individual to turn inward. A case example will make this point clearer. This example comes from the life of Dwight David Eisenhower, and illustrates the transformation of a career from competent to outstanding.[13]

Dwight Eisenhower's early career in the Army foreshadowed very little about his future development. During World War I, while some of his West Point classmates were already experiencing the war firsthand in France, Eisenhower felt "embedded in the monotony and unsought safety of the Zone of the Interior. . .that was intolerable punishment."[14]

Shortly after World War I, Eisenhower, then a young officer somewhat pessimistic about his career chances, asked for a transfer to Panama to work under General Fox Connor, a senior officer whom Eisenhower admired. The army turned down Eisenhower's request. This setback was very much on Eisenhower's mind when Ikey, his first-born son, succumbed to influenza. By some sense of responsibility for its own, the army transferred Eisenhower to Panama, where he took up his duties under General Connor with the shadow of his lost son very much upon him.

In a relationship with the kind of father he would have wanted to be, Eisenhower reverted to being the son he lost. In this highly charged situation, Eisenhower began to learn from his mentor. General Connor offered, and Eisenhower gladly took, a magnificent tutorial on the military. The effects of this relationship on Eisenhower cannot be measured quantitatively, but, in Eisenhower's own reflections and the unfolding of his career, one cannot overestimate its significance in the reintegration of a person shattered by grief.

As Eisenhower wrote later about Connor, "Life with General Connor was a sort of graduate school in military affairs and the humanities, leavened by a man who was experienced in his knowledge of men and their conduct. I can never adequately express my gratitude to this one gentleman. . . . In a lifetime of association with great and good men, he is the one more or less invisible figure to whom I owe an incalculable debt."[15]

Some time after his tour of duty with General Connor, Eisenhower's breakthrough occurred. He received orders to attend the Command and General Staff School at Fort Leavenworth, one of the most competitive schools in the army. It was a coveted appointment, and Eisenhower took advantage of the opportunity. Unlike his performance in high school and West Point, his work at the Command School was excellent; he was graduated first in his class.

Psychological biographies of gifted people repeatedly demonstrate the important part a mentor plays in developing an individual. Andrew Carnegie owned much to his senior, Thomas A. Scott. As head of the Western Division of the Pennsylvania Railroad, Scott recognized talent and the desire to learn in the young telegrapher assigned to him. By giving Carnegie increasing responsibility and by providing him with the opportunity to learn through close personal observation, Scott added to Carnegie's self-confidence and sense of achievement. Because of his own personal strength and achievement, Scott did not fear Carnegie's aggressiveness. Rather, he gave it full play in encouraging Carnegie's initiative.

Mentors take risks with people. They bet initially on talent they perceive in younger people. Mentors also risk emotional involvement in working closely with their juniors. The risks do not always pay off, but the willingness to take them appears crucial in developing leaders.

Can Organizations Develop Leaders?

The examples I have given of how leaders develop suggest the importance of personal influence and the one-to-one relationship. For organizations to encourage consciously the development of leaders as compared with managers would mean developing one-to-one relationships between junior and senior executives and, more important, fostering a culture of individualism and possibly elitism. The elitism arises out of the desire to identify talent and other qualities suggestive of the ability to lead and not simply to manage.

The Jewel Companies Inc. enjoy a reputation for developing talented people. The chairman and chief executive officer, Donald S. Perkins, is perhaps a good example of a person brought along through the mentor approach. Franklin J. Lunding, who was Perkins's mentor, expressed the philosophy of taking risks with young people this way:

> Young people today want in on the action. They don't want to sit around for six months trimming lettuce.[16]

This statement runs counter to the culture that attaches primary importance to slow progression based on experience and proved competence. It is a high-risk philosophy, one that requires time for the attachment between senior and junior people to grow and be meaningful, and one that is bound to produce more failures than successes.

The elitism is an especially sensitive issue. At Jewel the MBA degree symbolized the elite. Lunding attracted Perkins to Jewel at a time when business school graduates had little interest in retailing in general, and food distribution in particular. Yet the elitism seemed to pay off: not only did Perkins become the president at age 37, but also under the leadership of young executives recruited into Jewel with the promise of opportunity for growth and advancement, Jewel managed to diversify into discount and drug chains and still remain strong in food retailing. By assigning each recruit to a vice president who acted as sponsor, Jewel evidently tried to build a structure around the mentor approach to developing leaders. To counteract the elitism implied in such an approach, the company also introduced an "equalizer" in what Perkins described as "the first assistant philosophy." Perkins stated:

> Being a good first assistant means that each management person thinks of himself not as the order-giving, domineering boss, but as the first assistant to those who "report" to him in a more typical organizational sense. Thus we mentally turn our organizational charts upside-down and challenge ourselves to seek ways in which we can lead. . .by helping. . .by teaching. . .by listening. . .and by managing in the true democratic sense. . .that is, with the consent of the managed. Thus the satisfactions of leadership come from helping others to get things done and changed—and not from getting credit for doing and changing things ourselves.[17]

While this statement would seem to be more egalitarian than elitist, it does reinforce a youth-oriented culture since it defines the senior officer's job as primarily helping the junior person.

A myth about how people learn and develop that seems to have taken hold in the American culture also dominates thinking in business. The myth is that people learn best from their peers. Supposedly, the threat of evaluation and even humiliation recedes in peer relations because of the tendency for mutual identification and the social restraints on authoritarian behavior among equals. Peer training in organizations occurs in various forms. The use, for example, of task forces made up of peers from several interested occupational groups (sales, production, research, and finance) supposedly removes the restraints of authority on the individual's willingness to assert and exchange ideas. As a result, so the theory goes, people interact more freely, listen more objectively to criticism and other points of view and, finally, learn from this healthy interchange.

Another application of peer training exists in some large corporations, such as Philips, N.V., in Holland, where organization structure is built on the principle of joint responsibility of two peers, one representing the commercial end of the business and the other the technical. Formally, both hold equal responsibility for geographic operations or product groups, as the case may be. As a practical matter, it may turn out that one or the other of the peers dominates the management. Nevertheless, the main interaction is between two or more equals.

The principal question I would raise about such arrangements is whether they perpetuate the managerial orientation, and preclude the formation of one-to-one relationships between senior people and potential leaders.

Aware of the possible stifling effects of peer relationships on aggressiveness and individual initiative, another company, much smaller than Philips, utilizes joint responsibility of peers for operating units, with one important difference. The chief executive of this company encourages competition and rivalry among peers, ultimately appointing the one who comes out on top for increased responsibility. These hybrid arrangements produce some unintended consequences that can be disastrous. There is no easy way to limit rivalry. Instead, it permeates all levels of the operation and opens the way for the formation of cliques in an atmosphere of intrigue.

A large, integrated oil company has accepted the importance of developing leaders through the direct influence of senior on junior executives. One chairman and chief executive officer regularly selected one talented university graduate whom he appointed his special assistant, and with whom he would work closely for a year. At the end of the year, the junior executive would become available for assignment to one of the operating divisions, where he would be assigned to a responsibile post rather than a training position. The mentor relationship had acquainted the junior executive first-hand with the use of power, and with the important antidotes to the power disease called *hubris*—performance and integrity.

Working in one-to-one relationships, where there is a formal and recognized difference in the power of the actors, takes a great deal of tolerance for emotional interchange. This interchange, inevitable in close working arrangements, probably accounts for the reluctance of many executives to become involved in such relationships. *Fortune* carried an interesting story on the departure of a key executive, John W. Hanley, from the top management of Procter & Gamble, for the chief executive officer position at Monsanto.[18] According to this account, the chief executive and chairman of P&G passed over Hanley for appointment to the presidency and named another executive vice president to this post instead.

The chairman evidently felt he could not work well with Hanley who, by his own acknowledgement, was aggressive, eager to experiment and change practices, and constantly challenged his superior. A chief executive officer naturally has the right to select people with whom he feels congenial. But I wonder whether a greater capacity on the part of senior officers to tolerate the competitive impulses and behavior of their subordinates might not be healthy for corporations. At least a greater tolerance for interchange would not favor the managerial team player at the expense of the individual who might become a leader.

I am constantly surprised at the frequency with which chief executives feel threatened by open challenges to their ideas, as though the source of their authority, rather than their specific ideas, were at issue. In one case a chief executive officer, who was troubled by the agressiveness and sometimes outright rudeness of one of his talented vice presidents, used various indirect methods such as group meetings and hints from outside directors to avoid dealing with his subordinate. I advised the executive to deal head-on with what irritated him. I suggested that by direct, face-to-face confrontation, both he and his subordinate would learn to validate the distinction between the authority to be preserved and the issues to be debated.

To confront is also to tolerate aggressive interchange, and has the net effect of stripping away the veils of ambiguity and signaling so characteristic of managerial cultures, as well as encouraging the emotional relationship leaders need if they are to survive.

Notes

1. John D. Rockefeller, 3rd, *The Second American Revolution* (New York, Harper & Row, 1973), p. 72.

2. Theodore Levitt, "Management and the Post Industrial Society," *The Public Interest*, Summer 1976, p. 73.

3. Alfred P. Sloan, Jr., *My Years with General Motors* (New York, Doubleday, 1964), p. 429.

4. Ibid.

5. Ibid., p. 440.

6. Ibid., p. 91.

7. Ibid., p. 91.

8. Ibid., p. 93.

9. Stanley Hoffman and Inge Hoffman, "The Will for Grandeur: De Gaulle as Political Artist," *Daedalus*, Summer 1968, p. 849.

10. Abraham Zaleznik, Gene W. Dalton, and Louis B. Barnes, *Orientation and Conflict in Career*, (Boston, Division of Research, Harvard Business School, 1970), p. 316.

11. Ibid., p. 294.

12. William James, *Varieties of Religious Experience* (New York, Mentor Books, 1958).

13. This example is included in Abraham Zaleznik and Manfred F. R. Kets de Vries, *Power and the Corporate Mind* (Boston, Houghton Mifflin, 1975).

14. Dwight D. Eisenhower, *At Ease: Stories I Tell to Friends* (New York, Doubleday, 1967), p. 136.

15. Ibid., p. 187.

16. "Jewel Lets Young Men Make Mistakes," *Business Week*, January 17, 1970, p. 90.

17. "What Makes Jewel Shine So Bright," *Progressive Grocer*, September 1973, p. 76.

18. "Jack Hanley Got There by Selling Harder," *Fortune*, November 1976.

9 Understanding Leadership

W. C. H. PRENTICE

Many managers can motivate their employees to perform on the job by rewarding them adequately. But not many can motivate their subordinates to want to carry out the goals of the organization day in and day out for the same rewards. Those who can are leaders. The job of every leader is to create the desire to perform in each employee and to merge their performances into an integrated effective force. How do leaders do it? The author of this article likens the leader to a conductor who provides the setting for people to exercise their talents and the rules they must abide by, and then convinces them that they are "taking part in the making of a kind of music that could only be made under such a leader." If the leader succeeds, it will be because he or she understands that all people are complex and different. The more leaders can acknowledge the individual worth and talent of each person in their "orchestra" the more they are likely to enlist each member's genuine desire to achieve the common end. Leadership is not being nice to people. It is recognizing that people need an environment in which they can, in a sense, be nice to themselves.

Attempts to analyze leadership tend to fail because the would-be analyst misconceives the task. Leadership is usually not studied at all. Popularity, power, showmanship, and wisdom in long-range planning are studied instead. Some leaders have these things, but they are not of the essence of leadership.

Leadership is the accomplishment of a goal through the direction of human assistants. The person who successfully marshals human collaborators to achieve particular ends is a leader. A great leader is one who can do so day after day, and year after year, in a wide variety of circumstances.

The successful leader may not possess or display power and may not use force or the threat of harm. The person who leads well may not be popular; followers may never do what is wanted out of love or admiration for their boss. The good leader may not ever be a colorful person and may never use memorable devices to dramatize the purposes of the group or to focus attention on its leadership. As for the important matter of setting goals, the leader may actually possess little influence, or even little skill; a leader may merely carry out the plans of others.

The leader's *unique* achievement is a human and social one which stems from understanding fellow workers and the relationship of their individual goals to the group goal that must be carried out.

Problems and Illusions

It is not hard to state in a few words what successful leaders do that makes them effective. But it is much harder to tease out the components that determine their success. The usual method is to provide adequate recognition of each worker's function so that the worker can foresee the satisfaction of some major interest or motive in carrying out the group enterprise. Crude forms of leadership rely solely on single sources of satisfaction, that is, monetary rewards or the alleviation of fears about various kinds of insecurity. The task is adhered to because following orders will lead to a paycheck, and deviation will lead to unemployment.

No one can doubt that such forms of motivation are effective within limits. In a mechanical way they do attach the worker's self-interest to the interest of the employer or the group. But no one can doubt the weaknesses of such simple techniques. Human beings are not machines with a single set of push buttons. When their complex responses to love, prestige, independence, achievement, and group membership are unrecognized on the job, they perform at best as automata who bring far less than their maximum efficiency to the task, and at worst as rebellious slaves who consciously or unconsciously sabotage the activities they are supposed to be furthering.

It is ironic that our basic image of "the leader" is so often that of a military commander, because—most of the time, at least—military organizations are the purest example of an unimaginative application of simple reward and punishment as motivating devices. The invention in World War II of the term "snafu" (situation normal, all fouled up) merely epitomizes what literature about military life from Greece and Rome to the present day has amply recorded: in no other human endeavor is morale typically so poor, or goldbricking and waste so much in evidence.

In defense of the military, two observations are relevant:

1. The military undeniably has special problems. Because soldiers get killed and have to be replaced, there are important reasons for treating them uniformly and mechanically.
2. Clarity about duties and responsibilities, as maximized by the autocratic chain of command, is not only essential to warfare but has

> undoubted importance for most group enterprises. In fact, any departure from an essentially military type of leadership is still considered in some circles a form of anarchy.

We have all heard the cry, "somebody's got to be the boss," and I suppose no one would seriously disagree. But it is dangerous to confuse the chain of command or table of organization with a method of getting things done. It is instead comparable to the diagram of a football play which shows a general plan and how each individual contributes to it.

The diagram is not leadership. By itself it has no bearing one way or another on how well executed the play will be. Yet that very question of effective execution is the problem of leadership. Rewards and threats may help each player to carry out an assignment, but in the long run if success is to be continuing and if morale is to survive, each player must not only fully understand the part and its relation to the group effort; the player must also *want* to carry it out. The problem of every leader is to create these wants and to find ways to channel existing wants into effective cooperation.

Relations With People

When leaders succeed, it will be because they have learned two basic lessons: people are complex, and people are different. Human beings respond not only to the traditional carrot and stick used by the driver of a donkey but also to ambition, patriotism, love of the good and the beautiful, boredom, self-doubt, and many more dimensions and patterns of thought and feeling that make them human. But the strength and importance of these interests are not the same for all workers, nor is the degree to which they can be satisfied in their jobs. For example:

- ☐ One person may have a deep religious need, but that fact is quite irrelevant to the daily routine.
- ☐ Another may derive primary satisfaction in solving intellectual problems and never be led to discover how love for chess problems and mathematical puzzles can be applied to business.
- ☐ Or still another may need a friendly admiring relationship that is lacking at home and be constantly frustrated by the failure of a superior to recognize and take advantage of that need.

To the extent that the leaders' circumstances and skills permit them to respond to such individual patterns, they will be better able to create genuinely intrinsic interest in the work that they are charged with getting done. And in the last analysis an ideal organization should have workers at every level reporting to a manager whose dominion is small enough to enable this leader to know the workers as human beings.

Limits of the Golden Rule

Fortunately, the prime motives of people who live in the same culture are often very much alike, and there are some general motivational rules that work very well indeed. The effectiveness of Dale Carnegie's famous prescriptions in his *How to Win Friends and Influence People* is a good example.[1] Its major principle is a variation of the Golden Rule: "Treat others as you would like to be treated." While limited and oversimplified, such a rule is a great improvement over the primitive coercive approaches or the straight reward-for-desired-behavior approach.

But it would be a great mistake not to recognize that some of the world's most ineffective leadership comes from the "treat others as you would be treated" school. All of us have known unselfish people who earnestly wished to satisfy the needs of their fellows but who were nevertheless completely inept as executives (or perhaps even as friends or as husbands), because it never occurred to them that others had tastes or emotional requirements different from their own. We all know the tireless worker who recognizes no one else's fatigue or boredom, the barroom-story addict who thinks it jolly to regale the ladies with his favorites, the devotee of public service who tries to win friends and influence people by offering them tickets to lectures on missionary work in Africa, the miser who thinks everyone is after money, and so on.

Leadership really does require more subtlety and perceptiveness than is implied in the saying, "do as you would be done by."

The ones who lead us effectively must seem to understand our goals and purposes. They must seem to be in a position to satisfy them; they must seem to understand the implications of their own actions; they must seem to be consistent and clear in their decisions. The word "seem" is important here. If we do not apprehend would-be leaders as ones who have these traits, it will make no difference how able they may really be. We will still not follow their lead. If, on the other hand, we have been fooled and they merely seem to have these qualities, we will still follow them until we discover our error. In other words, it is the impression they make at any one time that will determine the influence they have on their followers.

Pitfalls of Perception

For followers to recognize their leaders as they really are may be as difficult as it is for the leaders to understand the followers completely. Some of the worst difficulties in relationships between superiors and subordinates come from misperceiving reality. So much of what we understand in the world around us is colored by the conceptions and prejudices we start with. My view of my employer or superior may be so colored by expectations based on the behavior of other bosses that facts may not appear in the same way to her and to me. Many failures of leadership can be traced to oversimplified misperceptions on the part of the worker or to failures of the superior to recognize the context or frame of reference within which leadership actions will be understood by the subordinate.

A couple of examples of psychological demonstrations from the work of S. E. Asch[2] will illustrate this point:

> If I describe a man as warm, intelligent, ambitious, and thoughtful, you get one kind of picture of him. But if I describe another person as cold, ambitious, thoughtful, and intelligent, you probably get a picture of a very different sort of man. Yet I have merely changed one word and the order of a couple of others. The kind of preparation that one adjective gives for those that follow is tremendously effective in determining what meaning will be given to them. The term "thoughtful" may mean thoughtful of others or perhaps rational when it is applied to a warm person toward whom we have already accepted a positive orientation. But as applied to a cold man the same term may mean brooding, calculating, plotting. We must learn to be aware of the degree to which one set of observations about a man may lead us to erroneous conclusions about his other behavior.
>
> Suppose that I show two groups of observers a film of an exchange of views between an employer and his subordinate. The scene portrays disagreement followed by anger and dismissal. The blame for the difficulty will be assigned very differently by the two groups if I have shown one a scene of the worker earlier in a happy, loving family breakfast setting, while the other group has seen instead a breakfast-table scene where the worker snarls at his family and storms out of the house. The altercation will be understood altogether differently by people who have had favorable or unfavorable glimpses of the character in question.

In business a worker may perceive an offer of increased authority as a dangerous removal from the safety of assured, though gradual, promotion. A change in channels of authority or reporting, no matter how valuable in increasing efficiency, may be thought of as a personal challenge or affront. The introduction of a labor-saving process may be perceived as a threat to one's job. An invitation to discuss company policy may be perceived as an elaborate trap to entice one into admitting heretical or disloyal views. A new fringe benefit may be regarded as an excuse not to pay higher salaries. And so on.

Too often the superior is entirely unprepared for these interpretations, and they seem stupid, dishonest, or perverse—or all three. But successful leaders will have been prepared for such responses. They will have known that many of their workers have been brought up to consider their employers as their natural enemies, and that habit has made it second nature for them to "act like an employee" in this respect and always to be suspicious of otherwise friendly overtures from above.

The other side of the same situation is as bad. The habit of acting like a boss can be destructive, too. For instance, much resistance to modern concepts of industrial relations comes from employers who think such ideas pose too great a threat to the long-established picture of themselves as business autocrats. Their image makes progress in labor relations difficult.

Troubles of a Subordinate

But another and still more subtle factor may intervene between employer and employee—a factor that will be recognized and dealt with by successful industrial leaders. That factor is the psychological difficulty of being a subordinate. It is not easy to be a subordinate. If I take orders from another, it limits the scope of my independent decision and judgment; certain areas are established within which I do what the other wishes instead of what I wish. To accept such a role without friction or rebellion, I must find in it a reflection of some form of order that goes beyond my own personal situation (i.e., my age, class, rank, and so forth), or perhaps find that the balance of dependence and independence actually suits my needs. These two possibilities lead to different practical consequences.

For one thing, it is harder to take orders from one whom I do not consider in some sense superior. It is true that one of the saddest failures in practical leadership may be the executive who tries so hard to be one of the employees that any vestige of awe that the workers might have had for their boss is destroyed, with the consequence that they begin to see the executive as a person like themselves and to wonder why they should take orders from such a person. Understanding leaders will not let their workers think that they consider the workers inferiors, but they may be wise to maintain a kind of psychological distance that permits them to accept their authority without resentment.

When one of two people is in a superior position and must make final decisions, the superior can hardly avoid frustrating the aims of the subordinate, at least on occasion. And frustration seems to lead to aggression. That is, thwarting brings out a natural tendency to fight back. It does not take much thwarting to build up a habit of being ready to attack or defend oneself when dealing with the boss.

The situation is made worse if the organization is such that open anger toward the boss is unthinkable, for then the response to frustration is itself frustrated, and a vicious cycle is started. Suggestion boxes, grievance committees, departmental rivalries, and other such devices may serve as lightning rods for the day-to-day hostility engendered by the frustrations inherent in being a subordinate. But in the long run an effective leader will be aware of the need to balance dependence with independence, constraint with autonomy, so that the inevitable psychological consequences of taking orders do not loom too large.

Better yet, the effective leader will recognize that many people are frightened by complete independence and need to feel the security of a system that prescribes limits to their freedom. This leader will try to adjust the amounts and kinds of freedom to fit the psychological needs of subordinates. Generally this means providing a developmental program in which employees can be given some sense of where they are going within the company, and the effective leader will make sure that the view is a realistic one. Here an analogy may be helpful:

> Nothing is more destructive of morale in any group situation than a phony democracy of the kind one finds in some families. Parents who announce that the children are going to participate share-and-share-alike in all decisions soon find that they cannot, in fact, let them, and when the program fails, the children are especially thwarted. They come to perceive each of the necessarily frequent decisions that are not made by vote or consultation as arbitrary. They develop a strong sense of injustice and rebellion.

In industry the same conditions hold. It is no good to pretend that certain decisions can be made by subordinates if in fact they cannot. To make dependency tolerable, the lines must be clearly drawn between those decisions that are the prerogative of the superior and those that can be made by or in consultation with the subordinate. Once those lines have been drawn, it is essential not to transgress them any more often than is absolutely necessary.

Ideally, subordinates should have an area within which they are free to operate without anyone looking over their shoulders. The superior should clarify the goals and perhaps suggest alternative ways of achieving them, but subordinates should feel free to make the necessary choices. That ideal may sound artificial to autocrats of "the old school," and, if it does, it will mean nothing even if they give lip service to it. If a worker knows that the boss likes plan A, he is not going to try plan B and risk his job if it fails. If he knows that his job rides on every major decision, he can only play safe by identifying himself in every case with his superior's views. But that makes him an automaton who can bring no additional intelligence to the organization nor free his superiors from any decisions. He earns the respect of no one—not even the boss who helped make him that way

Goals in Development

No decision is worth the name unless it involves the balancing of risks and returns. If it were a sure thing, we would not need someone's judgment about it. Mistakes are inevitable. What we must expect of employees is that they learn from their mistakes, not that they never make them. It should be the executive's concern to watch the long-term growth of employees to see that, as they learn, their successes increasingly outweigh their failures.

This concept of long-run growth is a vital part of continuing leadership. Each person must be permitted to know that a role in the group is subject to development and that its development is limited only by the person's contributions. Especially, the worker must see the leader as the individual most interested in and helpful toward the worker's growth. It is not enough to have interested personnel officers or other staff people who play no role in policy making. Despite all the assistance they can render in technical ways, they can never take the place of an interest on the part of the responsible executive.

Dealing With Tact

At just this point, one often finds misconceptions. No sensible person wishes to make of the executive a substitute for father or psychiatrist or even director of personnel. The executive's interest can and should be entirely impersonal and unsentimental. The employee might be told:

> There is nothing personal about this. Anyone in your post would get the same treatment. But as long as you work for me, I am going to see that you get every opportunity to use your last ounce of potential. Your growth and satisfaction are a part of my job. The faster you develop into a top contributor to this company, the better I will like it. If you see a better way to do your job, do it that way; if something is holding you back, come and see me about it. If you are right, you will get all the help I can give you plus the recognition you deserve.

No genuine growth of an employee will occur without some teaching. The superior must from time to time take cognizance of the successes and failures and make sure that the subordinate sees them and their consequences as he does. And at this point of assessment a gravely difficult aspect of leadership arises. How can criticism be impersonal and still effective? How can a decision or a method be criticized without the worker feeling that he or she is personally being demeaned?

The importance of adequate communication at this point is twofold. Not only may long-range damage be done to employee morale, but a quite specific short-range effect is often the employee's failure to do what is necessary to carry out the boss's alternative plan, since its failure might prove that the employee had been right in the first place. It is all too easy for a leader to produce antagonism and defensiveness by dealing impersonally with a problem and forgetting the human emotions and motives that are involved in it.

Interestingly enough, such failures seem to happen more often in office situations than anywhere else, and we might well wonder if we have not tended to insulate behavior in management from behavior outside—in the home, for instance. We do not assume that an order or a memorandum is the best way of making our wishes acceptable at home. Most reasonably bright people learn early in life how to get others to cooperate. It is second nature to create a personal and emotional setting that is right for the particular person (e.g., spouse, adult son, teenage daughter, or child) and for the particular request that is to be made.

More than that, we are likely to know which aspects of, say, a vacation plan to stress to make it seem attractive to the spouse who wants a change of scenery, the son who wants to fish, or the daughter who wants to ski. We are likely to learn, too, that one spouse with a hand in the decision-making process may be readily persuaded, whereas another may wish only to have a ready-made plan submitted for approval or disdain. Indeed, we probably respond to such differences at home with very little thought.

But in the office we lay aside our everyday intuitive skills in human relations and put on the mask of an employer or an executive. We try to handle our tasks with orders or directives impersonally aimed at whoever happens to be responsible for their execution, forgetting that effective mobilization of human resources always requires the voluntary participation of all. Leadership is an interaction among people. It requires followers with particular traits and particular skills and a leader who knows how to use them.

Secrets of a Conductor

The director of an orchestra may perhaps serve as a useful model for some of the important relationships which run through all leadership situations:

1. Obvious enough in this context, but not always remembered, is the fact that the musicians must have the requisite skills and training for their roles. Not all group failures are the boss's fault. Toscanini could not get great music from a high-school band.
2. A psychological setting must be established for the common task. A conductor must set up ground rules, signals, and tastes in such a way that the mechanics of getting a rehearsal started do not interfere with the musical purpose. Just as the conductor must establish agreement about promptness at rehearsals, talking or smoking between numbers, new versus old music, and a dozen other things that might otherwise come between the conductor and the musicians in their common aim, so every office or factory must have rules or customs which are clearly understood and easily followed.
3. Most important of all, the musicians must share satisfaction with their leader in the production of music or of music of a certain quality. Unless they individually achieve a sense of accomplishment or even fulfillment, the conductor's leadership has failed and great music will not be made. Some distinguished conductors have been petty tyrants; others play poker with their musicians and become godparents to their babies. These matters are essentially irrelevant. What the great conductor achieves is each instrumentalist's conviction that he or she is taking part in the making of a kind of music that could only be made under such a leader. Personal qualities and mannerisms may have a secondary importance; they may serve as reminders, reinstating and reinforcing the vital image of a person with the highest musical standards. But no one can become a Toscanini by imitating his mannerisms.

"Low-Pressure" Leadership

These simple facts are often overlooked. In industry we can find endless numbers of executives who merely mimic the surface characteristics of some successful colleague or superior without ever trying to find ways to enlist the active participation of their own staffs by showing them ways to personal fulfillment in the common task.

These leaders take the approach that a certain type of sales executive takes; and it is significant, I think, that the financial, manufacturing, and research staffs of many companies look on sales executives as a necessary evil, and would be horrified at the thought of bringing what they consider a "sales approach" into management. Their reason may never be clearly formulated, but it surely has something to do with an air of trickery and manipulation that surrounds *some* advertising, marketing, and selling. The sales executives and advertisers I refer to are often willing to seek and exploit a weak point in a customer's defenses and make a sale even when they suspect or perhaps know that the customer will live to regret the purchase.

Slick uses of social and psychological tricks can indeed result in persuading another to do your bidding, but they are unfit for a continuing human relationship. As every truly constructive sales executive knows, a business transaction should benefit both buyer and seller. And that means finding out the needs of the customer, making sure that in fact the customer understands them, and providing the customer with a product that will satisfy that need. Trained in such an approach, the seller should be the executive par excellence, carrying these means of selling over into administrative dealings.

By contrast, the tricky, fast-talking manipulator who is proud of outwitting customers, who counts on selling a man cigarettes by playing on his vanity or selling a woman cosmetics by playing on her ambition, might turn into an executive who treats workers as contemptuously as customers. If he enjoys hoodwinking workers by playing on their motives and their interests, they will soon discover that they are being toyed with, and the loyalty and confidence that are essential ingredients of effective leadership will be corroded away.

Conclusion

In the last resort, an executive must use skills and human insight as does an orchestra leader—to capture individual satisfactions in the common enterprise and to create fulfillment that holds the subordinate to the part. No collection of cute tricks of enticement or showmanship can do that.

Leadership, despite what we sometimes think, consists of a lot more than just "understanding people," "being nice to people," or not "pushing other people around." Democracy is sometimes thought to imply no division of authority, or to imply that everyone is the boss. Of course, that is nonsense, especially in business. But business leadership *can* be democratic in the sense of providing the maximum opportunity for growth to each worker without creating anarchy.

In fact, the orderly arrangement of functions and the accurate perception of a leader's role in that arrangement must always precede the development of abilities to the maximum. A leader's job is to provide that recognition of roles and functions within the group that will permit each member to satisfy and fulfill some major motive or interest.

Notes

1. Dale Carnegie, *How to Win Friends and Influence People* (New York, Simon & Schuster, 1936).

2. S. E. Asch, "Forming Impressions of Personality," *The Journal of Abnormal and Social Psychology,* 1946, Vol. 41, pp. 258–290.

10

How to Choose a Leadership Pattern

ROBERT TANNENBAUM and WARREN H. SCHMIDT

Once upon a time, managers made decisions—good ones naturally—and subordinates carried them out. But the fairy tale days of management, if they ever really existed, certainly are over now. With the increasing awareness of the values of participative management, managers are reluctant to deliver decisions from on high in the way "strong" leaders were supposed to. But, at the same time, managers don't know how much they ought to involve their subordinates in the decision-making process. With each decision, managers find themselves perplexed as to what course to follow. These authors present a framework that managers can use in trying to determine how participative they ought to be. They describe a range of behavior from making the decision and then announcing it to permitting the group to make decisions within prescribed limits. The authors conclude that through their understanding of themselves, their subordinates, and their companies' social environments, effective managers perceive which behavior is appropriate to a situation and can act accordingly.

> I put most problems into my group's hands and leave it to them to carry the ball from there. I serve merely as a catalyst, mirroring back the people's thoughts and feelings so that they can better understand them.
>
> It's foolish to make decisions oneself on matters that affect people. I always talk things over with my subordinates, but I make it clear to them that I'm the one who has to have the final say.
>
> Once I have decided on a course of action, I do my best to sell my ideas to my employees.
>
> I'm being paid to lead. If I let a lot of other people make the decisions I should be making, then I'm not worth my salt.
>
> I believe in getting things done. I can't waste time calling meetings. Someone has to call the shots around here, and I think it should be me.

Each of these statements represents a point of view about "good leadership." Considerable experience, factual data, and theoretical principles could be cited to support each statement, even though they seem to be inconsistent when placed together. Such contradictions point up the dilemma frequently facing the modern manager.

New Problem

The problem of how the modern manager can be "democratic" in relations with subordinates and at the same time maintain the necessary authority and control in the organization for which the manager is responsible has come into focus increasingly in recent years.

Earlier in the century this problem was not so acutely felt. The successful executive was generally pictured as possessing intelligence, imagination, initiative, the capacity to make rapid (and generally wise) decisions, and the ability to inspire subordinates. People tended to think of the world as being divided into leaders and followers.

New Focus

Gradually, however, from the social sciences emerged the concept of "group dynamics" with its focus on *members* of the group rather than solely on the leader. Research efforts of social scientists underscored the importance of employee involvement and participation in decision making. Evidence began to challenge the efficiency of highly directive leadership, and increasing attention was paid to problems of motivation and human relations.

Through training laboratories in group development that sprang up across the country, many of the newer notions of leadership began to exert an impact. These training laboratories were carefully designed to give people a first-hand experience in full participation and decision making. The designated "leaders" deliberately attempted to reduce their own power and to make group members as responsible as possible for setting their own goals and methods within the laboratory experience.

It was perhaps inevitable that some of the people who attended the training laboratories regarded this kind of leadership as being truly "democratic" and went home with the determination to build fully participative decision making into their own organizations. Whenever their bosses made a decision without convening a staff meeting, they tended to perceive this as authoritarian behavior. The true symbol of democratic leadership to some was the meeting—and the less directed from the top, the more democratic it was.

Some of the more enthusiastic alumni of these training laboratories began to get the habit of categorizing leader behavior as "democratic" *or* "authoritarian." The boss who made too many decisions alone was thought of as an authoritarian, and this manager's directive behavior was often attributed solely to personality.

New Need

The net result of the research findings and of the human relations training based upon them has been to call into question the stereotype of an effective leader. Consequently, the modern manager is often divided between two methods.

Often the manager is not quite sure how to behave; there are times when this executive is torn between exerting "strong" leadership and "permissive" leadership. Sometimes new knowledge pushes in one direction ("I should really get the group to help make this decision"), but at the same time experience pushes in another direction ("I really understand the problem better than the group and therefore I should make the decision"). The manager is not sure when a group decision is really appropriate or when holding a staff meeting serves merely as a device for avoiding decision-making responsibility.

The purpose of this chapter is to suggest a framework that managers may find useful in grappling with this dilemma. First, we look at the different patterns of leadership behavior that the manager can choose from in relating to subordinates. Then, we turn to some of the questions suggested by this range of patterns. For instance, how important is it for a manager's subordinates to know what type of leadership is being used in a situation? What factors should the manager consider in deciding on a leadership pattern? What difference do long-run objectives make as compared to immediate objectives?

Range of Behavior

Exhibit 1 presents the continuum or range of possible leadership behavior available to a manager. Each type of action is related to the degree of authority used by the boss and to the amount of freedom available to subordinates in reaching decisions. The actions seen on the extreme left characterize the manager who maintains a high degree of control while those seen on the extreme right characterize the manager who releases a high degree of control. Neither extreme is absolute; authority and freedom are never without their limitations.

Now let us look more closely at each of the behavior points occurring along this continuum.

The manager makes the decision and announces it.

In this case the boss identifies a problem, considers alternative solutions, chooses one of them, and then reports this decision to subordinates for

Exhibit 1. Continuum of Leadership Behavior

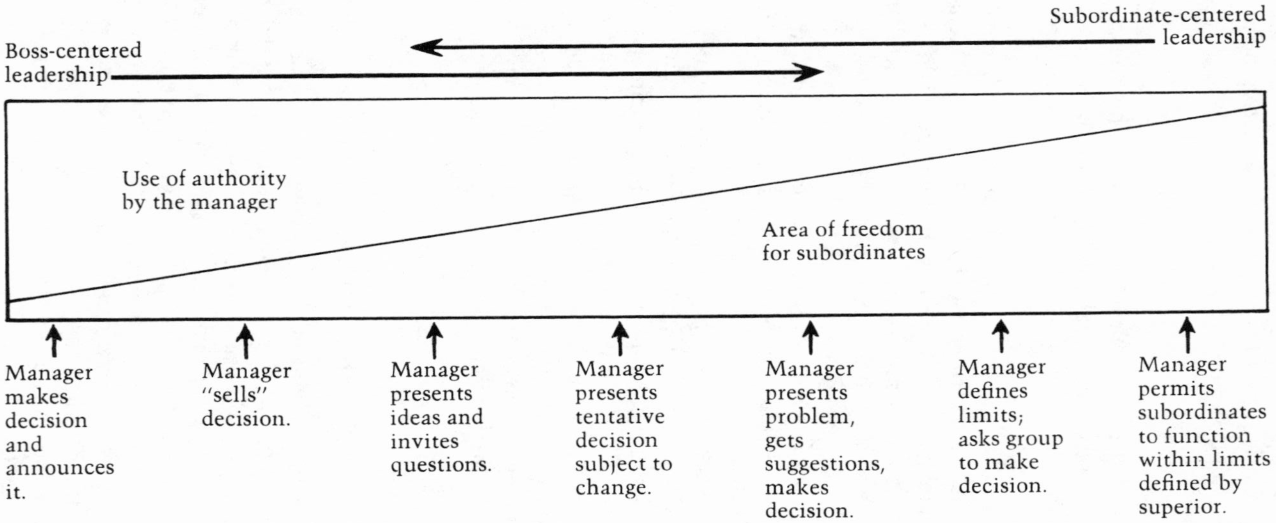

Boss-centered leadership

Subordinate-centered leadership

Use of authority by the manager

Area of freedom for subordinates

Manager makes decision and announces it.

Manager "sells" decision.

Manager presents ideas and invites questions.

Manager presents tentative decision subject to change.

Manager presents problem, gets suggestions, makes decision.

Manager defines limits; asks group to make decision.

Manager permits subordinates to function within limits defined by superior.

implementation. This manager may or may not give consideration to what he or she believes subordinates will think or feel about the decision; in any case, no opportunity is provided for them to participate directly in the decision-making process. Coercion may or may not be used or implied.

The manager "sells" a decision.

Here the manager, as before, takes responsibility for identifying the problem and arriving at a decision. However, rather than simply announcing it, the manager takes the additional step of persuading subordinates to accept it. In doing so, this executive recognizes the possibility of some resistance among those who will be faced with the decision and seeks to reduce this resistance by indicating, for example, what the employees have to gain from the decision.

The manager presents ideas, invites questions.

Here the boss who has arrived at a decision and who seeks acceptance of ideas provides an opportunity for subordinates to get a fuller explanation of the boss's thinking and intentions. After presenting the ideas, the manager invites questions so that associates can better understand what is to be accomplished. This "give and take" also enables both manager and subordinates to explore more fully the implications of the decision.

The manager presents a tentative decision subject to change.

This kind of behavior permits the subordinates to exert some influence on the decision. The initiative for identifying and diagnosing the problem remains with the boss. Before meeting with the staff, the manager has thought the problem through and arrived at a decision—but only a tentative one. Before finalizing it, the proposed solution is presented for the reaction of those who will be affected by it. The manager says in effect, "I'd like to hear what you have to say about this plan that I have developed. I'll appreciate your frank reactions, but will reserve for myself the final decision."

The manager presents the problem, gets suggestions, and then makes the decision.

Up to this point the boss has come before the group with a solution. Not so in this case. The subordinates now get the first chance to suggest solutions. The manager's initial role involves identifying the problem. The manager might, for example, say something of this sort: "We are faced with a number of complaints from newspapers and the general public on our service policy. What is wrong here? What ideas do you have for coming to grips with this problem?"

The function of the group becomes one of increasing the manager's repertory of possible solutions to the problem. The purpose is to capitalize on the knowledge and experience of those who are on the "firing line." From the expanded list of alternatives developed by manager and subordinates, the manager then selects the solution that seems most promising.[1]

The manager defines the limits and requests the group to make a decision.

At this point the manager passes to the group (possibly including the manager as a member) the right to make decisions. Before doing so, however, this leader defines the problem to be solved and boundaries within which the decision must be made.

An example might be the handling of a parking problem at a plant. The boss decides that this is something that should be worked on by the people involved, so they are called together and the existence of the problem is noted. Then the boss tells them:

"There is the open field just north of the main plant which has been designated for additional employee parking. We can build underground or surface multilevel facilities as long as the cost does not exceed $100,000. Within these limits we are free to work out whatever solution makes sense to us. After we decide on a specific plan, the company will spend the available money in whatever way we indicate."

The manager permits the group to make decisions within prescribed limits.

This represents an extreme degree of group freedom only occasionally encountered in formal organizations, as, for instance, in many research groups. Here the team of managers or engineers undertakes the identification and diagnosis of the problem, develops alternative procedures for solving it, and decides on one or more of these alternative solutions. The only limits directly imposed on the group by the organization are those specified by the superior of the team's boss. If the boss participates in the decision-making process, the boss attempts to do so with no more authority than any other member of the group. The boss makes an advance commitment to assist in implementing whatever decision the group makes.

Key Questions

As the continuum in Exhibit 1 demonstrates, there are a number of alternative ways in which a manager can relate to the group or individuals being supervised. At the extreme left of the range, the emphasis is on the manager—on what *the manager* is interested in, how *the manager* sees things, how *the manager* feels about them. As we move toward the subordinate-centered end of the continuum, however, the focus is increasingly on the subordinates—on what *they* are interested in, how *they* look at things, how *they* feel about them.

When business leadership is regarded in this way, a number of questions arise. Let us take four of special importance:

Can a boss ever relinquish responsibility by delegating it to someone else?

Our view is that the manager must expect to be held responsible by his or her superior for the quality of the decisions made, even though operationally these decisions may have been made on a group basis. The manager should, therefore, be ready to accept whatever risk is involved whenever the manager delegates decision-making power to subordinates. Delegation is not a way of "passing the buck." Also, it should be emphasized that the amount of freedom the boss gives to subordinates cannot be greater than the freedom which the boss has been given by a superior.

Should the manager participate with subordinates once responsibility has been delegated to them?

The manager should carefully think over this question and decide on a role prior to involving the subordinate group. The manager should ask if her or his presence will inhibit or facilitate the problem-solving process. There may be some instances when the manager should leave the group to let it solve the problem for itself. Typically, however, the boss has useful ideas to contribute, and should function as an additional member of the group. In the latter instance, it is important that the boss indicate clearly to the group that he or she is in a *member* role rather than in an authority role.

How important is it for the group to recognize what kind of leadership behavior the boss is using?

It makes a great deal of difference. Many relationship problems between boss and subordinate occur because the boss fails to make clear how his or her authority will be used. If, for example, the boss actually intends to make a certain decision alone, but the subordinate group gets the impression that this authority has been delegated, considerable confusion and resentment are likely to follow. Problems may also occur when the boss uses a "democratic" facade to conceal an already made decision which the manager hopes the group will accept as its own. The attempt to "make them think it was their idea in the first place" is a risky one. We believe that it is highly important for the manager to be honest and clear in describing what authority is being kept and what role the subordinates are being asked to assume in solving a particular problem.

Can you tell how "democratic" a manager is by the number of decisions subordinates make?

The sheer *number* of decisions is not an accurate index of the amount of freedom that a subordinate group enjoys. More important is the *significance* of the decisions which the boss entrusts to subordinates. Obviously a decision on how to arrange desks is of an entirely different order from a decision involving the introduction of new electronic data-processing equipment. Even though the widest possible limits are given in dealing with the first issue, the group will sense no particular degree of responsibility. For a boss to permit the group to decide equipment policy, even within rather narrow limits, would reflect the boss's greater degree of confidence in them.

Deciding How to Lead

Now let us turn from the types of leadership which are possible in a company situation to the question of what types are *practical* and *desirable*. What factors or forces should a manager consider in deciding how to manage? Three are of particular importance:

- ☐ Forces in the manager.
- ☐ Forces in the subordinates.
- ☐ Forces in the situation.

We should like briefly to describe these elements and indicate how they might influence a manager's action in a decision-making situation.[2] The strength of each of them will, of course, vary from instance to instance, but the manager who is sensitive to them can better assess the problems which face him or her and determine which mode of leadership behavior is most appropriate.

Forces in the Manager

The manager's behavior in any given instance will be influenced greatly by the many forces operating within the manager's personality. The manager will, of course, perceive leadership problems in a unique way on the basis of personal background, knowledge, and experience. Among the important internal forces affecting the manager will be the following:

1. *The manager's value system.* How strongly does the manager feel that individuals should have a share in making the decisions which affect them? Or, how convinced is the manager that the official who is paid to assume responsibility should personally carry the burden of decision making? The strength of convictions on questions like these will tend to move the manager to one end or the other of the continuum shown in Exhibit 1.

Managerial behavior will also be influenced by the relative importance that is attached to organizational efficiency, personal growth of subordinates, and company profits.[3]

2. *The manager's confidence in subordinates.* Managers differ greatly in the amount of trust they have in other people generally, and this carries over to the particular employees they supervise at a given time. In viewing the particular group of subordinates, the manager is likely to consider their knowledge and competence with respect to the problem. A central question the manager might ask himself or herself is: "Who is best qualified to deal with this problem?" Often the manager may, justifiably or not, have more confidence in personal capabilities than in those of subordinates.

3. *The manager's own leadership inclinations.* There are some managers who seem to function more comfortably and naturally as highly directive leaders. Resolving problems and issuing orders come easily to them. Other managers seem to operate more comfortably in a team role, where they are continually sharing many of their functions with their subordinates.

4. *The manager's feelings of security in an uncertain situation.* The manager who releases control over the decision-making process thereby reduces the predictability of the outcome. Some managers have a greater need than others for predictability and stability in their environment. This "tolerance for ambiguity" is being viewed increasingly by psychologists as a key variable in a person's manner of dealing with problems.

The manager brings these and other highly personal variables to each situation faced. If the manager can see them as forces which, consciously or unconsciously, influence his or her behavior, the manager can better understand what makes certain methods of acting personally preferable. And understanding this, the manager can often become more effective.

Forces in the Subordinate

Before deciding how to lead a certain group, the manager will also want to consider a number of forces affecting subordinates' behavior. The manager will want to remember that each employee is also influenced by many personality variables. In addition, each subordinate has a set of expectations about how the boss should act in relation to the subordinate (the phrase "expected behavior" is one we hear more and more often these days at discussions of leadership and teaching). The better the manager understands these factors, the more accurately the manager can determine what kind of managerial behavior will enable subordinates to act most effectively.

Generally speaking, the manager can permit subordinates greater freedom if the following essential conditions exist:

- ☐ If the subordinates have relatively high needs for independence. (As we all know, people differ greatly in the amount of direction that they desire.)

- ☐ If the subordinates have a readiness to assume responsibility for decision making. (Some see additional responsibility as a tribute to their ability; others see it as "passing the buck.")
- ☐ If they have a relatively high tolerance for ambiguity. (Some employees prefer to have clear-cut directives given to them; others prefer a wider area of freedom.)
- ☐ If they are interested in the problem and feel that it is important.
- ☐ If they understand and identify with the goals of the organization.
- ☐ If they have the necessary knowledge and experience to deal with the problem.
- ☐ If they have learned to expect to share in decision making. (Persons who have come to expect strong leadership and are then suddenly confronted with the request to share more fully in decision making are often upset by this new experience. On the other hand, persons who have enjoyed a considerable amount of freedom resent the boss who begins to make all the decisions.)

The manager will probably tend to make fuller use of personal authority if the above conditions do *not* exist; at times there may be no realistic alternative to doing a job singlehandedly.

The restrictive effect of many of the forces will, of course, be greatly modified by the general feeling of confidence which subordinates have in the boss. Where they have learned respect and trust, the boss is free to vary behavior. The boss will feel certain that subordinates do not perceive an authoritarian boss on those occasions when the boss makes decisions alone. Similarly, the boss will not be seen as using staff meetings to avoid decision-making responsibility. In a climate of mutual confidence and respect, people tend to feel less threatened by deviations from normal practice, which in turn makes possible a higher degree of flexibility in the whole relationship.

Forces in the Situation

In addition to the forces which exist in the manager and in subordinates, certain characteristics of the general situation will also affect the manager's behavior. Among the more critical environmental pressures that surround the manager are those which stem from the organization, the work group, the nature of the problem, and the pressures of time. Let us look briefly at each of these.

Type of Organization. Like individuals, organizations have values and traditions which inevitably influence the behavior of the people who work in them. The manager who is a newcomer to a company quickly discovers that certain kinds of behavior are approved while others are not. The newcomer also discovers that to deviate radically from what is generally accepted is likely to create problems.

These values and traditions are communicated in numerous ways—through job descriptions, policy pronouncements, and public statements by top executives. Some organizations, for example, hold to the notion that the desirable executive is one who is dynamic, imaginative, decisive, and persuasive. Other organizations put more emphasis upon the importance of the executive's ability to work effectively with people—human relations skills. The fact that superiors have a defined concept of what the good executive should be will very likely push the manager toward one end or the other of the behavioral range.

In addition to the above, the amount of employee participation is influenced by such variables as the size of the working units, their geographical distribution, and the degree of inter- and intra-organizational security required to attain company goals. For example, the wide geographical dispersion of an organization may preclude a practical system of participative decision making, even though this would otherwise be desirable. Similarly, the size of the working units or the need for keeping plans confidential may make it necessary for the boss to exercise more control than would otherwise be the case. Factors like these may limit considerably the manager's ability to function flexibly on the continuum.

Group Effectiveness. Before turning decision-making responsibility over to a subordinate group, the boss should consider how effectively its members work together as a unit.

One of the relevant factors here is the experience the group has had in working together. It can generally be expected that a group which has functioned for some time will have developed habits of cooperation and thus be able to tackle a problem more effectively than a new group. It can also be expected that a group of people with similar backgrounds and interests will work more quickly and easily than people with dissimilar backgrounds, because the communication problems are likely to be less complex.

The degree of confidence that the members have in their ability to solve problems as a group is also a key consideration. Finally, such group variables as cohesiveness, permissiveness, mutual acceptance, and commonality of purpose will exert subtle but powerful influence on the group's functioning.

The Problem Itself. The nature of the problem may determine what degree of authority should be delegated by the manager to subordinates. Obviously the manager will consider whether they have the kind of knowledge which is needed. It is possible to do them a real disservice by assigning a problem that their experience does not equip them to handle.

Since the problems faced in large or growing industries increasingly require knowledge of specialists from many different fields, it might be inferred that the more complex a problem, the more anxious a manager will be to get some assistance in solving it. However, this is not always the case. There will be times when the very complexity of the problem calls for one person to work it out. For example, if the manager has most of the background and factual data relevant to a given issue, it may be easier for the manager to think it through alone than to take the time to fill in the staff on all the pertinent background information.

The key question to ask, of course, is: "Have I heard the ideas of everyone who has the necessary knowledge to make a significant contribution to the solution of this problem?"

The Pressure of Time. This is perhaps the most clearly felt pressure on the manager (in spite of the fact that it may sometimes be imagined). The more that the manager feels the need for an immediate decision, the more difficult it is to involve other people. In organizations which are in a constant state of "crisis" and "crash programming" one is likely to find managers personally using a high degree of authority with relatively little delegation to subordinates. When the time pressure is less intense, however, it becomes much more possible to bring subordinates in on the decision-making process.

These, then, are the principal forces that impinge on the manager in any given instance and that tend to determine tactical behavior in relation to subordinates. In each case the manager's behavior ideally will be that which makes possible the most effective attainment of an immediate goal within the limits at hand.

Long-Run Strategy

As the manager works with the organization on the problems that come up day by day, the choice of a leadership pattern is usually limited. The manager must take account of the forces just described and, within the restrictions they impose, do the best possible. But as the manager looks ahead months or even years, thinking can be shifted from tactics to large-scale strategy. No longer need the manager be fettered by all of the forces mentioned, for many of them can be viewed as variables over which the manager has some control. The manager can, for example, gain new personal insights or skills, supply training for individual subordinates, and provide participative experiences for the employee group.

In trying to bring about a change in these variables, however, the manager is faced with a challenging question: At which point along the continuum *should* action be taken?

Attaining Objectives

The answer depends largely on what is to be accomplished. Let us suppose that the manager is interested in the same objectives that most modern managers seek to attain when they can shift their attention from the pressure of immediate assignments:

1 To raise the level of employee motivation.
2 To increase the readiness of subordinates to accept change.

3 To improve the quality of all managerial decisions.
4 To develop teamwork and morale.
5 To further the individual development of employees.

In recent years the manager has been deluged with a flow of advice on how best to achieve these longer-run objectives. It is little wonder that the manager is often both bewildered and annoyed. However, there are some guidelines that can usefully be followed in making a decision.

Most research and much of the experience of recent years give a strong factual basis to the theory that a fairly high degree of subordinate-centered behavior is associated with the accomplishment of the five purposes mentioned.[4] This does not mean that a manager should always leave all decisions to assistants. To provide the individual or the group with greater freedom than they are ready for at any given time may very well tend to generate anxieties and therefore inhibit rather than facilitate the attainment of desired objectives. But this should not keep the manager from making a continuing effort to confront subordinates with the challenge of freedom.

Conclusion

In summary, there are two implications in the basic thesis that we have been developing. The first is that the successful leader is one who is keenly aware of those forces which are most relevant to behavior at any given time. The manager accurately understands herself or himself, the individuals and group being dealt with, and the company and broader social environment in which the manager operates. And certainly the manager is able to assess the present readiness for growth of subordinates.

But this sensitivity or understanding is not enough, which brings us to the second implication. The successful leader is one who is able to behave appropriately in the light of these perceptions. If direction is in order, the manager is able to direct; if considerable participative freedom is called for, the manager is able to provide such freedom.

Thus, the successful manager can be primarily characterized neither as a strong leader nor as a permissive one. Rather, this manager is one who maintains a high batting average in accurately assessing the forces that determine what the most appropriate managerial behavior at any given time should be and in actually being able to behave accordingly. Being both insightful and flexible, the successful manager is less likely to see the problems of leadership as a dilemma.

Appendix: Retrospective Commentary

Since this article was first published in the *Harvard Business Review* in 1958, there have been many changes in organizations and in the world that have affected leadership patterns. While the article's continued popularity attests to its essential validity, we believe it can be reconsidered and updated to reflect subsequent societal changes and new management concepts.

The reasons for the article's continued relevance can be summarized briefly:

- The article contains insights and perspectives which mesh well with, and help clarify, the experiences of managers, other leaders, and students of leadership. Thus it is useful to individuals in a wide variety of organizations—industrial, governmental, educational, religious, and community.
- The concept of leadership the article defines is reflected in a continuum of leadership behavior (see Exhibit 1). Rather than offering a choice between two styles of leadership, democratic or authoritarian, it sanctions a range of behavior.
- The concept does not dictate to managers but helps them to analyze their own behavior. The continuum permits them to review their behavior within a context of other alternatives, without any style being labeled right or wrong.

(We have sometimes wondered if we have, perhaps, made it too easy for anyone to justify his or her style of leadership. It may be a small step between being nonjudgmental and giving the impression that all behavior is equally valid and useful. The latter was not our intention. Indeed, the thrust of our endorsement was for the manager who is insightful in assessing relevant forces within himself, others, and the situation, and who can be flexible in responding to these forces.)

In recognizing that our article can be updated, we are acknowledging that organizations do not exist in a vacuum but are affected by changes that occur in society. Consider, for example, the implications for organizations of these recent social developments:

- The youth revolution that expresses distrust and even contempt for organizations identified with the establishment.
- The civil rights movement that demands all minority groups be given a greater opportunity for participation and influence in the organizational processes.
- The ecology and consumer movements that challenge the right of managers to make decisions without considering the interest of people outside the organization.
- The increasing national concern with the quality of working life and its relationship to worker productivity, participation, and satisfaction.

These and other societal changes make effective leadership in this decade a more challenging task, requiring even greater sensitivity and flexibility than was needed in the 1950s. Today's manager is more likely to deal with employees who resent being treated as subordinates, who may be highly critical of any organizational system, who expect to be consulted and to exert influence, and who often stand on the edge of alienation from the institution that needs their loyalty and commitment. In addition, today's manager is frequently confronted by a highly turbulent, unpredictable environment.

In response to these social pressures, new concepts of management have emerged in organizations. Open-system theory, with its emphasis on subsystems' interdependency *and* on the interaction of an organization with its environment, has made a powerful impact on managers' approach to problems. Organization development has emerged as a new behavioral science approach to the improvement of individual, group, organizational, and interorganizational performance. New research has added to our understanding of motivation in the work situation. More and more executives have become concerned with social responsibility and have explored the feasibility of social audits. And a growing number of organizations, in Europe and in the United States, have conducted experiments in industrial democracy.

In light of these developments, we submit the following thoughts on how we would rewrite certain points in our original article.

The article described forces in the manager, subordinates, and the situation as givens, with the leadership pattern a resultant of these forces. We would now give more attention to the *interdependency* of these forces. For example, such interdependency occurs in: (a) the interplay between the manager's confidence in subordinates, their readiness to assume responsibility, and the level of group effectiveness; and (b) the impact of the behavior of the manager on that of subordinates, and vice versa.

In discussing the forces in the situation, we primarily identified organizational phenomena. We would now include forces lying outside the organization, and would explore the relevant interdependencies between the organization and its environment.

In the original article, we presented the size of the rectangle in Exhibit 1 as a given, with its boundaries already determined by external forces—in effect, a closed system. We would now recognize the possibility of the manager and/or subordinates taking the initiative to change those boundaries through interaction with relevant external forces—both within their own organization and in the larger society.

The article portrayed the manager as the principal and almost unilateral actor. The manager initiated and determined group functions, assumed responsibility, and exercised control. Subordinates made inputs and assumed power only at the will of the manager. Although the manager might have taken into account forces outside himself or herself, it was *the manager* who decided where to operate on the continuum—that is, whether to announce a decision instead of trying to sell an idea to subordinates, whether to invite questions, to let subordinates decide an issue, and so on. While the manager has retained this clear prerogative in many organizations, it has been challenged in others. Even in situations where the manager has retained it, however, the balance in the relationship between manager and subordinates at any given time is arrived at by interaction—direct or indirect—between the two parties.

Although power and its use by the manager played a role in our original article, we now realize that our concern with cooperation and collaboration, common goals, commitment, trust, and mutual caring limited our vision with respect to the realities of power. We did not attempt to deal with unions, other forms of joint worker action, or with individual workers' expressions of resistance. Today, we would recognize much more clearly the power available to *all* parties, and the factors that underlie the interrelated decisions on whether to use it.

In the original article, we used the terms "manager" and "subordinate." We are now uncomfortable with "subordinate" because of its demeaning, dependency-laden connotations and prefer "nonmanager." The titles "manager" and "nonmanager" make the terminological difference functional rather than hierarchical.

We assumed fairly traditional organizational structures in our original article. Now we would alter our formulation to reflect newer organizational modes which are slowly emerging, such as industrial democracy, intentional communities, and "phenomenarchy."[5] These new modes are based on observations such as the following:

- ☐ Both manager and nonmanagers may be governing forces in their group's environment, contributing to the definition of the total area of freedom.
- ☐ A group can function without a manager, with managerial functions being shared by group members.
- ☐ A group, as a unit, can be delegated authority and can assume responsibility within a larger organizational context.

Our thoughts on the question of leadership have prompted us to design a new behavior continuum (see Exhibit 2) in which the total area of freedom shared by manager and nonmanagers is constantly redefined by interactions between them and the forces in the environment.

The arrows in the exhibit indicate the continual flow of interdependent influence among systems and people. The points on the continuum designate the types of manager and nonmanager behavior that become possible with any given amount of freedom available to each. The new continuum is both more complex and more dynamic than the 1958 version, reflecting the organizational and societal realities of 1973.

Exhibit 2. Continuum of Manager-Nonmanager Behavior

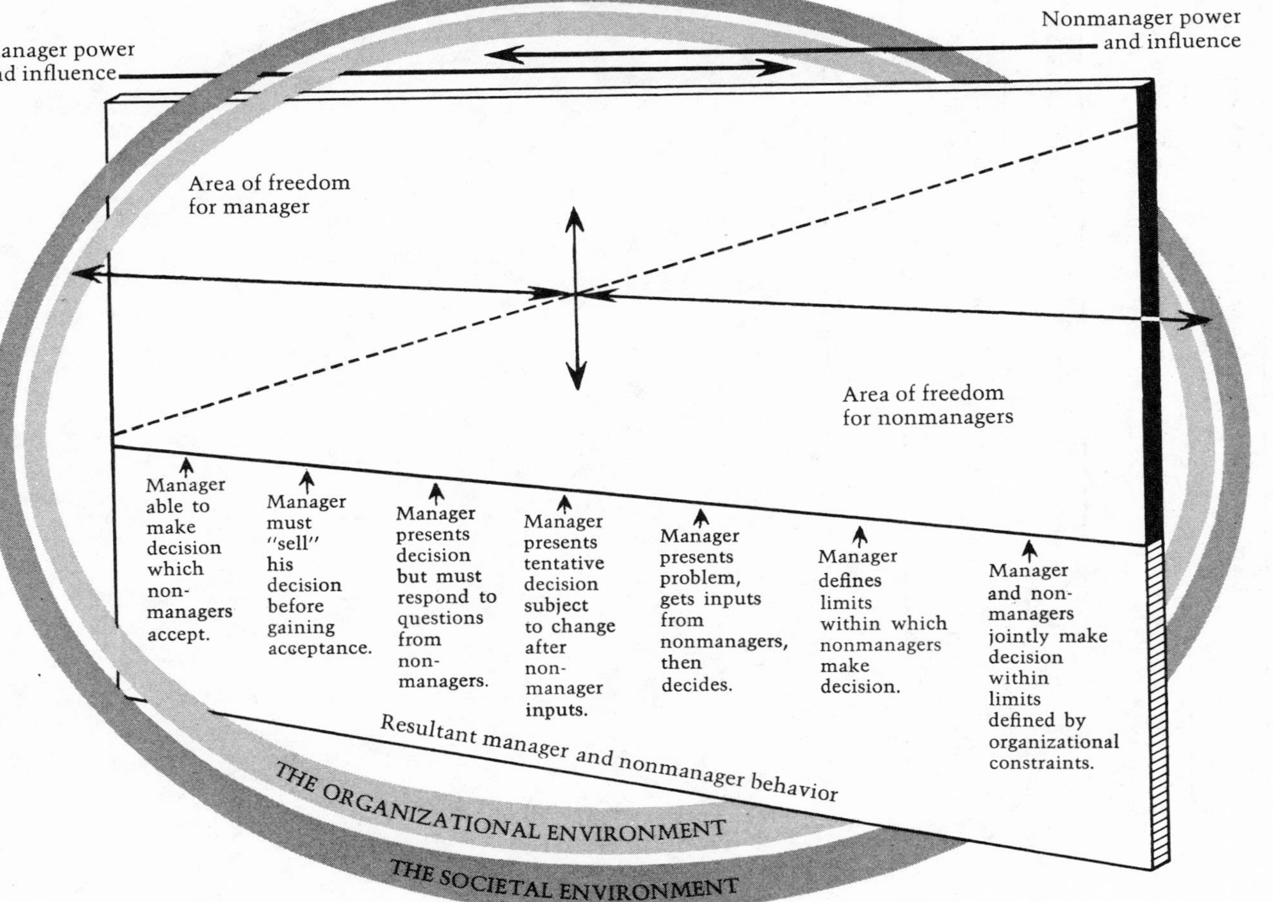
Manager power and influence
Nonmanager power and influence
Area of freedom for manager
Area of freedom for nonmanagers
Manager able to make decision which non-managers accept.
Manager must "sell" his decision before gaining acceptance.
Manager presents decision but must respond to questions from non-managers.
Manager presents tentative decision subject to change after non-manager inputs.
Manager presents problem, gets inputs from nonmanagers, then decides.
Manager defines limits within which nonmanagers make decision.
Manager and non-managers jointly make decision within limits defined by organizational constraints.
Resultant manager and nonmanager behavior
THE ORGANIZATIONAL ENVIRONMENT
THE SOCIETAL ENVIRONMENT

Notes

1. For a fuller explanation of this approach, see Leo Moore, "Too Much Management, Too Little Change," *HBR*, January–February 1956, p. 41.

2. See also Robert Tannenbaum and Fred Massarik, "Participation by Subordinates in the Managerial Decision-Making Process," *Canadian Journal of Economics and Political Science*, August 1950, p. 413.

3. See Chris Argyris, "Top Management Dilemma: Company Needs vs. Individual Development," *Personnel*, September 1955, pp. 123–134.

4. For example, see Warren H. Schmidt and Paul C. Buchanan, *Techniques That Produce Teamwork* (New London, Conn., Arthur C. Croft Publications, 1954); and Morris S. Viteles, *Motivation and Morale in Industry* (New York, Norton, 1953).

5. For a description of phenomenarchy, see Will McWhinney, "Phenomenarchy: A Suggestion for Social Redesign," *Journal of Applied Behavioral Science*, May 1973.

11

Business Leadership and a Creative Society

ABRAM T. COLLIER

What is the business of business? To some it is profits, to others it is satisfying the needs of a variety of constituencies including stockholders, customers, and employees of the company. To the author of this article "the business of business is discovery, innovation, and creativity." Because the society in which we live is a creative one, the task of leaders is to further the creative ideal in their organizations. To do this they need to recognize the power and strength that an organization can derive from the differences among people. To maintain order amid the chaos that diversity can create, executives need to foster understanding and respect for one another among individual members, as well as show them that the right to be creative carries obligations with it. Finally, as a creative society derives its power from its members' beliefs in the importance of their individual growth, leaders need to epitomize that growth.

High on the list of tasks facing the business administrator are those relating to the basic attitudes, interests, and objectives of the employees. Meeting antagonism and misunderstanding, as the administrator often does, the immediate reaction is to cry out: "How can I get across to my employees some understanding of the objectives I seek?" Well, that question may be important, but perhaps it should not have such priority. It might be better to ask first: "What, in truth, do I seek? What objectives do I have that my employees can also share?"

Some administrators, of course, have not bothered their heads with such intricate problems, feeling that "only results count" or "actions speak louder than words." But advertising and public relations executives have demonstrated how inadequate this view is; words and the things they connote are as much a part of our experience as the things that we perceive immediately and directly. And top-rank administrators such as Chester I. Barnard know also that one of the first and greatest functions of leadership is that the leader express for the group the ideals toward which they all, consciously or unconsciously, strive.

Winston Churchill's powerful "blood, sweat, and tears" speech in 1940 has now become a classic model in the political field of the way in which a leader can express the purpose of the people and rally them to common effort. Business executives, especially those of us concerned with personnel, productivity, and morale, have come to recognize the need for much the same kind of leadership, convinced that only in this way will employees ever have the satisfaction of really feeling they are identified with the enterprise for which they work.

But in seeking to exert such leadership we have already learned that there are some difficult problems of communication in the way. Take the many attempts that have been made in recent years, following the example of such companies as Du Pont, General Electric, and Republic Steel, to give supervisors and workers in business some understanding of the economic and political society in which we live. The general experience is that the terms "capitalism," "competition," "American way of life," "land of opportunity," and "free private enterprise," through excessive repetition, abuse, or otherwise, have lost much of their capacity to convey the meaning intended.

Moreover, where new symbols have been introduced for the old, they too have missed the mark. The editors of *Fortune*, for example, have characterized our society as the "permanent revolution," but we do not think of ourselves as revolutionaries—at least not of the black-bearded and bomb-carrying kind. Other attempts to call our society "open" or "free" have raised perplexing questions: Open for what? Free for what?

It seems to me that we business executives ought to aim at articulating an ideology that, in addition to being an accurate expression of management goals, is a little closer to the personal and even religious aspirations of the people than anything we have espoused in the past. Is it not possible that we have been thinking too much in terms of systems, of economics, of products, of laws? Perhaps these approaches should not have failed as they did; perhaps they can be improved. But in any event it seems to me that the fact of their failure (or, at best, their lack of any great success) should be accepted, and that the most profitable line of inquiry is to turn to a different sort of approach altogether.

The Creative Ideal

Accordingly, I put forward this simple proposition: that our society is a creative society; that its prime objective, as well as its great genius, is its creativeness; and that, as creative accomplishment is the actual day-to-day goal of modern business, it is also the keystone of our business philosophy.

I am thinking of creativeness in its widest and deepest sense. Thus, business does not exist merely to produce more goods and services, or better goods and services for more people, though that is no small part of its task. Business also, particularly in these days, affords the principal or the only means whereby individuals may gain the satisfaction of accomplishing something more than merely sustaining their own lives. Pleasure, power, and fame appear to be but by-products of the efforts we make to be useful members of society and to leave it with something more than it had when we arrived. Perhaps we leave only the grain of sand that Robert Frost said he wished to leave on the beach of history; but at least, if we do that, we can feel that we have fulfilled our role in living.

What I am suggesting is that the great goals of happiness, freedom, security—even goodness and truth—are values which should be viewed as subordinate to, and resulting from, a new and positive creative ideal. Our people in business and elsewhere seem to be driven by an urge to build; by a longing to explore and reach out; by a desire to realize, through people and for people, such things and experiences as humanity has never known before. In this light, our vaunted freedoms of thought and action, our sought-for freedoms from worry and want, and even our ethical standards of behavior (products as they are of other places and times) are not ends in themselves; rather, they emerge as important values just because they support and make possible a creative human society.

This is the modern heresy: It is not enough to be good, to lead a blameless life; we must also be creative.

The New and the Old

In one sense this ideal is modern in expression only. Seers in almost every age have been trying to tell us that the greatest individual satisfaction there is comes from a job well done. Samuel Johnson, for example, observed: "Life affords no higher pleasure than that of surmounting difficulties, passing from one step of success to another, forming new wishes and seeing them gratified." And Emerson said: "The *sum* of wisdom is that the time is never lost that is devoted to work."

In another sense, however, this ideal of ours shows some new, significantly new, aspects. Specifically, in American business it is now beginning to be recognized that *everyone* has the capacity for the satisfaction that comes from creative accomplishment. As science unleashes vast new sources of power, it appears possible for the first time in history for people of all types and classes to avoid the toil and suffering of hard labor and to experience the joys of work—a satisfaction which in times past was limited to the few.

Contrast this with the older view. We used to classify as creative only those accomplishments that certain individuals could achieve. The writer, the artist, the composer, the scientist—in other words, the rare people who had the genius to find and express new ideas or new truths—were considered the creative members of our society; the classic examples have been the Newtons, the Beethovens, the Kants, the Michelangelos, the Shakespeares. The magnitude of their work often crushed us by making us feel our own inadequacy.

Today, however, we are beginning to recognize that creative work may be accomplished collectively as well as individually. The great and small organizations that have built and operated our industrial plants, farms, transportation and communication networks, financial systems, and distributive organizations, all are examples of the creative genius which comes from the collective effort of administrators and workers, as well as specialists of all degrees.

Dimension of the Task

The first task of business leaders, therefore, is to create an environment in which there can flourish not only individual genius but, more important, the collective capacities of other people in the organization. Some difficult and searching questions must be answered if this task is to be accomplished. What are the basic positive forces operating in a creative business society? What generates their power? What keeps them in balance? What conditions their survival? What controls their direction?

To this end, I submit that the creative ideal depends on these concepts:

1. That the forces in business (and many other types of organization) are nurtured by the existence of *differences between individuals and groups*.
2. That these forces are kept in control and balance by the process of *individuals understanding each other*.
3. That a creative society depends for its survival upon the belief that *rights must be matched by obligations*.
4. That the directing force in a creative society is the *faith* of its members in *individual growth*.

The Power of Difference

In considering the importance of individual difference, it should first be noted that the goal of many societies—including the goal of communist society today and of almost every Utopia that has ever been conceived, from Plato to Aldous Huxley—has been to compel men to conform. The theory is that if everyone is induced to accept the same ideas of what is good and proper, conflicts between individuals and groups will disappear and humanity will live happily ever after.

By contrast, one of the cornerstones on which the creative society is built is the incontrovertible fact that people are different, that they cherish these differences, that the joy and fascination of life depends on the existence of differences, and that there are great social values in differences.

Driving Force

Every great ideal has its own theory of the nature of humankind. The wholly competitive or acquisitive society, which is gone (if it ever in fact existed), assumed that humans were motivated only by their own pleasure, that they were egoistic and greedy, and that their wants were insatiable. By assuming that the average person, the economic person, was moved by animal impulses, it was possible to work out satisfactory theoretical explanations of how people acted in the marketplace.

On the other hand, socialists have assumed, following the notions of Rousseau (and possibly the story of Genesis), that people were essentially good, self-sacrificing, considerate, and loving, but were corrupted by social institutions. On this basis socialists thought that if institutions were changed or destroyed and if nonconforming individuals and classes were eliminated, then all social problems would cease and the state could and would wither away.

But in a creative society neither of these views is adequate. We observe that people are both egoistic and self-sacrificing—and many things more. While people are, taken as a whole, driven by an urge to create and grow, their characteristics vary with their times, experiences, culture, inheritance, and with all the other circumstances in which they find themselves. To illustrate with a simple example:

> ☐ In the company with which I am associated we are using, as an aid in selection and placement, a test of personality or temperament in which the results are described not in imprecise words but in graphic form. Taking several major behavior characteristics, it plots with a fair degree of accuracy where a given individual falls on each of several temperament spectra. For instance, there is a spectrum of gregariousness in which the extreme extrovert falls at one end and the extreme introvert at the other; in between are those having various needs for sociability or a capacity to live within themselves.
>
> Thousands upon thousands of tests of this type have been made, and it is fair to say that in no two cases have the results—the combinations of characteristics on the several spectra—been exactly the same. Similarity of types may be observed, but every man and every woman is found to be unique. Furthermore, research into personality shows that people change their personalities, usually extremely slowly but sometimes dramatically. It also shows that behavior is not wholly a matter for the individual alone but depends in large part on the situation in which the individual finds himself. That is, the set of values according to which a person makes decisions may vary with external circumstances.

The driving force of difference—in individuals and in groups—seems well illustrated by the history of the United States and Canada (in contrast to some other countries). While no doubt we have strong forces in many companies, labor unions, churches, and schools which are trying to enforce a high degree of conformity to some particular viewpoint, practice, or belief, nevertheless those forces have been observably less dominant than the forces of individual integrity. In our business world, if an individual has felt personally more able to do a job better than someone else, the freedom to try has been there; indeed, the fact that the individual saw things differently has provided both the opportunity and the courage to try.

Moreover, there is good reason to believe that the differences between groups of people in the United States and Canada with respect to cultural, racial, and religious backgrounds have been a factor in the dynamic development of these countries. What does it mean that never before in history have so many diverse religious groups been able to live together with so little disharmony? Has our society progressed *in spite of* differences or *because of* them? Possibly the very existence of differences among various people and groups has given people the courage to disagree with prevailing opinions. Every discovery, every invention, every new industry, every new idea has come about because some person or some group of people has had the courage as well as the insight to disagree with the majority or do what the majority had not thought of doing before.

This is perhaps part of what David McCord Wright had in mind when he pointed out:

> Our dilemma. . .is that if we make men "free," they will become creative and from their creations will spring the probability of growth and the certainty of trouble.[1]

Diversity Rather Than Conflict

Differences do, of course, lead to trouble—to misunderstanding and conflict. Yet conflict is essential to constructive work. More than a generation ago Mary Parker Follett, a woman who has since become recognized for her many profound insights into the nature of business organizations, wrote:

> What people often mean by getting rid of conflict is getting rid of diversity, and it is of the utmost importance that these should not be considered the same. We may wish to abolish conflict, but we cannot get rid of diversity. We must face life as it is and understand that diversity is its most essential feature. . . .Fear of difference is dread of life itself. It is possible to conceive of conflict as not necessarily a wasteful outbreak of incompatibilities but a *normal* process by which socially valuable differences register themselves for the enrichment of all concerned.[2]

Creativeness in an organization depends to a large extent on people who are not too ready to agree. In our own experience, most of us abhor the attitude of "Well, if you're going to argue about it, let's do it your way." We have found that we must have diversity of opinion, firmly as well as fairly expressed, if our business is to make the wise decisions that will enable it to develop and grow.

If we accept difference, it necessarily follows that we are not sure we are right ourselves; we accept the notion that our conclusions about people and society must be treated only as working hypotheses and that there are realities beyond those of our immediate perceptions. It is sometimes forgotten how highly we esteem this concept in the physical sciences. The entire atomic world of neutrons and electrons has never been perceived directly; despite Hiroshima and Nagasaki, it is still a theory or a working hypothesis. The same hypothetical character pertains to all of our knowledge about genes—the transmission of traits from organisms to their offspring.

But if it is necessary to trust to more than our immediate perceptions in the physical sciences, it would seem even more important to do so in social, ethical, and political matters that deal with human beings. The observation of Yale's F. C. S. Northrop, that the ability to live in a world of both immediate perceptions and unperceived hypotheses is the essence of the genius of the West, would apply no less to our industrial and political society than to our scientific progress.

This means that we must subject our old concepts of right and wrong, of good and bad, to a radical change; things are no longer so black and white. Judge Learned Hand, philosopher as well as judge, has described the spirit of liberty as "the spirit that is not too sure that it is right." Tolerance for difference, for the viewpoint that we do not agree with, implies that we are not so sure of our own. We accept our principles of action as working hypotheses, realizing that something may happen to lead us to revise these opinions. While it often sounds as though some of our friends would never change their opinions (particularly on matters of ethics or politics), our great genius lies in the fact that we may talk loudly but, when the chips are down, we seem to act on the basis that all general rules of what is right and wrong must be tempered by common sense.

It can be reasonably contended that the great upheavals of modern history—its wars and its revolutions—are not so much the result of differences between people as of the feeling of a nation or a class that its capacity for creative expression is in some way threatened or thwarted. This was one cause of the Russian revolt of 1917, although the revolutionaries themselves later made the great and historic blunder of seeking to abolish conflict by abolishing difference rather than by accepting difference and in that way removing the barriers to creative work.

Nations such as ours, which have insisted on the freedom of their people to be different, have had to fight and may well fight again to preserve their right to disagree with one another. Yet, if the principle of difference is one of the cornerstones of creativeness, our society has little to fear *in the long run* from those who deny the privilege of difference to their own people.

Process of Understanding

If diversity is the first condition of the creative society, then understanding is the second. The Bible's exhortation, ''with all thy getting, get understanding,'' is particularly appropriate for modern industry. If for their dynamic creative power our businesses depend on continuing differences in viewpoint, for balance and braking power they must equally depend on understanding, on the felt necessity for securing agreement and cooperation.

In the sense that I am using the term, understanding refers both to self-understanding and understanding of others. Self-awareness as a desirable personal attribute is certainly not newer than the Socratic injunction, ''Know thyself''; but what is new in our time is the fact that thoughtful social scientists and hard-headed business executives are coming to see that self-awareness or self-understanding is directly related to an individual's capacity to do creative work with other people. Business people are beginning to think not only of the logics of business but also of what Pareto described as the nonlogics or the sentiments of people. They are beginning to see that their own behavior is a factor which influences the behavior of others, and that they are personally involved in more roles than one in every situation in which they play a part.

Let me illustrate from my own experience:

> □ For a short time, some years ago, I engaged in the general practice of law. Later I was employed as a lawyer by an insurance company. As a lawyer I found that my clients' problems were not mine; and no matter how hard I tried to solve them, I stood outside of the situation and was not involved in it. But when later I took an administrative position, I found that this detachment was no longer possible, even if I wanted it. I was personally involved in every important decision, and my behavior was affecting others. The shock of being forced to examine my own behavior was by no means small. What I needed to do, however, was no less than what all successful administrators are doing daily in every business.

In addition to self-awareness there is the need for understanding others. What we are learning today is not just that it is a ''good thing to see the other person's point of view,'' but also what it is that often makes it difficult to do so. We are learning that we cannot really understand another if we agree, nor can we understand if we disagree! When we feel either love or hate, we lose our power to see the world as others see it. We blur our own perceptions, and we cut off the normal flow of words which help us see into another's mind.

Communication Gateways

This conclusion has tremendous significance. If understanding the needs and desires of others is an essential for collective creative effort, it means that we can no longer be quick to evaluate people or their opinions as either good or bad. During the understanding process at least, we must throw our ethical judgments out the window.

Carl R. Rogers and F. J. Roethlisberger made this same point when in essence they said that the great barrier to communication is our tendency to evaluate, to approve or disapprove the statements that other people make.[3] For example:

☐ If you say to me, "I prefer Englishmen to the French," there is almost an overwhelming urge for me to say either "So do I" or "No, I think they are stuffy." We may then talk for hours without a meeting of the minds. If, on the other hand, I want to find out whether we really agree or disagree about this matter, if I want to listen intelligently and to understand what you mean, thus opening the gateway to communication, then I must restrain my natural inclination to presume what you mean and instead make an effort to draw you out. I might ask something like, "Do you mean Englishmen are more to be admired?" You may reply, "Yes, they are really facing up to their economic problems better than the French." And if I continue in that way, rephrasing your comments in question form to test out what you are *trying* to tell me, there is a much better chance that we can have a fruitful discussion.

This brief explanation of a gateway to understanding, of receiving communications, of listening, may sound extremely obvious and somewhat simple. We spend most of our time learning to express ourselves, which is difficult enough but still easier than listening. Indeed, it is fair to say that listening is one of the most difficult things in the world to do. When someone charges into your office and criticizes some action that you have taken, it is not easy to find out what is really on this person's mind when your first impulse is to say, "Go to hell." Or take the case where somebody asks you for your advice because of an inability to make a decision about a personal problem; most of us are inclined to comply with such a request without knowing what the real problem is, or without realizing that the decision will be sound only if it is personally made by the troubled person.

It takes real insight to be able to express in words what someone else is trying to tell us. It also takes great effort and even courage. If we put ourselves in someone else's position, if we try to express adequately the other's point of view, we may find that our own views become changed in the process. Professor Rogers says, "The risk of being changed is one of the most frightening prospects many of us can face."[4]

There are, of course, many other ways of securing understanding; some of them have been outlined by Stuart Chase in his popularization of social science, *Roads to Agreement*.[5] One is particularly worth mentioning:

> ☐ This way is modeled on the long-established custom of the Quaker business meeting. Quakers as a class are great individualists, but in handling the business affairs of their churches they act only with unanimity. They have no formal voting, no sense of a majority imposing its will on a reluctant minority. If a problem cannot be settled by unanimous agreement, they invoke periods of silence or put over the question until some future meeting. Some solution is usually forthcoming.

This rule of unanimity, it seems, is now being practiced by boards of directors and executive committees in businesses throughout the land. What a far cry this is from deciding what is the greatest good for the greatest number by a mechanical counting of hands! Where difference is accepted, it is possible also to accept the notion that a minority may be right.

Integration vs. Compromise

The concept of integration as opposed to compromise is also achieving a wider recognition. Integration may be called the means of solving a conflict of opinion in such a way that both sides prevail. The idea behind it is that the basic interests underlying many disputes are not inconsistent. For example:

> ☐ If two people in an office want to use the same desk, it may appear at first that a major conflict is in the making, which can be solved only if one or the other wins the decision. On investigation, however, it may appear that one of the persons wants the desk in order to have better light, whereas the other wants it in order to be near some friend. If these facts come out, it will be apparent that neither wants the desk as such and that it may well be possible to satisfy the basic interests of both.

In order to achieve integration, says Mary Parker Follett, we should "never, if possible, allow an either/or situation to be created . . . . There are almost always more than two alternatives in a situation and our job is to analyze the situation carefully enough for as many as possible to appear. A yes-or-no question is in itself a prejudgment."[6]

May there not be some relationship between these methods of reaching understanding and the spirit which is not too sure that it is right? Is there not some connection between these techniques of agreement and our capacity for collective creativeness? Can it not be said that in a creative society we must have both conflict and agreement?

Rights and Obligations

A third standard of a creative society, and an essential ingredient in our workaday world, has been foreshadowed by the previous discussion of difference and of understanding. It is the belief that human relationships are two-way matters and that rights are matched by obligations.

The "Double Plus"

Karl Marx predicted that in Western society it was inevitable that the rich would become richer and the poor would become poorer. This increasing division between the classes would, as he saw it, accelerate class warfare and the revolution. If our society had indeed been basically competitive and acquisitive, instead of creative and cooperative, Marx might well have been proved right. But the fact is that today, through our collective creativeness, the poor have become richer. Our society has been able to create wealth at a vastly greater rate than it has increased its population.

By and large, we have been able to maintain the viewpoint that our economic and political problem is not so much to redistribute the wealth that exists as to create more wealth for all. As the eminent economist Kenneth Boulding has written, "Economic life is not a 'zero-sum' poker game in which a fixed volume of wealth is circulated among the players, but a 'positive-sum' enterprise in which the accumulation of each person represents something he brings to the 'pot' rather than something he takes out."[7] In other words, we are engaged in a creative task of producing more and better things. We recognize that we share as we contribute, that no society can long give something for nothing (to the poor *or* the rich), and that we cannot do great work unless *everyone* shares both in the work and in its results.

This concept has been called by many names. Mutuality is one; give-and-take is another. Professor Charles I. Gragg of the Harvard Business School calls it the "double plus." As he sees it, business transactions and other relationships can be described in one of three ways:

1. There is first the kind of a transaction in which the plus is all on my side, leaving a big minus for you. If I take all the profit, however, through my power or my cleverness, then I have really lost the bargain, because you will come to distrust me and will refuse to do business with me for long.

2. The reverse situation is equally disastrous. If I, through an excess of altruism or with misguided notions of humanity, permit you to take the entire profit, with nothing for myself, I put you in the unhappy role of being

a recipient of my charity; moreover, I leave myself unable to do further business with anyone.

3. But there is still another and more satisfactory form. Only if you profit moderately and I profit moderately, only if there is a plus for you and a plus for me—a double plus—can we continue to deal with one another steadily and with confidence.

In our business lives we are beginning to see that by consciously fashioning our relationships with our employees, with our suppliers, with our customers—and, indeed, even with our competitors—we are not making suspicious and careful deals so much as common-sense arrangements that are carried on in this spirit of mutual give-and-take. That does not mean anything petty like back-scratching; every service and every kindness is not to be immediately returned, nor is every service to be performed in the hope of return. The correct attitude, rather, is a healthy respect for the well-being and personal integrity of the other person.

Profit for All

What does all this imply? Only in an atmosphere of profit (in the broad sense) to all parties can we meet the creative objectives that our society sets. If, in times past, we erred on the side of taking too much for ourselves, it is equally essential that we do not err in the future on the side of trying to do too much for others. A too-literal application of the Sermon on the Mount—the turn of the cheek—does small damage to us but great damage to the one who strikes the blow.

Why is it, otherwise, that the problem of providing for the aged worker has once more raised its head, when we thought a few years ago that we had safely tucked it away with compulsory retirement and pensioning at age 65? From the point of view of sympathy for the aged and of convenience in administering our business enterprises, the practice is as desirable today as it was 15 years ago. We have discovered, however, that many individuals who retire are hurt because they lose their sense of being creative, of being useful members of society. Moreover, when we contemplate that 11% of our population will be over 65 in another 20 years, we begin to realize that the real economic cost of compulsory retirement is not the money that goes into pensions but the lost productivity of these older people.

It seems that people, individually and in groups, must continue to be creative; if they are not, the individual or society, or both, will suffer. If we do not intend to keep people over 65 in business, some other way must be found to permit them to continue active membership in the world's work.

The same kind of thinking underlies our concern for other noncontributors to society. Society has been doing an increasingly successful job of minimizing sickness of almost all kinds, not so much out of solicitude for the feelings of persons who are ill as out of its own self-interest in having the benefit of their contribution. Programs undertaken with this motive quickly earn common respect, for the galling part of illness to the sufferer is the necessity of having to depend on others, of being no longer able to contribute.

We are concerned for similar reasons about the criminal and the indolent. It is true that we have not as yet learned enough to be confident of our ability to rehabilitate these people. But we have at least learned that it is no answer to judge them or to punish them; our first task is to understand them. We consider them "cured" only when they join the majority contributing commensurately to what they receive.

Why do business executives fight against the welfare state? Are business executives actually heartless and callous? Don't they recognize that the sick and the poor need the aid of the rest who are well and able? Of course they do. But their experience says to them that doctors do not give pills to everyone because a few are sick; that when a person is given something for nothing the person feels degraded; that a person who is well and able wants to earn the pay.

Business executives, who have learned from experience that paternalism has failed, hope that government will learn from their mistakes. Business executives have good reason for believing that government will not really serve the poor and sick until it stops regarding them as "little people" and undertakes instead the harder job of giving them an honest chance to do useful and creative work.

Faith in Human Growth

The fourth and last condition of maintaining and strengthening a creative society, the force that provides direction and control, is a clear faith in the growth and development of people. The machine age poses a great challenge to our willingness to demonstrate this faith. All of the new wealth we can produce with modern technology is of little avail if in the process people are reduced to the levels of the machines they tend. But fortunately we are not confronted with a Hobson's choice between wealth and people. We have found that the more we are able to train and develop people as individuals, leaving repetitive work to machines, the greater satisfactions they obtain and the more productive (in a material sense) they become.

Take a business with a large content of routine clerical work, for example, life insurance. In this business we stand on the threshold of a new era in adapting electronics to office workers' problems. When any business reaches this point, to be sure, management is bound to face the problem of securing the cooperation of people who may prefer things as they are. It may even have to face a problem of technological unemployment. But however real and thorny these difficulties are, they are insignificant compared to the human values that are gained. Instead of a business in which, say, 75% of the employees are engaged in routine tasks, the modern machine makes it possible for 75% to be engaged in tasks requiring skill and judgment. The machine eliminates human toil; but, much more important, it also provides opportunities for people to do only those tasks people alone can do.

New Concept of Organization

The development of the machine economy has numerous important implications for management. For one thing, it is fast bringing about a new concept of business organization. No longer can the boss know all the details and the intricacies of the operation. The boss is being forced more and more to rely on subordinates, to consult with them, to be guided by their joint conclusions—in short, to permit them to share and to grow in breadth of vision.

This in turn means, of course, a gradual abandonment of authoritarian principles. Administrators have begun to conceive of their role not as manipulators of labor but as coordinators of functions. Re-examining themselves and their jobs, they have discovered that they have no special claim to superior wisdom, no vested authority over the work and lives of others. They have found, rather, that they have a function to perform: to plan ahead, to coordinate the others, to secure their interest and cooperation.

Society will not, as a result, tend to become classless in any Marxian sense. Far from it. We may reasonably anticipate, however, that members of future "elites" will come to occupy positions of status and power less because of wealth, position, or birth and more because of the kind of contributions they make or because of the kind of functions they fulfill. Key positions will tend more and more to be occupied by those who are best able to conceive new ideas and the application of old ones, who are best able to communicate ideas and events, and who are best able to pull together people and things to achieve creative ends. Today's inheritance tax and management's increased interest in personnel development are fast speeding this process along.

Administrators as Teachers

In an important sense the role of the administrator seems destined to become more and more that of the instructor—the kind of teacher who understands pupils, accepts their differences, commands their respect, and inspires them to creative work of every kind. In such a role, administrators will have less of a problem of discipline to the degree that they are able to develop an environment for creative experience and to lead their students (their workers) to savor the satisfying taste of personal accomplishment. In so doing they will have gone far to eliminate the distinction between "schooling" and "education" which Mark Twain quite properly made when he quipped, "I have never let my schooling interfere with my education."

In their new role as teachers, administrators are learning that attitudes and viewpoints which affect behavior can frequently be communicated effectively only if they are reduced to concrete terms. In their efforts at training and development, particularly, they are recognizing the need to start from real case situations. Witness the growing attention to discussions of actual business problems rather than the oft-repeated clichés on general principles of management.

Abstract ideas, however, are not to be discarded simply because they so often fail to influence behavior. Indeed, as the mark of civilization they are necessary tools of communication which are quite adequate *if* both writer and reader start from the same premises. They are easily accepted, in other words, if they seem meaningful in relation to one's own experience. Aneurin Bevan's autobiography affords an example of this:

> □ Bevan's life as a young Welsh miner was filled with frustrations. Then he read Karl Marx. This experience "had all the impact of divine revelation. Everything fell in place. The dark places were lighted up and the difficult ways made easy."[8] Marx is most abstract, but nevertheless his words have had a great effect on people whose experience has led them to feel like chained and exploited men.

The moral of this fact has not been lost on business executives and politicians, who know that the only real and lasting bulwark against Marxism is in the experience of the large body of our workers and our citizens. If that experience is basically creative and satisfying—and it is management's task to see that it is so—the stultifying conformities of the socialist state will always be bitter to their taste.

But business executives and politicians, while often seeing what is the best *defense* against Marxism, have not been so quick to see what needs to be done in a *positive* way. Like Marxists, we too must have an appropriate body of abstract ideas—ideas that can constitute a simple article of faith but are also capable of profound extension, ideas that are consistent with experience but are also adaptable to new insights and new truths.

Perhaps this discussion will stimulate others to work out such ideas—each in a unique way, as a part of our individual differences, but all toward the same goal, in the spirit of mutuality. What I have written can be no more than a preface.

Conclusion

The problems of production, distribution, and finance are usually foreign to a worker's experience and interests. It is therefore just as silly for top management to hope that workers will be anxious to understand the problems of the business as it would be to fear that they are interested in gaining control of the business. What workers do appear to want is a chance to increase their usefulness and creativeness, a chance to develop their full potential as individuals within the scope of their environment and experience. It has become part of management's function to see not only that they have that chance but that the philosophy behind it is made articulate.

But the creative society is based on more than the relationship between management and workers, indispensable though that is in our industrial age. It depends on close relationships between all fields of human endeavor. Business is not "just business." The wall between business and the home, the community, the school, and the church has long since been stormed. Business is all people, places, and things; it is physics, economics, politics, sociology, psychology, philosophy, ethics, and aesthetics.

In the same broad sense, business is also religion. One of the recurring themes in most religions is that God is viewed as the Creator and that creativeness is one of His essential attributes. Another recurring theme is that the human spirit, the conscious "self," the unique ability to transcend material and animal limitations, is the essence of God in humankind. To suggest that creativeness may be a basic attribute of people in society is thus merely to relate these two ageless insights.

Moreover, it seems that a religious sense of wonder, humility, and faith helps us to see the vision of a boundless future built by the inherent capacities of people from all walks of life and of all races, creeds, natures, and backgrounds. It is a vision of cooperation, togetherness, and sharing the great adventure. It is a vision of independence and courage that explores the far reaches of the universe and probes deep into the essence of what we call humankind. It is, in short, a vision of a changing, growing, and infinitely exciting world which depends for its existence on the spirit that is not too sure it is right, on a deep-seated desire to open our minds and our hearts to the lives of others, on the practical sense of give-and-take, on our faith in the growth and development of ourselves and our fellow beings.

Appendix: Retrospective Commentary

The author of an article which is exhumed some years after publication has mixed feelings. In some ways he feels as though he were seeing a ghost. In other ways he feels like a father of a foundling who hears that the boy has grown up and won a prize at school: as a father he is proud, but his pride is limited by the knowledge that his own contribution was made in the very distant past.

Reviewing the results of these distant events, I believe I would not write the article much differently if I were to write it today. The events since 1953, I think, have not proved me wrong.

I still believe that the business of business is discovery, innovation, and creativity. I still believe the job of management is to maintain creativity with order—and order with creativity. I still believe creativity without order breeds chaos, and that order without creativity is a living death.

There is one aspect of the article, however, to which I might want to give greater emphasis if I were writing today—namely, the role of time. As the article suggests, difference, understanding, and mutuality are essential elements in a creative enterprise and should be accorded adequate time so they can be fully operative. Today I am perhaps more aware of the fact that everything has a price in time. Sometimes the price is too high. Sometimes diversity and understanding must be sacrificed to competitive pressures and other dangers.

I continue to believe that most things *can* be done—given sufficient time. The administrator can control, to a considerable extent, the rate of change within the organization, but the administrator finds it immeasurably more difficult to affect the rate of social change for a society as a whole. This latter rate continues to be agonizingly slow as race riots at home and the war in Vietnam so amply illustrate.

Nothing I say today, however, can change what I left on the *HBR* doorstep many years ago. If the foundling has survived, he speaks on his own. And if, gentle reader, you should disagree, please take it up with him, not me.

Notes

1. David McCord Wright, *The Impact of the Union* (New York, Harcourt, Brace, 1951), p. 274.

2. Mary Parker Follett, *Creative Experiences* (New York, Longmans, Green, 1924), pp. 300–301.

3. Carl R. Rogers and F. J. Roethlisberger, "Barriers and Gateways to Communication," *HBR*, July–August 1952, p. 46, and Chapter 8, this volume.

4. Ibid., p. 48.

5. Stuart Chase, *Roads to Agreement* (New York, Harper & Brothers, 1951), p. 45 ff.

6. Mary Parker Follett, *Dynamic Administration—The Collected Papers of Mary Parker Follett* (New York, Harper & Brothers, 1940), pp. 219–220.

7. Kenneth Boulding, "Religious Foundations of Economic Progress," *HBR*, May–June 1952, p. 36.

8. Aneurin Bevan, *In Place of Fear* (New York, Simon and Schuster, 1952), p. 19.

12
"Skyhooks"
With Special Implications for Monday Through Friday

O. A. OHMANN

For years managers have been concerned about their employees's blue-collar blues, and many researchers have investigated the degree to which workers in America's factories and plants were being demoralized by their jobs and whether the conditions in the plants or the nature of the jobs was at fault. More recently evidence has been mounting that many white-collar workers and even managers may also be disaffected by their work lives. The author of this article would say that the problem of demoralization at work is not peculiar to the level of worker or the job, rather its source is the depersonalization of work. As organizations grow and individuals lose their opportunities to express their individuality leaders need to provide them with "something to believe in, . . . something that will give meaning to the job." In the author's view a prime requirement for a leader is to provide employees with "skyhooks," the chance to share in a worthy objective that will integrate their life's experiences both within and outside of work. Whether the skyhooks are a renewed faith in industrial society or in God, the leader imparts to the organization that these skyhooks are of special significance and can provide a context that gives meaning to what people do at work.

During the last several years, while my principal job assignment has been management development, I have become increasingly impressed with the importance of intangibles in the art of administration. With the managerial revolution of the last generation and the transition from owner-manager to professional executive, there has appeared a growing literature on the science and art of administration. A shift in emphasis is noticeable in these writings over the past 30 years.

Following the early engineering approach typified by the work of Frederick Taylor and others, there next developed a search for the basic principles of organization, delegation, supervision, and control. More recently, as labor relations became more critical, the emphasis has shifted to ways of improving human relations. The approach to the problems of supervisory relationships was essentially a manipulative one. Textbooks on the techniques of personnel management mushroomed. Still later it became more and more apparent that the crux of the problem was the supervisor, and this resulted in a flood of "how to improve yourself" books. Meanwhile the complexities of the industrial community increased, and the discontents and tensions mounted.

It seems increasingly clear, at least to me, that while some administrative practices and personnel techniques may be better than others, their futility arises from the philosophical assumptions or value judgments on which this superstructure of manipulative procedure rests. We observe again and again that a manager with sound values and a stewardship conception of the role of boss can be a pretty effective leader even though the techniques used are unorthodox. I am convinced that workers have a fine sensitivity to spiritual qualities and want to work for a boss who believes in something and in whom they can believe.

This observation leads me to suspect that we may have defined the basic purposes and objectives of our industrial enterprise too narrowly, too selfishly, too materialistically. Bread alone will not satisfy workers. There are some indications that our people have lost faith in the basic values of our economic society, and that we need a spiritual rebirth in industrial leadership.

Certainly no people have ever had so much and enjoyed so little real satisfaction. Our economy has been abundantly productive, our standard of living is at an all-time peak, and yet we are a tense, frustrated, and insecure people full of hostilities and anxieties. Can it be that our *god of production* has feet of clay? Does industry need a new religion—or at least a better one than it has had?

I am convinced that the central problem is not the division of the spoils as organized labor would have us believe. Raising the price of prostitution does not make it the equivalent of love. Is our industrial discontent not in fact the expression of a hunger for a work life that has meaning in terms of higher and more enduring spiritual values? How can we preserve the wholeness of the personality if we are expected to worship God on Sundays and holidays and Mammon on Mondays through Fridays?

I do not imply that this search for real meaning in life is or should be limited to the hours on the job, but I do hold that the central values of our industrial society permeate our entire culture. I am sure we do not require a bill of particulars of the spiritual sickness of our time. The evidences of modern people's search for their souls are all about us. Save for the communist countries there has been a world-wide revival of interest in religion. The National Council of Churches reports that 59% of our total population (or 92 million) now claim church affiliation. The November 22, 1954 issue of *Barron's* devoted the entire front page to a review of a book by Barbara Ward, *Faith and Freedom.*[1]

Perhaps even more significant is the renaissance in the quality of religious thought and experience. Quite evidently our religion of materialism, science, and humanism is not considered adequate. People are searching for anchors outside themselves. They run wearily to the periphery of the spider web of their own reason and logic, and look for new "skyhooks"—for an abiding faith around which life's experiences can be integrated and given meaning.

Why "Skyhooks"?

Perhaps we should assume that this need for "skyhooks" is part of people's natural equipment—possibly a function of their intelligence—or, if you prefer, God manifesting Himself in His creatures. It seems to me, however, that the recent intensification of this need (or perhaps the clearer recognition of it) stems in part from certain broad social, economic, political, and philosophical trends. I shall not attempt a comprehensive treatment of these, but shall allude to only a few.

Abundance Without Satisfaction

I have already indicated that on the economic front we have won the battle of production. We have moved from an economy of scarcity to one of abundance. We have become masters of the physical world and have learned how to convert its natural resources to the satisfaction of our material wants. We are no longer so dependent and so intimately bound to the world of nature. In a way we have lost our feeling of being part of nature and with it our humble reverence for God's creation.

While the industrialization of our economy resulted in ever-increasing production, it also made of individual man a production number—an impersonal, de-skilled, interchangeable production unit, measured in so many cents per hour. For most employees, work no longer promotes the growth of personal character by affording opportunities for personal decision, exercise of judgment, and individual responsibility. A recent issue of *Nation's Business* quotes the modern British philosopher Alexander Lindsay on this point as follows:

> Industrialism has introduced a new division into society. It is the division between those who manage and take responsibility and those who are managed and have responsibility taken from them. This is a division more important than the division between the rich and poor.[2]

Certainly modern industrial workers have improved their material standards of living at the cost of becoming more and more dependent on larger and larger groups. Not only their dignity but also their security has suffered. And so they reach out for new "skyhooks"—for something to believe in, for something that will give meaning to their jobs.

Disillusionment With Science

A second trend which seems to bear some relation to our urgent need for a faith grows out of our disillusionment with science. As a result of the rapid advance of science, the curtains of ignorance and superstition have been pulled wide on all fronts of human curiosity and knowledge. Many of the bonds of our intellectual enslavement have been broken. Reason and scientific method were called on to witness the truth, the whole truth, and nothing but the truth. We were freed from the past—its traditions, beliefs, philosophies, its mores, morals, and religion. Science became our religion, and reason replaced emotion.

However, even before the atom bomb there was a growing realization that science did not represent the whole truth, that with all its pretensions it could be dead wrong, and, finally and particularly, that without proper moral safeguards the truth did not necessarily make you free. Atomic fission intensified the fear and insecurity of every one of us who contemplated the possibility of the concentration of power in the hands of men without morals. We want science to be in the hands of men who not only recognize their responsibility to man-made ethical standards (which are easily perverted) but have dedicated themselves to the eternal and absolute standards of God. Thus, while the evidence of material science has been welcomed, our own personal experiences will not permit us to believe that life is merely a whirl of atoms without meaning, purpose, beauty, or destiny.

Trend Toward Bigness

A third factor contributing to our insecurity is the trend toward bigness and the resulting loss of individuality. This is the day of bigger and bigger business—in every aspect of life. The small is being swallowed by the big, and the big by the bigger. This applies to business, to unions, to churches, to education, to research and invention, to newspapers, to our practice of the professions, to government, and to nations. Everything is getting bigger except the individual, and the individual is getting smaller and more insignificant and more dependent on larger social units. Whether we like it or not, this is becoming an administrative society, a planned and controlled society, with ever-increasing concentration of power. This is the day of collectivism and public-opinion polls. It is the day when the individual must be *adjusted to the group*—when the individual must above all else be sensitive to the feelings and attitudes of others, must get an idea of how others expect the individual to act, and then react to this.

This is the insecure world which David Riesman has described so well in his book *The Lonely Crowd*.[3] He pictures man as being no longer "tradition directed" as was primitive man, nor as in Colonial days is he "inner directed" as if by the gyroscope of his own ideals, but today he is "outer directed" as if by radar. He must constantly keep his antenna tuned to the attitudes and reactions of others to him. The shift has been from morals to morale and from self-reliance to dependence on one's peer group. However, the members of one's peer group are each responding to each other. Obviously these shifting sands of public opinion offer no stable values around which life can be consistently integrated and made meaningful. The high-water mark of adjustment in such a society is that the individual be socially accepted and above all else that he appear to be *sincere*.

This is certainly not a favorable environment for the development of steadfast character. It is essentially a neurotic and schizophrenic environment which breeds insecurity.

This socially dependent society also offers an ideal market for the wares of the "huckster," the propagandist, and the demagogue. Lacking a religious interpretation of the divine nature of people, these merchants in mass reaction have sought the least common denominator in human nature and have beamed the movies and newspapers at the ten-year mental level. One wonders if this approach to people does not make them feel that they have been sold short and that they are capable of much better than is expected of them. Has this demoralizing exposure of the cheapness of our values not intensified our search for something better to believe in?

On top of all these disturbing socioeconomic trends came the war. This certainly was materialism, science, and humanism carried to the logical conclusion. The war made us question our values and our direction. It left us less cocksure that we were right, and more fearful of ourselves as well as of others. It made us fearful of the power which we had gained, and led us to search our soul to determine whether we had the moral strength to assume the leadership role that had been given to us. We have been humbled in our efforts to play god and are about ready to give the job back. Note, however, that this is not a characteristic reaction to war. Typically wars have been followed by a noticeable deterioration of moral standards, of traditional values, and of social institutions.

Perhaps none of these rationalizations for our return to religion is entirely valid. I suspect that the search for some kind of overarching integrative principle or idea is the expression of a normal human need. Certainly history would indicate that people's need for a god is eternal even though it may be more keenly sensed in times of adversity. A religion gives a point of philosophical orientation around which life's experiences can be organized and digested. Without the equivalent, a personality cannot be whole and healthy. Short-term goals which need to be shifted with the changing tide do not serve the same integrative function as do the "skyhooks" which are fastened to eternal values. I do not personally regard the current religious revival as a cultural hangover, nor as a regression. Being a mystic I prefer instead to view the need for such a faith as the spark of the Creator in us to drive us on to achieve His will and our own divine destiny.

Why Monday Through Friday?

If we may grant for the moment that the modern person *is* searching for deeper meanings in life, we may then ask: What has this to do with industry? If people need "skyhooks," let them get them in church, or work out their own salvation. The business leaders of the past insisted that "business is business" and that it had little bearing on the individual's private life and philosophy.

There are several reasons why "skyhooks" must be a primary concern of the business administrator:

☐ For the individual the job is the center of life, and its values must be in harmony with the rest of life if the individual is to be a whole and healthy personality.

☐ This is an industrial society, and its values tend to become those of the entire culture.

☐ The public is insisting that business leaders are in fact responsible for the general social welfare—that the manager's responsibilities go far beyond those of running the business. They have delegated this responsibility to the business executive whether the executive wishes to play this role or not.

☐ Even if the administrator insists on a narrow definition of the administrative function as merely the production of goods and services as efficiently as possible, it is nevertheless essential that the administrator take these intangibles into account, since they are the real secrets of motivating an organization.

☐ Besides all this the administrator needs a better set of personal "skyhooks" if the administrator is to carry an ever-increasing load of responsibility without cracking up. The fact that so many administrators are taking time to rationalize, defend, and justify the private enterprise system is an outward indication of this need for more significant meanings.

Anything Wrong With Capitalism?

We may ask, then: What specifically is wrong with our capitalistic system of private enterprise? What is wrong with production or with trying to improve our present standard of living? What is wrong with a profit, or with private ownership of capital, or with competition? Is this not the true American way of life?

Nothing is necessarily wrong with these values. There are certainly worse motives than the profit motive. A refugee from communism is reported to have observed: "What a delight to be in the United States, where things are produced and sold with such a nice clean motive as making a profit."

I am not an economist, and it is beyond the scope of this article to attempt a revision of our economic theory. I am tempted, however, to make a couple of observations about these traditional economic concepts:

1 That while the values represented by them are not necessarily wrong, they are certainly pretty thin and do not challenge the best in people.
2 That many of the classical economic assumptions are outmoded and are no longer adequate descriptions of the actual operation of our present-day economy.

For example, the concept of economic man as being motivated by self-interest not only is outmoded by the best current facts of the social sciences but also fails to appeal to the true nobility of spirit of which we are capable.

The concept of the free and competitive market is a far cry from the highly controlled and regulated economy in which business must operate today. General Motors does not appear to want to put Chrysler out of business, and apparently the union also decided to take the heat off Chrysler rather than to press its economic advantage to the logical conclusion. The assumption that everyone is out to destroy competitors does not explain the sharing of technology through trade associations and journals. No, we also have tremendous capacity for cooperation when challenged by larger visions. We are daily denying the Darwinian notion of the "survival of the fittest"—which, incidentally, William Graham Sumner, one of the nineteenth-century apologists for our economic system, used for justifying unbridled self-interest and competition.

Certainly the traditional concept of private ownership of capital does not quite correspond to the realities of today's control of large blocks of capital by insurance companies and trusteed funds.

The notion of individual security through the accumulation of savings has largely given way to the collectivist means of group insurance, company annuities, and Social Security.

The concept that all profits belong to the stockholders is no longer enthusiastically supported by either the government or the unions, since both are claiming an increasing cut.

And so, while we may argue that the system of private enterprise is self-regulatory and therefore offers maximum individual freedom, the simple, cold fact is that it is in ever-increasing degree a managed or controlled economy—partly at the insistence of the voters, but largely as the result of the inevitable economic pressures and the trend toward bigness.[4]

Regardless of the rightness or wrongness of these changes in our system of enterprise, the changes have been considerable, and I doubt that classical economic theory can be used as an adequate rationale of its virtues. I am therefore not particularly optimistic about the efficacy of the current campaign to have business executives "save the private enterprise system and the American way of life" by engaging in wholesale economic education, much of which is based on outmoded concepts.

Much as economic theory needs revision, I fear that this is not likely to cure our ills. Nor do I believe that profit-sharing or any other device for increasing the workers' cut (desirable as these efforts may be) will give us what we really want. It is, rather, another type of sharing that is needed, a sharing of more worthy objectives, a sharing of the management function, and a sharing of mutual respect and Christian working relationships.

Goals and Purposes

What is wrong is more a matter of goals and purposes—of our assumptions about what we are trying to do and how we can dignify and improve ourselves in the doing. There is nothing wrong with production, but we should ask ourselves: *Production for what*? Do we use people for production or production for people? How can production be justified if it destroys personality and human values both in the process of its manufacture and by its end use? Clarence B. Randall of Inland Steel, in his book, *A Creed for Free Enterprise*, says:

> We have come to worship production as an end in itself, which of course it is not. It is precisely there that the honest critic of our way of life makes his attack and finds us vulnerable. Surely there must be for each person some ultimate value, some purpose, some mode of self-expression that makes the experience we call life richer and deeper.[5]

So far, so good, Mr. Randall. But now notice how he visualizes industry making its contribution to this worthy objective:

> To produce more and more with less and less effort is merely treading water unless we *thereby release time and energy for the cultivation of the mind and the spirit* and for the achievement of those ends for which Providence placed us on this earth.[6]

Here is the same old dichotomy—work faster and more efficiently so that you can finish your day of drudgery and cultivate your soul on your own time. In fact he says: "A horse with a very evil disposition can nevertheless pull the farmer's plow." No, I am afraid the job *is* the life. *This* is what must be made meaningful. We cannot assume that the end of production justifies the means. What happens to people in the course of producing may be far more important than the end product. Materialism is not a satisfactory "sky-hook." People are capable of better and want to do better. (Incidentally, I have the impression that Mr. Randall's practices line up very well with my own point of view even if his words do not.)

Perhaps we should ask: What is the really important difference between Russian communism and our system? Both worship production and are determined to produce more efficiently, and do. Both worship science. Both have tremendously improved the standard of living of their people. Both share the wealth. Both develop considerable loyalties for their system. (In a mere 40 years since Lenin started the communist revolution a third of the world's people have come to accept its allegiance.) True, in Russia capital is controlled by the state, while here it is theoretically controlled by individuals, although in actual practice, through absentee ownership, it is controlled to a considerable extent by central planning agencies and bureaus, both public and private.

No, the real difference is in the philosophy about people and how they may be used as means to ends. It is a difference in the assumptions made about the origin of rights—whether the individual is endowed with rights by the Creator and yields these only voluntarily to civil authority designated by the individual, or whether rights originate in force and in the will of the government. Is God a myth or the final and absolute judge to whom we are ultimately responsible? Are all standards of conduct merely human invention and relative, or absolute and eternal? Is humankind a meaningless happenstance of protoplasm or a divine creation with a purpose, with potential for improvement, and with a special destiny in the overall scheme of things? These are some of the differences—or at least I hope that they still are. And what a difference these intangible, perhaps mythical, "skyhooks" make. They are nevertheless the most real and worthwhile and enduring things in the world. The absence of these values permitted the Nazis to "process" people through the gas chambers in order to recover the gold in their teeth.

The Administrator Contributes

This, then, is part of our general cultural heritage and is passed on to us in many ways. However, it really comes to life in people—in their attitudes, aspirations, and behaviors. And in a managerial society this brings us back to the quality of the individual administrator. This manager interprets or crystallizes group values and objectives. This supervisor sets the climate within which these values either *do* or *do not* become working realities. This executive must define the goals and purposes of the group in larger and more meaningful perspective. This administrator integrates the smaller, selfish goals of individuals into larger, more social, and spiritual objectives for the group. This leader provides the vision without which the people perish. Conflicts are resolved by relating the immediate to the long range and more enduring values. In fact, we might say this *integrative function* is the core of the administrator's contribution.

The good ones have the mental equipment to understand the business and set sound long-term objectives, but the best ones have in addition the philosophical and character values which help them to relate the overall goals of the enterprise to eternal values. This is precisely the point at which deep-seated religious convictions can serve an integrative function, since they represent the most long-range of all possible goals.[7] Most really great leaders in all fields of human endeavor have been peculiarly sensitive to their historic role in human destiny. Their responsibility and loyalty are to some distant vision which gives calm perspective to the hot issues of the day.

This function of the administrator goes far beyond being a likable personality, or applying correct principles of organization, or being skillful in the so-called techniques of human relations. I am convinced that the difficulties which so many executives have with supervisory relationships cannot be remedied by cultivation of the so-called human relations skills. These difficulties spring, rather, from one's conception of the function or role of a boss, notions about the origin and nature of authority over others, the assumptions made about people and their worth, and a view of what administrator and staff are trying to accomplish together. To illustrate:

> ☐ If, for example, my personal goal is to get ahead in terms of money, position, and power; and if I assume that to achieve this I must best my competitors; that the way to do this is to establish a good production record; that my employees are means to this end; that they are replaceable production units which must be skillfully manipulated; that this can be done by appealing to the lowest form of immediate selfish interest; that the greatest threat to me is that my employees may not fully recognize my authority or accept my leadership—if these are my values, then I am headed for trouble—all supervisory techniques notwithstanding.

I wish I could be quite so positive in painting the picture of the right values and approaches to management. I suspect there are many, many different right answers. No doubt each company or enterprise will have to define its own long-term purposes and develop its own philosophy in terms of its history, traditions, and its real function in our economy. I am also certain that no one philosophy would be equally useful to all managers. The character of an organization is, to a large extent, set by the top executive or the top group, and it is inevitable that this be the reflection of the philosophy of these individuals. No one of us can operate with another's philosophy. I have also observed that in most enterprises the basic faith or spirit of the organization is a rather nebulous or undefined something which nevertheless has very profound meaning to the employees.

A Successful Executive

While recognizing the futility of advocating any one pattern of values, it occurs to me that it might, however, be suggestive or helpful if I told you something of the philosophy of one extremely successful executive I have pumped a good deal on this subject (for he is more inclined to live his values than to talk about them).

As near as I can piece it together, he believes that this world was not an accident but was created by God and that His laws regulate and control the universe and that we are ultimately *responsible to Him*. Humans, as

God's supreme creation, are in turn endowed with creative ability. Each individual represents a unique combination of talents and potentials. In addition, humans are the only animals endowed with freedom of choice and with a high capacity for making value judgments. With these gifts (of heredity and cultural environment) goes an obligation to give the best possible accounting of one's stewardship in terms of maximum self-development and useful service to one's fellows in the hope that one may live a rich life and be a credit to the Creator.

This executive also assumes that each individual possesses certain God-given rights of self-direction which only *the individual* can voluntarily delegate to others in higher authority, and that this is usually done in the interest of achieving some mutual cooperative good. The executive therefore assumes that his own authority as boss over others must be exercised with due regard for the attendant obligations to his employees and to the stockholders who have temporarily and voluntarily yielded their rights in the interest of this common undertaking. (Notice that the executive does not view this authority as originating with or derived from an immediate superior.) This delegated authority must, of course, be used to advance the common good rather than primarily to achieve the selfish ambitions of the leader at the expense of the led.

He further assumes that the voluntary association of employees in industry is for the purpose of increasing the creativity and productivity of all members of the group and thus of bringing about increased benefits to all who may share in the ultimate use of these goods and services. What is equally important, however, is that in the course of this industrial operation each individual should have an opportunity to develop the maximum potential of skills and that the working relationships should not destroy the individual's ability to achieve greatest maturity and richness of experience. The supervisor must set the working conditions and atmosphere which will make it possible for employees to achieve this dual objective of increasing productivity and maximizing self-development.

These goals can best be achieved by giving employees maximum opportunity to exercise their capacity for decision making and judgment within their assigned area of responsibility. The supervisor is then primarily a coach who must instruct, discipline, and motivate all the members of the group, making it possible for each to exercise any special talent in order to maximize the total team contribution. Profits are regarded as a measure of the group's progress toward these goals, and a loss represents not only an improper but even an immoral use of the talents of the group.

There is nothing "soft" about this operation. He sets high quality standards and welcomes stiff competition as an additional challenge to the group. Complete cooperation and dedication are expected—and received—from everyone. Incidentally, he views the activity of working together in this manner with others as being one of life's most rewarding experiences. He holds that this way of life is something which we have not yet fully learned, but its achievement is part of our divine destiny. He is firmly convinced that such conscientious efforts *will* be rewarded with success. He manages with a light touch that releases creativity, yet with complete confidence in the outcome.

This is probably a poor attempt at verbalizing the basic philosophy which this man lives so easily and naturally. I hope, however, that it has revealed something of his conception of his role or function as an executive, and his view of what he and his organization are trying to do together. With this account of his values I am sure that you would have no difficulty completing the description of his administrative practices and operating results. They flow naturally from his underlying faith, without benefit of intensive training in the principles and art of administration.

As you would suspect, people like to work for him—or with him. He attracts good talent (which is one of the real secrets of success). Those with shoddy values, selfish ambitions, or character defects do not survive—the organization is self-pruning. Those who remain develop rapidly because they learn to accept responsibility. He not only advocates but practices decentralization and delegation. His employees will admit that they have made mistakes, but usually add with a grin that they try not to make the same one twice. People respond to his leadership because he has faith in them and expects the best in them rather than the worst. He speaks well of the members of his organization, and they appear to be proud of each other and of their record of performance. He takes a keen interest in developing measurements of performance and in bettering previous records or competitive standards. He feels that no one has a right to "louse up a job"—a point on which he feels the stockholders and the Lord are in complete agreement.

While he does not talk much about "employee communications" or stress formal programs of this type, his practice is to spend a large proportion of his time in the field with his operating people rather than in his office. He is "people oriented," and he does a particularly good job of listening. The union committee members have confidence in his fairness, yet do a workmanlike job of bargaining. In administering salaries he seems to be concerned about helping the individual to contribute more so that a pay increase can be justified.

In his general behavior he moves without haste or hysteria. He is typically well organized, relaxed, and confident, even under trying circumstances. There is a high degree of consistency in his behavior and in the quality of his decisions because his basic values do not shift. Since he does not operate by expediency, others can depend on him; and this consistency makes for efficiency in the discharge of delegated responsibility. Those operating problems which do come to him for decision seem to move easily and quickly to a conclusion. His long-term values naturally express themselves in well-defined policies, and it is against this frame of reference that the decisions of the moment easily fall into proper perspective.

In policy-level discussions his contributions have a natural quality of objectivity because "self-concern" does not confuse. Others take him at face value because his motives are not suspect. When differences or conflicts do arise, his approach is not that of compromise; rather, he attempts to integrate the partisan views around mutually acceptable longer-range goals. The issues of the moment then seem to dissolve in a discussion of the best means to the achievement of the objective. I have no doubt that he also has some serious problems, but I have tried to give a faithful account of the impression which he creates. There is a *sense of special significance* about his operation which is shared by his associates.

This Is the Key

It is precisely this "sense of special significance" which is the key to leadership. We all know that there are many different ways of running a successful operation. I am certainly not recommending any particular set of administrative practices—although admittedly some are better than others. Nor am I suggesting that the set of values of the executive described in the preceding section should be adopted by others, or for that matter that they could be. What I am saying is that a person's real values have a subtle but inevitable way of being communicated, and they affect the significance of everything that is done.

These are the vague intangibles—the "skyhooks"—which are difficult to verbalize but easy to sense and tremendously potent in their influence. They provide a different, invisible, fundamental structure into which the experiences of every day are absorbed and given meaning. They are frequently unverbalized, and in many organizations they defy definition. Yet they are the most real things in the world.

The late Jacob D. Cox, Jr., former president of Cleveland Twist Drill Company, told a story that illustrates my point:

> Jimmy Green was a new union committee member who stopped in to see Mr. Cox after contract negotiations had been concluded. Jimmy said that in every other place he had worked, he had always gone home grouchy; he never wanted to play with the children or take his wife to the movies. And then he said, "But since I have been working here, all that has changed. Now when I come home, the children run to meet me and we have a grand romp together. It is a wonderful difference and I don't know why, but I thought you would like to know".[8]

As Mr. Cox observed, there must be a lot of Jimmy Greens in the world who want an opportunity to take part freely in a cooperative effort that has a moral purpose.

Appendix: Retrospective Commentary

Here is how "Skyhooks" came about. In a very real sense, I did not write it. It came as a stream of consciousness—but only after I had worked very hard for several weeks at putting my ideas together. I wrote the paper mainly to clear my own thinking, and to try it out for criticism on the Cleveland Philosophical Club. After much reading and thinking, I got absolutely nowhere. In desperation I was about to abandon the idea and write on a different subject. Deep inside my consciousness I said in effect to my silent partner within, "Look, if you want me to do this, you better help." About 2 a.m. that morning the ideas flowed in a continuous stream, and I put them down in shorthand notes as fast as I could.

The word "Skyhooks" for the title came in the heat of a discussion with a group of business executives attending the Institute of Humanistic Studies at Aspen, Colorado. As we debated the limits of the rational and scientific approach to life, it occurred to me that science appears rational on the surface, but at its very foundation typically lies a purely intuitive, nonrational assumption made by some scientist. He just hooked himself on a "piece of sky out there" and hung on. It was a complete leap of faith that led him.

In my studies of exceptional executives I had found a mystery not easily explainable by rational elements. These men, too, were hanging on skyhooks of their own—hidden and secret missions which went way beyond their corporate business objectives. Sometimes the mission was a "nutsy" one. Often it had long roots back in the executive's childhood and was emotional, intuitive, beyond rationality, selfless—but it stuck. For example, it might be like John F. Kennedy's determination to become President; reportedly he was doing it for his older brother, who had the ambition to be President but never made it because he was a war casualty.

Or perhaps the mission was like that of the president of one of our largest corporations. When he was 12 years old, his father died. He promised his mother he would help her work the farm in the hills so that his eight younger brothers could go through school. This is what he continued to do all of his life—helping other young people to make something of themselves. He was a great developer of managers.

I could fill a book with such examples. Many great executives I have known have something deep inside that supports them; something they trust when the going gets tough; something ultimate; something personal; something beyond reason—in short, a deep-rooted skyhook which brings them calm and confidence when they stand alone.

There is another interesting aspect to this question. In our rational, analytical, and highly successful Western culture, we have come to place great value on the material gains which represent the end results of our achievements. This is what our kids are complaining about: that we have gone overboard on material values and made a culture of *things*. But the *results* of our strivings are dead works; the life is in the *process* of achieving, in the leap of faith. David was great not when he slew Goliath, but when he decided to try.

So it seems to me that the skyhooks mystique is also characterized by a commitment to value the *process,* the working relationships with others, the spiritual bonds growing out of the faith in the God-potential deep within another person, and the basis of genuine community. The rest is the means, not the end.

In 1955, when my article was published, the generation gap had not been invented, and Marshall McLuhan had not alerted us to the fact that "the medium is the message." Yet a quick look backward reveals the considerable impact of youth and "McLuhanism" on our history and our future. The "McCarthy Kids" have ousted a President and his party, halted the military domination of our foreign policy, radically changed our educational and religious institutions, revised industry's approach to management recruiting, and made the Peace Corps type of job competitive with the "goodies" offered by business. Generalizing about the medium having greater impact than the message, they have pointed out that our values are dictated by our social systems—especially the technological, political, and managerial systems. More important than the things we create in industry, they say, is the *way* we create them—the kind of community we establish in our working together.

Without debating the merits of "pot" versus liquor, or anarchy versus order, I believe their emphasis on social process is introducing a new dimension into our corporate life and values.

"Skyhooks" was written for myself and not for publication. For a while I refused to give anybody a copy, but under pressure I duplicated a small number of copies for my friends, and they wanted copies for their friends. When the editor of *HBR* got his copy and asked, "How about publishing it?" I answered, "Only if you take it as it is; I don't want to revise it." I see little need for revising it now—except perhaps the reference (in the beginning paragraphs of this article) to the increase in membership in the institutional church. The search for ultimate values and meanings is keener than in 1955, but it is apparently no longer satisfied merely by church affiliation.

Notes

1. Barbara Ward, *Faith and Freedom* (New York, Norton, 1954).

2. John Kord Lagemann, "Job Enlargement Boosts Production," *Nation's Business,* December 1954, p. 36.

3. David Riesman, *The Lonely Crowd* (New Haven, Yale University Press, 1950).

4. See John Kenneth Galbraith, *American Capitalism* (Boston, Houghton Mifflin, 1952).

5. Clarence B. Randall, *A Creed for Free Enterprise* (Boston, Little, Brown, 1952), p. 16.

6. Ibid.

7. For further elaboration, see Gordon W. Allport, *The Individual and His Religion* (New York, Macmillan, 1953).

8. Jacob D. Cox, Jr., *Material Human Progress* (Cleveland, Cleveland Twist Drill Company, 1954), p. 104.

13
Leadership:
Sad Facts and Silver Linings

THOMAS J. PETERS

The typical CEO has endless interruptions and limited options for action. In addition, the CEO may not even hear about his or her choices, or any bad news that might require action, until it is almost too late. Finally, any decision will probably require months or years to implement fully. This author suggests that this gloomy picture has another side. In fact, each of these "sad facts" of managerial life can be turned into an opportunity to communicate values and to persuade, and they add up to a new notion of the chief executive's function.

You are executive vice president of a large corporation, challenged by competitors at home and abroad. During the past year, you have tried to get the organization moving on a much-needed overhaul of the product line. Today one of the task forces is to spend all day reviewing its key findings with you.

Twenty minutes into the presentation it is already clear that what it has come up with is a future product array with no apparent flexibility. You are being asked to bet several million dollars on a risky slate that is sure to be challenged in whole or in part long before even the first products hit the marketplace.

Then at 9:35 you are pulled out of the review to talk with the vice chairman about a product safety challenge that has just hit the local press. You get back to the meeting at 11:05 only to be pulled out again at 11:40: the president wants to verify the amount of capital spending in next year's budget before a luncheon with an outside board member. Finally, after returning at 12:35, you are pulled out for good at 2:15 to meet a major customer who has flown in unexpectedly to talk about a $20 million bid one of your major divisions just made. So, in the end, the six straight hours you had planned to give to that all-important product line issue were cut down to less than three.

The preceding situation would expose you to attack from two kinds of management thinkers. Decision-making theorists would chide you for failing to develop a wide range of options. Time effectiveness experts would criticize you for not going off-campus and devoting the full six-hour block to such a major issue.

There is, however, another side to the coin: the scenario just sketched is typical of the real world of senior management; it is, in fact, the norm.

Executives have sensed for years that this series of interruptions with the task at hand sandwiched in represents a true picture of the way they do business, but only recently has such a routine been thoroughly documented. In the early 1970s, when studying chief executives' use of time, Canadian researcher Henry Mintzberg noted that they moved in a fragmented fashion through a bewildering array of issues on any given day; in fact, fully half of their activities were completed in less than nine minutes.[1]

Moreover, he argued that such behavior was probably both appropriate and efficient. A chief executive officer provides a unique perspective and is a unique information source, Mintzberg pointed out. The CEO's ability to influence a large number of activities through brief contacts may, in fact, be a highly leveraged use of time. More recently, examining 25 major business decisions, Mintzberg found that, in every case, top management deliberation focused on only one option. They were all go–no-go issues; not a multiple choice question in the lot.

More than a decade ago, H. Edward Wrapp postulated in a much-quoted article that the successful manager "recognizes the futility of trying to push total packages or programs through the organization. . . . Avoiding debates on principles, he tries to piece together particles that may appear to be incidentals into a program that moves at least part way toward [his goals]."[2]

Without offering many prescriptions, other researchers, too, are challenging the conventional organizational wisdom concerning the supposed advantages of orderly decision-making processes and the supposed waste of time entailed by meetings, telephone conversations, unscheduled interruptions, and so on. The researchers do not deny the *rationality* of accepted notions about how a top executive ought to spend time, nor do they dismiss out of hand the values of orderly management.

Rather, by challenging the realism of advic ebased on a model so much less messy than the real world, they suggest that executive behavior that results from an ad hoc adaptation to shifting circumstances is not in itself irrational. Such behavior might, after all, prove to be the expression of a very different organizing principle.

Reckoning With Realities

Several of my colleagues and I have attempted to analyze the workings of advanced decision-making systems in some two dozen corporations in the United States and Western Europe. In general, our observations support the views of the realists against the less practical rationalizations of conventional organization theory. Our findings can be summarized under the following four headings:

1. *Senior managers will usually receive for review what amounts to a single option (one new product slate, one acquisition candidate, one major investment proposal), rather than a set of fully developed choices.* They usually face yes or no decisions rather than trade-offs. Rarely, moreover, does the proposal that they see include assessments of possible competitive responses or government constraints that will emerge over the long term.

2. *Senior management will spend most of its time fighting fires and may not come upon critical issues until late in the game.* It is unusual for senior management to get a look at proposals when the options are still wide open. Published scientific papers (the equivalent of polished proposals) typically suggest an "immaculate, rational, step-by-step approach to discovery," notes science historian Robert Merton;[3] the dead ends and assumptions left untested because of time constraints never show up in the finished product.

3. *Senior managers will be shielded from most bad news.* Obviously, the monthly or quarterly revenues and net income figures that top managers see are reasonably straightforward and timely; even by playing with receivables or speeding up deliveries, a division manager cannot hide bad news at this level for long. But *really* bad news—for example, on a share decline in a critical segment of a product line—can be concealed for months, sometimes for years.

4. *Most really important decisions emerge only after top managers have vacillated for months or years, apparently or actually; and the solution they choose at the end may well be indistinguishable from that proposed at the beginning of the search.* In practice, top managers typically respond to major issues with trial balloons. They seldom give public commitment to a choice before they are quite sure that: (a) its wisdom is no longer open to serious question and (b) the organization is agreeable.

Each of these observations seemingly casts a gloomy cloud over the potential for a rational organization theory. Yet I would argue that each can have a silver lining. The purpose of this article is to point out these silver linings and to suggest how senior executives can take advantage of them.

First, however, an important preliminary point. The four observations appear to be as characteristic of companies that perform well as of those that perform poorly. They are not, in other words, symptoms of some sort of organizational malaise that should be (or could be) "put right."

At first glance, the four observations offer no obvious encouragement to the senior executive who aspires to shape events and to leave a mark of excellence behind. Considered more thoughtfully, however, they do suggest a hopeful hypothesis: *perhaps* the seemingly disorderly bits of the choice process make available to the senior executive a set of opportunities to impart a thrust to, or to fine tune, the organization's sense of direction. I believe that this is indeed the case. Let us examine each observation in turn and try to discover its potential silver lining.

Not Enough Choices

Sad Fact No. 1. Senior managers get only one option.

Silver Lining. (a) The option is in accord with senior managers' preferences; (b) there are enough one-option choices in a given period to permit managers to shape them, over time, as a portfolio.

There is nothing wrong with one option, if it is an option the senior manager wants to see. This is an obvious statement, perhaps, but it has not-so-obvious implications. First, it assumes that the senior manager's main business is unearthing concerns, reminding people about past errors, setting directions, and building management capabilities. Chief executives have little enough time to spend "on the issues"—too little to spend it making complex trade-offs between action alternatives. Their real question, then, is less likely to be "Where are the other options?" than "Does this option contain the thrust we want to see?"

Suppose top managers are worried that their company is making a relatively high-cost product in a major line; it is making Oldsmobiles for a Chevrolet (or Honda) market. The new product slate comes up. Broadly, they want to know: Is it a low-cost slate? More important, is it clearly *different* from the slates of past years—different in the way they want to see? Top managers' yes or no decision on the proposal is in no sense a check on its optimality. It is, however, a check on its direction and a signal back to, say, division management that "We think you have (or have not) gotten the message."

Next consider this one-option agenda over six months or so. There may be a half-dozen decisions of note, which add up to a reasonably sizable portfolio of choices. Viewed in this light, the quarterly or annual slate of choices becomes an array of opportunities to communicate, reinforce, or adjust in a direction top management wishes to pursue.

Not Enough Time

Sad Fact No. 2. Time is fragmented; issues arrive late, fully staffed.

Silver Lining. (a) Each fragment can be used to convey preferences, so that the calendar or agenda as a whole provides an opportunity to set direction; (b) lateness is relative; each slight modification of the current option becomes a strong signal about what the next one should look like.

The point here is that fragmentation can, if properly managed, be a positive advantage. As Richard Neustadt wrote of Franklin Roosevelt:

> He had a strong feel for the cardinal fact of government: that presidents don't act on policies, programs or personnel in the abstract; they act in the concrete as they meet deadlines set by due dates, act on documents awaiting signatures, vacant posts awaiting appointees, officials seeking interviews, newsmen seeking answers, audiences waiting for a speech, etc.[4]

The fragments that compose the executive's working day can be used as a succession of opportunities to tackle bits of the issue stream. It is precisely the fragmented nature of their activity that permits top managers to fine tune, test, and retest the general strategic direction they are trying to impart to their companies over the longer term.

Moreover, fragmentation of time, properly exploited, can yield a rich variety of information. Within reason, the more views and visits in the top executive's schedule and the more numerous the interruptions and unscheduled encounters, the better informed the executive is likely to be. As Mintzberg observes, "The chief executive tolerates interruption because he does not wish to discourage the flow of current information."[5]

The potential danger is equally clear: the fragmentation of time multiplies opportunities for the executive to send inconsistent signals to the organization. To send effective signals to, say, the 25 to 75 key executives in an organization, the top management team must obviously be clear on the general message it wants to get across.

The second aspect of this fact of life is late exposure to issues. Senior managers must accept their fate as reviewers of completed staff work. Rarely does a rough draft, rife with contention over key assumptions or problem attributes, reach the executive suite.

Again, fragmentation, used effectively, can provide a partial answer. By their very position, top managers seldom deal with problems in isolation. They deal with a flow. Each brief exposure to an issue becomes an opportunity to express general concerns and to gradually sharpen the responses of the organization to reflect the same concerns. One CEO, in the midst of a strategic crisis, devoted a lot of time to a seemingly insignificant customer complaint because, as he explained afterward, it gave him a chance to demonstrate an approach to broad competitive issues that he was trying to instill throughout the organization.

Too Many Filters

Sad Fact No. 3. Bad news is normally hidden.

Silver Lining. Review and comment on details of good news offer a chance to shape attitudes and preferences, so that those down the line will share senior management's assumptions and priorities.

Inevitably, most news sent up the line to senior managers will be "good"; and, in any case, the chief executive is too far removed from daily operations to unerringly ask the crucial question that might open up a Pandora's box. True, the CEO can take advantage of the fragmentation of time to tap multiple sources of information and catch, by designed chance, a few reviews and analyses while debate is still focused on objectives and assumptions rather than on how to package a chosen option so the boss (or the finance staff) will buy it.

More important, however, is the opportunity that the good news presents. Much can be accomplished through a style of good-news review that zeros in on almost any sort of significant subpoint for special attention and comment. In dealing with the problem of how overextended and partially ignorant congressional representatives can quickly inform themselves on complex issues, political scientist Aaron Wildavsky makes a relevant point:

> Another way of handling complexity is to use actions on simpler items as indices of more complicated ones. Instead of dealing with the cost of a huge atomic installation, Congressmen may seek to discover how personnel and administrative costs or real estate transactions with which they have some familiarity are handled. The reader has probably heard of this practice under some such title as "straining at gnats." This practice may at times have greater validity than appears on the surface if it is used as a testing device, and if there is a reasonable connection between the competence shown in handling simple and complex items.[6]

Top managers regularly use forays into detail as a shield against surprise, and over time, they can learn a lot this way. More important, though, such attention conveys a sense of "how we deal with problems," and indicates the sort of understanding of issues that is expected of managers down the line. If, additionally, top managers' probings clearly reflect concern with a particular issue, the danger that their subordinates will lose sight of that issue will be slight.

Such irregular involvement with detail contrasts markedly with the exclusive use of staff for probing. Obviously, staff probes can be productive in some situations, but in others they may simply drive the bad news further into hiding. While using his staff as merciless probers, ITT's legendary chief executive Harold Geneen was a firm believer in face-to-face reviews because, as he put it, "You can tell by the tone of voice if a fellow is having a problem he hasn't reported yet."

A simple but often overlooked aspect of good-news review is the use of praise. An executive can use detailed good-news review deliberately to reinforce desired patterns of action or response. One CEO, when attending field reviews, always stopped in at a regional sales office or plant. He would dig into the records ahead of time, pick out an exemplary action by some sales executive or supervisor, and make a point of asking how this or that had been done so well.

The chief executive might then take up the idea in a memo that would be sent all around the company. Again, if in the course of a presentation a junior staff member came up with a particularly clever analysis that fitted in well with the CEO's current main concern—for example, looking at the competitor's position in a new way—the chief executive would interrupt the presentation and raise the possibility of introducing the idea into a large class of proposals or reviews.

Too Much Inertia

Sad Fact No. 4. Major choices take months or years to emerge.

Silver Lining. The process of choosing provides an opportunity to build a strong consensus for consistent implementing actions that will require only minimal correction over time. If enough choices are in the hopper, the lengthy sorting process will be punctuated by fairly frequent decisions that will support (or serve to test) top managers' chosen directions.

An instructive case in point concerns a large industrial products company, long dominated by engineers, that found itself threatened in frightening new ways. Overseas competitors' products were nicking sizable chunks from previously uncontested market segments. Cash-rich domestic competitors were investing in small companies making promising substitute products for some key lines. The threat was both diffuse and pervasive.

Gradually, over a three- to five-year period, the top team became convinced that its main task was to instill a marketing orientation. Early steps, all in the nature of trial balloons, included: (1) going outside to hire three senior marketers from companies with outstanding marketing reputations; (2) creating a top-level task force to assess the five-year competitive outlook; and (3) giving one of the new marketers a special new product group with a sizable budget to develop a product slate for one of the threatened market niches.

About 18 months later some more definite signals came of what was afoot: a major speech to security analysts outlining the company's new approach to marketing; irregular visits to important customers by the president and top team; the establishment of a monthly president's review, marked by several special sessions on competitive assessment and the beginning of share reporting in certain businesses; the creation of a large number of new assistant regional sales manager jobs and the hiring of highly paid MBAs to fill them. Finally, at about the three-year mark, the top team took some very conspicuous actions. It promoted two of the three marketers who had been recruited on the outside, together with two insiders, to the position of senior vice president, with realigned market responsibilities.

At the annual shareholders meeting the top team launched a new theme: "Our emerging role is to be preeminent in marketing." It brought out a slate of surprisingly good new products, striking back hard at competitors in one or two besieged market segments. Internally, it publicly introduced a new management information and cost system that had been implemented after three years of gradual, incremental development.

Thus, over a 36-month period, without much fanfare, the top team successfully shifted the institution's attention to the marketplace. Observers today, while noting that engineers still win a fair share of their battles, agree that the company has undergone a radical transformation.

Developing top management censensus in favor of such a major shift can be a delicate and time-consuming business. Bringing along one crucial member of a triumvirate (or at least effectively neutralizing his opposition) can take years. During such a process, even a decision about when to send up the next trial balloon may be politically loaded. As Peter Drucker wisely noted, "Priorities are easy; posteriorities—what jobs *not* to tackle—are tough." His point is consistent with a wide body of psychological research on building commitment and overcoming resistance to change: keeping a dissident actor from quick-triggering with a negative response is no easy chore.

The period of muddling about on the way to major change is not purely a matter of political maneuvering. At least as important is the "marinating time" it provides. In one company I know, the top 12 executives met weekly for several hours, over an 18-month period, in order to draft a modified change of charter for the company. They have used the resulting document, which they call their "Magna Carta," as the jumping-off point for a decade of substantial positive change. It is only two pages long. But it took this management group nearly two years to work through the critical issues involved and to come to terms with the new departures involved, although they had had a fairly good idea from the beginning what the shape of the outcome would be.

Revamping Management's Role

Each of the four seemingly discouraging facts of executive life can, as we have seen, be recast in positive terms. The results add up to a fresh conception of the top management task, one that fits both the disorderly facts of life and their recurrent silver linings. It rejects the traditional notion of the executive as dedicating large, discrete blocks of time to linear chunks called "planning," "deciding," or "implementing" and replaces it with something closer to a notion of the effective executive as a communicator, a persuader, and, above all, a consummate opportunist. The CEO is adept at grasping and taking advantage of each item in the random succession of time and issue fragments that crowd the day.

This reconception of the top management task requires hard thinking about what is and what is not achievable from the top. The CEO does not drive forklifts or install phones; management theory has long acknowledged that limitation. Research is beginning to suggest a further off-limits area—top managers cannot *solve* problems: their attention is fragmented; issues come to them late; and they are shielded from bad news. What they can do is: (1) generally shape business values and (2) educate by example.

Shaping Business Values

In his landmark study of top management activity, Philip Selznick concludes that the effective institutional leader "is primarily an expert in the promotion and protection of values."[7] Another recent study of leadership, by James McGregor Burns, contrasts lesser forms of management behavior with "transforming leadership," which, in the midst of the disorderly press of events, unleashes organizational energies through the promotion of new, overarching values.[8]

The same theme is echoed by Roy Ash, who created new institutional forms at Litton Industries and the U.S. Office of Management and Budget and is now in the process of reviving Addressograph-Multigraph. As he sees it, the really important change in a company lies in a process of "psychological transformation." One of Ash's recent notes to himself, as quoted in *Fortune,* clarifies his meaning. It reads, "Develop a much greater attachment of everybody to the bottom line—more agony and ecstasy."[9]

As descriptions of the top management task, these terms—institutional leadership, value promotion, transforming leadership—are surprisingly congenial to the disorderly, nonrational realities of most real-life management activity. In an untidy world, where goal setting, option selection, and policy implementation hopelessly fuzz together, the shaping of robust institutional values through a principle of ad hoc opportunism becomes preeminently the mission of the chief executive and his most senior colleagues.

The nature of this value-shaping process is not obvious. Among a group of chief executives (actually mayors) they studied, John Kotter and Paul Lawrence found that the more successful typically spent over a year carefully taking the pulse of key stakeholders, seeding ideas, and nursing along a consensus in favor of a few new directions. The less effective executives were those who plunged into major commitments before they had built adequate support.[10]

My own observations are wholly consistent with those of Kotter and Lawrence. The process of easing a larger organization into a major shift of values seems to require anywhere from three to eight years. A good example is the experience of Walter Spencer of Sherwin-Williams, who spent his first five years as CEO working to introduce a marketing orientation into a previously manufacturing-dominated institution. "When you take a 100-year-old company and change the culture of the organization, and try to do that in Cleveland's traditional business setting—well, it takes time; you just have to keep hammering away at everybody," Spencer told an interviewer from *Forbes*. "The changeover to marketing is probably irreversible now. It's not complete, but we've brought along a lot of young managers with that philosophy, and once you've taken a company this far, you can't go back."[11]

The literature of top management generally ignores the intricacies of effective value management, especially the aspect of timing. Yet almost any chief executive of a large enterprise knows how much time must be spent on patiently building support for initiatives. Only when crisis is imminent can the process be condensed, and even then some form of consensus-building is needed.

The art of value management, then, blends strategic foresight with a shrewd sense of timing and the political acumen necessary to build stable, workable coalitions. Fortunately, the practical exercise of these skills—as opposed to the textbook fantasies of rational problem solving—is actually enhanced by the untidiness of typical executive choice processes.

CEO as Exemplar

Top management's actions, over time, constitute the guiding, directing, and signaling process that shapes values in the near chaos of day-to-day operations. As Eli Ginzberg and Ewing Reilley have noted: "Those a few echelons from the top are always alert to the chief executive. Although they attach much importance to what he says, they will be truly impressed only by what he does."[12] Top management is at the apex of the symbolic signaling system, not the hard product delivery system. Because senior managers cannot act directly or promptly to resolve issues, their daily efforts must focus on the sending of effective and appropriate signals. Recounts one chief executive:

> The board's question at my first meeting was trivial: Could I get them speedier information about the installation of new machines? I used it as a simple teaching opportunity. I responded with the data requested but recast it in market share terms. My intent was to wean them away from thinking that the gross number was still an adequate measure of health. That little incident was my first easy opportunity to expose them to share issues.

The executive who sees the role in these terms is aware that symbol management is a source of both unparalleled opportunity and, for the unwary, of unparalleled risk. Knowing that subordinates will eventually make detailed interpretations of every activity ("With the investment bankers, was he? Maybe it's my division he wants to unload"), the chief executive will be scrupulously careful to avoid distracting signals. "People keep searching for clues," notes linguist Julius Roth. "The poorer and fewer the clues, the more desperate the search."[13]

Several business scholars and political scientists have suggested the image of the "leader as educator." Such a leader, in Selznick's words, must be able to "interpret the role of the enterprise, to perceive and develop models of thought and behavior, and to find general rather than merely partial, perspectives."[14]

Beyond that, the CEO needs to be able to articulate a vision in a compelling way. Warren Bennis underscores the point:

> If I were to give off-the-cuff advice to anyone trying to institute change, I would say, "How clear is the metaphor? How is that understood? How much energy are you devoting to it?" It's the imagery that creates the understanding, the compelling moral necessity that the new way is right. It was the beautiful writing of Darwin about his travels on the *Beagle*, rather than the content of his writing, that made the difference. The evolutionary idea had really been in the air for quite a while.[15]

If it is in shaping values that the senior executive can most efficiently use time, it is symbols that are the executive's primary value-shaping tools. As an educator, the CEO has quite an arsenal of pedagogical tricks of the trade available: manipulation of settings, varied repetition of signals, a range of sensitive responses to subtle feedback cues. Consider:

- ☐ Careful use of language, including insistently asked questions and attention to the minutiae of written proposals.
- ☐ Manipulation of settings, including the creation of forums and rules of debate designed to focus on critical concerns.
- ☐ Shifts of agenda and time allocation to signal, subtly but pervasively, a change in priorities.
- ☐ Consistent and frequent feedback and reinforcement, including the careful and selective interpretation of past results to stress a chosen theme.
- ☐ Selective seeding of ideas among various internal power groups, and cultivation of those that win support.

Collectively, these enable the CEO to intervene purposefully and effectively in what one philosopher called "the brute flow of random detail that adds up to everyday experience."

Concluding Note

Senior managers are used to hearing and reading advice about how they can combat sloppiness and introduce rationality or neatness into decision making. I have argued that "sloppiness" is normal, probably inevitable, and usually sensible. Organizations in the process of making important choices almost always look disorderly. But that apparent disorder can provide the latitude and the time required for the development of consensus; and without consensus, efforts at implementation will be doomed from the start.

The task of the senior executive, then, is not to impose an abstract order on an inherently disorderly process, but to become adept at the sorts of intervention by which it can be nudged in the desired direction and to some degree control its course.

Notes

1. Henry Mintzberg, "The Manager's Job: Folklore and Fact," *HBR*, July–August 1975, p. 49.

2. H. Edward Wrapp, "Good Managers Don't Make Policy Decisions," *HBR*, September–October 1967, p. 95.

3. Robert K. Merton, *Social Theory and Social Structure* (New York, The Free Press, 1968), p. 4.

4. Richard E. Neustadt, "Approaches to Staffing the Presidency," *American Political Science Review*, December 1963, p. 855.

5. Henry Mintzberg, *The Nature of Managerial Work* (New York, Harper & Row, 1973), p. 35.

6. Aaron Wildavsky, *The Politics of the Budgetary Process* (Boston, Little, Brown, 1964), p.12.

7. Philip Selznick, *Leadership in Administration* (Evanston, Ill., Row, Peterson, 1957), p. 28.

8. James McGregor Burns, *Leadership* (New York, Harper & Row, 1978).

9. Louis Kraar, "Roy Ash Is Having Fun at Addressogrief-Multigrief," *Fortune*, February 27, 1978, p. 47.

10. John P. Kotter and Paul R. Lawrence, *Mayors in Action* (New York, Wiley, 1974).

11. Harold Seneker, "Why Some CEOs Pop Pills (And Sometimes Quit)," *Forbes*, July 12, 1978, p. 70.

12. Eli Ginzberg and Ewing W. Reilley, *Effecting Change in Large Organizations* (New York, Columbia University Press, 1957), p. 42.

13. Julius A. Roth, *Timetables* (Indianapolis, Bobbs-Merrill, 1963), p. 7.

14. Selznick, p. 150.

15. Warren Bennis, *The Unconscious Conspiracy: Why Leaders Can't Lead* (New York, AMACOM, 1976), p. 93.

14

The Human Dilemmas of Leadership

ABRAHAM ZALEZNIK

Many managers might assume that people near the top of the organization have all their problems behind them. From others' points of view, these people have proved themselves in their functional areas and have displayed the leadership skills necessary to succeed to the top levels of the company. But, the author of this article maintains, success brings with it its own set of problems. People who achieve high-level positions often suffer from two kinds of anxiety that arise from unresolved inner conflicts that come to life when they approach the top. With success in an organization people often find themselves increasingly isolated from peers with whom they used to be quite friendly and from mentors who might see them as competitors. When executives feel status anxiety they feel "torn between the responsibilities of a newly acquired authority and the strong need to be liked." Executives on the rise can also succomb to competition anxiety, which can manifest itself either as fear of failure or as fear of success. To achieve success without crippling anxiety, the author holds that executives have to be responsible for their own development and become active to that end. The activity will help executives overcome the paralysis that anxiety can bring and take them further "on the road toward experiencing leadership as an adventure in learning."

About 20 years ago, the citizens of the United States and of the world became witnesses to a political drama that had all the ingredients of a first-class Greek tragedy. Were it not for the fact that the episode revealed some sense of the nature of power conflicts among influential men, one could safely have stopped reflections on the event at the point where its human interest ended and its deeper significance for leadership began. I am referring, of course, to the Adlai Stevenson episode that exploded on the public scene with an article in the *Saturday Evening Post* by Stewart Alsop and Charles Bartlett.[1]

I do not intend to go into a commentary on this article; rather, I want to use this episode to launch my reflections on the human dilemmas of leadership as they affect every person who works in a position of authority and responsibility. In the course of the Stevenson affair, we became privy to backstage rivalry among subordinates close to the President. We saw attempts at political homicide and character assassination through the use of "the leak" of so-called secret positions in the deliberations of high councils of government. We saw the President of the United States drop his guard, if only momentarily, to show us how difficult it is to make or hold friends while in the Presidency. And throughout the revelations, charges, and countercharges, we learned just what the medium of exchange can be in power conflicts; namely, prestige, personal integrity, friendship and loyalty, jealousy and egotism—all typical human sentiments likely to be found in any human encounter where people care about what they are doing.

In the professional literature on the job of the executive, one seldom finds much reference to or intelligent discussion of the dilemmas posed by the exercise of power and authority. The dramatists, novelists, biographers, and journalists attempt to portray these struggles in their works, but much is left to the sensitivity and intuition of the audience. And least of all are we ever invited to consider the underlying dynamics of leadership dilemmas and the different forms open to us for their resolution.

I should like to try to lift the veil somewhat on the nature of conflicts in exercising leadership. The two points I want to develop are:

1. The main source for the dilemmas leaders face can be found within themselves, in their own inner conflicts.

2. Dealing more intelligently with knotty decisions and the inevitable conflicts of interest existing among people in organizations presupposes that executives, at least the successful ones, are able to get their own house in order. It presupposes that the executive is able to resolve or manage inner conflicts so that actions are strongly grounded in reality, so that the executive is not constantly making and then undoing decisions to the service of mixed personal feelings and to the disservice and confusion of subordinates.

Tendency to Project

Most of us are accustomed by virtue of our training and inclinations to externalize conflicts and dilemmas. If an executive is immobilized in the face of a difficult problem, the tendency is to look to the outside for an explanation. The executive might be convinced of an inability to act for reason of possessing inadequate delegated authority. Or the executive might hesitate because of a perception that subordinates are holding out by providing too little information, confused positions, and mixed signals. In this case, the executive is likely to vent frustrations on their incompetence.

This generalized tendency to place conflicts in the outside world is part and parcel of a well-known mechanism of the mind called *projection.* A person projects when, unknowingly, a personal attitude is attributed to someone else. In the example just cited, the executive who despairs because subordinates are confused and who charges them with holding back and with indecision may well be reading a personal state of mind and attributing it to others.

It is just not within us to be able consistently to separate those issues which arise from our own concerns from those issues that reside in the realities of a situation. Let me cite another example:

□ The president of a large company became concerned with the possibility that his organization had failed to develop executive talent. This concern of his arose in connection with his own retirement. He organized a committee composed of assistants to vice presidents to study this problem and to report recommendations to him.

The president's forthcoming retirement was well known, and there was private speculation as to who among the vice presidents would be named as his successor. This succession obviously implied that several persons among the assistant vice presidents would be promoted. The task force met several times, but its discussions were not too productive or interesting. The group spent most of its time attempting to define what the president wanted the committee to do, instead of dealing with the issues the organization faced in attracting and developing executive talent.

In other words, they projected their own concerns and anxiety onto the president and attributed to him confused motives in undertaking the assessment of the company's needs in executive development. In reality the individuals themselves shared confused motivations. They were in intensive rivalry with one another over who among their immediate superiors would become president and how this change would affect their fate in the organization.

By centering attention on the inner conflicts of the executive, I do not mean to imply that conflicts are not based in the relations among individuals at work. The illustrations presented so far clearly indicate how vicious these relations may become. The point I am suggesting is that external conflicts in the form of power struggles and rivalry become more easily understood and subject to rational control under those conditions where the executive is able to separate internal conditions from those existing on the outside.

This process of separation is more easily said than done. Nevertheless, it is crucial for the exercise of leadership, and sometimes the separation is the very condition for survival. One wonders, for example, whether the failure to maintain this separation lay at the basis of the breakdown and subsequent suicide of such a brilliant man as James Forrestal. At the very least, by attending to internal conditions the executive can expect to be dealing with those situations most susceptible to rational control. It is in the long run a lot easier to control and change oneself than it is to control and change the world in which we live.

Forms of Inner Conflict

But before we examine some of the ways in which a person can learn to deal more competently with the inner life, we need to know something more about the nature of inner conflicts. Let us take two types that are quite prevalent among executives in organizations:

1 *Status anxiety.* This refers to those dilemmas frequently experienced by individuals at or near the top in their organizational world.
2 *Competition anxiety.* This refers to the feelings generated while climbing to the top.

These two prevalent types of anxiety, while resembling each other in a number of respects, are worth keeping separate for purposes of furthering understanding.

Status Anxiety

When an individual begins to achieve some success and recognition at work, there may be the sudden realization that a change has occurred within and in relations with associates. From a position of being the bright young person who receives much encouragement and support, this individual, almost overnight, is viewed as a contender by those who formerly acted as mentors. A similar change takes place in relations with persons who were peers. They appear cautious, somewhat distant, and constrained in their approach, where once the new success may have enjoyed the easy give-and-take of their friendship. The individual in question is then ripe for status anxiety—torn between the responsibilities of a newly acquired authority and the strong need to be liked.

There is a well-established maxim in the study of human behavior that describes this situation tersely and even poetically; namely, that "love flees authority." Where one individual has the capacity to control and affect the actions of another, either by virtue of differences in their positions, knowledge, or experience, then the feeling governing the relationship tends to be one of distance and (hopefully) respect, but not one ultimately of warmth and friendliness.

I do not believe that this basic dichotomy between respect or esteem and liking is easily changed. The executive who confuses the two is bound to get into trouble. Yet in our culture today we see all too much evidence of people seeking to obscure the difference. Much of the current ethos of success equates popularity and being liked with competence and achievement. In Arthur Miller's *Death of a Salesman,* Willie Loman in effect was speaking for our culture when he measured a person's achievement in the gradations of being liked, well liked, or very well liked.

Reaction and Recognition

In what ways do executives react when they are caught in the conflict between exercising authority and being liked?

Sometimes they seek to play down their authority and play up their likability by acting out the role of the "nice guy." This is sometimes called status stripping, where the individual tries in a variety of ways to discard all the symbols of status and authority. This ranges from proclaiming the open-door policy, where everyone is free to visit the executive any time, to the more subtle and less ritualistic means such as democratizing work by proclaiming equality of knowledge, experience, and position. And yet these attempts at status stripping fail sooner or later. The executive may discover that subordinates join in gleefully by stripping status and authority to the point where the executive becomes immobilized; is prevented from making decisions; is faced with the prospect of every issue from the most trivial to the most significant being dealt with in the same serious vein. In short, problem solving and work become terrorized in the acting out of status stripping.

The executive soon becomes aware of another aspect of the dilemma: Alarmingly, attempts to remove social distance in the interests of likability have not only reduced work effectiveness, but have resulted in an abortion of the intent to which the status-stripping behavior has been addressed. The executive discovers that subordinates gradually come to harbor deep and unspoken feelings of contempt, because the executive inadvertently has provided them with a negative picture of what rewards await them for achievement—a picture unpleasant to behold. In effect, the process of status stripping helps to destroy the incentives for achievement and in the extreme can produce feelings of helplessness and rage.

There is yet another side to the dilemma of status anxiety which is well worth examining. This side has to do with the hidden desire to "touch the peak." Executives frequently want to be near the source of power and to be accepted and understood by their bosses. Such motivations lead to excessive and inappropriate dependency bids, and to feelings of lack of autonomy on the part of the subordinate and of being leaned on too hard on the part of the superior. Under such conditions, communication between superior and subordinate tends to break down.

So far I have discussed the problem of status anxiety as an aspect of seeking friendship, warmth, and approval from subordinates and bosses. Status anxiety is also frequently generated by the fear of aggression and retaliation on the part of persons who hold positions of authority. Executives sometimes report feeling lonely and detached in their position. A closer look at the sense of loneliness reveals a feeling that one is a target for the aggression of others. This feeling occurs because the executive is called upon to take a position on a controversial issue and to support the stand. The executive must be able to take aggression with a reasonably detached view, or the anxiety can become intolerable.

If in your experience you have encountered an executive who seemed unable to take a stand on a problem, who seemed to equivocate or talk out of two sides of the mouth at once, then the chances are reasonably good that you have come upon someone in the throes of status anxiety. Sometimes this will appear in the form of hyperactivity—the case of the executive who flits from problem to problem or from work project to work project without really seeing an activity through to completion. In this case, the executive is utilizing the tactic of providing a shifting target so that other persons have difficulty in taking aim.

Constructive Approach

Now, in referring to aggression and the avoidance of aggression as aspects of status anxiety, I do not mean to imply hostile aggression. I mean to suggest instead that all work involves the release of aggressive energy. Solving problems and reaching decisions demand a kind of give-and-take where positions are at stake and where it is impossible for everyone concerned to be equally right all the time. But having to give way or to alter a position in the face of compelling argument is no loss. The executive who can develop a position, believe in it, support it to its fullest, and then back down, is a strong person.

It is just this type of person who does not suffer from status anxiety. This executive may love to provide a target because of the knowledge that this may be a very effective catalyst for first-class work accomplishment. This executive is secure enough to know that, in reality, nothing can be lost but much can be gained in the verve and excitement of interesting work. This type of executive is able to take aggression, and in fact encourage it, because the magical thinking that seems to equate position of authority with omnipotence has probably been abandoned. No one has the power to make everyone else conform to personal wishes, so it is no loss to learn that one has been wrong in the face of the arguments aggressively put forth by others. In fact, such ability to retract a stand results in heightened respect from others.

I am suggesting, in other words, that we should not be misled into equating the virtue of humility with executive behavior that appears modest, uncertain of a stand, and acquiescent toward others—behavior which frequently is feigned modesty to avoid becoming a target. True humility, in my opinion, is marked by the person who thinks through problems, is willing to be assertive, is realistic enough to encourage assertiveness from others, and is willing to acknowledge the superiority of ideas presented by others.

Competition Anxiety

The second main pattern of inner conflict that badly needs attention is what I have termed competition anxiety, a close kin of status anxiety. It goes without saying that the world of work is essentially a competitive one. Competition exists in the give-and-take of solving problems and making decisions. It also exists in the desire to advance into the more select and fewer positions at the top of a hierarchy. An executive who has difficulty in coming to terms with a competitive environment will be relatively ineffective.

From my observations of executives—and would-be executives—I have found two distinct patterns of competition anxiety: (1) the fear of failure and (2) the fear of success. Let us examine each in turn.

Fear of Failure

You have perhaps seen the fear of failure operate in the activities of the child, where this type of problem generally originates:

> ☐ The child may seem to become quite passive and unwilling to undertake work in school or to engage in sports with children his age. No amount of prodding by parents or teachers seems to activate his interests; in fact, prodding seems to aggravate the situation and induce even greater reluctance to become engaged in an activity. When this child progresses in school, he may be found to have considerable native talent, and sooner or later becomes tabbed as an "underachiever." He gets as far as he does thanks in large measure to the high quality of his native intelligence, but he does not live up to the promise which others observe in him.
>
> When this child grows up and enters a career, we may see the continuation of underachievement, marked by relative passivity and undistinguished performance. Where he may cast his lot is in the relative obscurity of group activity. Here he can bring his talents to bear in anonymous work. As soon as he becomes differentiated, he feels anxious and may seek to become immersed once again in group activity.

An important aspect of this pattern of response is the ingrained feeling that whatever the person undertakes is bound to fail. The person does not feel quite whole and lacks a strong sense of identity. The person is short on self-esteem and tends to quit before beginning in order to avoid confrontation with the fear of failure. Instead of risking failure this person is willing to assume anonymity, hence the sense of resignation and sometimes fatigue which that is communicated to intimates.

A closer study of the dilemma surrounding the fear of failure indicates that the person has not resolved feelings about competing. It may be that unrealistic standards of performance have been adopted or that the person is competing internally with unreachable objects. Therefore this individual resolves to avoid the game because it is lost before it starts.

If you recall James Thurber's characterization of Walter Mitty, you may get a clearer indication of the problem I am describing. Walter was a meek, shy man who seemed to have difficulty in mobilizing himself for even the simplest tasks. Yet in his inner world of fantasy, as Thurber portrays so humorously and touchingly, Walter Mitty is the grand captain of his destiny and the destiny of those who depend on him. He populates his inner world with images of himself as the pilot of an eight-engine bomber or the cool, skillful, nerveless surgeon who holds the life of his patient in his hands. Who could ever work in the world of mortals under standards that one had best leave to the gods!

You can observe from this description that fear of failure can be resolved only when the person is able to examine the inner competitive world, to judge its basis in reality, and to modify this structure in accordance with sensible standards.

Fear of Success

The fear of failure can be matched with its opposite, the fear of success. This latter pattern might be called the "Macbeth complex," since we have a ready illustration available in Shakespeare's *Macbeth*. The play can be viewed symbolically for our purposes:

> ☐ Macbeth was an ambitious man. It is interesting to note that the demon ambition is projected out in the form of the three witches and Macbeth's wife, who, Macbeth would lead us to believe, put the idea into his head to become king. But we do not believe for a minute that the ambition to become number one existed anywhere but within Macbeth himself. You remember that to become king, Macbeth killed Duncan, a nice old man who had nothing but feelings of admiration and gratitude for Macbeth.
>
> As the story unfolds, we find the crown resting uneasily on a tormented head. Macbeth is wracked with feelings of guilt for the misdeed he has committed and then with uneasy suspicion. The guilt is easy enough for us to understand, but the suspicion is a bit more subtle. Macbeth presents himself to us as a character who committed a foul deed to attain an ambition and is then suspicious that others are envious of him and seek to displace him in the number one position. So, there are few lieutenants to trust. And, paradoxically, the strongest subordinates become the ones least trusted and most threatening.

The play portrays in action the morbid cycle of the hostile-aggressive act followed by guilt and retribution. In addition, if we view the play symbolically, we can say that the individual, like Macbeth, may experience in fantasy the idea that one achieves position only through displacing someone else. Success, therefore, brings with it feelings of guilt and the urge to undo or to reverse the behavior that led to the success. If such concerns are strong enough—and they exist in all of us to some degree—then we may see implemented the fear of success.

The form of this implementation will vary. One prominent pattern it takes is in striving hard to achieve a goal, but just when the goal is in sight or within reach, the person commits self-sabotage, which can be viewed as a process of undoing—to avoid the success that may generate guilt. This process of self-sabotage is sometimes called snatching defeat out of the jaws of victory.

I am not certain just what Theodore H. White had in mind in *The Making of the President—1960,* portraying Nixon's defeat in the 1960 Presidential election, but he certainly conveys the impression that Nixon may have been going through a cycle such as the one described here—the fear of success. There were just too many errors of commission and omission that prevent us from passing off the election simply in terms of external events and forces, as important as these were.

Managing Inner Conflicts

To summarize the discussion thus far, I have called attention to the not easily accepted notion that conflicts of interest can and do exist within individuals and are not restricted to the relations among people in the ordinary conduct of affairs. I have said that the inner conflicts rooted in the emotional development of the individual are at the core of the leadership dilemma. It is misleading, in other words, to seek for causes of conflict exclusively in external forces.

Then, touching on a few of the inner conflicts of executives, I grouped them into two main types: (1) status anxiety and (2) competition anxiety. Both of these forms of inner conflict are rooted in the very process of human development in the strivings of individuals for some measure of autonomy and control over their environment. The forms happen to be especially crucial in the executive's world simply because the executive acts in the center of a network of authority and influence that at any point in time is subject to alteration. In fact, one can think of decision making and action in organizations as a continuing flow of influence interchanges where the sources of the power to influence are many. But whatever the external source through which any one person achieves power to influence, its final manifestations will reflect the inner emotional condition of the person.

Let us now see what guidelines exist for resolving and managing inner conflicts. There are six ideas I would like to suggest.

1. *The necessity of acknowledging and accepting the diversity of motivations.* The control of one's own responses and actions presupposes some accurate understanding of one's motivations. Everyone would like to believe

that the inner world is populated only by the socially nice drives and wishes. But this is not the case. It is fruitless to attempt to deny awareness of the less nice, but equally human, feelings that we all experience such as rivalry, dislike, rebelliousness, anger, and contempt. I am not urging executives to express these feelings impulsively. I am not of the school of thought that believes the catharsis of feelings in everyday relationships at work and at home is a good thing. But the awareness of how one is reacting in a situation is beneficial and permits more flexibility in thinking and action. Unless an executive establishes a close connection between the realms of thought and feeling, the two can exist in relative isolation from one another to the detriment of effectiveness as a manager. At the very least, such self-estrangement involves considerable costs in the waste of energy.

2. *The necessity of establishing a firm sense of identity.* The exercise of leadership requires a strong sense of identity—knowing who one is and who one is not. The myth of the value of being an "all-around person" is damaging to the strivings of an individual for self-identification and then for a place in the world. This active location and placement of one's self prevents the individual from being defined by others in uncongenial terms. It prevents being consigned to life within a sea of opinions. A sense of autonomy, separateness, or identity permits a freedom of action and thinking so necessary for leadership.

Not the least significant part of achieving a sense of identity is the creative integration of one's past. There is no tailor who can convert a hayseed into a city slicker—any more than a Park Avenue sophisticate can become a hick by spending a day on the farm. Coming to terms with being a hayseed or a Park Avenue sophisticate permits the development of a unique person who goes beyond the stereotypes that are offered models.

3. *The necessity of maintaining constancy and continuity in response.* Closely related to the need for a sense of identity is a constancy in how one represents and presents oneself to others. Constant alterations of oneself are confusing to work associates. These shifts are particularly damaging to subordinates who are entitled to the sense of security that comes from a feeling of reasonable continuity in the responses of their boss. For instance:

> ☐ I knew of one group of executives, many of whom had the practice of taking tranquilizers before a meeting with the president of the company. They claimed that they needed the tranquilizers to help them withstand the angry reactions the president demonstrated when people acted as though they had not thought through the ideas they were presenting. I think they were mistaken. They used the tranquilizers because they were very unsure as to just what the president would get angry about or when. If they had had some sense of the standards of performance to which the president reacted kindly or harshly, they would have been able to spend less time worrying and more time working.

4. *The necessity of becoming selective in activities and relationships.* Most executives believe that gregariousness and participation in many activities at work and in the community are of great value in their life. In a sense this belief is true. But I would urge that greater attention needs to be paid to selectivity. Without carefully selecting the matters to get involved in, the executive faces a drain on emotional energy that can become quite costly. Selectivity implies the capacity to say "no" without the sense that one has lost esteem. The capacity to say "no" also implies that one is so constituted that there is no need for esteem from diffuse persons and activities to enhance self-worth.

5. *The necessity of learning to communicate.* Conflict resolution, both inner and external, depends on the capacities of people to communicate. Communication is a complex process and one that requires careful thought and attention. Here are two suggestions for improving communication:

1 Try to develop a keen awareness of your own reactions (a point I referred to previously).
2 Try to make your opinions and attitudes known without wasteful delays. (An unexpressed reaction that simmers and then boils within is apt to explode at inappropriate times; this may lead to increased confusion and concern in the minds of listeners, to the detriment of information interchange.)

6. *The necessity of living within a cyclical life pattern.* The effective utilization of energy seems to involve a rhythmic pattern of alternating between different modes or cycles of response. The prototype of alternating modes is probably best found in the comparison of wakefulness and sleep. Wakefulness suggests activity, conscious attention to problems, and the tension of concentration and action. Sleep is the epitome of passivity in the adult as well as in the child; here concerns are withdrawn from the outside world to a state of inner bliss. In this passive state the organism is rejuvenated and made ready for a new cycle of activity.

This prototype can be applied to a wide range of events in the daily life of the executive. Building oneself into a rhythmic pattern, whether it be around work or play, talking or listening, being at work alone or in association with others, may be essential for dealing with the strains of a difficult role.

Summing Up

Training oneself to act and react in the ways just discussed may sound like a formidable task. Formidable it is, but perhaps the basic necessity is to overcome the sense of inertia to which we are all susceptible from time to time. While it sounds puritanical, the most elementary step necessary for achieving a mature orientation as an executive is to assume responsibility for one's own development. Basic to this responsibility is the experiencing of one's self in the active mode. (The sense of inertia referred to before is just the opposite; here life and events appear to occur apart from one's own intentions.) As soon as an executive is able to assume responsibility for personal experience and in the course of doing so overcomes the sense of inertia, the executive is on the road toward experiencing leadership as an adventure in learning.

Fortunately, increasing recognition by executives of the importance of their continuing development has made it possible for them, in conjunction with universities and institutes, to examine the dilemmas of leadership and to experiment with new approaches for their resolution.

Note

1. Stewart Alsop and Charles Bartlett, "In Time of Crisis," *Saturday Evening Post,* December 8, 1962, p. 15.

15

Management of Disappointment

ABRAHAM ZALEZNIK

While no one is immune to encounters with disappointment, people who want power and responsibility are especially vulnerable to episodes in which reality does not conform to their wishes or intentions. But, far from disappointment being a prelude to continued failure in their careers, these episodes may be occasions for accelerated personal growth and even the beginning of truly outstanding performance. The author discusses these immanent possibilities, illustrating his points with the reactions of well-known business and public leaders to the demands and stresses of responsibility.

Some years ago, *Life* magazine presented some unusually astute reflections on the leadership of President Johnson. Seen in the broadest possible perspective, these observations provoked a new set of questions about the motivation of leaders and, indirectly, fresh thinking about organizations, business as well as political.

The editors of *Life* began with the comment that President Johnson was not equally at home in each of the wide range of problems facing him. He would rather act on domestic problems than international issues; and if events forced him to look beyond our borders, he would much prefer to deal with the new nations, the "have nots" in Asia, Africa, and Latin America as compared with the "haves" of the established industrial societies in Europe. In brief, President Johnson was propelled by an identification with the underdog and, if left to his own devices, would attack the problems of poverty, disease, education, and related concerns which seem at their core to cause human suffering. The thrust of his intentions to lead invariably aimed at nurturing those for whom he felt strongly empathetic.

While these observations involve inevitably some oversimplification, they appear justified by the record of his Presidency. The editors of *Life* concluded with these comments:

> It can be argued—and is by many presidential scholars—that the man in the White House does not have a great deal of choice about the problems he gets or even how to deal with them. Perhaps that is so, but the Presidency still is a highly personal office. What pleases and placates, what intrigues and gratifies, what stimulates and flatters the man in the Oval Office subtly regulates the push and the priorities in the affairs of state that in the long run shape the era.[1]

Two points strike the reader of these editorial comments. The first is the rather tragic sense of leadership implied in the notion that events outside of one's control may not allow people to do those things which they dearly wish to do and for which their dispositions make them eminently suited. The second is the suggestion, even if only by inference, that we have here something more than a special situation or the idiosyncrasies of one man at one time and in one place.

We are not dealing with just the problems of political leaders, such as Johnson, although in many of the examples to follow I have used public figures, since their careers are well documented; if anything, we are more concerned with the problems of the head of a business. For this executive, particularly, there may be some important generalizations about leadership in the idea that people's inclinations channel them unknowingly in a certain direction. A chief executive may therefore be fortunate if personally comfortable and the least consciously controlled tendencies can be utilized. If we follow these leads, we soon delve into the borderland between personality and action in organizations.

It is my intention to take an excursion into this borderland, to leave the relatively safe, if somewhat arid, territory of organization theory which chooses to see management in terms divorced from the issues of personality. While, from a purely rational standpoint, a chief executive should be able to adjust the style and substance of actions to the problems which press for solution, the executive is above all else a human being. The strategies and policies offered in the executive's name, and the rationalistic terms with which they are advanced, often obscure the personal commitment in back of those formal programs. And, in fact, without the convictions drawn from personal commitment, the chief executive's attempts at persuasion and influence often leave others cold. On the other hand, while the conviction may be apparent, the direction of policy may appear so inconsistent and even unreal as to perplex subordinates and arouse wonder at the apparent displacement of personal concerns onto the business of the organization.

In effect, then, corporate executives may face paradoxical situations where they must live with themselves and be themselves while attempting to formulate realistic goals and means for implementing these goals.

Personal Equation

Almost four decades ago, a young businessman exemplified some of the hazards involved in this paradox. Charles Luckman came to the presidency of Lever Brothers evidently intent on making a personal impact on the company and on the business community. His career ended abruptly when it became clear that his efforts at personal role building had far outstripped the sound development of business strategy and structure.[2]

In more recent times, the career of John Connor, former president of Merck & Co., Inc. and Secretary of Commerce, illustrated another aspect of this paradox: the gap between personal initiatives and the practical opportunities offered by the power structure for expressing these initiatives. As *Fortune* commented in "The Paradoxical Predicament of John Connor":

> Jack Connor took office with an ebullience he has been hard put to maintain. Within the Commerce Department, Connor is something less than the complete boss: his chief lieutenants are answerable less to him than to the President, who appointed them, has the power to promote, and holds their political loyalties. And despite his resounding Cabinet title, Connor finds he has a lot less influence on policy than he was once accustomed to.[3]

This gap between what a leader wants to do and the practical possibilities of action within the realities of power relationships poses a severe test for the individual. In Connor's case, according to *Fortune*, he endured the frustrations by a sense of optimism: "Putting the best possible face on what could have only been a severe disappointment, Connor made no complaint."[4] But there is a limit to anyone's endurance, as indicated in Connor's later decision to resign his post and return to private enterprise.

For some executives, leadership is the conscious effort to suppress or subordinate their personal expression while meeting the standards and expectations others set. These executives usually do not provide remarkable case histories of business failure, but neither do they stand out as achievers. More significantly, they, along with a few intimates, measure the costs of unrealized hopes.

Where an individual expects, because of ability, position, or wealth, to exert influence over events, there is no escape from the personal commitment to action. And where such commitment is great, the potential for loss and disappointment is equally great.

Consider the case of Howard Hughes.

☐ In the spring of 1966, Hughes sold his holdings in Trans-World Airlines. While he realized enormous monetary gains in this transaction, he endured high personal costs because he gave up his intention to influence, if not control outright, one of the major international airlines. The decision to end a battle for corporate control implied a personal reappraisal of the potential gains and losses in continuing a set of tactics. That it was no simple outcome of investment logics was reflected in the comments of Charles Tillinghast, President of TWA, who explained Hughes' actions this way: "Perhaps he is a proud personality and wanted to divest voluntarily."[5]

As these illustrations suggest, the executive career turns on the subtle capacity to take personal risks in making decisions and putting them into action. This personal view of the executive career can, by extension, provide the ideas for understanding better what actually goes on in organizations and in the exercise of leadership. Someday this personal view may also provide a theory which can be articulated and used in building organization structures. In the meantime, we need to know considerably more about the many sides of an individual's leadership style.

In studying effective executives, one usually asks: What were the executive's experiences with success, and how were they built on during the executive's career? Psychological studies of creative people, including leaders, suggest that preoccupation with success may be less important than the role of disappointment in the evolution of a career.[6] Both the great strengths and weaknesses of gifted leaders often hinge on how they manage the disappointments which are inevitable in life.

The experience with disappointment is a catalytic psychological event that may foster growth or retardation in development. When the individual faces disappointment, emotional investments in people and activities need to be pulled back and reexamined before they are reinvested in a new outward direction. The key idea, however, is in the *facing* of disappointment. If disappointment and the pains attendant on it are denied or otherwise hidden from view, the chances are great that the individual will founder on the unresolved conflicts at the center of the experience with disappointment.

Leadership Style

In weighing ideas on the management of disappointment in the development of the executive career, we need to start with a clearer picture of the relationship between personality and leadership. This relationship involves the evolution of the individual's style of leadership. The concept of style refers to a widely noted observation that individuals who occupy the position of chief executive in similar organizations vary widely in the way they utilize the authority of their office.

The clearest illustration of this finding is offered in Richard E. Neustadt's study, *Presidential Power: The Politics of Leadership*.[7] In this book Neustadt compares Roosevelt, Truman, and Eisenhower in their responses to the problem of power in executive relations. For Eisenhower, the use of power was a highly charged and ambivalent experience. His style, therefore, featured formalization of relationships within a staff system. The job of the staff, headed by Sherman Adams, was to screen and decide issues before they reached the personal level of the President. When top subordinates could not reach consensus, Eisenhower inadvertently allowed his power to be diffused and eroded through alternating responses which seemed to favor one side and then the other, as illustrated in the controversy over the 1957 budget.

In contrast to Eisenhower, who sought harmony, consensus, and tranquillity in the exercise of his responsibilities, Franklin D. Roosevelt was a man bent on taking the initiative. He was intent on making new departures, and he exploited every power base available to him to rally support for his decisions. Thus:

> The first task of an executive, as he [Roosevelt] evidently saw it, was to guarantee himself an effective flow of information and ideas. . . . Roosevelt's persistent effort therefore was to check and balance information acquired through official channels with information acquired through a myriad of private, informal, and unorthodox channels and espionage networks. At times he seemed almost to pit his personal sources against his public sources.[8]

In doing this, however, he not only checked and balanced the flow and validity of his information but ensured for himself a position of the utmost centrality at every stage of the decision-making process. He could assess who wanted what and why. He could establish his priorities and make his choices guided by clear indications as to where and at whom his power should be directed in order to secure support. At the same time, Roosevelt's style of leadership not only was that of an initiator but involved the use of ambiguity in interpersonal relations. The use of ambiguity provided the means for maintaining his central position in the communications network and his flexibility in negotiation and decision making.

Similar observations about differences in style can be made about business leadership. Alfred P. Sloan, Jr. as head of General Motors functioned quite differently from his predecessor, William C. Durant.[9] Sloan was an organizer, while Durant was an entrepreneur. The entrepreneurial style of Durant was also quite different from the innovative pattern epitomized in the leadership of Henry Ford in the automotive industry. Ford's innovations depended on his ability to focus his goals, even to the point where they appeared to be fixations or obsessions. However much Ford operated with a one-track mind, he selected a profitable track that resulted in a major revolution in consumer behavior and industrial structure.

Differences in leadership style seem to revolve around differences in basic orientations to ideas, things, and people. Turning for help once again to Neustadt, we see how Roosevelt invested in ideas and political processes in a way that was free of conflicted attitudes toward people. For whatever reasons, Roosevelt was psychologically free to achieve his objectives through the use of all the bases of power available to him. He could *use* people. Consider:

> His [Roosevelt's] favorite technique was to keep grants of authority incomplete, jurisdictions uncertain, charters overlapping. The result of this competitive theory of administration was often confusion and exasperation on the operating level; but no other method could so reliably insure that in a large bureaucracy filled with ambitious men eager for power, the decisions and the power to make them would remain with the President.[10]

> Eisenhower's use of men tended to smother, not enhance, the competition roused by overlapping jurisdictions. Apparently this was intentional. . . . Eisenhower seemingly preferred to let subordinates proceed upon the lowest common denominators of agreement than to have their quarrels—and issues and details—pushed up to him.[11]

Patterns of investment in ideas, in things, and in people are relatively independent. An idea man may frequently experience personal conflict with people, but, as indicated in the case of Roosevelt, he may also be conflict-free in his relationships with others. A psychological study of Woodrow Wilson by Alexander and Juliette George[12] showed that Wilson's style of leadership reflected an emotional attachment to abstract ideas such as justice and democracy. But at an interpersonal level, Wilson had difficulty managing his competitive-aggressive strivings. He could work well with those few men, such as Colonel House, who flattered and openly adored him—or, interestingly enough, with those men who were his enemies. This polarization of relationships involving love and hate is more common than one would suppose and is found with considerable frequency among charismatic leaders.

Role of Conflict

To achieve psychological understanding of the motives underlying a leadership style, one must be prepared to deal with the unexpected. In human affairs, relationships seldom persist for the simple reasons that appear on the surface. The central problem in the case of leadership styles is to grasp the meanings of the behavior and the multiple causes of action.

The concepts of *meaning* and *cause* when applied to human activities have at least two points of reference. The first is the relation of the leader's acts to some problem or tension in his environment. For example, Sloan's actions in establishing a rational formal organization can be analyzed in relation to the problems of constructing a balance between centralized and decentralized functions within a company made up of complex marketing, engineering, and production strategies. The second point of reference for behavior is the inner world of the actor. Here we are concerned not only with the goals the individual seeks to achieve but also with the nature of the stimuli that constantly threaten the individual's capacity to tolerate painful sensations and experiences.

Studying the external meanings of behavior requires a historical examination of institutions and their environments. The internal meanings also require a historical study, but of the individual and the legacies of his development. Leadership style is essentially the outcome of the developmental process and can be defined, following the psychoanalytic concept of "character," as *the patterned modes of behavior with which an individual relates to external reality and to internal dispositions.*

One of the major contributions of psychoanalytic psychology has been to demonstrate the place of conflict in the development of the individual. Each stage in the life cycle involves personal conflict because the individual has the task of giving up one set of gratifications and searching for alternatives that take account simultaneously of biological, psychological, and social challenges. Failure to relinquish gratifications impedes development, while overly rapid learning establishes a gap between instinctual-emotional processes, on the one hand, and cognitive-rational capacities, on the other. This gap leads often to low tolerance for drives and emotions and to a highly rigid set of conditions for the exercise of competence.

Forrestal Tragedy

The life and tragic death of James Forrestal is a case in point. Forrestal built a successful career on Wall Street and in government service. Toward the latter part of his service as the first Secretary of Defense, he developed a series of symptoms which later, when he left his post, took the form of manic-depressive psychosis with paranoid delusions. He took his life while under treatment, an end not uncommon in this type of illness.

Throughout his life, Forrestal, according to one biographer,[13] developed his capacity for work, but at the expense of achieving intimacy in his family. Forrestal broke with his parental family after completing college, in effect renouncing his past. Such breaks with the past do not usually occur apart from basic disappointments in the individual's experience with his development and his position in the family.

In Forrestal's case, while the data permit only reasoned speculations, they suggest the kinds of disappointments one finds in a harsh mother-child relationship. As the result of a complex psychological process, the individual renounces nurturance and other tender emotional exchanges, and substitutes instead a burning ambition and drive to achieve. If such individuals have ability, as Forrestal clearly had in abundance, they may achieve leadership and success by any of the standards we use to evaluate performance. But these individuals are vulnerable to continuing disappointment that may lead to breakdown. For Forrestal, the major disappointment in his career in government was probably his failure to achieve a power base independent of the President of the United States. He may even have harbored strong ambitions for the Presidency—a position beyond his reach, given the political realities in our society.

Consequently, Forrestal's relationship with Truman became competitive and led to his replacement following the 1948 election. Forrestal fell ill immediately on the acceptance of his resignation and Louis Johnson's appointment as Secretary of Defense. As an active, ambitious man stripped of his power, he suffered a major deprivation with the severance of the channels formerly used in guiding his energies. Unfortunately, he had no alternative channels and no human relationship with which he could heal his wounds and rebuild his life.

Mastery Process

The end need not have been tragic. Many great men work through their disappointments and emerge with greater strength and a heightened capacity for leadership. Winston Churchill must have suffered a similar disappointment during World War I. The disastrous campaign at Gallipoli became Churchill's responsibility and interrupted abruptly the career of this ambitious and powerful man. But he mastered this disappointment to become a leader during the supreme crisis of World War II.

The process of mastery must have demanded the kind of psychological work which usually occurs in psychoanalysis. Here, the individual withdraws and refocuses energy and attention from the outer world to himself. The outcome, if successful, is reorganization of personality based on insight, and then the renewal of active concern with the use of one's energy in work.

We know all too little about the self-curative processes which occur for "great men" in their struggle with disappointment.[14] But Churchill must have been aided immeasurably by his range of talents, not the least of which was writing. In other words, he did not have all his eggs in one basket. He also found strength in his relationship with his wife.

Similar processes must have occurred in the emergence of Franklin D. Roosevelt as a great leader. The injury he suffered, and I refer now to psychological injury as a result of the polio attack, was the critical episode in his career. But, again unlike Forrestal, he had the psychological resources and the relationships for performing the curative work necessary in a personal crisis.

Two final examples will clarify the complex way disappointment acts in the adult years as the developmental crisis of a career. Disappointment is not simply a condition where the outer evidences of success are absent or where the failure to realize ambitions is the critical event:

☐ In his autobiographical writing John Stuart Mill described the onset of his late adolescent depression. He was reflecting on life and his ambitions, and asked himself this question: "Suppose that all your objects in life were realized; that all the changes in institutions and opinions which you were looking forward to could be completely effected at this very instant: would this be a great joy and happiness to you?"[15] His answer was negative, and the outcome of his personal honesty was an intense depression which lifted only after he was able to mourn and express the grief underlying the psychological loss connected with his disappointments in fantasy.

☐ Henry Ford seems to have experienced a similar disappointment in fantasy on the success of the Model T. That great achievement marked a turning point in his career. Where formerly he could channel energies and direct others, he became increasingly rigid and unrealistic in his thinking. He entertained omnipotent and somewhat paranoid ideas, as evidenced by the ill-fated venture on the Peace Ship and his acceptance and support of the anti-Semitic campaigns of the newspaper *The Dearborn Independent*.[16]

There are men who are spoiled by success and, as Sigmund Freud pointed out, develop symptoms only after major accomplishment.[17] To the naive observer, this consequence of achievement seems perverse or inexplicable. But it becomes comprehensible when analyzed in relation to the individual's investment in fantasies. To produce a car, become president of a company, or make a great scientific discovery is not a simple dream.[18] Such dreams may also contain the hopes for restoring the individual to some state of happiness. Or the individual may be enveloped by a sense of entitlement from which other persons are viewed as barriers to getting what are perceived as just deserts. These infantile wishes contained in the current actions of leaders are the most dangerous. Hell hath no fury like a person whose ambitions are frustrated because dreams cannot be realized no matter how hard the effort or how tangible the achievement. Ambitions which contain hopes for changing the past and reversing the psychological disappointments encountered in development are self-defeating. The best that any of us can do is to understand the past. It cannot be changed.

Attachment to Self

All human beings experience disappointment. If this hard fact of development were not so, it would be very difficult to explain the attractions of myth and legend. In myth we temporarily heal the wounds of disappointment and find ourselves restored to wishes once held and reluctantly abandoned in the interests of preserving attachment to reality and the objects we love. The psychology of the leader is therefore no different from that of other human beings in sharing an initial fate of injury and disappointment. But the psychology becomes different in the consequences of injury.

Most human beings accept disappointment and more or less content themselves with a collective engagement in which ritual and myth, along with work and human relationships, permit them to bear pain and loss. For creative people and those leaders endowed with special abilities, a sense of estrangement follows the early experiences with developmental conflicts. Like Narcissus, who caught his image in a reflecting pool and fell in love with this ideal self—in their childhood, leaders often direct their emotional investments inward. Their dreams and fantasies, translated as adults into ambitions, maintain their sense of being special. Very often these fantasies are part of an experience of destiny; their fate is to perform a great deed like Oedipus, who solved the riddle of the Sphinx, or the biblical Joseph, who interpreted the Pharaoh's dreams and predicted the famine.

The attachment to self leads to achievement, but only in conjunction with sharply developed talents. Without other qualities, such as the power to reason, to perceive the interplay of events in the environment, or to invent new solutions to old problems, the heightened sense of self would amount only to heightened frustration and, in the extreme, even madness. But the sense of self enters strongly into the personality of the leader and the ties others establish with the leader. What the leader does both with abilities and with investment in self is effectively the manifestation of what we call style, with its special consequences for institutional management.

Resource or Hazard?

The nature of policy and strategy in business organizations is a direct outcome of the actions of leaders. I do not believe it squares with reality to imagine that decisions are made in an impersonal way. They are made by people who think and act in relation to the influence of authority figures who themselves are, as I have tried to indicate, bound to a general process of human development.

In reaching decisions and charting a course for a corporation, considerable clarity of vision and accuracy in perception are necessary. The heightened sense of self that I have identified as a major factor in the psychology of leaders is both a resource and a hazard in corporate management and the fate of the individual. It is a resource in that the investment in self preserves the independence necessary to weigh opinions and advice of others. While it is good common sense to encourage subordinates to offer recommendations, in the final analysis a major policy cannot be advanced apart from the convictions of the chief executive. How does the executive achieve the conviction necessary to seal a decision? If the executive is dependent on others as a result of an impoverishment of self-confidence, it will be very difficult indeed to foster a position that will guide the destiny of the organization.

The problem of investment in self as a psychological quality of leadership is one of degree. Too little amounts to overdependence and often diffusion of purpose. The other extreme, overinvestment in self, poses problems as well, but in a more complex way than overdependence.

Freud, in his study "Group Psychology and the Analysis of the Ego,"[19] described the primal leader as an individual who loves no one but himself. This imagery suggests the autocrat who keeps subordinates equidistant from himself and relatively deprived of independent action. This primal leader is not an archaic figure in business management. He is not idealized now as he was in the late nineteenth and early twentieth centuries; nevertheless, he still persists with all his strengths and weaknesses in small enterprises as well as in large corporations. The autocrat provides a direction, and if he selects a correct path, he usually manages a successful enterprise. As a leader, he tends to select subordinates in his own image, and they reflect all his virtues and vices.

The hazard facing the autocrat stems from the tendency for new ideas, information, and vision to find limited acceptance. Subordinates tell the primal leader only what he wants to hear, and the opportunities for communication are limited by his distance. If an incorrect or outdated strategy continues to direct the organization, then the future is in doubt. Precisely this set of conditions occurred in the Ford Motor Company, leading to its decline in the industry and to serious financial losses from the 1920s until World War II.

Balance and Perspective. At a more personal level the problem the primal leader faces is maintaining balance and perspective through the inevitable disappointments when they occur—and especially those which he may experience at the height of his career. These disappointments may range from business setbacks to family problems—including the discovery that his sons and heirs are not made in his image and have distinct personalities and problems. The experience with these latter-day disappointments may produce a kind of psychic injury that reopens old wounds. The response may be rage and restitutive thought patterns that we recognize as a false sense of omnipotence and even delusions.

Evidently Harry Truman had some insight into the hazards of disappointment, particularly when a leader becomes aware of the limitations of the leader's power to control events and actions of others. Neustadt describes Truman's sympathetic anticipation of Eisenhower's problems with the Presidency. Truman said, "He'll sit here and he'll say, 'Do this! Do that!' And nothing will happen. Poor Ike—it won't be a bit like the Army. He'll find it very frustrating."[20] What Truman evidently recognized is that no matter how powerful the leader's position, the issue of influence is still problematic. Whether things get done is beyond the magical thinking that equates authority with influence.

The Narcissus-like leader who invests only in the self does not necessarily behave overtly like an autocrat, nor is this leader necessarily detached from others. Frequently one observes leaders who have close relationships with subordinates. We cannot conclude from superficial observation that the presence of these relationships indicates a balance between investment in self and others. Closer observation often shows that the ties are not in reality between two separate individuals who cooperate in a rational and purposive endeavor. Instead, the individuals position themselves around the leader as reflected images of the leader taken from the leader's infantile past. These executive structures then become dramatic reenactments of fantasies that existed to restore the self-esteem of the individual during early experiences with disappointment.

The structure and dynamics of these relationships have a variety of unconscious meanings that are carried forward into major episodes of corporate life. While the relationships may have adaptive value, they may also become central to the outbreak of pathological processes within the leader and other key executives in the organization. And again I suggest that the pathologies involve the reexperience of disappointment and loss when the relationships shift or, under the influence of reality, fail as restitutive episodes.

While subordinates may be related to a leader in ways which become significant in the reenactment of fantasies, there is still room for modification. I am reminded of the tragedy of King Lear, who had to drive away those individuals who loved him most because he could not tolerate the intensity of his love for his youngest daughter, Cordelia. The only figure who remained close to Lear and who would tell him the truth was his fool. But the only way the fool could exist and speak the truth was to take the position of the castrated object who himself posed no threat to the power of the leader.

With this observation our problem shifts. Why would anyone give up self-esteem to serve another, even though in a paradoxical way this person performs noble work in helping the narcissistic leader maintain a fragile hold on reality? To be the king's fool strikes me as an excessive price to pay for another man's contributions to society. There is still another way, and that is to maintain one's integrity, to speak the truth, and to let the chips fall where they may. Subordinates to narcissistic leaders sometimes succumb to their own restitutive fantasies as a way of rationalizing their position. We can be sure that where a close relationship persists, there are more reasons than we know to account for the willingness of people to maintain object ties.

Self-Examination Need

Business managers, whether they know it or not, commit themselves to a career in which they have to work on themselves as a condition for effective working on and working with other people. This fact of the business career is so often neglected that we would do well to re-examine the implications of the need to work on oneself as a condition for the exercise of power.

The analysis presented in this article suggests that a significant area for the personal and inner work on oneself is the experience with disappointment. The question we now have to explore is: How does an executive make the management of disappointment a catalytic experience for personal growth? Here are some leads and suggestions.

Preventive Aspects

First, as a preventive measure, examine carefully the personal goals in back of the decision to assume responsibility in a position. If the goals are themselves unrealistic, then major disappointment is inevitable.

A number of years ago, one man decided to change his career and take over a small enterprise. He told me that his reason for entering business was to put into practice the conceptions of good human relations in leadership to which he was personally dedicated. My question to him was this: How about going into business to manage a successful company and to make money? The intent of my question was not to insult his noble purposes but, rather, to suggest that the way one formulates personal goals has something to do with the way one will practice a profession. In other words, a noble intention may enlighten work, but it is no substitute for competence. The investment in noble purposes may even prevent success and finally set the stage for the traumatic experience with disappointment.

McGregor's Theories. A collection of essays by Douglas McGregor, published in 1966 following his death, offers by indirection some clues on how the clash between personal ideology and reality may obscure insight.[21]

McGregor pointed out the difference between what he called *Theory X* and *Theory Y*. According to persuasive arguments, many managers of complex organizations are acting on the basis of an outmoded conception of human nature and institutions. This conception, Theory X, sees man as a stubborn, recalcitrant being who has to be motivated to work in directions consonant with organizational goals. Believing in this conception of man produces a self-fulfilling prophecy. That is, the type of leadership fostered by this "mechanical" man is apt to produce stubborn, recalcitrant individuals who sabotage the organization rather than contribute to its well-being.

In advocating the opposite view, Theory Y, throughout his essays, McGregor proposed that leaders should change their ideas about human nature. The content of this altered view is supported, according to McGregor, by the findings of behavioral science, particularly psychology. McGregor appealed to managers to adopt a philosophy of leadership based on the assumption that individuals want to be self-actualizing and want to participate in harmony with their environment. In this view the leader is an agronomist who cultivates the organizational environment in which this more optimistic picture of man will be fulfilled.

The message is powerful and at the root of McGregor's considerable stature as a management theorist. Its appeal lies in its humaneness and in the subtle way it addresses itself to the underlying guilt which plagues people who exercise power in modern organizations. All too often, leaders are uneasy about the power they have over people and decisions. The uneasiness is accompanied by a sense of guilt and a desire for reassurance, love, and approval from associates. It is as though leaders listen for the voices outside themselves which will testify to their humanity in opposition to the disquieting inner voices that disapprove, depreciate, and accuse. In short, McGregor's message was designed to deal as much with a bad conscience as with the realities of work, authority, and decisions in organizations.

But how lasting and relevant are these external cures for a bad conscience? Whether in the name of religion or science, the cure is temporary as compared with the more arduous route of self-knowledge and mastery. Socrates' advice to "know thyself" is exceedingly relevant today for people of responsibility. Unfortunately, McGregor's theories avoid the inner conflicts and resolutions of leadership problems in their almost singular dedication to creating an ideal organization climate.

McGregor missed the point in the study of leadership because, while he was keen on talking to managers, he failed in a basic sense to identify with them. His identification was largely with subordinates; and in talking to managers, McGregor communicated the wish in all of us for benign and benevolent power figures. But to love and to be loved is not enough in the painful process of choice while exercising leadership.

McGregor did capture this idea in what must have been for him a period of intense stress. In his essay "On Leadership," written as he was about to leave the presidency of Antioch College, a position he held for six years, he said:

> Before coming to Antioch, I had observed and worked with top executives as an advisor in a number of organizations. I thought I knew how they felt about their responsibilities and what led them to behave as they did. I even thought I could create a role for myself that would enable me to avoid some of the difficulties they encountered. I was wrong! . . . I believed, for example, that a leader could operate successfully as a kind of advisor to his organization. I thought I could avoid being a "boss." Unconsciously, I suspect, I hoped to duck the unpleasant necessity of making difficult decisions, of taking responsibility for one course of action among many uncertain alternatives, of making mistakes and taking the consequences. I thought that maybe I could operate so that everyone would like me—that "good human relations" would eliminate all discord and disappointment. I could not have been more wrong. . . .[22]

The essay from which this quotation was taken appeared in May 1954. The subsequent essays, written while McGregor continued a distinguished career as Professor at M.I.T., suggest he had not assimilated the insight underlying his sense of disappointment. I suspect the insight got lost because McGregor was too hard on himself, as the brief quotation above suggests. In the later essays in this book, McGregor returns to the message through which he appealed to authority figures on behalf of subordinates.

Had he pursued the insight imbedded in the Antioch essay, he might have recognized that the essence of leadership is choice, a singularly individualistic act in which a person assumes responsibility for a commitment to direct an organization along a particular path. This leader might also have recognized that as much as a leader wishes to trust others, the soundness and validity of the positions subordinates come to communicate have to be judged. Otherwise, the leader is in danger of becoming a prisoner of the emotional commitments that subordinates demand, frequently at the expense of judging the correctness of policies and strategies.

McGregor's problem, I would suspect, developed out of his noble purposes. But nobility of purpose is not the first order of business in establishing one's position as chief executive of an organization. In the personal assessment of one's intention to lead, it is far better to assign the highest priority to discovering those things that need to be done, and then to devote oneself to engaging the commitments of others toward these goals. Of course, this does not rule out the possibility that historians can later look at this executive's work and discover the nobility which surrounded the leadership.

But no matter how hard one works on the preventive aspects, sooner or later disappointments occur, and the personal working through of these events then becomes the first order of business.

Facing Issues

My second suggestion is to face the disappointment squarely. The temptation and the psychology of individual response to disappointment is to avoid the pain of self-examination. If an avoidance pattern sets in, the individual will pay dearly for it later. Usually, avoidance occurs because this mode of response is the individual's habitual way of dealing with disappointment from childhood days on. It also seems clear that those people who are lucky enough to have learned from childhood days how to face loss are best equipped to deal with the personal issues that arise during experiences with disappointment in the executive career. Consider:

> ☐ One line manager in a large corporation worked closely with a vice president, who in the course of events in business life came out second best in a rivalry. The vice president resigned, and his department was left in a vulnerable position, without a leader, and with a loss of status. The line manager, who was in his early forties, had spent his entire working career with this large corporation. He had an excellent reputation, and the senior executives were genuinely hopeful that he would remain with the company.
>
> He thought the issue through and decided to resign, recognizing that his commitments to the deposed vice president were so strong that they would not permit him to reestablish ties with others and to work effectively without paying too high a personal price. He discovered that his experience and talents were indeed in high demand, and he made a successful transition to another corporation where, after demonstrating his competence, he became a vice president and senior executive in his own right.

The decision to remain or to leave was not the significant test of whether the line manager was actually facing the disappointment he had endured. Rather, the significant test came in his silent work of self-examination which he shared only with his wife, who matched his personal courage and willingness to take risks. In effect, this line manager learned to face events and to follow the principle of finance of writing off a loss and then setting forth on a new program.

Emotional Awareness

The key factor in mastering disappointment is the capacity to experience the emotions connected with the personal career losses.[23] The flight from the work leading to mastery is usually connected with the individual's limited capacity to tolerate painful emotions. The third suggestion, therefore, is to become intimately acquainted with one's own emotional reactions.

An example of the issues implicit in attempting to face the emotional reactions following disappointment is poignantly described in Volume II of *The Diaries of Harold Nicolson*.[24] Nicolson, a member of Parliament, held the post of Parliamentary Secretary in the Ministry of Information during the early years of World War II. Churchill asked for his resignation in connection with a series of top-level changes in the ministry resulting from public criticism and charges of mismanagement. Nicolson resigned, and the following day (July 19, 1941) he noted this entry in his diary:

> I wake up feeling that something horrible has happened, and then remember that I have been sacked from the Government. Go to the Ministry and start clearing out some of my private possessions. Then attend the Duty Room, probably for the last time. I meet Gerald Campbell in the passage. "I hear," he says, " that you have been thurtled?" * Everybody expresses dismay at my going.† I have a final drink in the Press Bar with Osbert Lancaster, and then lunch at the Travellers with Robin Maugham. He is as charming as he could be.
>
> But I mind more than I thought I should mind. It is mainly, I suppose, a sense of failure. I quite see that if the Labour leaders have been pressing to have my post, there is good cause why they should have it. But if I had more power and drive, I should have been offered Rab Butler's job at the Foreign Office,‡ which I should dearly have loved. As it is, I come back to the bench below the gangway having had my chance and failed to profit by it. Ever since I have been in the House I have been looked on as a might-be. Now I shall be a might-have-been. Always up till now I have been buoyed up by the hope of writing some good book or achieving a position of influence in politics. I now know that I shall never write a book better than I have written already, and that my political career is at an end. I shall merely get balder and fatter and more deaf as the years go by. This is an irritating thing. Success should come late in life in order to compensate for the loss of youth; I had youth and success together, and now I have old age and failure.§ Apart from all this, I mind leaving the Ministry where I did good work and had friends.
>
> This space indicates the end of my ambitions in life. "Omnium consensu capax imperii nisi imperasset." ¶

According to the editor of the diaries, it took Nicolson some time before he could assimilate the disappointment and plunge anew into lesser responsibilities. But Nicolson's apparent honesty, and his gifts as an observer and recorder of events, evidently helped him during a difficult personal crisis.

Studies of individuals who get into trouble and present themselves for treatment to a psychoanalyst frequently show that the roots of their difficulties lie in a limited capacity to tolerate emotions, especially those connected with loss and disappointment. The business executive is especially vulnerable because of the development of an unconscious strategy of forced activity or, more accurately, hyperactivity, as a defense against emotional awareness. The hyperactive executive is of course rewarded for hyperactivity, since, in the conventional understanding of how an executive should behave, busyness is generally considered a good thing.

However good it is in some respects, it is also bad if busyness serves to build and maintain the wall between the inner worlds of thought and feeling. In the treatment of such individuals who are in trouble, the most positive indicator of progress is the appearance of sadness and depression. As the individual consciously assimilates the depression and relates it to experiences with disappointment throughout development, the individual becomes capable of undoing the ineffective patterns and of substituting more effective ways of dealing with the demands and stresses of responsibility.

Conclusion

No one is immune to encounters with disappointment. More significantly, individuals who want power and responsibility or seek creative expression are especially vulnerable to episodes in which reality does not conform to one's wishes or intentions. As I have indicated in this article, far from disappointment being a prelude to continued failure in career, these critical episodes may actually be occasions for accelerated growth and even the beginning of truly outstanding performance.

But much depends on the quality of the psychological work the individual accomplishes under the stress of the sense of loss and bewilderment which frequently accompanies disappointment. As in all matters of personal development, the outcome turns on the quality of the person, the measure of courage mobilized, the richness of talents, and ability for constructive introspection.

It is no easy task to examine one's own motivations. In fact, the necessity seldom arises for many people until they meet an impasse in life. At this juncture, they are confronted with two sets of personal concerns: those connected directly with the present disappointments and those related to the experiences with disappointment in the past. Usually a crisis in the present reopens problems from the past, and, in this sense, the individual experiences a telescoping of time in which the psychological past and present tend to merge.

But the degree of telescoping is critical in judging the intensity of stress involved in the management of disappointment. It is usually difficult enough to solve a current problem, with all its demands for accurate observation and realistic thought. The difficulty increases, however, when the route to solving current problems involves examination of one's history with loss or deprivation. Here the most effective step the individual can take is to seek competent help.

In the course of examining reactions to disappointment, a subtle change may take place in the individual's perspectives and attitudes. While the individual may come to recognize the impossible quality of certain goals and wishes, and be willing to relinquish their demands on his behavior, at the same time uncharted possibilities for productive work and pleasure may be discovered. These immanent possibilities usually remain obscure so long as the individual is intent in questing for restitutive rewards to make up for felt losses of the past.

There is irony in all of human experience and no less in the solutions to the problem of disappointment. The deepest irony of all is to discover that one has been mourning losses that were never sustained, and yearning for a past that never existed, while ignoring one's own real capabilities for shaping the present.

Notes

1. *Life*, May 12, 1967, p. 46b.

2. See "The Case of Charles Luckman," *Fortune*, April 1950, p. 81.

3. "The Paradoxical Predicament of John Connor," *Fortune*, February 1966, p. 188.

4. Ibid., p. 152.

5. "Howard Hughes' Biggest Surprise," *Fortune*, July 1966, p. 119.

6. See Gregory Rochlin, *Griefs and Discontents* (Boston, Little, Brown, 1965).

7. Richard E. Neustadt, *Presidential Power: The Politics of Leadership* (New York, Wiley, 1960).

8. Neustadt, op. cit., p. 156.

9. See A. Chandler, *Strategy and Structure: Chapters in the History of Industrial Enterprises* (Cambridge, M.I.T. Press, 1962).

10. A. M. Schlesinger, Jr., *The Age of Roosevelt*, Vol. II: *The Coming of the New Deal* (Boston, Houghton Mifflin, 1959). Quoted in Neustadt, op. cit., p. 157.

11. Neustadt, op. cit., p. 161.

12. Alexander George and Juliette George, *Woodrow Wilson and Colonel House: A Personality Study* (New York, Dover, 1964).

13. A. A. Rogow, *James Forrestal: A Study of Personality, Politics, and Policy* (New York, Macmillan, 1963).

14. See, for example, Erik H. Erikson, *Young Man Luther* (New York, Norton, 1958).

15. See John Stuart Mill, *Autobiography* (New York, New American Library, 1964), p. 107.

16. See Anne Jardim, *The First Henry Ford: A Study in Personality and Business Leadership* (unpublished doctoral dissertation, Harvard Business School, 1967); see also Allan Nevins and F. F. Hill, *Ford: The Times, the Man, and the Company; Ford: Expansion and Challenge;* and *Ford: Decline and Rebirth* (New York, Scribner's, 1954 [Vol. I], 1957 [Vol. II], 1963 [Vol. III]).

17. See Sigmund Freud, "Those Wrecked by Success," in *The Standard Edition of the Complete Psychological Works of Sigmund Freud*, edited by J. Strachey (London, Hogarth, 1957), Vol. 14, pp. 316–331.

18. See Helen H. Tartakoff, "The Normal Personality in Our Culture and the Nobel Prize Complex," in *Psychoanalysis—A General Psychology, Essays in Honor of Heinz Hartman*, edited by R. M. Lowenstein, L. M. Newman, M. Schur, and A. J. Solnit (New York, International Universities Press, 1966).

19. See Sigmund Freud in Strachey, op. cit., Vol. 18, pp. 67–143.

20. Neustadt, op. cit., p. 22.

21. Douglas McGregor, *Leadership and Motivation* (Cambridge, The M.I.T. Press, 1966).

22. Ibid., p. 67.

23. See Elizabeth R. Zetzel, "Depression and the Incapacity to Bear It," in *Drives, Affects, Behavior,* edited by Rudolph M. Loewenstein (New York, International Universities Press, 1965), Vol. II.

24. Harold Nicolson, *The War Years, 1939–1945,* edited by Nigel Nicolson (New York, Atheneum Publishers, 1967).

* Nicolson was replaced as Parliamentary Secretary by Ernest Thurtle, Labour M.P. for Shoreditch, who retained the office till the end of the war. Duff Cooper was succeeded as Minister by Brendan Bracken.

† Duff Cooper wrote to him, "I think you have received very shabby treatment, and I find that everybody shares that view."

‡ R. A. Butler, Under-Secretary of State for Foreign Affairs since 1938, was now appointed Minister of Education, and was succeeded at the Foreign Office by Richard Law.

§ Nicolson was then 54.

¶ Tacitus on the Emperor Galba. "Had he never been placed in authority, nobody would ever have doubted his capacity for it."

PART THREE
UNDERSTANDING ORGANIZATIONAL POWER

AN OVERVIEW

In "The Effective Decision," an article that appears in the next section, Peter Drucker makes an observation that has relevance to the articles about power. Drucker comments that "in fact, no decision has been made unless carrying it out in specific steps has become someone's work assignment and responsibility. Until then, it is only a good intention." The same can be said of goals. Unless a manager has a way to carry out his or her goals they remain merely visions, things that remain to be realized someday. Realizing a vision, making it become more than just a good idea, requires that managers move their organizations to their purposes. In other words, managers need power. It's as simple as that.

The problem with this simple fact of life is that "power" is such a loaded word. To many people power is by definition evil and those who want it necessarily suspect. To make accepting the fact that they need power easier, it's helpful for managers to see that not all power is oppressive. Power can be enabling. Without physical power, people cannot move physical objects, and without organizational power, executives cannot accomplish their goals.

In "Power Failure in Management Circuits," Rosabeth Moss Kanter shows, through many examples, how it is powerlessness in organizations, not power, that corrupts. In her studies of organizations, Kanter has found three typically powerless positions which force their incumbents to act in ways that we normally associate with oppressive power. People in the three positions—first-line supervisors, staff, and, surprisingly, chief executive officers—are powerless because they are often cut off from resources, support, and information that they need to get things done.

Powerlessness creates other problems for organizations that can't be resolved by structural means as the ones Kanter describes can. These are the power problems that arise from the personal powerlessness that some people feel. Regardless of their position, some executives will act in oppressive ways because they need to heighten their own self-esteem. Abraham Zaleznik comments in "Power and Politics in Organizational Life" that it is because personalities are so intractable that managers who want to achieve their ends have to use political means to do so at times. Managers wanting to influence their organizations need to change the structure but with the recognition that their own emotional conflicts and those of others can impede clear thinking.

The most effective managers in moving their organizations are those who have gained a measure of maturity. They are the ones, as David C. McClelland and David H. Burham describe in "Power Is the Great Motivator," who use power to positively influence the organization rather than for their own ends.

But because as we've seen many managers don't have the requisite power to act, managers need to acquire power other than what they have through formal authority alone. John P. Kotter describes various methods of influence open to managers, how they can use them, and what their advantages and drawbacks are. He cautions, however, in "Power, Dependence, and Effective Management" that the most effective managers are those who, among other things, "are sensitive to what others consider legitimate behavior in acquiring and using power."

Robert N. McMurry hits the same note in "Power and the Ambitious Executive" when he describes the personal style that managers need to affect others. McMurry lists 15 qualities, from using caution in taking counsel to being open-minded and receptive to opinions that differ from their own, that politically astute managers have.

Regardless of his or her informal influence or personal style, however, without the support of a boss, in most organizations a manager's attempts to make changes will be useless. In "Managing Your Boss," John J. Gabarro and John P. Kotter comment that effective managers see their relationships with their bosses as an area they need to manage like any other. They take great efforts to make sure that the relationship meets both parties' needs. By securing a mutually satisfying relationship with their bosses, managers are in a good position to get the resources they need to effect organizational change.

It is especially important for general managers to be adept at managing this relationship. As Hugo Uyterhoeven points out in "General Managers in the Middle," general managers have to accomplish a great deal through the efforts of superiors, subordinates, and peers all of whom place differing and shifting demands on them. In maneuvering the various relationships to effect change, it is imperative that managers understand that they might be perceived as seeking power for their own ends. One of the ways they can guard against this perception is to establish an atmosphere of trust in the organization. As Louis B. Barnes shows in "Managing the Paradox of Organizational Trust," trust is a precious commodity that managers can easily create but just as easily destroy by falling prey to some simple assumptions about the way the world works."

Finally, in this section, Roger Harrison maintains in "Understanding your Organization's Character," that any change a manager makes to implement his or her goals needs to be consonant with the ideology of the organization. Without this understanding, regardless of the worthwhileness of their visions or the purity of their motives, managers will meet resistance from members of the organization.

16

Power Failure in Management Circuits

ROSABETH MOSS KANTER

When one thinks of "power," one often assumes that a person is the source of it and that some mystical charismatic element is at work. Of course, with some people this is undoubtedly so; they derive power from how other people perceive them. In organizations, however—says this author—power is not so much a question of people but of positions. Drawing a distinction between productive and oppressive power, the author maintains that the former is a function of having open channels to supplies, support, and information; the latter is a function of these channels being closed. She then describes three positions that are classically powerless: first-line supervisors, staff professionals, and, surprisingly, chief executive officers. These positions can be powerless because of difficulties in maintaining open lines of information and support. Seeing powerlessness in these positions as dangerous for organizations, she urges managers to restructure and redesign their organizations to eliminate pockets of powerlessness.

Power is America's last dirty word. It is easier to talk about money—and much easier to talk about sex—than it is to talk about power. People who have it deny it; people who want it do not want to appear to hunger for it; and people who engage in its machinations do so secretly.

Yet, because it turns out to be a critical element in effective managerial behavior, power should come out from undercover. Having searched for years for those styles or skills that would identify capable organization leaders, many analysts, like myself, are rejecting individual traits or situational appropriateness as key and finding the sources of a leader's real power.

Access to resources and information and the ability to act quickly make it possible to accomplish more and to pass on more resources and information to subordinates. For this reason, people tend to prefer bosses with "clout." When employees perceive their manager as influential upward and outward, their status is enhanced by association and they generally have high morale and feel less critical or resistant to their boss.[1] More powerful leaders are also more likely to delegate (they are too busy to do it all themselves), to reward talent, and to build a team that places subordinates in significant positions.

Powerlessness, in contrast, tends to breed bossiness rather than true leadership. In large organizations, at least, it is powerlessness that often creates ineffective, desultory management and petty, dictatorial, rules-minded managerial styles. Accountability without power—responsibility for results without the resources to get them—creates frustration and failure. People who see themselves as weak and powerless and find their subordinates resisting or discounting them tend to use more punishing forms of influence. If organizational power can "ennoble," then, recent research shows, organizational powerlessness can (with apologies to Lord Acton) "corrupt."[2]

So perhaps power, in the organization at least, does not deserve such a bad reputation. Rather than connoting only dominance, control, and oppression, *power* can mean efficacy and capacity—something managers and executives need to move the organization toward its goals. Power in organizations is analogous in simple terms to physical power: it is the ability to mobilize resources (human and material) to get things done. The true sign of power, then, is accomplishment—not fear, terror, or tyranny. Where the power is "on," the system can be productive; where the power is "off," the system bogs down.

But saying that people need power to be effective in organizations does not tell us where it comes from or why some people, in some jobs, systematically seem to have more of it than others. In this article I want to show that to discover the sources of productive power, we have to look not at the *person*—as conventional classifications of effective managers and employees do—but at the *position* the person occupies in the organization.

Where Does Power Come From?

The effectiveness that power brings evolves from two kinds of capacities: first, access to the resources, information, and support necessary to carry out a task; and, second, ability to get cooperation in doing what is necessary. (Exhibit 1 identifies some symbols of an individual manager's power.)

Both capacities derive not so much from a leader's style and skill as from his or her location in the formal and informal systems of the organization—in both job definition and connection to other important people in the company. Even the ability to get cooperation from subordinates is strongly defined by the manager's clout outward. People are more responsive to bosses who look as if they can get more for them from the organization.

Exhibit 1. Some Common Symbols of a Manager's Organizational Power (Influence Upward and Outward)

To what extent a manager can—
Intercede favorably on behalf of someone in trouble with the organization
Get a desirable placement for a talented subordinate
Get approval for expenditures beyond the budget
Get above-average salary increases for subordinates
Get items on the agenda at policy meetings
Get fast access to top decision makers
Get regular, frequent access to top decision makers
Get early information about decisions and policy shifts

We can regard the uniquely organizational sources of power as consisting of three "lines":

1. *Lines of supply.* Influence outward, over the environment, means that managers have the capacity to bring in the things that their own organizational domain needs—materials, money, resources to distribute as rewards, and perhaps even prestige.
2. *Lines of information.* To be effective, managers need to be "in the know" in both the formal and the informal sense.
3. *Lines of support.* In a formal framework, a manager's job parameters need to allow for nonordinary action, for a show of discretion or exercise of judgment. Thus managers need to know that they can assume innovative, risk-taking activities without having to go through the stifling multilayered approval process. And, informally, managers need the backing of other important figures in the organization whose tacit approval becomes another resource they bring to their own work unit as well as a sign of the manager's being "in."

Note that productive power has to do with *connections* with other parts of a system. Such systemic aspects of power derive from two sources—job activities and political alliances:

1. Power is most easily accumulated when one has a job that is designed and located to allow *discretion* (nonroutinized action permitting flexible, adaptive, and creative contributions), *recognition* (visibility and notice), and *relevance* (being central to pressing organizational problems).
2. Power also comes when one has relatively close contact with *sponsors* (higher-level people who confer approval, prestige, or backing), *peer networks* (circles of acquaintanceship that provide reputation and information, the grapevine often being faster than formal communication channels),

and *subordinates* (who can be developed to relieve managers of some of their burdens and to represent the manager's point of view).

When managers are in powerful situations, it is easier for them to accomplish more. Because the tools are there, they are likely to be highly motivated and, in turn, to be able to motivate subordinates. Their activities are more likely to be on target and to net them successes. They can flexibly interpret or shape policy to meet the needs of particular areas, emergent situations, or sudden environmental shifts. They gain the respect and cooperation that attributed power brings. Subordinates' talents are resources rather than threats. And, because powerful managers have so many lines of connection and thus are oriented outward, they tend to let go of control downward, developing more independently functioning lieutenants.

The powerless live in a different world. Lacking the supplies, information, or support to make things happen easily, they may turn instead to the ultimate weapon of those who lack productive power—oppressive power: holding others back and punishing with whatever threats they can muster.

Exhibit 2 summarizes some of the major ways in which variables in the organization and in job design contribute to either power or powerlessness.

Exhibit 2. Ways Organizational Factors Contribute to Power or Powerlessness

Factors	Generates *Power* When Factor Is	Generates *Powerlessness* When Factor Is
Rules inherent in the job	Few	Many
Predecessors in the job	Few	Many
Established routines	Few	Many
Task variety	High	Low
Rewards for reliability/predictability	Few	Many
Rewards for unusual performance/innovation	Many	Few
Flexibility around use of people	High	Low
Approvals needed for nonroutine decisions	Few	Many
Physical location	Central	Distant
Publicity about job activities	High	Low
Relation of tasks to current problem areas	Central	Peripheral
Focus of tasks	Outside work unit	Inside work unit
Interpersonal contact in the job	High	Low
Contact with senior officials	High	Low
Participation in programs, conferences, meetings	High	Low

Exhibit 2. **(*Continued*)**

Factors	Generates *Power* When Factor Is	Generates *Powerlessness* When Factor Is
Participation in problem-solving task forces	High	Low
Advancement prospects of subordinates	High	Low

Positions of Powerlessness

Understanding what it takes to have power and recognizing the classic behavior of the powerless can immediately help managers make sense out of a number of familiar organizational problems that are usually attributed to inadequate people:

- ☐ The ineffectiveness of first-line supervisors.
- ☐ The petty interest protection and conservatism of staff professionals.
- ☐ The crises of leadership at the top.

Instead of blaming the individuals involved in organizational problems, let us look at the positions people occupy. Of course, power or powerlessness in a position may not be all of the problem. Sometimes incapable people *are* at fault and need to be retrained or replaced. (See the appendix for a discussion of another special case, women.) But where patterns emerge, where the troubles associated with some units persist, organizational power failures could be the reason. Then, as Volvo President Pehr Gyllenhammar concludes, we should treat the powerless not as "villains" causing headaches for everyone else but as "victims."[3]

First-Line Supervisors

Because an employee's most important work relationship is with his or her supervisor, when many of them talk about "the company," they mean their immediate boss. Thus a supervisor's behavior is an important determinant of the average employee's relationship to work and is in itself a critical link in the production chain.

Yet I know of no U.S. corporate management entirely satisfied with the performance of its supervisors. Most see them as supervising too closely and not training their people. In one manufacturing company where direct laborers were asked on a survey how they learned their job, on a list of seven possibilities "from my supervisor" ranked next to last. (Only company training programs ranked worse.) Also, it is said that supervisors do not translate company policies into practice—for instance, that they do not carry out the right of every employee to frequent performance reviews or to career counseling.

In court cases charging race or sex discrimination, first-line supervisors are frequently cited as the "discriminating official."[4] And, in studies of innovative work redesign and quality of work life projects, they often appear as the implied villains; they are the ones who are said to undermine the program or interfere with its effectiveness. In short, they are often seen as "not sufficiently managerial."

The problem affects white-collar as well as blue-collar supervisors. In one large government agency, supervisors in field offices were seen as the source of problems concerning morale and the flow of information to and from headquarters. "Their attitudes are negative," said a senior official. "They turn people against the agency; they put down senior management. They build themselves up by always complaining about headquarters, but prevent their staff from getting any information directly. We can't afford to have such attitudes communicated to field staff."

Is the problem that supervisors need more management training programs or that incompetent people are invariably attracted to the job? Neither explanation suffices. A large part of the problem lies in the position itself—one that almost universally creates powerlessness.

First-line supervisors are "people in the middle," and that has been seen as the source of many of their problems.[5] But by recognizing that first-line supervisors are caught between higher management and workers, we only begin to skim the surface of the problem. There is practically no other organizational category as subject to powerlessness.

First, these supervisors may be at a virtual dead end in their careers. Even in companies where the job used to be a stepping stone to higher-level management jobs, it is now common practice to bring in MBAs from the outside for those positions. Thus moving from the ranks of direct labor into supervision may mean, essentially, getting "stuck" rather than moving upward. Because employees do not perceive supervisors as eventually joining the leadership circles of the organization, they may see them as lacking the high-level contacts needed to have clout. Indeed, sometimes turnover among supervisors is so high that workers feel they can outwait—and outwit—any boss.

Second, although they lack clout, with little in the way of support from above, supervisors are forced to administer programs or explain policies that they have no hand in shaping. In one company, as part of a new personnel program supervisors were required to conduct counseling interviews with employees. But supervisors were not trained to do this and were given no incentives to get involved. Counseling was just another obligation. Then managers suddenly encouraged the workers to bypass their supervisors or to put pressure on them. The personnel staff brought them together and told them to demand such interviews as a basic right. If supervisors had not felt powerless before, they did after that squeeze from below, engineered from above.

The people they supervise can also make life hard for them in numerous ways. This often happens when a supervisor has risen up from the ranks. Peers that have not made it are resentful or derisive of their former colleague, whom they now see as trying to lord it over them. Often it is easy for workers to break rules and let a lot of things slip.

Yet, first-line supervisors are frequently judged according to rules and regulations while being limited by other regulations in what disciplinary actions they can take. They often lack the resources to influence or reward people; after all, workers are guaranteed their pay and benefits by someone other than their supervisors. Supervisors cannot easily control events; rather, they must react to them.

In one factory, for instance, supervisors complained that performance of their job was out of their control: they could fill production quotas only if they had the supplies, but they had no way to influence the people controlling supplies.

The lack of support for many first-line managers, particularly in large organizations, was made dramatically clear in another company. When asked if contact with executives higher in the organization who had the potential for offering support, information, and alliances diminished their own feelings of career vulnerability and the number of headaches they experienced on the job, supervisors in five out of seven work units responded positively. For them *contact* was indeed related to a greater feeling of acceptance at work and membership in the organization.

But in the two other work units where there was greater contact, people perceived more, not less, career vulnerability. Further investigation showed that supervisors in these business units got attention only when they were in trouble. Otherwise, no one bothered to talk to them. To these particular supervisors, hearing from a higher-level manager was a sign not of recognition or potential support but of danger.

It is not surprising, then, that supervisors frequently manifest symptoms of powerlessness: overly close supervision, rules-mindedness, and a tendency to do the job themselves rather than to train their people (since job skills may be one of the few remaining things they feel good about). Perhaps this is why they sometimes stand as roadblocks between their subordinates and the higher reaches of the company.

Staff Professionals

Also working under conditions that can lead to organizational powerlessness are the staff specialists. As advisers behind the scenes, staff people must sell their programs and bargain for resources, but unless they get themselves entrenched in organizational power networks, they have little in the way of favors to exchange. They are seen as useful adjuncts to the primary tasks of the organization but inessential in a day-to-day operating sense. This disenfranchisement occurs particularly when staff jobs consist of easily routinized administrative functions which are out of the mainstream of the currently relevant areas and involve little innovative decision making.

Furthermore, in some organizations, unless they have had previous line experience, staff people tend to be limited in the number of jobs into which they can move. Specialists' ladders are often very short, and professionals are just as likely to get "stuck" in such jobs as people are in less prestigious clerical or factory positions.

Staff people, unlike those who are being groomed for important line positions, may be hired because of a special expertise or particular background. But management rarely pays any attention to developing them into more general organizational resources. Lacking growth prospects themselves and working alone or in very small teams, they are not in a position to develop others or pass on power to them. They miss out on an important way that power can be accumulated.

Sometimes staff specialists, such as house counsel or organization development people, find their work being farmed out to consultants. Management considers them fine for the routine work, but the minute the activities involve risk or something problematic, they bring in outside experts. This treatment says something not only about their expertise but also about the status of their function. Since the company can always hire talent on a temporary basis, it is unclear that the management really needs to have or considers important its own staff for these functions.

And, because staff professionals are often seen as adjuncts to primary tasks, their effectiveness and therefore their contribution to the organization are often hard to measure. Thus visibility and recognition, as well as risk taking and relevance, may be denied to people in staff jobs.

Staff people tend to act out their powerlessness by becoming turf-minded. They create islands within the organization. They set themselves up as the only ones who can control professional standards and judge their own work. They create sometimes false distinctions between themselves as experts (no one else could possibly do what they do) and lay people, and this continues to keep them out of the mainstream.

One form such distinctions take is a combination of disdain when line managers attempt to act in areas the professionals think are their preserve and of subtle refusal to support the managers' efforts. Or staff groups battle with each other for control of new "problem areas," with the result that no one really handles the issue at all. To cope with their essential powerlessness, staff groups may try to elevate their own status and draw boundaries between themselves and others.

When staff jobs are treated as final resting places for people who have reached their level of competence in the organization—a good shelf on which to dump managers who are too old to go anywhere but too young to retire—then staff groups can also become pockets of conservatism, resistant to change. Their own exclusion from the risk-taking action may make them resist *anyone's* innovative proposals. In the past, personnel departments, for example, have sometimes been the last in their organization to know about innovations in human resource development or to be interested in applying them.

Top Executives

Despite the great resources and responsibilities concentrated at the top of an organization, leaders can be powerless for reasons that are not very different from those that affect staff and supervisors: lack of supplies, information, and support.

We have faith in leaders because of their ability to make things happen in the larger world, to create possibilities for everyone else, and to attract resources to the organization. These are their supplies. But influence outward—the source of much credibility downward—can diminish as environments change, setting terms and conditions out of the control of the leaders. Regardless of top management's grand plans for the organization, the environment presses. At the very least, things going on outside the organization can deflect a leader's attention and drain energy. And, more detrimental, decisions made elsewhere can have severe consequences for the organization and affect top management's sense of power and thus its operating style inside.

In the go-go years of the mid-1960s, for example, nearly every corporation officer or university president could look—and therefore feel—successful. Visible success gave leaders a great deal of credibility inside the organization, which in turn gave them the power to put new things in motion.

In the past few years, the environment has been strikingly different and the capacity of many organization leaders to do anything about it has been severely limited. New "players" have flexed their power muscles: the Arab oil bloc, government regulators, and congressional investigating committees. And managing economic decline is quite different from managing growth. It is no accident that when top leaders personally feel out of control, the control function in corporations grows.

As powerlessness in lower levels of organizations can manifest itself in overly routinized jobs where performance measures are oriented to rules and absence of change, so it can at upper levels as well. Routine work often drives out nonroutine work. Accomplishment becomes a question of nailing down details. Short-term results provide immediate gratifications and satisfy stockholders or other constituencies with limited interests.

It takes a powerful leader to be willing to risk short-term deprivations in order to bring about desired long-term outcomes. Much as first-line supervisors are tempted to focus on daily adherence to rules, leaders are tempted to focus on short-term fluctuations and lose sight of long-term objectives. The dynamics of such a situation are self-reinforcing. The more the long-term goals go unattended, the more a leader feels powerless and the greater the scramble to prove that he or she is in control of daily events at least. The more he is involved in the organization as a short-term Mr. Fix-it, the more out of control of long-term objectives he is, and the more ultimately powerless he is likely to be.

Credibility for top executives often comes from doing the extraordinary: exercising discretion, creating, inventing, planning, and acting in nonroutine ways. But since routine problems look easier and more manageable, require less change and consent on the part of anyone else, and lend themselves to instant solutions that can make any leader look good temporarily, leaders may avoid the risky by taking over what their subordinates should be doing. Ultimately, a leader may succeed in getting all the trivial problems dumped on his or her desk. This can establish expectations even for leaders attempting more challenging tasks. When Warren Bennis was president of the University of Cincinnati, a professor called him when the heat was down in a classroom. In writing about this incident, Bennis commented, "I suppose he expected me to grab a wrench and fix it."[6]

People at the top need to insulate themselves from the routine operations of the organization in order to develop and exercise power. But this very insulation can lead to another source of powerlessness—lack of information. In one multinational corporation, top executives who are sealed off in a large, distant office, flattered and virtually babied by aides, are frustrated by their distance from the real action.[7]

At the top, the concern for secrecy and privacy is mixed with real loneliness. In one bank, organization members were so accustomed to never seeing the top leaders that when a new senior vice president went to the branch offices to look around, they had suspicion, even fear, about his intentions.

Thus leaders who are cut out of an organization's information networks understand neither what is really going on at lower levels nor that their own isolation may be having negative effects. All too often top executives design "beneficial" new employee programs or declare a new humanitarian policy (e.g., "Participatory management is now our style") only to find the policy ignored or mistrusted because it is perceived as coming from uncaring bosses.

The information gap has more serious consequences when executives are so insulated from the rest of the organization or from other decision makers that, as Nixon so dramatically did, they fail to see their own impending downfall. Such insulation is partly a matter of organizational position and, in some cases, of executive style.

For example, leaders may create closed inner circles consisting of "doppelgängers," people just like themselves, who are their principal sources of organizational information and tell them only what they want to know. The reasons for the distortions are varied: key aides want to relieve the leader of burdens, they think just like the leader, they want to protect their own positions of power, or the familiar "kill the messenger" syndrome makes people close to top executives reluctant to be the bearers of bad news.

Finally, just as supervisors and lower-level managers need their supporters in order to be and feel powerful, so do top executives. But for them sponsorship may not be so much a matter of individual endorsement as an issue of support by larger sources of legitimacy in the society. For top executives the problem is not to fit in among peers; rather, the question is whether the public at large and other organization members perceive a common interest which they see the executives as promoting.

If, however, public sources of support are withdrawn and leaders are open to public attack or if inside constituencies fragment and employees see their interests better aligned with pressure groups than with organizational leadership, then powerlessness begins to set in.

When common purpose is lost, the system's own politics may reduce the capacity of those at the top to act. Just as managing decline seems to create a much more passive and reactive stance than managing growth, so does mediating among conflicting interests. When what is happening outside and inside their organizations is out of their control, many people at the top turn into decline managers and dispute mediators. Neither is a particularly empowering role.

Thus when top executives lose their own lines of supply, lines of information, and lines of support, they too suffer from a kind of powerlessness. The temptation for them then is to pull in every shred of power they can and to decrease the power available to other people to act. Innovation loses out in favor of control. Limits rather than targets are set. Financial goals are met by reducing "overhead" (people) rather than by giving people the tools and discretion to increase their own productive capacity. Dictatorial statements come down from the top, spreading the mentality of powerlessness farther until the whole organization becomes sluggish and people concentrate on protecting what they have rather than on producing what they can.

When everyone is playing "king of the mountain," guarding turf jealously, then king of the mountain becomes the only game in town.

To Expand Power, Share It

In no case am I saying that people in the three hierarchical levels described are always powerless, but they are susceptible to common conditions that can contribute to powerlessness. Exhibit 3 summarizes the most common symptoms of powerlessness for each level and some typical sources of that behavior.

I am also distinguishing the tremendous concentration of economic and political power in large corporations themselves from the powerlessness that can beset individuals even in the highest positions in such organizations. What grows with organizational position in hierarchical levels is not necessarily the power to accomplish—productive power—but the power to punish, to prevent, to sell off, to reduce, to fire, all without appropriate concern

Exhibit 3. Common Symptoms and Sources of Powerlessness for Three Key Organizational Positions

Position	Symptoms	Sources
First-line supervisors	Close, rules-minded supervision	Routine, rules-minded jobs with little control over lines of supply
	Tendency to do things oneself, blocking of subordinates' development and information	Limited lines of information
	Resistant, underproducing subordinates	Limited advancement or involvement prospects for oneself/subordinates
Staff professionals	Turf protection, information control	Routine tasks seen as peripheral to "real tasks" of line organization
	Retreat into professionalism	Blocked careers
	Conservative resistance to change	Easy replacement by outside experts
Top executives	Focus on internal cutting, short-term results, "punishing"	Uncontrollable lines of supply because of environmental changes
	Dictatorial top-down communications	Limited or blocked lines of information about lower levels of organization
	Retreat to comfort of like-minded lieutenants	Diminished lines of support because of challenges to legitimacy (e.g., from the public or special interest groups)

for consequences. It is that kind of power—oppressive power—that we often say corrupts.

The absence of ways to prevent individual and social harm causes the polity to feel it must surround people in power with constraints, regulations, and laws that limit the arbitrary use of their authority. But if oppressive power corrupts, then so does the absence of productive power. In large organizations, powerlessness can be a bigger problem than power.

David C. McClelland makes a similar distinction between oppressive and productive power:

> The negative . . . face of power is characterized by the dominance-submission mode: if I win, you lose. . . . It leads to simple and direct means of feeling powerful [such as being aggressive]. It does not often lead to effective social leadership for the reason that such a person tends to treat other people as pawns. People who feel they are pawns tend to be passive and useless to the leader who gets his satisfaction from dominating them. Slaves are the most inefficient form of labor ever devised by man. If a leader wants to have far-reaching influence, he must make his followers feel powerful and able to accomplish things on their own. . . . Even the most dictatorial leader does not succeed if he has not instilled in at least some of his followers a sense of power and the strength to pursue the goals he has set.[8]

Organizational power can grow, in part, by being shared. We do not yet know enough about new organizational forms to say whether productive power is infinitely expandable or where we reach the point of diminishing returns. But we do know that sharing power is different from giving or throwing it away. Delegation does not mean abdication.

Some basic lessons could be translated from the field of economics to the realm of organizations and management. Capital investment in plants and equipment is not the only key to productivity. The productive capacity of nations, like organizations, grows if the skill base is upgraded. People with the tools, information, and support to make more informed decisions and act more quickly can often accomplish more. By empowering others, a leader does not decrease personal power; instead the leader may increase it—especially if the whole organization performs better.

This analysis leads to some counterintuitive conclusions. In a certain tautological sense, the principal problem of the powerless is that they lack power. Powerless people are usually the last ones to whom anyone wants to entrust more power, for fear of its dissipation or abuse. But those people are precisely the ones who might benefit most from an injection of power and whose behavior is likely to change as new options open up to them.

Also, if the powerless bosses could be encouraged to share some of the power they do have, their power would grow. Yet, of course, only those leaders who feel secure about their own power outward—their lines of supply, information, and support—can see empowering subordinates as a gain rather than a loss. The two sides of power (getting it and giving it) are closely connected.

There are important lessons here for both subordinates and those who want to change organizations, whether executives or change agents. Instead of resisting or criticizing a powerless boss, which only increases the boss's feeling of powerlessness and need to control, subordinates instead might concentrate on helping the boss become more powerful. Managers might make pockets of ineffectiveness in the organization more productive not by training or replacing individuals but by structural solutions such as opening supply and support lines.

Similarly, organizational change agents who want a new program or policy to succeed should make sure that the change itself does not render any other level of the organization powerless. In making changes, it is wise to make sure that the key people in the level or two directly above and in neighboring functions are sufficiently involved, informed, and taken into account, so that the program can be used to build their own sense of power also. If such involvement is impossible, then it is better to move these people out of the territory altogether than to leave behind a group from whom some power has been removed and who might resist and undercut the program.

In part, of course, spreading power means educating people to this new definition of it. But words alone will not make the difference; managers will need the real experience of a new way of managing.

Here is how the associate director of a large corporate professional department phrased the lessons that he learned in the transition to a team-oriented, participatory, power-sharing management process:

> Get in the habit of involving your own managers in decision making and approvals. But don't abdicate! Tell them what you want and where you're coming from. Don't go for a one-boss grass roots "democracy." Make the management hierarchy work for you in participation. . . .
>
> Hang in there, baby, and don't give up. Try not to "revert" just because everything seems to go sour on a particular day. Open up—talk to people and tell them how you feel. They'll want to get you back on track and will do things to make that happen—because they don't really want to go back to the way it was. . . . Subordinates will push you to "act more like a boss," but their interest is usually more in seeing someone else brought to heel than getting bossed themselves.

Naturally, people need to have power before they can learn to share it. Exhorting managers to change their leadership styles is rarely useful by itself. In one large plant of a major electronics company, first-line production supervisors were the source of numerous complaints from managers who saw them as major roadblocks to overall plant productivity and as insufficiently skilled supervisors. So the plant personnel staff undertook two pilot programs to increase the supervisors' effectiveness. The first program was based on a traditional competency and training model aimed at teaching the specific skills of successful supervisors. The second program, in contrast, was designed to empower the supervisors by directly affecting their flexibility, access to resources, connections with higher-level officials, and control over working conditions.

After an initial gathering of data from supervisors and their subordinates, the personnel staff held meetings where all the supervisors were given tools for developing action plans for sharing the data with their people and collaborating on solutions to perceived problems. But then, in a departure from common practice in this organization, task forces of supervisors were formed to develop new systems for handling job and career issues common to them and their people. These task forces were given budgets, consultants, representation on a plantwide project steering committee alongside managers at much higher levels, and wide latitude in defining the nature and scope of the changes they wished to make. In short, lines of supply, information, and support were opened to them.

As the task forces progressed in their activities, it became clear to the plant management that the hoped-for changes in supervisory effectiveness were taking place much more rapidly through these structural changes in power than through conventional management training; so the conventional training was dropped. Not only did the pilot groups design useful new procedures for the plant, astonishing senior management in several cases with their knowledge and capabilities, but also, significantly, they learned to manage their own people better.

Several groups decided to involve shop-floor workers in their task forces; they could now see from their own experience the benefits of involving subordinates in solving job-related problems. Other supervisors began to experiment with ways to implement "participatory management" by giving subordinates more control and influence without relinquishing their own authority.

Soon the "problem supervisors" in the "most troubled plant in the company" were getting the highest possible performance ratings and were considered models for direct production management. The sharing of organizational power from the top made possible the productive use of power below.

One might wonder why more organizations do not adopt such empowering strategies. There are standard answers: that giving up control is threatening to people who have fought for every shred of it; that people do not want to share power with those they look down on; that managers fear losing their own place and special privileges in the system; that "predictability" often rates higher than "flexibility" as an organizational value; and so forth.

But I would also put skepticism about employee abilities high on the list. Many modern bureaucratic systems are designed to minimize dependence on individual intelligence by making routine as many decisions as possible. So it often comes as a genuine surprise to top executives that people doing the more routine jobs could, indeed, make sophisticated decisions or use resources entrusted to them in intelligent ways.

In the same electronics company just mentioned, at the end of a quarter the pilot supervisory task forces were asked to report results and plans to senior management in order to have their new budget requests approved. The task forces made sure they were well prepared, and the high-level executives were duly impressed. In fact, they were *so* impressed that they kept interrupting the presentations with compliments, remarking that the supervisors could easily be doing sophisticated personnel work.

At first the supervisors were flattered. Such praise from upper management could only be taken well. But when the first glow wore off, several of them became very angry. They saw the excessive praise as patronizing and insulting. "Didn't they think we could think? Didn't they imagine we were capable of doing this kind of work? " one asked. "They must have seen us as just a bunch of animals. No wonder they gave us such limited jobs."

As far as these supervisors were concerned, their abilities had always been there, in latent form perhaps, but still there. They as individuals had not changed—just their organizational power.

Appendix: Women Managers Experience Special Power Failures

The traditional problems of women in management are illustrative of how formal and informal practices can combine to engender powerlessness. Historically, women in management have found their opportunities in more routine, low-profile jobs. In staff positions, where they serve in support capacities to line managers but have no line responsibilities of their own, or in supervisory jobs managing "stuck" subordinates, they are not in a position either to take the kinds of risks that build credibility or to develop their own team by pushing bright subordinates.

Such jobs, which have few favors to trade, tend to keep women out of the mainstream of the organization. This lack of clout, coupled with the greater difficulty anyone who is "different" has in getting into the information and support networks, has meant that merely by organizational situation women in management have been more likely than men to be rendered structurally powerless. This is one reason those women who have achieved power have often had family connections that put them in the mainstream of the organization's social circles.

A disproportionate number of women managers are found among first-line supervisors or staff professionals; and they, like men in those circumstances, are likely to be organizationally powerless. But the behavior of other managers can contribute to the powerlessness of women in management in a number of less obvious ways.

One way other managers can make a woman powerless is by patronizingly overprotecting her: putting her in "a safe job," not giving her enough to do to prove herself, and not suggesting her for high-risk, visible assignments. This protectiveness is sometimes born of "good" intentions to give her every chance to succeed (why stack the deck against her?). Out of managerial concerns, out of awareness that a woman may be up against situations that men simply do not have to face, some very well-meaning managers protect their female managers ("It's a jungle, so why send her into it? ").

Overprotectiveness can also mask a manager's fear of association with a woman should she fail. One senior bank official at a level below vice president told me about his concerns with respect to a high-performing, financially experienced woman reporting to him. Despite *his* overwhelmingly positive work experiences with her, he was still afraid to recommend her for other assignments because he felt it was a personal risk. "What if other managers are not as accepting of women as I am? " he asked. "I know I'd be sticking my neck out; they would take her more because of my endorsement than her qualifications. And what if she doesn't make it? My judgment will be on the line."

Overprotection is relatively benign compared with rendering a person powerless by providing obvious signs of lack of managerial support. For example, allowing someone supposedly in authority to be bypassed easily means that no one else has to take him or her seriously. If a woman's immediate supervisor or other managers listen willingly to criticism of her and show they are concerned every time a negative comment comes up and that they assume she must be at fault, then they are helping to undercut her. If managers let other people know that they have concerns about this person or that they are testing her to see how she does, then they are inviting other people to look for signs of inadequacy or failure.

Furthermore, people assume they can afford to bypass women because they "must be uninformed" or "don't know the ropes." Even though women may be respected for their competence or expertise, they are not necessarily seen as being informed beyond the technical requirements of the job. There may be a grain of historical truth in this. Many women come to senior management positions as "outsiders" rather than up through the usual channels.

Also, because until very recently men have not felt comfortable seeing women as businesspeople (business clubs have traditionally excluded women), they have tended to seek each other out for informal socializing. Anyone, male or female, seen as organizationally naive and lacking sources of "inside dope" will find personal lines of information limited.

Finally, even when women are able to achieve some power on their own, they have not necessarily been able to translate such personal credibility into an organizational power base. To create a network of supporters out of individual clout requires that a person pass on and share power that subordinates and peers be empowered by virtue of their connection with that person. Traditionally, neither men nor women have seen women as capable of sponsoring others, even though they may be capable of achieving and succeeding on their own. Women have been viewed as the *recipients* of sponsorship rather than as the sponsors themselves.

(As more women prove themselves in organizations and think more self-consciously about bringing along young people, this situation may change. However, I still hear many more questions from women managers about how they can benefit from mentors, sponsors, or peer networks than about how they themselves can start to pass on favors and make use of their own resources to benefit others.)

Viewing managers in terms of power and powerlessness helps explain two familiar stereotypes about women and leadership in organizations: that no one wants a woman boss (although studies show that anyone who has ever had a woman boss is likely to have had a positive experience), and that the reason no one wants a woman boss is that women are "too controlling, rules-minded, and petty."

The first stereotype simply makes clear that power is important to leadership. Underneath the preference for men is the assumption that, given the current distribution of people in organizational leadership positions, men are more likely than women to be in positions to achieve power and, therefore, to share their power with others. Similarly, the "bossy woman boss" stereotype is a perfect picture of powerlessness. All of those traits are just as characteristic of men who are powerless, but women are slightly more likely, because of circumstances I have mentioned, to find themselves powerless than are men. Women with power in the organization are just as effective—and preferred—as men.

Recent interviews conducted with about 600 bank managers show that, when a woman exhibits the petty traits of powerlessness, people assume that she does so "because she is a woman." A striking difference is that, when a man engages in the same behavior, people assume the behavior is a matter of his own individual style and characteristics and do not conclude that it reflects on the suitability of men for management.

Notes

1. Donald C. Pelz, "Influence: A Key to Effective Leadership in the First-Line Supervisor," *Personnel*, November 1952, p. 209.

2. See Rosabeth Moss Kanter, *Men and Women of the Corporation* (New York, Basic Books, 1977), pp. 164–205; and David Kipnis, *The Powerholders* (Chicago, University of Chicago Press, 1976).

3. Pehr G Gyllenhammar, *People at Work* (Reading, Mass., Addison-Wesley, 1977), p. 133.

4. William E. Fulmer, "Supervisory Selection: The Acid Test of Affirmative Action," *Personnel,* November–December 1976, p. 40.

5. See Rosabeth M. Kanter and Barry A. Stein, "Life in the Middle: Getting In, Getting Up, and Getting Along," in *Life in Organizations*, edited by Rosabeth M. Kanter and Barry A. Stein (New York, Basic Books, 1979).

6. Warren Bennis, *The Unconscious Conspiracy: Why Leaders Can't Lead* (New York, AMACOM, 1976).

7. See Rosabeth Moss Kanter, "How the Top Is Different," in *Life in Organizations,* op. cit.

8. David C. McClelland, *Power: The Inner Experience* (New York, Irvington Publishers, 1975), p. 263. Quoted by permission.

17

Power and Politics in Organizational Life

ABRAHAM ZALEZNIK

The competition for power is characteristic of all political structures. And, whatever else they may be, business organizations are political structures in that they provide both a base for the development of executive careers and a platform for the expression of individual interests and motives. People in positions of authority, however, "differ from 'ordinary' humans," says this author, "in that they have the capacity to impose their personal defenses onto the stage of corporate life. Fortunately, the relationships are susceptible to intelligent management," and it is to the nature of this intelligence that the discussion is devoted.

There are few business activities more prone to a credibility gap than the way in which executives approach organizational life. A sense of disbelief occurs when managers purport to make decisions in rationalistic terms while most observers and participants know that personalities and politics play a significant if not an overriding role. Where does the error lie? In the theory which insists that decisions should be rationalistic and nonpersonal? Or in the practice which treats business organizations as political structures?

Whatever else organizations may be (problem-solving instruments, sociotechnical systems, reward systems, and so on), they are political structures. This means that organizations operate by distributing authority and setting a stage for the exercise of power. It is no wonder, therefore, that individuals who are highly motivated to secure and use power find a familiar and hospitable environment in business.

At the same time, executives are reluctant to acknowledge the place of power both in individual motivation and in organizational relationships. Somehow, power and politics are dirty words. And in linking these words to the play of personalities in organizations, some managers withdraw into the safety of organizational logics.

As I suggest in this article, frank recognition of the importance of personality factors and a sensitive use of the strengths and limitations of people in decisions on power distributions can improve the quality of organizational life.

Political Pyramid

Organizations provide a power base for individuals. From a purely economic standpoint, organizations exist to create a surplus of income over costs by meeting needs in the marketplace. But organizations also are political structures which provide opportunities for people to develop careers and therefore provide platforms for the expression of individual interests and motives. The development of careers, particularly at high managerial and professional levels, depends on accumulation of power as the vehicle for transforming individual interests into activities which influence other people.

Scarcity and Competition

A political pyramid exists when people compete for power in an economy of scarcity. In other words, people cannot get the power they want just for the asking. Instead, they have to enter into the decisions on how to distribute authority in a particular formal organization structure. Scarcity of power arises under two sets of conditions:

1 Where individuals gain power in absolute terms at someone else's expense.
2 Where there is a gain comparatively—not literally at someone else's expense—resulting in a relative shift in the distribution of power.

In either case, the psychology of scarcity and comparison takes over. Human beings tend to make comparisons as a basis for their sense of self-esteem. They may compare themselves with other people and decide that a personal absolute loss or the shift in proportional shares of authority reflects an attrition in a personal power base. They may also compare their positions relative to others against personal standards and feel a sense of loss. This tendency to compare is deeply ingrained in people, especially since they experience early in life the effects of comparisons in the family where—in an absolute sense—time and attention, if not love and affection, go to the most dependent member.

Corporate acquisitions and mergers illustrate the effects of both types of comparisons. In the case of one merger, the president of the acquired company resigned rather than accept the relative displacement in rank which occurred when the president no longer could act as a chief executive officer. Two vice presidents vied for the position of executive vice president. Because of their conflicting ambitions, the expedient of making them equals drove the competition underground, but not for long. The vice president with the weaker power base soon resigned in the face of a personal inability to consolidate a workable definition of personal responsibilities. The weaker vice president's departure resulted in increased power for the remaining vice president and the gradual elimination of "rival camps" which had been covertly identified with the main contenders for power.

The fact that organizations are pyramids produces a scarcity of positions the higher one moves in the hierarchy. This scarcity, coupled with inequalities, certainly needs to be recognized. While it may be humane and socially desirable to say that people are different rather than unequal in their potential, nevertheless executive talent is in short supply. The end result should be to move the more able people into the top positions and to accord them the pay, responsibility, and authority to match their potential.

On the other side, the strong desires of equally able people for the few top positions available means that someone will either have to face the realization of unfulfilled ambition or have to shift interest to another organization.[1]

Constituents and Clients

Besides the conditions of scarcity and competition, politics in organizations grows out of the existence of constituencies. A superior may be content with shifts in the allocation of resources and consequently power, but this superior represents subordinates who, for their own reasons, may be unhappy with the changes. These subordinates affirm and support their boss. They can also withdraw affirmation and support, and consequently isolate the superior with all the painful consequences this entails.

While appointments to positions come from above, affirmation of position comes from below. The only difference between party and organizational politics is in the subtlety of the voting procedure. Consider:

□ In a large consumer products corporation, one division received almost no capital funds for expansion while another division, which had developed a new marketing approach for products common to both, expanded dramatically. The head of the static division found personal power diminished considerably, as reflected in how seriously this head's subordinates took efforts at influence (e.g., in programs to increase the profit return from existing volume).

This manager initiated one program after another with little support from subordinates because of a lack of ability to make a claim for capital funds. The flow of capital funds in this corporation provided a measure of power gains and losses in both an absolute and a relative sense.

Power and Action

Still another factor which heightens the competition for power that is characteristic of all political structures is the incessant need to use whatever power one possesses. Corporations have an implicit "banking" system in power transactions. The initial "capitalization" which makes up an individual's power base consists of three elements:

1. The quantity of formal authority vested in one's position relative to other positions.
2. The authority vested in one's expertise and reputation for competence (a factor weighted by how important the expertise is for the growth areas of the corporation as against the historically stable areas of its business).
3. The attractiveness of one's personality to others (a combination of personal respect as well as liking, although these two sources of attraction are often in conflict).

This capitalization of power reflects the total esteem with which others regard the individual. By a process which is still not too clear, the individual internalizes all of the sources of power capital in a manner parallel to the way he develops a sense of self-esteem. The individual knows he or she has power, assesses it realistically, and is willing to risk personal esteem to influence others.

A critical element here is the risk in the uses of power. The individual must perform *and* get results. If the individual fails to do either, an attrition occurs in the personal power base in direct proportion to the doubts other people entertained in their earlier appraisals of the individual.

What occurs here is an erosion of confidence which ultimately leads the individual to self-doubt and undermines the psychological work which led in the first place to self-internalizing authority as a prelude to action. (While, as I have suggested, the psychological work that an individual goes through to consolidate esteem capital is a crucial aspect of power relations, I shall have to reserve careful examination of this problem until a later date. The objective now is to examine from a political framework the problems of organizational life.)

What distinguishes alterations in the authority structure from other types of organizational change is their direct confrontation with the political character of corporate life. Such confrontations are real manipulations of power as compared with the indirect approaches which play on ideologies and attitudes. In the first case, the potency and reality of shifts in authority have an instantaneous effect on what people do, how they interact, and how they think about themselves. In the second case, the shifts in attitude are often based on the willingness of people to respond the way authority figures want them to; ordinarily, however, these shifts in attitude are but temporary expressions of compliance.

One of the most common errors executives make is to confuse compliance with commitment. Compliance is an attitude of acceptance when a directive from an authority figure asks for a change in an individual's position, activities, or ideas. The individual complies or "goes along" usually because he is indifferent to the scope of the directive and the changes it proposes. If compliance occurs out of indifference, then one can predict little difficulty in translating the intent of directives into actual implementation.[2]

Commitment, on the other hand, represents a strong motivation on the part of an individual to adopt or resist the intent of a directive. If the individual is committed personally to a change, then the individual will use ingenuity to interpret and implement the change in such a way as to assure its success. If he or she decides to fight or block the change, the individual may act compliant but reserve other times and places to negate the effects of directives. For example:

> ☐ In one large company, the top management met regularly for purposes of organizational planning. The executives responsible for implementing planning decisions could usually be counted on to carry them out when they had fought hard and openly in the course of reaching such decisions. When they seemed to accept a decision, giving all signs of compliance, the decision usually ended up as a notation in the minutes. Surface compliance occurred most frequently when problems involved loyalties in subordinates.
>
> In one instance, a division head agreed to accept a highly regarded executive from another division to meet a serious personnel shortage in the organization. When the time came to effect the transfer, however, this division general manager refused, with some justification, on the grounds that bringing someone in from outside would demoralize the staff. This manager used compliance initially to respond to the problem of personally perceived "family" loyalty commitments. Needless to say, the existence of these loyalties was the major problem to be faced in carrying out organizational planning.

Compliance as a tactic to avoid changes and commitment as an expression of strong motivation in dealing with organizational problems are in turn related to how individuals define their interests. In the power relations among executives, the so-called areas of common interest are usually reserved for the banalities of human relationships. The more significant areas of attention usually force conflicts of interest, especially competition for power, to the surface.

Interest Conflicts

Organizations demand, on the one hand, cooperative endeavor and commitment to common purposes. The realities of experience in organizations, on the other hand, show that conflicts of interest exist among people who ultimately share a common fate and are supposed to work together. What makes business more political and less ideological and rationalistic is the overriding importance of conflicts of interest.

If individuals are told that their job scopes are reduced in either absolute or proportional terms for *the good of the corporation,* they face a conflict. Should they acquiesce for the idea of common good or fight in the service of their self-interest? Rational people will fight (how constructively depends on the absence of neurotic conflicts and on ego strength). Their willingness to fight increases as they come to realize the intangible nature of what people think is good for the organization. And, in point of fact, their willingness may serve the interests of corporate purpose by highlighting issues and stimulating careful thinking before the reaching of final decisions.

Secondary Effects

Conflicts of interest in the competition for resources are easily recognized, as for example, in capital budgeting or in allocating money for research and development. But these conflicts can be subjected to bargaining procedures which all parties to the competition validate by their participation.

The secondary effects of bargaining do involve organizational and power issues. However, the fact that these power issues *follow* debate on economic problems rather than *lead* it creates a manifest content which can be objectified much more readily than in areas where the primary considerations are the distributions of authority.

In such cases, which include developing a new formal organization structure, management succession, promotions, corporate mergers, and entry of new executives, the conflicts of interest are severe and direct simply because there are no objective measures of right or wrong courses of action. The critical question which has to be answered in specific actions is: Who gets power and position? This involves particular people with their strengths and weaknesses and a specific historical context in which actions are understood in symbolic as well as rational terms. To illustrate:

☐ A large corporation, General Motors in fact, inadvertently confirmed what every seasoned executive knows: that coalitions of power to overcome feelings of rivalry and the play of personal ambitions are fragile solutions. The appointment of Edward Cole to the presidency followed by Semon Knudsen's resignation shattered the illusion that the rational processes in business stand apart or even dominate the human emotions and ties that bind people to one another. If any corporation prides itself on rationality, General Motors is it. To have to experience so publicly the inference that major corporate life, particularly at the executive levels, is not so rational after all, can be damaging to the sense of security people get from belief in an idea as it is embodied in a corporate image.

The fact that Knudsen subsequently was discharged from the presidency of Ford (an event I discuss later in this article) suggests that personalities and the politics of corporations are less aberrations and more conditions of life in large organizations.

But just as General Motors wants to maintain an image, many executives prefer to ignore what this illustration suggests: that organizations are political structures which feed on the psychology of comparison. To know something about the psychology of comparison takes us into the theory of self-esteem in both its conscious manifestations and its unconscious origins. Besides possibly enlightening us in general and giving a more realistic picture of people and organizations, there are some practical benefits in such knowledge. These benefits include:

☐ Increased freedom to act more directly; instead of trying to "get around" a problem, one can meet it.

☐ Greater objectivity about people's strengths and limitations, and, therefore, the ability to use them more honestly as well as effectively.

☐ More effective planning in organizational design and in distribution of authority; instead of searching for the "one best solution" in organization structure, one accepts a range of alternatives and then gives priority to the personal or emotional concerns that inhibit action.

Power Relations

Organizational life within a political frame is a series of contradictions. It is an exercise in rationality, but its energy comes from the ideas in the minds of power figures the content of which, as well as their origins, are only dimly perceived. It deals with sources of authority and their distribution; yet it depends in the first place on the existence of a balance of power in the hands of an individual who initiates actions and gets results. It has many rituals associated with it, such as participation, democratization, and the sharing of power; yet the real outcome is the consolidation of power around a central figure to whom other individuals make emotional attachments.

Faulty Coalitions

The formal organization structure implements a coalition among key executives. The forms differ, and the psychological significance of various coalitions also differs. But no organization can function without a consolidation of power in the relationship of a central figure with a select group. The coalition need not exist between the chief executive and immediate subordinates or staff. It may indeed bypass the second level as in the case of Presidents of the United States who do not build confident relationships within their cabinets, but instead rely on members of the executive staff or on selected individuals outside the formal apparatus.

The failure to establish a coalition within the executive structure of an organization can result in severe problems, such as paralysis in the form of inability to make decisions and to evaluate performance, and in-fighting and overt rivalry within the executive group.

When a coalition fails to develop, the first place to look for causes is the chief executive's problems in creating confident relationships. The causes are many and complex, but they usually hinge around the nature of the chief executive's defenses and what the executive needs to avoid as a means of alleviating stress. For example:

> □ The "palace revolt," which led to Semon Knudsen's departure from Ford Motor Company, is an illustration of the failure in the formation of a coalition. While it is true that Henry Ford II named Knudsen president of the company, Knudsen's ultimate power as a newcomer to an established power structure depended on forming an alliance. The particular individual with whom an alliance seemed crucial was Lee Iacocca. For some reason, Knudsen and Iacocca competed for power and influence instead of using cooperatively a power base to which both contributed as is the case with most workable coalitions. In the absence of a coalition, the alternate postures of rivalry and battle for control erupted. Ford ultimately responded by weighing his power with one side over the other.

As I have indicated, it is not at all clear why in Knudsen's case the coalition failed to develop. But in any failure the place to look is in the personalities of the main actors and in the nature of their defenses which make certain coalitions improbable no matter how strongly other realities indicate their necessity.

But defensiveness on the part of a chief executive can also result in building an unrealistic and unworkable coalition, with the self-enforced isolation which is its consequence. One of the most frequently encountered defensive maneuvers which leads to the formation of unrealistic coalitions or to the isolation of the chief executive is the fear of rivalry.

A realistic coalition matches formal authority and competence with the emotional commitments necessary to establish and maintain the coalition. The fear of rivals on the part of chief executives, or the jealousy on the part of subordinates of the chief executive's power, can at the extreme result in paranoid distortions. People become suspicious of one another, and through selective perceptions and projections of their own fantasies create a world of plots and counterplots.

The displacement of personal concerns onto substantive material in decision making is potentially the most dangerous form of defensiveness. The need for defenses arises because people become anxious about the significance of evaluations within existing power coalitions. But perhaps even more basic is the fear and the rivalry to which all coalitions are susceptible given the nature of investments people make in power relations. While it is easy to dismiss emotional reactions like these as neurotic distortions, their prevalence and impact deserve careful attention in all phases of organizational life.

Unconscious Collusions

All individuals and consequently groups experience areas of stress which mobilize defenses. The fact that coalitions embody defensive maneuvers on those occasions where stress goes beyond the usual level of tolerance is not surprising. An even more serious problem, however, occurs when the main force that binds people in a structure is the need to defend against or to act out the conflicts which individuals cannot tolerate alone.

Where coalitions represent the aggregation of power with conscious intention of using the abilities of members for constructive purposes, collusions represent predominance of unconscious conflict and defensive behavior. In organizational life, the presence of collusions and their causes often becomes the knot which has to be unraveled before any changes can be implemented.

The collusion of latent interests among executives can become the central theme and sustaining force of an organization structure of top management. For a collusion to take hold, the conflicts of the "power figure" have to be communicated and sensed by others as an overriding need which seeks active expression in the form of a theme. The themes vary just as do the structures which make a collusion. Thus one common theme is the need to control; another is the need to be admired and idealized; and still another is the need to find a scapegoat to attack in response to frustrations in solving problems.

If people could hold on to and keep within themselves areas of personal conflict, there would be far fewer collusions in organizational life. But it is part of the human condition for conflicts and needs to take over life situations. As a result, we find numerous instances of collusions controlling the behavior of executives. To illustrate:

☐ A multidivisional corporation found itself with a revolution on its hands. The president was sensitive to the opinions of a few outside board members representing important stockholder interests. He was so concerned that he would be criticized by these board members, he demanded from vice presidents full information on their activities and complete loyalty to him. Over a period of years, he moved divisional chief executives to corporate headquarters so he could assure himself of their loyalty. Other executives joined in to gratify the president's need for control and loyalty.

The result of this collusion, however, was to create a schism between headquarters and field operations. Some of the staff members in the field managed to inform the board members of the lack of attention to and understanding of field problems. Discontent grew to such an extent that the board placed the president on early retirement.

Subsequently, the new president, with the support of the board, decentralized authority and appointed new division heads who were to make their offices in divisional headquarters with full authority to manage their respective organizations. One of the lingering problems of the new president was to dissolve the collusion at headquarters without wholesale firing of vice presidents.

Just as power distributions are central to the tasks of organizational planning, so the conservation of power is often the underlying function of collusions. Thus:

☐ A manufacturing vice president of a medium-sized company witnessed over a period of 15 years a procession of changes in top management and ownership. He had managed to retain his job because he made himself indispensable in the management of the factory.

To each new top management, he stressed the importance of "home rule" as a means of assuring loyalty and performance in the plant. He also tacitly encouraged each supervisor to go along with whatever cliques happened to form and dominate the shop floor.

However, over time a gradual loss of competitive position, coupled with open conflict among cliques in the form of union disputes, led to the dismissal of the vice president. None of his successors could reassert control over the shop, and the company eventually moved or liquidated many of the operations in this plant.

"Life Dramas"

Faulty coalitions and unconscious collusions, as I have illustrated, can result from the defensive needs of a chief executive. These needs, which often appear as a demand on others to bolster the self-esteem of the chief executive, are tolerated to a remarkable degree and persist for a long time before harmful effects become apparent to outside stockholders, bankers, or boards of directors which ultimately control the distributions of power in organizations. Occasionally, corporations undergo critical conflicts in organizational politics which cannot be ignored in the conscious deliberations which affect how power gets distributed or used.

Intertwined with the various expressions of power conflicts in organizations are three underlying "life dramas" deserving careful attention:

The *first* portrays stripping the powers of a *parental figure*.

The *second* portrays the predominance of *paranoid thinking,* where distortions of reality result from the surfacing of conflicts which formerly had been contained in collusions.

The *third* portrays a *ritualistic ceremonial* in which real power issues are submerged or isolated in compulsive behavior but at the cost of real problem solving and work.

Parental Figure

The chief executive in a business, along with the heads of states, religious bodies, and social movements, becomes an object for other people. The term "object" should be understood, in a psychological sense, as a person who is the recipient of strong emotional attachments from others. It is obvious that a chief executive is the *object* because the chief executive controls so many of the levers which ultimately direct the flow of rewards and punishments. But there is something to say beyond this obvious calculation of rewards and punishments as the basis for the emotional attachments between leader and led as *object* and *subject*.

Where a leader displays unusual attributes in personal intuitive gifts, cultivated abilities, or deeper personal qualities, the leader's fate as the *object* is governed by powerful emotions. I hesitate to use the word "charismatic" to describe such a leader, partially because it suggests a mystique but also because, in its reference to the "great" person as charismatic leader, it expands to superhuman proportions what really belongs to the psychology of everyday life.

What makes for strong emotional attachments is as much in the need of the *subject* as in the qualities of the *object*. In other words, the personalities of leaders take on proportions which meet what subordinates need and even demand. If leaders in fact respond with the special charisma that is often invested in them at the outset, then they are parties to a self-fulfilling prophecy. Of course, the qualities demanded have to be present in some nascent form ready to emerge as soon as the emotional currents become real in authority relationships.

The emotional attachments I am referring to usually contain mixtures of positive and negative feelings. If the current were only of one kind, such as either admiration or hostility, then the authority relationship would be simpler to describe as well as to manage. All too often, the way positive feelings blend into the negative sets off secondary currents of emotion which intensify the relationships.

On the one side, subordinates cannot help but have fantasies of what they would do if they held the No. 1 position. Such fantasies, besides providing fleeting pleasures and helping one to regulate ambitions, also provide channels for imaginative and constructive approaches to solving problems. It is only a short step from imagining what one would do as chief executive to explaining to the real chief executive the ideas which have been distilled from this flight into fantasy. If the chief executive senses envy in back of the thoughts, the chief executive may become frightened and choke off ideas which can be used quite constructively.

Critical Episode. But suppose a situation arises where not one but several subordinates enjoy the same fantasy of being No. 1? Suppose also that subordinates feel deprived in their relationship with the chief executive? Suppose finally that facing the organization there are substantive problems which are more or less out of control. With these three conditions, and depending on the severity of the real problems besetting the enterprise, the stage is set for a collusion which, when acted out, becomes a critical episode of displacing the parental figure. To demonstrate:

> □ In November 1967, the directors of the Interpublic Group, a $700 million complex in advertising and public relations, moved for the resignation of the leader and chief executive officer, Marion Harper, Jr. Briefly, Harper had managed over a period of 18 years to build the world's largest conglomerate in market services, advertising, and information on the base of a personally successful agency career. In expanding from this base, Harper made acquisitions, started new companies, and widened his orbit into international branches and companies.
>
> As often happens, the innovator and creative person is careless in controlling what he has built so that financial problems become evident. In Harper's case, he appeared either unwilling or unable to recognize the seriousness of his financial problems and, in particular, the significance of allowing cash balances to go below the minimum required in agreements with lending institutions.
>
> Harper seemed careless in another, even more telling, way. Instead of developing a strong coalition among his executive group, he relied on individual ties to him in which he clearly dominated the relationship. If any of the executives ''crossed'' him, Harper would exile the offender to one of the ''remote'' branches or place him on partial retirement.
>
> When the financial problems became critical, the aggrieved executives who had once been dependent on Harper and then cast out, formed their own coalition, and managed to garner the votes necessary to, in effect, fire Harper. Although little information is available on the aftermath of this palace revolution, the new coalition had its own problems—which, one would reasonably judge, included contentions for power.

A cynic viewing this illustration of the demise of a parental figure could conclude that if one seeks to maintain power by dominance, then one had best go all the way. This means that to take some but not all of the power away from rebellious offspring sets the stage for a cabal among the deprived. With a score to settle, they await only the right circumstances to move in and depose the aggressor.

While this cynical view has its own appeal, it ignores the deeper issues of why otherwise brilliant people fail to recognize the realistic needs for coalitions in the relationships of superior and subordinates. To answer this question, we would need to understand how powerful people operate with massive blind spots which limit vision and the ability to maneuver in the face of realistic problems.

The one purpose that coalitions serve is to guard against the effects of blind spots, since it is seldom the case that two people have identical limitations in their vision and ability to respond. The need to control and dominate in a personalistic sense is perhaps the most serious of all possible blind spots which can affect chief executives, because they make it difficult for people to help them, while creating grievances which sooner or later lead to attacks on them.

The unseating of a chief executive by a coalition of subordinates seldom reduces the emotional charge built up in the uncertain attachments to the ousted leader. A new head has to emerge and establish a confident coalition. Until the contentions for power subside and the guilt reactions attached to deposing the leader dissolve, individuals remain vulnerable to their own blind spots and unconscious reactions to striving for power.

The references to a parental figure in the preceding discussion may appear to exaggerate the meaning of power conflicts. In whatever ways it exaggerates, it also condenses a variety of truths about coalitions among executives. The chief executive is the central *object* in a coalition because the chief executive occupies a position analogous to parents in the family. The chief executive is at the nucleus of a political structure whose prototype is the family in which jealousy, envy, love, and hate find original impetus and expression.

It would be a gross error to assume that in making an analogy between the family and formal organizations the parental role is strictly paternal. There are also characteristics of the mother figure in certain types of chief executives and combinations of mother-father in the formation of executive coalitions.

Chief executives can also suffer from depersonalization in their roles and as a result become emotionally cold and detached. The causes of depersonalization are complex but, in brief, have some connections to the narrow definitions of rationality which exclude the importance of emotions in guiding communication as well as thought.

For the purpose of interpreting how defensive styles affect the behavior of leaders, there is some truth to the suggestion that the neutrality and lack of warmth characteristic of some leaders is a result of an ingrained fear of becoming the *object* for other people—for to become the *object* arouses fears that subordinates will become envious and compete for power.

Paranoid Thinking

This is a form of distortion in ideas and perception to which all human beings are susceptible from time to time. For those individuals who are concerned in their work with the consolidation and uses of power, the experience with suspiciousness, the attribution of bad motives to others, jealousy, and anxiety (characteristics of paranoid thinking), may be more than a passing state of mind.

In fact, such ideas and fantasies may indeed be communicated to others and may even be the main force which binds men into collusions. Organizational life is particularly vulnerable to the effects of paranoid thinking because it stimulates comparisons while it evokes anticipations of added power or fears of diminished power.

To complicate matters even more and to suggest just how ambiguous organizational decisions become, there may be some truth and substance in back of the suspicions, distrust, and jealousies which enflame thinking. Personality conflicts do affect decisions in allocating authority and responsibility, and an individual may not be distorting at all to sense exclusion or denial of an ambition based on some undercurrents in relationships with others. To call these sensitivities paranoid thinking may itself be a gross distortion. But no matter how real the events, the paranoid potential is still high as a fallout of organizational life.

Paranoid thinking goes beyond suspiciousness, distrust, and jealousy. It may take the form of grandiose ideas and overestimation of one's power and control. This form of distortion leads to swings in mood from elation to despair, from a sense of omnipotence to helplessness. Again, when acted out, the search for complete control produces the tragedies which the initial distortions attempt to overcome. The tragedy of Jimmy Hoffa is a good case in point. Consider:

> ☐ From all indications, Hoffa performed brilliantly as president of the teamsters' union. He was a superb organizer and bargainer, and in many ways a highly moral and even prudish man. There is little evidence to support allegations that he used his office to enrich himself.
>
> Hoffa's troubles stemmed from his angry reactions when he could not get his way in managing the union's pension fund and from his relations with the government. In overestimating his power, Hoffa fell victim to the illusion that no controls outside himself could channel his actions. One of the results of the issue is that Hoffa served a sentence in Lewisburg Penitentiary for jury tampering.
>
> It is interesting to note that Hoffa's successor delegated considerable authority to regional officers, a step that removed him from direct

comparisons with Hoffa and served to cement a coalition of top officers in the teamsters.

Executives, too, can be victims of their successes just as much as of their failures. If past successes lead to the false sense of omnipotence which goes unchecked in, say, the executive's control of the board of directors, then the executive and the organization become the victims of changing times and competitive pressures along with the weakening in perception and reasoning which often accompanies aging.

One could speculate with some reason that paranoid distortions are the direct result of senility and the inability to accept the fact of death. While intellectually aware of the inevitability of death, gifted executives can sometimes not accept emotionally the ultimate in the limitations of power. The disintegration of personality in the conflict between the head and the heart is what we come to recognize as the paranoid potential in all forms of our collective relations.

Ritualistic Ceremonial

Any collective experience, such as organizational life with its capacity for charging the atmosphere in the imagery of power conflicts, can fall victim to rigidities. The rigidities I have in mind consist mainly of the formation and elaboration of structures, procedures, and other ceremonials which create the illusion of solving problems but in reality only give people something to act on to discharge valuable energies.

The best example of a ritualistic approach to real problems is the ever-ready solution of bringing people together in a committee on the naive grounds that the exchange of ideas is bound to produce a solution. There are even fads and fashions to ritualism as in the sudden appearance of favorite words like "brainstorming" or "synergism."

It is not that bringing people together to discuss problems is bad. Instead, it is the naive faith which accompanies such proposals, ultimately deflecting attention from where it properly belongs. Thus:

☐ In one research organization, professionals faced severe problems arising from personal jealousies as well as differences of opinion on the correct goals and content for the research program. Someone would periodically suggest that the problems could not be solved unless people came together, preferably for a weekend away from the job, to share ideas and really get down to the "nitty-gritty" of the problem. (It is interesting to note that no one ever defines the "nitty-gritty.") The group would indeed follow such suggestions and typically end the weekend with a feeling of euphoria brought on by considerable drinking and a sumptuous meal.

The most concrete proposal for action was in the idea that the basic problem stemmed from the organization's increased size so that people

> no longer knew one another and their work. The solution which appeared, only shortly to disappear, was to publish a laboratory newsletter that would keep people abreast of their colleagues' newest ideas.

In a more general vein, ritualism can be invoked to deal with any real or fancied danger, with uncertainty, ambivalent attitudes, or a sense of personal helplessness. Rituals are used even in the attempt to manipulate people. That power relations in organizations should become a fertile field for ritualism should not surprise anyone.

As I have tried to indicate, the problems of organizational life involve the dangers associated with losses of power; the uncertainties are legion especially in the recognition that there is no one best way to organize and distribute power, and yet any individual must make a commitment to some form of organization.

Ambivalent attitudes, such as the simultaneous experience of love and hate, are also associated with authority relationships, particularly in how superior-subordinate become the subject and object for the expression of dependency reactions. In addition, the sense of helplessness is particularly sensitized in the events which project gains and losses in power and status.

Finally, superior and subordinate in any power structure are constantly tempted to manipulate each other as a way of gaining control over one's environment, and the more so when there is a lack of confidence and credibility in the organization's efforts to solve problems in realistic ways.

The negative effects of ritualism are precisely in the expenditure of energy to carry out the rituals and also in the childlike expectation that the magic formulas of organizational life substitute for diagnosing and solving real problems. When the heads of organizations are unsure of the bases for the exercise of power and become defensive, the easy solution is to play for time by invoking rituals which may temporarily relieve anxiety.

Similarly, when executives fail to understand the structure and potential of the power coalitions they establish (either consciously or unconsciously), they increasingly rely on rituals to deflect attention away from their responsibilities. And, when leaders are timid men incapable of initiating or responding, the spontaneous reaction is to use people to act out rituals. Usually, the content and symbolism in the rituals provide important clues about the underlying defensiveness of the executive.

Obsessional Leaders. The gravitational pull to ceremonials and magic is irresistible. In positions of power, obsessional leaders use in their public performances the mechanisms of defense which originate in their private conflicts. These defenses include hyper-rationality, the isolation of thought and feeling, reactive behavior in turning anger into moral righteousness, and passive control of other people as well as their own thought processes.

Very frequently, particularly in this day and age of psychologizing conflict, obsessive leaders "get religion" and try to convert others into some new state of mind. The use of sensitivity training with its attachment to "openness" and "leveling" in power relations seems to be the current favorite.

What these leaders do not readily understand is the fallacy of imposing a total solution for the problem of power relations where reality dictates at best the possibility of only partial and transient solutions. To force openness through the use of group pressure in T-groups and to expect to sustain this pressure in everyday life is to be supremely ritualistic. People intelligently resist saying everything they think to other people because they somehow have a deep recognition that this route leads to becoming overextended emotionally and, ultimately, to sadistic relationships.

Intelligent Uses of Power. The choice fortunately is not between ritualistic civility and naive openness in human relationships, particularly where power is concerned. In between is the choice of defining those partial problems which can be solved and through which bright people can learn something about the intelligent uses of power.

We should not lose sight of the basic lesson that people in positions of power differ from "ordinary" human beings mainly in their capacity to impose their personal defenses onto the stage of corporate life. Fortunately, the relationships are susceptible to intelligent management, and it is to the nature of this intelligence that I wish to address the conclusion of this chapter.

Coming Full Circle

The main job of organizational life, whether it concerns developing a new political pyramid, making new appointments to executive positions, or undergoing management succession at top levels, is to bring talented individuals into location for the legitimate uses of power. This is bound to be a highly charged event in corporate relationships because of the real changes in power distributions and the emotional reactions people experience along with the incremental gains and losses of power.

The demand, on the one hand, is for objectivity in assessing people and needs (as opposed to pseudorationality and rationalizing). This objectivity, on the other hand, has to be salvaged from the impact of psychological stresses which impel people to act out fantasies associated with power conflicts. The stresses of change in power relations tend to increase defensiveness to which counterreactions of rationalizing and of mythmaking serve no enduring purpose except perhaps to drive underground the concerns which make people react defensively in the first place.

Stylistic Biases

Thought and action in the politics of organizational life are subject to the two kinds of errors commonly found in practical life: the errors of omission and those of commission. It is both what people do and what they neglect to do that result in the negative effects of action outweighing the positive. But besides the specific errors of omission and commission (the tactical aspects of action), there are also the more strategic aspects which have to be evaluated. The strategic aspects deal both with the corporate aims and objectives and with the style of the leaders who initiate change.

In general, leaders approach change with certain stylistic biases over which they may not have too much control. There is a preferred approach to power problems which derives from the personality defenses of the leader and as well as from the realities of the situation. Of particular importance as stylistic biases are the preferences for partial, as contrasted with total, approaches and the preferences for substance over form.

Partial vs. Total. The partial approaches attempt to define and segregate problems which become amenable to solution by directive, negotiation, consensus, and compromise.

The total approaches usually escalate the issues in power relations so that implicitly people act as though it were necessary to undergo major conversions. The conversions can be directed toward personality structure, ideals, and beliefs, or toward values which are themselves connected to important aspects of personal experience.

When conversions become the end products of change, then one usually finds the sensitization of concerns over such matters as who dominates and who submits, who controls and who is being controlled, who is accepted and who is rejected. The aftermath of these concerns is the heightening of fantasy and defense at the expense of reality.

It may come as something of a disappointment to readers who are favorably disposed to psychology to consider the possibility that while organizations do have an impact on the attitudes of their constituent members, they cannot change personality structures or carry out therapeutic procedures. People may become more effective while working in certain kinds of organizations, but only when effectiveness is not dependent on the solution of neurotic conflict.

The advocates of total approaches seem to miss this point in their eagerness to convert people and organizations from one set of ideals to another. It becomes a good deal wiser, if these propositions are true, to scale down and make concrete the objectives that one is seeking to achieve.

A good illustration is in the attention given to decentralization of authority. Decentralization can be viewed in the image of conversion to certain ideals about who should have power and how this power should be used responsibly, or through an analytical approach to decide selectively where power is ill-placed and ill-used and to work on change at these locations. In other words, the theory of the partial approach to organizations asserts priorities and depends on good diagnostic observation and thought.

Substance vs. Form. Leaders can also present a stylistic bias in their preference for substance or form. Substance, in the language of organizations, is the detail of goals and performance—that is, who has to do what with whom to meet specific objectives. Form directs attention to the relationship of "who to whom" and attempts to achieve goals by specifying how the people should act in relation to each other.

There is no way in which matters of form can be divorced from substance. But students of organization should at least be clear that attention to form *ahead of* substance threatens a person's sense of what is reasonable in undertaking actions. Attention to form may also present an implicit attack on one's conception of one's independence and freedom from constraint.

Making form secondary to substance has another virtue: it can secure agreement on priorities without the need of predetermining who will have to give way in the ultimate give-and-take of the negotiations that must precede decisions on organization structure.

The two dimensions of bias, shown in the Exhibit 1 matrix, along with the four cells which result, clarify different executive approaches to power. The two dimensions define the executive's cognitive biases in: (1) selection of goals (partial vs. total), and (2) orientation toward action (form vs. substance).

In the *bureaucratic* approach—that is, partial goals and attachment to form as a mode of acting—the emphasis is on procedure and the establishment of precedent and rule to control the uses of power.

The appeal of this approach is its promise of certainty in corporate relationships and in the depersonalization of power. The weaknesses of the bureaucratic approach are too familiar to need detailing here. Its major defect, however, is its inability to separate the vital from the trivial. It more easily commands energy over irrelevant issues because the latent function of the bureaucratic approach is to bypass conflict.

My contention here is that few important problems can be attended to without conflict of ideas and interests. Eventually organizations become stagnant because the bureaucratic approaches seldom bring together power and the vital issues which together make organizations dynamic.

The *conversion* approach (total-form) is notable through the human relations and sensitivity training movements as well as ideological programs, such as the Scanlon Plan and other forms of participative management. The popularity of "management by objectives" bears some scrutiny as a conversion movement directed toward power figures.

Another "total" approach which differs from conversion in its emphasis on substance is *compliance* with the directives of the powerful leader. This is the arena of the authoritarian personality (in both the leader, who has the power, and in the led, who seek submission), for whom personal power gets expressed in some higher goal that makes it possible for ends to justify means. The ideals may, for example, be race, as with dictator Adolf

Exhibit 1. Cognitive Management Styles in Organizational Life

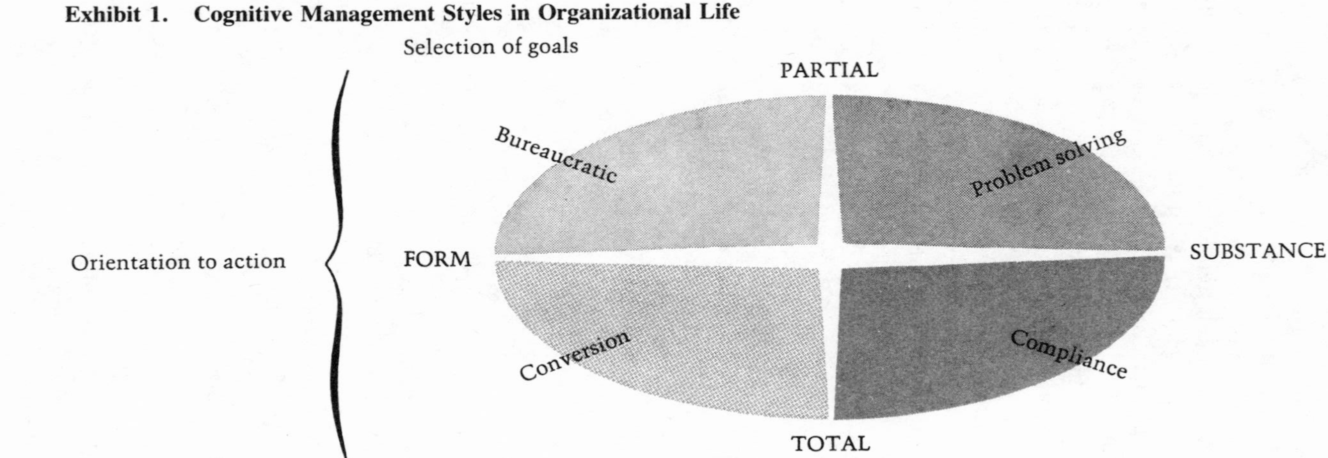

Hitler, or religion, as with Father Charles Coughlin, a dictator-type of the depression. In business, the illustrations are of a technological variety as with Frederick Winslow Taylor's "scientific management" and Henry Ford's automobile and assembly line.

Almost any technology can assume the proportions of the total approach if it is advanced by a charismatic leader and has deep emotional appeal. This explains the popularity of "management information systems," "value analysis," and "program planning and budgeting" which lead to a belief that the system itself is based on order, rationality, and control; therefore, the belief in turn helps to counteract the fears of chaos and lack of control which make people willing to demand total dependence and compliance in power relations. The effects of this fear on how people seek to arrange power relations in business, government, and the community cannot be overestimated.

Problem-Solving Approach

It should be perfectly obvious by now that my favored approach to organizational life combines the biases in Exhibit 1 of the partial substantive quadrant which I have designated "problem solving." From observation of competent business executives, we know it is precisely their ability to define problems worthy of thought and action and to use their organization to evolve solutions which characterize their style.

The contrary notion that executives are primarily caretakers, mediators, and seekers of consensus is more a myth than an accurate portrayal of how the competent ones attach themselves to power. To have power and not direct it to some substantive end that can be attained in the real world is to waste energy. The difficulties with the problem-solving approach are in risking power in favor of a substantive goal.

While there are no absolute right answers in problem solving, there are ways of evaluating the correctness of a program and plan. With a favorable average, the executive finds his power base enhanced and his ability to take risks increased.

The problem-solving approach to organization structure operates according to certain premises:

1. That organization structure is an instrument rather than an end. This means that a structure should be established or modified quickly instead of stringing out deliberations as though there actually exists a best and single solution for the problem of allocating power.
2. That organization structure can be changed but should not be tinkered with. This means that members of an executive organization can rely on a structure and can implement it without the uncertainty which comes from the constant modification of the organization chart.
3. That organization structure expresses the working coalition attached to the chief executive. In other words, the coalition has to be estab-

lished de facto for the structure to mean anything. If the structure is out of line with the coalition, there will be an erosion of power and effectiveness. If no coalition exists in the minds of participants, putting it on paper in the form of an organization chart is nothing more than an academic exercise and a confusing one at that.

4. That organization structure represents a blend of people and job definitions, but the priority is in describing the structure to accommodate competent people. The reason for this priority lies in the fact that competent executives are hard to find. Therefore, as an action principle, one should ensure the effective uses of the scarcest resources rather than conform to some ideal version of power relations.

5. That organization structure is a product of negotiation and compromise among executives who hold semiautonomous power bases. The more the power base of an executive is his or her demonstrated competence, the greater his or her autonomy of power and therefore capacity to determine the outcome in the allocations of power.

The basic criticism of the problem-solving approach is in the danger of defining issues narrowly and ultimately undermining the moral-ethical basis of leadership. This criticism is valid, but as with so many problems in practical affairs, it can be overcome only by leaders who can see beyond the limits of immediate contingencies. In fact, I have tried to show throughout this article how the limitations of leaders, in both their cognitive and emotional capacities, become the causes of power problems.

We have therefore come full circle in this analysis: because power problems are the effects of personality on structure, the solutions demand thinking which is free from the disabilities of emotional conflicts. This insight is often the margin between enduring with what exists or taking those modest steps which align competence with institutional authority in the service of human needs.

Notes

1. See Abraham Zaleznik, "The Management of Disappointment," *HBR*, November–December 1967, p. 59, and Chapter 11, this volume.

2. See Chester Barnard, *The Function of the Executive* (Cambridge, Mass., Harvard University Press, 1938), p. 167.

18

Power Is the Great Motivator

DAVID C. MCCLELLAND and DAVID H. BURNHAM

Good managers, those who get the best out of their subordinates and who thereby produce positive results for their organizations, are the keys to an organization's success. It is not surprising then that much research and thought have gone into trying to define just what motivates a good manager and how to describe the good characteristics so they can be objectively measured and identified. In this article, the authors describe a motivation pattern that empirical research has discovered most good managers share. Good managers are not motivated by a need for personal aggrandizement, or by a need to get along with subordinates, but rather by a need to influence others' behavior for the good of the whole organization. In other words, good managers want power. On its own, however, power can lead to authoritarianism, so it needs to be tempered by maturity and a high degree of self-control. The authors maintain that workshops can help a manager discover whether he or she has the correct motivation profile to be a good manager. Workshops can help most managers become good or better.

What makes or motivates a good manager? The question is so enormous in scope that anyone trying to answer it has difficulty knowing where to begin. Some people might say that a good manager is one who is successful; and by now most business researchers and business executives themselves know what motivates people who successfully run their own small businesses. The key to their success has turned out to be what psychologists call "the need for achievement," the desire to do something better or more efficiently than it has been done before. Any number of books and articles summarize research studies explaining how the achievement motive is necessary for people to attain success on their own.[1]

Author's Note. All the case material in this article is disguised.

But what has achievement motivation got to do with good management? There is no reason on theoretical grounds why a person who has a strong need to be more efficient should make a good manager. While it sounds as if everyone ought to have the need to achieve, in fact, as psychologists define and measure achievement motivation, it leads people to behave in very special ways that do not necessarily lead to good management.

For one thing, because they focus on personal improvement, on doing things better by themselves, achievement-motivated people want to do things themselves. For another, they want concrete short-term feedback on their performance so that they can tell how well they are doing. Yet a manager, particularly one of or in a large complex organization, cannot perform all the tasks necessary for success alone. The manager must lead others so that they will do things for the organization. Also, feedback on subordinates' performance may be a lot vaguer and more delayed than it would be if the manager were doing everything personally.

The manager's job seems to call more for someone who can influence people than for someone who does things better alone. In motivational terms, then, we might expect the successful manager to have a greater "need for power" than need to achieve. But there must be other qualities beside the need for power that go into the makeup of a good manager. Just what these qualities are and how they interrelate is the subject of this article.

To measure the motivations of managers, good and bad, we studied a number of individual managers from different large U.S. corporations who were participating in management workshops designed to improve their managerial effectiveness. (The workshop techniques and research methods and terms used are described in the appendix.)

The general conclusion of these studies is that the top manager of a company must possess a high need for power, that is, a concern for influencing people. However, this need must be disciplined and controlled so that it is directed toward the benefit of the institution as a whole and not toward the manager's personal aggrandizement. Moreover, the top manager's need for power ought to be greater than personal need for being liked by people.

Now let us look at what these ideas mean in the context of real individuals in real situations and see what comprises the profile of the good manager. Finally, we will look at the workshops themselves to determine how they go about changing behavior.

Measuring Managerial Effectiveness

First, what does it mean when we say that a good manager has a greater need for "power" than for "achievement"? To get a more concrete idea, let us consider the case of Ken Briggs, a sales manager in a large U.S. corporation who joined one of our managerial workshops (see the appendix).

Some six or seven years ago, Ken Briggs was promoted to a managerial position at corporate headquarters, where he had responsibility for salespeople who service his company's largest accounts.

In filling out his questionnaire at the workshop, Ken showed that he correctly perceived what his job required of him, namely, that he should influence others' success more than achieve new goals himself or socialize with his subordinates. However, when asked with other members of the workshop to write a story depicting a managerial situation, Ken unwittingly revealed through his fiction that he did not share those concerns. Indeed, he discovered that his need for achievement was very high—in fact over the 90th percentile—and his need for power was very low, in about the 15th percentile. Ken's high need to achieve was no surprise—after all, he had been a very successful sales executive—but obviously his motivation to influence others was much less than his job required. Ken was a little disturbed but thought that perhaps the measuring instruments were not too accurate and that the gap between the ideal and his score was not as great as it seemed.

Then came the real shocker. Ken's subordinates confirmed what his stories revealed: he was a poor manager, having little positive impact on those who worked for him. Ken's subordinates felt that they had little responsibility delegated to them, that he never rewarded but only criticized them, and that the office was not well organized, but confused and chaotic. On all three of these scales, his office rated in the 10th to 15th percentile relative to national norms.

As Ken talked the results over privately with a workshop leader, he became more and more upset. He finally agreed, however, that the results of the survey confirmed feelings he had been afraid to admit to himself or others. For years, he had been miserable in his managerial role. He now knew the reason: He simply did not want to nor had he been able to influence or manage others. As he thought back, he realized that he had failed every time he had tried to influence his staff, and he felt worse than ever.

Ken had responded to failure by setting very high standards—his office scored in the 98th percentile on this scale—and by trying to do most things himself, which was close to impossible; his own activity and lack of delegation consequently left his staff demoralized. Ken's experience is typical of those who have a strong need to achieve but low power motivation. They may become very successful sales executives and, as a consequence, may be promoted into managerial jobs for which they, ironically, are unsuited.

If achievement motivation does not make a good manager, what motive does? It is not enough to suspect that power motivation may be important; one needs hard evidence that people who are better managers than Ken Briggs do in fact possess stronger power motivation and perhaps score higher in other characteristics as well. But how does one decide who is the better manager?

Real-world performance measures are hard to come by if one is trying to rate managerial effectiveness in production, marketing, finance, or research and development. In trying to determine who the better managers were in Ken Briggs's company, we did not want to rely only on the opinions of their superiors. For a variety of reasons, superiors' judgments of their subordinates' real-world performance may be inaccurate. In the absence of some standard measure of performance, we decided that the next best index of a manager's effectiveness would be the climate the manager creates in the office, reflected in the morale of subordinates.

Almost by definition, a good manager is one who, among other things, helps subordinates feel strong and responsible, who rewards them properly for good performance, and who sees that things are organized in such a way that subordinates feel they know what they should be doing. Above all, managers should foster among subordinates a strong sense of team spirit, of pride in working as part of a particular team. If a manager creates and encourages this spirit, subordinates certainly should perform better.

In the company Ken Briggs works for, we have direct evidence of a connection between morale and performance in the one area where performance measures are easy to come by—namely, sales. In April 1973, at least three employees from this company's 16 sales districts filled out questionnaires that rated their office for organizational clarity and team spirit (see the appendix). Their scores were averaged and totaled to give an overall morale score for each office. The percentage gains or losses in sales for each district in 1973 were compared with those for 1972. The difference in sales figures by district ranged from a gain of nearly 30% to a loss of 8%, with a median gain of around 14%. Exhibit 1 shows the average gain in sales performance plotted against the increasing averages in morale scores.

In Exhibit 1 we can see that the relationship between sales and morale is surprisingly close. The six districts with the lowest morale early in the year showed an average sales gain of only around 7% by year's end (although there was wide variation within this group), whereas the two districts with the highest morale showed an average gain of 28%. When morale scores rise above the 50th percentile in terms of national norms, they seem to lead to better sales performance. In Ken Briggs's company, at least, high morale at the beginning is a good index of how well the sales division actually performed in the coming year.

And it seems very likely that the manager who can create high morale among sales executives can also do the same for employees in other areas (production, design, and so on), leading to better performance. Given that high morale in an office indicates that there is a good manager present, what general characteristics does this manager possess?

A Need for Power

In examining the motive scores of over 50 managers of both high and low morale units in all sections of the same large company, we found that most of the managers—over 70%—were high in power motivation compared with

Exhibit 1. Correlation Between Morale Score and Sales Performance for a Large U.S. Corporation

Average percent gain in sales by district from 1972 to 1973

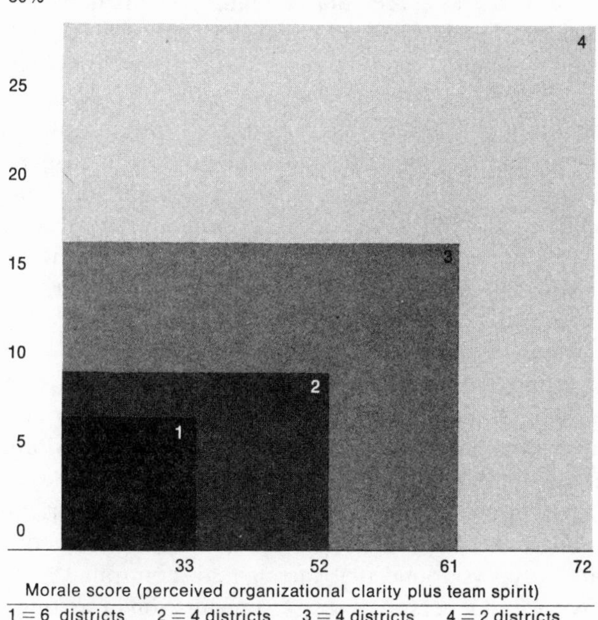

men in general. This finding confirms the fact that power motivation is important for management. (Remember that as we use the term "power motivation," it refers not to dictatorial behavior, but to a desire to have impact, to be strong and influential.) The better managers, as judged by the morale of those working for them, tended to score even higher in power motivation. But the most important determining factor of high morale turned out not to be how their power motivation compared to their need to achieve but whether it was higher than their need to be liked. This relationship existed for 80% of the better sales managers as compared with only 10% of the poorer managers. And the same held true for other managers in nearly all parts of the company.

In the research, product development, and operations divisions, 73% of the better managers had a stronger need for power than a need to be liked (or what we term "affiliation motive") as compared with only 22% of the poorer managers. Why should this be so? Sociologists have long argued that, for a bureaucracy to function effectively, those who manage it must be universalistic in applying rules. That is, if they make exceptions for the particular needs of individuals, the whole system will break down.

The manager with a high need for being liked is precisely the one who wants to stay on good terms with everybody, and, therefore, is the one most likely to make exceptions in terms of particular needs. If a male employee asks for time off to stay home with his sick wife to help look after her and the kids, the affiliative manager agrees almost without thinking, because he feels sorry for the man and agrees that his family needs him.

When President Ford remarked in pardoning ex-President Nixon that he had "suffered enough," he was responding as an affiliative manager would, because he was empathizing primarily with Nixon's needs and feelings. Sociological theory and our data both argue, however, that the person whose need for affiliation is high does not make a good manager. This kind of person creates poor morale because of a lack of understanding that other people in the office will tend to regard exceptions to the rules as unfair to themselves, just as many U.S. citizens felt it was unfair to let Richard Nixon off and punish others less involved than he was in the Watergate scandal.

Socialized Power

But so far our findings are a little alarming. Do they suggest that the good manager is one who cares for power and is not at all concerned about the needs of other people? Not quite, for the good manager has other characteristics which must still be taken into account.

Above all, the good manager's power motivation is not oriented toward personal aggrandizement but toward the institution being served. In another major research study, we found that the signs of controlled action or inhibition that appear when a person exercises imagination in writing stories tell a great deal about the kind of power that person needs.[2] We discovered that, if a high power motive score is balanced by high inhibition, stories about power tend to be altruistic. That is, the heroes in the story exercise power on behalf of someone else. This is the "socialized" face of power as distinguished from the concern for personal power, which is characteristic of individuals whose stories are loaded with power imagery but which show no sign of inhibition or self-control. In our earlier study, we found ample evidence that these latter individuals exercise their power impulsively. They are more rude to other people, they drink too much, they try to exploit others sexually, and they collect symbols of personal prestige such as fancy cars or big offices.

Individuals high in power and in control, on the other hand, are more institution minded; they tend to get elected to more offices, to control their drinking, and to want to serve others. Not surprisingly, we found in the workshops that the better managers in the corporation also tend to score high on both power and inhibition.

Profile of a Good Manager

Let us recapitulate what we have discussed so far and have illustrated with data from one company. The better managers we studied are high in power motivation, low in affiliation motivation, and high in inhibition. They care about institutional power and use it to stimulate their employees to be more productive. Now let us compare them with affiliative managers—those in whom the need for affiliation is higher than the need for power—and with the personal power managers—those in whom the need for power is higher than for affiliation but whose inhibition score is low.

In the sales division of our illustrative company, there were managers who matched the three types fairly closely. Exhibit 2 shows how their subordinates rated the offices they worked in on responsibility, organizational clarity, and team spirit. There are scores from at least three subordinates for each manager, and several managers are represented for each type, so that the averages shown in the exhibit are quite stable. Note that the manager who is concerned about being liked by people tends to have subordinates who feel that they have very little personal responsibility, that organizational procedures are not clear, and that they have little pride in their work group.

In short, as we expected, affiliative managers make so many ad hominem and ad hoc decisions that they almost totally abandon orderly procedures. Their disregard for procedure leaves employees feeling weak, irre-

Exhibit 2. Average Scores on Selected Climate Dimensions by Subordinates of Managers With Different Motive Profiles

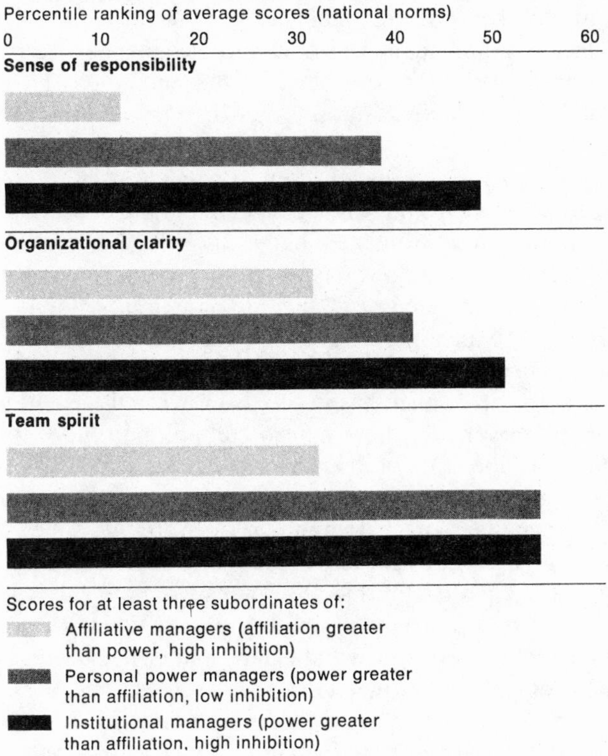

Percentile ranking of average scores (national norms)

0 10 20 30 40 50 60

Sense of responsibility

Organizational clarity

Team spirit

Scores for at least three subordinates of:

Affiliative managers (affiliation greater than power, high inhibition)

Personal power managers (power greater than affiliation, low inhibition)

Institutional managers (power greater than affiliation, high inhibition)

sponsible, and without a sense of what might happen next, of where they stand in relation to their manager, or even of what they ought to be doing. In this company, the group of affiliative managers portrayed in Exhibit 2 were below the 30th percentile in morale scores.

The managers who are motivated by a need for personal power are somewhat more effective. They are able to create a greater sense of responsibility in their divisions and, above all, a greater team spirit. They can be thought of as managerial equivalents of successful tank commanders such as General Patton, whose own daring inspired admiration in his troops. But notice how in Exhibit 2 these men are still only in the 40th percentile in the amount of organizational clarity they create, as compared to the high power, low affiliation, high inhibition managers, whom we shall term "institutional."

Managers motivated by personal power are not disciplined enough to be good institution builders, and often their subordinates are loyal to them as individuals rather than to the institution they both serve. When a personal power manager leaves, disorganization often follows. Subordinates' strong group spirit, which the manager has personally inspired, deflates. The subordinates do not know what to do for themselves.

Of the managerial types, the "institutional" manager is the most successful in creating an effective work climate. Exhibit 2 shows that subordinates feel that they have more responsibility. Also, this kind of manager creates high morale because this manager produces the greatest sense of organizational clarity and team spirit. If such a manager leaves, another manager can more readily step in because the employees have been encouraged to be loyal to the institution rather than to a particular person.

Managerial Styles

Since it seems undeniable from Exhibit 2 that either kind of power orientation creates better morale in subordinates than a "people" orientation, we must consider that a concern for power is essential to good management. Our findings seem to fly in the face of a long and influential tradition of organizational psychology, which insists that authoritarian management is what is wrong with most businesses in this country. Let us say frankly that we think the bugbear of authoritarianism has in fact been wrongly used to downplay the importance of power in management. After all, management is an influence game. Some proponents of democratic management seem to have forgotten this fact, urging managers to be primarily concerned with people's human needs rather than with helping them to get things done.

But a good deal of the apparent conflict between our findings and those of other behavioral scientists in this area arises from our talking about *motives* and behaviorists often talking about *actions*. What we are saying is that managers must be interested in playing the influence game in a controlled way. That does not necessarily mean that they are or should be authoritarian in action. On the contrary, it appears that power-motivated managers make their subordinates feel strong rather than weak. The true authoritarian in action would have the reverse effect, making people feel weak and powerless.

Thus another important ingredient in the profile of a manager is managerial style. In the illustrative company, 63% of the better managers (those whose subordinates had higher morale) scored higher on the democratic or coaching styles of management as compared with only 22% of the poorer managers, a statistically significant difference. By contrast, the latter scored higher on authoritarian or coercive management styles. Since the better managers were also higher in power motivation, it seems that, in action, they express their power motivation in a democratic way, which is more likely to be effective.

To see how motivation and style interact, let us consider the case of George Prentice, a manager in the sales division of another company. George had exactly the right motive combination to be an institutional manager. He was high in the need for power, low in the need for affiliation, and high in inhibition. He exercised power in a controlled, organized way. His stories reflected this fact. In one, for instance, he wrote, "The men sitting around the table were feeling pretty good; they had just finished plans for reorganizing the company; the company has been beset with a number of organizational problems. This group, headed by a hard-driving, brilliant young executive, has completely reorganized the company structurally with new jobs and responsibilities. . . ."

This described how George himself was perceived by the company, and shortly after the workshop he was promoted to vice president in charge of all sales. But George was also known to his colleagues as a monster, a tough guy who would "walk over his grandmother" if she stood in the way of his advancement. He had the right motive combination and, in fact, was more interested in institutional growth than in personal power, but his managerial style was all wrong. Taking his cue from some of the top executives in the corporation, he told people what they had to do and threatened them with dire consequences if they didn't do it.

When George was confronted with his authoritarianism in a workshop, he recognized that this style was counterproductive—in fact, in another part of the study we found that it was associated with low morale—and he subsequently changed to acting more like a coach, which was the scale on which he scored the lowest initially. George saw more clearly that his job was not to force other people to do things but to help them to figure out ways of getting their job done better for the company.

The Institutional Manager

One reason it was easy for George Prentice to change managerial style was that in his imaginative stories he was already having thoughts about helping others, characteristic of people with the institution-building motivational pattern. In further examining institution builders' thoughts and actions, we found they have four major characteristics:

1. They are more organization-minded; that is, they tend to join more organizations and to feel responsible for building up these organizations.

Furthermore, they believe strongly in the importance of centralized authority.

2. They report that they like to work. This finding is particularly interesting, because our research on achievement motivation has led many commentators to argue that achievement motivation promotes the "Protestant work ethic." Almost the precise opposite is true. People who have a high need to achieve like to get out of work by becoming more efficient. They would like to see the same result obtained in less time or with less effort. But managers who have a need for institutional power actually seem to like the discipline of work. It satisfies their need for getting things done in an orderly way.

3. They seem quite willing to sacrifice some of their own self-interest for the welfare of the organization they serve. For example, they are more willing to make contributions to charities.

4. They have a keen sense of justice. It is almost as if they feel that if a person works hard and sacrifices for the good of the organization, he should and will get a just reward for his effort.

It is easy to see how each of these four concerns helps a person become a good manager, concerned about what the institution can achieve.

Maturity. Before we go on to look at how the workshops can help managers to improve their managerial style and recognize their own motivations, let us consider one more fact we discovered in studying the better managers at George Prentice's company. They were more mature (see the appendix). Mature people can be most simply described as less egotistic. Somehow their positive self-image is not at stake in what they are doing. They are less defensive, more willing to seek advice from experts, and have a longer range view. They accumulate fewer personal possessions and seem older and wiser. It is as if they have awakened to the fact that they are not going to live forever and have lost some of the feeling that their own personal future is all that important.

Many U.S. business executives fear this kind of maturity. They suspect that it will make them less hard driving, less expansion-minded, and less committed to organizational effectiveness. Our data do not support their fears. These fears are exactly the ones George Prentice had before he went to the workshop. Afterward he was a more effective manager, not despite his loss of some of the sense of his own importance, but because of it. The reason is simple: his subordinates believed afterward that he genuinely was more concerned about the company than about himself. Where once they respected his confidence but feared him, they now trust him. Once he supported their image of him as a "big man" by talking about the new Porsche and the new Honda he had bought; when we saw him recently he said, almost as an aside, "I don't buy things anymore."

Changing Managerial Style

George Prentice was able to change his managerial style after learning more about himself in a workshop. But does self-knowledge generally improve managerial behavior?

Some people might ask, "What good does it do to know, if I am a manager, that I should have a strong power motive, not too great a concern about being liked, a sense of discipline, a high level of maturity, and a coaching managerial style? What can I do about it?" The answer is that workshops for managers that give information to them in a supportive setting enable them to change.

Consider the results shown in Exhibit 3, where "before" and "after" scores are compared. Once again we use the responses of subordinates to give some measure of the effectiveness of managers. To judge by their subordinates' responses, the managers were clearly more effective afterward. The subordinates felt that they were given more responsibility, that they received more rewards, that the organizational procedures were clearer, and that morale was higher. These differences are all statistically significant.

But what do these differences mean in human terms? How did the managers change? Sometimes they decided they should get into another line of work. This happened to Ken Briggs, for example, who found that the reason he was doing so poorly as a manager was because he had almost no

Exhibit 3. Average Scores on Selected Climate Dimensions by Over 50 Sales People Before and After Their Managers Were Trained

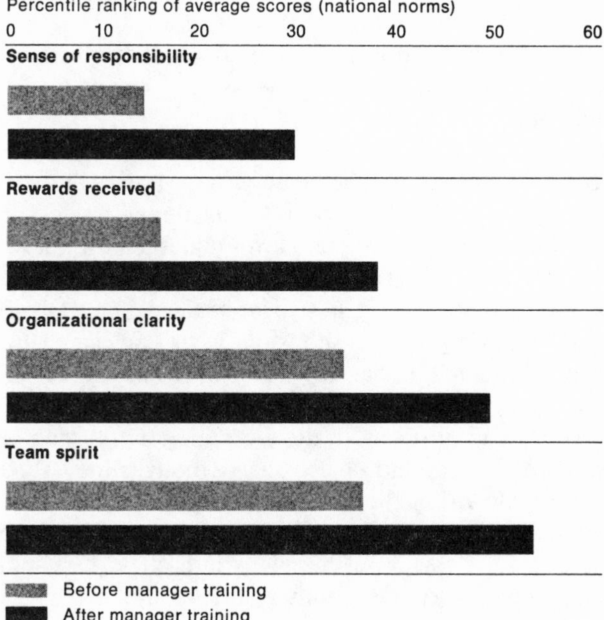

interest in influencing others. He understood how he would have to change if he were to do well in his present job, but in the end decided, with the help of management, that he would prefer to work back into his first love, sales.

Ken Briggs moved into "remaindering," to help retail outlets for his company's products get rid of last year's stock so that they could take on each year's new styles. He is very successful in this new role; he has cut costs, increased dollar volume, and in time has worked himself into an independent role selling some of the old stock on his own in a way that is quite satisfactory to the business. And he does not have to manage anybody anymore.

In George Prentice's case, less change was needed. He was obviously a very competent person with the right motive profile for a top managerial position. When he was promoted, he performed even more successfully than before because he realized the need to become more positive in his approach and less coercive in his managerial style.

But what about a person who does not want to change jobs and discovers a lack of the right motive profile to be a manager?

The case of Charlie Blake is instructive. Charlie was as low in power motivation as Ken Briggs, his need to achieve was about average, and his affiliation motivation was above average. Thus he had the affiliative manager profile, and, as expected, the morale among his subordinates was very low. When Charlie learned that his subordinates' sense of responsibility and perception of a reward system were in the 10th percentile and that team spirit was in the 30th, he was shocked. When shown a film depicting three managerial climates, Charlie said he preferred what turned out to be the authoritarian climate. He became angry when the workshop trainer and other members in the group pointed out the limitations of this managerial style. He became obstructive in the group process and objected strenuously to what was being taught.

In an interview conducted much later, Charlie said, "I blew my cool. When I started yelling at you for being all wrong, I got even madder when you pointed out that, according to my style questionnaire, you bet that that was just what I did to my salespeople. Down underneath I knew something must be wrong. The sales performance for my division wasn't so good. Most of it was due to me anyway and not to my salespeople. Obviously their reports that they felt very little responsibility was delegated to them and that I didn't reward them at all had to mean something. So I finally decided to sit down and try to figure what I could do about it. I knew I had to start being a manager instead of trying to do everything myself and blowing my cool at others because they didn't do what I thought they should. In the end, after I calmed down on the way back from the workshop, I realized that it is not so bad to make a mistake; it's bad not to learn from it."

After the course, Charlie put his plans into effect. Six months later, his subordinates were asked to rate him again. He attended a second workshop to study these results and reported, "On the way home I was very nervous. I knew I had been working with those guys and not selling so much myself, but I was very much afraid of what they were going to say about how things were going in the office. When I found out that the team spirit and some of those other low scores had jumped from around 30th to the 55th percentile, I was so delighted and relieved that I couldn't say anything all day long."

When he was asked how he acted differently from before, he said, "In previous years when the corporate headquarters said we had to make 110% of our original goal, I had called the salespeople in and said, in effect, 'This is ridiculous; we are not going to make it, but you know perfectly well what will happen if we don't. So get out there and work your tail off.' The result was that I worked 20 hours a day and they did nothing.

"This time I approached it differently. I told them three things. First, they were going to have to do some sacrificing for the company. Second, working harder is not going to do much good because we are already working about as hard as we can. What will be required are special deals and promotions. You are going to have to figure out some new angles if we are to make it. Third, I'm going to back you up. I'm going to set a realistic goal with each of you. If you make that goal but don't make the company goal, I'll see to it that you are not punished. But if you do make the company goal, I'll see to it that you will get some kind of special rewards."

When the salespeople challenged Charlie saying he did not have enough influence to give them rewards, rather than becoming angry Charlie promised rewards that were in his power to give—such as longer vacations.

Note that Charlie has now begun to behave in a number of ways that we found to be characteristic of the good institutional manager. He is, above all, higher in power motivation, the desire to influence his salespeople, and lower in his tendency to try to do everything himself. He asks the staff to sacrifice for the company. He does not defensively chew them out when they challenge him but tries to figure out what their needs are so that he can influence them. He realizes that his job is more one of strengthening and supporting his subordinates than of criticizing them. And he is keenly interested in giving them just rewards for their efforts.

The changes in his approach to his job have certainly paid off. The sales figures for his office in 1973 were up more than 16% over 1972 and up still further in 1974 over 1973. In 1973 his gain over the previous year ranked seventh in the nation; in 1974 it ranked third. And he wasn't the only one in his company to change managerial styles. Overall sales at his company were up substantially in 1973 as compared with 1972, an increase which played a large part in turning the overall company performance around from a $15 million loss in 1972 to a $3 million profit in 1973. The company continued to improve its performance in 1974 with an 11% further gain in sales and a 38% increase in profits.

Of course not everyone can be reached by a workshop. Henry Carter managed a sales office for a company which had very low morale (around the 20th percentile) before he went for training. When morale was checked some six months later, it had not improved. Overall sales gain subsequently reflected this fact since it was only 2% above the previous year's figures.

Oddly enough, Henry's problem was that he was so well liked by everybody that he felt little pressure to change. Always the life of the party, he is particularly popular because he supplies other managers with special hard-to-get brands of cigars and wines at a discount. He uses his close ties with everyone to bolster his position in the company, even though it is known that his office does not perform well compared with others.

His great interpersonal skills became evident at the workshop when he did very poorly at one of the business games. When the discussion turned to why he had done so badly and whether he acted that way on the job, two prestigious participants immediately sprang to his defense, explaining away Henry's failure by arguing that the way he did things was often a real help to others and the company. As a result, Henry did not have to cope with such questions at all. He had so successfully developed his role as a likeable, helpful friend to everyone in management that, even though his salespeople performed badly, he did not feel under any pressure to change.

Checks and Balances

What have we learned from Ken Briggs, George Prentice, Charlie Blake, and Henry Carter? Principally, we have discovered what motive combination makes an effective manager. We have also seen that change is possible if a person has the right combination of qualities.

Oddly enough, the good manager in a large company does not have a high need for achievement, as we define and measure that motive, although there must be plenty of that motive somewhere in his organization. The top managers shown here have a high need for power and an interest in influencing others, both greater than their interest in being liked by people. The manager's concern for power should be socialized—controlled so that the institution as a whole, not only the individual, benefits. People and nations with this motive profile are empire builders; they tend to create high morale and to expand the organizations they head.

But there is also danger in this motive profile; empire building can lead to imperialism and authoritarianism in companies and in countries.

The same motive pattern which produces good power management can also lead a company or a country to try to dominate others, ostensibly in the interest of organizational expansion. Thus it is not surprising that big business has had to be regulated from time to time by federal agencies. And it is most likely that international agencies will perform the same regulative function for empire-building countries.

For an individual, the regulative function is performed by two characteristics that are part of the profile of the very best managers—a greater emotional maturity, where there is little egotism, and a democratic, coaching managerial style. If an institutional power motivation is checked by maturity, it does not lead to an aggressive, egotistic expansiveness.

For countries, this checking means that they can control their destinies beyond their borders without being aggressive and hostile. For individuals, it means they can control their subordinates and influence others around them without resorting to coercion or to an authoritarian management style. Real disinterested policymaking has a vital role to play at the top of both countries and companies.

Summarized in this way, what we have found out through empirical and statistical investigations may just sound like good common sense. But the improvement over common sense is that now the characteristics of the good manager are objectively known. Managers of corporations can select those who are likely to be good managers and train those already in managerial positions to be more effective with more confidence.

Appendix: Workshop Techniques

The case studies and data on companies used in this article were derived from a number of workshops we conducted where executives came to learn about their managerial styles and abilities as well as how to change them. The workshops had a dual purpose, however. They provided an opportunity for us to study which motivation pattern, whether it be a concern for achievement, power, people, or a combination thereof, makes the best managers.

When the managers first arrived at the workshops, they were asked to fill out a questionnaire about their job. Each participant analyzed the job, explaining what he or she thought it required. The managers were asked to write a number of stories to pictures of various work situations. The stories were coded for the extent to which an individual was concerned about achievement, affiliation, or power, as well as for the amount of inhibition or self-control they revealed. The results were then matched against national norms. The differences between a person's job requirements and motivational patterns can often help assess whether the person is either in the right job, is a candidate for promotion to another job or is likely to be able to adjust to fit the present position.

At the workshops and in this article, we use the technical terms "need for achievement," "need for power," and "need for affiliation" as defined in the books *The Achieving Society* and *Power: The Inner Experience*. The terms refer to measurable factors in groups and individuals. Briefly, these characteristics are measured by coding an individual's spontaneous thoughts for the frequency with which the individual thinks about doing something better or more efficiently than before (need for achievement), about establishing or maintaining friendly relations with others (need for affiliation), or about having impact on others (need for power). (When we talk about power, we are not talking about dictatorial power, but about the need to be strong and influential.) As used here, therefore, the motive labels are precise terms, referring to a particular method of defining and measuring, much as "gravity" is used in physics, or "gross national product" is used in economics.

To find out what kind of managerial style the participants had, we gave them a questionnaire in which they had to choose how they would handle various realistic work situations in office settings. Their answers were coded for six different management styles or ways of dealing with work situations. The styles depicted were democratic, affiliative, pacesetting, coaching, coercive, and authoritarian. The managers were asked to comment on the effectiveness of each style and to name the style that they prefer.

One way to determine how effective managers are is to ask the people who work for them. Thus, to isolate the characteristics that good managers have, we surveyed at least three subordinates of each manager at the workshop to see how they answered questions about their work situations that revealed characteristics of their supervisors along several dimensions, namely: (1) the amount of conformity to rules required, (2) the responsibility they feel they are given, (3) the emphasis the department places on standards of performance, (4) the degree to which they feel rewards are given for good work as opposed to punishment for something that goes wrong, (5) the degree of organizational clarity in the office, and (6) its team spirit.[3] The managers who received the highest morale scores (organizational clarity plus team spirit) from their subordinates were determined to be the best managers, possessing the most desirable motive patterns.

The subordinates were also surveyed six months after the managers returned to their offices to see if the morale scores rose after the workshop.

One other measure was obtained from the participants to find out which managers had another characteristic deemed important for good management: maturity. Scores were obtained for four stages in the progress toward maturity by coding the stories which the managers wrote for such matters as their attitudes toward authority and the kinds of emotions displayed over specific issues.

People in Stage I are dependent on others for guidance and strength. Those in Stage II are interested primarily in autonomy, in controlling themselves. In Stage III, people want to manipulate others; in Stage IV, they lose their egotistic desires and wish to selflessly serve others.[4]

The conclusions presented in this article are based on workshops attended by over 500 managers from over 25 different U.S. corporations. However, the data in the exhibits are drawn from just one of these companies for illustrative purposes.

Notes

1. For instance, see David C. McClelland and David H. Burnham, *The Achieving Society* (New York, Van Nostrand, 1961) and David C. McClelland, David H. Burnham, and David Winter, *Motivating Economic Achievement* (New York, Free Press, 1969).

2. David C. McClelland, William N. Davis, Rudolf Kalin, and Erie Warner, *The Drinking Man* (New York, The Free Press, 1972).

3. Based on G. H. Litwin and R. A. Stringer, *Motivation and Organizational Climate* (Boston, Division of Research, Harvard Business School, 1966).

4. Based on work by Abigail Stewart reported in David C. McClelland, *Power: The Inner Experience* (New York, Irvington Publishers, 1975).

19

Power, Dependence, and Effective Management

JOHN P. KOTTER

Americans have probably always been suspicious of power—the United States was born out of a rebellion against it, and our political processes seem to confirm that distrust. We have equated power with exploitation and corruption. But, the author of this article asserts, the negative aspects of power have blinded people to its positive points, to its uses, and to the fact that, without it, people cannot accomplish very much anywhere. And that is especially true in management. The author maintains that, as organizations have grown more complex, it has become more difficult, if not impossible, for managers to achieve their ends either independently or through persuasion and formal authority alone. They increasingly need power to influence other people on whom they are dependent. Furthermore, he says, effective managers tend to be very successful at developing four different types of power, which they use along with persuasion to influence others. And they do so, the author concludes, with maturity, great skill, and a sensitivity to the obligations and risks involved.

Americans, as a rule, are not very comfortable with power or with its dynamics. We often distrust and question the motives of people who we think actively seek power. We have a certain fear of being manipulated. Even those people who think the dynamics of power are inevitable and needed often feel somewhat guilty when they themselves mobilize and use power.

Author's Note. This article is based on data from a clinical study of a highly diverse group of 26 organizations including large and small, public and private, manufacturing and service organizations. The study was funded by the Division of Research at the Harvard Business School. As part of the study process, the author interviewed about 250 managers.

Simply put, the overall attitude and feeling toward power, which can easily be traced to the nation's very birth, is negative. In his enormously popular *Greening of America,* Charles Reich reflects the views of many when he writes, "It is not the misuse of power that is evil; the very existence of power is evil."[1]

One of the many consequences of this attitude is that power as a topic for rational study and dialogue has not received much attention, even in managerial circles. If you doubt this, all you need do is flip through some textbooks, journals, or advanced management course descriptions. The word *power* rarely appears.

This lack of attention to the subject of power merely adds to the already enormous confusion and misunderstanding surrounding the topic of power and management. And this misunderstanding is becoming increasingly burdensome because in today's large and complex organizations the effective performance of most managerial jobs requires one to be skilled at the acquisition and use of power.

From my own observations, I suspect that a large number of managers—especially the young, well-educated ones—perform significantly below their potential because they do not understand the dynamics of power and because they have not nurtured and developed the instincts needed to effectively acquire and use power.

In this article I hope to clear up some of the confusion regarding power and managerial work by providing tentative answers to three questions:

1 Why are the dynamics of power necessarily an important part of managerial processes?
2 How do effective managers acquire power?
3 How and for what purposes do effective managers use power?

I will not address questions related to the misuse of power, but not because I think they are unimportant. The fact that some managers, some of the time, acquire and use power mostly for their own aggrandizement is obviously a very important issue that deserves attention and careful study. But that is a complex topic unto itself and one that has already received more attention than the subject of this article.

Recognizing Dependence in the Manager's Job

One of the distinguishing characteristics of a typical manager is how dependent he is on the activities of a variety of other people to perform his job effectively.[2] Unlike doctors and mathematicians, whose performance is more directly dependent on their own talents and efforts, a manager can be dependent in varying degrees on superiors, subordinates, peers in other parts of the organization, the subordinates of peers, outside suppliers, customers, competitors, unions, regulating agencies, and many others.

These dependency relationships are an inherent part of managerial jobs because of two organizational facts of life: division of labor and limited resources. Because the work in organizations is divided into specialized divisions, departments, and jobs, managers are made directly or indirectly dependent on many others for information, staff services, and cooperation in general. Because of their organization's limited resources, managers are also dependent on their external environments for support. Without some minimal cooperation from suppliers, competitors, unions, regulatory agencies, and customers, managers cannot help their organizations survive and achieve their objectives.

Dealing with these dependencies and the manager's subsequent vulnerability is an important and difficult part of a manager's job because, while it is theoretically possible that all of these people and organizations would automatically act in just the manner that a manager wants and needs, such is almost never the case in reality. All the people on whom a manager is dependent have limited time, energy, and talent, for which there are competing demands.

Some people may be uncooperative because they are too busy elsewhere, and some because they are not really capable of helping. Others may well have goals, values, and beliefs that are quite different and in conflict with the manager's and may therefore have no desire whatsoever to help or cooperate. This is obviously true of a competing company and sometimes of a union, but it can also apply to a boss who is feeling threatened by a manager's career progress or to a peer whose objectives clash with the manager's.

Indeed, managers often find themselves dependent on many people (and things) whom they do not directly control and who are not "cooperating." This is the key to one of the biggest frustrations managers feel in their jobs, even in the top ones, which the following example illustrates:

☐ After nearly a year of rumors, it was finally announced in May 1974 that the president of ABC Corporation had been elected chairman of the board and that Jim Franklin, the vice president of finance, would replace him as president. While everyone at ABC was aware that a shift would take place soon, it was not at all clear before the announcement who would be the next president. Most people had guessed it would be Phil Cook, the marketing vice president.

Nine months into his job as chief executive officer, Franklin found that Phil Cook (still the marketing vice president) seemed to be fighting him in small and subtle ways. There was never anything blatant, but Cook just did not cooperate with Franklin as the other vice presidents did. Shortly after being elected, Franklin had tried to bypass what he saw as a potential conflict with Cook by telling him that he would understand if Cook would prefer to move somewhere else where he could be a CEO also. Franklin said that it would be a big loss to the company but that he would be willing to help Cook in a number of ways if he wanted to look for a presidential opportunity elsewhere. Cook had thanked him but had said that family and community commitments would prevent him from relocating and all CEO opportunities were bound to be in a different city.

Since the situation did not improve after the tenth and eleventh months, Franklin seriously considered forcing Cook out. When he thought about the consequences of such a move, Franklin became more and more aware of just how dependent he was on Cook. Marketing and sales were generally the keys to success in their industry, and the company's sales force was one of the best, if not the best, in the industry. Cook had been with the company for 25 years. He had built a strong personal relationship with many of the people in the sales force and was universally popular. A mass exodus just might occur if Cook were fired. The loss of a large number of sales executives, or even a lot of turmoil in the department, could have a serious effect on the company's performance.

After one year as chief executive officer, Franklin found that the situation between Cook and himself had not improved and had become a constant source of frustration.

As a person gains more formal authority in an organization, the areas of vulnerability increase and become more complex rather than the reverse. As the previous example suggests, it is not at all unusual for the president of an organization to be in a highly dependent position, a fact often not apparent to either the outsider or to the lower level manager who covets the president's job.

A considerable amount of the behavior of highly successful managers that seems inexplicable in light of what management texts usually tell us managers do becomes understandable when one considers a manager's need for, and efforts at, managing relationships with others.[3] To be able to plan, organize, budget, staff, control, and evaluate, managers need some control over the many people on whom they are dependent. Trying to control others solely by directing them and on the basis of the power associated with one's position simply will not work—first, because managers are always dependent on some people over whom they have no formal authority, and second, because virtually no one in modern organizations will passively accept and completely obey a constant stream of orders from someone just because he or she is the "boss."

Trying to influence others by means of persuasion alone will not work either. Although it is very powerful and possibly the single most important method of influence, persuasion has some serious drawbacks too. To make it work requires time (often lots of it), skill, and information on the part of the persuader. And persuasion can fail simply because the other person chooses not to listen or does not listen carefully.

This is not to say that directing people on the basis of the formal power of one's position and persuasion are not important means by which successful managers cope. They obviously are. But, even taken together, they are not usually enough.

Successful managers cope with their dependence on others by being sensitive to it, by eliminating or avoiding unnecessary dependence, and by establishing power over those others. Good managers then use that power to help them plan, organize, staff, budget, evaluate, and so on. *In other words, it is primarily because of the dependence inherent in managerial jobs that the dynamics of power necessarily form an important part of a manager's processes.*

An argument that took place during a middle management training seminar I participated in a few years ago helps illustrate further this important relationship between a manager's need for power and the degree of dependence on others:

> ☐ Two participants, both managers in their thirties, got into a heated disagreement regarding the acquisition and use of power by managers. One took the position that power was absolutely central to managerial work, while the other argued that it was virtually irrelevant. In support of their positions, each described a very "successful" manager. In one of these examples, the manager seemed to be constantly developing and using power, while in the other, such behavior was rare. Subsequently, both seminar participants were asked to describe their successful managers' jobs in terms of the dependence *inherent* in those jobs.
>
> The young manager who felt power was unimportant described a staff vice president in a small company who was dependent only on the immediate subordinates, peers, and boss. This person, Joe Phillips, had to depend on his subordinates to do their jobs appropriately, but, if necessary, he could fill in for any of them or secure replacement for them rather easily. He also had considerable formal authority over them; that is, he could give them raises and new assignments, recommend promotions, and fire them. He was moderately dependent on the other four vice presidents in the company for information and cooperation. They were likewise dependent on him. The president had considerable formal authority over Phillips but was also moderately dependent on him for help, expert advice, the service his staff performed, other information, and general cooperation.
>
> The second young manager—the one who felt power was very important—described a service department manager, Sam Weller, in a large, complex, and growing company who was in quite a different position. Weller was dependent not only on his boss for rewards and information, but also on 30 other individuals who made up the divisional and corporate top management. And while his boss, like Phillips's was mod-

> erately dependent on him too, most of the top managers were not. Because Weller's subordinates, unlike Phillips's, had people reporting to them, Weller was dependent not only on his subordinates but also on his subordinates' subordinates. Because he could not himself easily replace or do most of their technical jobs, unlike Phillips, he was very dependent on all these people.
>
> In addition, for critical supplies, Weller was dependent on two other department managers in the division. Without their timely help, it was impossible for his department to do its job. These departments, however, did not have similar needs for Weller's help and cooperation. Weller was also dependent on local labor union officials and on a federal agency that regulated the division's industry. Both could shut his division down if they wanted.
>
> Finally, Weller was dependent on two outside suppliers of key materials. Because of the volume of his department's purchase relative to the size of these two companies, he had little power over them.
>
> Under these circumstances, it is hardly surprising that Sam Weller had to spend considerable time and effort acquiring and using power to manage his many dependencies, while Joe Phillips did not.

As this example also illustrates, not all management jobs require an incumbent to be able to provide the same amount of successful power-oriented behavior. But most management jobs today are more like Weller's than Phillips's. And, perhaps more important, the trend over the past two or three decades is away from jobs like Phillips's and toward jobs like Weller's. So long as our technologies continue to become more complex, the average organization continues to grow larger, and the average industry continues to become more competitive and regulated, that trend will continue; as it does so, the effective acquisition and use of power by managers will become even more important.

Establishing Power in Relationships

To help cope with the dependency relationships inherent in their jobs, effective managers create, increase, or maintain four different types of power over others.[4] Having power based in these areas puts the manager in a position both to influence those people on whom he or she is dependent when necessary and to avoid being hurt by any of them.

Sense of Obligation

One of the ways that successful managers generate power in their relationships with others is to create a sense of obligation in those others. When the manager is successful, the others feel that they should—rightly—allow the manager to influence them within certain limits.

Successful managers often go out of their way to do favors for people who they expect will feel an obligation to return those favors. As can be seen in the following description of a manager by a subordinate, some people are very skilled at identifying opportunities for doing favors that cost them very little but that others appreciate very much:

☐ Most of the people here would walk over hot coals in their bare feet if my boss asked them to. He has an incredible capacity to do little things that mean a lot to people. Today, for example, in his junk mail he came across an advertisement for something that one of my subordinates had in passing once mentioned that he was shopping for. So my boss routed it to him. That probably took 15 seconds of his time, and yet my subordinate really appreciated it. To give you another example, two weeks ago he somehow learned that the purchasing manager's mother had died. On his way home that night, he stopped off at the funeral parlor. Our purchasing manager was, of course, there at the time. I bet he'll remember that brief visit for quite a while.

Recognizing that most people believe that friendship carries with it certain obligations ("A friend in need . . ."), successful managers often try to develop true friendships with those on whom they are dependent. They will also make formal and informal deals in which they give something up in exchange for certain future obligations.

Belief in a Manager's Expertise

A second way successful managers gain power is by building reputations as "experts" in certain matters. Believing in the manager's expertise, others will often defer to the manager on those matters. Managers usually establish this type of power through visible achievement. The larger the achievement and the more visible it is, the more power the manager tends to develop.

One of the reasons that managers display concern about their "professional reputations" and their "track records" is that they have an impact on others' beliefs about their expertise. These factors become particularly important in large settings, where most people have only secondhand information about most other people's professional competence, as the following shows:

☐ Herb Randley and Bert Kline were both 35-year-old vice presidents in a large research and development organization. According to their closest associates, they were equally bright and competent in their technical fields and as managers. Yet Randley had a much stronger professional reputation in most parts of the company, and his ideas generally carried much more weight. Close friends and associates claim the reason that Randley is so much more powerful is related to a number of tactics that he has used more than Kline has.

Randley has published more scientific papers and managerial articles than Kline. Randley has been more selective in the assignments he has worked on, choosing those that are visible and that require his strong suits. He has given more speeches and presentations on projects that are his own achievements. And in meetings in general, he is allegedly forceful in areas where he has expertise and silent in those where he does not.

Identification With a Manager

A third method by which managers gain power is by fostering others' unconscious identification with them or with ideas they "stand for." Sigmund Freud was the first to describe this phenomenon, which is most clearly seen in the way people look up to "charismatic" leaders. Generally, the more a person finds a manager both consciously and (more important) unconsciously an ideal person, the more that person will defer to that manager.

Managers develop power based on others' idealized views of them in a number of ways. They try to look and behave in ways that others respect. They go out of their way to be visible to their employees and to give speeches about their organizational goals, values, and ideals. They even consider, while making hiring and promotion decisions, whether they will be able to develop this type of power over the candidates:

☐ One vice president of sales in a moderate-size manufacturing company was reputed to be so much in control of his sales force that he could get them to respond to new and different marketing programs in a third of the time taken by the company's best competitors. His power over his employees was based primarily on their strong identification with him and what he stood for. Emigrating to the United States at age 17, this person worked his way up "from nothing." When made a sales manager in 1965, he began recruiting other young immigrants and sons of immigrants from his former country. When made vice president of sales in 1970, he continued to do so. In 1975, 85% of his sales force was made up of people whom he hired directly or who were hired by others he brought in.

Perceived Dependence on a Manager

The final way that an effective manager often gains power is by feeding others' beliefs that they are dependent on the manager either for help or for not being hurt. The more they perceive they are dependent, the more most people will be inclined to cooperate with such a manager.

There are two methods that successful managers often use to create perceived dependence.

Finding and Acquiring Resources. First, the manager identifies and secures (if necessary) resources that another person requires to perform a job, that

that person does not possess, and that are not readily available elsewhere. These resources include such things as authority to make certain decisions; control of money, equipment, and office space; access to important people; information and control of information channels; and subordinates. Then the manager takes action so that the other person correctly perceives that the manager has such resources and is willing and ready to use them to help (or hinder) the other person. Consider the following extreme—but true—example.

When young Tim Babcock was put in charge of a division of a large manufacturing company and told to "turn it around," he spent the first few weeks studying it from afar. He decided that the division was in disastrous shape and that he would need to take many large steps quickly to save it. To be able to do that, he realized he needed to develop considerable power fast over most of the division's management and staff. He did the following:

- ☐ He gave the division's management two hours' notice of his arrival.
- ☐ He arrived in a limousine with six assistants.
- ☐ He immediately called a meeting of the 40 top managers.
- ☐ He outlined briefly his assessment of the situation, his commitment to turn things around, and the basic direction he wanted things to move in.
- ☐ He then fired the four top managers in the room and told them that they had to be out of the building in two hours.
- ☐ He then said he would personally dedicate himself to sabotaging the career of anyone who tried to block his efforts to save the division.
- ☐ He ended the 60-minute meeting by announcing that his assistants would set up appointments for him with each of them starting at 7:00 A.M. the next morning.

Throughout the critical six-month period that followed, those who remained at the division generally cooperated energetically with Mr. Babcock.

Affecting Perceptions of Resources. A second way effective managers gain these types of power is by influencing other persons' perceptions of the manager's resources.[5] In settings where many people are involved and where the manager does not interact continuously with those he or she is dependent on, those people will seldom possess "hard facts" regarding what relevant resources the manager commands directly or indirectly (through others), what resources the manager will command in the future, or how prepared the manager is to use those resources to help or hinder them. They will be forced to make their own judgments.

Insofar as a manager can influence people's judgments, the manager can generate much more power than one would generally think in light of the reality of the manager's resources.

In trying to influence people's judgments, managers pay considerable attention to the "trappings" of power and to their own reputations and images. Among other actions, they sometimes carefully select, decorate, and arrange their offices in ways that give signs of power. They associate with people or organizations that are known to be powerful or that others perceive as powerful. Managers selectively foster rumors concerning their own power. Indeed, those who are particularly skilled at creating power in this way tend to be very sensitive to the impressions that all their actions might have on others.

Formal Authority

Before discussing how managers use their power to influence others, it is useful to see how formal authority relates to power. By *formal authority*, I mean those elements that automatically come with a managerial job—perhaps a title, an office, a budget, the right to make certain decisions, a set of subordinates, a reporting relationship, and so on.

Effective managers use the elements of formal authority as resources to help them develop any or all of the four types of power previously discussed, just as they use other resources (such as their education). Two managers with the same formal authority can have very different amounts of power entirely because of the way they have used that authority. For example:

- ☐ By sitting down with employees who are new or with people who are starting new projects and clearly specifying who has the formal authority to do what, one manager creates a strong sense of obligation in others to defer to the manager's authority later.
- ☐ By selectively withholding or giving the high-quality service the department can provide other departments, other managers are made to see clearly that they are dependent on the manager of that department.

On its own, then, formal authority does not guarantee a certain amount of power; it is only a resource that managers can use to generate power in their relationships.

Exercising Power to Influence Others

Successful managers use the power they develop in their relationships, along with persuasion, to influence people on whom they are dependent to behave in ways that make it possible for the managers to get their jobs done effectively. They use their power to influence others directly, face to face, and in more indirect ways.

Exhibit 1. Methods of Influence

Face-to-Face Methods	What They Can Influence	Advantages	Drawbacks
Exercise obligation-based power.	Behavior within zone that the other perceives as legitimate in light of the obligation.	Quick. Requires no outlay of tangible resources.	If the request is outside the acceptable zone, it will fail; if it is too far outside, others might see it as illegitimate.
Exercise power based on perceived expertise.	Attitudes and behavior within the zone of perceived expertise.	Quick. Requires no outlay of tangible resources.	If the request is outside the acceptable zone, it will fail; if it is too far outside, others might see it as illegitimate.
Exercise power based on identification with a manager.	Attitudes and behavior that are not in conflict with the ideals that underlie the identification.	Quick. Requires no expenditure of limited resources.	Restricted to influence attempts that are not in conflict with the ideals that underlie the identification.
Exercise power based on perceived dependence.	Wide range of behavior that can be monitored.	Quick. Can often succeed when other methods fail.	Repeated influence attempts encourage the other to gain power over the influencer.
Coercively exercise power based on perceived dependence.	Wide range of behavior that can be easily monitored.	Quick. Can often succeed when other methods fail.	Invites retaliation. Very risky.

Exhibit 1. (*Continued*)

Face-to Face Methods	What They Can Influence	Advantages	Drawbacks
Use persuasion.	Very wide range of attitudes and behavior.	Can produce internalized motivation that does not require monitoring. Requires no power or outlay of scarce material resources.	Can be very time-consuming. Requires other person to listen.
Combine these methods.	Depends on the exact combination.	Can be more potent and less risky than using a single method.	More costly than using a single method.

Indirect Methods	What They Can Influence	Advantages	Drawbacks
Manipulate the other's environment by using any or all of the face-to-face methods.	Wide range of behavior and attitudes.	Can succeed when face-to-face methods fail.	Can be time-consuming. Is complex to implement. Is very risky, especially if used frequently.
Change the forces that continuously act on the individual: Formal organizational arrangements. Informal social arrangements. Technology. Resources available. Statement of organizational goals.	Wide range of behavior and attitudes on a continuous basis.	Has continuous influence, not just a one-shot effect. Can have a very powerful impact.	Often requires a considerable power outlay to achieve.

Face-to-Face Influence

The chief advantage of influencing others directly by exercising any of the types of power is speed. If the power exists and the manager correctly understands the nature and strength of it, the manager can influence the other person with nothing more than a brief request or command:

- Jones thinks Smith feels obligated to him for past favors. Furthermore, Jones thinks that his request to speed up a project by two days probably falls within a zone that Smith would consider legitimate in light of his own definition of his obligation to Jones. So Jones simply calls Smith and makes his request. Smith pauses for only a second and says yes, he'll do it.
- Manager Johnson has some power based on perceived dependence over manager Baker. When Johnson tells Baker that she wants a report done in 24 hours, Baker grudgingly considers the costs of compliance, of noncompliance, and of complaining to higher authorities. He decides that doing the report is the least costly action and tells Johnson he will do it.
- Young Porter identifies strongly with Marquette, an older manager who is not his boss. Porter thinks Marquette is the epitome of a great manager and tries to model himself after him. When Marquette asks Porter to work on a special project "that could be very valuable in improving the company's ability to meet new competitive products," Porter agrees without hesitation and works 15 hours per week above and beyond his normal hours to get the project done and done well.

When used to influence others, each of the four types of power has different advantages and drawbacks. For example, power based on perceived expertise or on identification with a manager can often be used to influence attitudes as well as someone's immediate behavior and thus can have a lasting impact. It is very difficult to influence attitudes by using power based on perceived dependence, but if it can be done, it usually has the advantage of being able to influence a much broader range of behavior than the other methods do. When exercising power based on perceived expertise, for example, one can only influence attitudes and behavior within that narrow zone defined by the "expertise."

The drawbacks associated with the use of power based on perceived dependence are particularly important to recognize. A person who feels dependent on a manager for rewards (or lack of punishments) might quickly agree to a request from the manager but then not follow through—especially if the manager cannot easily find out if the person has obeyed or not. Repeated influence attempts based on perceived dependence also seem to encourage the other person to try to gain some power to balance the manager's. And perhaps most important, using power based on perceived dependence in a coercive way is very risky. Coercion invites retaliation.

For instance, in the example in which Tim Babcock took such extreme steps to save the division he was assigned to "turn around," his development and use of power based on perceived dependence could have led to mass resignation and the collapse of the division. Babcock fully recognized this risk, however, and behaved as he did because he felt there was simply *no other way* that he could gain the very large amount of quick cooperation needed to save the division.

Effective managers will often draw on more than one form of power to influence someone, or they will combine power with persuasion. In general, they do so because a combination can be more potent and less risky than any single method, as the following description shows:

> ☐ "One of the best managers we have in the company has lots of power based on one thing or another over most people. But he seldom if ever just tells or asks someone to do something. He almost always takes a few minutes to try to persuade them. The power he has over people generally induces them to listen carefully and certainly disposes them to be influenced. That, of course, makes the persuasion process go quickly and easily. And he never risks getting the other person mad or upset by making what that person thinks is an unfair request or command."

It is also common for managers not to coercively exercise power based on perceived dependence by itself, but to combine it with other methods to reduce the risk of retaliation. In this way, managers are able to have a large impact without leaving the bitter aftertaste of punishment alone.

Indirect Influence Methods

Effective managers also rely on two types of less direct methods to influence those on whom they are dependent. In the first way, they use any or all of the face-to-face methods to influence other people, who in turn have some specific impact on a desired person.

Product manager Stein needed plant manager Billings to "sign off" on a new product idea (Product X) which Billings thought was terrible. Stein decided that there was no way he could logically persuade Billings because Billings just would not listen to him. With time, Stein felt, he could have broken through that barrier. But he did not have that time. Stein also realized that Billings would never, just because of some deal or favor, sign off on a product he did not believe in. Stein also felt it not worth the risk of trying to force Billings to sign off, so here is what he did:

> ☐ On Monday, Stein got Reynolds, a person Billings respected, to send Billings two market research studies that were very favorable to Product X, with a note attached saying, "Have you seen this? I found them rather surprising. I am not sure if I entirely believe them, but still. . . ."

> On Tuesday, Stein got a representative of one of the company's biggest customers to mention casually to Billings on the phone that he had heard a rumor about Product X being introduced soon and was "glad to see you guys are on your toes as usual."
>
> On Wednesday, Stein had two industrial engineers stand about three feet away from Billings as they were waiting for a meeting to begin and talk about the favorable test results on Product X.
>
> On Thursday, Stein set up a meeting to talk about Product X with Billings and invited only people whom Billings liked or respected and who also felt favorably about Product X.
>
> On Friday, Stein went to see Billings and asked him if he was willing to sign off on Product X. He was.

This type of manipulation of the environments of others can influence both behavior and attitudes and can often succeed when other influence methods fail. But it has a number of serious drawbacks. It takes considerable time and energy, and it is quite risky. Many people think it is wrong to try to influence others in this way, even people who, without consciously recognizing it, use this technique themselves. If they think someone is trying, or has tried, to manipulate them, they may retaliate. Furthermore, people who gain the reputation of being manipulators seriously undermine their own capacities for developing power and for influencing others. Almost no one, for example, will want to identify with a manipulator. And virtually no one accepts, at face value, a manipulator's sincere attempts at persuasion. In extreme cases, a reputation as a manipulator can completely ruin a manager's career.

A second way in which managers indirectly influence others is by making permanent changes in an individual's or a group's environment. They change job descriptions, the formal systems that measure performance, the extrinsic incentives available, the tools, people, and other resources that the people or groups work with, the architecture, the norms or values of work groups, and so on. If the manager is successful in making the changes, and the changes have the desired effect on the individual or group, that effect will be sustained over time.

Effective managers recognize that changes in the forces that surround a person can have great impact on that person's behavior. Unlike many of the other influence methods, this one doesn't require a large expenditure of limited resources or effort on the part of the manager on an ongoing basis. Once such a change has been successfully made, it works independently of the manager.

This method of influence is used by all managers to some degree. Many, however, use it sparingly simply because they do not have the power to change the forces acting on the person they wish to influence. In many organizations, only the top managers have the power to change the formal measurement systems, the extrinsic incentives available, the architecture, and so on.

Generating and Using Power Successfully

Managers who are successful at acquiring considerable power and using it to manage their dependence on others tend to share a number of common characteristics:

1. They are sensitive to what others consider to be legitimate behavior in acquiring and using power. They recognize that the four types of power carry with them certain "obligations" regarding their acquisition and use. A person who gains a considerable amount of power based on perceived expertise is generally expected to be an expert in certain areas. If it ever becomes publicly known that the person is clearly not an expert in those areas, such a person will probably be labeled a "fraud" and will not only lose power but will suffer other reprimands too.

A person with whom a number of people identify is expected to act like an ideal leader. If this person clearly lets people down, that power will not only be lost, but ex-followers will be righteously angry. Many managers who have created or used power based on perceived dependence in ways that their employees have felt unfair, such as in requesting overtime work, have ended up with unions.

2. They have good intuitive understanding of the various types of power and methods of influence. They are sensitive to what types of power are easiest to develop with different types of people. They recognize, for example, that professionals tend to be more influenced by perceived expertise than by other forms of power. They also have a grasp of all the various methods of influence and what each can accomplish, at what costs, and with what risks. (See Exhibit 1.) They are good at recognizing the specific conditions in any situation and then at selecting an influence method that is compatible with those conditions.

3. They tend to develop all the types of power, to some degree, and they use all the influence methods mentioned in Exhibit 1. Unlike managers who are not very good at influencing people, effective managers usually do not think that only some of the methods are useful or that only some of the methods are moral. They recognize that any of the methods, used under the right circumstances, can help contribute to organizational effectiveness with few dysfunctional consequences. At the same time, they generally try to avoid those methods that are more risky than others and those that may have dysfunctional consequences. For example, they manipulate the environment of others only when absolutely necessary.

4. They establish career goals and seek out managerial positions that allow them to successfully develop and use power. They look for jobs, for

example, that use their backgrounds and skills to control or manage some critically important problem or environmental contingency that an organization faces. They recognize that success in that type of job makes others dependent on them and increases their own perceived expertise. They also seek jobs that do not demand a type or a volume of power that is inconsistent with their own skills.

5. They use all of their resources, formal authority, and power to develop still more power. To borrow Edward Banfield's metaphor, they actually look for ways to "invest" their power where they might secure a high positive return.[6] For example, by asking a person for two important favors, a manager might be able to finish a construction program one day ahead of schedule. That request may cost most of the obligation-based power the manager has over that person, but in return the manager may significantly increase perceived expertise as a manager of construction projects in the eyes of everyone in the organization.

Just as in investing money, there is always some risk involved in using power this way; it is possible to get a zero return for a sizable investment, even for the most powerful manager. Effective managers do not try to avoid risks. Instead, they look for prudent risks, just as they do when investing capital.

6. Effective managers engage in power-oriented behavior in ways that are tempered by maturity and self-control.[7] They seldom, if ever, develop and use power in impulsive ways or for their own aggrandizement.

7. Finally, they also recognize and accept as legitimate that, in using these methods, they clearly influence other people's behavior and lives. Unlike many less effective managers, they are reasonably comfortable in using power to influence people. They recognize, often only intuitively, what this chapter is all about—that their attempts to establish power and use it are an absolutely necessary part of the successful fulfillment of their difficult managerial role.

Notes

1. Charles A. Reich, *The Greening of America: How the Youth Revolution Is Trying to Make America Liveable* (New York, Random House, 1970).

2. See Leonard R. Sayles, *Managerial Behavior: Administration in Complex Organization* (New York, McGraw-Hill, 1964) as well as Rosemary Stewart, *Managers and Their Jobs* (London, Macmillan, 1967) and *Contrasts in Management* (London, McGraw-Hill, 1976).

3. I am talking about the type of inexplicable differences that Henry Mintzberg has found; see his article "The Manager's Job: Folklore and Fact," *HBR*, July–August 1975, p. 49.

4. These categories closely resemble the five developed by John R. P. French and Bertram Raven; see "The Base of Social Power" in *Group Dynamics: Research and Theory*, edited by

Dorwin Cartwright and Alvin Zandler (New York, Harper & Row, 1968), Chapter 20. Three of the categories are similar to the types of "authority"-based power described by Max Weber in *The Theory of Social and Economic Organization* (New York, Free Press, 1947).

5. For an excellent discussion of this method, see Richard E. Neustadt, *Presidential Power* (New York, Wiley, 1960).

6. See Edward C. Banfield, *Political Influence* (New York, Free Press, 1965), Chapter 11.

7. See David C. McClelland and David H. Burnham, "Power Is the Great Motivator," *HBR*, March–April 1976, p. 100, and Chapter 18 of this volume.

20
Power and the Ambitious Executive

ROBERT N. McMURRY

The methods of holding top-management power in a company strike many people as devious and Machiavellian. They involve calculated alliances, compromises, and "deals"—and often they fly in the face of practices advocated by experts on organizational behavior. From the standpoint of the beleaguered and harrassed executive, however, there may be no substitute for them—if he or she wants to survive at the top.

The most important and unyielding necessity of organizational life is not better communications, human relations, or employee participation, but power. I define *power* as the capacity to modify the conduct of other employees in a desired manner, together with the capacity to avoid having one's own behavior modified in undesired ways by other employees. Executives must have power because, unfortunately, many employees resent discipline; to these employees, work is something to be avoided. In their value systems "happiness" is the ultimate goal. For the organization to be made productive, such persons must be subjected to discipline.

Without power there can be no authority; without authority, there can be no discipline; without discipline, there can be difficulty in maintaining order, system, and productivity. An executive without power is, therefore, all too often a figurehead—or worse, headless. The higher an executive is in the management hierarchy, the greater the need for power. This is because power tends to weaken as it is disseminated downward.

Gaining and Keeping Power

If the executive owns the business, that fact may ensure power. If the executive does not, and sometimes even when the executive does, power must be acquired and held by means which are essentially political. Of critical importance, since most of the executive's power is derived or delegated, it must be dependable. Nothing is more devastating to an executive than to lose support and backing in moments of crisis. For this reason the development of continuing power is the most immediate and nagging concern of many professional managers.

How can chief executives and other managers who possess little or no equity in a business consolidate enough power to protect their jobs and enforce their dictates when necessary? The eight recommendations which follow are the fruit of 30 years of observation of a great number of executives managing a variety of enterprises.

A number of these conclusions conflict with the findings of other writers. The most that can be said in defense of my recommendations is that they did not spring from an ivory tower. They are based on strategies and tactics employed by demonstrably successful executives who lacked financial control of their enterprises. The executives were working pragmatists. Their prime criterion of a desirable course of action was: Will it work? While the strategies presented here are not infallible, they have proven their worth more often than not in the hard and competitive world of business.

The executive should take all possible steps to ensure personal compatibility with superiors.

In the case of the chief executive, this means compatibility with the owners and/or their representatives, such as bankers, lawyers, and family members; in the case of other managers, senior executives and owners are the key groups. The point is that though a manager may have all the skills, experience, and personal attributes the managerial position requires, if personal values and goals are not reasonably consonant with those of the persons who hold power and the manager is not acceptable to them personally, the manager's tenure will probably be brief.

To protect against subsequent disillusionment and conflict, the prospective manager should, before joining the company, endeavor to become acquainted with the prospective superior or superiors informally. This could be done at dinner with them, on the golf course, or on a trip. At such a meeting the superior's values, standards, prejudices, and expectations can be learned. If any significant evidence of incompatibility emerges, the prospect should call off negotiations—incompatibility tends to worsen rather than improve with continued contact.

If at all possible, the manager's spouse should meet the superior, also under informal conditions, since compatibility with the spouse can play an important part in the new person's acceptance. Likewise, if it can be arranged for the manager's spouse to meet the chief's spouse, early in the course of negotiations, that should be done. Compatibility between these two can be very advantageous; incompatibility can be fatal.

Whether coming to the company from outside or being promoted from within, the executive should obtain an employment contract.

While many owners and senior executives protest that they never make such agreements and that it is against their policy to do so, the prospective manager must insist that every policy is subject to change and that there is no deal without one. A failure to win out at this most critical juncture can be fatal. The reason is not so much that failure strips away any vestige of job security and power but that it indicates to those in command that the prospect is somewhat docile and submissive and probably can be pushed about at their whim.

This is particularly true where the executive's primary assignment is to salvage and rehabilitate a sick or failing operation or to initiate and pioneer a new and radically different field of activity that no one in the business knows much about. The compensation may be alluring, the status attractively elevated, and the challenge exciting. But the risks have to be great. If worse comes to worst and the executive is removed, there will be a tidy sum to last the six months or longer that will be needed to find a new job.

On taking a major assignment, the executive should obtain from superiors a clear, concise, and unambiguous statement in writing of duties, responsibilities, reporting relationships, and scope of authority.

Such a document is absolutely essential if the manager is not later to make the humiliating and frustrating discovery that the parameters of the job have been changed, often without notice. The manager may have been led to believe at the outset that certain responsibilities and commensurate authority to carry them out pertained to the job. Later the manager may learn that no such authority came with the job and that some of the people who were thought of as subordinates in effect are not. The manager may discover a certain powerlessness, with all authority having been taken. If, after protesting, the manager cannot substantiate charges with a written commitment, the word is likely to be: "You have misunderstood our original agreement."

The executive should take exceptional care to find subordinates who combine technical competence with reliability, dependability, and loyalty.

As many a top executive has sorrowfully learned, the manager is constantly vulnerable to sabotage by underlings. This is especially the case when the manager comes in from outside and "does not know where the bodies are buried." It is for this reason that extreme care should be taken in the choice of immediate subordinates.

In theory, each superior, regardless of level in the management hierarchy, should have a strong, competent number-two executive who is ready and willing to step in should the superior be promoted, retire, leave the company, or for any reason be unable to continue to function. Some executives do just this. But in practice the policy can be hazardous, at least in terms of the senior person's job security.

An aggressive, ambitious, upwardly mobile number-two person is dangerous to any chief, weak or strong. For one thing, the number-two executive is often very difficult to control. This executive has a personal array of goals and objectives which may or may not be consistent with those of the superior and/or the company. Since the second executive is usually inner directed and possesses strong convictions, the number-two executive is often difficult to divert from set personal goals designed to be self-beneficial (and secondarily to benefit the company). The risk is considerably lessened if the chief has only one strong subordinate, for one is easier to watch and constrain.

Moreover, since the strong subordinate tends to be an individualist, this second lieutenant is more apt to be in conflict with peers. There is a compulsive need to achieve *personal* goals regardless of the needs or expectations of the others or of the welfare of the enterprise as a whole. This influence may not only be divisive but may also tend to fragment the enterprise to induce a centrifugal effect in it. This is why such businesses as advertising and consulting are so notoriously prone to fragmentation; they attract too many entrepreneurs.

Strong, decisive, qualified people are rarely willing to remain for more than a brief time in a secondary role. Their impatience is accentuated if, for any reason, they do not respect their superior or feel frustrated in their careers. Sometimes they conclude that their greatest opportunity lies not in seeking advancement by moving to another company but by undermining and eventually supplanting their present superior.

In consequence, the politically astute top executive seeks subordinates who not only have the requisite technical skills but who are also to some degree passive, dependent, and submissive. Their "loyalty" is often a euphemism for docility. They tend to be security-conscious and prone to form a dependent relationship with their chief. If the chief has held the current position for many years, this building of a submissive group has usually taken place slowly by a process of trial and error. But when coming in from outside or taking over as the result of a merger, the chief is often prone (and is usually well advised) to bring associates from the outside or to give preferment to personal acquaintances who have worked with the chief before.

A useful defensive tactic for the executive is to select a compliant board of directors.

Of course, the chief executive is the one most immediately concerned with this ploy, but second- and third-level managers, too, may have a vital interest in this matter. In recent years, changes in directors' responsibilities have made it somewhat more difficult to stack the board in the old-fashioned sense. But its membership and operation can still be influenced in a significant way.

Inside directors tend usually to be more malleable than outside directors. Few will be courageous enough to cross swords with the chief executive. While board members by law are the stockholders' representatives and thus are the holders of ultimate power in the business, in practice this is often little more than a polite fiction. In many instances they have largely abdicated their management or even corporate supervisory responsibilities.

Sometimes the directors are too busy to interfere in operations. Not infrequently they have little equity in the business and, hence, are disinterested in it. Sometimes they have been chosen principally because they are "big names" who add status and respectability to the company but can devote little time to its affairs. Much as some observers and authorities dislike such tendencies, they are the realities. The top-management group that knows how to use and exploit power will make sure that it, too, enjoys the blessings of a compliant board.

In business, as in diplomacy, the most important stratagem of power is for the executive to establish alliances.

The more alliances the executive can build, the better. Several kinds of relationships can be established:

☐ *With superiors.* The executive can make personal contact with and develop a relationship with the owner of the business or, where the ownership is widely diversified, with the more influential stockholders. One chief executive I know has lunch once each month with the widow of the founder of his company. As long as she is convinced that he is a "wonderful man," he has both power and tenure.

Where banks, insurance companies, or mutual funds have a controlling voice in the company, the executive can seek to gain favor with their key executives. If certain directors are unusually dominant, the executive does everything possible to win their favor and support. This does not necessarily mean obsequious and sycophantic behavior in relationships with them. On the contrary, the executive may regularly stand up to them and confront them directly.

The key to success in a relationship of this nature is the ascertainment of the other person's expectations. If the man or woman whose support the executive hopes to win likes tigers, he or she gets a tiger; if the person prefers a mouse, more aggressive impulses are restrained. Above all, the executive studies each person's prejudices and values and is careful never to offend them.

☐ *With peers.* The adroit manager also builds allegiances with equals. While these people may not be direct sources of power, they can often be valuable as supplementary means of support and intelligence. Included among contacts should be prominent industry figures. Since government intervention in business is increasing daily, acquaintance with senators, members of Congress, and major department heads in government can also be helpful. (The owners of a company doing business with the Defense Department will think twice before sacking an executive who is on intimate terms with the Secretary or a deputy.)

One good means of ensuring support from peers is to identify common goals and objectives toward which all can strive. An even more powerful step is to find a common enemy—an antibusiness government official, let us say, or a hostile labor leader. Often influential rivals for power or even disgruntled subordinates can be neutralized by being taken into groups having common goals or enemies.

☐ *With subordinates.* I have already mentioned the importance of selecting dependent subordinates in whose selfish interest it is to support their chief. Such persons may also be useful as sources of internal intelligence. The information they provide is not always completely accurate or reliable, but it can be cross-checked against data from a variety of other sources.

The executive should recognize the power of the purse.

The executive knows that the best control to exercise over subordinates is fiscal. Hence the executive seeks as quickly as possible to be in a position to approve all budgets. Nothing is as effective in coping with a recalcitrant staff as the power to cut off financial support for their projects. On the other hand, nothing so often promotes gratitude and cooperation as fiscal support of subordinates' favorite projects.

The executive should understand the critical importance of clear and credible channels of communication upward from all levels of personnel and downward from the executive to them.

Without such channels the executive is an isolate who does not know what is transpiring in the enterprise. Executive commands will be heard only partially by subordinates; they will be infrequently understood and rarely acted on. The executive should recognize that many of the staff have strong motives to hide the truth and to block or distort executive downward communication.[1]

To overcome deficiencies of communication, the executive must learn not to depend too much on a hierarchy of assistants (many of whom are not communication centers at all, but barriers to it). Where possible, people will be addressed directly in periodic "State of the Company" reports to them and encouraging direct feedback from them by soliciting anonymous questions and expressions of dissatisfaction. The executive must supplement formal channels of upward and downward communication by all available means, such as work councils, opinion polls, interviews with natural leaders, and community surveys.

Personal Style

The place of a chief or other top executive in a business in which the chief has little or no equity is somewhat analogous to that of a diplomat working in an unfriendly, if not openly hostile, country. There may be much overt status and prestige, but little real power. Certain goals must be accomplished, but there is little true leverage to apply to those people who must be influenced. In view of this, sometimes indirect, oblique, Machiavellian stratagems must be used to gain ends.

Observation of many politically astute executives in action indicates that most of them utilize supplementary ploys in coping with and influencing owners, associates, employees, and other groups. They know that an executive-politician must:

☐ *Use caution in taking counsel.* This leader may take the views of others into account, but the leader knows the decisions must be personal. Advice is useful, but unless its limits are recognized, it can easily become pressure.

☐ *Avoid too close superior-subordinate relationships.* While friendliness with subordinates is a must, the executive is never intimate with them. Personal feelings must never be a basis for action concerning them. The door may be "open"—but not too far.

☐ *Maintain maneuverability.* The executive is never committed completely and irrevocably. If conditions change, the altered circumstances can gracefully be adapted to and the course can be changed without loss of face.

☐ *Use passive resistance when necessary.* When under pressure to take action personally regarded as inadvisable, the executive can stall. To resist such demands openly is likely to precipitate a crisis. Therefore the executive initiates action, but in such a manner that the undesired program suffers from endless delays and ultimately dies on the vine.

☐ *Not hesitate to be ruthless when expedient.* No one really expects the boss to be "nice" at all times. If he or she is, the boss will be considered to be a softy or a patsy and no longer deserving of respect. (A surprisingly large segment of the population has a strong need to be submissive. Hence these people are more comfortable under a ruthless superior. This can be clearly seen in the rank and file of many labor organizations.)

☐ *Limit what is to be communicated.* Many things should not be revealed. For instance, bad news may create costly anxieties or uncertainties among the troops; again, premature announcements of staff changes may give rise to schisms in the organization.

☐ *Recognize that there are seldom any secrets in an organization.* The boss must be aware that anything revealed "in confidence" will probably be the property of everyone in the establishment the next morning.

☐ *Learn never to place too much dependence on a subordinate unless it is clearly to the latter's personal advantage to be loyal.* Although some people are compulsively conscientious, most are not. Most give lip service to the company or the boss, but when the crunch comes, their loyalty is exclusively to themselves and their interests.

☐ *Be willing to compromise on small matters.* The boss does this in order to obtain power for further movement. Nothing is more often fatal to executive power than stubbornness in small matters.

☐ *Be skilled in self-dramatization and be a persuasive personal sales executive.* The boss is essentially an actor, capable of influencing audiences emotionally as well as rationally. The boss first ascertains the audience's wants and values and then proceeds to confirm them, thus absolutely ensuring the hearer's acceptance of the message.

☐ *Radiate self-confidence.* The boss must give the impression of mastery of the task at hand and of being completely in command of the situation, even though the boss may not be sure at all.

☐ *Give outward evidence of status, power, and material success.* Most people measure a leader by the degree of pomp and circumstance surrounding the leader. (This is why the king lives in a palace and the Pope in the Vatican.) Too much modesty and democracy in the way of life may easily be mistaken for a lack of power and influence. For example, most subordinates take vicarious pride in being able to say, "That's my boss who lives in the mansion on the hill and drives a Rolls Royce."

☐ *Avoid bureaucratic rigidity in interpreting company rules.* To win and hold the allegiance of subordinates, an executive must be willing to "bend the rules" from time to time and make exceptions, even when they are not wholly justified.

☐ *Remember to give praise as well as censure.* Frequently, because of being under pressure from superiors, the executive takes out frustrations on subordinates by criticizing them, sometimes unreasonably. This executive must remember that, if their loyalty is to be won and held, they merit equal amounts of praise and reassurance.

☐ *Be open-minded and receptive to differing opinions.* If the executive makes people feel that anyone who disagrees with him or her is, ipso facto, wrong, personal power will suffer. Listening to dissent is the principal means by which the executive can experience corrective contact with reality and receive warning that the course being followed will lead to trouble. Also, openness to disagreement helps the executive to use power fairly—or, more accurately, use it in a manner that will be perceived as fair by subordinates.

Conclusion

The position of a top executive who has little or no equity in the business is often a perilous one, with little inherent security. If things go well, this chief's tenure is usually ensured; if they go badly, all too often this chief is made the scapegoat. Since many of the factors that affect the executive's performance are beyond control, the executive is constantly subject to the threat of disaster. The only hope for survival under these conditions is to gain and retain power by tactics that are in a large measure political and means that are, in part at least, Machiavellian.

Such strategies are not always noble and high-minded. But neither are they naive. From the selfish standpoint of the beleaguered and harrassed executive, they have one primary merit: they enhance chances of survival.

Note

1. For a fuller explanation of this point, see Robert N. McMurry, "Clear Communications for Chief Executives," *HBR*, March–April 1965, p. 131.

21
Managing Your Boss

JOHN J. GABARRO and JOHN P. KOTTER

Good managers recognize that a relationship with a boss involves mutual dependence and that, if it is not managed well, they cannot be effective in their jobs. They also recognize that the boss-subordinate relationship is not like the one between a parent and a child, in that the burden for managing the relationship should not and cannot fall entirely on the boss. Bosses are only human; their wisdom and maturity are not always greater than their subordinates'. Effective managers see managing the relationship with the boss as part of their job. As a result, they take time and energy to develop a relationship that is consonant with both persons' styles and assets and that meets the most critical needs of each.

To many the phrase *managing your boss* may sound unusual or suspicious. Because of the traditional top-down emphasis in organizations, it is not obvious why you need to manage relationships upward—unless, of course, you would do so for personal or political reasons. But in using the expression *managing your boss*, we are not referring to political maneuvering or apple polishing. Rather, we are using the term to mean the process of consciously working with your superior to obtain the best possible results for you, your boss, and the company.

Recent studies suggest that effective managers take time and effort to manage not only relationships with their subordinates but also those with their bosses.[1] These studies show as well that this aspect of management, essential though it is to survival and advancement, is sometimes ignored by otherwise talented and aggressive managers. Indeed, some managers who actively and effectively supervise subordinates, products, markets, and technologies, nevertheless assume an almost passively reactive stance vis-à-vis their bosses. Such a stance practically always hurts these managers and their companies.

If you doubt the importance of managing your relationship with your boss or how difficult it is to do so effectively, consider for a moment the following sad but telling story:

Frank Gibbons was an acknowledged manufacturing genius in his industry and, by any profitability standard, a very effective executive. In 1973, his strengths propelled him into the position of vice president of manufacturing for the second largest and most profitable company in its industry. Gibbons was not, however, a good manager of people. He knew this, as did others in his company and his industry. Recognizing this weakness, the president made sure that those who reported to Gibbons were good at working with people and could compensate for his limitations. The arrangement worked well.

In 1975, Philip Bonnevie was promoted into a position reporting to Gibbons. In keeping with the previous pattern, the president selected Bonnevie because he had an excellent track record and a reputation for being good with people. In making that selection, however, the president neglected to notice that, in his rapid rise through the organization, Bonnevie himself had never reported to anyone who was poor at managing subordinates. Bonnevie had always had good-to-excellent bosses. He had never been forced to manage a relationship with a difficult boss. In retrospect, Bonnevie admits he had never thought that managing his boss was a part of his job.

Fourteen months after he started working for Gibbons, Bonnevie was fired. During that same quarter, the company reported a net loss for the first time in seven years. Many of those who were close to these events say that they don't really understand what happened. This much is known, however: while the company was bringing out a major new product—a process that required its sales, engineering, and manufacturing groups to coordinate their decisions very carefully—a whole series of misunderstandings and bad feelings developed between Gibbons and Bonnevie.

For example, Bonnevie claims Gibbons was aware of and had accepted Bonnevie's decision to use a new type of machinery to make the new product; Gibbons swears he did not. Furthermore, Gibbons claims he made it clear to Bonnevie that introduction of the product was too important to the company in the short run to take any major risks.

As a result of such misunderstandings, planning went awry: a new manufacturing plant was built that could not produce the new product designed by engineering, in the volume desired by sales, at a cost agreed on by the executive committee. Gibbons blamed Bonnevie for the mistake. Bonnevie blamed Gibbons.

Of course, one could argue that the problem here was caused by Gibbons's inability to manage his subordinates. But one can make just as strong a case that the problem was related to Bonnevie's inability to manage his boss. Remember, Gibbons was not having difficulty with any other subordinates. Moreover, given the personal price paid by Bonnevie (being fired and having his reputation within the industry severely tarnished), there was little consolation in saying the problem was that Gibbons was poor at managing subordinates. Everyone already knew that.

We believe that the situation could have turned out differently had

Bonnevie been more adept at understanding Gibbons and at managing his relationship with him. In this case, an inability to manage upward was unusually costly. The company lost $2 to $5 million, and Bonnevie's career was, at least temporarily, disrupted. Many less costly cases like this probably occur regularly in all major corporations, and the cumulative effect can be very destructive.

Misreading the Boss-Subordinate Relationship

People often dismiss stories like the one we just related as being merely cases of personality conflict. Because two people can on occasion be psychologically or temperamentally incapable of working together, this can be an apt description. But more often, we have found, a personality conflict is only a part of the problem—sometimes a very small part.

Bonnevie did not just have a different personality from Gibbons, he also made or had unrealistic assumptions and expectations about the very nature of boss-subordinate relationships. Specifically, he did not recognize that his relationship to Gibbons involved *mutual dependence* between two *fallible* human beings. Failing to recognize this, a manager typically either avoids trying to manage his or her relationship with a boss or manages it ineffectively.

Some people behave as if their bosses were not very dependent on them. They fail to see how much the boss needs their help and cooperation to do his or her job effectively. These people refuse to acknowledge that the boss can be severely hurt by their actions and needs cooperation, dependability, and honesty from them.

Some see themselves as not very dependent on their bosses. They gloss over how much help and information they need from the boss in order to perform their own jobs well. This superficial view is particularly damaging when a manager's job and decisions affect other parts of the organization, as was the case in Bonnevie's situation. A manager's immediate boss can play a critical role in linking the manager to the rest of the organization, in making sure the manager's priorities are consistent with organizational needs, and in securing the resources the manager needs to perform well. Yet some managers need to see themselves as practically self-sufficient, as not needing the critical information and resources a boss can supply.

Many managers, like Bonnevie, assume that the boss will magically know what information or help their subordinates need and provide it to them. Certainly, some bosses do an excellent job of caring for their subordinates in this way, but for a manager to expect that from all bosses is dangerously unrealistic. A more reasonable expectation for managers to have is that modest help will be forthcoming. After all, bosses are only human. Most really effective managers accept this fact and assume primary responsibility for their own careers and development. They make a point of seeking the information and help they need to do a job instead of waiting for their bosses to provide it.

In light of the foregoing, it seems to us that managing a situation of mutual dependence among fallible human beings requires the following:

- ☐ That you have a good understanding of the other person and yourself, especially regarding strengths, weaknesses, work styles, and needs.
- ☐ That you use this information to develop and manage a healthy working relationship—one which is compatible with both persons' work styles and assets, is characterized by mutual expectations, and meets the most critical needs of the other person. And that is essentially what we have found highly effective managers doing.

Understanding the Boss and Yourself

Managing your boss requires that you gain an understanding of both the boss and his context as well as your own situation and needs. All managers do this to some degree, but many are not thorough enough.

The Boss's World

At a minimum, you need to appreciate your boss's goals and pressures, strengths and weaknesses. What are your boss's organizational and personal objectives, and what are the pressures, especially those from the boss's and others at that level? What are your boss's long suits and blind spots? What is his or her preferred style of working? Does the boss like to get information through memos, formal meetings, or phone calls? Does your boss thrive on conflict or try to minimize it?

Without this information, a manager is flying blind when dealing with his boss, and unnecessary conflicts, misunderstandings, and problems are inevitable.

Goals and Pressures. In one situation we studied, a top-notch marketing manager with a superior performance record was hired into a company as a vice president "to straighten out the marketing and sales problems." The company, which was having financial difficulties, had been recently acquired by a larger corporation. The president was eager to turn it around and gave the new marketing vice president free rein—at least initially. Based on his previous experience, the new vice president correctly diagnosed that greater market share was needed and that strong product management was required to bring that about. As a result, he made a number of pricing decisions aimed at increasing high-volume business.

When margins declined and the financial situation did not improve, however, the president increased pressure on the new vice president. Believing that the situation would eventually correct itself as the company gained back market share, the vice president resisted the pressure.

When by the second quarter margins and profits had still failed to improve, the president took direct control over all pricing decisions and put all items on a set level of margin, regardless of volume. The new vice president began to find himself shut out by the president, and their relationship deteriorated. In fact, the vice president found the president's behavior bizarre. Unfortunately, the president's new pricing scheme also failed to increase margins, and by the fourth quarter both the president and the vice president were fired.

What the new vice president had not known until it was too late was that improving marketing and sales had been only *one* of the president's goals. His most immediate goal had been to make the company more profitable—quickly.

Nor had the new vice president known that his boss was invested in this short-term priority for personal as well as business reasons. The president had been a strong advocate of the acquisition within the parent company, and his personal credibility was at stake.

The vice president made three basic errors. He took information supplied to him at face value, he made assumptions in areas where he had no information, and—most damaging—he never actively tried to clarify what his boss's objectives were. As a result, he ended up taking actions that were actually at odds with the president's priorities and objectives.

Managers who work effectively with their bosses do not behave this way. They seek out information about the boss's goals and problems and pressures. They are alert for opportunities to question the boss and others around him to test their assumptions. They pay attention to clues in the boss's behavior. Although it is imperative they do this when they begin working with a new boss, effective managers also do this on an ongoing basis because they recognize that priorities and concerns change.

Strengths, Weaknesses, and Work Style. Being sensitive to a boss's work style can be crucial, especially when the boss is new. For example, a new president who was organized and formal in his approach replaced a man who was informal and intuitive. The new president worked best when he had written reports. He also preferred formal meetings with set agendas.

One of his division managers realized this need and worked with the new president to identify the kinds and frequency of information and reports the president wanted. This manager also made a point of sending background information and brief agendas for their discussions. He found that with this type of preparation their meetings were very useful. Moreover, he found that with adequate preparation his new boss was even more effective at brainstorming problems than his more informal and intuitive predecessor had been.

In contrast, another division manager never fully understood how the new boss's work style differed from that of his predecessor. To the degree that he did sense it, he experienced it as too much control. As a result, he seldom sent the new president the background information he needed, and the president never felt fully prepared for meetings with the manager. In fact, the president spent much of his time when they met trying to get information that he felt he should have had before his arrival. The boss experienced these meetings as frustrating and inefficient, and the subordinate often found himself thrown off guard by the questions that the president asked. Ultimately, this division manager resigned.

The difference between the two division managers just described was not so much one of ability or even adaptability. Rather, the difference was that one of the men was more sensitive to his boss's work style than the other and to the implications of his boss's needs.

You and Your Needs

The boss is only one-half of the relationship. You are the other half, as well as the part over which you have more direct control. Developing an effective working relationship requires, then, that you know your own needs, strengths and weaknesses, and personal style.

Your Own Style. You are not going to change either your basic personality structure or that of your boss. But you can become aware of what it is about you that impedes or facilitates working with your boss and, with that awareness, take actions that make the relationship more effective.

For example, in one case we observed, a manager and superior ran into problems whenever they disagreed. The boss's typical response was to harden a position and overstate it. The manager's reaction was then to raise the ante and intensify the forcefulness of the argument. In doing this, the manager channeled anger into sharpening attacks on the logical fallacies in the boss's assumptions. The boss in turn would become even more adamant about holding the original position. Predictably, this escalating cycle resulted in the subordinate avoiding whenever possible any topic of potential conflict with the boss.

In discussing this problem with peers, the manager discovered that this reaction to the boss was a typical reaction to counterarguments—but with a difference. The response would overwhelm peers, but not the boss. Because attempts to discuss this problem with the boss were unsuccessful, the only way to change the situation was to deal with instinctive reactions. Whenever the two reached an impasse, the manager would check personal impatience and suggest that they break up and think about it before getting together again. Usually when they renewed their discussion, they had digested their differences and were more able to work them through.

Gaining this level of self-awareness and acting on it are difficult but not impossible. For example, by reflecting over past experiences, a young manager discovered a personal ineptitude for dealing with difficult and emotional issues where people were involved. By reason of disliking those issues and realizing that instinctive responses to them were seldom very good, this manager developed a habit of touching base with the boss whenever such a problem arose. Their discussions always surfaced ideas and approaches the manager had not considered. In many cases, they also identified specific actions the boss could take to help.

Dependence on Authority Figures. Although a superior-subordinate relationship is one of mutual dependence, it is also one in which the subordinate is typically more dependent on the boss than the other way around. This dependence inevitably results in the subordinate feeling a certain degree of frustration, sometimes anger, when actions or options are constrained by the boss's decisions. This is a normal part of life and occurs in the best of relationships. The way in which a manager handles these frustrations largely depends on the manager's predisposition toward dependence on authority figures.

Some people's instinctive reaction under these circumstances is to resent the boss's authority and to rebel against the boss's decisions. Sometimes a person will escalate a conflict beyond what is appropriate. Seeing the boss almost as an institutional enemy, this type of manager will often, without being conscious of it, fight with the boss just for the sake of fighting. This manager's reactions to being constrained are usually strong and sometimes impulsive. This manager sees the boss as someone who, by virtue of role, is a hindrance to progress, an obstacle to be circumvented or at best tolerated.

Psychologists call this pattern of reactions counterdependent behavior. Although a counterdependent person is difficult for most superiors to manage and usually has a history of strained relationships with superiors, this sort of manager is apt to have even more trouble with a boss who tends to be directive or authoritarian. When the manager acts on personal negative feelings, often in subtle and nonverbal ways, the boss sometimes *does* become the enemy. Sensing the subordinate's latent hostility, the boss will lose trust in the subordinate or the subordinate's judgment and behave less openly.

Paradoxically, a manager with this type of predisposition is often a good manager of subordinates. This manager will often go out of the way to get support for them and will not hesitate to go to bat for them.

At the other extreme are managers who swallow their anger and behave in a very compliant fashion when the boss makes what they know to be a poor decision. These managers will agree with the boss even when a disagreement might be welcome or when the boss would easily alter his decision if given more information. Because they bear no relationship to the specific situation at hand, their responses are as much an overreaction as those of counterdependent managers. Instead of seeing the boss as an enemy, these people deny their anger—the other extreme—and tend to see the boss as if he or she were an all-wise parent who should know best, should take responsibility for their careers, train them in all they need to know, and protect them from overly ambitious peers.

Both counterdependence and overdependence lead managers to hold unrealistic views of what a boss is. Both views ignore that most bosses, like everyone else, are imperfect and fallible. They don't have unlimited time, encyclopedic knowledge, or extrasensory perception; nor are they evil enemies. They have their own pressures and concerns that are sometimes at odds with the wishes of the subordinate—and often for good reason.

Altering predispositions toward authority, especially at the extremes, is almost impossible without intensive psychotherapy (psychoanalytic theory and research suggest that such predispositions are deeply rooted in a person's personality and upbringing). However, an awareness of these extremes and the range between them can be very useful in understanding where your own predispositions fall and what the implications are for how you tend to behave in relation to your boss.

If you believe, on the one hand, that you have some tendencies toward counterdependence, you can understand and even predict what your reactions and overreactions are likely to be. If, on the other hand, you believe you have some tendencies toward overdependence, you might question the extent to which your overcompliance or inability to confront real differences may be making both you and your boss less effective.

Developing and Managing the Relationship

With a clear understanding of both your boss and yourself, you can—usually—establish a way of working together that fits both of you, that is characterized by unambiguous mutual expectations, and that helps both of you to be more productive and effective. We have already outlined a few things such a relationship consists of, which are itemized in Exhibit 1, and here are a few more.

Compatible Work Styles

Above all else, a good working relationship with a boss accommodates differences in work style. For example, in one situation we studied, a manager (who had a relatively good relationship with his superior) realized that during meetings his boss would often become inattentive and sometimes brusque. The subordinate's own style tended to be discursive and exploratory. He would often digress from the topic at hand to deal with background factors, alternative approaches, and so forth. His boss, instead, preferred to discuss problems with a minimum of background detail and became impatient and distracted whenever his subordinate digressed from the immediate issue.

Recognizing this difference in style, the manager became terser and more direct during meetings with his boss. To help himself do this, before meetings with the boss he would develop brief agendas that he used as a guide. Whenever he felt that a digression was needed, he explained why. This small shift in his own style made these meetings more effective and far less frustrating for them both.

Exhibit 1. Managing the Relationship With Your Boss

Make sure you understand your boss and his or her context, including:
- His or her goals and objectives
- The pressures on him or her
- His or her strengths, weaknesses, blind spots
- His or her preferred work style

Assess yourself and your needs, including:
- Your own strengths and weaknesses
- Your personal style
- Your predisposition toward dependence on authority figures

Develop and maintain a relationship that:
- Fits both your needs and styles
- Is characterized by mutual expectations
- Keeps your boss informed
- Is based on dependability and honesty
- Selectively uses your boss's time and resources

Subordinates can adjust their styles in response to their bosses' preferred method for receiving information. Peter Drucker divides bosses into "listeners" and "readers." Some bosses like to get information in report form so that they can read and study it. Others work better with information and reports presented in person so that they can ask questions. As Drucker points out, the implications are obvious. If your boss is a listener, you brief the boss in person, *then* follow it up with a memo. If your boss is a reader, you cover important items or proposals in a memo or report, *then* discuss them.

Other adjustments can be made according to a boss's decision-making style. Some bosses prefer to be involved in decisions and problems as they arise. These are high-involvement managers who like to keep their hands on the pulse of the operation. Usually their needs (and your own) are best satisfied if you touch base with them on an ad hoc basis. A boss who has a need to be involved will become involved one way or another, so there are advantages to including this boss at your initiative. Other bosses prefer to delegate—they don't want to be involved. They expect you to come to them with major problems and inform them of important changes.

Creating a compatible relationship also involves drawing on each other's strengths and making up for each other's weaknesses. Because he knew that his boss—the vice president of engineering—was not very good at monitoring employees' problems, one manager we studied made a point of doing it himself. The stakes were high: The engineers and technicians were all union members, the company worked on a customer-contract basis, and the company had recently experienced a serious strike.

The manager worked closely with his boss, the scheduling department, and the personnel office to ensure that potential problems were avoided. He also developed an informal arrangement through which his boss would review with him any proposed changes in personnel or assignment policies before taking action. The boss valued his advice and credited his subordinate for improving both the performance of the division and the labor-management climate.

Mutual Expectations

The subordinate who passively assumes that he or she knows what the boss expects is in for trouble. Of course, some superiors will spell out their expectations very explicitly and in great detail. But most do not. And although many corporations have systems that provide a basis for communicating expectations (such as formal planning processes, career planning reviews, and performance appraisal reviews), these systems never work perfectly. Also, between these formal reviews expectations invariably change.

Ultimately, the burden falls on the subordinate to find out what the boss's expectations are. These expectations can be both broad (regarding, for example, what kinds of problems the boss wishes to be informed about and when) as well as very specific (regarding such things as when a particular project should be completed and what kinds of information the boss needs in the interim).

Getting a boss who tends to be vague or nonexplicit to express expectations can be difficult. But effective managers find ways to get that information. Some will draft a detailed memo covering key aspects of their work and then send it to their bosses for approval. They then follow this up with a face-to-face discussion in which they go over each item in the memo. This discussion often surfaces virtually all of the boss's relevant expectations.

Other effective managers will deal with an inexplicit boss by initiating an ongoing series of informal discussions about "good management" and "our objectives." Still others find useful information more indirectly through those who used to work for the boss and through the formal planning systems in which the boss makes commitments to a superior. Which approach you choose, of course, should depend on your understanding of your boss's style.

Developing a workable set of mutual expectations also requires that you communicate your own expectations to the boss, find out if they are realistic, and influence the boss to accept the ones that are important to you. Being able to influence the boss to value your expectations can be particularly important if the boss is an overachiever. Such a boss will often set unrealistically high standards that need to be brought into line with reality.

A Flow of Information

How much information a boss needs about what a subordinate is doing will vary significantly depending on the boss's style, the current situation, and the confidence the boss has in the subordinate. But it is not uncommon for a boss to need more information than the subordinate would naturally supply or for the subordinate to think the boss knows more than the boss really does. Effective managers recognize that they probably underestimate what the boss needs to know and make sure they find ways to keep the boss informed through a process that fits the boss's style.

Managing the flow of information upward is particularly difficult if the boss does not like to hear about problems. Although many would deny it, bosses often give off signals that they want to hear only good news. They show great displeasure—usually nonverbally—when someone tells them about a problem. Ignoring individual achievement, they may even evaluate more favorably subordinates who do not bring problems to them.

Nevertheless—for the good of the organization, boss, and subordinate—a superior needs to hear about failures as well as successes. Some subordinates deal with a good-news-only boss by finding indirect ways to deliver the necessary information, such as a management information system in which there is no messenger to be killed. Others see to it that potential problems, whether in the form of good surprises or bad news, are communicated immediately.

Dependability and Honesty

Few things are more disabling to a boss than an undependable subordinate whose work cannot be trusted. Almost no one is intentionally undependable, but many managers are inadvertently so because of oversight or uncertainty about the boss's priorities. A commitment to an optimistic delivery date may please a superior in the short term but be a source of displeasure if not honored. It's difficult for a boss to rely on a subordinate who repeatedly slips deadlines. As one president put it (describing a subordinate): "When he's great, he's terrific, but I can't depend on him. I'd rather he be more consistent even if he delivered fewer peak successes—at least I could rely on him."

Nor are many managers intentionally dishonest with their bosses. But it is so easy to shade the truth a bit and play down concerns. Current concerns often become future surprise problems. It's almost impossible for bosses to work effectively if they cannot rely on a fairly accurate reading from their subordinates. Because it undermines credibility, dishonesty is perhaps the most troubling trait a subordinate can have. Without a basic level of trust in a subordinate's word, a boss feels compelled to check all of a subordinate's decisions, which makes it difficult to delegate.

Good Use of Time and Resources

Your boss is probably as limited in time, energy, and influence as you are. Every request you make of the boss uses up some of these resources. For this reason, common sense suggests drawing on these resources with some selectivity. This may sound obvious, but it is surprising how many managers use up their boss's time (and some of their own credibility) over relatively trivial issues.

In one instance, a vice president went to great lengths to get his boss to fire a meddlesome secretary in another department. His boss had to use considerable effort and influence to do it. Understandably, the head of the other department was not pleased. Later, when the vice president wanted to tackle other more important problems that required changes in the scheduling and control practices of the other department, he ran into trouble. He had used up many of his own as well as his boss's blue chips on the relatively trivial issue of getting the secretary fired, thereby making it difficult for him and his boss to meet more important goals.

Whose Job Is It?

No doubt, some subordinates will resent that on top of all their other duties, they also need to take time and energy to manage their relationships with their bosses. Such managers fail to realize the importance of this activity and how it can simplify their jobs by eliminating potentially severe problems. Effective managers recognize that this part of their work is legitimate. Seeing themselves as ultimately responsible for what they achieve in an organization, they know they need to establish and manage relationships with everyone on whom they are dependent, and that includes the boss.

Note

1. See, for example, John J. Gabarro, "Socialization at the Top: How CEOs and Their Subordinates Develop Interpersonal Contacts," *Organizational Dynamics,* Winter 1979; and John P. Kotter, *Power in Management* (New York, AMACOM, 1979).

22
General Managers in the Middle

HUGO E. R. UYTERHOEVEN

Having a boss's responsibility without a boss's authority; functioning as a specialist and a generalist at the same time; meeting the conflicting demands of superiors, subordinates, and peers while still getting the job done—these exacting requirements sound like part of a manager's nightmare. But, according to this author, they are daily facets of general management at middle levels of an organization, where risk and opportunity go hand in hand. While these general management positions are increasingly common in divisionalized corporations, they are often misunderstood by both middle managers and their superiors. In this article, the author discusses the demanding requirements of the job from a top-management and a middle-management perspective, and shows how it represents an opportunity for individual and corporate growth.

Traditionally, the job of general manager has been equated with that of a company's chief executive. General manager and boss have been thought of synonymously. Yet, increasingly, corporate organizations are providing for general management positions at levels below the chief executive; and, as a result, the number of general managers at the middle level is rising.

The middle-level general manager phenomenon (i.e., a general manager who is responsible for a particular business unit at the intermediate level of the corporate hierarchy) is a direct outgrowth of the movement toward a divisional form of organization. For example, while the *functional* organization requires only one general manager, the *divisional* organization provides for a variety of business units, each requiring a general manager. Often the process of divisionalization extends several levels down into the organization (i.e., group, division, department), further increasing the need for general managers at lower levels.

The shift from functional to divisional organization occurred in the United States largely during the last two decades and is currently taking place in Europe. It is a worldwide phenomenon necessitated by the greater product-line diversity as well as the growing international operations of a vast majority of the larger corporations.

Although the divisional organization is now a familiar phenomenon, little attention has been directed at obtaining a clear understanding of the middle-level general management position. Of course, one approach would be to refer to what is known about the top-level general manager, but this knowledge is not really applicable—the two positions are significantly different. Furthermore, general management at the middle organizational level is, in a number of respects, more difficult.

In this article, I shall attempt to (a) define the characteristics and responsibilities of the middle-level general manager's job and (b) draw the implications for the individual assigned to it (hereafter referred to as "middle manager") as well as for the employing company.

Managing Relationships

The middle manager, like most managers, accomplishes goals largely by managing relationships. There are few things a manager can do alone; the support, cooperation, or approval of a large number of people are needed. As the textbooks say, the manager "gets things done through others."

Managing relationships at the middle level in the organization, however, is a threefold task, requiring the middle manager to act as subordinate, equal, and superior:

- Upward, relating to the boss as a subordinate, taking orders.
- Downward, relating to the team as a superior, giving orders.
- Laterally, often relating to peers in the organization as an equal; for example, the middle manager may have to secure cooperation from a pooled sales force or solicit assistance from corporate staff services.

Thus the middle manager wears three hats in fulfilling the general management role. In contrast, the top-level general manager acts primarily as a superior—this alone is a significant difference between the two positions.

Managing the triple set of relationships is most demanding; it is analogous to a baseball player having to excel simultaneously in hitting, fielding, and pitching. The middle manager must be able not only to manage all three relationships, but also to shift quickly and frequently from one to another.

In view of these conflicting and changing demands, it is often difficult for the middle manager to arrive at a consistent pattern of behavior. Moreover, the process of satisfying the requirements of one set of relationships may reduce effectiveness in managing another. For instance, middle managers who follow orders from headquarters to the letter may thereby, in the eyes of subordinates, either weaken their authority or appear unreasonable and unresponsive. Consider this illustration from an internationally divisionalized company:

> ☐ Headquarters restricted the freedom of one division manager to purchase from the outside, an order which threatened to undermine his authority as a general manager. He was torn between the dilemma of (a) asserting his authority with his subordinates by ignoring or fighting headquarters' orders or (b) weakening his image as a superior by following headquarters' orders. Being a good subordinate would have weakened him as a superior; yet, by being a strong superior, he would have been a disloyal subordinate. As it turned out, the general manager held prolonged negotiations with a peer in the pooled sales force to arrive at a mutually satisfactory solution, but this made the general manager appear inconclusive and indecisive to his subordinates.

In order to successfully manage such multiple relationships, and their often conflicting and changing demands, middle managers should recognize the full scope of their job. For instance, they should:

1. Make the network of relationships explicit. To whom do they have to relate? What are the key relationships?
2. Identify, in their specific situation, the triple set of requirements. What is expected of them as good subordinates? What is required to be effective colleagues and equals? And what does it take to provide leadership as superiors? This analysis should force middle managers to focus not only on their own goals and abilities but also on those of their "opposite numbers" at all three levels.
3. Recognize the difficulty of achieving consistent behavior in view of conflicting demands and be willing to wear three hats at the same time. Success will involve the balancing of all three roles. Sometimes it requires trade-offs. Under such complex circumstances, it helps to proceed explicitly.
4. Communicate their understanding of the job to others in the organization with whom they must relate. (These others should bear in mind that, singly, they are part of but one of the multiple relationship sets that the managers have to manage; their expectations and responses should take this into account.)

A Playing Coach

In some respects, middle managers are the leaders of their units who delegate, guide, and plan; in other respects, however, they have specific operating responsibilities and must "roll up their sleeves" to achieve output and to meet their targets. Therefore, they are both delegators and doers, both strategists and operators, or, to use another sports analogy, both coaches and players. In contrast, their superiors are usually coaches and their subordinates are normally players.

Continuing the analogy, sports experience indicates that it is easier to excel either as coaches or as players and that playing-coach jobs are clearly the most difficult—the skills of successful players are different from those of successful coaches, but playing coaches must possess the skills of both. Likewise, the dual role of middle managers combines different skills and actions. On the one hand, they need a broad overview, detachment, and a long-run perspective. On the other hand, they need detailed knowledge and experience, the ability to involve themselves directly and deeply, and a sense of urgency.

Acting both as players and as coaches, middle managers must constantly balance the two roles and sometimes make trade-offs. Are they going to be too much like players, too involved in operating details and in doing things themselves? Or are they becoming too much like coaches by staying aloof, by delegating too much, by not getting sufficiently involved? It is easy to misperceive one's role, especially in regard to the latter. For example:

> ☐ Top management in a large divisionalized corporation assigned a promising middle manager to a recent acquisition. Charged with enthusiasm for his new position, the manager saw himself as primarily a delegator, an organization builder whose job was to oversee the installation of parent company procedures and guide the acquisition's integration with staff services of the parent. He had not considered becoming directly involved in operating details or concentrating attention on increasing sales, both of which his immediate superior, the former owner/manager, saw as primary responsibilities of the middle-management position.

This question of balance—of asking oneself, "To what extent do I get involved in actual operations and to what extent do I delegate?"—is most delicate. And the balancing of the two roles is, of course, also influenced by the demands, expectations, and abilities of middle managers' superiors and subordinates. The choice is not entirely free.

The Bilingual Manager

In keeping with their dual roles, middle managers usually receive abstract guidance from their superiors in the form of goals that they must translate into concrete action.

If, for example, a company's chief executive sets the goal of a certain percentage increase in earnings per share (and mentions it to financial analysts, thereby making it an even stronger commitment), how is the goal achieved? The chief executive will communicate it to the group vice president, who will salute and pass it on to the divisional general manager, who, in turn, will salute and pass it on to the middle manager. The latter will salute, turn around, and find nobody to pass the goal on to. To use Harry Truman's famous dictum, the buck stops here.

The buck stops at the middle manager, who must assume the bilingual role of translating the strategic language of superiors into the operational language of subordinates in order to get results. The middle manager must turn the abstract guidance of, say, more earnings per share or meeting the budget into the concrete action required to achieve the results.

Often the middle manager is presented these abstract goals carrying the label, "difficult but achievable." While such labels may have a motivating purpose, they are basically a euphemism for the following proposition: top management knows the results it wants to see, has no idea how to achieve them, and assigns the middle manager the twofold duty of figuring out how to perform the task and then getting it done (i.e., the boss tells what is wanted, not how it should be accomplished).

Strategy Considerations

There are several reasons for the foregoing results-oriented procedure. One explanation is that the middle manager, being closest to the action, has most of the data and hence is in the best position to make the decisions relevant to translating goals into action. A second explanation states that it is a superior's privilege to push decision making down and let subordinates sweat it out. Why should a superior take risks when subordinates can take them instead?

The implications of top management's approach, however, are more important than the explanations. First of all, middle-level general managers are provided with much broader *de facto* responsibility than is usually codified in job descriptions or organization charts. The job is, in fact, invested with responsibilities for corporate strategy. It is important, therefore, that managers go beyond the formal definitions of their jobs, functioning broadly enough so that they deal explicitly with the full scope of their real responsibilities. A narrow understanding of their roles, by contrast, may cause them to ignore critical tasks; they cannot assume responsibilities they do not recognize.

But with responsibility goes risk, particularly where the goals are abstract and the charter is unclear. The risk is further compounded by the many constraints, external as well as organizational, within which the middle manager operates. However, along with risk goes opportunity. As Harry Truman put it, "If you can't stand the heat, get out of the kitchen." To be a strategist rather than just an order taker is exciting, even without the job's ceremonial attributes.

Formulating strategy for translating abstract goals into concrete action requires the ability to develop plans. In doing so, middle managers must take into account external factors of an economic, political, marketing, technological, or competitive nature. Moreover, in line with their dual roles, they must achieve congruence between the goals of subordinates (whose commitment is essential) and the goals imposed by superiors (whose approval they seek).

This strategic task is both intellectual and administrative in nature, and the communication of plans is as critical as their development. Often, communication is most effectively accomplished not through proclamation but, rather, through "teaching" the general management point of view during day-to-day activities.

Summing up, to translate goals into action middle-level general managers must:

- ☐ Define their jobs realistically and broadly.
- ☐ Assume full responsibility for translating the abstract goals into concrete action through strategic decision making and planning, taking into account both external and organizational factors.
- ☐ Effectively communicate their decisions and plans to both superiors and subordinates.

From Action to Measurement

Middle managers must be able to translate not only from abstract guidance into concrete action but also from concrete action into abstract measurement. Their superiors measure success in terms of results and are less interested in *how* it has been accomplished. Consequently, middle managers' performances are most often appraised by matching the abstract results of their actions with the abstract guidance that they have been given.

This fact of organizational life sometimes leads to misunderstanding. In one company, for example, a middle manager was unable to meet his goals, and invoked his actions to show why. Top management, however, perceived the explanations as excuses. Concrete action was not part of its measurement system.

In terms of the total equation, there can be real problems when the signals from abstract measurement contradict those from abstract guidance. Where this occurs, the translation process frequently gets reversed. Instead of starting with the abstract guidance (goals) to develop specific action, the middle manager starts with the abstract measurement (required results) and translates backward to his plan of action. Here are two illustrations:

- ☐ In one company, top management emphasized the need for its divisions to have ample productive capacity. In the measurement of performance, however, excess capacity was looked on unfavorably. As a result, division managers added capacity very cautiously, achieving high plant-utilization ratios at the expense of lost sales (which did not show up in the measurement system).
- ☐ And in another company, top management stressed the need for new product and market development; yet the middle managers were measured on the basis of short-term profitability. With R&D and mar-

keting expenses reducing short-term profitability, pressures to achieve the latter created an obvious reluctance to incur the former.

Translating action into measurement involves the same skills as translating goals into action. One language is operational and involves a variety of dimensions, whereas the other is abstract and is often in terms of a single dimension. The required ability is to relate these two different languages. And when measurement and goals are contradictory, middle managers must be able to tread a thin line between the two, sometimes making trade-offs.

Furthermore, they must cope with an additional problem: the language of corporate measurement is sometimes inadequate for measuring and guiding the activities of their subordinates. While top management typically measures middle managers on the basis of profit and loss, middle managers have to evaluate their subordinates in terms of different quantitative measures (such as costs, production and sales volume, number of rejects, etc.) as well as qualitative judgments (such as adequacy of the plant layout, effectiveness of the R&D effort, comprehensiveness of the marketing activities). These measures not only are different in kind and more numerous, but also require greater expertise and more intimate knowledge of specifics.

Responsibility/Authority

Middle managers typically assume full responsibility for their units and are evaluated on the results of the total operation. There is no way to shift the blame as might be done in a functionally organized setup, where marketing could claim that production did not deliver on time or production could point the finger at marketing for not bringing in enough orders.

Like the chief executive, middle managers have to account for the performance of others. Unlike the chief executive, however, they have only limited authority in the pursuit of their goals. They often need cooperation from equals, say, in a centralized R&D department; and they receive solicited, or unsolicited, guidance from superiors. Thus responsibility and authority do not overlap. The former exceeds the latter.

While textbooks state categorically that such an imbalance is wrong and that responsibility should be backed up with the necessary authority, the responsibility/authority discrepancy is an inevitable fact of life where divisionalization penetrates the organization. To function effectively in this imperfect world, middle managers must meet two requirements:

1. In spite of the limited authority, they must be willing to accept full responsibility and take action accordingly. At the same time, they should recognize that they cannot do everything themselves, that they must cooperate and coordinate with others. The ability to manage multiple relationships is critical here.
2. While they always have the opportunity to "go to court," to appeal

to their superiors when cooperation from equals is not forthcoming, they should rely on this route only as a last resort or when the issue is clear-cut—preventive settlements, even if they involve compromises, may be preferable. By going to court, they are asking somebody higher up to take the risk. The fact that this "somebody" has attained a higher position probably attests that the superior is good at keeping a low profile and is unlikely to be receptive unless middle managers pick their fights wisely, carefully, and infrequently.

Inevitable Politics

Discrepancies between responsibility and authority, coupled with all of the previously discussed factors—multiple relationships, the playing-coach role, translation from goals to action and back to results—necessarily result in a structure that requires managers to coexist in a political atmosphere. There are different interests and interest groups, conflicting goals and ambitions, and positions of power and weakness.

Moreover, this coexistence is not necessarily peaceful. Career objectives and prestige, as well as positions of influence, are at stake, and the general manager in the middle is an easy and accessible target—malcontent soldiers do not pick on the general directly; they go for the officers.

The position of the middle manager is further exposed by a measurement system requiring direct and frequent responses. To meet goals, the middle manager needs cooperation and assistance and is therefore vulnerable to sabotage. In a political sense, the manager is up for reelection continuously and thus must possess a political sensitivity as well as the constitution to stomach pressures and conflicts. Awareness of the configuration of the power structure and the direction of political winds is a must. Unfortunately, in this potentially volatile atmosphere, managers often fail to ask an obvious but key question: "Who are my friends and who are my enemies?"

A Major Transition

The middle manager's job is usually an individual's first try at general management. Typically selected on the basis of outstanding achievement as a functional specialist, the new manager's previous experience is not transferable to this new terrain. The new position represents a major transition. Fred Borch, General Electric's chairman of the board and chief executive officer, considers the step from functional to general management to be the greatest challenge of a manager's entire career.

Indeed, the skills and activities which led to success in a manager's functional career—whether marketing, manufacturing, engineering, R&D, control, or finance—are usually those of specialization, of deep involvement in a narrow area. The specialist knows more and more about less and less.

In the medical and legal professions, specialization is the usual route to excellence and eminence. The manager, too, during the early phases of a career, follows this pattern; a track record is established by excelling in a particular specialty. But unlike the doctor and the lawyer, the manager's career progression pattern is brutally shifted.

Having earned spurs as a specialist, the manager is given a new and drastically different challenge, that of excelling as a generalist. Instead of knowing more and more about less and less, the manager now shifts to knowing less and less about more and more.

This transition, in turn, represents a major risk. Previously, each step up the functional specialization ladder led to familiar challenges which required proven skills. Now, the challenges are new and the skills unproven. Not all managers will be able to make this transition; not all will possess the required general management skills; and in spite of earlier successes, not all will successfully meet the new challenge.

Overcoming Resentment

In making the major and risky transition, the middle manager, as noted earlier, does not always face a friendly working environment; rather, the promotion may have caused resentment. Some may consider themselves better qualified, because of age or seniority; they may view the new middle manager's capabilities and background as insufficient for the job. Others may resent the promoted individual as a representative of an "educated elite."

Yet the new middle manager needs the support of those very people who may resent the appointment. Their cooperation is essential; there will be constant obstacles until cooperation is achieved. In overcoming this possible handicap of resentment, administrative skills and experience are of utmost importance. Unfortunately, however, these skills are typically the new middle manager's short suit; the neophyte is more often long on technical abilities and experience, which are obviously less relevant to the task.

Acclimating to New Terrain

Since promotions do not always occur within the same department, the middle manager often comes from another segment of the organization. The newcomer will probably be unfamiliar with the unit's history, opportunities, and problems. And obtaining facts or information to accurately diagnose the situation will not be easy, for the following reasons:

- ☐ While superiors have assessed the unit's performance in terms of its abstract results, the middle manager has to evaluate it in terms of concrete action. The latter is much harder to determine than the former.
- ☐ The middle manager will have to be acquainted not only with the "formal" organization of the unit, but with its "informal" structure as well. While the formal structure can be found in manuals and organization charts, the informal one has to be discovered through daily activities and interpersonal relationships.

☐ Politics may color the facts given. Certain information may be deliberately withheld, while other aspects may be overemphasized.

In summary, the newcomer's fact-finding mission is difficult and hazardous. The new manager will be required to sift through information that is often contradictory, tough to evaluate, and not always obvious.

Furthermore, the new arrival will be dealing with strangers, and thus will have to establish new relationships. This is a particularly difficult challenge to the neophyte general manager who also is possibly resented as a newcomer. Since relationships cannot be ordered from above, the middle manager will have to earn the respect and confidence of new counterparts not by virtue of the uniform worn, but instead by the quality of the manager's daily activities.

Managerial Acrobatics. Without essential facts and established relationships, it is difficult for a middle manager to get off to a fast start. Yet the new manager often walks into a situation that requires quick and decisive action. In this event a balance will have to be struck between (a) an early commitment based on inadequate facts and nonexisting relationships and (b) indecision while facts and relationships are established.

The first course of action is often preferred, since it establishes a manager's authority and image. It may also be a response to pressures that are pushing for an early commitment. The risks, however, are great. Before proceeding on such a path, it is worthwhile to pause and consider the long-run implications of action that precedes the establishment of facts and relationships. What, for example, are the chances of making major mistakes? While it is often argued that the wrong action is preferable to no action at all, it is important for the middle manager to get off to a good start, not just a fast one. Things that start badly usually get worse.

Experimental Leadership

In making the transition, a middle manager often functions as an agent of change. The assignment may have come from top management to bring about changes in the manager's new unit, or personal ambition may push this new boss to develop fresh approaches. This implies experimentation and a process of learning through trial and error. Experimentation, however, means vulnerability. The middle manager's unit, for instance, may have been chosen as the experimental laboratory for the entire organization; and, since an experiment is easier to defeat than a long-established policy, the forces of resistance mentioned earlier may be encouraged to mount opposition, or even sabotage. Where the agent of change is an inexperienced newcomer, it is particularly easy to shift blame to such a neophyte's shoulders.

Experimental leadership rarely permits one to move ahead at great speed in a single direction. It involves slow testing and occasional backtracking that may be viewed by subordinates as indecision and defeat. Thus, they may interpret experimental leadership as lack of leadership, withholding their support and blaming their leader for inexperience or ignorance.

Under this handicap, success may be difficult to achieve. Top executives, in such circumstances, may not always come to the rescue. They may be watching rather than supporting the experiment. This is their privilege. From their vantage point, why should they stake their reputations, possibly their careers, on the uncertain outcome of an experiment?

Thus it is unrealistic to expect rescue from above. More importantly, to judge the soundness and results of an experimental change, whether initiated from above or by the middle manager, an objective and neutral superior is needed. He can also act as a mutually acceptable arbiter where conflicts arise, as in situations of limited authority.

The middle manager may be better served in the long run by having such a neutral, higher-level arbiter rather than a prejudiced ally. In the former instance, cooperation and support can be obtained through candid and open negotiation; the availability of an objective judge encourages reasonable attitudes from all parties concerned. In the latter instance, resistance from others will go "underground," which obviously makes the task of obtaining cooperation and support more difficult. A case from one large company illustrates this point:

> ☐ One of the divisions had to rely heavily on a centralized R&D department for its custom-made product innovations. Conflicts arose between the market-oriented division and the technology-oriented R&D department, so the division manager took the case to superiors. A new, marketing-oriented group vice president overwhelmingly ruled in favor of the division. Subsequently, the R&D department's contributions declined because of alleged "technical difficulties" and "conflicting demands from other divisions."

Challenge and Opportunity

The preceding description of the characteristics of the middle-management position portrays it as a major challenge, as indeed it is. Why would anyone want to accept such an ill-defined, open-ended, risky assignment? Yet, as I pointed out earlier, with risk goes opportunity; and with open-endedness goes a job of considerably broader scope than what is stated in the formal job description.

Why is it not possible, then, to design this job by including all the positive elements and eliminating all the drawbacks? The answer is that the drawbacks are inherent in a divisional organizational structure—they can be excluded only by eliminating the structure itself.

A divisional structure, however, is essential to the conduct of large-scale operations for a diverse range of products in a variety of countries. It also permits a large number of managers to assume general management responsibilities early in their careers, sometimes in their early or middle thirties after less than 10 years of business experience. In contrast, the functional organization usually offers an individual manager a first attempt at general management only after the age of 50, after some 25 to 30 years of business experience.

The choice, then, is between having a broad opportunity to assume an imperfect general management job at an early age and having a very limited opportunity to hold a "perfect" general management job late in one's career. To put it in the context of Churchill's famous statement: early in a person's career, the middle-management job is the worst assignment except for all the others. Moreover, the advantages and opportunities are many, both for the company and for the aspiring executives:

☐ The chance to run one's own show at a young age, rather than having to wait for a quarter of a century, should increase the probability of advancement, as well as make a business career more exciting.

☐ The shift from specialist to generalist early in one's career is less perilous, and failure is less painful, than if the shift occurs later. A manager who has spent some 25 years as a specialist is apt to be firmly set and will find it difficult to make a major change. A younger manager, on the other hand, should still be flexible and able to adapt more easily to a different set of job requirements. Failure is also easier to take—and to overcome—early in one's career than it is later on. (Putting a 25-year track record on the line is a major risk and one that might well destroy someone's entire career.)

☐ The early shift from specialist to generalist is also less risky from the company's viewpoint. When a manager who has been a specialist for a quarter of a century is selected for the president's job, the total conduct of the company is entrusted to someone with no record in general management. It is not at all certain that a successful engineering, marketing, manufacturing, or finance vice president will turn into a first-rate general manager. In the divisional organization, however, the middle manager typically manages one of several profit centers. Thus risk is greatly reduced by entrusting to an unproven general manager only a small segment of the total enterprise.

☐ A large number of general management slots in an organization enables a corporation to attract and retain many capable managers and avoids an elimination contest for a company's single general management position. This large reservoir of general managers can be transferred and promoted as new opportunities arise. Since the scarcest resource of a company is usually competent management, overcoming this hurdle may eventually constitute a major competitive advantage.

☐ The middle-management phenomenon is conducive to management development and training. A manager can start in a small profit center, establish a track record there, transfer to a larger unit, and so on. Thus both the breadth and the challenge of the general management job can be increased as the manager moves up in the ranks. The individual's confidence and versatility will also be enhanced, fostering personal career development as well as strengthening corporate competence.

☐ Middle managers are close to the action. Leadership and coordination, therefore, take place on the battlefield rather than from distant headquarters. Decisions are made more quickly by better informed people, who can more closely monitor an action's impact and ensure its proper implementation.

Conclusion

There are some important implications that can be drawn from the characteristics of the middle-level general management job; and they affect not only the person who holds it but superiors as well.

One common pitfall is that superiors tend to judge middle managers in terms of their own jobs. They believe that middle managers have the same opportunities, prerogatives, and power that they do and therefore should shoulder similar responsibility. This same belief is frequently shared by the middle managers themselves.

As I have attempted to show, however, the middle manager's job is quite different from that of the top-level general manager. The job itself is demanding enough. It should not be made more difficult by an incorrect understanding of its scope and characteristics.

Top management often fails to recognize that imperfection is a fact of life in the middle-management job. Furthermore, formal job descriptions frequently reflect sacred dogmas like overlapping authority and responsibility. Such ostrich-like attitudes create unrealistic expectations among all parties involved. Unrealistic expectations inevitably produce disenchantments and failures. Reality, even though it may not correspond to the demands of theoretical elegance, must be faced. If reality imposes imperfection, as it does, then imperfection must be recognized and accepted, rather than swept under the rug.

Need for Ratification

Given the job's characteristics, the middle manager can govern effectively only with the consent of those being governed. While the manager is formally promoted or demoted by a superior, the jury usually consists of subordinates and peers. By giving or withholding their support, they greatly influence the middle manager's career.

This need for ratification is easily overlooked or underestimated by the middle manager, who may approach the job with supreme confidence in personal abilities, viewing the new appointment as evidence of recognized importance and talents. Where change is required, the new manager may be self-appointed as the new leader destined to bring order out of chaos and turn failure into success.

At the same time, the newcomer may see his subordinates as old-timers who have failed in the past to meet the challenge. Hence the new arrival may doubt their abilities and downgrade their importance. A middle manager who approaches the job by overestimating personal importance and underestimating that of subordinates is erecting a self-imposed barrier to ratification. This person is creating the conditions for a self-fulfilling prophecy—with the manager being the ultimate victim.

Accommodation and Compromise

Another important implication for the middle manager is the necessity of finding the way in a maze of accommodation and compromise. Quick decisions, a straightforward course of action, or completely rational and logical solutions are not always possible. What is judged as necessary must be brought within the realm of what is possible.

Often it is difficult to adjust to such a complex challenge. While the neophyte may have made a mark as a technical expert whose previous successes were based on purely rational solutions to technical problems, optimization may not be the most successful approach in the new role. Rarely do perfect solutions exist for the middle manager. There are *viable* solutions, however, and they require constant accommodation and compromise.

Job Strategy

Given the difficulty and challenge of general management at middle organizational levels, the job should be approached as explicitly as possible. The middle manager must attempt to define the following:

- ☐ The scope of the multiple relationships within the organizational structure as well as the specific important personal relationships.
- ☐ The "playing coach" role.
- ☐ The "bilingual" task of translating goals to action and action to measurement.
- ☐ The implications of having full responsibility while holding limited authority.
- ☐ The "political" environment in which the manager has to survive from a position of limited power and great vulnerability.

Just as companies formulate corporate strategy by matching their resources to their environment, so can the middle manager formulate job strategy by identifying the total organizational environment and match this with personal strengths and weaknesses as well as personal values.

Looking at the job in strategic terms should help the manager face varied daily challenges, overcome frustrations, and develop a consistent pattern of behavior. Obviously, a job strategy should be not a ceremonial proclamation but, instead, a plan of action which the middle manager internalizes to guide daily actions.

A managerial record, like a judicial one, is established through the cumulative impact of a series of decisions, many of which set precedents. If these decisions can be related not only to the specific demands of each separate issue but also to an overall philosophy and master plan, their internal consistency and cumulative impact will establish a strong and cohesive organizational fabric. This is the landmark of an effective and successful manager.

23

Managing the Paradox of Organizational Trust

LOUIS B. BARNES

Even though many managers might agree that trust in an organization is more important to its functioning than, say, authority or power, it seems that organizational trust is not always easy to develop. Why is something so important so difficult to build and to maintain? This article is about trust, what it is, and how people in organizations destroy it by holding and acting on three fairly simple and accepted assumptions. The difficulty about these assumptions, which on their own are relatively harmless, is that combined they create a self-reinforcing atmosphere of pervasive mistrust. The author shows how the simple assumptions become destructive and indicates that the way to break out of the pattern is to behave in what are seemingly inappropriate, or paradoxical, ways. The startling thing is that even though trust is easily destroyed, it is often easily created and maintained—if we don't fall prey to simplistic ways of thinking.

Several years ago, the largest subsidiary in a giant international complex found itself with a new president, a bright young marketing manager named Jones from one of the subsidiary's divisions. Jones soon let it be known that the old days of delegation were over and that he was going to create a strong, centralized head office with himself as its driving force. On more than one occasion, Jones made it clear that he had little respect for either the previous management or some of the managers still in the company. He introduced specific cost, measurement, and reporting procedures; a number of managers and staff members were fired, took early retirement, or resigned. As Jones set his policies in motion, other old-timers were immobilized or by-passed.

Jones spent a good deal of time in the field, and every three months he took a team of headquarters staff with him to area plan-and-review sessions that cynics labeled "jump for Jonesie" shows, "rock 'em, sock 'em" binges, and "point the finger" days. Along with his periodic outbursts about the shortcomings of certain subordinates or reports, Jones's tough-spoken demands for tight budgets, detailed action plans, and short-term goals set the tone for management meetings.

As time went on, opposition to Jones appeared within both the company and the parent organization, but it remained underground because his company's measurable benefits seemed to outweigh the obvious costs of his behavior. The performance figures looked good. With increased inflation, cost cutting, and rising demand, the so-called bottom line showed the company to be very successful. Balanced against these positive indicators, high dissatisfaction, high turnover, postponed investments, and little evidence of succession planning all seemed negligible.

After several long, serious strikes in three of the subsidiary's key plants, however, top management finally became concerned with Jones's hard-line approach. Shortly after the last strike, senior managers in the parent company began to review their options—and about a year later replaced Jones with a senior manager from the parent company. No one within the subsidiary appeared capable of taking the job at that time.

This story may sound dramatic, but I suggest that the Manager Joneses of the world are legion. Sometimes the battle lines are more subtly drawn than in this case; sometimes managers are the masters and sometimes the victims, but almost invariably at one time or another managers fall into Jones-like situations.

Like all people, managers behave according to their assumptions of how the world works—whether, for instance, it is a kind or a cruel place. Disastrous behavior such as Jones's follows when a manager's assumptions about the world establish a dangerous and self-defeating pattern.

The pattern develops, I believe, when managers hold three simple assumptions that, in combination, prevent trust from forming. Even though managers like Jones will state that it is trust more than either power or hierarchy that really makes an organization function effectively, these same managers all too often find themselves operating in and sometimes creating an atmosphere of pervasive *mis*trust in their companies.

Using Manager Jones as representative of all of us at times, I want to explore this mistrust—so subtle, so prevalent, and yet so unproductive—and then to describe how the three assumptions people make daily can create this destructive atmosphere.

I will briefly describe the three "harmless" assumptions, show how they appear in a managerial context, and then explore some alternative approaches and assumptions. In presenting these alternatives, I argue in favor of two fragile but important concepts—namely, tentative trust and paradoxical action.

Too often we fail to go beyond our initial reactions in order to look at an issue's deeper levels and thus avoid the time and the tension that such work entails. Then, as Manager Jones did, later on we pay the price. To see how this happens, let's begin with the assumptions as Manager Jones might have experienced them.

Three Harmless Assumptions

The three assumptions are, first, that important issues naturally fall into two opposing camps, exemplified by either/or thinking; second, that hard data and facts are better than what appear to be soft ideas and speculation, exemplified in the "hard drives out soft" rule; and finally, that the world in general is an unsafe place, exemplified by a person's having a pervasive mistrust of the universe around him or her. These assumptions can often be useful and necessary. Separately, they seem so natural that we don't see them as harmful. As a matter of fact, we often see them as healthy; in certain situations, for instance, we think only a fool would *not* be mistrustful.

Nevertheless, when managers combine all three assumptions at the same time, which we do very naturally as well, the assumptions may benefit us in the short run—but be very destructive in the long. Now let's look at them in turn.

Do or Die

A person holds assumption 1 when *either/or* thinking dominates choices and decision making. Like the rest of us, Manager Jones had to turn complex sets of alternatives into useful prime choices. Under conditions of uncertainty, Jones relied on experience and instinct to help him limit the alternatives, make choices, and then implement them. Using analysis and discussion, managers typically narrow their alternatives into such options as make or buy, act or react, centralize or decentralize, expand or retrench, and reward or punish.

But the problem with this way of thinking is more serious than that it limits options. People often become emotionally attached to a symbol or choice and see it as either good or bad. We set up the alternatives as adversaries and turn them into unions *versus* management, blacks *versus* whites, government *versus* business, theory *versus* practice, and us *versus* them (whoever they are). Despite Lincoln's reminder that a house divided against itself cannot stand, American tradition and history have taught us to separate issues into their two most obvious alternatives—and then to pronounce one of them "good" and the other "bad." It seems that part of what Manager Jones created in those around him was this either/or mentality. By his own definition, his choices were good. Others were to be criticized and attacked.

Even when it occurs, however, either/or thinking by itself is not destined for disaster. The real problem is that the assumption builds certain future expectations. For Manager Jones, these expectations prevented him from stepping outside of each either/or dichotomy to look again at the ingredients—to find an unseen paradoxical alternative or ingenious recombination. In Jones's case, for instance, he never sought to reintegrate the old-timers into his new management scheme. Because he saw them as having caused the problems, that would have seemed absurd at the time. Yet, paradoxically, they might have helped Jones overcome his subsequent turnover, morale, and strike problems.

Other examples of either/or ingredients illustrate the problem as well as a resolution. For example:

> ☐ For several generations now, people have viewed the management versus union dichotomy as a fact of life. One is good while the other is bad, depending on your perspective. If not enemies, the two have been at least antagonistic adversaries bound mainly by a legal contract. In many companies, this view leads to daily frictions between workers and supervisors. These can escalate into formal grievances. Under such conditions, even honest cooperative gestures are seen as dishonest or hostile. In one company, management tried to start some "improvement meetings" with workers. But because of past union-management experiences, the meetings were doomed before they started.
>
> Yet in other companies, workers and managers have bargained hard on some issues and achieved shop floor cooperation on others, beyond the legalities of the contract. They were both bound to but not always limited by the contract.

Are these latter situations an exception to the rule? Probably they are, simply because the rule in most companies seems based on the more prevalent either/or assumption and its traditions. It is easier to take a firm position and act as if us or them, right or wrong, and good or bad were the major real-life options. But again, the villain here is not the either/or assumption itself. It is the distortion that occurs when people assume they need to defend their positions while also adopting the other two assumptions.

A Bird in the Hand . . .

Assumption 2 is the principle that *hard is better than soft*, which means that hard drives out soft.* We saw it in Jones; we see it in ourselves. The idea goes as follows. Once Jones began to make either/or choices, he almost "had to" show their superiority and defend them; at least, that's the way he saw it. And to defend his position, he needed hard facts rather than soft feelings,

---

**Author's Note.* George F. F. Lombard of the Harvard Business School first called my attention to this assumption some years ago as a variant on Gresham's Law that "bad money drives out good money." I have since heard of other similar variations such as one coined by Warren Bennis, recent president of the University of Cincinnati, as Bennis's Principle: "routine work drives out nonroutine work." In the same spirit, I suppose, "hard drives out soft" deserves to be known as Lombard's Law, which is what some of us have affectionately called it in recent years.

hard numbers rather than soft words, and hard data and concrete steps rather than abstract possibilities. It meant short-term action taking rather than long-term planning, "tell it like it is" statements rather than speculative explorations.

Consequently, Jones became a tough wheeler-dealer manager who needed to win out over the other side. As "they" became the opposition, having the best defense meant having a good offense. In Jones's case, as in many of our own situations, it is easy to see how the dangerous link between the first and second assumptions gets fused.

Holding this second assumption easily leads a person to a hard-nosed, buccaneer management style that turns doubt into action and stirs the hearts of those who idolize such uncompromising figureheads as General George S. Patton, Harold Geneen of ITT, the Ayatollah Khomeini, or the late John Wayne's macho cowboy roles. Such leaders at least *act* as if they know what they're doing. And the shoot-from-the-hip style is not restricted to management; the hard/soft assumption shows up in the hard-nosed skepticism of science and in the lawyer's quest for hard evidence. In the best competitive tradition, people who hold this assumption "get things done," despite later consequences.

Yet both proponents and opponents of hard-is-better-than-soft can make profound mistakes in its name. Both can propel an either/or position a long way toward a disaster of the extremes, as the following example shows:

> ☐ When John F. Kennedy took office in 1961, he was confronted with the CIA's plans for the Bay of Pigs invasion. Although Kennedy seemed to have early doubts about the invasion and even though a few advisers like Arthur Schlesinger, Jr., and Chester Bowles expressed reservations, Kennedy went along with the arguments for an attack as presented by Allan Dulles of the CIA, some joint chief of staff members, and other highly qualified advisers.
>
> Schlesinger later wrote about the hard-drives-out-soft mood of those meetings in his book *A Thousand Days*: "Moreover, the advocates of the adventure had a rhetorical advantage. They could strike virile poses and talk of tangible things—fire power, air strikes, landing craft, and so on. To oppose this plan, one had to invoke intangibles—the moral position of the United States, the response of the United Nations, 'world public opinion,' and other such odious concepts.
>
> "But just as the members of the White House Staff who sat in the Cabinet Room failed in their job of protecting the President, so the representatives of the State Department failed in protecting the diplomatic interests of the nation. I could not help feeling that the desire to prove to the CIA and the Joint Chiefs that they were not soft-headed idealists but were really tough guys too influenced State's representatives at the Cabinet table."[1]

The Bay of Pigs example illustrates the power of the hard-is-better-than-soft assumption in combination with its either/or companion. When opposing sides are formed, people feel almost compelled to choose one or the other—and to find tangible ways of defending their choices. The side that usually seems most convincing is the one that is supported by hard evidence and defended by hard tactics, which have both an intellectual and an emotional appeal for the tough-minded and the would-be tough-minded, like Jones.

The danger with people's tendencies to make hard-nosed choices is that, as in the Bay of Pigs discussions, such choices quickly acquire their own momentum. To stop the snowball—to try to reexamine the options—means violating the either/or and hard/soft assumptions, while seeming, as Schlesinger says, to be a "soft-headed idealist." As many managers know, in most tough-guy contexts it can be very hard to appear soft.

Pitting himself and his hard-line approach against both old-line practices and old-time managers, Jones exemplified the tough-guy manager. However, he personified a third assumption as well.

Nice Guys Finish Last

The third harmless assumption forms a basis for and helps contaminate the other two. It holds that the world is a dangerous place requiring that a person adopt a position of *pervasive mistrust* to survive. When held, this assumption dominates the atmosphere and blots out situational factors. Like the other two assumptions, mistrust can be very useful when our safety or well-being is at stake. On other occasions, however, our own mistrust helps set the stage for either/or thinking and hard-drives-out-soft behavior.

According to those who had known him in earlier years, Manager Jones had been taunted in childhood for being weak. To avoid the appearance of weakness, he adopted an aggressive posture and an air of superskepticism, which fit his view of the world. He was bright enough to be a rising star in a company where mutual trust among managers was considered important. Jones, himself, was considered trustworthy by his superiors in the sense of being a predictable producer.

As Jones set one subordinate faction against another, however, and as hard began to drive out soft, the parent company managers saw how destructive Jones's sense of mistrust was and how absent and important the softer, more caring side of trust had become. Not surprisingly, key subordinates reciprocated Jones's lack of caring, which led them to indulge in inconsistent and unpredictable behavior. As a result, any earlier bases for organizational trust disappeared.

Jones's assumption of pervasive mistrust as reinforced by his either/or and hard-drives-out-soft viewpoints. The situation deteriorated even more as Jones's subordinates took sides and added fuel to the fires of mistrust. It took the company more than five years to move out of what was by then commonly acknowledged to be a very difficult situation. This experience suggests how much harder it is to drive out hard with soft than vice versa, even though it can be done over time. It also suggests that we should examine the tenacious roots of trust and mistrust more closely. For this, the work of Erik H. Erikson is instructive (see Appendix A).

Although Erikson's work rests on rich clinical evidence, it seems reasonable to ask, "What do early trust-mistrust patterns have to do with managers like Jones?" In response, researchers would generally agree that we never fully conquer old anxieties or doubts; when we encounter difficult new situations, we often reexperience old tensions. Thus the early major dilemmas of the human life cycle can often return in later years when we meet new tension-filled settings and experiences.

In addition—and most important for managers—even though our earliest and most basic assumptions about trust and mistrust are formed in early infancy, they are affected by new situations and by how a person feels about the immediate situation. Consequently, the trust versus mistrust dilemma constantly confronts us as we face new situations, new people, new adversities, and even new successes.

In this fashion, much of our initial behavior in these new situations is an effort to search for, test out, and initiate a tentative sense of trust or mistrust. When other people see this initial behavior as *both* predictable and caring, they develop an expectation of future hope, which accompanies trust. Such early search behavior also invites similar responses from others.

This exchange creates the giving and getting-in-return behavior that Erikson pictures and which pervades all cultures in what sociologists call the norm of reciprocity. Its universal pattern gives us (and Jones) a way to check out and test for the presence of trust. When we try to give something, we have a chance to see what we get in return. If the exchange is unsuccessful, for whatever reason, we usually assume it is a situation in which mistrust prevails.

To further show how the trust/mistrust assumption works, though, let me briefly describe three studies by other behavioral scientists.

The first, by James Driscoll, shows how satisfaction in organizations is determined more by the degree of trust present than by either levels of participation or people's inherent trust. In other words, Driscoll suggests that with trust, the immediate environment is more important than either one's background or one's participation in decisions.[2]

The second study of trust and mistrust is Dale Zand's simulation of managerial problem solving, and the third is R. Wayne Boss's replication of Zand's study done some years later.[3] Both studies examine how high-trust and low-trust conditions affect the quality of managerial problem solving involving a company president and three vice presidents. Each study set up teams with sets of instructions; some teams' instructions were filled with high-trust assumptions, others' had low-trust assumptions. The surprising thing in these studies is how easily the simple instructions given to each set created these trust differences. Zand's instructions for the high-trust teams, all of whom were managers attending a course, read as follows (note the words I have italicized):

> You have learned *from your experience* during the past two years that *you can trust* the other members of the top management team. You and the other top managers *openly express your differences and your feelings of encouragement or of disappointment*. You and the others *share all relevant information and freely explore ideas and feelings that may be in or out of your defined responsibility*. The result has been a *high level of give and take and mutual confidence in each other's support and ability*.[4]

According to Zand, the instructions given to the low-trust groups were "worded to induce a decrease in trust." This was epitomized by the president perceiving the vice presidents as potentially competitive.

The key difference in the two sets may be the specific cues about the give-and-take reciprocity among managers. In the high-trust teams, the norms of reciprocity included expressing differences of opinion, stating feelings of encouragement and disappointment, sharing information, exploring ideas outside of one's own function, providing high give and take, and giving support. For the low-trust teams the opposite was implied.

Both the Zand and the Boss studies indicate that high trust was the key factor in problem-solving effectiveness. Moreover, in his replication study, Boss reports a surprising finding (italics mine):

> *The fact that trust was the overriding variable was not initially apparent to the subjects*. When participants were asked to explain the reasons for the obvious differences in team effectiveness, they offered a number of plausible explanations. . . . When told of the different instructions, the group members reacted with amazement and relief. *They were amazed that they had not perceived what seemed to them after the fact to be obvious*.[5]

What does all this tell us about the soft assumption of trust?

1. Our concerns about trust apparently begin very early and recur throughout our lives.
2. Trust seems important for both effective performance and high satisfaction.
3. Trust may be easier both to create and to destroy, under some conditions, than we have assumed (it depends on how norms of reciprocity develop and take hold).
4. Managers may gloss over the crucial role of trust and mistrust assumptions and fall back on more convenient explanations for behavior in their companies, such as personality differences and the boss's actions.
5. Perhaps most important, our assumptions of trust and mistrust come at us from both past and present situations.

We may not be able to do much about the past, but we do have some control over present and future actions. In new situations, once we question the inevitability of pervasive mistrust, then the either/or and hard/soft assumptions also stand on shakier ground. Indeed, if we question all three assumptions enough, it becomes apparent that they no longer need to combine to our detriment. But what can we use to replace them?

Alternative Approaches

So far I've discussed how—even though separately each may be very useful—long-term problems arise when managers combine the three harmless assumptions. The same is true when we combine their most obvious alternatives, which, in good either/or fashion, happen to come from their exact opposites. Manager Jones would most likely reject the idea that pervasive trust (the obvious alternative to pervasive mistrust) could possibly replace his assumption. His experience has taught him otherwise. And he would surely (and with reason) reject the idea that a prolonged-tolerance-for-ambiguity or a soft-is-better-than-hard viewpoint is a suitable replacement for any more rigorous stance.

Even though Jones might reject these obvious alternatives, others do not. For some people, the concepts of pervasive trust, prolonged ambiguity, and soft-overwhelming-hard fit together and have great appeal. With almost religious fervor, like flower children or sensitivity training converts, they promote their causes to proclaim the new utopias. Typically, that fervor is all it takes for their more mistrustful adversaries to draw new lines and define new battlegrounds.

Ultimately, holders of opposing viewpoints emerge and throw loaded overstatements at the other side, as both parties get drawn into defending fixed positions.

Over the years the management pendulum swings back and forth from liberal to conservative, from centralization to decentralization, from harsh layoff periods to expensive benefit programs, and from severe survival controls to expanded product development and cries for creativity. A major problem is that early dialogue between the opposing viewpoints often triggers defensive thinking within each position, as happened in Jonestown, Watergate, and Iran. In each case, typically—and tragically—either/or, mistrust, and hard-drives-out-soft prevail in the short term.

At the same time, people in organizations can and do learn. What appears to be pendulum behavior isn't merely that. Opposites sometimes converge or change as they develop. Sometimes new managers and new situations phase new assumptions into old issues. Sometimes a wise, experienced manager can rise above a repeated false dichotomy and furnish the impetus for finding new approaches. Such approaches, however, require people adept at a third path, not just a middle way, as well as specific steps toward organizational trust and constructive reciprocities. To do this, managers need to abandon the three assumptions and their opposites in favor of less rigid, more creative combinations.

Things Aren't Always as They Seem

Another example, as follows, might help to illustrate how this third way can work:

> ☐ The faculty and administration of a small college were torn by argument and dissension. The veteran president had recently resigned, and a search committee had chosen a woman with a distinguished academic record as the new president. Not long after the new president arrived, the dean of faculty also resigned.
>
> After conferring with the executive committee of the faculty, the new president appointed a young, recently tenured faculty member as the acting dean of faculty. She also announced three short-term goals: improving the enrollment picture, improving the financial situation, and building new trust. She resisted strong pressures to produce a specific "mission" statement, saying that as soon as she did, it would polarize the college community into those who agreed with the statement and those who didn't. She also chose to keep the new dean of faculty as an acting dean so that he could be tested in his new role while she and the faculty learned to work with him and with each other.
>
> During their first year of working together, the new president and the acting dean took supportive but active roles in faculty discussions, helped to pass legislation that greatly simplified the cumbersome committee structure, improved the enrollment and financial pictures, and tried to strengthen faculty work relationships.
>
> Specifically, the new dean worked hard to reinvolve a number of senior faculty members who were described by others as "burned out" and "losers" of earlier faculty battles. He did this by going to them for advice on important matters, frequently seeking them out in their offices, refusing to let them withdraw, helping them to get money for such mundane tasks as manuscript typing and library research, sending them to conferences on innovative practices in their own fields, asking them to chair short-term task forces, and seeking and finding financial help for them to start new research.
>
> At the start of the second year of the acting dean's appointment, the president still refused to appoint him as the permanent dean until the official search committee was set up and made its own report and recommendation. The acting dean agreed: "I have everything to gain by not having the official title and authority. This way I can still get help from everyone and don't have to act like an official dean." Nevertheless, within a few months a search committee did recommend that his title be made official.

> A number of knowledgeable sources have since reported that the college is progressing excellently.

As managers, the new president and her acting dean posed a puzzle to most of their constituents. She was new, an outsider, and wouldn't take a firm position on educational policy; he was young and had little administrative experience. In an institution where protocol, tradition, and gestures of strong leadership had been important, neither administrator leaned on them. Where mistrust had been rampant, she set out to assume and to build trust. In an effort to demonstrate that there was still leadership in the faculty ranks as well, he set out to revitalize burned-out faculty members.

In effect, the president and the dean refused to adopt either set of simple hard or soft assumptions. Instead they assumed a condition of tentative trust and worked toward a set of *and/also* rather than either/or expectations. They did this by behaving in ways that explored, listened, and confronted while exemplifying care for the school and its people. In effect they began reciprocities that could lead to organizational trust.

In doing so, the president and dean created a sense of shared hope for the future. Both gave ample evidence of caring for the school and its individual members. After identifying a set of crucial problems—enrollment, finances, trust, a demoralized faculty, little support for faculty projects, and low student and faculty initiative—both confronted them. As new leaders, they worked on old issues in new ways and surprised some people. They did not initially set forth a master plan or mission. She chose a relatively inexperienced person as dean. They both tried to build and rebuild faculty leadership instead of drawing attention to their own. And even after the acting dean had convinced the faculty of his competence, the president refused to push for his permanent appointment until the faculty also took responsibility for it.

As a result, the either/or power struggles that had existed between the previous administration and the faculty moved toward a set of and/also expectations. The new administration, the senior faculty, the junior faculty, the students, and the subfactions built a new leadership network where the quality of students rose, student turnover and attrition declined, programs expanded, and finances improved. Paradoxically, the president and dean accomplished the expected, or hoped-for, results by creatively pursuing the unexpected—at least in the eyes of many constituents.

These seemingly inappropriate about-faces are what I call paradoxical actions. In using the word *paradox* in this way, I'm borrowing from philosopher W. V. Quine's notion that paradox is "any conclusion that at first sounds absurd but that has an argument to sustain it," although these arguments are often buried, ignored, or brushed over quickly.[6] Paradoxical actions are the "absurd" steps, such as listening hard to the other person when one is trying to win an argument, that break up and bridge false dichotomies. They create working links toward trust where there were few or none before.

Paradoxical Actions . . .

The mysteriousness of paradox has fascinated poets, scientists, philosophers, and laymen for thousands of years. Paradoxical puzzles can both pose unanswerable questions and lead to insightful creative answers; Kierkegaard called paradox the "source of the thinker's passion." The reconciliation of apparent contradictions underlies some of the most truly creative discoveries of science, not to mention most religions, while the suggested unity of opposites permeates the works of great writers, like O'Neill and Conrad. Most important, partly because it is based on an unfamiliar logic or rationale, a paradox's true workings always seem to be just beyond our understanding.

Once we see these same paradoxical situations as and/also propositions rather than either/or contradictions, the reconciliations seem relatively obvious. That awareness, though, doesn't always help us find the underlying unities the next time we face a set of apparent opposites. Manager Jones is not the only one who finds it difficult to break old reciprocities or the patterns that reinforce them. Sometimes, however, change requires the very opposite of what appears to be logically appropriate behavior.

At the same time, paradoxical actions are not foreign to many a modern manager. To buy when others are selling, to ask questions when others expect answers, or to give new autonomy when subordinates expect tighter controls are all actions that make sense under certain conditions. And, without highlighting it, some of the most popular management concepts of recent years have relied on paradox. The work of McGregor, Blake and Mouton, and Lawrence and Lorsch all entail paradoxes (see Appendix B).

In a sense, these real and theoretical examples highlight the almost unnoticed role of paradox in organizational behavior. In similar fashion, I suspect, most readers overlook the crucial role that paradox plays in their own more creative actions. And yet, acting paradoxically constitutes one way to get beyond tentative trust rather than adopting the extremes of pervasive trust or pervasive mistrust.

Likewise, a manager who avoids either/or thinking or its mushy opposite, prolonged ambiguity, must consciously adopt an and/also viewpoint whereby ingredients are kept separate but are not assumed to be in conflict. Finally, and most difficult, managers need to replace the hard versus soft behavior with paradoxical actions that *cope* with new information, *confront* important discrepancies, and *care* for individual people and issues. The goal is not to do one or the other; it is to weave them into a pattern of separate behaviors that sets the basis for new reciprocal patterns.

. . . and Norms of Reciprocity

Earlier, I suggested that the fragile toughness of trust is a crucial factor in blending extremist hard- and soft-line assumptions into an organizational bonding that holds a company's disparate parts together. Trust that is too tentative, emotional, and fragile will fall back into pervasive mistrust. Trust that is too tenacious, impervious, and tough becomes inflexibly shaped into a pattern of pervasive trust. Organizations with too much mistrust become overly differentiated, with people succumbing to either/or expectations and hard-drives-out-soft behavior. Organizations with too much trust become overly integrated, with people lapsing into prolonged ambiguity and soft-is-better-than-hard behavior. Both extremist patterns depend on emotions more than on data and self-awareness. Both also build up ineffective reciprocity patterns.

The three-path diagram in Exhibit 1 displays the points I've made so far plus another path that is based on the more modest assumption of tentative trust. The diagram also suggests that the patterns persist because people reinforce them: that is, attack/defend/withdraw behavior follows from an assumption of pervasive mistrust and win/lose expectations. Such behavior begins a cycle that repeats itself until it becomes a norm of reciprocity and degenerates into a continuing self-oriented need pattern. Obeying a distorted golden rule, people do to others what they perceive is being done to them. Beginning with a pervasive sense of mistrust, they shift eventually into a set of destructive reciprocities and finally to even more divisive and self-oriented needs. As emotions run high, the cycle continues, engendering even more mistrust.

The three-path diagram also suggests that norms of reciprocity need not result in rigid patterns and structures. One way to break those norms, which are perceived as natural by the time they are frozen, is to seek for and initiate paradoxical actions. New norms cannot be set into motion unless the old ones are broken. And the old ones cannot be broken unless paradoxical insights and actions help break old patterns. Some of this paradoxical behavior is subtle and difficult to capture. It hinges on words, gestures, and maybe most of all on careful listening for new clues and knowledge.

But even more, paradoxical actions begin to set up new relationships and in that sense lead to the unexpected. Such actions suggest that, in Lewis Carroll's words, "things aren't always as they seem." Consider one final example where a major company president, reflecting on a turbulent year of employee relations, notes:

> Some of our problems are our own fault. We lost contact with our own employees. Managements in large companies say that they get too big to stay in personal contact with their employees. We swallowed that. Now, however, I think that the opposite is true. The larger we get, the *more* important it is for us to emphasize personal contact by top management down through all levels. We've been doing it all wrong. We stumbled over our own assumptions.

In essence, to prevent mistrust beliefs or their extreme opposites from becoming frozen, we sometimes need, unlike our friend Manager Jones, to live and to create paradoxical actions. We need to know and act as though some things are both certain and uncertain. We need to polarize and synthesize, to see questions in answers, to be both inside and outside of situations, to learn while teaching, and to find unity in opposites as well as opposites in

Exhibit 1. The Assumptions and the Patterns They Create

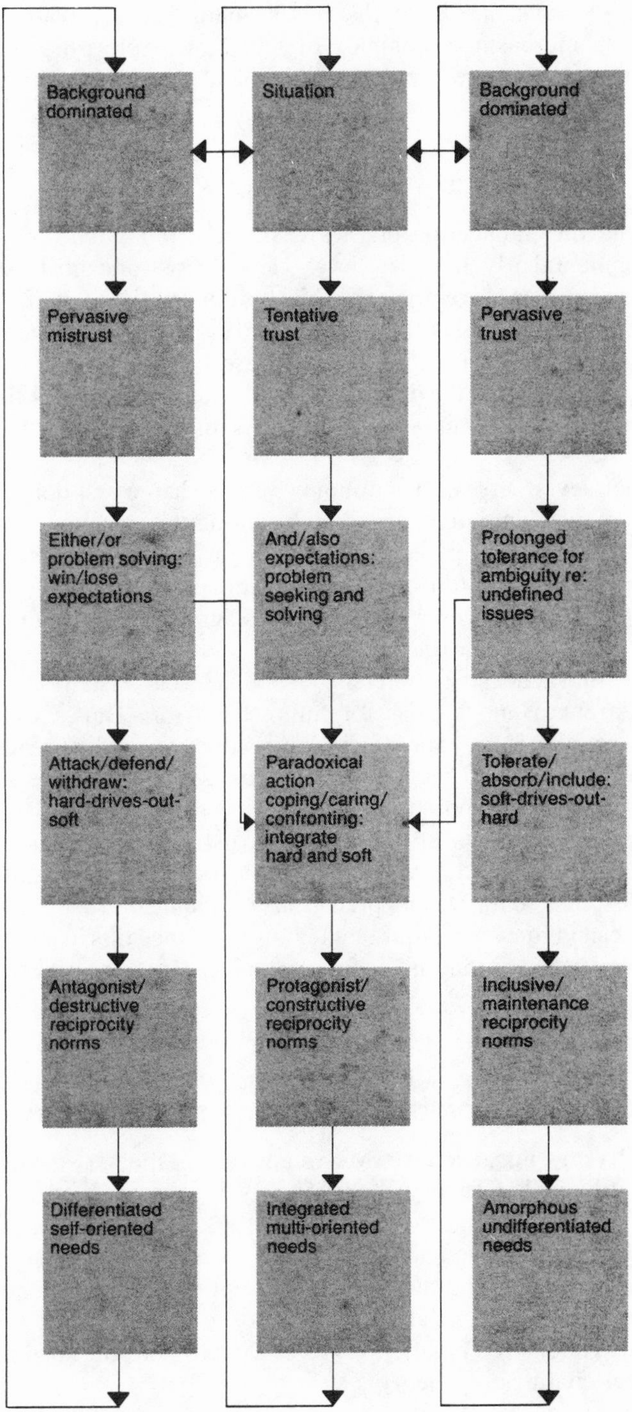

Background dominated	Situation	Background dominated
Pervasive mistrust	Tentative trust	Pervasive trust
Either/or problem solving: win/lose expectations	And/also expectations: problem seeking and solving	Prolonged tolerance for ambiguity re: undefined issues
Attack/defend/withdraw: hard-drives-out-soft	Paradoxical action coping/caring/confronting: integrate hard and soft	Tolerate/absorb/include: soft-drives-out-hard
Antagonist/destructive reciprocity norms	Protagonist/constructive reciprocity norms	Inclusive/maintenance reciprocity norms
Differentiated self-oriented needs	Integrated multi-oriented needs	Amorphous undifferentiated needs

unity. Interestingly enough, excellent managers, though they are not used to talking these ways, *are* used to thinking paradoxically. Our hope for dealing with an increasingly complex organizational future lies in understanding—and making more explicit—the implicit truth in this way of thinking.

Appendix A: Trust Versus Mistrust

Since 1950 and the publication of Erik Erikson's *Childhood and Society*, many developmental psychologists have viewed trust and mistrust as the cornerstones of human development. Erikson divides the human life cycle into eight stages and suggests that each period is a time for a major developmental dilemma or crisis. The first of these crises is the trust versus mistrust crisis, which faces the human infant on entering a world of confusion and complexity. The determining relationship is, of course, with the infant's mother.

The other seven crises are autonomy versus shame and doubt (during the first year or two), initiative versus guilt (during the remaining preschool years), industry versus inferiority (during the early school years), identity versus identity confusion (during adolescence), intimacy versus isolation (during young adulthood), generativity versus stagnation (during adulthood), and integrity versus despair (during old age).

Working through and tentatively resolving each crisis brings an accompanying strength and a basis for future behavior. Thus viewed very roughly, for example, the young child who works through the autonomy crisis achieves an expected virtue of self-control, which provides a behavioral base for holding on and letting go.

Although Erikson sets up the trust/mistrust dilemma in an either/or form, he is careful to add that variations of the same problem continue on through life despite a tentative and precarious balancing of trust and mistrust during the crucial infancy period. If that tentative balance tilts in the direction of trust, Erikson suggests that the infant gains a basis for expecting the virtue of hope in the future, which in turn lays the groundwork for giving-and-receiving behavior.[7]

Appendix B: Paradox in Management Theories

More than 20 years ago, Douglas McGregor wrote about two sets of assumptions that he called Theory X and Theory Y. Theory X corresponded with our first three assumptions, the hard ones. But Theory Y was not just Theory X's opposite, although that is what many observers concluded. McGregor did not intend the two sets of assumptions to be forced into the hard versus soft mold. He meant Theory Y to be an integrative set of assumptions, not Theory X's polar opposite. As McGregor notes in describing the paradoxical qualities of Theory Y:

> The central principle of Theory Y is that of integration; the creation of conditions such that the members of the organization can achieve their own goals best by directing their goals toward the success of the enterprise. . . . The concept of integration and self-control [also] carries the implication that the organization will be more effective in achieving its economic objectives if adjustments are made in significant ways to the needs and goals of its members.[8]

In other words, McGregor is suggesting that each party could meet its own goals best by paradoxically directing them largely toward the goals of the other party. Much to McGregor's disappointment, this was not the way many people came to see Theory Y.

Likewise, five years later, Robert R. Blake and Jane S. Mouton developed the managerial grid. Building on others' thinking, including McGregor's, they originated the concept of organization development and built it around five styles of management. By using the concern for production and the concern for people as two polar extremes, they identified two of the styles (9,1 and 1,9) with these extremes, another style (1,1) as low on both concerns, and two other styles (5,5 and 9,9) as trying to take both production and people concerns into account. Blake and Mouton's major contribution, I believe, was to distinguish the middle path compromise position of 5,5 from the paradoxical fusion style of 9,9. As they wrote about the 9,9 style:

> Unlike the other basic approaches, it is assumed in the 9,9 managerial style that there is no necessary and inherent conflict between the organization purpose of production requirements and the needs of people. Under 9,9, effective integration of people with production is possible by involving them and their ideas in determining the conditions and strategies of work.[9]

In their writings on differentiation and integration, Paul R. Lawrence and Jay W. Lorsch described another paradox dealing with organizational structure. Lawrence and Lorsch found that active and uncertain organizational environments require specialized and differentiated functions within the organization. However, high differentiation also requires stronger, more elaborate integration efforts to help coordinate the parts of the organization. The paradox lies in the idea that the most effective companies in turbulent environments had both high differentiation and high integration. As Lawrence and Lorsch observe:

> The finding still leaves us with a curious contradiction. If, as we have found, differentiation and integration work at cross purposes within each organization, how can two (of the studied) organizations achieve high degrees of both? The best approach to explaining this apparent paradox becomes evident. . . . If organizations have groups of highly differentiated managers who are able to work together effectively, these managers must have strong capacities to deal with interdepartmental con-

flicts. . . . Effective integration . . . means that these conflicts must be resolved to the approximate satisfaction of all parties and to the general good of the enterprise.[10]

Notes

1. Arthur W. Schlesinger, Jr., *A Thousand Days: John F. Kennedy in the White House* (Boston, Houghton Mifflin, 1965), p. 255.

2. James W. Driscoll, "Trust and Participation in Organizational Decision Making as Predictors of Satisfaction," *Academy of Management Journal*, 1973, vol. 21, no. 1, p. 44.

3. Dale Zand, "Trust and Managerial Problem Solving," *Administrative Science Quarterly*, June 1972, p. 229; and R. Wayne Boss, "Trust and Managerial Problem Solving Revisited," *Group and Organizational Studies*, September 1978, p. 331.

4. Zand, "Trust and Managerial Problem Solving," p. 234.

5. Boss, "Trust and Managerial Problem Solving Revisited," p. 338.

6. W. V. Quine, *The Ways of Paradox* (Cambridge, Mass., Harvard University Press, 1976), p. 1.

7. Erik H. Erikson, *Childhood and Society* (New York, Norton, 1950).

8. Douglas McGregor, *The Human Side of Enterprise* (New York, McGraw-Hill, 1960), p. 49.

9. Robert R. Blake and Jane S. Mouton, *The Managerial Grid* (Houston, Gulf Publishing, 1964), p. 142; and Robert R. Blake, Jane S. Mouton, Louis B. Barnes, and Larry E. Greiner, "Breakthrough in Organization Development," *HBR*, November–December 1964, p. 133.

10. Paul R. Lawrence and Jay W. Lorsch, *Organization and Environment* (Boston, Harvard Business School Division of Research, 1967), p. 53.

24 Understanding Your Organization's Character

ROGER HARRISON

The character of an organization, according to this author, is rooted in its ideological orientation. He postulates four separate ideologies that determine (a) the compatibility of an organization's interests with those of its members and (b) an organization's ability to deal with the external environment. He argues, moreover, that the failure to understand ideological differences often causes conflict between organizations as well as within them. After discussing the different ideologies and the types of organizations they embody, the author presents an overall framework for determining the optimum ideological fit of organizational interests and human interests.

The failure to recognize the ideological issues that underlie organizational conflict is common among managers and administrators. Usually the issues are recognized only when they are blatant and the lines of struggle are drawn, as in labor-management relationships. But by then the conflict may well have developed to the point where a constructive resolution is virtually impossible.

While the term "organization ideologies" is perhaps unfortunately ambiguous, it is the best name I can apply to the systems of thought that are central determinants of the character of organizations. An organization's ideology affects the behavior of its people, its ability to effectively meet their needs and demands, and the way it copes with the external environment. Furthermore, much of the conflict that surrounds organization change is really ideological struggle (an idea that is certainly not new to political science but one about which behavioral scientists have, until recently, been curiously quiet).

For example, during the commissioning and start-up stages of a U.S. chemical plant in Europe, it became apparent that the Americans and local nationals involved had rather different ideas about decision making and commitment to decisions. Consider the approach of each group:

- ☐ The Americans tended to operate within what I later describe as a task-oriented ideology. In problem-solving meetings they believed that everyone who had relevant ideas or information should contribute to the debates, and that in reaching a decision the greatest weight should be given to the best-informed and most knowledgeable people. They strove, moreover, for a clear-cut decision; and once the decision was made, they usually were committed to it even if they did not completely agree with it.
- ☐ Some of the nationals, however, came to the project from very authoritarian organizations and tended to operate from a power-oriented ideological base (this is also described later). Each individual seemed to be trying to exert as much control as possible and to accept as little influence from others as possible. The person in a position of authority seemed to ignore the ideas of juniors and the advice of staff experts. The person who was not in a position of authority kept rather quiet in meetings and seemed almost happy when there was an unclear decision or no decision at all. This person would then proceed the way he had wanted to all along.

The task-oriented people regarded the foregoing behavior as uncooperative and, sometimes, as devious or dishonest. The power-oriented people, however, interpreted the task-oriented individuals' emphasis on communication and cooperation as evidence of softness and fear of taking responsibility.

Each group was engaging in what it regarded as normal and appropriate practice and tended to regard the other as difficult to work with or just plain wrong. That the differences were ideological was dimly realized only by the more thoughtful participants. The remainder tended to react to each other as wrongheaded *individuals*, rather than as adherents of a self-consistent and internally logical way of thinking and explaining their organizational world.

In this article I present a theory that identifies four distinct, competing organization iedologies and their meaning for the business executive. But, first, let me attempt to further clarify the concept. Here are the most obvious functions that an organization ideology performs:

- ☐ Specifies the goals and values toward which the organization should be directed and by which its success and worth should be measured.
- ☐ Prescribes the appropriate relationships between individuals and the organization (i.e., the "social contract" that legislates what the organization should be able to expect from its people, and vice versa).

☐ Indicates how behavior should be controlled in the organization and what kinds of control are legitimate and illegitimate.

☐ Depicts which qualities and characteristics of organization members should be valued or vilified, as well as how these should be rewarded or punished.

☐ Shows members how they should treat one another—competitively or collaboratively, honestly or dishonestly, closely or distantly.

☐ Establishes appropriate methods of dealing with the external environment—aggressive exploitation, responsible negotiation, proactive exploration.

Values and Ideologies

An organization ideology, however, is more than a set of prescriptions and prohibitions. It also establishes a rationale for these "do"s and "don't"s. This rationale explains the behavior of an organization's members as well as the working of the external environment (in the latter case, by telling members how to expect other people and organization systems to behave).

The rationale of an organization ideology is similar to what behavioral scientists call "organization theory." The difference is that behavioral scientists try with varying degrees of success to keep their values from influencing their organization theories; people, for the most part, do not try to keep their values from influencing their organization ideologies. (This is one reason why education about organization behavior is likely to be so emotionally loaded; if you change a man's organization theory, he usually ends up questioning his values as well.)

Among people in organizations, ideas of "what is" and "what ought to be" merge into one another and are—or are made to appear—consistent. Here is an example:

The ideology of a large U.S. manufacturer of consumer products prescribed that work should be organized in the way that produced the most profit. If this meant that some organization members had boring jobs which offered little opportunity for satisfaction and pride in their work, then it was unfortunate but ideologically irrelevant. According to the rationale of this ideology, a majority of people did not have much aptitude or desire for responsibility and decision making, anyhow, and those who did would rise by natural selection to more responsible, satisfying jobs.

Some young managers, however, had rather more egalitarian personal values. They uneasily suspected that there were more boring jobs than there were apathetic people to fill them. They were very excited about a group of research studies which attempted to show that giving employees more responsibility and involvement in decision making actually led to improved performance. But in my discussions with the managers, I found that the studies' instrumental value in improving organization effectiveness was not the cause of their popularity; rather, they were welcomed because they helped the managers reconcile their personal values with the dictum of the prevailing ideology that work should, above all, be organized to produce the best economic result. (I have, in fact, found that behavioral research findings are usually accepted or rejected on such ideological grounds instead of on the probability of their being true.)

A Conceptual Framework

There is a considerable body of thought in political science which holds that attempts to resolve ideological struggle are unwarranted interferences with the natural course of history and as such are doomed to be ineffectual.

I do not feel that this theory has been adequately tested, particularly in regard to organization change and development. The first step in testing it is to develop ways of discovering and understanding ideological conflicts when they arise in organizations.

In the remainder of this article I present a conceptual framework for doing this. It postulates four organization ideologies: (1) power orientation; (2) role orientation; (3) task orientation; and (4) person orientation. These ideologies are seldom found in organizations as pure types, but most organizations tend to center on one or another of them. I shall describe and contrast them in their pure form to emphasize their differences, and then indicate what I believe to be the strengths and weaknesses of each. After this I shall apply the conceptual model to some common conflicts in modern organization life.

Power Orientation

An organization that is power-oriented attempts to dominate its environment and vanquish all opposition. It is unwilling to be subject to any external law or power. And within the organization those who are powerful strive to maintain absolute control over subordinates.

The power-oriented organization is competitive and jealous of its territory (whether this be markets, land area, product lines, or access to resources). It seeks to expand its control at the expense of others, often exploiting weaker organizations. Even a weak power-oriented organization takes satisfaction in being able to dominate others that are still weaker. Such organizations always attempt to bargain to their own advantage and readily find justification for abrogating agreements which are no longer self-serving.

Some modern conglomerates project images of power ideology. They buy and sell organizations and people as commodities, in apparent disregard of human values and the general welfare. They seem to have voracious appetites for growth, which is valued for its own sake. Competition to acquire other companies and properties is ruthless and sometimes outside the law. Within the organization, the law of the jungle often seems to prevail among executives as they struggle for personal advantage against their peers.

There is, however, a softer form of the power orientation that is often found among old established firms, particularly those with a background of family ownership. Here the employees may be cared for rather than exploited, especially those that are old and loyal. Externally, the proprietors may hold to a code of honor, especially when dealing with others like themselves. This is the power orientation with a velvet glove. But when the benevolent authority is crossed or challenged, from either within or without, the iron fist is very likely to appear again. In such cases, the test of power orientation is how hard a person or organization will fight for power and position when these are at issue.

Role Orientation

An organization that is role-oriented aspires to be as rational and orderly as possible. In contrast to the willful autocracy of the power-oriented organization, there is a preoccupation with legality, legitimacy, and responsibility.

It is useful to see role orientation as having developed partly in reaction to power orientation. Competition and conflict, for example, are regulated or replaced by agreements, rules, and procedures. Rights and privileges are carefully defined and adhered to. While there is a strong emphasis on hierarchy and status, it is moderated by the commitment to legitimacy and legality. The different attitudes of the power and role orientations toward authority might be likened to the differences between a dictatorship and a constitutional monarchy.

Predictability of behavior is high in the role-oriented organization, and stability and respectability are often valued as much as competence. The correct response tends to be more highly valued than the effective one. Procedures for change tend to be cumbersome; therefore the system is slow to adapt to change.

Most commercial organizations are too constricted by market demands to afford the extreme rigidity of a pure role orientation or the worst excesses of its tendency to place procedural correctness before task effectiveness. Some businesses, however, which either control their markets or operate in areas that are highly regulated by law, exhibit a considerable degree of role orientation. The rationality, impersonality, and adherence to procedure of many banks, insurance companies, public utilities, and social work organizations are cases in point. Their role orientation leaves the customer, the public, or the client with little alternate choice in dealing with them.

Task Orientation

In the organization that is task-oriented, achievement of a superordinate goal is the highest value. The goal need not be economic; it could be winning a war, converting the heathen, reforming a government, or helping the poor. The important thing is that the organization's structure, functions, and activities are all evaluated in terms of their contribution to the superordinate goal.

Nothing is permitted to get in the way of accomplishing the task. If established authority impedes achievement, it is swept away. If outmoded roles, rules, and regulations hinder problem solving, they are changed. If individuals do not have the skills or technical knowledge to perform a task, they are retrained or replaced. And if personal needs and social considerations threaten to upset effective problem solving, they are suppressed in the interests of "getting on with the job."

There is no ideological commitment to authority, respectability, and order as such. Authority is considered legitimate only if it is based on appropriate knowledge and competence; it is not legitimate if it is based solely on power or position. And there is little hesitation to break rules and regulations if task accomplishment is furthered by doing so.

There is nothing inherently competitive about task orientation. The organization structure is shaped and changed to meet the requirements of the task or function to be performed. Emphasis is placed on rapid, flexible organization response to changed conditions. Collaboration is sought if it will advance the goal; allies are chosen on the basis of mutual goals and values; and there is little "advantage seeking" in relationships with other organizations.

The task orientation is most readily found in those small organizations whose members have come together because of some shared value, task, or goal. Examples are social service organizations, research teams, and high-risk businesses. Often, however, internal conflict and external stress drive these organizations toward power and role orientations.

Large organizations that operate in highly complex, shifting environments offer more durable examples. Companies involved with dynamic markets or fast-changing, complex technology frequently establish project teams or "task forces." These groups of specialists are selected to solve a particular problem and often operate in a very flexible and egalitarian manner until the problem is solved. The units are then disbanded, and the members join other teams to work on new problems. Although the larger organization in which it operates may be basically role- or power-oriented, the project team or task force often exhibits a relatively pure task orientation. Moreover, these groups have been so successful that some organizations are trying to install a task-oriented ideology throughout their operations.

Some of the aerospace industries have probably gone the furthest in this direction, TRW Systems being a notable example. Although I do not know of any large organization that could be classed as "pure" in its task orientation, the success of such task-oriented programs as MBO is a sign of the growing interest among managers. Parenthetically, the most frequent reason for the failure of MBO is probably that task-oriented managers try to install it in power- or role-oriented organizations.

Person Orientation

Unlike the other three types, the person-oriented organization exists primarily to serve the needs of its members. The organization itself is a device through which the members can meet needs that they could not otherwise satisfy by themselves. Just as some organizations continually evaluate the worth of individual members as tools and accept or reject them accordingly, so the person-oriented organizations are evaluated as tools by their members. For this reason, some of these organizations may have a very short life; they are disposable when they cease to provide a system for members to "do their own thing."

Authority in the role- or power-oriented sense is discouraged. When it is absolutely necessary, authority may be assigned on the basis of task competence, but this practice is kept to the bare minimum. Instead, individuals are expected to influence each other through example, helpfulness, and caring.

Consensus methods of decision making are preferred; people are generally not expected to do things that are incongruent with their own goals and values. Thus roles are assigned on the basis of personal preference and the need for learning and growth. Moreover, the burden of unrewarding and unpleasant tasks is shared equally.

Illustrations of person orientation are small groups of professionals who have joined together for research and development. Some consulting companies, too, seem to be designed primarily as vehicles for members. It is typical of such organizations that growth, expansion, and maximization of income and profit are not primary considerations. Rather, the organizations, hopefully, are conducted to make enough money to survive and provide their members with a reasonable living as well as an opportunity to do meaningful and enjoyable work with congenial people.

There seem to be increasing pressures from the members of modern industrial organizations to move toward person orientation. Young professionals are pushing their companies for opportunities to work on interesting, worthwhile (congruent with their own values) projects. Engineers and scientists, for example, have refused to work on projects for the military and have been successful in getting transfers to nondefense-related activities. Job recruiters find that college graduates are often more interested in opportunities to learn and grow than they are in their chances for organization advancement. Such signs of social change illustrate why person orientation must be considered an ideological force to be reckoned with, even though there are few contemporary organizations that operate in total congruence with its principles.

Strengths and Weaknesses

An organization ideology obviously has a profound effect on organization effectiveness. It determines how (a) decisions are made, (b) human resources are used, and (c) the external environment is approached. An organization ideology tends to be internally viable when the people within the system want and need the prescribed incentives and satisfactions that reward good performance. It tends to be externally viable when the organization it embodies is a microcosm of the external environment and rewards the same skills, values, and motivations.

External Viability

Usually, as an organization increases in size, its operational environment becomes more complex. Most arenas in which large companies operate change rapidly and/or have many features that require an integrated response. World-wide markets and rapidly changing technology, for example, make heavy demands on the information-processing and decision-making capabilities of organizations.

The power-oriented organization is not well adapted to flexible response and effective information processing in such environments. Since decisions are made at the top, the information has to pass through many people who screen out the "irrelevant" data. Moreover, some may distort the message to their own advantage (aggressive competition is part of the ideology). And when conditions change rapidly, the time lag introduced by the filtering process may unduly delay organization response.

The role-oriented organization is also insufficiently flexible to easily adapt to rapid external changes. In order to achieve the security that is one of its highest values, it must perpetuate rather rigid roles and reporting relationships. This gives stability but means that even the most powerful individuals may be unable to produce needed changes quickly.

In times of change, established procedures often do not apply, and the information channels become overloaded with problems that require higher-level decisions. Consider what happened in the commissioning and start-up example referred to at the beginning of this article:

Because equipment was not working properly, many actions which ordinarily would have been dealt with by standard operating procedures required top-management decisions. But the ordinary channels would not carry the necessary volume of information, and the quality of decision making and problem solving suffered accordingly. However, when control was shifted to teams of experts clustered around each plant (a task-oriented system) the problems were handled more smoothly.

Change-Oriented Structures. The task-oriented organization's greatest strength is dealing with complex and changing environments. Decentralized control shortens communication channels and reduces time lags, distortion, and attenuation of messages.

Both the power- and role-oriented organizations associate control with a *position* in the organization; neither provides for rapid and rational reassignment of appropriate *persons* to positions of influence. In contrast, the task-oriented ideology clears the way for a very flexible system of control—one that can shift rapidly over time as differing resources are required by external problems.

Probably the best example of this system in operation is the project team or task force that is formed to identify, diagnose, and solve a particular problem. Even some rather bureaucratic organizations make use of these temporary systems for emergency problem solving. The task force leader is selected for his or her combination of technical expertise and ability to manage a small group in an egalitarian manner.

The temporary work system is a particularly characteristic response of the task-oriented organization to environmental change. These temporary systems can be activated quickly, provided with the necessary mix of skills and abilities, and disbanded again when the need is past. Their use provides what is, in effect, a continuously variable organization structure.

The person-oriented organization, too, is well adapted to dealing with complexity and change. It also features a fluid structure and short lines of communication and control.

Coping With Threat. In a highly competitive environment where organizations are frequently confronted with overt threats and hostility, the strengths and weaknesses of ideological types form a different pattern.

For example, while the power-oriented organization is not well suited to handle complexity and change, its structure and decision-making processes are admirably suited for swift decision making and rapid-action follow-through under high-risk conditions. It tends to promote tough, aggressive people who can lead the organization in a dangerous, competitive environment.

The task-oriented organization usually takes longer to respond, but the response is more likely to be based on adequate data and planning. In contrast to the power-oriented structure, which is aggressively directed from the top, it tends to enlist the full commitment of organization members at all levels.

The role-oriented organization does not deal successfully with sudden increases in threat because it relies heavily on established operational procedures. Consequently, its structure is too cumbersome to react quickly in cases of overt threat.

And the person-oriented organization has difficulty directing its members' activities in unison until the danger is so clear and present that it may be too late. The person-oriented structure, however, does offer some advantages—its members are committed and have a high concern for one another's welfare.

Probably the most viable organization in a hostile, threatening environment would have a combination of the power and task orientations. This is a difficult marriage, however, because the desire for personal power is often incompatible with the required willingness to relinquish control to those with the most knowledge and ability for the task at hand.

Internal Viability

The power-oriented organization is an excellent structure for attaching many eyes, ears, hands, and feet to one brain. It exercises tight internal control and integration. As mentioned earlier, the system works well when problems take the form of overt challenges that can be comprehended and solved by one or a few intelligent, courageous people at the top.

But when the power-oriented organization becomes large and complex, this control tends to break down. Under these conditions the role-oriented ideology is more effective. It provides rules and procedures that allow a high degree of internal integration with little active intervention from the top.

It is obviously more difficult to achieve internal cohesion under a task- or person-oriented ideology. For example, if the work is done by temporary project teams, how are their efforts to be coordinated to a common goal? When a problem-solving team comes up with a solution and then disbands, how is its work to be given impact and continuity in the rest of the organization? Some stable and central structure is needed to provide coordination, long-range planning, and continuity of effort. If it is too stable, however, it may become role-oriented (rigid and hard to change) or power-oriented (recentralizing control). The personal power and security needs of individual members may foster such developments.

These dilemmas of internal structure have led to various compromise solutions such as the "matrix organization." The term "matrix" is used because the actual working groups *cut horizontally across* the normal functional-pyramidal organization, bringing together selected individuals from different functions and different levels to work in a relatively autonomous, egalitarian group. Structural stability is provided by a fixed *role-oriented* framework organized on functional lines. Personnel are readily detachable from the functions for varying periods of time during which they join a *task-oriented* work unit or project team. They are directed by the work unit; but their pay, career prospects, and promotions emanate from the role-oriented part of the system.

Matrix forms of organizations have been used with success in highly technical businesses operating in a fast-changing environment. Again, TRW Systems is perhaps the oldest and most comprehensive example. Considerable experimentation with matrix forms has also taken place in the chemical industry, both in the United States and abroad.

Although the matrix system can be effective, it often suffers from attempts of the role-oriented functions to overcontrol the task-oriented functions. The resulting conflict is usually won by the former, which has greater permanence and more resources. One reason for this difficulty is that organizations try to operate partially task-oriented structures without commitment to the ideology. Role-oriented people cannot be plugged into a task-oriented system without conflict.

Effective Motivation. While the power-oriented organization provides a chance for a few aggressive people to fight their way to the top, it offers little security to the ordinary person. It is most viable in situations where people are deprived and powerless and have to accept a bad bargain as better than none. For example, the power-oriented organization thrives in underdeveloped countries.

The power-oriented organization also has the problem of using too much of its energy to police people. Reliance on rewards and punishments tends to produce surface compliance and covert rebellion. Where the quantity and quality of work can be observed (as on an assembly line), inspection and discipline may keep the system working. But if the power does not command loyalty as well, the system usually breaks down. A simple example is the sabotage of hard-to-test aspects of car assembly by disgruntled workers.

The role-oriented ideology tries to deal with the difficulty of supervising complex decision-making and problem-solving tasks by rationalization and simplification. Each job is broken into smaller elements, rules are established, and performance is observed. When conditions change, however, the members are likely to continue carrying out the same (now ineffective) procedures.

The power- and role-oriented organizations simply do not provide for the development and utilization of internal commitment, initiative, and independent judgment on the part of members at other than the highest levels. Nevertheless, in societies where most people's aspirations are just to get by, or at most to achieve a measure of economic security, the power- and role-oriented organizations are able to function adequately.

In affluent societies, however, where security is more widely assured, people begin to look for deeper satisfactions in their work. They attempt to change tightly controlled work assignments and rigid internal structures. When trends toward task orientation ("useful," "meaningful" work) and person orientation (interesting work, self-expression, and "doing one's own thing") begin to develop in the wider society, internal pressures for change develop within power- and role-oriented organizations.

Unfortunately, not all people can function productively in a flexible and egalitarian structure. Some people *are* dependent, apathetic, or insecure. They do need external incentives to work and directives or rules to guide their activities.

Furthermore, the task-oriented ideology has its own ways of exploiting the individual. When the person's knowledge and skills become obsolete for the task at hand, an individual is expected to step gracefully aside to make room for someone who is better qualified. Status and recognition depend almost entirely on task contribution; if the problems facing the organization change suddenly, this can produce cruel reversals of an individual's personal fortune and work satisfaction.

The person-oriented organization seems to be specially created to fit the work situation to the motives and needs of the independent, self-directed individual. It is flexible to this person's demands, whereas the power-oriented organization is controlling; it gives scope for individual expression, whereas the role-oriented organization programs every move; it is concerned about personal needs, whereas the task-oriented organization uses people as instruments for "higher" ends. Unfortunately, as discussed above, the person-oriented organization is less likely to be effective in the external environment than organizations based on the other ideologies.

Toward Resolving Conflict

One basic tension runs throughout the ideologies and organization types discussed thus far. It is the conflict between (a) the values and structural qualities which advance the interests of people and (b) the values and structural qualities which advance the interests of organizations.

I can identify six interests, all mentioned previously, which are currently the subject of ideological tension and struggle. Three of these are primarily interests of people, and three are primarily interests of organizations. The three interests of people are:

1. Security against economic, political, or psychological deprivation.
2. Opportunities to voluntarily commit one's efforts to goals that are personally meaningful.
3. The pursuit of one's own growth and development, even where this may conflict with the immediate needs of the organization.

The three interests of organizations are:

1. Effective response to threatening and dangerous complex environments.
2. Dealing rapidly and effectively with change and complex environments.
3. Internal integration and coordination of effort toward organization needs and goals, including the subordination of individual needs to the needs of the organization.

These are obviously not all the interests at issue, but in my opinion they are among the most salient.

Exhibit 1 shows the position of each ideology vis-à-vis each interest and indicates, as does the preceding analysis, that the four ideologies have quite dissimilar profiles. Each ideology thus "fits" the needs of a given organization and its members differently. For example, a small organization operating in a rapidly changing technical field and employing people who desire personal growth and autonomy might find its best fit with either the task or person orientation (this depends, of course, on how competitive its markets are and what financial shape it is in). A very large organization

Exhibit 1. Interests of People and the Organization Under Four Orientations

A. Interests of people

Orientation	Security Against Economic, Political, and Psychological Deprivation	Opportunities for Voluntary Commitment to Worthwhile Goals	Opportunities to Pursue One's Own Growth and Development Independent of Organization Goals
Power orientation	Low: At the pleasure of the autocrat	Low: Unless one is in a sufficiently high position to determine organization goals	Low: Unless one is in a sufficiently high position to determine organization goals
Role orientation	High: Secured by law, custom, and procedure	Low: Even if, at times, one is in a high position	Low: Organization goals are relatively rigid and activities are closely prescribed
Task orientation	Moderate: Psychological deprivation can occur when an individual's contributions are redundant	High: A major basis of the individual's relationship to the organization	Low: The individual should not be in the organization if he does not subscribe to some of its goals
Person orientation	High: The individual's welfare is the major concern	High: But only if the individual is capable of generating his own goals	High: Orientation goals are determined by individual needs

B. Interests of the organization

Orientation	Effective Response to Dangerous, Threatening Environments	Dealing Rapidly and Effectively With Environmental Complexity and Change	Internal Integration and Coordination of Effort—If Necessary, at the Expense of Individual Needs
Power orientation	High: The organization tends to be perpetually ready for a fight	Moderate to low: Depends on size; pyramidal communication channels are easily overloaded	High: Effective control emanates from the top

Exhibit 1. (*Continued*)

B. Interests of the organization

Orientation	Effective Response to Dangerous, Threatening Environments	Dealing Rapidly and Effectively With Environmental Complexity and Change	Internal Integration and Coordination of Effort—If Necessary, at the Expense of Individual Needs
Role orientation	Moderate to low: The organization is slow to mobilize to meet increases in threat	Low: Slow to change programmed procedures; communication channels are easily overloaded	High: Features a carefully planned rational system of work
Task orientation	Moderate to high: The organization may be slow to make decisions but produces highly competent responses	High: Flexible assignment of resources and short communication channels facilitate adaptation	Moderate: Integrated by common goal; but flexible, shifting structure may make coordination difficult
Person orientation	Low: The organization is slow to become aware of threat and slow to mobilize effort against it	High: But response is erratic; assignment of resources to problems depends greatly on individual needs and interests	Low: A common goal is difficult to achieve and activities may shift with individual interests

operating a slowly changing technology in a restricted market and employing people who desire stability and security might find that a role orientation would provide the best balance.

For most organizations, however, there is no perfect fit with any one of the four ideologies. The "ideal" ideology would possess some power orientation to deal smartly with the competition, a bit of role orientation for stability and internal integration, a charge of task orientation for good problem solving and rapid adaption to change, and enough person orientation to meet the questions of new recruits who want to know why they should be involved at all unless their *individual* needs are met.

But, unfortunately, this mixture of ideologies *and their consequences* for people and organizations will inevitably result in conflict, and its subsequent wear and tear on organizations and their members. Trying to mix ideologies may also prevent each type from producing the advantages that are unique to it.

On the other hand, I do not think that the most viable organizations and the maximum satisfaction of human needs will result from monolithic structures which are ideologically homogeneous. It seems to me that we must learn to create and maintain organizations that contain within them the same diversity of ideologies and structures as are found in the complex environments in which the organizations must live and grow. This means that organizations may have to be composed of separate *parts* that are ideologically homogeneous within themselves yet still quite different from each other.

Such organizations will be very effective in dealing with complex environments and maximizing satisfactions for different types of people, but they will be subject to more internal conflict and ideological struggle than most current organizations could tolerate. For example, instead of a "company spirit" there will be several "company spirits," all different and very likely antagonistic. In this environment of conflicting but mutually interdependent parts, the management—not the resolution—of conflict will be a task of the greatest importance. One can imagine, in fact, that the most important job of top managers will not be directing the business, but, instead, managing the integration of its parts.[1]

Concluding Note

Whether people confront or avoid them, ideological issues will continue to sharpen of their own accord, both inside and outside the organization. As long as we continue to raise and educate our children permissively, the pressure from younger members of the organization for greater person orientation will increase. As operational environments become more turbulent and more technical, the attractions of task orientation will make themselves felt. Yet every change in organizations means some degree of power redistribution and with it some shift in rewards—such shifts will always be resisted by those with the most to lose, usually the older members of the organization who have a higher status. Thus I believe that ideological conflict will increase within organizations, whether that conflict is dealt with openly or not.

By dealing with such conflict openly, however, business executives may find ways to manage it in the service of both the organization and its members and also to use tension creatively as well as competitively. Hidden conflict, on the other hand, tends to eat away at the strength of an organization and then to erupt when it is most dangerous to organization health.

In writing this article, I have attempted to render these inevitable ideological differences more conceptually clear. The next step is to develop a common language and set of norms that support both the open confrontation of such issues and the strategies for dealing with them in our organizations.

Note

1. See Paul R. Lawrence and Jay W. Lorsch, "New Management Job: The Integrator," *HBR*, November–December 1967, p. 142.

PART FOUR
THE SKILLS OF AN EFFECTIVE EXECUTIVE

AN OVERVIEW

In the first article in this section, Robert L. Katz takes a different approach from many of the authors so far, in defining what a good manager is. In "The Skills of an Effective Administrator," Katz asserts that it is more useful to look at what executives do than what they are. In describing what they do he maintains that technical, human, and conceptual skills can be learned and that effective executives "are not necessarily born; they may be developed."

Regardless of how managers acquire them, however, it's legitimate to wonder how these skills and the ones discussed in the previous sections affect how executives actually perform their jobs. If, as Henry Mintzberg does in "The Manager's Job: Folklore and Fact," we adopt the view that managers don't control, plan, coordinate, and organize per se but instead play a variety of roles, we need to ask whether the roles they play require the manager have personal, leadership, and political skills. For instance, in playing Mintzberg's information role, managers scan their lines of information, which Kanter has shown effective managers need, or in the same role, find resources through information channels, which Kotter describes managers doing to acquire power.

One of the ways managers stay in control of their jobs is through delegating (which we could say is part of a leader's role) some of it to subordinates. As James C. Harrison, Jr. suggests in "How to Stay on Top of the Job," managers ought to choose a delegation method depending on the task and the amount of time the executive has to stay involved.

But how do the skills affect the ability to delegate? Letting go of a task, even though they cannot pass on accountability, requires a manager have not only knowledge of and trust in his or her subordinates but also be able to tolerate the periods of uncertainty between the time the job is delegated and when it is performed. Executives have to keep their hands in, but that does not mean taking control.

A similar process is necessary when managers muddle with a purpose, as H. Edward Wrapp maintains they need to do in "Good Managers Don't Make Policy Decisions." Successful managers take bits and pieces of information and mold them into patterns that they continually reform and reconceptualize. Looking at this process as requiring one of the skills, we can hypothesize that to muddle successfully, and not draw premature conclusions, a manager needs to have a strong sense of self.

In making good decisions, as Peter Drucker describes in "The Effective Decision," managers follow a distinct series of steps from classifying the problem to deciding which option will fulfill the problem's boundary conditions. To make "right" decisions, managers have to go out and look for themselves at what is going on in their organizations. But looking is useless if the manager cannot perceive reality though eyes unclouded by wishful thinking and patterns of thought built upon old concepts and expectations.

This clear vision is also essential when managers have to sift the qualitative data their subordinates bring them. And as Larry E. Greiner, D. Paul Leitch, and Louis B. Barnes make clear in "Putting Judgments Back into Decisions," qualitative judgments are "critical in evaluating the performance of lower levels in today's organizations."

One of the things we saw leaders do is transmit something of value to the members of their organizations. When they make ethical decisions, as Laura L. Nash describes them doing in "Ethics Without the Sermon," managers reveal their values and their willingness to pursue a theoretical inquiry for the good of the organization as well as expand peoples' expectations of corporate behavior.

Finally, the skills of self-examination and exploration that are crucial to an individuals' growth are at the heart of the management process itself. As Richard Tanner Pascale says toward the end of his article "Zen and the Art of Management," in which he explores the subtle nuances in interpersonal communications that Japanese managers implicitly recognize, "I submit that a nontrivial set of management problems might be better understood if viewed from the other side of our Western fence. Undoubtedly, a very high degree of personal development is necessary to embrace both of these outlooks, to know when each is appropriate and to acquire the skills which each requires."

25
Skills of an Effective Administrator

ROBERT L. KATZ

Ever since organizations and management have been the subject of study people have been energetically trying to identify the personality traits of the ideal executive. This article was written to direct attention away from that effort and toward a more useful question: What observable skills does an effective executive demonstrate? The author points out that management's real concern should be for what a person can do rather than what a person is. He identifies three basic skills—technical, human, and conceptual—that every successful manager must have in varying degrees according to the level of management at which he or she is operating. With the three-skill approach the author challenges the notion that good managers are born. Undoubtedly, certain people are more richly endowed at birth with these skills than others, but with practice and training most managers can better their performance and be more effective in their jobs.

Although the selection and training of good administrators is widely recognized as one of American industry's most pressing problems, there is surprisingly little agreement among executives or educators on what makes a good administrator. The executive development programs of some of the nation's leading corporations and colleges reflect a tremendous variation in objectives.

At the root of this difference is industry's search for the traits or attributes which will objectively identify the "ideal executive" who is equipped to cope effectively with any problem in any organization. As one observer of U.S. industry recently noted:

> The assumption that there is an executive type is widely accepted, either openly or implicitly. Yet any executive presumably knows that a com-

Author's Note. This article is based on a study prepared under a grant from the Alfred P. Sloan Foundation.

> pany needs all kinds of managers for different levels of jobs. The qualities most needed by a shop superintendent are likely to be quite opposed to those needed by a coordinating vice president of manufacturing. The literature of executive development is loaded with efforts to define the qualities needed by executives, and by themselves these sound quite rational. Few, for instance, would dispute the fact that a top manager needs good judgment, the ability to make decisions, the ability to win respect of others, and all the other well-worn phrases any management man could mention. But one has only to look at the successful managers in any company to see how enormously their particular qualities vary from any ideal list of executive virtues.[1]

Yet this quest for the executive stereotype has become so intense that many companies, in concentrating on certain specific traits or qualities, stand in danger of losing sight of their real concern: *What a person can accomplish.*

It is the purpose of this article to suggest what may be a more useful approach to the selection and development of administrators. This approach is based not on what good executives *are* (their innate traits and characteristics), but rather on what they *do* (the kinds of skills which they exhibit in carrying out their jobs effectively). As used here, a *skill* implies an ability which can be developed, not necessarily inborn, and which is manifested in performance, not merely in potential. So the principal criterion of skillfulness must be effective action under varying conditions.

This approach suggests that effective administration rests on *three basic developable skills* which obviate the need for identifying specific traits and which may provide a useful way of looking at and understanding the administrative process. This approach is the outgrowth of firsthand observation of executives at work coupled with study of current field research in administration.

In the sections which follow, an attempt is made to define and demonstrate what these three skills are; to suggest that the relative importance of the three skills varies with the level of administrative responsibility; to present some of the implications of this variation for selection, training, and promotion of executives; and to propose ways of developing these skills.

Three-Skill Approach

It is assumed here that an administrator is one who (a) directs the activities of other persons and (b) undertakes the responsibility for achieving certain objectives through these efforts. Within this definition, successful administration appears to rest on three basic skills, which we will call *technical, human,* and *conceptual*. It would be unrealistic to assert that these skills are not interrelated, yet there may be real merit in examining each one separately, and in developing them independently.

Technical Skill

As used here, technical skill implies an understanding of, and proficiency in, a specific kind of activity, particularly one involving methods, processes, procedures, or techniques. It is relatively easy for us to visualize the technical skill of the surgeon, the musician, the accountant, or the engineer when each is performing his or her own special function. Technical skill involves specialized knowledge, analytical ability within that specialty, and facility in the use of the tools and techniques of the specific discipline.

Of the three skills described in this article, technical skill is perhaps the most familiar because it is the most concrete, and because, in our age of specialization, it is the skill required of the greatest number of people. Most of our vocational and on-the-job training programs are largely concerned with developing this specialized technical skill.

Human Skill

As used here, human skill is the leader's ability to work effectively as a group member and to build cooperative effort within the team. As *technical* skill is primarily concerned with working with "things" (processes or physical objects), so *human* skill is primarily concerned with working with people. This skill is demonstrated in the way the individual perceives (and recognizes the perceptions of) superiors, equals, and subordinates, and in subsequent personal behavior.

The person with highly developed human skill is aware of personal attitudes, assumptions, and beliefs about other individuals and groups; this skill comes with the ability to see the usefulness and limitations of these feelings. By accepting the existence of different viewpoints, perceptions, and beliefs, this person is skilled in understanding what others really mean by their words and behavior. This person is equally skillful in communicating to others, in their own contexts, what is meant by *his or her* behavior.

Such a person works to create an atmosphere of approval and security in which subordinates feel free to express themselves without fear of censure or ridicule, by encouraging them to participate in the planning and carrying out of those things which directly affect them. This person is sufficiently sensitive to the needs and motivations of others in the organization so that the possible reactions to, and outcomes of, various courses of action that may be undertaken can be judged. Having this sensitivity, the person is able and willing to *act* in a way which takes these perceptions by others into account.

Real skill in working with others must become a natural, continuous activity, since it involves sensitivity not only at times of decision making but also in the day-by-day behavior of the individual. Human skill cannot be a "sometime thing." Techniques cannot be randomly applied, nor can personality traits be put on or removed like an overcoat. Because everything which an executive says and does (or leaves unsaid or undone) has an effect on associates, the true self will, in time, show through. Thus, to be effective, this skill must be naturally developed and unconsciously, as well as consistently, demonstrated in the individual's every action. It must become an integral part of the whole being.

Because human skill is so vital a part of everything the administrator does, examples of inadequate human skill are easier to describe than are highly skillful performances. Perhaps consideration of an actual situation would serve to clarify what is involved:

> ☐ When a new conveyor unit was installed in a shoe factory where workers had previously been free to determine their own work rate, the production manager asked the industrial engineer who had designed the conveyor to serve as foreman, even though a qualified foreman was available. The engineer, who reported directly to the production manager, objected, but under pressure he agreed to take the job "until a suitable foreman could be found," even though this was a job of lower status than his present one. Then this conversation took place:
>
> **Production manager.** *I've had a lot of experience with conveyors. I want you to keep this conveyor going at all times except for rest periods, and I want it going at top speed. Get these people thinking in terms of 2 pairs of shoes a minute, 70 dozen pairs a day, 350 dozen pairs a week. They are all experienced operators on their individual jobs, and it's just a matter of getting them to do their jobs in a little different way. I want you to make that base rate of 250 dozen pair a week work!* [*Base rate was established at slightly under 75% of the maximum capacity. This base rate was 50% higher than under the old system.*]
>
> **Engineer.** *If I'm going to be foreman of the conveyor unit, I want to do things my way. I've worked on conveyors, and I don't agree with you on first getting people used to a conveyor going at top speed. These people have never seen a conveyor. You'll scare them. I'd like to run the conveyor at one-third speed for a couple of weeks and then gradually increase the speed.*
>
> *I think we should discuss setting the base rate* [*production quota before incentive bonus*] *on a daily basis instead of a weekly basis.* [*Workers had previously been paid on a daily straight piecework basis.*]
>
> *I'd also suggest setting a daily base rate at 45 or even 40 dozen pair. You have to set a base rate low enough for them to make. Once they know they can make the base rate, they will go after the bonus.*
>
> **Production manager.** *You do it your way on the speed; but remember it's the results that count. On the base rate, I'm not discussing it with you; I'm telling you to make the 250 dozen pair a week work. I don't want a daily base rate.*[2]

Here is a situation in which the production manager was so preoccupied with getting the physical output that he did not pay attention to the people through whom that output had to be achieved. Notice, first, that he made the engineer who designed the unit serve as foreman, apparently hoping to force the engineer to justify his design by producing the maximum output. However, the production manager was oblivious to (a) the way the engineer perceived this appointment, as a demotion, and (b) the need for the engineer to be able to control the variables if he was to be held responsible for maximum output. Instead the production manager imposed a production standard and refused to make any changes in the work situation.

Moreover, although this was a radically new situation for the operators, the production manager expected them to produce immediately at well above their previous output—even though the operators had an unfamiliar production system to cope with, the operators had never worked together as a team before, the operators and their new foreman had never worked together before, and the foreman was not in agreement with the production goals or standards. By ignoring all these human factors, the production manager not only placed the engineer in an extremely difficult operating situation but also, by refusing to allow the engineer to "run his own show," discouraged the very assumption of responsibility he had hoped for in making the appointment.

Under these circumstances, it is easy to understand how the relationship between these two men rapidly deteriorated, and how production, after two months' operation, was at only 125 dozen pairs per week (just 75% of what the output had been under the old system).

Conceptual Skill

As used here, conceptual skill involves the ability to see the enterprise as a whole; it includes recognizing how the various functions of the organization depend on one another, and how changes in any one part affect all the others; and it extends to visualizing the relationship of the individual business to the industry, the community, and the political, social, and economic forces of the nation as a whole. Recognizing these relationships and perceiving the significant elements in any situation, the administrator should then be able to act in a way which advances the overall welfare of the total organization.

Hence, the success of any decision depends on the conceptual skill of the people who make the decision and those who put it into action. When, for example, an important change in marketing policy is made, it is critical that the effects on production, control, finance, research, and the people involved be considered. And it remains critical right down to the last executive who must implement the new policy. If each executive recognizes the overall relationships and significance of the change, he or she is almost certain to be more effective in administering it. Consequently the chances for succeeding are greatly increased.

Not only does the effective coordination of the various parts of the business depend on the conceptual skill of the administrators involved, but so also does the whole future direction and tone of the organization. The attitudes of a top executive color the whole character of the organization's response and determine the "corporate personality" which distinguishes one company's ways of doing business from another's. These attitudes are a reflection of the administrator's conceptual skill (referred to by some as "creative ability"—the way the administrator perceives and responds to the direction in which the business should grow, company objectives and policies, and stockholders' and employees' interests.

Conceptual skill, as defined above, is what Chester I. Barnard, former president of the New Jersey Bell Telephone Company, is implying when he says: ". . . the essential aspect of the [executive] process is the sensing of the organization as a whole and of the total situation relevant to it."[3] Examples of inadequate conceptual skill are all around us. Here is one instance:

> ☐ In a large manufacturing company which had a long tradition of job-shop type operations, primary responsibility for production control had been left to the foremen and other lower-level supervisors. "Village" type operations with small working groups and informal organizations were the rule. A heavy influx of orders following World War II tripled the normal production requirements and severely taxed the whole manufacturing organization. At this point, a new production manager was brought in from outside the company, and he established a wide range of controls and formalized the entire operating structure.
>
> As long as the boom demand lasted, the employees made every effort to conform with the new procedures and environment. But when demand subsided to prewar levels, serious labor relations problems developed, friction was high among department heads, and the company found itself saddled with a heavy indirect labor cost. Management sought to reinstate its old procedures; it fired the production manager and attempted to give greater authority to the foremen once again. However, during the four years of formalized control, the foremen had grown away from their old practices, many had left the company, and adequate replacements had not been developed. Without strong foreman leadership, the traditional job-shop operations proved costly and inefficient.

In this instance, when the new production controls and formalized organizations were introduced, management did not foresee the consequences of this action in the event of a future contraction of business. Later, when conditions changed and it was necessary to pare down operations, management was again unable to recognize the implications of its action and reverted to the old procedures, which, under the circumstances, were no longer appropriate. This compounded *conceptual* inadequacy left the company at a serious competitive disadvantage.

Because a company's overall success is dependent on its executives' conceptual skill in establishing and carrying out policy decisions, this skill is the unifying, coordinating ingredient of the administrative process, and of undeniable overall importance.

Relative Importance

We may notice that, in a very real sense, conceptual skill embodies consideration of both the technical and human aspects of the organization. Yet the concept of *skill*, as an ability to translate knowledge into action, should enable one to distinguish between the three skills of performing the technical activities (technical skill), understanding and motivating individuals and groups (human skill), and coordinating and integrating all the activities and interests of the organization toward a common objective (conceptual skill).

This separation of effective administration into three basic skills is useful primarily for purposes of analysis. In practice, these skills are so closely interrelated that it is difficult to determine where one ends and another begins. However, just because the skills are interrelated does not imply that we cannot get some value from looking at them separately, or by varying their emphasis. In playing golf the action of the hands, wrists, hips, shoulders, arms, and head are all interrelated; yet in improving one's swing it is often valuable to work on one of these elements separately. Also, under different playing conditions the relative importance of these elements varies. Similarly, although all three are of importance at every level of administration, the technical, human, and conceptual skills of the administrator vary in relative importance at different levels of responsibility.

At Lower Levels

Technical skill is responsible for many of the great advances of modern industry. It is indispensable to efficient operation. Yet it has greatest importance at the lower levels of administration. As the administrator moves further and further from the actual physical operation, this need for technical skill becomes less important, provided that there are skilled subordinates and the administrator can help them solve their own problems. At the top, technical skill may be almost nonexistent, and the executive may still be able to perform effectively if human and conceptual skills are highly developed. For example:

☐ In one large capital-goods producing company, the controller was called on to replace the manufacturing vice president, who had been stricken suddenly with a severe illness. The controller had no previous production experience, but he had been with the company for more than 20 years and knew many of the key production personnel intimately. By setting up an advisory staff, and by delegating an unusual amount of authority to his department heads, he was able to devote himself to coordination of the various functions. By so doing, he produced a highly efficient team. The results were lower costs, greater productivity, and higher morale than the production division had ever before experienced. Management had gambled that this man's ability to work with people was more important than his lack of a technical production background, and the gamble paid off.

Other examples are evident all around us. We are all familiar with those "professional managers" who are becoming the prototypes of our modern executive world. These people shift with great ease, and with no apparent loss in effectiveness, from one industry to another. Their human and conceptual skills seem to make up for their unfamiliarity with the new job's technical aspects.

At Every Level

Human skill, the ability to work with others, is essential to effective administration at every level. One recent research study has shown that human skill is of paramount importance at the supervisor level, pointing out that the chief function of the supervisor as an administrator is to attain collaboration of people in the work group.[4] Another study reinforces this finding and extends it to the middle-management group, adding that the administrator should be primarily concerned with facilitating communication in the organization.[5] And still another study, concerned primarily with top management, underscores the need for self-awareness and sensitivity to human relationships by executives at that level.[6] These findings would tend to indicate that human skill is of great importance at every level, but notice the difference in emphasis.

Human skill seems to be most important at lower levels, where the number of direct contacts between administrators and subordinates is greatest. As we go higher and higher in the administrative echelons, the number and frequency of these personal contacts decrease, and the need for human skill becomes proportionately, although probably not absolutely, less. At the same time, conceptual skill becomes increasingly more important with the need for policy decisions and broad-scale action. The human skill of dealing with individuals then becomes subordinate to the conceptual skill of integrating group interests and activities into a whole.

In fact, a recent research study by Professor Chris Argyris of Yale University has given us the example of an extremely effective plant manager who, although possessing little human skill as defined here, was nonetheless very successful.

This manager, the head of a largely autonomous division, made his supervisors, through the effects of his strong personality and the "pressure" he applied, highly dependent on him for most of their "rewards, penalties, authority, perpetuation, communication, and identification."

As a result, the supervisors spent much of their time competing with one another for the manager's favor. They told him only the things they thought he wanted to hear, and spent much time trying to find out his desires. They depended on him to set their objectives and to show them how to reach them. Because the manager was inconsistent and unpredictable in his behavior, the supervisors were insecure and continually engaged in interdepartmental squabbles which they tried to keep hidden from the manager.

Clearly, human skill as defined here was lacking. Yet, by the evaluation of his superiors and by his results in increasing efficiency and raising profits and morale, this manager was exceedingly effective. Professor Argyris suggests that employees in modern industrial organizations tend to have a "built-in" sense of dependence on superiors which capable and alert people can turn to advantage.[7]

In the context of the three-skill approach, it seems that this manager was able to capitalize on this dependence because he recognized the interrelationships of all the activities under his control, identified himself with the organization, and sublimated the individual interests of his subordinates to *his* (the organization's) interest, set his goals realistically, and showed his subordinates how to reach these goals. This would seem to be an excellent example of a situation in which strong conceptual skill more than compensated for a lack of human skill.

At the Top Level

Conceptual skill, as indicated in the preceding sections, becomes increasingly critical in more responsible executive positions where its effects are maximized and most easily observed. In fact, recent research findings lead to the conclusion that at the top level of administration this conceptual skill becomes the most important ability of all. As Herman W. Steinkraus, president of Bridgeport Brass Company, said:

> One of the most important lessons which I learned on this job [the presidency] is the importance of coordinating the various departments into an effective team, and, secondly, to recognize the shifting emphasis from time to time of the relative importance of various departments to the business.[8]

It would appear, then, that at lower levels of administrative responsibility, the principal need is for technical and human skills. At higher levels, technical skill becomes relatively less important while the need for conceptual skill increases rapidly. At the top level of an organization, conceptual skill becomes the most important skill of all for successful administration. A chief executive may lack technical or human skills and still be effective if there are subordinates who have strong abilities in these directions. But if the chief executive's conceptual skill is weak, the success of the whole organization may be jeopardized.

Implications for Action

This three-skill approach implies that significant benefits may result from redefining the objectives of executive development programs, from reconsidering the placement of executives in organizations, and from revising procedures for testing and selecting prospective executives.

Executive Development

Many executive development programs may be failing to achieve satisfactory results because of their inability to foster the growth of these administrative skills. Programs which concentrate on the mere imparting of information or the cultivation of a specific trait would seem to be largely unproductive in enhancing the administrative skills of candidates.

A strictly informative program was described to me recently by an officer and director of a large corporation who had been responsible for the executive-development activities of his company, as follows:

> What we try to do is to get our promising young men together with some of our senior executives in regular meetings each month. Then we give the young fellows a chance to ask questions to let them find out about the company's history and how and why we've done things in the past.

It was not surprising that neither the senior executives nor the young men felt this program was improving their administrative abilities.

The futility of pursuing specific traits becomes apparent when we consider the responses of an administrator in a number of different situations. In coping with these varied conditions, this executive may appear to demonstrate one trait in one instance—for example, dominance when dealing with subordinates—and the directly opposite trait under another set of circumstances—for example, submissiveness when dealing with superiors. Yet in each instance the administrator may be acting appropriately to achieve the best results. Which, then, can we identify as a desirable characteristic? Here is a further example of this dilemma:

☐ A Pacific Coast sales manager had a reputation for decisiveness and positive action. Yet when he was required to name an assistant to understudy his job from among several well-qualified subordinates, he deliberately avoided making a decision. His associates were quick to observe what appeared to be obvious indecisiveness.

But after several months had passed, it became clear that the sales manager had very unobtrusively been giving the various salesmen opportunities to demonstrate their attitudes and feelings. As a result, he was able to identify strong sentiments for one man whose subsequent promotion was enthusiastically accepted by the entire group.

In this instance, the sales manager's skillful performance was improperly interpreted as "indecisiveness." Their concern with irrelevant traits led his associates to overlook the adequacy of his performance. Would it not have been more appropriate to conclude that his human skill in working with others enabled him to adapt effectively to the requirements of a new situation?

Cases such as these would indicate that it is more useful to judge an administrator on the results of performance than on apparent traits. Skills are easier to identify than are traits and are less likely to be misinterpreted. Furthermore, skills offer a more directly applicable frame of reference for executive development, since any improvement in an administrator's skills must necessarily result in more effective performance.

Still another danger in many existing executive development programs lies in the unqualified enthusiasm with which some companies and colleges have embraced courses in "human relations." There would seem to be two inherent pitfalls here: (1) Human relations courses might only be imparting information or specific techniques, rather than developing the individual's human skill. (2) Even if individual development does take place, some companies, by placing all of their emphasis on human skill, may be completely overlooking the training requirements for top positions. They may run the risk of producing people with highly developed human skill who lack the conceptual ability to be effective top-level administrators.

It would appear important, then, that the training of a candidate for an administrative position be directed at the development of those skills which are most needed at the level of responsibility for which she or he is being considered.

Executive Placement

This three-skill concept suggests immediate possibilities for the creating of management teams of individuals with complementary skills. For example, one medium-size midwestern distributing organization has as president a man of unusual conceptual ability but extremely limited human skill. However, he has two vice presidents with exceptional human skill. These three men make up an executive committee which has been outstandingly successful, the skills of each member making up for deficiencies of the others. Perhaps the plan of two-person complementary conference leadership proposed by Robert F. Bales, in which the one leader maintains "task leadership" while the other provides "social leadership," might also be an example in point.[9]

Executive Selection

In trying to predetermine a prospective candidate's abilities on a job, much use is being made these days of various kinds of testing devices. Executives are being tested for everything from "decisiveness" to "conformity." These tests, as a recent article in *Fortune* points out, have achieved some highly questionable results when applied to performance on the job.[10] Would it not be much more productive to be concerned with skills of doing rather than with a number of traits which do not guarantee performance?

This three-skill approach makes trait testing unnecessary and substitutes for it procedures which examine a person's ability to cope with the actual problems and situations that will be found on the job. These procedures, which indicate what a person can *do* in specific situations, are the same for selection and for measuring development. They are described in the section on developing executive skills which follows.

This approach suggests that executives should *not* be chosen on the basis of their apparent possession of a number of behavior characteristics or traits, but on the basis of their possession of the requisite skills for the specific level of responsibility involved.

Developing the Skills

For years many people have contended that leadership ability is inherent in certain chosen individuals. We talk of "born leaders," "born executives," "born salespeople." It is undoubtedly true that certain people, naturally or innately, possess greater aptitude or ability in certain skills. But research in psychology and physiology would also indicate, first, that those having strong aptitudes and abilities can improve their skill through practice and training, and, secondly, that even those lacking the natural ability can improve their performance and overall effectiveness.

The *skill* conception of administration suggests that we may hope to improve our administrative effectiveness and to develop better administrators for the future. This skill conception implies *learning by doing*. Different people learn in different ways, but skills are developed through practice and through relating learning to one's own personal experience and background. If well done, training in these basic administrative skills should develop executive abilities more surely and more rapidly than through unorganized experience. What, then, are some of the ways in which this training can be conducted?

Technical Skill

Development of technical skill has received great attention for many years by industry and educational institutions alike, and much progress has been made. Sound grounding in the principles, structures, and processes of the individual specialty, coupled with actual practice and experience during which the individual is watched and helped by a superior, appear to be most effective. In view of the vast amount of work which has been done in training people in the technical skills, it would seem unnecessary in this article to suggest more.

Human Skill

Human skill, however, has been much less understood, and only recently has systematic progress been made in developing it. Many different approaches to the development of human skill are being pursued by various universities and professional people today. These are rooted in such disciplines as psychology, sociology, and anthropology.

Some of these approaches find their application in "applied psychology," "human engineering," and a host of other manifestations requiring technical specialists to help the business executive with human problems. As a practical matter, however, the executive must develop personal human skill, rather than lean on the advice of others. To be effective, the executive must develop a personal point of view toward human activity, so that the executive will (a) recognize personal feelings and sentiments in a situation; (b) have an attitude about personal experiences which will enable reevaluation and learning from them; (c) develop ability in understanding what others by their actions and words (explicit or implicit) are trying to communicate to the executive; and (d) develop ability in successfully communicating ideas and attitudes to others.[11]

This human skill can be developed by some individuals without formalized training. Others can be individually aided by their immediate superiors as an integral part of the "coaching" process to be described later. This aid depends for effectiveness, obviously, on the extent to which the superior possesses the human skill.

For larger groups, the use of case problems coupled with impromptu role playing can be very effective. This training can be established on a formal or informal basis, but it requires a skilled instructor and organized sequence of activities.[12] It affords as good an approximation to reality as can be provided on a continuing classroom basis and offers an opportunity for critical reflection not often found in actual practice. An important part of the procedure is the self-examination of the trainee's own concepts and values, which may enable personal development of more useful attitudes about oneself and about others. With the change in attitude, hopefully, there may also come some active skill in dealing with human problems.

Human skill has also been tested in the classroom, within reasonable limits, by a series of analyses of detailed accounts of actual situations involving administrative action, together with a number of role-playing opportunities in which the individual is required to carry out the details of self-proposed action. In this way an individual's understanding of the total situation and personal ability to do something about it can be evaluated.

On the job, there should be frequent opportunities for a superior to observe an individual's ability to work effectively with others. These may appear to be highly subjective evaluations and to depend for validity on the human skill of the rater. But does not every promotion, in the last analysis, depend on someone's subjective judgment? And should this subjectivity be berated, or should we make a greater effort to develop people within our organizations with the human skill to make such judgments effectively?

Conceptual Skill

Conceptual skill, like human skill, has not been very widely understood. A number of methods have been tried to aid in developing this ability, with varying success. Some of the best results have always been achieved through the "coaching" of subordinates by superiors.[13] This is no new idea. It implies that one of the key responsibilities of the executive is to help subordinates to develop their administrative potentials. One way a superior can help "coach" a subordinate is by assigning a particular responsibility, and then responding with searching questions or opinions, rather than giving answers, whenever the subordinate seeks help. When Benjamin F. Fairless, now chairman of the board of the United States Steel Corporation, was president of the corporation, he described his coaching activities:

> When one of my vice presidents or the head of one of our operating companies comes to me for instructions, I generally counter by asking him questions. First thing I know, he has told me how to solve the problem himself.[14]

Obviously, this is an ideal and wholly natural procedure for administrative training, and applies to the development of technical and human skill, as well as to that of conceptual skill. However, its success must necessarily rest on the abilities and willingness of the superior to help the subordinate.

Another excellent way to develop conceptual skill is through trading jobs, that is, by moving promising young people through different functions of the business but at the same level of responsibility. This gives the person the chance literally to "be in the other's shoes."

Other possibilities include: special assignments, particularly the kind which involve inter-departmental problems; and management boards, such as the McCormick Multiple Management plan, in which junior executives serve as advisers to top management on policy matters.

For larger groups, the kind of case-problems course described above, only using cases involving broad management policy and interdepartmental coordination, may be useful. Courses of this kind, often called "General Management" or "Business Policy," are becoming increasingly prevalent.

In the classroom, conceptual skill has also been evaluated with reasonable effectiveness by presenting a series of detailed descriptions of specific complex situations. In these the individual being tested is asked to set forth a course of action which responds to the underlying forces operating in each situation and which considers the implications of this action on the various functions and parts of the organization and its total environment.

On the job, the alert supervisor should find frequent opportunities to observe the extent to which the individual is able to relate self and job to the other functions and operations of the company.

Like human skill, conceptual skill, too, must become a natural part of the executive's makeup. Different methods may be indicated for developing different people, by virtue of their backgrounds, attitudes, and experience.

But in every case that method should be chosen which will enable the executive to develop individual personal skill in visualizing the enterprise as a whole and in coordinating and integrating its various parts.

Conclusion

The purpose of this article has been to show that effective administration depends on three basic personal skills, which have been called *technical, human,* and *conceptual*. The administrator needs: (a) sufficient technical skill to accomplish the mechanics of the particular job for which he or she is responsible; (b) sufficient human skill in working with others to be an effective group member and to be able to build cooperative effort within the team she or he leads; (c) sufficient conceptual skill to recognize the interrelationships of the various factors involved in the situation, which will lead him or her to take that action which is likely to achieve the maximum good for the total organization.

The relative importance of these three skills seems to vary with the level of administrative responsibility. At lower levels, the major need is for technical and human skills. At higher levels, the administrator's effectiveness depends largely on human and conceptual skills. At the top, conceptual skill becomes the most important of all for successful administration.

This three-skill approach emphasizes that good administrators are not necessarily born; they may be developed. It transcends the need to identify specific traits in an effort to provide a more useful way of looking at the administrative process. By helping to identify the skills most needed at various levels of responsibility, it may prove useful in the selection, training, and promotion of executives.

Appendix: Retrospective Commentary

When this article was first published in 1955, there was a great deal of interest in trying to identify a set of ideal personality traits that would readily distinguish potential executive talent. The search for these traits was vigorously pursued in the hope that the selection and training of managers could be conducted with greater reliability.

This article was an attempt to focus attention on demonstrable skills of performance rather than on innate personality characteristics. And, while describing the three kinds of administrative skill (technical, human, and conceptual), it also attempted to highlight the importance of conceptual skill as a uniquely valuable managerial capability, long before the concept of corporate strategy was well defined or popularly understood.

It still appears useful to think of managerial ability in terms of these three basic, observable skills. It also still appears that the relative importance of these skills varies with the administrative level of the manager in the organization. However, my experience over the past 20 years, in working with senior executives in a wide variety of industries, suggests that several specific points require either sharp modification or substantial further refinement.

Human Skill

I now believe that this kind of skill could be usefully subdivided into (a) leadership ability within the manager's own unit and (b) skill in intergroup relationships. In my experience, outstanding capability in one of these roles is frequently accompanied by mediocre performance in the other.

Often, the most internally efficient department managers are those who have committed themselves fully to the unique values and criteria of their specialized functions, without acknowledging that other departments' differing values have any validity at all. For example, production managers may be most efficient if they put all their emphasis on obtaining a high degree of reliability in their production schedule. They would then resist any external pressures that place a higher priority on criteria other than delivering the required output on time. Or sales managers may be most efficient if they put all their emphasis on maintaining positive relationships with customers. They would then resist all pressures that would emphasize other values, such as ease of production or selling the highest gross margin items. In each case, managers will probably receive strong support from subordinates, who share the same values. But they will encounter severe antagonism from other departments with conflicting values.

To the extent that two departments' values conflict with each other, skillful intergroup relationships require some equivocation. But compromise is often perceived by departmental subordinates as a "sellout." Thus managers are obliged to choose between gaining full support from subordinates or enjoying full collaboration with peers and/or superiors. Having both is rarely possible. Consequently, I would revise my original evaluation of human skill to say now that internal *intragroup* skills are essential in lower and middle management roles and that *intergroup* skills become increasingly important in successively higher levels of management.

Conceptual Skill

In retrospect, I now see that what I called conceptual skill depends entirely on a specific way of thinking about an enterprise. This "general management point of view," as it has come to be known, involves always thinking in terms of the following: relative emphases and priorities among conflicting objectives and criteria; relative tendencies and probabilities (rather than certainties); rough correlations and patterns among elements (rather than clear-cut cause-and-effect relationships).

I am now far less sanguine about the degree to which this way of thinking can be developed on the job. Unless a person has learned to think this way early in life, it is unrealistic to expect a major change on reaching executive status. Job rotation, special interdepartmental assignments, and working with case problems certainly provide opportunities for a person to enhance previously developed conceptual abilities. But I question how easily this way of thinking can be inculcated after a person passes adolescence. In this sense, then, conceptual skill should perhaps be viewed as an *innate* ability.

Technical Skill

In the original article, I suggested that specific technical skills are unimportant at top management levels. I cited as evidence the many professional managers who move easily from one industry to another without apparent loss of effectiveness.

I now believe this mobility is possible only in very large companies, where the chief executive has extensive staff assistance and highly competent, experienced technical operators throughout the organization. An old, established, large company has great operational momentum that enables the new chief executive to concentrate on strategic issues.

In smaller companies, where technical expertise is not as pervasive and seasoned staff assistance is not as available, I believe the chief executive has a much greater need for personal experience in the industry. The chief executive not only needs to know the right questions to ask subordinates; enough industry background is also needed to know how to evaluate the answers.

Role of the Chief Executive

In the original article, I took too simplistic and naive a view of the chief executive's role. My extensive work with company presidents and my own personal experience as a chief executive have given me much more respect for the difficulties and complexities of that role. I now know that every important executive action must strike a balance among so many conflicting values, objectives, and criteria that it will *always* be suboptimal from any single viewpoint. *Every* decision or choice affecting the whole enterprise has negative consequences for some of the parts.

The chief executive must try to perceive the conflicts and trace accurately their likely impact throughout the organization. Reluctantly, but wittingly, the CEO may have to sacrifice the interests of a single unit or part for the good of the whole. The chief needs to be willing to accept solutions that are adequate and feasible in the total situation rather than what, from a single point of view, may be elegant or optimum.

The chief executive must not only be an efficient operator, but also an effective strategist. It is the CEO's responsibility to provide the framework and direction for overall company operations. This executive must continually specify where the company will place its emphasis in terms of products, services, and customers. The chief must define performance criteria and determine what special competencies the company will emphasize. The chief executive also needs to set priorities and timetables. He or she must establish the standards and controls necessary to monitor progress and to place limits on individual actions. She or he must bring into the enterprise additional resources when they are needed.

Moreover, the chief executive must change management style and strike different balances among personal skills as conditions change or as the organization grows in size and complexity. The *remedial* role (saving the organization when it is in great difficulty) calls for drastic human action and emphasizes conceptual and technical skills. The *maintaining* role (sustaining the organization in its present posture) emphasizes human skills and requires only modest technical or strategic changes. But the *innovative* role (developing and expanding the organization) demands high competence in both conceptual and intergroup skills, with the technical contribution provided primarily by subordinates.

In my view, it is impossible for anyone to perform well in these continually changing roles without help. Yet because effective management of the total enterprise involves constant suboptimizing, it is impossible for the chief executive to get unanimous or continuous support from subordinates. By being overly friendly or supportive, the chief's effectiveness or objectivity may be compromised. Yet somewhere in the organization, the CEO needs to have a well-informed, objective, understanding, and supportive sounding board with whom doubts, fears, and aspirations can be freely discussed. Sometimes this function can be supplied by an outside director, the outside corporate counsel, or the company auditor. But such a confidant requires just as high a degree of conceptual and human skills as the chief executive; and to be truly helpful, this confidant must know all about the company's operations, key personnel, and industry. This role has been largely overlooked in discussions of organizational requirements, but in my view, its proper fulfillment is essential to the success of the chief executive and the enterprise.

Conclusion

I now realize more fully that managers at all levels require some competence in each of the three skills. Even managers at the lowest levels must continually use all of them. Dealing with the external demands on managers' units requires conceptual skill; the limited physical and financial resources available to them tax their technical skills; and the capabilities and demands of the persons with whom they deal make it essential that they possess human skill. A clear idea of these skills and of ways to measure managers' competence in each category still appears to me to be a most effective tool for top management, not only in understanding executive behavior, but also in the selection, training, and promotion of managers at all levels.

Notes

1. Perrin Stryker, "The Growing Pains of Executive Development," *Advanced Management*, August 1954, p. 15.

2. From a mimeographed case in the files of the Harvard Business School; copyrighted by the President and Fellows of Harvard College.

3. Chester I. Barnard, *Functions of the Executive* (Cambridge, Mass., Harvard University Press, 1948), p. 235.

4. A. Zaleznik, *Foreman Training in a Growing Enterprise* (Boston, Division of Research, Harvard Business School, 1951).

5. Harriet O. Ronken and Paul R. Lawrence, *Administering Changes* (Boston, Division of Research, Harvard Business School, 1952).

6. Edmund P. Learned, David H. Ulrich, and Donald R. Booz, *Executive Action* (Boston, Division of Research, Harvard Business School, 1950).

7. Chris Argyris, *Executive Leadership* (New York, Harper & Brothers, 1953); see also "Leadership Pattern in the Plant," *HBR*, January–February 1954, p. 63.

8. Herman W. Steinkraus, "What Should a President Do?," *Dun's Review*, August 1951, p. 21.

9. Robert F. Bales, "In Conference," *HBR*, March–April 1954, p. 44.

10. William H. Whyte, Jr., "The Fallacies of 'Personality' Testing," *Fortune*, September 1954, p. 117.

11. For a further discussion of this point, see F. J. Roethlisberger, "Training Supervisors in Human Relations," *HBR*, September 1951, p. 47.

12. See, for example, A. Winn, "Training in Administration and Human Relations," *Personnel*, September 1953, p. 139; see also, Kenneth R. Andrews, "Executive Training by the Case Method," *HBR*, September 1951, p. 58.

13. For a more complete development of the concept of "coaching," see Myles L. Mace, *The Growth and Development of Executives* (Boston, Division of Research, Harvard Business School, 1950).

14. "What Should a President Do?," *Dun's Review*, July 1951, p. 14.

26

The Manager's Job: Folklore and Fact

HENRY MINTZBERG

Just what does the manager do? For years the manager, the heart of the organization, has been assumed to be like an orchestra leader, controlling the various parts of the organization with the ease and precision of a Seiji Ozawa. However, when one looks at the few studies that have been done—covering managerial positions from the president of the United States to street gang leaders—the facts show that managers are not reflective, regulated workers, informed by their massive MIS systems, scientific, and professional. The evidence suggests that they play a complex, intertwined combination of interpersonal, informational, and decisional roles. The author's message is that if managers want to be more effective, they must recognize what their job really is and then use the resources at hand to support rather than hamper their own nature. Understanding their jobs as well as understanding themselves takes both introspection and objectivity on the managers' part. At the end of the article the author includes a set of self-study questions to help provide that insight.

If you ask managers what they do, they will most likely tell you that they plan, organize, coordinate, and control. Then watch what they do. Don't be surprised if you can't relate what you see to these four words.

When they are called and told that one of their factories has just burned down, and they advise the caller to see whether temporary arrangements can be made to supply customers through a foreign subsidiary, is this planning, organizing, coordinating, or controlling? How about when presenting a gold watch to a retiring employee? Or when attending a conference to meet people in the trade? Or on returning from that conference, when telling one of the employees about an interesting product idea picked up there?

The fact is that these four words, which have dominated management vocabulary since the French industrialist Henri Fayol first introduced them in 1916, tell us little about what managers actually do. At best, they indicate some vague objectives managers have when they work.

The field of management, so devoted to progress and change, has for more than half a century not seriously addressed *the* basic question: What do managers do? Without a proper answer, how can we teach management? How can we design planning or information systems for managers? How can we improve the practice of management at all?

Our ignorance of the nature of managerial work shows up in various ways in the modern organization—in the boast by successful managers that they never spent a single day in a management training program; in the turnover of corporate planners who never quite understood what it was the manager wanted; in the computer consoles gathering dust in the back room because the managers never used the fancy on-line MIS some analyst thought they needed. Perhaps most important, our ignorance shows up in the inability of our large public organizations to come to grips with some of their most serious policy problems.

Somehow, in the rush to automate production, to use management science in the functional areas of marketing and finance, and to apply the skills of the behavioral scientist to the problem of worker motivation, the manager—that person in charge of the organization or one of its subunits—has been forgotten.

My intention in this article is simple: to break you away from Fayol's words and introduce you to a more supportable, and what I believe to be a more useful, description of managerial work. This description derives from my review and synthesis of the available research on how various managers have spent their time.

In some studies, managers were observed intensively ("shadowed" is the term some of them used); in a number of others, they kept detailed diaries of their activities; in a few studies, their records were analyzed. All kinds of managers were studied—foremen, factory supervisors, staff managers, field sales managers, hospital administrators, presidents of companies and nations, and even street gang leaders. These "managers" worked in the United States, Canada, Sweden, and Great Britain. Appendix A is a brief review of the major studies that I found most useful in developing this description, including my own study of five American chief executive officers.

A synthesis of these findings paints an interesting picture, one as different from Fayol's classical view as a cubist abstract is from a Renaissance painting. In a sense, this picture will be obvious to anyone who has ever spent a day in a manager's office, either in front of the desk or behind it. Yet, at the same time, this picture may turn out to be revolutionary, in that it throws into doubt so much of the folklore that we have accepted about the manager's work.

I first discuss some of this folklore and contrast it with some of the discoveries of systematic research—the hard facts about how managers spend their time. Then I synthesize these research findings in a description of ten roles that seem to describe the essential content of all managers' jobs. In a concluding section, I discuss a number of implications of this synthesis for those trying to achieve more effective management, both in classrooms and in the business world.

Some Folklore and Facts About Managerial Work

There are four myths about the manager's job that do not bear up under careful scrutiny of the facts.

Folklore 1. *The manager is a reflective, systematic planner.* The evidence on this issue is overwhelming, but not a shred of it supports this statement.

Fact. *Study after study has shown that managers work at an unrelenting pace, that their activities are characterized by brevity, variety, and discontinuity, and that they are strongly oriented to action and dislike reflective activities.* Consider this evidence:

- ☐ Half the activities engaged in by the five chief executives of my study lasted less than nine minutes, and only 10% exceeded one hour.[1] A study of 56 U.S. foremen found that they averaged 583 activities per eight-hour shift, an average of 1 every 48 seconds.[2] The work pace for both chief executives and foremen was unrelenting. The chief executives met a steady stream of callers and mail from the moment they arrived in the morning until they left in the evening. Coffee breaks and lunches were inevitably work related, and ever-present subordinates seemed to usurp any free moment.
- ☐ A diary study of 160 British middle and top managers found that they worked for a half hour or more without interruption only about once every two days.[3]
- ☐ Of the verbal contacts of the chief executives in my study, 93% were arranged on an ad hoc basis. Only 1% of the executives' time was spent in open-ended observational tours. Only 1 out of 368 verbal contacts was unrelated to a specific issue and could be called general planning. Another researcher finds that "in *not one single case* did a manager report the obtaining of important external information from a general conversation or other undirected personal communication."[4]
- ☐ No study has found important patterns in the way managers schedule their time. They seem to jump from issue to issue, continually responding to the needs of the moment.

Is this the planner that the classical view describes? Hardly. How, then, can we explain this behavior? The manager is simply responding to the pressures of the job. I found that my chief executives terminated many of their own activities, often leaving meetings before the end, and interrupted their desk work to call in subordinates. One president not only placed his desk so that he could look down a long hallway but also left his door open when he was alone—an invitation for subordinates to come in and interrupt him.

Clearly, these managers wanted to encourage the flow of current information. But more significantly, they seemed to be conditioned by their own work loads. They appreciated the opportunity cost of their own time, and they were continually aware of their ever-present obligations—mail to be answered, callers to attend to, and so on. It seems that no matter what they are doing, managers are plagued by the possibilities of what they might do and what they must do.

When managers must plan, they seem to do so implicitly in the context of daily actions, not in some abstract process reserved for two weeks in the organization's mountain retreat. The plans of the chief executives I studied seemed to exist only in their heads—as flexible, but often specific, intentions. The traditional literature notwithstanding, the job of managing does not breed reflective planners; managers are real-time responders to stimuli, individuals who are conditioned by their job to prefer live to delayed action.

Folklore 2. *The effective manager has no regular duties to perform.* Managers are constantly being told to spend more time planning and delegating, and less time seeing customers and engaging in negotiations. These are not, after all, the true tasks of the manager. To use the popular analogy, the good manager, like the good conductor, carefully orchestrates everything in advance, then sits back to enjoy the fruits of the labor, responding occasionally to an unforeseeable exception.

But here again the pleasant abstraction just does not seem to hold up. We had better take a closer look at those activities managers feel compelled to engage in before we arbitrarily define them away.

Fact. *In addition to handling exceptions, managerial work involves performing a number of regular duties, including ritual and ceremony, negotiations, and processing of soft information that links the organization with its environment.* Consider some evidence from the research studies:

- ☐ A study of the work of the presidents of small companies found that they engaged in routine activities because their companies could not afford staff specialists and were so thin on operating personnel that a single absence often required the president to substitute.[5]
- ☐ One study of field sales managers and another of chief executives

suggest that it is a natural part of both jobs to see important customers, assuming the managers wish to keep those customers.[6]

☐ Someone, only half in jest, once described the manager as that person who sees visitors so that everyone else can get the work done. In my study, I found that certain ceremonial duties—meeting visiting dignitaries, giving out gold watches, presiding at Christmas dinners—were an intrinsic part of the chief executive's job.

☐ Studies of managers' information flow suggest that managers play a key role in securing "soft" external information (much of it available only to them because of their status) and in passing it along to their subordinates.

Folklore 3. *The senior manager needs aggregated information, which a formal management information system best provides.* Not too long ago, the words *total information system* (MIS) were everywhere in the management literature. In keeping with the classical view of the manager as that individual perched on the apex of a regulated, hierarchical system, the literature's manager was to receive all his important information from a giant, comprehensive MIS.

But lately, as it has become increasingly evident that these giant MIS systems are not working—that managers are simply not using them—the enthusiasm has waned. A look at how managers actually process information makes the reason quite clear. Managers have five media at their command—documents, telephone calls, scheduled and unscheduled meetings, and observational tours.

Fact. *Managers strongly favor the verbal media—namely, telephone calls and meetings.* The evidence comes from every single study of managerial work. Consider the following:

☐ In two British studies, managers spent an average of 66% and 80% of their time in verbal (oral) communication.[7] In my study of five American chief executives, the figure was 78%.

☐ These five chief executives treated mail processing as a burden to be dispensed with. One came in Saturday morning to process 142 pieces of mail in just over three hours, to "get rid of all the stuff." This same manager looked at the first piece of "hard" mail he had received all week, a standard cost report, and put it aside with the comment, "I never look at this."

☐ These same five chief executives responded immediately to 2 of the 40 routine reports they received during the five weeks of my study and to four items in the 104 periodicals. They skimmed most of these periodicals in seconds, almost ritualistically. In all, these chief executives of good-sized organizations initiated on their own—that is, not

> in response to something else—a grand total of 25 pieces of mail during the 25 days I observed them.

An analysis of the mail the executives received reveals an interesting picture—only 13% was of specific and immediate use. So now we have another piece in the puzzle: not much of the mail provides live, current information—the action of a competitor, the mood of a government legislator, or the rating of last night's television show. Yet this is the information that drove the managers, interrupting their meetings and rescheduling their workdays.

Consider another interesting finding. Managers seem to cherish "soft" information, especially gossip, hearsay, and speculation. Why? The reason is its timeliness; today's gossip may be tomorrow's fact. The manager who is not accessible to be told by telephone that the biggest customer was seen golfing with the main competitor may read about a dramatic drop in sales in the next quarterly report. But then it's too late.

To assess the value of historical, aggregated, "hard" MIS information, consider two of the manager's prime uses for information—to identify problems and opportunities[8] and to build personal mental models of surrounding things (e.g., how the organization's budget system works, how customers buy the product, how changes in the economy affect the organization, and so on). Every bit of evidence suggests that the manager identifies decision situations and builds models not with the aggregated abstractions an MIS provides, but with specific tidbits of data.

Consider the words of Richard Neustadt, who studied the information-collecting habits of Presidents Roosevelt, Truman, and Eisenhower:

> It is not information of a general sort that helps a President see personal stakes; not summaries, not surveys, not the *bland amalgams*. Rather . . . it is the odds and ends of *tangible detail* that pieced together in his mind illuminate the underside of issues put before him. To help himself he must reach out as widely as he can for every scrap of fact, opinion, gossip, bearing on his interests and relationships as President. He must become his own director of his own central intelligence.[9]

The manager's emphasis on the verbal media raises two important points:

1. Verbal information is stored in the brains of people. Only when people write this information down can it be stored in the files of the organization—whether in metal cabinets or on magnetic tape—and managers apparently do not write down much of what they hear. Thus the strategic data bank of the organization is not in the memory of its computers but in the minds of its managers.

2. The manager's extensive use of verbal media helps to explain reluctance to delegate tasks. When we note that most of the manager's important information comes in verbal form and is stored in his or her head, we can well appreciate the reluctance. It is not as if a dossier can be handed

over to someone; the time must be taken to "dump memory"—to tell that someone all that is known about the subject. But this could take so long that the manager may find it easier to do the task personally. Thus the manager is damned by a personal information system to a "dilemma of delegation"—to do too much personally or to delegate to subordinates with inadequate briefing.

Folklore 4. *Management is, or at least is quickly becoming, a science and a profession.* By almost any definitions of *science* and *profession*, this statement is false. Brief observation of any manager will quickly lay to rest the notion that managers practice a science. A science involves the enaction of systematic, analytically determined procedures or programs. If we do not even know what procedures managers use, how can we prescribe them by scientific analysis? And how can we call management a profession if we cannot specify what managers are to learn? For after all, a profession involves "knowledge of some department of learning or science" (*Random House Dictionary*).[10]

Fact. *The managers' programs—to schedule time, process information, make decisions, and so on—remain locked deep inside their brains.* Thus, to describe these programs, we rely on words like *judgment* and *intuition*, seldom stopping to realize that they are merely labels for our ignorance.

I was struck during my study by the fact that the executives I was observing—all very competent by any standard—are fundamentally indistinguishable from their counterparts of a hundred years ago (or a thousand years ago, for that matter). The information they need differs, but they seek it in the same way—by word of mouth. Their decisions concern modern technology, but the procedures they use to make them are the same as the procedures of the nineteenth-century manager. Even the computer, so important for the specialized work of the organization, has apparently had no influence on the work procedures of general managers. In fact, the manager is in a kind of loop, with increasingly heavy work pressures but no aid forthcoming from management science.

Considering the facts about managerial work, we can see that the manager's job is enormously complicated and difficult. The manager is overburdened with obligations; yet delegation of tasks is not easy. As a result, the manager is driven to overwork and is forced to do many tasks superficially. Brevity, fragmentation, and verbal communication characterize the work. Yet these are the very characteristics of managerial work that have impeded scientific attempts to improve it. As a result, the management scientist has concentrated efforts on the specialized functions of the organization, where analysis of procedures and quantification of relevant information is easier.[11]

But the pressures of the manager's job are becoming worse. Where before the manager needed only to respond to owners and directors, now subordinates with democratic norms continually reduce the manager's freedom to issue unexplained orders, and a growing number of outside influences (consumer groups, government agencies, and so on) expect attention. And the manager has had nowhere to turn for help. The first step in providing the manager with some help is to find out what the job really is.

Back to a Basic Description of Managerial Work

Now let us try to put some of the pieces of this puzzle together. Earlier, I defined the manager as that person in charge of an organization or one of its subunits. Besides chief executive officers, this definition would include vice presidents, bishops, supervisors, hockey coaches, and prime ministers. Can all of these people have anything in common? Indeed they can. For an important starting point, all are vested with formal authority over an organizational unit. From formal authority comes status, which leads to various interpersonal relations, and from these comes access to information. Information, in turn, enables the manager to make decisions and strategies for the unit.

The manager's job can be described in terms of various "roles," or organized sets of behaviors identified with a position. My description, shown in Exhibit 1, comprises ten roles. As we shall see, formal authority gives rise to the three interpersonal roles, which in turn give rise to the three informational roles; these two sets of roles enable the manager to play the four decisional roles.

Exhibit 1. The Manager's Roles

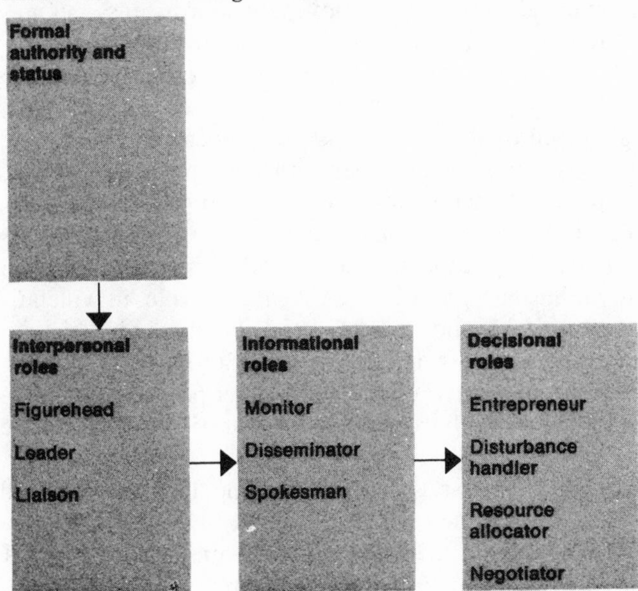

Interpersonal Roles

Three of the manager's roles arise directly from formal authority and involve basic interpersonal relationships.

1. First is the *figurehead* role. By virtue of the position as head of an organizational unit, every manager must perform some duties of a ceremonial nature. The president greets the touring dignitaries, the supervisor attends the wedding of a lathe operator, and the sales manager takes an important customer to lunch.

The chief executives of my study spent 12% of their contact time on ceremonial duties; 17% of their incoming mail dealt with acknowledgments and requests related to their status. For example, a letter to a company president requested free merchandise for a crippled schoolchild; diplomas were put on the desk of the school superintendent for signature.

Duties that involve interpersonal roles may sometimes be routine, involving little serious communication and no important decision making. Nevertheless, they are important to the smooth functioning of an organization and cannot be ignored by the manager.

2. Because of being in charge of an organizational unit, the manager is responsible for the work of the people of that unit. These actions constitute the *leader* role. Some of these actions involve leadership directly—for example, in most organizations the manager is normally responsible for hiring and training his or her own staff.

In addition, there is the indirect exercise of the leader role. Every manager must motivate and encourage employees, somehow reconciling their individual needs with the goals of the organization. In virtually every contact the manager has with employees, subordinates seeking leadership clues probe the manager's actions: "Does he approve?" "How would she like the report to turn out?" "Is he more interested in market share than high profits?"

The influence of the manager is most clearly seen in the leader role. Formal authority vests the manager with great potential power; leadership determines in large part how much of it will be realized.

3. The literature of management has always recognized the leader role, particularly those aspects of it related to motivation. In comparison, until recently it has hardly mentioned the *liaison* role, in which the manager makes contacts outside the vertical chain of command. This is remarkable in light of the finding of virtually every study of managerial work that managers spend as much time with peers and other people outside their units as they do with their own subordinates—and, surprisingly, very little time with their own superiors.

In Rosemary Stewart's diary study, the 160 British middle and top managers spent 47% of their time with peers, 41% of their time with people outside their unit, and only 12% of their time with their superiors. For Robert H. Guest's study of U.S. foremen, the figures were 44%, 46%, and 10%.

Exhibit 2. The Chief Executives' Contacts[a]

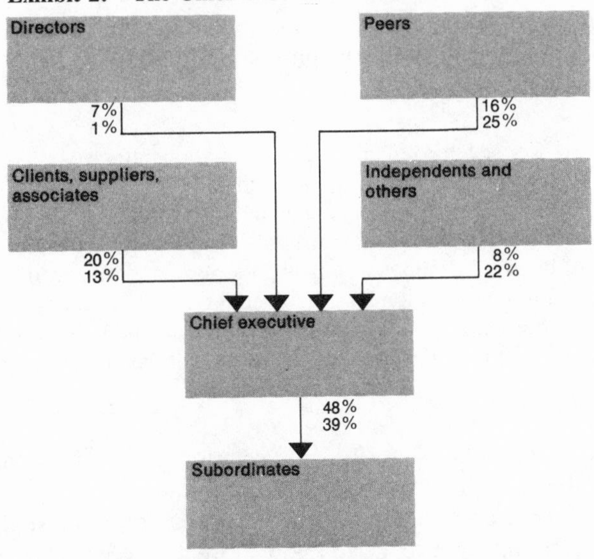

[a]The top figure indicates the proportion of total contact time spent with each group and the bottom figure, the proportion of mail from each group.

The chief executives of my study averaged 44% of their contact time with people outside their organizations, 48% with subordinates, and 7% with directors and trustees.

The contacts the five CEOs made were with an incredibly wide range of people: subordinates; clients, business associates, and suppliers; and peers—managers of similar organizations, government and trade organization officials, fellow directors on outside boards, and independents with no relevant organizational affiliations. The chief executives' time with and mail from these groups is shown in Exhibit 2. Guest's study of foremen shows, likewise, that their contacts were numerous and wide ranging, seldom involving fewer than 25 individuals, and often more than 50.

As we shall see shortly, the manager cultivates such contacts largely to find information. In effect, the liaison role is devoted to building up the manager's own external information system—informal, private, verbal, but, nevertheless, effective.

Informational Roles

By virtue of interpersonal contacts, both with subordinates and with a network of contacts, the manager emerges as the nerve center of the organizational unit. The manager may not know everything, but the manager typically knows more than any member of the staff.

Studies have shown this relationship to hold for all managers, from street gang leaders to U.S. presidents. In *The Human Group*, George C. Homans explains how, because they were at the center of the information flow in their own gangs and were also in close touch with other gang leaders, street gang leaders were better informed than any of their followers.[12] And Richard Neustadt describes the following account from his study of Franklin D. Roosevelt:

> The essence of Roosevelt's technique for information-gathering was competition. "He would call you in," one of his aides once told me, "and he'd ask you to get the story on some complicated business, and you'd come back after a couple of days of hard labor and present the juicy morsel you'd uncovered under a stone somewhere, and *then* you'd find out he knew all about it, along with something else you *didn't* know. Where he got this information from he wouldn't mention, usually, but after he had done this to you once or twice you got damn careful about *your* information."[13]

We can see where Roosevelt "got this information" when we consider the relationship between the interpersonal and informational roles. As leader, the manager has formal and easy access to every member of the staff. Hence, as noted earlier, the manager tends to know more about his or her own unit than anyone else does. In addition, liaison contacts expose the manager to external information to which subordinates often lack access. Many of these contacts are with other managers of equal status, who are themselves nerve centers in their own organization. In this way, the manager develops a powerful data base of information.

The processing of information is a key part of the manager's job. In my study, the chief executives spent 40% of their contact time on activities devoted exclusively to the transmission of information; 70% of their incoming mail was purely informational (as opposed to requests for action). The manager does not leave meetings or hang up the telephone in order to get back to work. In large part, communication *is* the work. Three roles describe these informational aspects of managerial work.

1. As *monitor*, the manager perpetually scans the environment for information, interrogates liaison contacts and subordinates, and receives unsolicited information, much of it as a result of the network of personal contacts the manager has developed. Remember that a good part of the information the manager collects in the monitor role arrives in verbal form, often as gossip, hearsay, and speculation. By virtue of contacts, the manager has a natural advantage in collecting this soft information for the organization.

2. The manager must share and distribute much of this information. Information gleaned from outside personal contacts may be needed within the organization. In the *disseminator* role, the manager passes some of the privileged information directly to subordinates, who would otherwise have

no access to it. When subordinates lack easy contact with one another, the manager will sometimes pass information from one to another.

3. In the *communicator* role, the manager sends some information to people outside the unit—a president makes a speech to lobby for an organization cause, or a supervisor suggests a product modification to a supplier. In addition, as part of the role as communicator, every manager must inform and satisfy the influential people who control the organizational unit. For the supervisor, this may simply involve keeping the plant manager informed about the flow of work through the shop.

The president of a large corporation, however, may spend a great amount of time dealing with a host of influences. Directors and shareholders must be advised about financial performance; consumer groups must be assured that the organization is fulfilling its social responsibilities; and government officials must be satisfied that the organization is abiding by the law.

Decisional Roles

Information is not, of course, an end in itself; it is the basic input to decision making. One thing is clear in the study of managerial work: the manager plays the major role in the unit's decision-making system. As its formal authority, only the manager can commit the unit to important new courses of action; and as its nerve center, only the manager has full and current information to make the set of decisions that determines the unit's strategy. Four roles describe the manager as decision-maker.

1. As *entrepreneur*, the manager seeks to improve the unit, to adapt it to changing conditions in the environment. In the monitor role, the president is constantly on the lookout for new ideas. When a good one appears, the president initiates a development project that may be personally supervised or delegated to an employee (perhaps with the stipulation that the president must approve the final proposal).

There are two interesting features about these development projects at the chief executive level.

First, these projects do not involve single decisions or even unified clusters of decisions. Rather, they emerge as a series of small decisions and actions sequenced over time. Apparently, the chief executive prolongs each project so that it can be fitted bit by bit into a busy, disjointed schedule and so that the president can gradually come to comprehend the issue, if it is a complex one.

Second, the chief executives I studied supervised as many as 50 of these projects at the same time. Some projects entailed new products or processes; others involved public relations campaigns, improvement of the cash position, reorganization of a weak department, resolution of a morale problem in a foreign division, integration of computer operations, various acquisitions at different stages of development, and so on.

The chief executive appears to maintain a kind of inventory of the development projects that are to be personally supervised—projects that are at various stages of development, some active and some in limbo. Like a juggler, the president keeps a number of projects in the air; periodically, one comes down, is given a new burst of energy, and is sent back into orbit. At various intervals, the chief puts new projects on-stream and discards old ones.

2. While the entrepreneur role describes the manager as the voluntary initiator of change, the *disturbance handler* role depicts the manager involuntarily responding to pressures. Here change is beyond the manager's control. Action is a must because the pressures of the situation are too severe to be ignored: strike looms, a major customer has gone bankrupt, or a supplier reneges on a contract.

It has been fashionable, I noted earlier, to compare the manager to an orchestra conductor, just as Peter F. Drucker wrote in *The Practice of Management*:

> The manager has the task of creating a true whole that is larger than the sum of its parts, a productive entity that turns out more than the sum of the resources put into it. One analogy is the conductor of a symphony orchestra, through whose effort, vision and leadership individual instrumental parts that are so much noise by themselves become the living whole of music. But the conductor has the composer's score; he is only interpreter. The manager is both composer and conductor.[14]

Now consider the words of Leonard R. Sayles, who has carried out systematic research on the manager's job:

> [The manager] is like a symphony orchestra conductor, endeavouring to maintain a melodious performance in which the contributions of the various instruments are coordinated and sequenced, patterned and paced, while the orchestra members are having various personal difficulties, stage hands are moving music stands, alternating excessive heat and cold are creating audience and instrument problems, and the sponsor of the concert is insisting on irrational changes in the program.[15]

In effect, every manager must spend a good part of the time responding to high-pressure disturbances. No organization can be so well run, so standardized, that it has considered every contingency in the uncertain environment in advance. Disturbances arise not only because poor managers ignore situations until they reach crisis proportions, but also because good managers cannot possibly anticipate all the consequences of the actions they take.

3. The third decisional role is that of *resource allocator*. To the man-

ager falls the responsibility of deciding who will get what in the organizational unit. Perhaps the most important resource the manager allocates is his or her own time. Access to the manager constitutes exposure to the unit's nerve center and decision-maker. The manager is also charged with designing the unit's structure, that pattern of formal relationships that determines how work is to be divided and coordinated.

Also, in the role as resource allocator, the manager authorizes the important decisions of the unit before they are implemented. By retaining this power, the manager can ensure that decisions are interrelated; all must pass through a single brain. To fragment this power is to encourage discontinuous decision making and a disjointed strategy.

There are a number of interesting features about the manager's authorizing others' decisions. First, despite the widespread use of capital budgeting procedures—a means of authorizing various capital expenditures at one time—executives in my study made a great many authorization decisions on an ad hoc basis. Apparently, many projects cannot wait or simply do not have the quantifiable costs and benefits that capital budgeting requires.

Second, I found that the chief executives faced incredibly complex choices. They had to consider the impact of each decision on other decisions and on the organization's strategy. They had to ensure that the decision would be acceptable to those who influence the organization, as well as ensure that resources would not be overextended. They had to understand the various costs and benefits as well as the feasibility of the proposal. They also had to consider questions of timing. All this was necessary for the simple approval of someone else's proposal. At the same time, however, delay could lose time, while quick approval could be ill considered and quick rejection might discourage the subordinate who had spent months developing a pet project.

One common solution to approving projects is to pick the person instead of the proposal. That is, those projects are authorized that are presented to the manager by people whose judgment is trusted. But the manager cannot always use this simple dodge.

4. The final decisional role is that of *negotiator*. Studies of managerial work at all levels indicate that managers spend considerable time in negotiations: the president of the football team is called in to work out a contract with the holdout superstar; the corporation president leads the company's contingent to negotiate a new strike issue; the supervisor argues a grievance problem to its conclusion with the shop steward. As Leonard Sayles puts it, negotiations are a "way of life" for the sophisticated manager.

These negotiations are duties of the manager's job; perhaps routine, they are not to be shirked. They are an integral part of the job, for only the manager has the authority to commit organizational resources in "real time," and only the manager has the nerve center information that important negotiations require.

The Integrated Job

It should be clear by now that the ten roles I have been describing are not easily separable. In the terminology of the psychologist, they form a gestalt, an integrated whole. No role can be pulled out of the framework and the job be left intact. For example, a manager without liaison contacts lacks external information. As a result, this manager can neither disseminate the information employees need nor make decisions that adequately reflect external conditions. (In fact, this is a problem for the new person in a managerial position, since the neophyte cannot make effective decisions until a network of contacts has been built up.)

Here lies a clue to the problems of team management.[16] Two or three people cannot share a single managerial position unless they can act as one entity. This means that they cannot divide up the ten roles unless they can very carefully reintegrate them. The real difficulty lies with the informational roles. Unless there can be full sharing of managerial information—and, as I pointed out earlier, it is primarily verbal—team management breaks down. A single managerial job cannot be arbitrarily split, for example, into internal and external roles, for information from both sources must be brought to bear on the same decisions.

To say that the ten roles form a gestalt is not to say that all managers give equal attention to each role. In fact, I found in my review of the various research studies that:

- ☐ Sales managers seem to spend relatively more of their time in the interpersonal roles, presumably a reflection of the extrovert nature of the marketing activity.
- ☐ Production managers give relatively more attention to the decisional roles, presumably a reflection of their concern with efficient work flow.
- ☐ Staff managers spend the most time in the informational roles, since they are experts who manage departments that advise other parts of the organization.

Nevertheless, in all cases the interpersonal, informational, and decisional roles remain inseparable.

Toward More Effective Management

What are the messages for management in this description? I believe, first and foremost, that this description of managerial work should prove more important to managers than any prescription they might derive from it. That is to say, *the manager's effectiveness is significantly influenced by insight into his or her own work.* Performance depends on how well the pressures and dilemmas of the job are understood and responded to. Thus managers who can be introspective about their work are likely to be effective at their jobs. Appendix B offers 14 groups of self-study questions for managers. Some may sound rhetorical; none is meant to be. Even though the questions cannot be answered simply, the manager should address them.

Let us take a look at three specific areas of concern. For the most part, the managerial logjams—the dilemma of delegation, the data base centralized in one brain, the problems of working with the management scientist—revolve around the verbal nature of the manager's information. There are great dangers in centralizing the organization's data bank in the minds of its managers. When they leave, they take their memory with them. And when subordinates are out of convenient verbal reach of the manager, they are at an informational disadvantage.

1. *The manager is challenged to find systematic ways to share privileged information.* A regular debriefing session with key subordinates, a weekly memory dump on the dictating machine, the maintaining of a diary of important information for limited circulation, or other similar methods may ease the logjam of work considerably. Time spent disseminating this information will be more than regained when decisions must be made. Of course, some will raise the question of confidentiality. But managers would do well to weigh the risks of exposing privileged information against having subordinates who can make effective decisions.

If there is a single theme that runs through this article, it is that the pressures of the job drive the manager to be superficial in his actions—to overload himself with work, encourage interruption, respond quickly to every stimulus, seek the tangible and avoid the abstract, make decisions in small increments, and do everything abruptly.

2. *Here again, the manager is challenged to deal consciously with the pressures of superficiality by giving serious attention to the issues that require it, by stepping back from tangible bits of information in order to see a broad picture, and by making use of analytical inputs.* Although effective managers have to be adept at responding quickly to numerous and varying problems, the danger in managerial work is that they will respond to every issue equally (and that means abruptly) and that they will never work the tangible bits and pieces of informational input into a comprehensive picture of their world.

As I noted earlier, the manager uses these bits of information to build models of his or her world. But the manager can also avail himself of the models of the specialists. Economists describe the functioning of markets, operations researchers simulate financial flow processes, and behavioral scientists explain the needs and goals of people. The best of these models can be searched out and learned.

In dealing with complex issues, the senior manager has much to gain from a close relationship with the management scientists of the organization. They have something important that the senior manager lacks—time to probe complex issues. An effective working relationship hinges on the resolution of what a colleague and I have called "the planning dilemma."[17] Managers have the information and the authority; analysts have the time and the technology. A successful working relationship between the two will be effected when the manager learns to share information and the analyst learns to adapt to the manager's needs. For the analyst, adaptation means worrying less about the elegance of the method and more about its speed and flexibility.

It seems to me that analysts can help the top manager especially to schedule time, feed in analytical information, monitor projects under the top manager's supervision, develop models to aid in making choices, design contingency plans for disturbances that can be anticipated, and conduct "quick-and-dirty" analysis for those that cannot. But there can be no cooperation if the analysts are out of the mainstream of the manager's information flow.

3. *The manager is challenged to gain control of personal time by turning obligations into advantages and by turning wishes into obligations.* The chief executives of my study initiated only 32% of their own contacts (and another 5% by mutual agreement). And yet to a considerable extent they seemed to control their time. There were two key factors that enabled them to do so.

First, the manager has to spend so much time discharging obligations that if they were viewed as just that, the manager would leave no mark on the organization. The unsuccessful manager blames failure on the obligations; the effective manager turns obligations to personal advantage. A speech is a chance to lobby for a cause; a meeting is a chance to reorganize a weak department; a visit to an important customer is a chance to extract trade information.

Second, the manager frees some time to do those things that the manager—perhaps no one else—thinks important by turning them into obligations. Free time is made, not found, in the manager's job; it is forced into the schedule. Hoping to leave some time open for contemplation or general planning is tantamount to hoping that the pressures of the job will go away. The manager who wants to innovate initiates a project and obligates others to report back; the manager who needs certain environmental information establishes channels that will automatically yield information; the manager who has to tour facilities has made a public commitment.

The Educator's Job

Finally, a word about the training of managers. Our management schools have done an admirable job of training the organization's specialists—management scientists, marketing researchers, accountants, and organizational development specialists. But for the most part they have not trained managers.[18]

Management schools will begin the serious training of managers when skill training takes a serious place next to cognitive learning. Cognitive learning is detached and informational, like reading a book or listening to a lecture. No doubt much important cognitive material must be assimilated by the manager-to-be. But cognitive learning no more makes managers than it does swimmers. The latter will drown the first time they jump into the water if their coach never takes them out of the lecture hall, gets them wet, and gives them feedback on their performance.

In other words, we are taught a skill through practice plus feedback, whether in a real or a simulated situation. Our management schools need to identify the skills managers use, select students who show potential in these skills, put the students into situations where these skills can be practiced, and then give them systematic feedback on their performance.

My description of managerial work suggests a number of important managerial skills—developing peer relationships, carrying out negotiations, motivating subordinates, resolving conflicts, establishing information networks and subsequently disseminating information, making decisions in conditions of extreme ambiguity, and allocating resources. Above all, the manager needs to be introspective about the work so that on-the-job learning may continue.

Many of the manager's skills can, in fact, be practiced, using techniques that range from role playing to videotaping real meetings. And our management schools can enhance the entrepreneurial skills by designing programs that encourage sensible risk taking and innovation.

No job is more vital to our society than that of the manager. It is the manager who determines whether our social institutions serve us well or whether they squander our talents and resources. It is time to strip away the folklore about managerial work, and time to study it realistically so that we can begin the difficult task of making significant improvements in its performance.

Appendix A: Research on Managerial Work

Considering its central importance to every aspect of management, there has been surprisingly little research on the manager's work, and virtually no systematic building of knowledge from one group of studies to another. In seeking to describe managerial work, I conducted my own research and also scanned the literature widely to integrate the findings of studies from many diverse sources with my own. These studies focused on two very different aspects of managerial work. Some were concerned with the characteristics of the work—how long managers work, where, at what pace and with what interruptions, with whom they work, and through what media they communicate. Other studies were more concerned with the essential content of the work—what activities the managers actually carry out, and why. Thus, after a meeting, one researcher might note that the manager spent 45 minutes with three government officials in their Washington office, while another might record that the manager presented the company's stand on some proposed legislation in order to change a regulation.

A few of the studies of managerial work are widely known, but most have remained buried as single journal articles or isolated books. Among the more important ones I cite (with full references in the footnotes) are the following:

- ☐ Sune Carlson developed the diary method to study the work characteristics of nine Swedish managing directors. Each kept a detailed log of activities. Carlson's results are reported in his book *Executive Behaviour*. A number of British researchers, notably Rosemary Stewart, have subsequently used Carlson's method. In *Managers and Their Jobs*, she describes the study of 160 top and middle managers of British companies during four weeks, with particular attention to the differences in their work.
- ☐ Leonard Sayles's book *Managerial Behavior* is another important reference. Using a method he refers to as "anthropological," Sayles studied the work content of middle- and lower-level managers in a large U.S. corporation. Sayles moved freely in the company, collecting whatever information struck him as important.
- ☐ Perhaps the best-known source is *Presidential Power*, in which Richard Neustadt analyzes the power and managerial behavior of Presidents Roosevelt, Truman, and Eisenhower. Neustadt used secondary sources—documents and interviews with other parties—to generate his data.
- ☐ Robert H. Guest, in *Personnel*, reports on a study of the foreman's working day. Fifty-six U.S. foremen were observed and each of their activities recorded during one eight-hour shift.
- ☐ Richard C. Hodgson, Daniel J. Levinson, and Abraham Zaleznik studied a team of three top executives of a U.S. hospital. From that study they wrote *The Executive Role Constellation*. These researchers addressed in particular the way in which work and socioemotional roles were divided among the three managers.
- ☐ William F. Whyte, from his study of a street gang during the Depression, wrote *Street Corner Society*. His findings about the gang's leadership, which George C. Homans analyzed in *The Human Group*, suggest some interesting similarities of job content between street gang leaders and corporate managers.

My own study involved five American CEOs of middle- to large-sized organizations—a consulting firm, a technology company, a hospital, a consumer goods company, and a school system. Using a method called "structural observation," during one intensive week of observation for each executive I recorded various aspects of every piece of mail and every verbal contact.

My method was designed to capture data on both work characteristics and job content. In all, I analyzed 890 pieces of incoming and outgoing mail and 368 verbal contacts.

Appendix B: Self-Study Questions for Managers

1. Where do I get my information, and how? Can I make greater use of my contacts to get information? Can other people do some of my scanning for me? In what areas is my knowledge weakest, and how can I get others to provide me with the information I need? Do I have powerful enough mental models of those things I must understand within the organization and in its environment?

2. What information do I disseminate in my organization? How important is it that my subordinates get my information? Do I keep too much information to myself because dissemination of it is time-consuming or inconvenient? How can I get more information to others so they can make better decisions?

3. Do I balance information collecting with action taking? Do I tend to act before information is in? Or do I wait so long for all the information that opportunities pass me by and I become a bottleneck in my organization?

4. What pace of change am I asking my organization to tolerate? Is this change balanced so that our operations are neither excessively static nor overly disrupted? Have we sufficiently analyzed the impact of this change on the future of our organization?

5. Am I sufficiently well informed to pass judgment on the proposals that my subordinates make? Is it possible to leave final authorization for more of the proposals with subordinates? Do we have problems of coordination because subordinates in fact now make too many of these decisions independently?

6. What is my vision of direction for this organization? Are these plans primarily in my own mind in loose form? Should I make them explicit in order to guide the decisions of others in the organization better? Or do I need flexibility to change them at will?

7. How do my subordinates react to my managerial style? Am I sufficiently sensitive to the powerful influence my actions have on them? Do I fully understand their reactions to my actions? Do I find an appropriate balance between encouragement and pressure? Do I stifle their initiative?

8. What kind of external relationships do I maintain, and how? Do I spend too much of my time maintaining these relationships? Are there certain types of people whom I should get to know better?

9. Is there any system to my time scheduling, or am I just reacting to the pressures of the moment? Do I find the appropriate mix of activities, or do I tend to concentrate on one particular function or one type of problem just because I find it interesting? Am I more efficient with particular kinds

of work at special times of the day or week? Does my schedule reflect this? Can someone else (in addition to my secretary) take responsibility for much of my scheduling and do it more systematically?

10. Do I overwork? What effect does my work load have on my efficiency? Should I force myself to take breaks or to reduce the pace of my activity?

11. Am I too superficial in what I do? Can I really shift moods as quickly and frequently as my work patterns require? Should I attempt to decrease the amount of fragmentation and interruption in my work?

12. Do I orient myself too much toward current, tangible activities? Am I a slave to the action and excitement of my work, so that I am no longer able to concentrate on issues? Do key problems receive the attention they deserve? Should I spend more time reading and probing deeply into certain issues? Could I be more reflective? Should I be?

13. Do I use the different media appropriately? Do I know how to make the most of written communication? Do I rely excessively on face-to-face communication, thereby putting all but a few of my subordinates at an informational disadvantage? Do I schedule enough of my meetings on a regular basis? Do I spend enough time touring my organization to observe activity at first hand? Am I too detached from the heart of my organization's activities, seeing things only in an abstract way?

14. How do I blend my personal rights and duties? Do my obligations consume all my time? How can I free myself sufficiently from obligations to ensure that I am taking this organization where I want it to go? How can I turn my obligations to my advantage?

Notes

1. All the data from my study can be found in Henry Mintzberg, *The Nature of Managerial Work* (New York, Harper & Row, 1973).

2. Robert H. Guest, "Of Time and the Foreman," *Personnel*, May 1956, p. 478.

3. Rosemary Stewart, *Managers and Their Jobs* (London, Macmillan, 1967); see also Sune Carlson, *Executive Behaviour* (Stockholm, Strömbergs, 1951), the first of the diary studies.

4. Francis J. Aguilar, *Scanning the Business Environment* (New York, Macmillan, 1967), p. 102.

5. Unpublished study by Irving Choran, reported in Mintzberg, op. cit.

6. Robert T. Davis, *Performance and Development of Field Sales Managers* (Boston, Division of Research, Harvard Business School, 1957); George H. Copeman, *The Role of the Managing Director* (London, Business Publications, 1963).

7. Stewart, op. cit.; Tom Burns, "The Directions of Activity and Communication in a Departmental Executive Group," *Human Relations*, 1954, vol. 7, no. 1, p. 73.

8. H. Edward Wrapp, "Good Managers Don't Make Policy Decisions," *HBR*, September–October 1967, p. 91; Wrapp refers to this as spotting opportunities and relationships in the stream of operating problems and decisions; in his article Wrapp raises a number of excellent points related to this analysis.

9. Richard E. Neustadt, *Presidential Power* (New York, Wiley, 1960), pp. 153–154; italics added.

10. For a more thorough, though rather different, discussion of this issue, see Kenneth R. Andrews, "Toward Professionalism in Business Management," *HBR*, March–April 1969, p. 49.

11. C. Jackson Grayson, Jr., in "Management Science and Business Practice," *HBR*, July–August 1973, p. 41, explains in similar terms why, as chairman of the Price Commission, he did not use those very techniques that he himself promoted in his earlier career as a management scientist.

12. George C. Homans, *The Human Group* (New York, Harcourt, Brace & World, 1950), based on the study by William F. Whyte entitled *Street Corner Society*, rev. ed. (Chicago, University of Chicago Press, 1955).

13. Neustadt, op. cit., p. 157.

14. Peter F. Drucker, *The Practice of Management* (New York, Harper & Row, 1954), pp. 341–342.

15. Leonard R. Sayles, *Managerial Behavior* (New York, McGraw-Hill, 1964), p. 162.

16. See Richard C. Hodgson, Daniel J. Levinson, and Abraham Zaleznik, *The Executive Role Constellation* (Boston, Division of Research, Harvard Business School, 1965), for a discussion of the sharing of roles.

17. James S. Hekimian and Henry Mintzberg, "The Planning Dilemma," *The Management Review*, May 1968, p. 4.

18. See J. Sterling Livingston, "Myth of the Well-Educated Manager," *HBR*, January–February 1971, p. 79.

27
How to Stay on Top of the Job

JAMES C. HARRISON, JR.

As all executives are well aware, the amount they can accomplish in a job is directly proportional to the amount they delegate to others. But with delegation comes a major problem. Even though executives can delegate a particular task they cannot delegate the responsibility connected to it. How much can they delegate and still keep on top of their jobs? The author describes nine different methods of delegating from previewing direction and questioning subordinates while the job is in progress to delegating by interdependence and correlation. He describes when it's appropriate to use the different styles, when to combine them, and how to know when to compromise. Ultimately, however, which style is most appropriate depends on the job being delegated and the amount of time the executive can spend in overseeing his obligations. Regardless, whenever they delegate, executives must keep their hands in whatever the task is.

Think of four executives you know. How many of them delegate responsibility to a subordinate the same way you do? One? Two? More than likely, *none* of them does.

Styles of delegation can range all the way from the executive who turns over an assignment carte blanche, to the executive who treats a subordinate as an "assistant to," giving a minimum of authority and responsibility. To be sure, most executives are familiar with and probably share the common business tenet that "the delegation of responsibility for performance should never be conferred without the delegation of authority for directing the performance." But what about the act of delegation itself? Specifically:

☐ How much responsibility can an executive delegate to a subordinate?

☐ When delegation proves unfruitful, can an executive excuse himself by placing the blame on the delegated-to subordinate?

☐ Does the delegating executive have equal responsibility for the failure?

☐ If so, how can an executive use delegation to reduce the demands on time, develop subordinates, and still keep on top of every job?

☐ In sum, what do executives really mean by the word *delegation*?

The plain fact is that some executives are able to use delegation successfully and others are not. And the differences in practice that go to make up delegation undoubtedly relate to the indication that there is a good deal of confusion among executives as to exactly what delegation is.

Two Extremes

Example 1. Following the Presidential election, an Associated Press dispatch, carrying the by-line of Jack Bell and bearing the dateline Washington, D.C., dealt with the question of whether the new Cabinet, under the direction of John F. Kennedy, would imitate its predecessor's custom of "calling turns and making policies." Bell doubted such would be the case, after having evaluated the new President's past behavior: "He hasn't tackled as mammoth a task as the presidency, but he has kept personally *on top of jobs* he has filled as a member of the House and a member of the Senate."[1]

Example 2. I happened to be present when a company president called a hurried conference with his staff following a meeting of the firm's board of directors. The board had been very critical of a recent decline in sales and profits, and had strongly intimated to the president that the fault lay not in the capabilities of the staff but in a lack of energetic application of their talents. The president concluded his post-mortem with this admonishment:

> I don't intend to subject myself to such humiliation again. You men are paid to do your jobs; it's not up to me to do them for you. I don't know how you spend your time, and I don't intend to try to find out. You know your responsibilities, and these figures bear out that you haven't discharged them properly. All I can say, men, is that if the next report doesn't show a marked improvement, I can't guarantee that all of us in this room will be together when another conference of this nature takes place.

For the sake of mutual understanding, even at the risk of belaboring the obvious, permit me to compare these two events. In both situations, there was a "delegation of responsibility." The fact that President Kennedy kept "personally on top of jobs" is, by nature of the wording, indication that he was not the sole performer. The company president conveyed his delegation with the words, "You know your responsibilities"; for, given the hierarchical organization of a business, such responsibilities could exist for his staff only by his transfer of them from himself to the staff.

But there are great differences in the styles of delegation used by these two men. The key to these differences in practice lies in their interpretations of the word *delegation*. Thus:

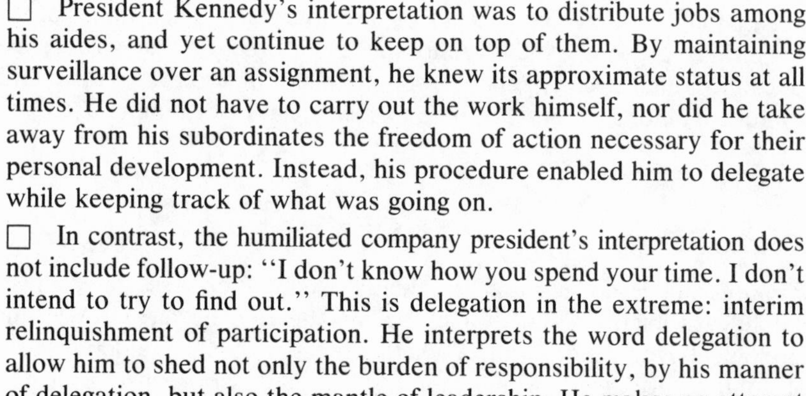

- ☐ President Kennedy's interpretation was to distribute jobs among his aides, and yet continue to keep on top of them. By maintaining surveillance over an assignment, he knew its approximate status at all times. He did not have to carry out the work himself, nor did he take away from his subordinates the freedom of action necessary for their personal development. Instead, his procedure enabled him to delegate while keeping track of what was going on.
- ☐ In contrast, the humiliated company president's interpretation does not include follow-up: "I don't know how you spend your time. I don't intend to try to find out." This is delegation in the extreme: interim relinquishment of participation. He interprets the word delegation to allow him to shed not only the burden of responsibility, by his manner of delegation, but also the mantle of leadership. He makes no attempt to stay on top of the job; he wants only to get out from under it.

Yet the company president undoubtedly does not believe that he is shirking his duties, and his personal sense of responsibility is, no doubt, equal to that felt by President Kennedy under his style of delegation. The difference between these two men, again, is not in their zeal or conscience; it lies in their *interpretation* of the word *delegation*—in a situation where interpretation is the key to the successful practice of it.

Root of Confusion

Why are there such differences in interpretation and, consequently, differences in practice? All Americans have a common language, presumably, so where does the confusion in meaning originate?

The search for answers to such questions has given birth to the scientific study of the meanings of words, called semantics. Semantics has as a basis the idea that words are not things in themselves, but are symbols of things. Consequently, one's interpretation of a word is not as flawless as might be one's examination of the object represented by the word.

In effect, the meaning of the word is no more correct than the symbolization it possesses for the hearer or reader. In spite of Gertrude Stein's reiteration that "a rose is a rose is a rose," a rose is *not* a rose if the person reading or hearing the phrase associates the word rose with a peony. This same kind of confusion can arise with the word *delegation*. No matter what the intent of the speaker or writer, its meaning is what the hearer or reader receives.

The dictionary does not settle the matter. *Webster's New International Dictionary* defines delegation as the "act of delegating, or investing with authority to act for another." But what is meant by "investing with authority"? Here is the root of the problem.

The key semantic, and consequently behavioral, difficulty arises in defining what degree of authority and what type of behavior are to be invested. For the amount of power or the kind of power to be given is not an inherent or specified part of the written definition. *Rather, the degree of authority is dependent on the extent to which a person is allowed to substitute one behavior for another.* And this is usually—in daily business practice—a matter of subjective interpretation and operating behavior on the part of the delegator. Consider:

- ☐ If, for example, delegation allows unrestricted substitution, then the company president is justified in the attitude he has adopted. Having invested his subordinates with authority (if such investiture can be unrestricted), he has unburdened himself of the particular responsibility.
- ☐ On the other hand, if delegation allows only a restricted substitution, then President Kennedy's method is the only possible approach. Because his subordinates acted with limited authority, he himself had to stay "on top of jobs," for he had to bridge the gap between the power they were given and the power necessary to complete the task at hand. That is, he had to participate with them in order to provide, when required, for the variance between the amount of authority delegated and the full power demanded in the final action.

Is the amount of substitution of behavior, the delegation of either unlimited or limited authority, merely a matter of personal choice? Can any executive divest himself of full authority in an action which comes within the sphere of his jurisdiction? Does the act of delegation have certain specific definable goals? Can styles of delegation be tailored to meet these goals?

Scope of Obligation

The decisive answer to these questions, and to the confusion over the meaning of delegation, is one word: *accountability*. An executive can delegate responsibility, that is, obligation. The executive can hold another person accountable as the delegator of responsibility to do a certain job. But this act by no means diminishes the measure of the executive's own accountability to superiors. The executive can no more be divorced from this liability than be excused from blame in the event of a subordinate's failure, or take full credit for the success. *The executive, not the subordinate, possesses the full obligation.*

Thus, in every single act of delegating there are two sets of correlative and equal responsibilities: (1) the obligations which the delegate has to the principal, and (2) the obligations for which the principal is accountable to those represented.

The obligation in the principal's case is not solely that of setting action in motion, such as by assigning the work to a subordinate. Far from it. The principal's responsibility is for final results, irrespective of the style or type of delegation. The same holds true for a subordinate if the latter in turn delegates the job down the line.

A president, for example, is a delegate of the board of directors assigned to the task of increasing sales and profits. The president, in turn, since this assignment is not done alone, delegates specific aspects of this responsibility to members of the staff. Because of this delegation, they are obligated to the president to produce the desired results. However—and this is the emphatic point—the president cannot delegate to them accountability to the board; this is the president's alone.

Nor can assistants delegate to their assistants their accountability to the president. The proper discharge of their responsibilities will pay off the obligation imposed on them, but a failure on their part will not make the president blameless for the outcome as far as the board is concerned. The assignment may have been more than a one-person job, but the accountability for its successful completion is *a one-person burden*. Only the labors can be shared.

Keeping on Top

If one must delegate and yet retain full accountability for the results, then some sort of supervision is necessary. How can a busy executive keep on top of every job that must be turned over to others? The ease that an executive will have in doing this job depends on the style of delegation selected.

Many executives, such as the company president cited earlier, behave as if keeping on top means only that they should watch what is going on, as spectators. But in this guise a person is actually not an executive; the person is not, as is demanded in his or her title, working through others. Rather, the person has simply turned a job over to others, retaining only all the confining characteristics of a helpless onlooker. The person can really be an *executive* only when working through others; only when they are extensions of the executive; only when the executive is well enough informed of their efforts to protect personal accountability, to be certain of the outcome.

Many executives hold "orientation" sessions. Here the nature of the problem is spelled out, dissected, and apportioned among the potential solvers. Yet this practice merely justifies the role of the spectator. Such a procedure amounts to no more than the president's saying: "*Now* you know your responsibilities. . . ." The executives may have known their responsibilities, but, judging by the results, the president certainly did not know his or hers, or was more a gambler than an executive. Certainly, an orientation session is necessary; the problem has to be spelled out and apportioned. But the crucial error occurs when an executive participates no further and merely awaits the end result. Keeping on top of what is going on means more than simply knowing what is going on; it means keeping a hand in the actions as well.

Keeping a Hand In

But to delegate and at the same time remember one's own full accountability requires self-discipline. Let me give you a very personal example. At one time I headed an advertising agency. One day there came to our door an account which was very foreign to my experience: publicizing a series of evangelistic meetings conducted by Billy Graham. On the advice of his friends, he was making his first public appearance outside his adopted home of Charlotte, North Carolina. The account was placed with our agency by a committee of local citizens whose sole responsibility to Graham consisted of engaging advertising services, setting the dates of meetings, and stipulating the amount of money to be expended on the campaign.

I knew that the head of our art department was a running mate of the members of the sponsoring committee and, realizing my own inexperience with this type of account, "delegated" the task to the artist. I dismissed the matter from my mind until Graham's business manager (whose name I have since forgotten) came into the agency prior to the first evangelistic meeting. I sent for the artist, and he showed up with layouts far more suitable as illustrations for religious works than as a mass appeal to the audience that Graham hoped to reach. Well, shamefacedly, I banished the artist along with his works to their northern-lighted quarters, and begged for another day of grace. The business manager granted it, but with some memorable parting words:

> Mr. Harrison, may I give you a little advice? A good executive has to delegate, just as you have done in this case. And the power to delegate enables a man to multiply his abilities many times. But, in order to do this, he must learn one basic rule: *to keep his hand in* whatever he delegates.

Most executives *do* want to multiply their abilities by spreading the actual work to be done among subordinates. But to do this successfully requires that an executive remember that *accountability* cannot be delegated. In sum, an executive must select delegating behavior that will concurrently allow:

- ☐ Spreading the physical work among aides.
- ☐ Seeing to it that the job is done correctly.
- ☐ Having enough time to take corrective action should something go wrong.
- ☐ Developing subordinate's talents and abilities.

It is combining these four elements into practice that most executives find difficult. Yet only by selecting a style of delegation that includes these four elements can an executive keep a hand in sufficiently to protect accountability.

Auditing Progress

But just how can an executive keep a hand in every job, considering the multiplicity of demands on time and energies? Obviously, such limitations prevent a complete sharing of the assignment. However, time is not so short (and, in fact, cannot be) that it prevents an active participation in every delegated job.

Such participation is possible, not by supervising every detail of the job, but by periodic audits of what is going on. Though the captain of a ship has other duties that prohibit personally steering the boat himself, the captain still has to make intermittent comparisons between the ship's present position and planned destination. True, such checks do not guarantee constant, undeviating, continuous direction of the ship's course. They do, nevertheless, enable the captain to make corrections with a minimum of lost time, effort, and results.

However, *auditing*, like delegation, can denote many different kinds of specific activities. So rather than fall into semantic traps, let us define auditing by looking at some methods that successful executives use to audit progress. From time to time I have observed various styles of delegation which business executives use to protect their accountability. Each of these methods has as a goal the four elements outlined above, and stresses active executive participation in the delegated activity, giving ample opportunity for correction before it is too late.

Now I confess that in only rare instances did I find uncompromising adherence to any single one of these methods for auditing delegation. Rather, the choice of a particular device depended on the nature of the responsibility delegated. The same executive would use several of them concurrently, each for different individual assignments. Conditions, not the executives, determined the selection of a specific plan of delegation. But more about this later. First, here are the methods of delegation.

1. *Previewing direction.* In this method, an executive gives a subordinate the problem and asks for a written synopsis of a plan of action at a specified time. By this process the executive receives at the very start the subordinate's interpretation of the problem, a definite and concrete line of attack, and a detailed plan of procedure that can be corrected or adjusted.

2. *Questioning on progress.* This is the most informal, the most revealing, and the most time-consuming style of delegation emphasizing executive participation. It requires that an executive send for or go to a

subordinate at or during the most propitious stages of development for the project in question. This method requires deft timing and a clear attitude of friendly interest. The executive cannot risk the appearance of "checking up," lest the subordinate's self-confidence be destroyed. This method is inconvenient because it requires an executive to stop work at the most inopportune moments, takes time to carry out, and interrupts the subordinate. Yet the executive does maintain a maximum grasp of what is going on.

3. *Demanding reports.* This method requires that the subordinate submit periodic progress reports, with or without specific deadlines. It can be the most pleasant of all audits, since it saves the time of all concerned. Yet it can also be the least satisfying method because its effectiveness depends on the subordinate's writing ability, the inclusion in the report of all facts necessary for judgment of progress (usually making the report unwieldy), and mutually understood measurements of development and progress which allow the accountable executive to be aware of deviations from an apparent pathway to the desired goal. In sum, this method relies heavily on the subordinate's talents and the executive's clarity in putting across ideas from the start. It may be doubly difficult to use if the project is complex.

4. *Scheduling conferences.* By scheduling oral reports or conferences for definite dates in the future, this style of delegation attempts to alleviate the complications of method 3, while at the same time gaining the merits of the informal questioning used in method 2. It is most useful when the project to be audited is one which has a series of events that can be planned and timed in advance. Success is contingent on a carefully planned chronology of developments, an assumption that the forecasts or scheduled events will actually materialize at the times anticipated, and a presumption that the original plan of attack decided on is the only feasible approach. The drawbacks consist of the pressure imposed by time, a blind conformance to a prearranged method of attack, and a prohibition of creative experimentation by the calendar-bound subordinate.

5. *Setting deadlines.* This method of delegation sets a time limit for completing delegated assignments. It is fairer than scheduling conferences in advance, since it abolishes all of the drawbacks except for the pressure imposed by time. But it also entails a maximization of certain potential liabilities.

These include loss of all time and materials consumed in the event of an impractical or unworkable solution, denial of all possible interim help and advice the delegator could have given his subordinate, and setback in the morale of the work force if failure should result.

Against these must be weighed freedom of thought and action extended to the delegated-to person, development of the subordinates' talents through the thrust of full and unrestrained authority, and minimizing interruptions of the work of the delegating executive.

Obviously, the only difference between this method and that employed by the company president in our vignette is the length of time during which there is, for all intents and purposes, complete abandonment of executive control. Naturally, the shorter the period, the better. This style of delegation is warranted only when the subordinate has proved an ability to perform successfully, the subordinate's mode of performance is identical to that of the delegating executive, or the task is so perfunctory that the path to its completion is unmistakable.

6. *Checking results.* This method, unlike method 2, can be used only when the particular project has tangible results while in progress. It is the most accurate, the most convenient for all concerned, and the least trouble to the subordinate.

The real test in using this method is in the self-discipline of the delegating executive, since it is imperative that progress (or lack of it) be witnessed firsthand. This style requires available time to travel to and make an inspection of the progress, a knack of showing interest in the progress instead of reflecting suspicion on the abilities of the delegate (as in method 2), and an ability and temperament to make constructive suggestions, as well as to leave behind an aura of encouragement.

7. *Measuring by crosscurrents.* Few problems are separate entities. The solution of one problem is usually reflected in other phases of an enterprise. For example, relieving a bottleneck in filling orders will automatically minimize the number and vociferousness of the complaints from the shipping department. In fact, the great majority of business problems are made known, not by their noticeable presence, but by their hindrance to other activities.

These crosscurrents of work flow provide measuring devices and warning signals, if an executive is attuned to them. This style of watchful delegation is effective where there is no damaging delay due to time lags in the crosscurrent warning signals, and where there is a dependable and direct relationship between the warning sign and its designated cause, and isolation and control of all other factors that filter into the crosscurrent.

8. *Delegating by interdependence.* This method can be used when the start of one activity begins with the culmination of another, or when the solution of a problem in one department becomes a problem in another, much like a relay race. Though devoid of intermediate participation by the top executive and consequently subject to inherent dangers, this style of delegation redeems itself on the strength of the adage: "Two heads are better than one." In effect, the report of progress is automatically given by the start of the next phase in the sequence. The delegated subordinates check on each other, for any one's performance is dependent on the others.

Such chains are quite often the case in business, as when the production, sales, and advertising departments are charged with increasing the volume of goods sold. Production must come forth with a product which sales thinks it can merchandise successfully; sales must invent a strategy in its area of marketing which will lend the greatest support to advertising; and advertising must originate a campaign designed to promote the salability of the product and to accelerate the effectiveness of the sales strategy. The responsibility and compliance of one group are, under such an alignment, mutually dependent on and therefore limited by the efforts of the others. The top executive has a built-in audit of progress.

Naturally, delegating by interdependence relies for favorable outcome on a marked degree of departmental interdependency for final results, separate and distinct functional responsibilities for each department involved, and sharp lines of demarcation whose boundaries, while contiguously dependent in that they circumscribe departments whose progress can be measured by their own results and not by the shortcomings of others.

9. *Delegating by correlation.* In contrast to the preceding method, this one depends on parallel activities: two or more departments predicate their plans on the fact that all the others will complete their roles successfully and simultaneously. The chief advantage over delegation by interdependence is a reliance on *concurrent* employment of efforts, so that all related (but departmentalized) goals will materialize at the same time. By the same token, the main disadvantage is that such a parallel relationship of results will end up in failure for all if there is a failure for one. This type of delegating arrangement can be employed whenever a successful conclusion can be pinpointed in time. For example:

☐ A bakery might be faced, in its wrapping area, with the problem of adapting machines to the use of a new wrapping film. A deadline of three weeks is given. During this same interval, the sales department is to formulate merchandising plans to introduce the bread in its "new dress." The same length of time is granted to the advertising department to prepare, and have ready to go, a specific promotion and media plan. Thus, on a stated date, all three responsibilities must be fulfilled: the bread must appear in its new wrapper, the merchandising must begin, and the advertising must appear.

Obviously, delegating by correlation needs to take into account assurance of satisfactory results, assumption of scheduled performance, and willingness of the top executive to accept accountability in the event of failure in any or all departments.

Combining Methods

As must be clear to the reader by now, all these styles of delegation can be easily combined. For example:

☐ Delegating by correlation can be supplemented by scheduling conferences in order to obtain reports.

☐ Delegating by interdependence can also include demanding reports of the subordinates.

- ☐ Measuring crosscurrents may be made more accurate by checking of results.
- ☐ The method of previewing direction offers an effective start to setting deadlines.
- ☐ The system of demanding reports may be improved by questioning on progress as well.

In many instances more than two of the methods may be combined. One successful method for delegating and still keeping a hand in might combine previewing directions, scheduling conferences, checking results, and also delegating by interdependence.

Selecting a Style

As noted earlier, the successful executives I observed allowed the situation, the particular project, to dictate their choice of a style of delegation. In addition, they considered the effectiveness of any one method insofar as inherent advantages or disadvantages made the particular delegating process easier or more difficult. Finally, they made their selection with a view to the amount of time, money, and effort needed to keep on top of the job optimally, weighed against the value of perfect performance within a given span of time. In effect, they appeared to ask themselves, unconsciously, two sets of questions:

- ☐ What do I need to know in order to check the progress of this particular job and when do I need to know it most? How effectively do each of the styles of delegation adaptable to this project give me the optimum information?
- ☐ What compromise, if any, must I make between the optimum style of delegation and other effective methods because of limits of time, effort, or money? Or, in other words, how important is it to do this project perfectly?

Measuring Points

The terms of the specific information needed are usually defined by the project itself. These terms may consist of personal observations, physical measurements, or end results. They may be posed as general judgments or may refer to specifics such as personnel, sales volume, units, and so on—in sum, whatever measurements are applicable to the nature of the job.

In addition, however, there is the problem of when it is best to make these measurements. That is, the problem of finding those crucial times in the project which will indicate clearly the absence or presence of progress toward the desired end result. Obviously, a busy executive cannot check all aspects of any one job. If this were possible, there would be no need to delegate. Therefore, an executive must also narrow down these measuring points to only those areas and times which will give a maximum insight into the project.

In any job, the natural place to find such measuring points is between the different phases or steps of the project. For example, the artist working under me in the Billy Graham promotion example had to work in stages. He would have developed his ideas in a number of steps: (1) general idea or theme; (2) rough layouts depicting the theme; (3) copy expounding the theme; (4) finished layouts; (5) finished artwork; and (6) pasteups for reproductions. I could have selected any one or all of these points for auditing his progress. And a correction at any early stage would have prevented wasted time and effort in the steps that followed. Each phase gave me the opportunity for corrective action, to keep my hand in and at the same time to protect my accountability.

In sum, I had to decide what I wanted to know as well as the optimum time for having this information and making my audit.

In many cases, the specific method to be used for participating in the delegated job is predetermined by the job itself. In the Billy Graham campaign, for example, the only measuring stick was my reaction to the ideas themselves. The only way I could make this measure was to go and look at the work in progress. A report could not substitute for my "seeing for myself," and only a method of auditing progress which allowed me to do this would have been suitable.

On the other hand, in many other kinds of business situations an executive could use quite different methods almost equally well. A written report giving product performance statistics could be just as good (if not better) as going to see the product in action. In such situations, the executive must rank the different methods according to the degree to which they provide the optimum amount of information about the project for purposes of keeping a hand in. But in making this evaluation an executive must not be beguiled by the method that seems most comfortable. The executive must evaluate the device according to the needs of the situation.

Necessity for Compromise

Three tentative evaluations will have now been made by an executive selecting a style of delegation: the specific terms of the information needed; the crucial measuring points; and the optimum method of auditing. Yet these three elements are not always harmonious, nor can the executive always be certain that the time or money is available to carry them through effectively. The final selection of a method of auditing, then, is a matter of compromise, a matter of weighing the following five considerations and resolving them to a solution:

- ☐ How important is this job? What are the costs of imperfect final results?

- ☐ How much time and money will it take to make the optimum measurements and audit?
- ☐ Do I have this much time? Must I make the time available?
- ☐ Can I interrupt this project to make an evaluation? For how long? How important is the deadline for completion?
- ☐ How much faith do I have in the man carrying out this project?

Such conflicts demand adherence to the principle of "first things first." For example, if the job is so important that the executive cannot risk failure, then, of course, control is the primary objective. In such a situation, a relatively time-consuming method giving good control may, in the end, be a small price for seeing to it that the job is completed successfully—may be cheap in light of the costs of failure. Even drawing time and effort away from other projects may be less costly in the long run.

In another case, the executive's primary goal may be to reduce personal time on a particular project in order to spend effort elsewhere. To do this, the executive must select a method that will, with the least amount of time, still give the optimum information needed to protect accountability. The crucial point in making such a selection usually comes in deciding which measuring points can be bypassed with the least danger. That is, how long can the executive afford not to look into a given project?

Such a decision can best be made by considering each stage or part of the job in terms of the degree that this particular phase carries the project to an irreversible decision—that is, a decision which could destroy the project or bring it short of its mark. Obviously, once such an irreversible phase is over, it is too late. The executive must decide how long before such an irreversible phase is reached that an audit is necessary. And this decision must certainly consider the costs of making changes at any given phase.

Though an executive's primary objective may be to minimize the amount of time spent in auditing delegation, the decision is not that simple. Rather, the objective should be to minimize the amount of time needed to gather the optimum information that must be had in order to protect the executive's accountability. The executive does this by selecting the style of delegation that not only uses the least amount of time, but helps to keep a hand in the job most efficiently. The happiest compromise ensures that the executive is protecting personal overall accountability as completely as possible, even if this occasionally means that the executive has to spend more time than originally planned.

If an executive is constrained by the fact that the project cannot be interrupted for evaluation, then a style of delegation must be selected that allows a hand to be kept in from the very beginning. At the least, a plan must be devised to get as much information as early as possible. In essence, the executive will have to adopt a style which is optimum within the restriction imposed by a crash project.

One final caveat: many times the strongest restriction on choosing a style of delegation does not relate to the job itself, but to the person delegated to carry out the job. If the project is one in which there are a number of inherent pitfalls, perhaps closer supervision is needed for one subordinate than for another. Similarly, the executive must consider the effects that any style of delegation will have on a subordinate's morale and development. And many times the critical restraint on the executive will be the need to select a style that will best help train the subordinate to carry out delegation effectively.

Each of the five considerations, then, can serve as a constraint on the selection of a given style of delegation. These considerations, by dictating what is most important about the particular project, determine the direction of any compromise. As constraints, they serve as a center around which the executive can resolve all the considerations into a solution—that is, a personal style of delegation for the project in question.

Conclusion

An executive can never delegate accountability. Though an assistant can be vested with full responsibility and complete authority, the executive, nevertheless, cannot escape final full accountability for the results. The only recourse for seeing to it that things go right is through executive participation—maintaining enough contact with every job so that the executive is "on top of it" by "keeping a hand in."

This article suggests a number of styles of delegation which accomplish this goal. Their purpose is to advise the executive of the status of an assignment in time to take corrective steps before failure either renders success hopeless or becomes unnecessarily costly.

However, the selection of one style or a combination of them is not a matter of arbitrary choice. Rather, it is dictated, first, by the type of job to be delegated and, secondly, by the amount of time an executive can invest in protecting accountability. The weighing of these two factors, resolved one against the other, determines the optimum style of delegation to be selected.

Note

1. *Chronicle*, Augusta, Ga., January 22, 1961; italics added.

28

Good Managers Don't Make Policy Decisions

H. EDWARD WRAPP

The successful general manager neither spells out detailed objectives nor makes master plans for his or her organization. The author believes a successful manager seldom makes forthright statements of policy. He or she is an opportunist, who tends to muddle through problems—although muddling with a purpose. The manager is enmeshed in many operating matters and cannot be limited to "the big picture."

Although these and other characteristics of top executives described in this article do run counter to much of the literature and teaching of management, Mr. Wrapp can support his heresies with a rich background of experience and observation. For many years he has watched the long-range planning phenomenon at close range. In addition to having once been a corporate executive himself, he has worked on a large variety of consulting assignments in business and gathered numerous cases on management.

The upper reaches of management are a land of mystery and intrigue. Very few people have ever been there, and the present inhabitants frequently send back messages that are incoherent both to other levels of management and to the world in general. This may account for the myths, illusions, and caricatures that permeate the literature of management—for example, such widely held notions as these:

- ☐ Life gets less complicated as a manager reaches the top of the pyramid.
- ☐ The manager at the top level knows everything that's going on in

---

Author's Note. This article is based on a talk delivered at the Executive Program Club luncheon in Chicago, April 27, 1967. A similar version of it will be published as a Selected Paper later this year by the Graduate School of Business, University of Chicago.

the organization, can command whatever resources that may be needed, and therefore can be more decisive.

☐ The general manager's day is taken up with making broad policy decisions and formulating precise objectives.

☐ The top executive's primary activity is conceptualizing long-range plans.

☐ In a large company, the top executive may be seen meditating about the role of the organization in society.

I suggest that none of these versions alone, or in combination, is an accurate portrayal of what a general manager does. Perhaps students of the management process have been overly eager to develop a theory and a discipline. As one executive I know puts it, "I guess I do some of the things described in the books and articles, but the descriptions are lifeless, and my job isn't."

What common characteristics, then, do successful executives exhibit *in reality*? I identify here five skills or talents which, in my experience, seem especially significant. (For details on the method used in reaching these conclusions, see the appendix.)

Keeping Well Informed

First, my heroes have a special talent for keeping themselves informed about a wide range of operating decisions being made at different levels in the company. As they move up the ladder, they develop a network of information sources in many different departments. They cultivate these sources and keep them open no matter how high they climb in the organization. When the need arises, they bypass the lines on the organization chart to seek more than one version of a situation.

In some instances, especially when they suspect the executives would not be in total agreement with their decision, their subordinates will elect to inform them in advance, before they announce a decision. In these circumstances, the executives are in a position to defer the decision, or redirect it, or even block further action. However, they do not insist on this procedure. Ordinarily they leave it up to the members of their organizations to decide at what stage they inform the executives.

Top-level managers are frequently criticized by writers, consultants, and lower levels of management for continuing to enmesh themselves in operating problems, after promotion to the top, rather than withdrawing to the "big picture." Without any doubt, some managers to get lost in a welter of detail and insist on making too many decisions. Superficially, good managers may seem to make the same mistake—but their purposes are different. They know that only by keeping well informed about the decisions being made can they avoid the sterility so often found in those who isolate themselves from operations. If they follow the advice to free themselves from operations, they may soon find themselves subsisting on a diet of abstractions, leaving the choice of what to eat in the hands of their subordinates. As Kenneth Boulding puts it: "The very purpose of a hierarchy is to prevent information from reaching higher layers. It operates as an information filter, and there are little wastebaskets all along the way."[1]

What kinds of action do successful executives take to keep their information live and accurate? Here is an example:

☐ One company president that I worked with sensed that his vice presidents were insulating him from some of the vital issues being discussed at lower levels. He accepted a proposal for a formal management development program primarily because it afforded him an opportunity to discuss company problems with middle managers several layers removed from him in the organization. By meeting with small groups of these men in an academic setting, he learned much about their preoccupations, and also about those of his vice presidents. And he accomplished his purposes without undermining the authority of line managers.

Focusing Time and Energy

The second skill of good managers is that they know how to save their energy and hours for those few particular issues, decisions, or problems to which they should give their personal attention. They know the fine and subtle distinction between keeping fully informed about operating decisions and allowing the organization to force them into participating in these decisions or, even worse, making them. Recognizing that they can bring their special talents to bear on only a limited number of matters, they choose those issues which they believe will have the greatest long-term impact on the company, and on which their special abilities can be most productive. Under ordinary circumstances they will limit themselves to three or four major objectives during any single period of sustained activity.

What about the situations they elect *not* to become involved in as decision makers? They make sure (using the skill first mentioned) that the organization keeps them informed about these situations at various stages; they do not want to be accused of indifference to such issues. They train their subordinates not to bring the matters to them for a decision. The communication to them from below is essentially one of: "Here is our sizeup, and here's what we propose to do." Reserving their hearty encouragement for those projects which hold superior promise of a contribution to total corporate strategy, they simply acknowledge receipt of information on other matters. When they see a problem where the organization needs their help, they find a way to transmit their know-how short of giving orders—usually by asking perceptive questions.

Playing the Power Game

To what extent do successful top executives push their ideas and proposals through the organization? The rather common notion that the "prime mover" continually creates and forces through new programs, like a powerful majority leader in a liberal Congress, is in my opinion very misleading.

Successful managers are sensitive to the power structure in the organization. In considering any major current proposal, they can plot the position of the various individuals and units in the organization on a scale ranging from complete, outspoken support down to determined, sometimes bitter, and oftentimes well-cloaked opposition. In the middle of the scale is an area of comparative indifference. Usually, several aspects of a proposal will fall into this area, and *here is where they know they can operate*. They assess the depth and nature of the blocs in the organization. Their perception permits them to move through what I call *corridors* of comparative indifference. They seldom challenge when a corridor is blocked, preferring to pause until it has opened up.

Related to this particular skill is their ability to recognize the need for a few trial-balloon launchers in the organization. They know that the organization will tolerate only a certain number of proposals which emanate from the apex of the pyramid. No matter how sorely they may be tempted to stimulate the organization with a flow of their own ideas, they know they must work through idea people in different parts of the organization. As they study the reactions of key individuals and groups to the trial balloons these people send up, they are able to make a better assessment of how to limit the emasculation of the various proposals. For seldom do they find a proposal which is supported by all quarters of the organization. The emergence of strong support in certain quarters is almost sure to evoke strong opposition in others.

Value of Sense of Timing

Circumstances like these mean that a good sense of timing is a priceless asset for a top executive. Let me illustrate:

☐ A vice president had for some time been convinced that the company lacked a sense of direction and needed a formal long-range planning activity to fill the void. Up to the time in question, soft overtures to other top executives had been rebuffed. And then there was an opening.

A management development committee proposed a series of weekend meetings for second-level officers in the company. After extensive debate, but for reasons not announced, the president rejected this proposal. The members of the committee openly resented what seemed to them an arbitrary rejection.

The vice president, sensing a tense situation, suggested to the president that the same officers who were to have attended the weekend management development seminars be organized into a long-range planning committee. The timing of the suggestion was perfect. The president, looking for a bone to toss to the committee, acquiesced immediately, and the management development committee in its next meeting enthusiastically endorsed the idea.

This vice president had been conducting a kind of continuing market research to discover how to sell the long-range planning proposal. Previous probes of the "market" had told the vice president that the president's earlier rejections of the proposal were not so final as to preclude an eventual shift in the corridors of attitude I have mentioned. The vice president caught the committee in a conciliatory mood, and the proposal rode through with colors flying.

As good managers stand at a point in time, they can identify sets of goals they are interested in, albeit the outline of them may be pretty hazy. Their timetables, which are also pretty hazy, suggest that some goals must be accomplished sooner than others, and that some may be safely postponed for several months or years. They have a still hazier notion of how they can reach these goals. They assess key individuals and groups. They know that each has its own set of goals, some of which they understand rather thoroughly and others about which they can only speculate. They know also that these individuals and groups represent blocks to certain programs or projects, and that these points of opposition must be taken into account. As the day-to-day operating decisions are made, and as proposals are responded to both by individuals and by groups, they perceive more clearly where the corridors of comparative indifference are. They take action accordingly.

The Art of Imprecision

The fourth skill of successful managers is knowing how to satisfy the organization that it has a sense of direction *without ever actually getting themselves committed publicly to a specific set of objectives*. This is not to say that they do not have objectives—personal and corporate, long-term and short-term. They are significant guides to their thinking, and they modify them continually as they better understand the resources they are working with, the competition, and the changing market demands. But as the organization clamors for statements of objectives, these are samples of what they get back from these managers:

Our company aims to be number one in its industry.

Our objective is growth with profit.

We seek the maximum return on investment.

Management's goal is to meet its responsibilities to stockholders, employees, and the public.

In my opinion, statements such as these provide almost no guidance to the various levels of management. Yet they are quite readily accepted as objectives by large numbers of intelligent people.

Maintaining Viability

Why do good managers shy away from precise statements of their objectives for the organization? The main reason is that they find it impossible to set down specific objectives which will be relevant for any reasonable period into the future. Conditions in business change continually and rapidly, and corporate strategy must be revised to take the changes into account. The more explicit the statement of strategy, the more difficult it becomes to persuade the organization to turn to different goals when needs and conditions shift.

The public and the stockholders, to be sure, must perceive the organization as having a well-defined set of objectives and a clear sense of direction. But in reality good top managers are seldom so certain of the direction which should be taken. Better than anyone else, they sense the many, many threats to their company—threats which lie in the economy, in the actions of competitors, and, not least, within their own organization.

They also know that it is impossible to state objectives clearly enough so that everyone in the organization understands what they mean. Objectives get communicated only over time by a consistency or pattern in operating decisions. Such decisions are more meaningful than words. In instances where precise objectives are spelled out, the organization tends to interpret them so they fit its own needs.

Subordinates who keep pressing for more precise objectives are in truth working against their own best interests. Each time the objectives are stated more specifically, a subordinate's range of possibilities for operating are reduced. The narrower field means less room to roam and to accommodate the flow of ideas coming up from the subordinate's part of the organization.

Avoiding Policy Straitjackets

Successful managers' reluctance to be precise extends into the area of policy decisions. They seldom make a forthright statement of policy. They may be aware that in some companies there are executives who spend more time in arbitrating disputes caused by stated policies than in moving the company forward. The management textbooks contend that well-defined policies are the sine qua non of a well-managed company. My research does not bear out this contention. For example:

☐ The president of one company with which I am familiar deliberately leaves the assignments of his top officers vague and refuses to define policies for them. He passes out new assignments with seemingly no pattern in mind and consciously sets up competitive ventures among

> his subordinates. His methods, though they would never be sanctioned by a classical organization planner, are deliberate—and, incidentally, quite effective.

Since able managers do not make policy decisions, does this mean that well-managed companies operate without policies? Certainly not. But the policies are those which evolve over time from an indescribable mix of operating decisions. From any single operating decision might have come a very minor dimension of the policy as the organization understands it; from a series of decisions comes a pattern of guidelines for various levels of the organization.

Skillful managers resist the urge to write a company creed or to compile a policy manual. Preoccupation with detailed statements of corporate objectives and departmental goals and with comprehensive organization charts and job descriptions—this is often the first symptom of an organization which is in the early stages of atrophy.

The "management by objectives" school, so widely heralded in recent years, suggests that detailed objectives be spelled out at all levels in the corporation. This method is feasible at lower levels of management, but it becomes unworkable at the upper levels. The top manager must think out objectives in detail, but ordinarily some of the objectives must be withheld, or at least communicated to the organization in modest doses. A conditioning process which may stretch over months or years is necessary in order to prepare the organization for radical departures from what it is currently striving to attain.

Suppose, for example, that a president is convinced the company must phase out of the principal business it has been in for 35 years. Although making this change of course is one objective, the president may well feel unable to disclose the idea even to the vice presidents, whose total know-how is in the present business. A blunt announcement that the company is changing horses would be too great a shock for most of them to bear. And so the president begins moving toward this goal but without a full disclosure to the management group.

A detailed spelling out of objectives may only complicate the task of reaching them. Specific, detailed statements give the opposition an opportunity to organize its defenses.

Muddling With a Purpose

The fifth, and most important, skill bears little relation to the doctrine that management is (or should be) a comprehensive, systematic, logical, well-programmed science. Of all the heresies set forth here, this should strike doctrinaires as the rankest of all!

Successful managers, in my observation, recognize the futility of trying to push total packages or programs through the organization. They are willing to take less than total acceptance in order to achieve modest progress toward their goals. Avoiding debates on principles, they try to piece together particles that may appear to be incidentals into a program that moves at least part of the way toward their objectives. Their attitudes are based on optimism and persistence. Over and over they say to themselves, "There must be some parts of this proposal on which we can capitalize."

Whenever they identify relationships among the different proposals before them, they know that they present opportunities for combination and restructuring. It follows that they have wide-ranging interests and curiosity. The more things they know about, the more opportunities they will have to discover parts which are related. This process does not require great intellectual brilliance or unusual creativity. The wider ranging their interests, the more likely that they will be able to tie together several unrelated proposals. They are skilled as analysts, but even more talented as conceptualizers.

If managers have built or inherited a solid organization, it will be difficult for them to come up with ideas which no one in the company ever thought of before. Their most significant contribution may be that they can see relationships which no one else has seen. Take this example:

☐ A division manager had set as one of the objectives, at the start of a year, an improvement in product quality. At the end of the year, in reviewing progress toward this objective, the manager could identify three significant events which had brought about a perceptible improvement.

First, the head of the quality control group, a veteran manager who was doing only an adequate job, asked early in the year for assignment to a new research group. This opportunity permitted the division manager to install a promising young engineer in this key spot.

A few months later, opportunity number two came along. The personnel department proposed a continuous program of checking the effectiveness of training methods for new employees. The proposal was acceptable to the manufacturing group. The division manager's only contribution was to suggest that the program should include a heavy emphasis on employees' attitudes toward quality.

Then a third opportunity arose when one of the division's best customers discovered that the wrong material had been used for a large lot of parts. The heat generated by this complaint made it possible to institute a completely new system of procedures for inspecting and testing raw materials.

As the division manager reviewed the year's progress on product quality, these were the three most important developments. None of them could have been predicted at the start of the year, but the manager was quick to see the potential in each as it popped up in the day-to-day operating routines.

Exploitation of Change

Good managers can function effectively only in an environment of continual change. A *Saturday Review* cartoonist has caught the idea as he pictures an executive seated at a massive desk instructing his secretary to "send in a deal; I feel like wheelin'." Only with many changes in the works can managers discover new combinations of opportunities and open up new corridors of comparative indifference. Their stimulation to creativity comes from trying to make something useful of the proposals or ideas in front of them. They will try to make strategic change a way of life in the organization and continually review the strategy even though current results are good.

Charles Lindblom has written an article with an engaging title, "The Science of Muddling Through."[2] In this paper he describes what he calls "the rational comprehensive method" of decision making. The essence of this method is that the decision maker, for each problem, proceeds deliberately, one step at a time, to collect complete data; to analyze the data thoroughly; to study a wide range of alternatives, each with its own risks and consequences; and, finally, to formulate a detailed course of action. Lindblom immediately dismisses "the rational comprehensive method" in favor of what he calls "successive limited comparisons." He sees the decision maker as comparing the alternatives which are open in order to learn which most closely meets the objectives the decision maker has in mind. Since this is not so much a rational process as an opportunistic one, he sees the manager as a muddler, but a muddler with a purpose.

H. Igor Ansoff, in his book *Corporate Strategy*,[3] espouses a similar notion as he describes what he calls the "cascade approach." In his view, possible decision rules are formulated in gross terms and are successively refined through several stages as the emergence of a solution proceeds. This process gives the appearance of solving the problem several times over, but with successively more precise results.

Both Lindblom and Ansoff are moving us closer to an understanding of how managers really think. The process is not highly abstract; rather, the manager searches for a means of drawing into a pattern the thousands of incidents which make up the day-to-day life of a growing company.

Contrasting Pictures

It is interesting to note, in the writings of several students of management, the emergence of the concept that, rather than making decisions, the leader's principal task is maintaining operating conditions which permit the various decision-making systems to function effectively. The supporters of this theory, it seems to me, overlook the subtle turns of direction which the leader can provide. He cannot add purpose and structure to the balanced judgments of subordinates if he simply rubberstamps their decisions. He must weigh the issues and reach his own decision.

Richard M. Cyert and James G. March contend that in real life managers do not consider all the possible courses of action, that their search ends once they have found a satisfactory alternative. In my sample, good managers are not guilty of such myopic thinking. Unless they mull over a wide range of possibilities, they cannot come up with the imaginative combinations of ideas which characterize their work.

Many of the articles about successful executives picture them as great thinkers who sit at their desks drafting master blueprints for their companies. The successful top executives I have seen at work do not operate this way. Rather than produce a full-grown decision tree, they start with a twig, help it grow, and ease themselves out on the limbs only after they have tested to see how much weight the limbs can stand.

In my picture, general managers sit in the midst of continuous streams of operating problems. Their organizations present them with a flow of proposals to deal with the problems. Some of these proposals are contained in voluminous, well-documented, formal reports; some are as fleeting as the walk-in visit from a subordinate whose latest inspiration came during the morning's coffee break. Knowing how meaningless it is to say, "This is a finance problem," or, "That is a communications problem," managers feel no compulsion to classify their problems. They are, in fact, undismayed by problems that defy classification. As the late Gary Steiner, in one of his speeches, put it, the manager "has a high tolerance for ambiguity."

In considering each proposal, the general manager tests it against at least three criteria:

1 Will the total proposal—or, more often, will some part of the proposal—move the organization toward the objectives which the general manager has in mind?
2 How will the whole or parts of the proposal be received by the various groups and subgroups in the organization? Where will the strongest opposition come from, which group will furnish the strongest support, and which group will be neutral or indifferent?
3 How does the proposal relate to programs already in process or currently proposed? Can some parts of the proposal under consideration be added on to a program already under way, or can they be combined with all or parts of other proposals in a package which can be steered through the organization?

The Making of a Decision

As another example of a general manager at work, let me describe the train of events which led to a parent company president's decision to attempt to consolidate two of his divisions:

☐ Let us call the executive Mr. Brown. One day the manager of Division A came to him with a proposal that her division acquire a certain company. That company's founder and president—let us call him Mr. Johansson—had a phenomenal record of inventing new prod-

> ucts, but earnings in his company had been less than phenomenal. Johansson's asking price for his company was high when evaluated against the earnings record.
>
> Not until Brown began to speculate on how Johansson might supply fresh vigor for new products in Division A did it appear that perhaps a premium price could be justified. For several years Brown had been unsuccessful in stimulating the manager of that division to see that she must bring in new products to replace those which were losing their place in the market.
>
> The next idea which came to Brown was that Johansson might invent not only for Division A but also for Division B. As Brown analyzed how this might be worked out organizationally, he began to think about the markets being served by Divisions A and B. Over the years, several basic but gradual changes in marketing patterns had occurred, with the result that the marketing considerations which had dictated the establishment of separate divisions no longer prevailed. Why should the company continue to support the duplicated overhead expenses in the two divisions?
>
> As Brown weighed the issues, he concluded that by consolidating the two divisions, he could also shift responsibilities in the management groups in ways that would strengthen them overall.

If we were asked to evaluate Brown's capabilities, how would we respond? Putting aside the objection that the information is too sketchy, our tendency might be to criticize Brown. Why did he not identify the changing market patterns in his continuing review of company position? Why did he not force the issue when the division manager failed to do something about new product development? Such criticism would reflect "the rational comprehensive method" of decision making.

But, as I analyze the gyrations in Brown's thinking, one characteristic stands out. He kept searching for the follow-on opportunities which he could fashion out of the original proposal, opportunities which would stand up against the three criteria earlier mentioned. In my book, Brown would rate as an extremely skillful general manager.

Conclusion

To recapitulate, general managers possess five important skills. They know how to:

1. *Keep open many pipelines of information.* No one will quarrel with the desirability of an early warning system which provides varied viewpoints on an issue. However, very few managers know how to practice this skill, and the books on management add precious little to our understanding of the techniques which make it practicable.

2. *Concentrate on a limited number of significant issues.* No matter how skillful the managers are in focusing their energies and talents, they are inevitably caught up in a number of inconsequential duties. Active leadership of an organization demands a high level of personal involvement, and personal involvement brings with it many time-consuming activities which have an infinitesimal impact on corporate strategy. Hence this second skill, while perhaps the most logical of the five, is by no means the easiest to apply.

3. *Identify the corridors of comparative indifference.* Are there inferences here that good managers have no ideas of their own, that they stand by until their organizations propose solutions, that they never use their authority to force a proposal through the organization? Such inferences are not intended. The message is that a good organization will tolerate only so much direction from the top; good managers therefore are adept at sensing how hard they can push.

4. *Give the organization a sense of direction with open-ended objectives.* In assessing this skill, keep in mind that I am talking about top levels of management. At lower levels, managers should be encouraged to write down their objectives, if for no other reason than to ascertain if they are consistent with corporate strategy.

5. *Spot opportunities and relationships in the stream of operating problems and decisions.* Lest it be concluded from the description of this skill that good managers are more improvisers than planners, let me emphasize that they are planners and encourage planning by subordinates. Interestingly, though, professional planners may be irritated by good general managers. Most of them complain about general managers' lack of vision. They devise a master plan, but the president (or other operating executive) seems to ignore it, or to give it minimum acknowledgment by borrowing bits and pieces for implementation. They seem to feel that the power of a good master plan will be obvious to everyone, and its implementation automatic. But general managers know that even if the plan is sound and imaginative, the job has only begun. The long, painful task of implementation will depend on the general managers' skill, not that of the planner.

Practical Implications

If this analysis of how skillful general managers think and operate has validity, then it should help us see several problems in a better light.

☐ *Investment analysis.* The investment community is giving increasing attention to sizing up the management of a company being appraised. Thus far, the analysts rely mainly on results or performance rather than on a probe of management skills. But current performance can be affected by many variables, both favorably and unfavorably, and is a dangerous base for predicting what the management of a company will produce in the future. Testing the key managers of a company against the five skills described holds promise for evaluating the caliber of a management group.

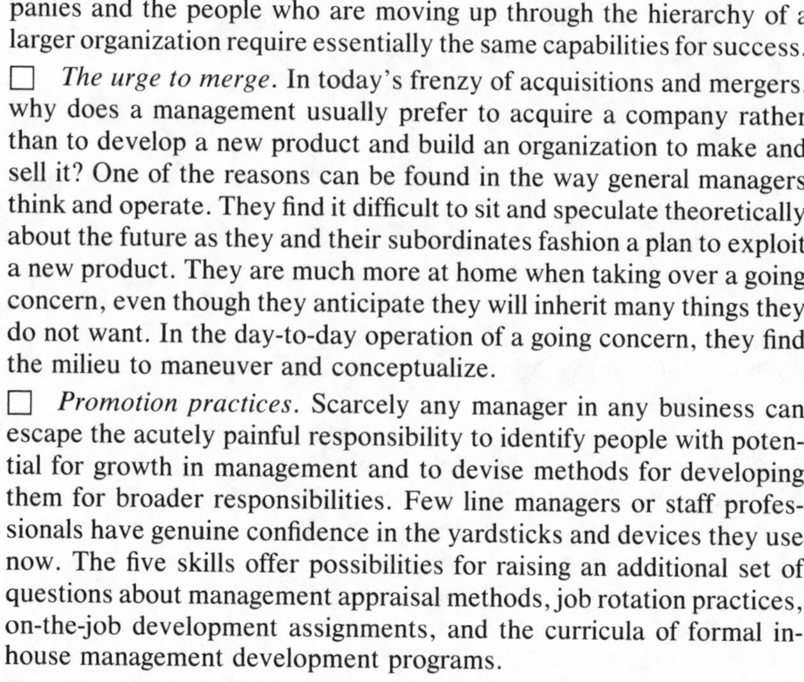

Incidentally, I believe that managers who are building their own companies and the people who are moving up through the hierarchy of a larger organization require essentially the same capabilities for success.

□ *The urge to merge.* In today's frenzy of acquisitions and mergers, why does a management usually prefer to acquire a company rather than to develop a new product and build an organization to make and sell it? One of the reasons can be found in the way general managers think and operate. They find it difficult to sit and speculate theoretically about the future as they and their subordinates fashion a plan to exploit a new product. They are much more at home when taking over a going concern, even though they anticipate they will inherit many things they do not want. In the day-to-day operation of a going concern, they find the milieu to maneuver and conceptualize.

□ *Promotion practices.* Scarcely any manager in any business can escape the acutely painful responsibility to identify people with potential for growth in management and to devise methods for developing them for broader responsibilities. Few line managers or staff professionals have genuine confidence in the yardsticks and devices they use now. The five skills offer possibilities for raising an additional set of questions about management appraisal methods, job rotation practices, on-the-job development assignments, and the curricula of formal inhouse management development programs.

One group of distinguished executives ignores with alarming regularity the implications of the five skills. These are the presidents of multidivision companies who "promote" successful division managers to the parent company level as staff officers. Does this recurring phenomenon cast doubt on the validity of my theory? I think not. To the contrary, strong supporting evidence for my thesis can be found in the results of such action. What happens is that line managers thus "promoted" often end up on the sidelines, out of the game for the rest of their careers. Removed from the tumult of operations, the environment which I contend is critical for their success, many of them just wither away in their high-status posts as senior counselors and never become effective.

Appendix: Basis of Conclusions in This Article

I have reached the conclusions outlined here after working closely with many managers in many different companies. In truth, the managers were not preselected with research in mind. Never did I tell the individuals that they were being studied, nor was I in fact studying their behavior. Research was not the purpose of our relationship. We were collaborating to solve some real problem.

Researching the management process when the manager is aware of being studied sometimes produces strange results. Rarely is a good executive able to think objectively about the management process as it is exemplified in his own methods. When an executive tries to explain to a researcher or writer, there is a tendency to feel compelled to develop rational, systematic explanations of how the executive does the job—explanations which in my opinion are largely fictional.

A manager cannot be expected to describe personal methods even if the manager understands them. They border on manipulation, and the stigma associated with manipulation can be fatal. If the organization ever identifies the manager as a manipulator, the job becomes more difficult. No one willingly submits to manipulation, and those around organize to protect themselves. And yet every good manager does have to manipulate.

My definition of a good manager is a simple one: under competitive industry conditions, the manager is able to move the organization significantly toward the set goals, whether measured by higher return on investment, product improvement, development of management talent, faster growth in sales and earnings, or some other standard. Bear in mind that this definition does not refer to the administrator whose principal role is to maintain the status quo in a company or in a department. Keeping the wheels turning in a direction already set is a relatively simple task, compared to that of directing the introduction of a continuing flow of changes and innovations, and preventing the organization from flying apart under the pressure.

Notes

1. From a speech at a meeting sponsored by the Crowell Collier Institute of Continuing Education in New York, as reported in *Business Week*, February 18, 1967, p. 202.

2. Charles Lindblom, "The Science of Muddling Through," *Readings in Managerial Psychology*, edited by Harold J. Leavitt and Louis R. Pondy (Chicago, University of Chicago Press, 1964), p. 61.

3. H. Igor Ansoff, *Corporate Strategy* (New York, McGraw-Hill, 1965).

29 The Effective Decision

PETER F. DRUCKER

Regardless of the content of their jobs, all executives carry out one common process. They make decisions. But although decision making defines the executive job, most executives probably don't make that many decisions per se. Most of the time executives—effective ones at any rate—are going through the essential steps of the decision-making process, steps that have to be taken before a decision is made. The essential steps include classifying the problem, defining it, specifying those conditions the answer must satisfy, and determining what the right decision, not just the acceptable one, would have to be to fulfill those conditions. The last step in the process is implementing the decision. If it is not implemented, even the decision that has passed through the other four stages remains merely a good idea.

Effective executives do not make a great many decisions. They concentrate on what is important. They try to make the few important decisions on the highest level of conceptual understanding. They try to find the constants in a situation, to think through what is strategic and generic rather than to "solve problems." They are, therefore, not overly impressed by speed in decision making; rather, they consider virtuosity in manipulating a great many variables a symptom of sloppy thinking. They want to know what the decision is all about and what the underlying realities are which it has to satisfy. They want impact rather than technique. And they want to be sound rather than clever.

Effective executives know when a decision has to be based on principle and when it should be made pragmatically, on the merits of the case. They know the trickiest decision is that between the right and the wrong compromise, and they have learned to tell one from the other. They know that the most time-consuming step in the process is not making the decision but putting it into effect. Unless a decision has "degenerated into work," it is

Author's Note. This article is derived from a chapter in my book, *The Effective Executive*, published by Harper & Row, Publishers, Inc.

not a decision; it is at best a good intention. This means that, while the effective decision itself is based on the highest level of conceptual understanding, the action commitment should be as close as possible to the capacities of the people who have to carry it out. Above all, effective executives know that decision making has its own systematic process and its own clearly defined elements.

Sequential Steps

The elements do not by themselves "make" the decisions. Indeed, every decision is a risk-taking judgment. But unless these elements are the stepping-stones of the executive's decision process, he will not arrive at a right, and certainly not at an effective, decision. Therefore, in this article I shall describe the sequence of steps involved in the decision-making process. There are six such steps:

1 *The classification of the problem.* Is it generic? Is it exceptional and unique? Or is it the first manifestation of a new genus for which a rule has yet to be developed?
2 *The definition of the problem.* What are we dealing with?
3 *The specifications which the answer to the problem must satisfy.* What are the "boundary conditions"?
4 *The decision as to what is "right," rather than what is acceptable, in order to meet the boundary conditions.* What will fully satisfy the specifications *before* attention is given to the compromises, adaptations, and concessions needed to make the decision acceptable?
5 *The building into the decision of the action to carry it out.* What does the action commitment have to be? Who has to know about it?
6 *The feedback which tests the validity and effectiveness of the decision against the actual course of events.* How is the decision being carried out? Are the assumptions on which it is based appropriate or obsolete?

Let us take a look at each of these individual elements.

The Classification

The effective decision maker asks: Is this a symptom of a fundamental disorder or a stray event? The generic always has to be answered through a rule, a principle. But the truly exceptional event can only be handled as such and as it comes.

Strictly speaking, the executive might distinguish among four, rather than between two, different types of occurrences.

First, there is the truly generic event, of which the individual occurrence is only a symptom. Most of the "problems" that come up in the course of the executive's work are of this nature. Inventory decisions in a business, for instance, are not "decisions." They are adaptations. The problem is generic. This is even more likely to be true of occurrences within manufacturing organizations. For example:

☐ A product control and engineering group will typically handle many hundreds of problems in the course of a month. Yet, whenever these are analyzed, the great majority prove to be just symptoms—and manifestations—of underlying basic situations. The individual process control engineer or production engineer who works in one part of the plant usually cannot see this. He might have a few problems each month with the couplings in the pipes that carry steam or hot liquids, and that's all.

Only when the total workload of the group over several months is analyzed does the generic problem appear. Then it is seen that temperatures or pressures have become too great for the existing equipment and that the couplings holding the various lines together need to be redesigned for greater loads. Until this analysis is done, process control will spend a tremendous amount of time fixing leaks without ever getting control of the situation.

The second type of occurrence is the problem which, while a unique event for the individual institution, is actually generic. Consider:

☐ The company that receives an offer to merge from another, larger one, will never receive such an offer again if it accepts. This is a nonrecurrent situation as far as the individual company, its board of directors, and its management are concerned. But it is, of course, a generic situation which occurs all the time. Thinking through whether to accept or to reject the offer requires some general rules. For these, however, the executive has to look to the experience of others.

Next there is the exceptional event that the executive must distinguish. To illustrate:

☐ The huge power failure that plunged into darkness the whole of Northeastern North America from the St. Lawrence to Washington in November 1965 was, according to first explanations, a truly exceptional situation. So was the thalidomide tragedy which led to the birth of so many deformed babies in the early 1960s. The probability of either of these events occurring, we were told, was one in ten million or one in a hundred million, and concatenations of these events were as unlikely ever to recur again as it is unlikely, for instance, for the chair on which I sit to disintegrate into its constituent atoms.

Unique events are rare, however. Whenever one appears, the decision maker has to ask: Is this a true exception or only the first manifestation of a new genus? And this—the early manifestation of a new generic problem—is the fourth and last category of events with which the decision process deals. Thus:

> ☐ We know now that both the Northeastern power failure and the thalidomide tragedy were only the first occurrences of what, under conditions of modern power technology or of modern pharmacology, are likely to become fairly frequent occurrences unless generic solutions are found.

All events but the unique require a generic solution. They require a rule, a policy, or a principle. Once the right principle has been developed, all manifestations of the same generic situation can be handled pragmatically—that is, by adaptation of the rule to the concrete circumstances of the case. Unique events, however, must be treated individually. The executive cannot develop rules for the exceptional.

The effective decision maker spends time determining which of the four different types of the above situations are being faced. The decision maker knows that the wrong decision will be made if the situation is classified incorrectly.

By far the most common mistake of the decision maker is to treat a generic situation as if it were a series of unique events—that is, to be pragmatic when lacking the generic understanding and principle. The inevitable result is frustration and futility. This was clearly shown, I think, by the failure of most of the policies, both domestic and foreign, of the Kennedy Administration. Consider:

> ☐ For all the brilliance of its members, the Administration achieved fundamentally only one success, and that was in the Cuban missile crisis. Otherwise, it achieved practically nothing. The main reason was surely what its members called "pragmatism"—namely, the Administration's refusal to develop rules and principles, and its insistence on treating everything "on its merits." Yet it was clear to everyone, including the members of the Administration, that the basic assumptions on which its policies rested—the valid assumptions of the immediate postwar years—had become increasingly unrealistic in international, as well as in domestic, affairs in the 1960s.

Equally common is the mistake of treating a new event as if it were just another example of the old problem to which, therefore, the old rules should be applied:

> ☐ This was the error that snowballed the local power failure on the New York–Ontario border into the great Northeastern blackout. The

power engineers, especially in New York City, applied the right rule for a normal overload. Yet their own instruments had signaled that something quite extraordinary was going on which called for exceptional, rather than standard, countermeasures.

By contrast, the one great triumph of President Kennedy in the Cuban missile crisis rested on acceptance of the challenge to think through an extraordinary, exceptional occurrence. As soon as he accepted this, his own tremendous resources of intelligence and courage effectively came into play.

The Definition

Once a problem has been classified as generic or unique, it is usually fairly easy to define. "What is this all about?" "What is pertinent here?" "What is the key to this situation?" Questions such as these are familiar. But only the truly effective decision makers are aware that the danger in this step is not the wrong definition; it is the plausible but incomplete one. For example:

☐ The American automobile industry held to a plausible but incomplete definition of the problem of automotive safety. It was this lack of awareness—far more than any reluctance to spend money on safety engineering—that eventually, in 1966, brought the industry under sudden and sharp Congressional attack for its unsafe cars and then left the industry totally bewildered by the attack. It simply is not true that the industry has paid scant attention to safety.

On the contrary, it has worked hard at safer highway engineering and at driver training, believing these to be the major areas for concern. That accidents are caused by unsafe roads and unsafe drivers is plausible enough. Indeed, all other agencies concerned with automotive safety, from the highway police to the high schools, picked the same targets for their campaigns. These campaigns have produced results. The number of accidents on highways built for safety has been greatly lessened. Similarly, safety-trained drivers have been involved in far fewer accidents.

But although the ratio of accidents per thousand cars or per thousand miles driven has been going down, the total number of accidents and the severity of them have kept creeping up. It should therefore have become clear long ago that something would have to be done about the small but significant probability that accidents will occur despite safety laws and safety training.

This means that future safety campaigns will have to be supplemented by engineering to make accidents themselves less dangerous. Whereas cars have been engineered to be safe when used correctly, they will also have to be engineered for safety when used incorrectly.

There is only one safeguard against becoming the prisoner of an incomplete definition: check it again and again against *all* the observable facts, and throw out a definition the moment it fails to encompass any of them.

The effective decision maker always tests for signs that something is atypical or something unusual is happening. The decision maker always asks: Does the definition explain the observed events, and does it explain all of them? The decision maker always writes out what the definition is expected to make happen—for instance, make automobile accidents disappear—and then tests regularly to see if this really happens. Finally, the decision maker goes back and thinks the problem through again whenever something is atypical, when there are phenomena the decision maker's explanation does not really explain, or when the course of events deviates, even in details, from expectations.

These are in essence the rules Hippocrates laid down for medical diagnosis well over 2,000 years ago. They are the rules for scientific observation first formulated by Aristotle and then reaffirmed by Galileo 300 years ago. These, in other words, are old, well-known, time-tested rules, which an executive can learn and apply systematically.

The Specifications

The next major element in the decision process is defining clear specifications as to what the decision has to accomplish. What are the objectives the decision has to reach? What are the minimum goals it has to attain? What are the conditions it has to satisfy? In science these are known as "boundary conditions." A decision, to be effective, needs to satisfy the boundary conditions. Consider:

> ☐ "Can our needs be satisfied," Alfred P. Sloan, Jr. presumably asked himself when he took command of General Motors in 1922, "by removing the autonomy of our division heads?" His answer was clearly in the negative. The boundary conditions of his problem demanded strength and responsibility in the chief operating positions. This was needed as much as unity and control at the center. Everyone before Sloan had seen the problem as one of personalities—to be solved through a struggle for power from which one man would emerge victorious. The boundary conditions, Sloan realized, demanded a solution to a constitutional problem—to be solved through a new structure: decentralization which balanced local autonomy of operations with central control of direction and policy.

A decision that does not satisfy the boundary conditions is worse than one which wrongly defines the problem. It is all but impossible to salvage the decision that starts with the right premises but stops short of the right conclusions. Furthermore, clear thinking about the boundary conditions is needed to know when a decision has to be abandoned. The most common cause of failure in a decision lies not in its being wrong initially. Rather, it is a subsequent shift in the goals—the specifications—which makes the prior right decision suddenly inappropriate. And unless the decision maker has kept the boundary conditions clear, so as to make possible the immediate replacement of the outflanked decision with a new and appropriate policy, the decision maker may not even notice that things have changed. For example:

> ☐ Franklin D. Roosevelt was bitterly attacked for his switch from conservative candidate in 1932 to radical President in 1933. But it wasn't Roosevelt who changed. The sudden economic collapse which occurred between the summer of 1932 and the spring of 1933 changed the specifications. A policy appropriate to the goal of national economic recovery—which a conservative economic policy might have been—was no longer appropriate when, with the Bank Holiday, the goal had to become political and social cohesion. When the boundary conditions changed, Roosevelt immediately substituted a political objective (reform) for his former economic one (recovery).

Above all, clear thinking about the boundary conditions is needed to identify the most dangerous of all possible decisions: the one in which the specifications that have to be satisfied are essentially incompatible. In other words, this is the decision that might—just might—work if nothing whatever goes wrong. A classic case is President Kennedy's Bay of Pigs decision:

> ☐ One specification was clearly Castro's overthrow. The other was to make it appear that the invasion was a "spontaneous" uprising of the Cubans. But these two specifications would have been compatible with each other only if an immediate island-wide uprising against Castro would have completely paralyzed the Cuban army. And while this was not impossible, it clearly was not probable in such a tightly controlled police state.

Decisions of this sort are usually called "gambles." But actually they arise from something much less rational than a gamble—namely, a hope against hope that two (or more) clearly incompatible specifications can be fulfilled simultaneously. This is hoping for a miracle; and the trouble with miracles is not that they happen so rarely, but that they are, alas, singularly unreliable.

Everyone can make the wrong decision. In fact, everyone will sometimes make a wrong decision. But no executive needs to make a decision which, on the face of it, seems to make sense but, in reality, falls short of satisfying the boundary conditions.

The Decision

The effective executive has to start out with what is "right" rather than what is acceptable precisely because there always has to be compromise in the end. But if the executive does not know what will satisfy the boundary conditions, the decision maker cannot distinguish between the right compromise and the wrong compromise—and may end up by making the wrong compromise. Consider:

☐ I was taught this when I started in 1944 on my first big consulting assignment. It was a study of the management structure and policies of General Motors Corporation. Alfred P. Sloan, Jr., who was then chairman and chief executive officer of the company, called me to his office at the start of my assignment and said: "I shall not tell you what to study, what to write, or what conclusions to come to. This is your task. My only instruction to you is to put down what you think is right as you see it. Don't you worry about our reaction. Don't you worry about whether we will like this or dislike that. And don't you, above all, concern yourself with the compromises that might be needed to make your conclusions acceptable. There is not one executive in this company who does not know how to make every single conceivable compromise without any help from you. But he can't make the *right* compromise unless you first tell him what right is."

The effective executive knows that there are two different kinds of compromise. One is expressed in the old proverb: "Half a loaf is better than no bread." The other, in the story of the Judgment of Solomon, is clearly based on the realization that "half a baby is worse than no baby at all." In the first instance, the boundary conditions are still being satisfied. The purpose of bread is to provide food, and half a loaf is still food. Half a baby, however, does not satisfy the boundary conditions. For half a baby is not half of a living and growing child.

It is a waste of time to worry about what will be acceptable and what the decision maker should or should not say so as not to evoke resistance. (The things one worries about seldom happen, while objections and difficulties no one thought about may suddenly turn out to be almost insurmountable obstacles.) In other words, the decision maker gains nothing by starting out with the question: "What is acceptable?" For in the process of answering it, the decision maker usually gives away the important things and loses any chance to come up with an effective—let alone the right—answer.

The Action

Converting the decision into action is the fifth major element in the decision process. While thinking through the boundary conditions is the most difficult step in decision making, converting the decision into effective action is usually the most time-consuming one. Yet a decision will not become effective unless the action commitments have been built into it from the start. In fact, no decision has been made unless carrying it out in specific steps has become someone's work assignment and responsibility. Until then, it is only a good intention.

The flaw in so many policy statements, especially those of business, is that they contain no action commitment—to carry them out is no one's specific work and responsibility. Small wonder then that the people in the organization tend to view such statements cynically, if not as declarations of what top management is really *not* going to do.

Converting a decision into action requires answering several distinct questions: Who has to know of this decision? What action has to be taken? Who is to take it? What does the action have to be so that the people who have to do it *can* do it? The first and the last of these questions are too often overlooked—with dire results. A story that has become a legend among operations researchers illustrates the importance of the question, "Who has to know?":

☐ A major manufacturer of industrial equipment decided several years ago to discontinue one of its models that had for years been standard equipment on a line of machine tools, many of which were still in use. It was, therefore, decided to sell the model to present owners of the old equipment for another three years as a replacement, and then to stop making and selling it. Orders for this particular model had been going down for a good many years. But they shot up immediately as customers reordered against the day when the model would no longer be available. No one had, however, asked, "Who needs to know of this decision?"

Consequently, nobody informed the purchasing clerk who was in charge of buying the parts from which the model itself was being assembled. His instructions were to buy parts in a given ratio to current sales—and the instructions remained unchanged.

Thus, when the time came to discontinue further production of the model, the company had in its warehouse enough parts for another 8 to 10 years of production, parts that had to be written off at a considerable loss.

The action must also be appropriate to the capacities of the people who have to carry it out. Thus:

☐ A large U.S. chemical company found itself, in recent years, with fairly large amounts of blocked currency in two West African countries. To protect this money, top management decided to invest it locally in businesses which (a) would contribute to the local economy, (b) would not require imports from abroad, and (c) would if successful be the kind that could be sold to local investors if and when currency remittances became possible again. To establish these businesses, the company developed a simple chemical process to preserve a tropical fruit—a staple crop in both countries—which, up until then, had suffered serious spoilage in transit to its Western markets.

The business was a success in both countries. But in one country the local manager set the business up in such a manner that it required highly skilled and technically trained management of a kind not easily available in West Africa. In the other country the local manager thought through the capacities of the people who would eventually have to run the business. Consequently, he worked hard at making both the process and the business simple, and at staffing his operation from the start with local nationals right up to the top management level.

A few years later it became possible again to transfer currency from these two countries. But, though the business flourished, no buyer could be found for it in the first country. No one available locally had the necessary managerial and technical skills to run it, and so the business had to be liquidated at a loss. In the other country so many local entrepreneurs were eager to buy the business that the company repatriated its original investment with a substantial profit.

The chemical process and the business built on it were essentially the same in both places. But in the first country no one had asked: "What kind of people do we have available to make this decision effective? And what can they do?" As a result, the decision itself became frustrated.

This action commitment becomes doubly important when people have to change their behavior, habits, or attitudes if a decision is to become effective. Here, the executive must make sure not only that the responsibility for the action is clearly assigned, but that the people assigned are capable of carrying it out. Thus the decision maker has to make sure that the measurements, the standards for accomplishment, and the incentives of those charged with the action responsibility are changed simultaneously. Otherwise, the organization people will get caught in a paralyzing internal emotional conflict. Consider these two examples:

□ When Theodore Vail was president of the Bell Telephone System 60 years ago, he decided that the business of the Bell System was service. This decision explains in large part why the United States (and Canada) has today an investor-owned, rather than a nationalized, telephone system. Yet this policy statement might have remained a dead letter if Vail had not at the same time designed yardsticks of service performance and introduced these as a means to measure, and ultimately to reward, managerial performance. The Bell managers of that time were used to being measured by the profitability (or at least by the cost) of their units. The new yardsticks resulted in the rapid acceptance of the new objectives.

☐ In sharp contrast is the recent failure of a brilliant chairman and chief executive to make effective a new organization structure and new objectives in an old, large, and proud U.S. company. Everyone agreed that the changes were needed. The company, after many years as leader of its industry, showed definite signs of aging. In many markets newer, smaller, and more aggressive competitors were outflanking it. But contrary to the action required to gain acceptance for the new ideas, the chairman—in order to placate the opposition—promoted prominent spokesmen of the old school into the most visible and highest salaried positions—in particular into three new executive vice presidencies. This meant only one thing to the people in the company: "They don't really mean it." If the greatest rewards are given for behavior contrary to that which the new course of action requires, then everyone will conclude that this is what the people at the top really want and are going to reward.

Only the most effective executive can do what Vail did—build the execution of the decision into the decision itself. But every executive can think through what action commitments a specific decision requires, what work assignments follow from it, and what people are available to carry it out.

The Feedback

Finally, information monitoring and reporting have to be built into the decision to provide continuous testing, against actual events, of the expectations that underlie the decisions. Decisions are made by people. People are fallible; at best, their works do not last long. Even the best decision has a high probability of being wrong. Even the most effective one eventually becomes obsolete.

This surely needs no documentation. And every executive always builds organized feedback—reports, figures, studies—into the decision to monitor and report on it. Yet far too many decisions fail to achieve their anticipated results, or indeed ever to become effective, despite all these feedback reports. Just as the view from the Matterhorn cannot be visualized by studying a map of Switzerland (one abstraction), a decision cannot be fully and accurately evaluated by studying a report. That is because reports are of necessity abstractions.

Effective decision makers know this and follow a rule which the military developed long ago. The commander who makes a decision does not depend on reports to see how it is being carried out. The commander—or an aide—goes and looks. The reason is not that effective decision makers (or effective commanders) distrust subordinates. Rather, the reason is that they learned the hard way to distrust abstract "communications."

With the coming of the computer this feedback element is even more important, for the decision maker will in all likelihood be even further removed from the scene of action. Unless the decision maker accepts, as a matter of course, that a personal visit to the scene of action is beneficial, the decision maker will be increasingly divorced from reality. All a computer can handle is abstractions. And abstractions can be relied on only if they are constantly checked against concrete results. Otherwise, they are certain to mislead.

To go and look is also the best, if not the only way, for an executive to test whether the assumptions on which a decision has been made are still valid or whether they are becoming obsolete and need to be thought through again. And the executive always has to expect the assumptions to become obsolete sooner or later. Reality never stands still very long.

Failure to go out and look is the typical reason for persisting in a course of action long after it has ceased to be appropriate or even rational. This is true for business decisions as well as for governmental policies. It explains in large measure the failure of Stalin's cold war policy in Europe, but also the inability of the United States to adjust its policies to the realities of a Europe restored to prosperity and economic growth, and the failure of the British to accept, until too late, the reality of the European Common Market. Moreover, in any business I know, failure to go out and look at customers and markets, at competitors and their products, is also a major reason for poor, ineffectual, and wrong decisions.

The decision maker needs organized information for feedback. The decision maker needs reports and figures. But unless feedback is built around direct exposure to reality—unless there is the discipline to go out personally and look—the decision maker condemns himself to a sterile dogmatism.

Concluding Note

Decision making is only one of the tasks of an executive. It usually takes but a small amount of time. But to make the important decisions is the *specific* executive task. Only an executive makes such decisions.

An *effective* executive makes these decisions as a systematic process with clearly defined elements and in a distinct sequence of steps. Indeed, to be expected (by virtue of position or knowledge) to make decisions that have significant and positive impact on the entire organization, its performance, and its results characterizes the effective executive.

30

Putting Judgment Back Into Decisions

LARRY E. GREINER, D. PAUL LEITCH, and LOUIS B. BARNES

Do modern information systems, which provide management with computer-generated indexes of performance, help managers to make sound judgments about an organization's effectiveness? An extensive study made by the authors in a large organization raises serious doubts. The evidence from the study indicates that informed managers still rely much more on qualitative than quantitative criteria in appraising performance, even when the quantitative measures are available and in use. Furthermore, those managers who use more subjective data tend to agree more with one another than those who depend on highly quantified information. The findings have significant implications for management training and for the planning of information systems.

Top managers are currently inundated with reams of information concerning the performance of organizational units under their supervision. Behind this information explosion lies a seemingly logical assumption made by information specialists and frequently accepted by line managers: If top management can be supplied with more "objective" and "accurate" *quantified* information, they will make "better" judgments about the performance of their operating units.

But how valid is this assumption? A research study we have recently completed indicates that quantified performance information may have a more limited role than is currently assumed or envisioned; in fact, managers rely more on subjective information than they do on so-called "objective" statistics in assessing the overall performance of lower level units.

Authors' Note. We are grateful to the Internal Revenue Service and the Division of Research, Harvard Business School, for supporting this study.

The Human Factor

Despite the increasing desire for and trend toward the quantification of performance results, most managers are the first to admit that their performance assessments begin and end with human judgment. Managers determine what kinds of performance information to collect; and later, when this information is in front of them, they study the data, make up their minds, and decide what to do. For example, here is how a vice president of finance in a large steel company describes the importance of human judgment in assessing organization performance:

> We have capital budgets, we have fixed budgets, we have variable budgets, we have standard costs. We have the full assortment. None of our controls is 100% effective. None replaces subjective judgment.[1]

There are several reasons why managerial judgment is critical in evaluating the performance of lower level units in today's organizations:

- ☐ Organizations are becoming so large and complex that, as yet, no universal mathematical formulas exist for encompassing all of the variables that reflect the total performance of a particular subunit.
- ☐ Events within and around an organization change so rapidly that indicators of "good" performance last year may not be appropriate this year.
- ☐ Managers are frequently aware of nonquantifiable factors which information specialists don't usually hear about or record on their standard forms.
- ☐ Ultimately, it is managers, not computers, that must make decisions based on their assessments of performance. If a manager makes a "biased" judgment of performance, then the manager's actions are also likely to be "biased."

In this article, we describe the purpose and methods of our study. Then we present the major findings, which at times are coupled with some broad implications for management. We conclude with more specific suggestions for improving the quality of performance judgments in organizations.

In particular, we consider these important questions that bear on the judgmental process:

- ☐ How important relatively are quantitative and qualitative criteria to managers in making judgments of performance? (If quantitative criteria are less important than assumed, then the organization may be able to redirect the activities of computers and staff analysts to use them more efficiently.)

☐ Are managers consistent from one day to the next in their judgments?

☐ Do managers agree more on current effectiveness than they do on changes in effectiveness over time?

☐ Can managers actually agree with each other in assessing the performance of organizational units beneath them? (If they can't, then they are likely to give off conflicting signals to lower levels.)

☐ Must managers agree on specific criteria if they are to agree in their overall judgments about performance?

☐ Does a manager's position in the organization affect judgments of performance? (If it does, misunderstandings among managerial levels are likely to ensue.)

How the Study Was Made

We conducted our investigation in a large government agency, the Internal Revenue Service. Although the IRS is not a business organization, it does contain many elements common to most large, complex organizations. More than 60,000 people are employed by the IRS in either the national office headquarters or the 7 regional and 58 district offices, or the 7 computer service centers. The IRS organization is also divided functionally into several major divisions, with each division having a representative group at all regional and most district offices. The measurement of performance is a key concern of IRS managers; many statistical indicators of performance are regularly collected, including indexes of costs, output, and morale.

Top management in the IRS became interested in having a study made partly out of curiosity about the reliability of their performance assessments of district operations. Despite their access to many quantitative performance measures, they readily acknowledged that their overall assessments of district performance depended, in the final analysis, on subjective judgment. At the national office level, managers were interested in knowing if they agreed with their counterparts at the regional level, and vice versa. In addition, managers at all levels were curious about the degree to which they relied on quantitative versus qualitative information in forming their judgments.

The study focused on three types of performance evaluation mentioned most frequently in initial interviews with IRS managers at the national and regional levels:

1 The current effectiveness of divisional subunits within a district. (This is important because it provides early signs of problems in the making.)

2 The performance improvement of these units over the preceding 18 months. (This adds perspective to the judgments of current effectiveness, especially when a currently high-performing unit is slipping or a low-performing unit is improving.)
3 Specific reasons for a unit's performance improvement, or lack of it. (This provides more precise clues for taking corrective action. For example, corrective action might be quite different if the reason were judged to be an uncontrollable "natural disaster" rather than a "lack of leadership.")

The Judging Procedure

To investigate how the IRS top managers evaluated these three performance dimensions, we formed 15 panels, representing 5 headquarters divisions and 10 regional divisions; see Exhibit 1. Each panel consisted of 2 to 5 managers acting as judges. Insofar as possible, judges were selected for their familiarity with the performance of their particular divisions at the district level and for their reputed "objectivity" in assessing subunit performance.

The procedure we used to study the performance judgments of these 15 panels is described in Exhibit 2. We have covered this method in some detail because, as we shall suggest later, other organizations may be interested in undertaking similar studies. (This is the first study, as far as we know, that has designed and utilized a methodology for systematically examining managerial judgments of subunit performance.)

When each judge had completed the procedure described in Exhibit 2, the judge sent the data cards directly to us for analysis. Our analytical procedure was based largely on a mathematical technique called correlation analysis. First, we totaled the number of times that each judge chose one unit over another. From these totals we computed for each judge a rank order of those units evaluated; the unit chosen most over other units received a rank of "1," and so forth down the list. Then this rank order was correlated against the rank orders for the other judges in each panel. This produced a "level of agreement" *within* each of the 15 panels.

Additional correlations were also computed *between* panels by comparing an overall rank order for each panel (based on an average of individual rank orders) with the overall rank order for other panels. Perfect agreement between rank orders, as measured by a statistical correlation, as +1.00, while perfect disagreement was −1.00. There is no fixed rule for determining an "acceptable" correlation of agreement, although the following guideline tends to be commonly used in research:

+.9 or −.9 = high correlation.
+.7 or −.7 = substantial correlation.
+.5 or −.5 = moderate correlation.
+.3 or −.3 = low correlation.

Exhibit 1. Location of Judges' Panels

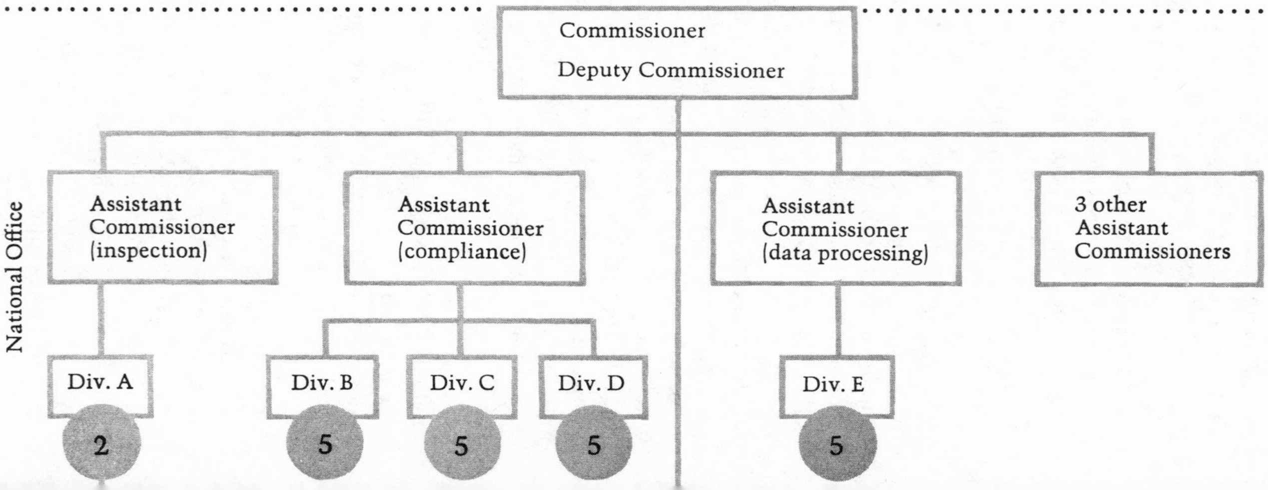

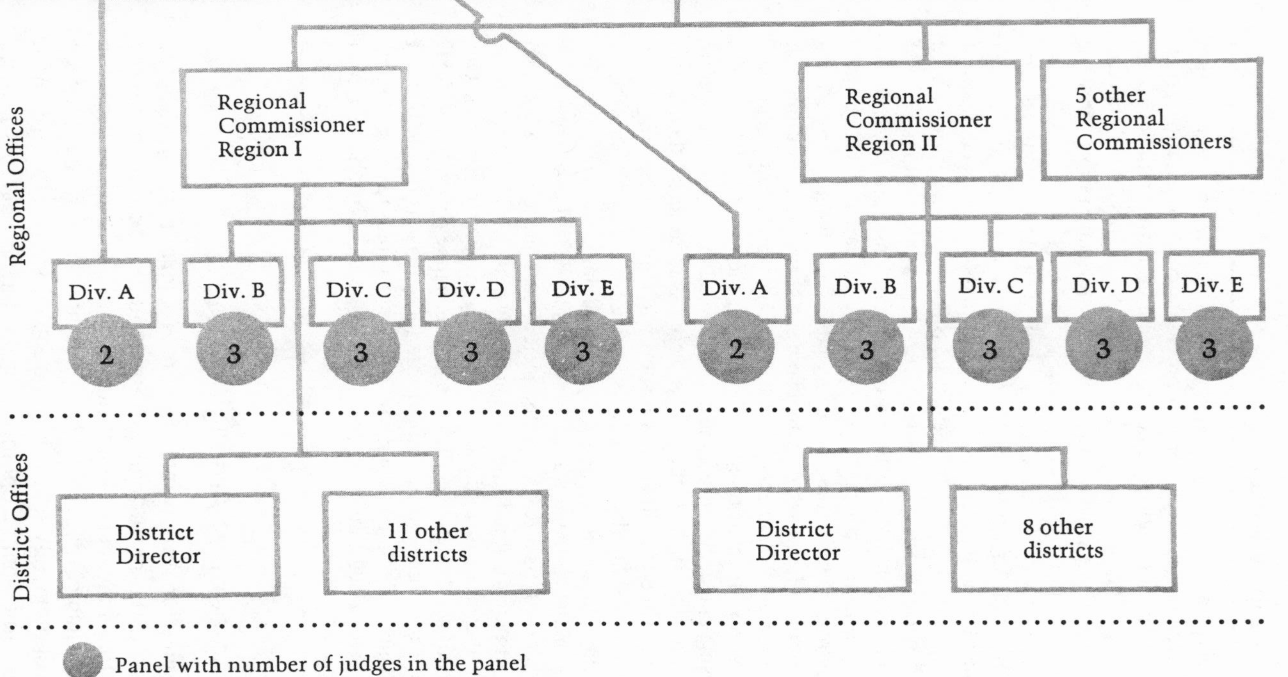
Regional Offices
District Offices
Regional Commissioner Region I
Regional Commissioner Region II
5 other Regional Commissioners
Div. A
2
Div. B
3
Div. C
3
Div. D
3
Div. E
3
Div. A
2
Div. B
3
Div. C
3
Div. D
3
Div. E
3
District Director
11 other districts
District Director
8 other districts
Panel with number of judges in the panel

Exhibit 2. Steps in the Judging Procedure

Step 1. Each judge received a folder containing a range of performance information on each unit to be evaluated. This was done to provide a common starting point. The information covered an 18-month time period. Some of it was statistical (e.g., productivity indexes), and some was more subjective (such as ''personnel management'' conditions). Each judge was asked to study this information thoroughly for two days, then put it away and not look at it again.

Step 2. Each judge received two identical decks of cards. One deck was to be used for judging overall current effectiveness, while the other was for judging overall performance improvement over 18 months. Each card within a deck listed a pair of comparable divisional units from two different district offices (e.g., Division A from District I as compared with Division A, District 2). All possible combinations of district pairs were covered in each deck. Numerous precautions were taken in the construction of each deck to prevent bias. For example, the order in which pairs were presented was determined by a random number table so as to delete any effects due to order of presentation. Also, each unit appeared the same number of times on the left side as it did on the right side of each card so as to cancel effects of placement.

Steps 3–4. Each judge was instructed to circle the unit on each card which had the higher performance, using one deck for judging current effectiveness and the second deck for evaluating improvement. Half the judges were asked to make their effectiveness judgments first, while the other half made their improvement judgments first. This was done to counter any biasing effects arising from making one type of judgment before the other. In addition, judges were asked not to confer with other judges, so as to ensure that each judge was making an independent assessment.

Steps 5–6. Three days after Steps 3 & 4 were completed, each judge was given two more decks of cards, both identical in format to the first two decks. The instructions were to repeat exactly the procedure followed in making the first judgments. Our intent here was to find out if judgments were stable from one time period to the next.

Step 7. As a final step, each judge was asked to write three reasons on the back of each card in the improvement deck to explain why one unit was picked over another. From this information, we hoped to learn more about the specific criteria that each judge was using.

Agreement Among Managers

A basic and critical question for any management is: Can our managers agree with one another about the performance of units under their supervision? Pessimists contend that managers cannot mentally assimilate and agree on all the complex performance data available, or that managers are such an idiosyncratic lot psychologically that it is impossible for them to agree with one another. On the other hand, optimists argue that managers are quite adept at simplifying complex information, being far more logical and objective than the pessimists might believe.

Our findings strongly support the optimists. While we cannot answer the agreement question for *all* organizations, Exhibit 3 does reveal that the particular managers we studied were, in general, able to reach a substantial level of agreement in their overall judgments of *both* current effectiveness and performance improvement. There was also a high correlation between their first-day and third-day judgments on both performance measurements.

The critical reader should ask, of course, if high agreement was merely a product of common "bias" among the judges within each panel. If such a bias did exist, this would be disturbing because IRS managers, while in overall agreement, could be making inaccurate assessments. One check on the amount of bias was to examine the extent of agreement between each divisional panel at the regional level and its counterpart panel at the national office. These panels all reported to different bosses and were separated by large physical distances. Under these conditions of limited authority and interaction we felt that high agreement between national and regional office panels could not be explained in terms of a commonly shared bias.

The findings indeed revealed considerable agreement between regional and national office panels from each of the five divisions: an average of +.75 for their current effectiveness judgments and +.65 for their performance improvement judgments. Therefore, we think it reasonable to infer that common bias was not a strong contributing factor toward high agreement.

The improvement evaluation is obviously a complex assessment which includes many subjective considerations and also requires a longer time perspective. Yet IRS managers seemed to find themselves on relatively the same historical wavelength. This finding is important because a manager's awareness of performance trends is often what tempers action-taking plans. Lack of agreement about trends could produce not only inappropriate actions, but also conflicting decisions from different managers.

At the same time, we should point out that a considerable range existed between panels with the lowest and highest levels of internal agreement. For current-effectiveness judgments, the lowest agreement panel had an internal correlation of +.16 while the highest agreement panel had +.99. For performance-improvement judgments, the internal correlation was +.10 for the lowest agreement panel and +1.00 for the highest panel. Thus, a large majority of panels revealed substantial internal agreement, while a few

Exhibit 3. Level of Overall Agreement

	Current Effectiveness	Performance Improvement Over 18 Months
Average correlation of agreement within 15 panels	+.76	+.71
Average correlation of agreement between day 1 and day 3 judgments for 50 judges	+.90	+.83

panels revealed much disagreement. This suggests the importance of discovering the factors that block agreement on some panels and the factors that cause high agreement on others.

Effect of Distance

We found two important organizational variables which seemed to distinguish between high- and low-agreement panels. The most potent variable appeared to be "organizational distance." Exhibit 4 shows not only that members of national office panels (two levels removed from districts) agreed less with one another in comparison with judges on regional office panels (one level removed), but also that their judgments were less stable from day 1 to day 3.

We prefer the term "organizational distance" to "physical distance" because the Region I office and its 12 districts were located within 600 miles of Washington, while the Region II office and its 9 districts were situated more than 1,300 miles away. Yet national office panels did not reach any more agreement about the closer Region I districts than they did about the more remote Region II districts. It appears that sitting close to the top of the organizational pyramid is not necessarily the easiest or best vantage point for assessing field unit performance. Undoubtedly, certain information disappears in the gap between levels, never reaching the top.

For us, these findings raise doubts about concentrating too much decision-making power at the top of large organizations when the decision to be made is based on the evaluations of performance. They also cause one to question an overreliance on centralized information systems. Centralized systems, because of their remoteness and need for uniformity, may be particularly insensitive to what is happening in each field unit.

Exhibit 4. Relationship Between Organizational Distance and Level of Overall Agreement

	Current Effectiveness	Performance Improvement Over 18 Months
Average correlation of agreement within:		
5 national office panels	+.53	+.41
10 regional office panels	+.84	+.81
Average correlation of agreement between day 1 and day 3 judgments for:		
22 national judges	+.80	+.71
28 regional office judges	+.93	+.87

The Effect of Size

A second important, but less pronounced, organizational variable was the size of functional divisions. Exhibit 5 reveals that panels from the two largest agency divisions (A and B), each of which employed more than twice as many people as any other division, reached lower levels of agreement. These large division panels, regardless of their level in the organization, seemed to have particular difficulty in assessing performance improvement over time.

Managers in large divisions are often physically and organizationally separated; they also become more specialized in their job functions. As a result, their communications are likely to be less frequent and conducted from narrower frames of reference. Further evidence of this communications breakdown was found in that large division panels from the national office agreed with their counterpart panels at the regional offices only at the level of +.46 when judging performance improvement, while national and regional panels from small divisions agreed with each other at a much higher level, +.83, in judging improvement. Apparently, the communications pipeline between national and regional levels was more open in small divisions.

Both Exhibit 4 and Exhibit 5 make clear that the performance judgments of IRS managers are affected by their positions in the organizations. We suspect that the same findings apply to other large organizations as well. If a manager is located at headquarters, he is less likely to agree with his colleagues. In addition, if he is in a large division, he is less likely to agree not only with his peers at headquarters but also with managers at the next lower level in his division. Judgments of current effectiveness probably will not be as strongly affected by these organizational forces as are judgments of performance improvement.

Exhibit 5. Relationship Between Organization Size and Level of Overall Agreement

	Current Effectiveness	Performance Improvement Over 18 Months
Average correlation of agreement within:		
6 large division panels	+.73	+.48
9 small division panels	+.82	+.86
Average correlation of agreement between day 1 and day 3 judgments for:		
22 large division judges	+.83	+.73
28 small division judges	+.92	+.89

Lower level managers, because they can agree more with each other, may be able to teach higher level managers a few of their trade secrets. Some clues to these trade secrets became more obvious when we focused on the specific criteria used by high-agreement panels.

Criteria for Judgment

While broader organizational forces (distance and size) produced variations in judgment, the specific criteria used by judges also contributed to differences in agreement. An analysis was made of the criteria filled out by judges on the reverse sides of their "performance improvement" cards.

As a first step, we arranged for an independent group of IRS analysts in Washington to categorize the criteria reported by the 50 judges. This group of analysts individually rated each of the reasons given by the judges on a 5-point scale: a rating of 4 or 5 was given to highly qualitative criteria, a 3 to mixed qualitative and quantitative criteria, and a 1 or 2 to highly quantitative criteria. One example of a qualitative criterion was "management is setting challenging goals," while a quantitative one was "time spent per average case."

Exhibit 6 shows the ranking of the 10 most frequently mentioned criteria. The phrasing of these criteria was done by the IRS national office analysts, who inferred the categories from a variety of specific phrases found on the judges' cards. Some categories are unique to IRS operations, but they indicate general types of criteria that could apply to other organizations as well.

Important here is the fact that a large majority of items (7 of 10) are qualitative (rated 4 or 5 on the rating scale), although two strongly quantitative criteria (rated 1) were also mentioned by the judges. The most important criterion was "quality and effectiveness of management"; it was used by judges in 13 of the 15 panels.

From this initial categorizing process, we found that 92 different criteria were used by the entire group of judges. These criteria divided themselves into 39% qualitative, 22% mixed, and 39% quantitative, based on the ratings assigned by the IRS analysts. Of significant interest here is the fact that such a high percentage of qualitative criteria were used. The IRS devotes considerable manpower and money to quantifying performance results; yet these numerical results played a more limited role than we suspected.

Number of Factors

Next we compared the criteria used by four high-agreement panels (those panels with an internal correlation of +.84 or better) with the criteria used by four low-agreement panels (those with an internal correlation of +.30 or lower). Here we did not find any significant difference in the total number

Exhibit 6. Most Frequently Mentioned Criteria

Rank		Rating on 5-Point Scale[a]
1	Quality and effectiveness of management	4
2	Productivity measurements	1
3	Manpower utilization	4
4	Overall improvement, status quo, or decline	3
5	Inventory level of uncollected TDAs (taxpayer delinquent accounts)	1
6	Progress and achievement of established objectives and planned programs	4
7	Morale	4
8	Management participation and concern in local problem solving	5
9	Potential available and use to which potential is put	4
10	Improved quality and composition and balance of fieldwork	5

[a]1: Highly quantitative; 2: more quantitative than qualitative; 3: mixed quantitative and qualitative; 4: more qualitative than quantitative; and 5: highly qualitative.

of criteria used; that is, low-agreement panels did not appear to be confusing themselves with too many criteria. High-agreement panels averaged 11.8 different criteria per panel, and low-agreement panels, 12.8. One high-agreement panel used as few as 7 criteria, while another used 20. Approximately the same range of total criteria (6 to 20) was found among low-agreement panels.

Points of Agreement

An important distinction was discovered in the extent of *common* criteria used by high-agreement panels. Exhibit 7 reveals that 44% of the criteria used in each high-agreement panel were commonly used by *every* judge within that panel. Only 12% of the criteria used in low-agreement panels were common to every judge.

We conclude from Exhibit 7 that lack of agreement about specific criteria probably results in lack of agreement about the overall performance of a unit. At the same time, we should point out that "perfect" agreement of specific criteria is not essential; a high percentage of criteria (41%) were unique to individual judges in high-agreement panels. Apparently, many judges took somewhat different reasoning paths to arrive at essentially the same end result.

A broad implication here is that, while managements should work to-

Exhibit 7. Consensus About Criteria

Level of Agreement	Used by All Members	Used by Some but Not All Members	Used by Only One Member
Four high-agreement panels	44%	15%	41%
Four low-agreement panels	12	17	71

ward agreement on criteria for evaluating overall performance, they should also leave some latitude for each manager to select individual reasons. All too many managements spend endless meeting hours trying to agree on a limited number of criteria. According to our findings, this costly and often frustrating task may not be necessary.

Qualitative Criteria

One very significant finding was that high-agreement panels used considerably more qualitative than quantitative criteria in making their decisions. Exhibit 8 shows that 69% of the criteria used by high-agreement panels were qualitative, compared to only 20% for low-agreement panels. Low-agreement panels used 68% quantitative criteria yet could reach only an overall agreement level of no better than +.31. Furthermore, we found that the only criteria which low-agreement panels could completely agree on with *quantitative* criteria; there was far less agreement on qualitative criteria. This suggests that if managers want to be more in line with their colleagues in assessing total performance, they need to use not only *a greater proportion of qualitative criteria, but also develop more consensus on the specific qualitative criteria to be used.*

Why would qualitative evidence be relied on so heavily by high-agreement panels, and why might these criteria lead them to greater overall agreement? As we interpret our findings, there are at least three reasons:

1. Qualitative factors probably give more *concrete, more sensitive,* and *more current* clues to the underlying strengths of a unit; whereas statistics, despite their apparent preciseness, are usually averages or aggregates that fail to portray the complex events behind them.
2. Qualitative criteria present clearer leads for required corrective action; whereas statistical results may give little indication of *why* events happened as they did.
3. Qualitative criteria tend to be broader because they are not tied to particular measurable points; whereas quantitative criteria, just because they have to be particularized to certain narrow segments of field operations in order to be measured, may result in very diverse inferences being drawn from them in judging overall performance.

Exhibit 8. Type of Criteria and Level of Overall Agreement

Level of Agreement	Types of Criteria Used: Quantitative	Mixed	Qualitative
Four high-agreement panels	17%	14%	69%
Four low-agreement panels	68	12	20

Applying the Results

Up to this point, we have mentioned some general implications of our findings, now we would like to draw them together and offer some specific suggestions for action.

- ☐ Most important is the need to recognize that managers—not computers, numbers, or information systems—are the critical element in the assessment of subunit performance.

  Statistical reports have increasingly taken on the revered status of "objectivity," while managerial judgments have too often been sidetracked as overly "subjective" or "opinionated." Thus we find organizations building larger headquarters staffs to process ever larger amounts of statistical performance information, much of which is never used.

- ☐ All organizations ought to be vitally concerned with studying how their managers actually assess subunit performance. While organizations frequently spend large sums of money generating more and more information about subunit performance, they seldom consider what information is actually used or needed by their managers. Nor do they always recognize the importance of achieving a high level of agreement among top managers about subunit performance. If managers cannot agree, there is something amiss, either with the company's information system or with the managers and their organizational environment.

  We therefore suggest that organizations take periodic "X rays" of their judgmental process. The study methodology used in the IRS is one useful approach. The findings can be used both for training managers to reach more informed judgments about subunit performance, and for designing information systems which will provide more help to managers in making their judgments.

- ☐ Management training should use research findings derived from the actual company environment to design programs that fit the needs of its particular management group. To do this, the key management group participating in the study could be brought together to hear and discuss the significant findings.

The critical questions before these managers should be: (a) Why do we have these results? (b) What do we do about them? The answers, of course, will vary with each organization and its unique findings. But the general thrust of actions afterward should be more informed and constructive.

For example, a top management group may decide to pay greater attention to the judgments of its field managers. Or agreement may be reached to place greater and more explicit emphasis on qualitative criteria. Or the present information system may be altered to provide data on those criteria which are most frequently used, while eliminating data on those which are not heavily used.

The next step would be to discuss the findings within smaller functional groupings. It would be useful for those groups in lowest agreement to sit down and discuss why they see subunits from such different perspectives. They may discover, in the process of this examination, that they fail to discuss their observations sufficiently with each other. Or they may find that each is using too diverse a set of criteria, and that more consensus needs to be reached on particular criteria.

☐ The formal information system must be designed to complement these changes if they are to be put into practice. For instance, it makes little sense for a company computer to continue providing data on 50 variables when its managers are in substantial agreement after using data on only 15 variables.

A real challenge for some organizations is to build more qualitative information into their formal systems. One method used in some companies is to request a written narrative with each submission of statistics from the field. Another method is to hold periodic, in-depth discussions involving several managers form different levels so that each can contribute whatever qualitative data are available to him.

Organizations might also consider the possibility of incorporating a judgmental procedure, such as the one used in this study, into an organization's on-going process of performance assessment. Managements need to consider the challenge of systematically recording managerial judgments as much as they systematize statistical results. Lower level managers can attest to their feelings of frustration when one upper level manager tells one of them that he or she is doing a "good" job while another upper level manager downgrades her or him. On the other hand, if this same manager knows that five upper level managers systematically agree in ranking the unit at the "tail-end" of the pack, the manager cannot as easily rationalize the results.

Our suggestion at this early stage, however, is to experiment with, but not institutionalize, a more systematic judging procedure, perhaps in only one division of a large company. Every formal system, if taken too seriously and rigidly, can become more of a hindrance than a help.

There are always bugs to be worked out of these systems before giving them wider application.

Conclusion

A major task of any management is to know what is *actually* taking place within its organization. One critical, but seldom examined, function is the manner in which key managers assess the performance of units under their supervision. In the absence of knowledge, numerous myths and assumptions have abounded. Particularly noticeable is a growing mistrust of the reliability of managerial judgments. Signs of this mistrust are reflected in current trends toward more statistics, more computers, more information specialists, and more centralized information systems—the IRS, where this study was conducted, being no exception.

Yet the findings of this study seriously dispute many of these newer trends and assumptions. Notably:

1 Managers can generally agree with each other about the current effectiveness and performance trends of subunits under them.
2 Their judgments seem to be quite stable from one day to the next.
3 Managers who agree most with their colleagues tend to come from levels closest to the field; work in smaller divisions; use more commonly shared criteria; and rely more on qualitative than on quantitative criteria.

These conclusions must be qualified to the extent that they are based on *one study in a single nonbusiness organization*. Therefore, we should treat them more as propositions to be tested further, rather than as final answers.

However, we believe these findings place a new challenge before every management: to seek new ways of studying, assisting, and restoring confidence in the performance judgments of their managers. This will not occur magically. First, a concerned management will have to investigate and identify its current practices for judging performance. Then, it will have to use the study findings to train its managers in improving their judgmental practices. Finally, it will have to strive to make its information system a more helpful servant rather than an irrelevant master.

Note

1. Letter from Robert Jacobs, "From the Thoughtful Businessman," *HBR*, January–February 1967, p. 48.

31

Ethics Without the Sermon

LAURA L. NASH

"Like some Triassic reptile, the theoretical view of ethics lumbers along in the far past of Sunday School and Philosophy I, while the reality of practical business concerns is constantly measuring a wide range of competing claims on time and resources against the unrelenting and objective marketplace." So writes the author of this article as she introduces a procedure to test pragmatically the ethical content and human fallout of everyday decisions in business and other organizational settings. First you have to define the problem as you see it, then (insofar as possible) examine it as outsiders might see it. You explore where your loyalties lie and consider both your intentions in making the decision and whom your action might affect. You proceed to the consequences of disclosing your action to those you report to or respect, and then analyze the symbolic meaning to all affected. In her conclusion the author attacks the sticky question of the proper moral standpoint of the organization as a whole.

As if via a network TV program on the telecommunications satellite, declarations such as these are being broadcast throughout the land:

☐ *Scene 1.* Annual meeting, Anyproducts Inc.; John Q. Moneypockets, chairman and CEO, speaking: "Our responsibility to the public has always come first at our company, and we continue to strive toward serving our public in the best way possible in the belief that good ethics is good business. . . . Despite our forecast of a continued recession in the industry through 1982, we are pleased to announce that 1981's earnings per share were up for the twenty-sixth year in a row."

☐ *Scene 2.* Corporate headquarters, Anyproducts Inc.; Linda Diesinker, group vice president, speaking: "Of course we're concerned

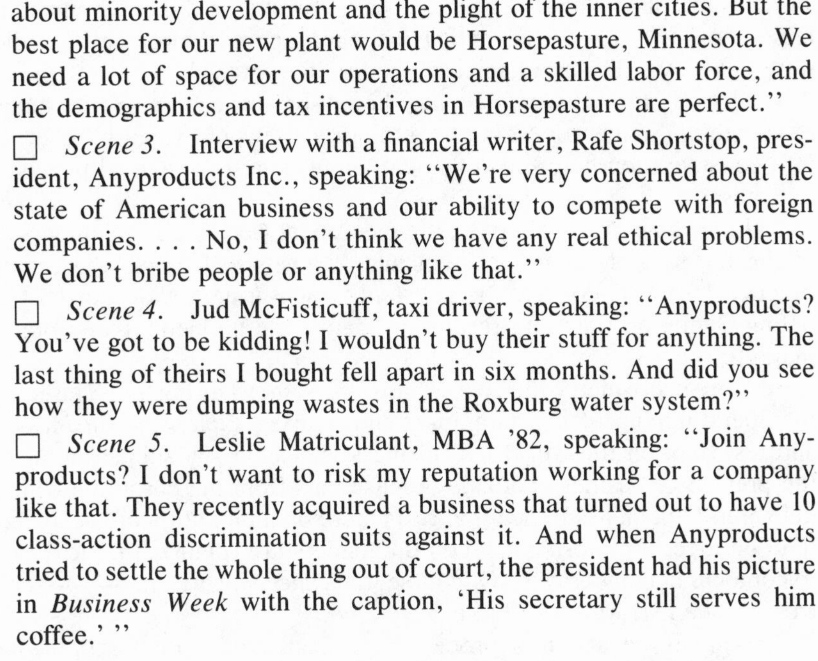

about minority development and the plight of the inner cities. But the best place for our new plant would be Horsepasture, Minnesota. We need a lot of space for our operations and a skilled labor force, and the demographics and tax incentives in Horsepasture are perfect."

☐ *Scene 3.* Interview with a financial writer, Rafe Shortstop, president, Anyproducts Inc., speaking: "We're very concerned about the state of American business and our ability to compete with foreign companies. . . . No, I don't think we have any real ethical problems. We don't bribe people or anything like that."

☐ *Scene 4.* Jud McFisticuff, taxi driver, speaking: "Anyproducts? You've got to be kidding! I wouldn't buy their stuff for anything. The last thing of theirs I bought fell apart in six months. And did you see how they were dumping wastes in the Roxburg water system?"

☐ *Scene 5.* Leslie Matriculant, MBA '82, speaking: "Join Anyproducts? I don't want to risk my reputation working for a company like that. They recently acquired a business that turned out to have 10 class-action discrimination suits against it. And when Anyproducts tried to settle the whole thing out of court, the president had his picture in *Business Week* with the caption, 'His secretary still serves him coffee.' "

Whether you regard it as an unchecked epidemic or as the first blast of Gabriel's horn, the trend toward focusing on the social impact of the corporation is an inescapable reality that must be factored into today's managerial decision making. But for the executive who asks, "How do we as a corporation examine our ethical concerns?" the theoretical insights currently available may be more frustrating than helpful.

As the first scene in this article implies, many executives firmly believe that corporate operations and corporate values are dynamically intertwined. For the purposes of analysis, however, the executive needs to uncoil the business-ethics helix and examine both strands closely.

Unfortunately, the ethics strand has remained largely inaccessible, for business has not yet developed a workable process by which corporate values can be articulated. If ethics and business are part of the same double helix, perhaps we can develop a microscope capable of enlarging our perception of both aspects of business administration—what we do and who we are.

Sidestepping Triassic Reptiles

Philosophy has been sorting out issues of fairness, injury, empathy, self-sacrifice, and so on for more than 2,000 years. In seeking to examine the ethics of business, therefore, business logically assumes it will be best served by a "consultant" in philosophy who is already familiar with the formal discipline of ethics.

As the philosopher begins to speak, however, a difficulty immediately arises; corporate executives and philosophers approach problems in radically different ways. The academician ponders the intangible, savors the paradoxical, and embraces the peculiar; he or she speaks in a special language of categorical imperatives and deontological viewpoints that must be taken into consideration before a statement about honesty is agreed to have any meaning.

Like some Triassic reptile, the theoretical view of ethics lumbers along in the far past of Sunday School and Philosophy I, while the reality of practical business concerns is constantly measuring a wide range of competing claims on time and resources against the unrelenting and objective marketplace.

Not surprisingly, the two groups are somewhat hostile. The jokes of the liberal intelligentsia are rampant and weary: "*Ethics and Business*—the shortest book in the world." "Business and ethics—a subject confined to the preface of business books." Accusations from the corporate cadre are delivered with an assurance that rests more on an intuition of social climate than on a certainty of fact: "You do-gooders are ruining America's ability to compete in the world." "Of course, the cancer reports on ——— [choose from a long list] were terribly exaggerated."

What is needed is a process of ethical inquiry that is immediately comprehensible to a group of executives and not predisposed to the utopian, and sometimes anticapitalistic, bias marking much of the work in applied business philosophy today. So I suggest, as a preliminary solution, a set of 12 questions that draw on traditional philosophical frameworks but that avoid the level of abstraction normally associated with formal moral reasoning.

I offer the questions as a first step in a very new discipline. As such, they form a tentative model that will certainly undergo modifications after its parts are given some exercise. Exhibit 1 poses the 12 questions.

To illustrate the application of the questions, I will draw especially on a program at Lex Service Group, Ltd., whose top management prepared a statement of financial objectives and moral values as a part of its strategic planning process.[1] Lex is a British company with operations in the United Kingdom and the United States. Its sales total about $1.2 billion. In 1978 its structure was partially decentralized, and in 1979 the chairman's policy group began a strategic planning process. The intent, according to its statement of values and objectives, was "to make explicit the sort of company Lex was, or wished to be."

Neither a paralegal code nor a generalized philosophy, the statement consisted of a series of general policies regarding financial strategy as well as such aspects of the company's character as customer service, employee-shareholder responsibility, and quality of management. Its content largely reflected the personal values of Lex's chairman and CEO, Trevor Chinn, whose private philanthropy is well known and whose concern for social welfare has long been echoed in the company's personnel policies.

In the past, pressure on senior managers for high profit performance had obscured some of these ideals in practice, and the statement of strategy was a way of radically realigning various competing moral claims with the financial objectives of the company. As one senior manager remarked to me, "The values seem obvious, and if we hadn't been so gross in the past we wouldn't have needed the statement." Despite a predictable variance among Lex's top executives as to the desirability of the values outlined in the statement, it was adopted with general agreement to comply and was scheduled for reassessment at a senior managers' meeting one year after implementation.

The 12 Questions

1. *Have you defined the problem accurately?*

How one assembles the facts weights an issue before the moral examination ever begins, and a definition is rarely accurate if it articulates one's loyalties rather than the facts. The importance of factual neutrality is readily seen, for example, in assessing the moral implications for producing a chemical agent for use in warfare. Depending on one's loyalties, the decision to make the substance can be described as serving one's country, developing products, or killing babies. All of the above may be factual statements, but none is neutral or accurate if viewed in isolation.

Similarly, the recent controversy over marketing U.S.-made cigarettes in Third World countries rarely noted that the incidence of lung cancer in underdeveloped nations is quite low (from one-tenth to one-twentieth the rate for U.S. males) due primarily to the lower life expectancies and earlier predominance of other diseases in these nations. Such a fact does not decide the ethical complexities of this marketing problem, but it does add a crucial perspective in the assignment of moral priorities by defining precisely the injury that tobacco exports may cause.

Extensive fact gathering may also help defuse the emotionalism of an issue. For instance, local statistics on lung cancer incidence reveal that the U.S. tobacco industry is not now "exporting death," as has been charged. Moreover, the substantial and immediate economic benefits attached to tobacco may be providing food and health care in these countries. Nevertheless, as life expectancy and the standards of living rise, a higher incidence of cigarette-related diseases appears likely to develop in these nations. Therefore, cultivation of the nicotine habit may be deemed detrimental to the long-term welfare of these nations.

According to one supposedly infallible truth of modernism, technology is so complex that its results will never be fully comprehensible or predictable. Part of the executive's frustration in responding to question 1 is the real possibility that the "experts" will find no grounds for agreement about the facts.

As a first step, however, defining fully the factual implications of a decision determines to a large degree the quality of one's subsequent moral position. Pericles' definition of true courage rejected the Spartans' blind obedience in war in preference to the courage of the Athenian citizen who, he said, was able to make a decision to proceed in full knowledge of the probable danger. A truly moral decision is an informed decision. A decision that is based on blind or convenient ignorance is hardly defensible.

One simple test of the initial definition is question 2.

2. *How would you define the problem if you stood on the other side of the fence?*

The contemplated construction of a plant for Division X is touted at the finance committee meeting as an absolute necessity for expansion at a cost saving of at least 25%. With plans drawn up for an energy-efficient building and an option already secured on a 99-year lease in a new industrial park in Chippewa County, the committee is likely to feel comfortable in approving the request for funds in a matter of minutes.

The facts of the matter are that the company will expand in an appropriate market, allocate its resources sensibly, create new jobs, increase Chippewa County's tax base, and most likely increase its returns to the shareholders. To the residents of Chippewa County, however, the plant may mean the destruction of a customary recreation spot, the onset of severe traffic jams, and the erection of an architectural eyesore. These are also facts of the situation, and certainly more immediate to the county than utilitarian justifications of profit performance and rights of ownership from an impersonal corporation whose headquarters are 1,000 miles from Chippewa County and whose executives have plenty of acreage for their own recreation.

The purpose of articulating the other side, whose needs are understandably less proximate than operational considerations, is to allow some mechanism whereby calculations of self-interest (or even of a project's ultimate general beneficence) can be interrupted by a compelling empathy for those who might suffer immediate injury or mere annoyance as a result of a corporation's decisions. Such empathy is a necessary prerequisite for shouldering voluntarily some responsibility for the social consequences of corporate operations, and it may be the only solution to today's overly litigious and anarchic world.

There is a power in self-examination: With an exploration of the likely consequences of a proposal, taken from the viewpoint of those who do not immediately benefit, comes a discomfort or an embarrassment that rises in proportion to the degree of the likely injury and its articulation. Like Socrates as gadfly, who stung his fellow citizens into a critical examination of their

Exhibit 1. Twelve Questions for Examining the Ethics of a Business Decision

1 Have you defined the problem accurately?
2 How would you define the problem if you stood on the other side of the fence?
3 How did this situation occur in the first place?
4 To whom and to what do you give your loyalty as a person and as a member of the corporation?
5 What is your intention in making this decision?
6 How does this intention compare with the probable results?
7 Whom could your decision or action injure?
8 Can you discuss the problem with the affected parties before you make your decision?
9 Are you confident that your position will be as valid over a long period of time as it seems now?
10 Could you disclose without qualm your decision or action to your boss, your CEO, the board of directors, your family, society as a whole?
11 What is the symbolic potential of your action if understood? if misunderstood?
12 Under what conditions would you allow exceptions to your stand?

conduct when they became complacent, the discomfort of the alternative definition is meant to prompt a disinclination to choose the expedient over the most responsible course of action.

Abstract generalities about the benefits of the profit motive and the free market system are, for some, legitimate and ultimate justifications, but when unadorned with alternative viewpoints, such arguments also tend to promote the complacency, carelessness, and impersonality that have characterized some of the more injurious actions of corporations. The advocates of these arguments are like the reformers in Nathaniel Hawthorne's short story "Hall of Fantasy" who "had got possession of some crystal fragment of truth, the brightness of which so dazzled them that they could see nothing else in the whole universe."

In the example of Division X's new plant, it was a simple matter to define the alternate facts; the process rested largely on an assumption that certain values were commonly shared (no one likes a traffic jam, landscaping pleases more than an unadorned building, and so forth). But the alternative definition often underscores an inherent disparity in values or language. To some, the employment of illegal aliens is a criminal act (fact 1); to others, it is a solution to the 60% unemployment rate of a neighboring country (fact 2). One country's bribe is another country's redistribution of sales commissions.

When there are cultural or linguistic disparities, it is easy to get the facts wrong or to invoke a pluralistic tolerance as an excuse to act in one's own self-interest: "That's the way they do things over there. Who are we to question their beliefs?" This kind of reasoning can be both factually inaccurate (many generalizations about bribery rest on hearsay and do not represent the complexities of a culture) and philosophically inconsistent (there are plenty of beliefs, such as those of the environmentalist, which the same generalizers do not hesitate to question).

3. *How did this situation occur in the first place?*

Lex Motor Company, a subsidiary of Lex Service Group Ltd., had been losing share at a 20% rate in a declining market; and Depot B's performance was the worst of all. Two nearby Lex depots could easily absorb B's business, and closing it down seemed the only sound financial decision. Lex's chairman, Trevor Chinn, hesitated to approve the closure, however, on the grounds that putting 100 people out of work was not right when the corporation itself was not really jeopardized by B's existence. Moreover, seven department managers, who were all within five years of retirement and had had 25 or more years of service at Lex, were scheduled to be made redundant.

The values statement provided no automatic solution, for it placed value on both employees' security and shareholders' interest. Should they close Depot B? At first Chinn thought not: Why should the little guys suffer disproportionately when the company was not performing well? Why not close a more recently acquired business where employee service was not so large a factor? Or why not wait out the short term and reduce head count through natural attrition?

As important as deciding the ethics of the situation was the inquiry into its history. Indeed, the history gave a clue to solving the dilemma: Lex's traditional emphasis on employee security *and* high financial performance had led to a precipitate series of acquisitions and subsequent divestitures when the company had failed to meet its overall objectives. After each rationalization, the people serving the longest had been retained and placed at Depot B, so that by 1980 the facility had more managers than it needed and a very high proportion of long-service employees.

So the very factors that had created the performance problems were making the closure decision difficult, and the very solution that Lex was inclined to favor again would exacerbate the situation further!

In deciding the ethics of a situation it is important to distinguish the symptoms from the disease. Great profit pressures with no sensitivity to the cycles.in a particular industry, for example, may force division managers to be ruthless with employees, to short-weight customers, or even to fiddle with cash flow reports in order to meet headquarters' performance criteria.

Dealing with the immediate case of lying, quality discrepancy, or strained labor relations—when the problem is finally discovered—is only a temporary solution. A full examination of how the situation occurred and what the traditional solutions have been may reveal a more serious discrepancy of values and pressures, and this will illuminate the real significance and ethics of the problem. It will also reveal recurring patterns of events that in isolation appear trivial but that as a whole point up a serious situation.

Such a mechanism is particularly important because very few executives are outright scoundrels. Rather, violations of corporate and social values usually occur inadvertently because no one recognizes that a problem exists until it becomes a crisis. This tendency toward initial trivialization seems to be the biggest ethical problem in business today. Articulating answers to my first three questions is a way of reversing that process.

4. *To whom and what do you give your loyalties as a person and as a member of the corporation?*

Every executive faces conflicts of loyalty. The most familiar occasions pit private conscience and sense of duty against corporate policy, but equally frequent are the situations in which one's close colleagues demand participation (tacit or explicit) in an operation or a decision that runs counter to company policy. To whom or what is the greater loyalty—to one's corporation? superior? family? society? self? race? sex?

The good news about conflicts of loyalty is that their identification is a workable way of smoking out the ethics of a situation and of discovering the absolute values inherent in it. As one executive in a discussion of a Harvard case study put it, "My corporate brain says this action is O.K., but my noncorporate brain keeps flashing these warning lights."

The bad news about conflicts of loyalty is that there are few automatic answers for placing priorities on them. "To thine own self be true" is a murky quagmire when the self takes on a variety of roles, as it does so often in this complex modern world.

Supposedly, today's young managers are giving more weight to individual than to corporate identity, and some older executives see this tendency as being ultimately subversive. At the same time, most of them believe individual integrity is essential to a company's reputation.

The U.S. securities industry, for example, is one of the most rigorous industries in America in its requirements of honesty and disclosure. Yet in the end, all its systematic precautions prove inadequate unless the people involved also have a strong sense of integrity that puts loyalty to these principles above personal gain.

A system, however, must permit the time and foster the motivation to allow personal integrity to surface in a particular situation. An examination of loyalties is one way to bring this about. Such an examination may strengthen reputations but also may result in blowing the whistle (freedom of thought carries with it the risk of revolution). But a sorting out of loyalties can also bridge the gulf between policy and implementation or among various interest groups whose affiliations may mask a common devotion to an aspect of a problem—a devotion on which consensus can be built.

How does one probe into one's own loyalties and their implications? A useful method is simply to play various roles out loud, to call on one's loyalty to family and community (for example) by asking, "What will I say when my child asks me why I did that?" If the answer is "That's the way the world works," then your loyalties are clear and moral passivity inevitable. But if the question presents real problems, you have begun a demodulation of signals from your conscience that can only enhance corporate responsibility.

5. *What is your intention in making this decision?*

6. *How does this intention compare with the likely results?*

These two questions are asked together because their content often bears close resemblance and, by most calculations, both color the ethics of a situation.

Corporation Buglebloom decides to build a new plant in an underdeveloped minority-populated district where the city has been trying with little success to encourage industrial development. The media approve and Buglebloom adds another star to its good reputation. Is Buglebloom a civic leader and a supporter of minorities or a canny investor about to take advantage of the disadvantaged? The possibilities of Buglebloom's intentions are endless and probably unfathomable to the public; Buglebloom may be both canny investor and friend of minority groups.

I argue that despite their complexity and elusiveness, a company's intentions *do* matter. The "purity" of Buglebloom's motives (purely profit-seeking or purely altruistic) will have wide-reaching effects inside and outside the corporation—on attitudes toward minority employees in other parts of the company, on the wages paid at the new plant, and on the number of other investors in the same area—that will legitimize a certain ethos in the corporation and the community.

Sociologist Max Weber called this an "ethics of attitude" and contrasted it with an "ethics of absolute ends." An ethics of attitude sets a standard to ensure a certain action. A firm policy at headquarters of not cheating customers, for example, may also deter salespeople from succumbing to a tendency to lie by omission or purchasers from continuing to patronize a high-priced supplier when the costs are automatically passed on in the selling price.

What about the ethics of result? Two years later, Buglebloom wishes it had never begun Project Minority Plant. Every good intention has been lost in the realities of doing business in an unfamiliar area, and Buglebloom now has dirty hands: Some of those payoffs were absolutely unavoidable if the plant was to open, operations have been plagued with vandalism and language problems, and local resentment at the industrialization of the neighborhood has risen as charges of discrimination have surfaced. No one seems to be benefiting from the project.

The goodness of intent pales somewhat before results that perpetrate great injury or simply do little good. Common sense demands that the "responsible" corporation try to align the two more closely, to identify the probable consequences and also the limitations of knowledge that might lead to more harm than good. Two things to remember in comparing intention and results are that knowledge of the future is always inadequate and that overconfidence often precedes a disastrous mistake.

These two precepts, cribbed from ancient Greece, may help the corporation keep the disparities between intent and result a fearsome reality to consider continuously. The next two questions explore two ways of reducing the moral risks of being wrong.

7. *Whom could your decision or action injure?*

The question presses whether injury is intentional or not. Given the limits of knowledge about a new product or policy, who and how many will come into contact with it? Could its inadequate disposal affect an entire community? two employees? yourself? How might your product be used if it happened to be acquired by a terrorist radical group or a terrorist military police force? Has your distribution system or disposal plan ensured against such injury? Could it ever?

If not, there may be a compelling moral justification for stopping production. In an integrated society where business and government share certain values, possible injury is an even more important consideration than potential benefit. In policymaking, a much likelier ground for agreement than benefit is avoidance of injury through those "universal nos"—such as no mass death, no totalitarianism, no hunger or malnutrition, no harm to children.

To exclude *at the outset* any policy or decision that might have such results is to reshape the way modern business examines its own morality. So often business formulates questions of injury only after the fact in the form of liability suits.

8. *Can you engage the affected parties in a discussion of the problem before you make your decision?*

If the calculus of injury is one way of responding to limitations of knowledge about the probable results of a particular business decision, the participation of affected parties is one of the best ways of informing that consideration. Civil rights groups often complain that corporations fail to invite participation from local leaders during the planning stages of community development projects and charitable programs. The corporate foundation that builds a tennis complex for disadvantaged youth is throwing away precious resources if most children in the neighborhood suffer from chronic malnutrition.

In the Lex depot closure case I have mentioned, senior executives agonized over whether the employees would choose redundancy over job transfer and which course would ultimately be more beneficial to them. The managers, however, did not consult the employees. There were more than 200 projected job transfers to another town. But all the affected employees, held by local ties and uneasy about possibly lower housing subsidies, refused relocation offers. Had the employees been allowed to participate in the redundancy discussions, the company might have wasted less time on relocation plans or might have uncovered and resolved the fears about relocating.

The issue of participation affects everyone. (How many executives feel that someone else should decide what is in *their* best interest?) And yet it is a principle often forgotten because of the pressure of time or the inconvenience of calling people together and facing predictably hostile questions.

9. *Are you confident that your position will be as valid over a long period of time as it seems now?*

As anyone knows who has had to consider long-range plans and short-term budgets simultaneously, a difference in time frame can change the meaning of a problem as much as spring and autumn change the colors of a tree. The ethical coloring of a business decision is no exception to this generational aspect of decision making. Time alters circumstances, and few corporate value systems are immune to shifts in financial status, external political pressure, and personnel. (One survey now places the average U.S. CEO's tenure in office at five years.)

At Lex, for example, the humanitarianism of the statement of objectives and values depended on financial prosperity. The values did not fully anticipate the extent to which the U.K. economy would undergo a recession, and the resulting changes had to be examined, reconciled, and fought if the company's values were to have any meaning. At the Lex annual review, the managers asked themselves repeatedly whether hard times were the ultimate test of the statement or a clear indication that a corporation had to be able to "afford" ethical positions.

Ideally, a company's articulation of its values should anticipate changes of fortune. As the hearings for the passage of the Foreign Corrupt Practices Act of 1977 demonstrated, doing what you can get away with today may not be a secure moral standard, but short-term discomfort for long-term sainthood may require irrational courage or a rational reasoning system or, more likely, both. These 12 questions attempt to elicit a rational system. Courage, of course, depends on personal integrity.

Another aspect of the ethical time frame stretches beyond the boundaries of question 9 but deserves special attention, and that is the timing of the ethical inquiry. When and where will it be made?

We do not normally invoke moral principles in our everyday conduct. Some time ago the participants in a national business ethics conference had worked late into the night preparing the final case for the meeting, and they were very anxious the next morning to get the class under way. Just before the session began, however, someone suggested that they all donate a dollar apiece as a gratuity for the dining hall help at the institute.

Then just as everyone automatically reached into his or her pocket, another person questioned the direction of the gift. Why tip the person behind the counter but not the cook in the kitchen? Should the money be given to each person in proportion to salary or divided equally among all? The participants laughed uneasily—or groaned—as they thought of the diversion of precious time from the case. A decision had to be made.

With the sure instincts of efficient managers, the group chose to forgo further discussion of distributive justice and, yes, appoint a committee. The committee doled out the money without further group consideration, and no formal feedback on the donation was asked for or given.

The questions offered here do not solve the problem of making time for the inquiry. For suggestions about creating favorable conditions for examining corporate values, drawn from my field research, see the appendix.

10. *Could you disclose without qualm your decision or action to your boss, your CEO, the board of directors, your family, or society as a whole?*

The old question, "Would you want your decision to appear on the front page of the *New York Times*?" still holds. A corporation may maintain that there's really no problem, but a survey of how many "trivial" actions it is reluctant to disclose might be interesting. Disclosure is a way of sounding those submarine depths of conscience and of searching out loyalties.

It is also a way of keeping a corporate character cohesive. The Lex group, for example, was once faced with a very sticky problem concerning a small but profitable site with unpleasant (though in no way illegal) working conditions, where two men with 30 years' service worked. I wrote up the case for a Lex senior managers' meeting on the promise to disguise it heavily because the executive who supervised the plant was convinced that, if the chairman and the personnel director knew the plant's true location, they would close it down immediately.

At the meeting, however, as everyone became involved in the discussion and the chairman himself showed sensitivity to the dilemma, the executive disclosed the location and spoke of his own feelings about the situation. The level of mutual confidence was apparent to all, and by other reports it was the most open discussion the group had ever had.

The meeting also fostered understanding of the company's values and their implementation. When the discussion finally flagged, the chairman spoke up. Basing his views on a full knowledge of the group's understanding of the problem, he set the company's priorities. "Jobs over fancy conditions, health over jobs," Chinn said, "but we always *must disclose*." The group decided to keep the plant open, at least for the time being.

Disclosure does not, however, automatically bring universal sympathy. In the early 1970s, a large food store chain that repeatedly found itself embroiled in the United Farm Workers (UFW) disputes with the Teamsters over California grape and lettuce contracts took very seriously the moral implications of a decision whether to stop selling these products. The company endlessly researched the issues, talked to all sides, and made itself available to public representatives of various interest groups to explain its position and to hear out everyone else.

When the controversy started, the company decided to support the UFW boycott, but three years later top management reversed its position. Most of the people who wrote to the company or asked it to send representatives to their local UFW support meetings, however, continued to condemn the chain even after hearing its views, and the general public apparently never became aware of the company's side of the story.

11. *What is the symbolic potential of your action if understood? if misunderstood?*

Jones Inc., a diversified multinational corporation with assets of $5 billion, has a paper manufacturing operation that happens to be the only major industry in Stirville, and the factory has been polluting the river on which it is located. Local and national conservation groups have filed suit against Jones Inc. for past damages, and the company is defending itself. Meanwhile, the corporation has adopted plans for a new waste-efficient plant. The legal battle is extended and local resentment against Jones Inc. gets bitter.

As a settlement is being reached, Jones Inc. announces that, as a civic-minded gesture, it will make 400 acres of Stirville woodland it owns available to the residents for conservation and recreation purposes. Jones's intention is to offer a peace pipe to the people of Stirville, and the company sees the gift as a symbol of its own belief in conservation and a way of signaling that value to Stirville residents and national conservation groups. Should Jones Inc. give the land away? Is the symbolism significant?

If the symbolic value of the land is understood as Jones Inc. intends, the gift may patch up the company's relations with Stirville and stave off further disaffection with potential employees as the new plant is being built. It may also signal to employees throughout the corporation that Jones Inc. places a premium on conservation efforts and community relations.

If the symbolic value is misunderstood, however, or if completion of the plant is delayed and the old one has to be put back in use—or if another Jones operation is discovered to be polluting another community and becomes a target of the press—the gift could be interpreted as nothing more than a cheap effort to pay off the people of Stirville and hasten settlement of the lawsuit.

The Greek root of our word *symbol* means both signal and contract. A business decision—whether it is the use of an expense account or a corporate donation—has a symbolic value in signaling what is acceptable behavior within the corporate culture and in making a tacit contract with employees and the community about the rules of the game. How the symbol is actually perceived (or misperceived) is as important as how you intend it to be perceived.

12. *Under what conditions would you allow exceptions to your stand?*

If we accept the idea that every business decision has an important symbolic value and a contractual nature, then the need for consistency is obvious. At the same time, it is also important to ask under what conditions the rules of the game may be changed. What conflicting principles, circumstances, or time constraints would provide a morally acceptable basis for making an exception to one's normal institutional ethos? For instance, how does the cost of the strategy to develop managers from minority groups over the long term fit in with short-term hurdle rates? Also to be considered is what would mitigate a clear case of employee dishonesty.

Questions of consistency—if you would do X, would you also do Y?—are yet another way of eliciting the ethics of the company and of oneself, and can be a final test of the strength, idealism, or practicality of those values. A last example from the experience of Lex illustrates this point and gives temporary credence to the platitude that good ethics is good business. An article in the Sunday paper about a company that had run a series of racy ads, with pictures of half-dressed women and promises of free merchandise to promote the sale of a very mundane product, sparked an extended examination at Lex of its policies on corporate inducements.

One area of concern was holiday giving. What was the acceptable limit for a gift—a bottle of whiskey? a case? Did it matter only that the company did not *intend* the gift to be an inducement, or did the mere possibility of inducement taint the gift? Was the cut-off point absolute? The group could agree on no halfway point for allowing some gifts and not others, so a new value was added to the formal statement that prohibited the offering or receiving of inducements.

The next holiday season Chinn sent a letter to friends and colleagues who had received gifts of appreciation in the past. In it he explained that, as a result of Lex's concern with "the very complex area of business ethics," management had decided that the company would no longer send any gifts, nor would it be appropriate for its employees to receive any. Although the letter did not explain Lex's reasoning behind the decision, apparently there was a large untapped consensus about such gift giving: By return mail Chinn received at least 20 letters from directors, general managers, and chairmen of companies with which Lex had done business congratulating him for his decision, agreeing with the new policy, and thanking him for his holiday wishes.

The "Good Puppy" Theory

The 12 questions are a way to articulate an idea of the responsibilities involved and to lay them open for examination. Whether a decisive policy is also generated or not, there are compelling reasons for holding such discussions:

- ☐ The process facilitates talk as a group about a subject that has traditionally been reserved for the privacy of one's conscience. Moreover, for those whose consciences twitch but don't speak in full sentences, the questions help sort out their own perceptions of the problem and various ways of thinking about it.
- ☐ The process builds a cohesiveness of managerial character as points of consensus emerge and people from vastly different operations discover that they share common problems. It is one way of determining the values and goals of the company, and that is a key element in determining corporate strategy.
- ☐ It acts as an information resource. Senior managers learn about other parts of the company with which they may have little contact.
- ☐ It helps uncover ethical inconsistencies in the articulated values of the corporation or between these values and the financial strategy.
- ☐ It helps uncover sometimes dramatic differences between the values and the practicality of their implementation.
- ☐ It helps the CEO understand how the senior managers think, how they handle a problem, and how willing and able they are to deal with complexity. It reveals how they may be drawing on the private self to the enhancement of corporate activity.
- ☐ In drawing out the private self in connection with business and in exploring the significance of the corporation's activities, the process derives meaning from an environment that is often characterized as meaningless.
- ☐ It helps improve the nature and range of alternatives.
- ☐ It is cathartic.

The process is also reductive in that it limits the level of inquiry. For example, the 12 questions ask what injury might result from a decision and what good is intended, but they do not ask the meaning of *good* or whether the result is "just."

Socrates asked how a person could talk of pursuing the good before knowing what the good is; and the analysis he visualized entailed a lifelong process of learning and examination. Do the 12 short questions, with their explicit goal of simplifying the ethical examination, bastardize the Socratic ideal? To answer this, we must distinguish between personal philosophy and participation as a corporate member in the examination of a *corporate* ethos, for the 12 questions assume some difference between private and corporate "goodness."

This distinction is crucial to any evaluation of my suggested process for conducting an ethical inquiry and needs to be explained. What exactly do we expect of the "ethical," or "good," corporation? Three examples of goodness represent prevailing social opinions, from that of the moral philosopher to the strict Friedmaniac.

1. The most rigorous moral analogy to the good corporation would be the "good man." An abstract, philosophical ideal having highly moral connotations, the good man encompasses an intricate relation of abstractions such as Plato's four virtues (courage, godliness or philosophical wisdom, righteousness, and prudence). The activities of this kind of good corporation imply a heavy responsibility to collectively know the good and to resolve to achieve it.

2. Next, there is the purely amoral definition of good, as in a "good martini" —an amoral fulfillment of a largely inanimate and functional purpose. Under this definition, corporate goodness would be best achieved by the unadorned accrual of profits with no regard for the social implications of the means whereby profits are made.

3. Halfway between these two views lies the good as in "good puppy"—here goodness consists primarily of the fulfillment of a social contract that centers on avoiding social injury. Moral capacity is perceived as present, but its potential is limited. A moral evaluation of the good puppy is possible but exists largely in concrete terms; we do not need to identify the puppy's intentions as utilitarian to understand and agree that its "ethical" fulfillment of the social contract consists of not soiling the carpet or biting the baby.

It seems to me that business ethics operates most appropriately for the corporate person when it seeks to define and explore corporate morality at the level of the good puppy. The good corporation is expected to avoid perpetrating irretrievable social injury (and to assume the costs when it unintentionally does injury) while focusing on its purpose as a profit-making organization. Its moral capacity does not extend, however, to determining by itself what will improve the general social welfare.

The good puppy inquiry operates largely in concrete experience; just as the 12 questions impose a limit on our moral expectations, so too they impose a limit (welcome, to some) on our use of abstraction to get at the problem.

The situations for testing business morality remain complex. But by avoiding theoretical inquiry and limiting the expectations of corporate goodness to a few rules for social behavior that are based on common sense, we can develop an ethic that is appropriate to the language, ideology, and institutional dynamics of business decision making the consensus. This ethic can also offer managers a practical way of exploring those occasions when their corporate brains are getting warning flashes from their noncorporate brains.

Shared Conditions of Some Successful Ethical Inquiries

Fixed time frame	Understanding and identifying moral issues takes time and causes ferment, and the executive needs an uninterrupted block of time to ponder the problems.
Unconventional location	Religious groups, boards of directors, and professional associations have long recognized the value of the retreat as a way of stimulating fresh approaches to regular activities. If the group is going to transcend normal corporate hierarchies, it should hold the discussion on neutral territory so that all may participate with the same degree of freedom.
Resource person	The advantage of bringing in an outsider is not that he or she will impose some preconceived notion of right and wrong on management but that he or she will serve as a midwife for bringing the values already present in the institution out into the open. The resource person can generate closer examination of the discrepancies between values and practice and draw on a wider knowledge of instances and intellectual frameworks than the group can. The resource person may also take the important role of arbitrator—to ensure that one person does not dominate the session with his or her own values and that the dialogue does not become impossibly emotional.
Participation of CEO	In most corporations the chief executive still commands an extra degree of authority for the intangible we call corporate culture, and the discussion needs the perspective of and legitimization by that authority if it is to have any seriousness of purpose and consequence. One of the most interesting experi-

ments in examining corporate policy I have observed lacked the CEO's support and within a year it died on the vine.

Credo

Articulating the corporation's values and objectives provides a reference point for group inquiry and implementation. Ethical codes, however, when drawn up by the legal department, do not always offer a realistic and full representation of management's beliefs. The most important ethical inquiry for management may be the very formulation of such a statement, for the *process* of articulation is as useful as the values agreed on.

Homegrown topics

In isolating an ethical issue, drawing on your own experience is important. Philosophical business ethics has tended to reflect national social controversies, which though relevant to the corporation may not always be as relevant—not to mention as easily resolved—as some internal issues that are shaping the character of the company to a much greater degree. Executives are also more likely to be informed on these issues.

Resolution

In all the programs I observed except one, there was a point at which the inquiry was slated to have some resolution: either a vote on the issue, the adoption of a new policy, a timetable for implementation, or the formulation of a specific statement of values. The one program observed that had no such decision-making structure was organized simply to gather information about the company's activities through extrahierarchical channels. Because the program had no tangible goals or clearly articulated results, its benefits were impossible to measure.

Note

1. The process is modeled after ideas in Kenneth R. Andrews's book *The Concept of Corporate Strategy* (Homewood, Ill., Richard D. Irwin, 1980, revised edition) and in Richard F. Vancil's article "Strategy Formulation in Complex Organizations," *Sloan Management Review*, Winter 1976, p. 4.

32
Zen and the Art of Management

RICHARD TANNER PASCALE

For many in the West, the term Zen connotes puzzling aspects of Eastern culture. This article attempts to unlock these puzzles as they apply to management of organizations. In the most exhaustive study to date of Japanese-managed companies in the United States and Japan, the author finds that when technology and government factors are equal, the Japanese companies' U.S. subsidiaries do not outperform their American counterparts (despite what has been reported in the U.S. press). Furthermore, and contrary to the conventional wisdom, American managers use a participative decision-making style as often as Japanese managers do. The author explores nuances of the administrative process that appear to account for more effective organizational functioning. He concludes that the arts employed by successful Japanese and American managers include subtle ways of dealing with others in the organization, such as permitting a certain situation to remain ambiguous instead of striving for a premature conclusion. While American managers are often as skillful in these areas as the Japanese, an Eastern perspective makes many of these tools more tangible and their potential more evident.

For 20 years or more students of management have labored to minimize its mystique, reduce our dependence on "gut feel," and establish a more scientific basis for managerial behavior. All the while, practitioners have been cautious in embracing these pursuits; casting a wary eye on "textbook" solutions, they assert that management is an art as much as a science.

Author's Note. The ideas presented in this article are drawn from my book, *The Art of Japanese Management*, published by Simon and Schuster in 1981. I wish to thank the National Commission on Productivity and the Weyerhaeuser Foundation for support of the research that formed the basis for this article, and Anthony G. Athos for his helpful comments on the manuscript.

Yet even the most skeptical admit that some benefit has accrued from these efforts. All realms of management, from finance to human relations, have felt the impact of analytical inquiry.

One common theme in this evolution of a "management science" has been the desire to make explicit the tools and processes that managers have historically employed intuitively. With just such a goal in mind, I embarked in 1974 on a study of Japanese-managed companies in the United States and Japan. The purpose was to ascertain what elements of the communications and decision-making processes contributed to the reported high performance of Japanese companies.

A number of respected observers of Japanese ways had attributed their success in part to such practices as "bottom-up" communication, extensive lateral communication across functional areas, and a pronounced use of participative- (or consensus-) style decision making that supposedly leads to higher quality decisions and implementation. The research consisted of interviews of and questionnaires administered to more than 215 managers and 1,400 workers in 26 companies and 10 industries.

I made communication audits of the number of telephone calls and face-to-face contacts initiated and received by managers of Japanese companies in Japan, of their subsidiaries in the United States, and of near-identical American companies matched on an industry-by-industry basis. I took pains to document the size and length of meetings and the volume of formal correspondence and informal notes, to observe the frequency of interaction in managerial office areas, and to obtain managers' perceptions of the nature and quality of the decision making and implementation process.

What did I find? First, Japanese-managed businesses in both countries are not much different from American-owned companies: They use the telephone to about the same degree and write about the same number of letters. In their decision-making processes, both in their U.S. subsidiaries and in Japan, the Japanese do not use a participative style any more than Americans do. Actually, I discovered only two significant differences between Japanese and American companies:[1]

1. Three times as much communication was initiated at lower levels of management in the Japanese companies, then percolated upward.
2. While managers of Japanese companies rated the quality of their decision making the same as did their American counterparts, they perceived the quality of *implementation* of those decisions to be better.

These findings puzzled me. How could the style of decision making (in particular, the degree of participation) and quality of decisions be the same in the two groups, yet the quality of implementation be different? Evidently, the greater reliance by the Japanese on bottom-up communication played a role, but the causal relationship remained unclear.

A senior executive at Sony provided a clue. "To be truthful," the Japanese manager said, "probably 60% of the decisions I make are my decisions. But I keep my intentions secret. In discussions with subordinates, I ask questions, pursue facts, and try to nudge them in my direction without disclosing my position. Sometimes I end up changing my position as the result of the dialogue. But whatever the outcome, they feel a part of the decision. Their involvement in the decision also increases their experience as managers."

Many others, American as well as Japanese, alluded in interviews to the same technique. "It does not make so much difference," reflected an American who ran a ball-bearing plant in New Hampshire, "if decisions are top down as it does how the top-down decision maker goes about touching bases. If he begins with an open question, he can often guide his subordinates to a good solution."

In these statements, and in others like them, is the genesis of this paper. The important discovery of this research was not, as expected, that Japanese do some things differently and better. While that is true to a limited extent, the more significant finding is that successful managers, *regardless of nationality*, share certain common characteristics that are related to subtleties of the communications process.

The term Zen in the title of this article is used figuratively to denote these important nuances in interpersonal communication often enshrouded in a veil of mystique. The phenomenon does not correspond to the analytical dimension of consecutive deductive responses. Nor is it directly akin to the human relations dimension that highlights the virtues of problem confrontation, participation, and openness. I refer to this Zen-like quality as the *implicit* dimension. It is as distinct from the other, better-known dimensions of management as time is from the other three dimensions of physical space.

In trying to explain the implicit dimension, I find that the traditional language of management gets in the way. To work around the difficulty, it is helpful to explore this dimension through the lens of the Eastern metaphor. After many interviews with American and Japanese managers, I have come to believe that the perspective imbedded in Eastern philosophy, culture, and values helps make the implicit dimension more visible. Whereas Japanese managers find certain insights within easy reach of their Eastern way of thinking, American managers, while often just as skillful, must swim upstream culturally, so to speak.

Ambiguity as a Managerial Tool

Much of the lore of management in the West regards ambiguity as a symptom of a variety of organizational ills whose cure is larger doses of rationality, specificity, and decisiveness. But is ambiguity sometimes desirable?

Ambiguity may be thought of as a shroud of the unknown surrounding certain events. The Japanese have a word for it, *ma*, for which there is no

English translation. The word is valuable because it gives an explicit place to the unknowable aspect of things. In English we may refer to an empty space between the chair and the table; the Japanese don't say the space is empty but "full of nothing." However amusing the illustration, it goes to the core of the issue. Westerners speak of what is unknown primarily in reference to what is known (like the space between the chair and the table), while most Eastern languages give honor to the unknown in its own right. Consider this Tao verse:

Thirty spokes are made one by holes in a hub
Together with the vacancies between them, they comprise a wheel.
The use of clay in moulding pitchers
Comes from the hollow of its absence;
Doors, windows, in a house
Are used for their emptiness:
Thus we are helped by what is not
To use what is.[2]

Of course, there are many situations that managers find themselves in where being explicit and decisive is not only helpful but necessary. There is considerable advantage, however, in having a dual frame of reference—recognizing the value of both the clear and the ambiguous. The point to bear in mind is that in certain situations ambiguity may serve better than absolute clarity.

When executives have access to too much data for human processing, they need to simplify. If they have examined, say, different pricing schemes for 12 months and have identified all the choices available to them, the time has probably come to decide on one of them. "Deciding" in these circumstances has the benefit of curtailing the wheel spinning, simplifying things, and resolving anxiety for themselves and others.

But there is another kind of problem—for example, merging the production and engineering departments—where experience may suggest that the issue is more complicated than the bare facts indicate. Frequently the issue crops up around changes that arouse human feelings. Under these circumstances the notion of ambiguity is useful. Rather than grasping for a solution, the administrator may take the interim step of "deciding" how to proceed. The process of "proceeding" in turn generates further information; you move toward your goal through a sequence of tentative steps rather than bold-stroke actions. The distinction is between having enough data to *decide* and having enough data to *proceed*.

If an executive's perception of the problem and the means of implementation involve groups of persons at different levels of the organization with different mandates (like unions and professional groups) and the distribution of power is such that full control is lacking, successful implementation usually requires tentativeness. The notion of ambiguity helps make tentativeness legitimate.

Ambiguity has two important connotations for management. First, it is a useful concept in thinking about how we deal with others, orally and in writing. Second, it provides a way of legitimizing the loose rein that a manager permits in certain organizational situations where agreement needs time to evolve or where further insight is needed before conclusive action can be taken.

Cards off the Table

To watch a skilled manager use ambiguity is to see an art form in action. Carefully selecting words, constructing a precise tension between the oblique and the specific, the manager picks the way across difficult terrain. In critiquing a subordinate's work, for example, the executive occasionally finds it desirable to come close enough to the point to ensure that the subordinate gets the message but not so close as to "crowd" the subordinate and cause defensiveness.

A Japanese manager conducts the dialogue in circles, widening and narrowing them to correspond to the subordinate's sensitivity to the feedback. The manager may say, "I'd like you to reflect a bit further on your proposal." Translated into Western thought patterns, this sentence would read, "You're dead wrong and you'd better come up with a better idea."[3] The first approach keeps the subordinate's pride intact.

Part of our drive for the explicit stems from the Western notion that it's a matter of honor to "get the cards on the table." This attitude rests on the assumption that, no matter how much it hurts, it's good for you; and the sign of a good manager is the ability to give and take negative feedback.

No doubt there is a good deal of merit in this conventional wisdom. But between the mythology of our management lore and our foibles as human beings often lies the true state of things. It is desirable to get the facts and know where one stands. But it is also human to feel threatened, particularly when personal vulnerability is an issue.

There is no reason to believe that Westerners have less pride than the Japanese or feel humiliation less poignantly than the Japanese do. An American Management Association survey indicates that issues involving self-respect mattered greatly to more than two-thirds of the persons sampled.[4] Eastern cultures are sensitive to the concept of "face"; Westerners, however, regard it as a sign of weakness. Yet look back on instances in organizations where an individual, publicly embarrassed by another, hurt himself and the organization just to even the score. The evidence suggests that explicitly crowding a person into a corner may in many instances be not only unwarranted but also counterproductive.

Delivering oneself of the need to "speak the truth" often masks a self-serving sense of brute integrity. "Clearing the air" can be more helpful to the "clearer" than to others who are starkly revealed. The issue of brute integrity is not just an outcome of a certain cultural tendency to speak plainly and bluntly, nor is it wholly explainable in terms of our assumptions about authority and hierarchy and the relationships between bosses and subordinates. At a deeper level, it has a sexist component. In our culture, simple, straightforward, simplistic confrontation—a kind of high noon shoot-'em-out—is mixed with notions of what masculinity is. Unfortunately, shoot-'em-outs work best when the other guy dies. If you have to work with that person on a continuing basis, macho confrontations complicate life immensely.

In contrast, ambiguity, in reference to sensitivity and feelings, is alleged in the Western world to be female. But if we set aside the stereotypes and contemplate the consequences of these two modes of behavior on organizational life, we may discover that primitive notions of masculinity work no better in the office over the long term than they do in bed.

Are brute integrity and explicit communication worth the price of the listener's goodwill, open-mindedness, and receptivity to change? Explicit communication is a cultural assumption, not a linguistic imperative. Many executives develop the skills necessary to vary their position along the spectrum from explicitness to ambiguity.

More "Ura" Than "Omote"

Earlier I noted the value of ambiguity in permitting time and space for certain situations to take clearer shape or reach an accommodation of their own. A certain looseness in the definition of the relationship between things can permit a workable arrangement to evolve, whereas premature action may freeze things into rigidity. For example, one of the most persistent afflictions in American organizations is the penchant to make formal announcements. Most things one does announce themselves.

The Japanese manager comes culturally equipped with a pair of concepts, *omote* (in front) and *ura* (behind the scenes). These ideas correspond to the Latin notions of de jure and de facto, with one important distinction: the Japanese think of *ura* as constituting *real life*; *omote* is the ceremonial function for the benefit of others. The Japanese relegate the making of announcements to a secondary place that follows after all the action has taken place behind the scenes.

"You Americans are fond of announcing things," said one Japanese manager in the study. "It sets everything astir. The other day we decided to try out having our personnel department handle certain requests that traditionally had been handled by the production people. Our American vice president insisted on announcing it. Well, the production department had always handled its own personnel affairs and got its back up. Rumors commenced about whether the personnel people were in ascendence, building an empire, and so forth. Given the tentativeness of the system we were trying out, why not just begin by quietly asking that certain matters be referred to personnel? Before long, the informal organization will accustom itself to the new flow. Clearly you can't do this all the time, but some of the time it certainly works."

To announce what you want to happen, you have to make statements concerning a lot of things that you don't know about yet. If certain processes and relationships are allowed to take their own shape first, however, your announcement will probably have to be made just once because you will only be confirming what has already happened. Consider how differently attempts at organizational change might proceed if they embraced the Eastern orientation. Instead of turning the spotlight on the intended move, parading the revised organization charts and job descriptions, management would reassign tasks incrementally, gradually shift boundaries between functions, and issue the announcement only when the desired change had become a de facto reality. In some situations this is the better way.

"Impossible!" some will argue. "People resist change. Only by announcing your intentions can you bring the organization into line." But is it really "into line?" Unquestionably, decrees have their part to play in some organizational actions. But more often than not, the sudden lurch to a new order belies an informal process of resistance that works with enduring effectiveness. One has only to look at the Department of Health, Education, and Welfare for an illustration of this phenomenon. A congressional mandate and 20 years' worth of frustrated presidents have not greatly altered the character of the three distinct bureaus comprising that agency.

The notion of achieving gradual change, rather than launching a head-on assault, runs deep in Eastern culture. It provides a manager with a context for thinking about outflanking organizational obstacles and in time letting them wither away. "It is well to persist like water," counsels the Tao saying. "For back it comes, again and again, wearing down the rigid strength which cannot yield to withstand it."[5]

With such an orientation one can accept the inevitability of obstacles rather than view them with righteous indignation—as some Western managers are inclined to do. And as the Tao saying suggests, acceptance does not convey fatalistic resignation. Rather, it points toward the value of patiently flowing with a solution while in due time it overcomes the obstacles in its path.

To Get Recognition, Give It Away

One way of thinking about the rewards employees receive is in terms of a triad: promotion, remuneration, and recognition. Of the three forms of reward, the first two are relatively unresponsive in the day-to-day operation of an organization. Promotions and wage hikes seldom come oftener than six months apart. On a daily basis, recognition is the reward most noticed and sought after. In the American Management Association survey to which I alluded earlier, 49% of the respondents indicated that recognition for what they did was their most important reward.

Recognition may become an increasingly important "fringe benefit" since a central problem facing American society is how to reward people in a period of slowed growth when employees win promotions and raises less often. Enriching our understanding of recognition and the role it plays may provide some helpful guidance.

Recognition is a powerful operating incentive. People who live in organizations develop uncanny sensitivity to where it is flowing. If you ask a person to change, one of the most relevant rewards you can provide in return is recognition. If, on the contrary, you try to induce change but you are seen as unwilling to share the recognition, you are not apt to get very far. It is an ironic axiom of organization that if you are willing to give up recognition, in return you gain increased power to bring about effective change.

The Eastern frame of thinking embodies the dual nature of recognition, as this Tao proverb shows:

A wise man has a simple wisdom
Which other men seek.
Without taking credit
Is accredited.
Laying no claim
Is acclaimed.[6]

We are all acquainted with "expressed" recognition, the big prize that modern organizational knights vie for. "B.L.T." is the recognition sandwich . . . "bright lights and trumpets," that is. When you receive a B.L.T., everybody knows about it. But Eastern thinking reminds us of a second variety, which might be called implied recognition. It is subtle but no less tangible, and it is acquired over time.

In its positive form it is the reputation of being trustworthy, skilled in making things happen in the organization, and accomplished in getting things done through people. In its negative manifestation a person is regarded as using people, prone to cutting corners, and out for oneself. Implied recognition can be given in a variety of ways that may seem insignificant, except to the recipient. An effort to seek another's opinion, for example, communicates respect for the other's insight. So does an invitation to participate in a significant meeting from which the person might otherwise have been excluded.

The phenomenon of implied recognition generally plays an important role in organizations that run smoothly. Problems arise when organizations overemphasize incentives that rivet attention on expressed recognition and undermine regard for implied recognition. As a result, all the members of the "team" try to grab the ball and nobody blocks. They seldom win consistently. But why grab from others what they will give you voluntarily? When you make sure you get the credit you deserve, in the long run you get less of it than you would otherwise.

Eastern perspective provides a further insight. It reminds us that the real organization you are working for is the organization called yourself. The problems and challenges of the organization that you are working for "out there" and the one "in here" are not two separate things. They grow toward excellence together. The sense of the "implied" for accommodation and timing and the sense of the "expressed" for the jugular must be woven together like strands in a braided rope, alternatively appearing and disappearing from sight but part of the whole. Good executives master the art *and* the science of management—not just one or the other.

Leaders Go Straight—Around the Circle

Western concepts of leadership embrace a number of images—strength, firmness, determination, and clarity of vision. In American management lore, leaders are seen as lonely figures capable of decisive action in the face of adversity.[7] Eastern thinking views leadership in significantly different ways. Whereas Western leaders are supposedly selected from among those who are outstanding, Eastern culture values leaders who stand "in" rather than stand "out."

In Judeo-Christian cultures, words very nearly possess sacredness. People are willing to sacrifice for, live by, and die for words. We cling to them and make them swell with meaning; they are shafts of light that give form to our experiential darkness. Anthony G. Athos of the Harvard Business School notes the distinction between two everyday words, choice and decision. Managers, we are taught, "make decisions"; lovers "choose." The former term implies mastery; the latter conveys a difficult selection among choices, in which we can gain some things only by giving up others.[8]

Athos's insight is particularly important for managers because the word "decision" and the phrase "decision making" conjure up an extensive mythology of meaning. Good decision makers, our mythology tells us, have command of the facts, are aware of the options, and select from among them the best one.

The Japanese, however, do not even have a term for decision making in the Western sense. This linguistic curiosity reflects something deeper, a tendency of the culture to acknowledge the ambivalence experienced when our mastery of situations is imperfect. Faced with difficult trade-offs, Japanese "choose" one over the other; Westerners like to think they "decide."

The lore of Eastern management more fully acknowledges the inevitable sense of incompleteness that stems from having to choose. It sensitizes its managers to the illusions of mastery and trains them to suspect the accompanying belief that anything is ever truly decided. Whereas the mythology of Western management tends to cast solutions as fixed and final, Eastern philosophical tradition emphasizes individual accommodation to a continuously unfolding set of events.

Think of the consequences of these outlooks as managers of these two cultures go about living up to their cultural imperatives. Eastern managers accept ambivalence. When faced with the necessity to "juggle," they do so with reassurance that the experience is congruent with what management is all about. Faced with the same set of events, some American managers may feel uneasy. This problem is exacerbated by the absence of cultural underpinnings for thinking about certain activities in which mastery of the situation is either impossible or downright undesirable. (Also, their language is not attuned to expression of this mode of thinking.)

The Western notion of mastery is closely linked with deep-seated assumptions about the self. The professional life of some Westerners, and certainly many who move into management positions, is dedicated to strengthening the ego in an effort to assert and maintain control over their environment and their destiny. In contrast, the Eastern frame of reference views pragmatically appropriate limitations of the ego as a virtue.

To the Easterner, overt strength is not unequivocally a desired attribute. This notion of strength may be likened to the endurance of coral reefs that survive the massive forces of sea and wind during typhoons. Reefs do not attempt to resist the sea like defiant walls of steel and concrete. Instead, the reef extends wedges out in a seaward direction. The waves deflect off these wedges, one against the other. Consequently their power, rather than directed at the reef, is turned against itself. The reef does not insist on standing higher than the sea. In times of typhoon, the waves wash over the reef. And it survives.

Let things flow. "Success is going straight—around the circle," says the Chinese adage. How often in organizations does the forcing of events precipitate needless resistance and even crisis? Yet the Western notion of leadership, fueled by the high value placed on logical, purposive, goal-blinded action, impels many to leap before they look.[9]

Dam up a river. In time the water rises until a trickle finds its way around the obstruction, gradually increasing in flow and force until its original course is resumed. Managers, of course, do not have to watch torrents of frustration and energy needlessly build up behind an organizational obstruction. But perhaps the solution is not always to dynamite away the obstruction; sometimes it is to trace a way around it with a light touch, enough to get a trickle flowing. Let the flow of events do the rest of the work. By embracing an alternative concept of leadership, managers can choose, where appropriate, to seek a contributing place in the flow of things rather than impose a false sense of mastery over events.

For Employees, Idiosyncracies vs. Systems

The typical Western organization prides itself on having made a science of the secular virtues of efficiency and impartiality. In trying to cope with the slowed growth and economic uncertainty of recent years, organizations have intensified the emphasis on efficiency. A different set of forces has put emphasis on impartiality—among them the regulations aimed at eliminating discrimination of all kinds. The dilemma is how to treat people as equal without treating them as the same. Many organizations appear to be insensitive to this distinction. As a result they, like white bread or pure sugar, become bland and somewhat unhealthful; all the vital human elements seem to get refined away.

I should acknowledge that many Western executives show deep concern for the people working for them. In a survey of American managers, psychologist Jay Hall found that those most highly rated in interpersonal skills were generally regarded as the most competent by their bosses. "Good managers," Hall wrote, "use an integrative style of management in which production goals and people's needs are equally important."[10]

Obviously, organizations need efficient systems to accomplish their tasks. But enough is enough, and more may be too much. The human touch is often lacking, and its absence breeds isolation and detachment. Lonely people perform instrumental functions as if they truly were interchangeable parts in a great machine. The explanation, I suppose, is that the increasing physical density of workers in our landscaped offices and automated factories has nothing to do with the psychic distances. Hard-edged procedures enhance this sense of aloneness.

Japanese companies, despite their evident prowess at adopting Western technology, have not followed the Western pattern where trade-offs between human relationships and secular efficiencies are concerned. Of more than 600 American employees of Japanese corporations interviewed in my study (including 100 managers and 500 workers) almost all expressed an awareness of the more personalized approach of their employers. The Japanese have a word describing a special quality of master potters who make the "perfect" bowl. The bowl is endowed with an ever-so-slight imperfection—a constant reminder of the object's relation to the humanity of the maker. The master knows that the perfection of mass-produced bowls is less satisfying than ones that lean a little. In this context, it might be said that Japanese companies lean a little.

The Japanese distinguish between our notion of "organization" and their notion of "the company." In their minds, the term organization refers only to the system; their concept of the company includes its underlying character as well. A company's character describes a shared sense of values long held by members and enforced by group norms. The result is an institutional way of doing things that is different from what efficiency alone would require. The "company" may accomplish the same tasks as an "organization" does, but it occupies more space, moves with more weight, and reflects a commitment to larger ends than just the accomplishment of a mission.

In Japan, companies are thought of as taking all of an employee. (In the United States the prevailing notion is that they take a piece of an employee.) The relationship is akin to the binding force of the family. Lacking such a philosophy, Western organizations tend to rely on what bureaucracies do best—championing "systems solutions"—rather than deal with the idiosyncratic requirements of human nature. The result can isolate people into the lonely illusion of objectivity.

Is the Bottom Line the Measure?

From the Japanese vantage point, the sense of incompleteness in our working lives stems from a divergence between what many people seek and what most Western organizations provide. Most people bring three kinds of needs to their organizational existence: a need to be rewarded for what they achieve, a need to be accepted as a unique person, and a need to be appreciated not only for the function performed but also as a human being. The term "reward," as used here, refers to the tangible payments one receives from an organization (such as salary and promotions) in exchange for services provided.

I use this narrow, rather instrumental definition of rewards to distinguish it from "acceptance" and "appreciation," which represent other kinds of benefits sought. In this context, acceptance refers to the quality of being known in a human sense rather than simply valued for the function one performs. The worker feels acceptance when people and organizations know him for who he is and make allowance for that uniqueness in their relationship with him. Appreciation goes a step further, conveying not only an acknowledgment by others of a person's distinctness but also a valuation of it in a positive and supportive way.

In an effort to express their commitment to people, the Japanese companies in the United States that I studied spent on average more than three times as much per employee on social and recreational facilities and activities than their American counterparts ($48.85 per employee per year versus $14.85). Some of these programs were probably largely symbolic, but many also fostered increased off-the-job contact among employees. The benefit was to "personalize" the particular company.

Perhaps a more direct vehicle for providing acceptance and appreciation is the Japanese policy of supporting spans of control at the supervisory level. This practice resulted in twice as much contact between workers and their supervisors as in American companies, measured by employees per first-line supervisor (30.1 versus 13.5). The supervisors in Japanese-managed companies more often worked alongside the subordinates, engaged in personal counseling more extensively, and permitted more interaction among workers than the American companies did.[11]

What was the outcome? The evidence is sufficiently mixed to gratify both skeptics and advocates. There was no difference in production; the average output per unit of labor was about the same. Moreover, the Japanese companies experienced somewhat higher levels of tardiness and absenteeism. In respect to job satisfaction, the results were more favorable for Japanese-managed businesses in the United States. Their managers and workers expressed much more satisfaction with their jobs than did their counterparts in American companies.

Why bother, it might be asked, if the result has no impact on the bottom line? By Eastern standards the bottom line misses the point. It was Socrates (not an Eastern philosopher) who observed that "man is the measure of all things." Eastern perspective brings his meaning into fuller view. To the Eastern mind, it is "man," not the "bottom line," that is the ultimate measure of all things. He is not the source of all things, as some who view man in total command of his destiny might proclaim. Nor is he the objectified contributor to all things, as some organizations appear to presume in weighing his contributions against their costs.

A Japanese, while concerned with the bottom line, is not single-minded about it as many Westerners are. Rather, he proceeds with a dual awareness—that there is a second ledger in which "success" is debited or credited in terms of his contribution to the quality of relationships that ensue. So the professional manager defines his role not only as one who accomplishes certain organizational tasks but also as an essential intermediary in the social fabric.

Are Feathers More Effective Than Sledgehammers?

This discussion has utilized Eastern ideas as a metaphor for exploring the process of management. One central theme is that it is not just particular notions—such as ambiguity or implied recognition—that can be helpful but the cultural context underlying these notions as well. I have tried to suggest that a combination of culture, words, philosophy, and values provides each of us with a particular outlook. The Eastern outlook is adopted not because it is "best" but because it sheds a different light on certain aspects of management. The Eastern perspective provides not so much a new set of tools (for, as I have noted repeatedly, many skilled American managers use these tools) but rather legitimacy for using these tools in some situations where they are appropriate.

From the Eastern vantage point, process is where managers live. This vantage point dwells on the chemistry of human relationships, as well as on the mechanics of human accomplishment, and it provides a way of thinking that assigns a particular value to human needs as well as to systems and economic requirements. Appreciation of the underpinnings of this outlook is fundamental to the thrust of this article. For if they are bounded by our traditional set of Western assumptions, many of the ideas here become empty techniques.

Management assumptions act as fences—keeping some things in and other things out of our awareness. As we have seen, there are many fences, not of wood but shaped by our words, values, and management ideology. I submit that a nontrivial set of management problems might be better understood if viewed from the other side of our Western fence. Undoubtedly, a very high degree of personal development is necessary to embrace both of these outlooks, to know when each is appropriate and to acquire the skills which each requires.

This suggests a cautionary note for the Western manager: in addition to approaching things purposively, defining problems crisply, and identifying his objectives explicitly (which are desirable but not necessarily sufficient traits to manage all problems skillfully), the manager may also wish to bear in mind that our Western world view diminishes our sensitivity and skill in managing certain kinds of problems. Such insight may enable us to avoid using sledgehammers when feathers will do. Eastern ideas provide a metaphor for the acquisition of such skill. "Truth lurks in metaphors."[12]

Notes

1. For a detailed report of these findings see my article "Communications and Decision Making Across Cultures: Japanese and American Comparisons," *Administrative Science Quarterly*, March 1978.

2. Witter Bynner, *The Way of Life According to Lao Tzu* (New York, Capricorn Books, 1944), p. 30.

3. Frank Gibney, "The Japanese and Their Language," *Encounter*, March 1975, p. 33.

4. G. McLean Preston and Katherine Jillson, "The Manager and Self-Respect," *AMA Survey Report* (New York, AMACOM, 1975).

5. Bynner, op. cit., p. 74.

6. Ibid., pp. 28 and 38.

7. For a discussion of the myths versus the realities of management behavior and leadership, see Leonard Sayles, *Managerial Behavior* (New York, McGraw-Hill, 1964), especially pp. 41–45; also see Henry Mintzberg, "The Manager's Job: Folklore and Fact," *HBR*, July–August 1975, p. 49.

8. Anthony G. Athos, "Choice and Decision," unpublished working paper, 1973.

9. For a discussion of this "flowing" phenomenon in a Western context, see James D. Thompson, *Organizations in Action* (New York, McGraw-Hill, 1967), p. 149.

10. Jay Hall, "What Makes a Manager Good, Bad, or Average?," *Psychology Today*, August 1976, p. 52.

11. Richard Tanner Pascale and Mary Ann Maguire, "The Company and the Worker: Japanese and American Comparisons," Graduate School of Business, Stanford University, 1977.

12. Anthony G. Athos, "Satan Is Left-Handed," *Association of Humanistic Psychology Newsletter*, December 1975.

About the Authors

Louis B. Barnes *is professor of organizational behavior at the Harvard Business School. He has been a frequent contributor to* the HBR *on subjects ranging from organizational transitions to judgmental decision making and executive power networks. Professor Barnes is currently engaged in research on unstructured and complicated executive decision processes, focusing partly on what distinguishes more successful from less successful processes.*

Fernando Bartolomé *obtained his L.I.B. (master in law) from Zaragoza University, his M.B.A. from Navarra University in Spain, and his Ph.D. in business administration from Harvard University in 1972. While completing his doctorate he taught at the University of Los Andes in Bogotá and Sir George Williams University in Montreal. Upon graduation from the Harvard Business School in 1972, Dr. Bartolomé joined the faculty of INSEAD (the European Institute of Business Administration) in Fontainebleau, France, where he is currently professor of business administration. At the present time, Dr. Bartolomé is Visiting Professor of Business Administration at the Harvard Business School. Dr. Bartolomé has lectured widely in Europe, the United States, and Latin America and has worked as consultant and teacher with a number of firms, among them Rank Xerox, Nestle, Esso Europe, Imperial Oil, Hewlett-Packard, Schlumberger, and IBM. His research interests have focused on the interaction between the professional and private lives of executives. His publications include* Professional Lives vs. Private Lives—Shifting Patterns of Managerial Commitment *(with Paul Evans, published by Organizational Dynamics in the spring of 1979) and* Must Success Cost So Much? *(with Paul Evans), a book on the effects of professional life on private life (published in Europe in 1980 and in the United States in 1981 by Basic Books).*

Paul Brouwer *graduated from Hope College in 1934. He received a masters degree from Northwestern University in 1937 and in 1946 Dr. Brouwer graduated from the University of Chicago with a Ph.D. in Human Growth and*

Development. Dr. Brouwer retired in 1976 from Rohrer, Hibler and Replogle, where he was corporate psychologist, partner, and manager, concluding 32 years of working with individual executives and with their organizations. In 1972 Dr. Brouwer co-edited Managing Through Insights *and in 1977 co-authored* Performance Appraisal and Human Development. *Dr. Brouwer's latest book,* The Managerial Challenge, *was published in 1981.*

***David H. Burnham** has an M.B.A. from Harvard Business School. He lives in Cohasset, Massachusetts, and is a management consultant working in the United States, Great Britain, and the Far East. Since the publication of* Power Is the Great Motivator *Mr. Burnham has been involved with helping managers to improve the performance and job satisfaction of their subordinates.*

***Abram Collier** is the retired chairman of New England Mutual Life Insurance Company. His book,* Management, Men and Values, *was published by Harper & Row in 1962. In 1978 Collier was designated Businessman of the Year by the Harvard Business School Association of Boston.*

***Peter F. Drucker** is a writer, especially on political and economic subjects. His many books include* The Practice of Management *(1954),* The Effective Executive *(1960),* The Age of Discontinuity *(1969),* Management: Tasks, Responsibilities, Practices *(1974);* Managing in Turbulent Times *(1980),* The Changing World of the Executive *(essays) (1982). He is also co-author of* Song of the Bush: Japanese Paintings *(1979). Mr. Drucker is an editorial columnist for the* Wall Street Journal *and a frequent contributor to magazines. Mr. Drucker also is a management consultant, specializing in economic and business policy and in top management organization. He has been consultant to several of the country's largest companies as well as to leading companies abroad; to agencies of the U.S. government and to several governments in the free world such as Canada and Japan; and to public service institutions such as universities and hospitals. Mr. Drucker has been Clarke Professor of Social Science and Management at Claremont Graduate School, Claremont, California, since 1971. He is also professorial lecturer in Oriental art at Pomona College, one of the Claremont Colleges. From 1950 to 1972 Mr. Drucker was professor of management at the Graduate Business School of New York University, which he still serves as Distinguished University Lecturer.*

***Paul A. Lee Evans** is associate professor of organizational behavior at INSEAD. He has a Ph.D. in management and organizational psychology from the Sloan School of Management at M.I.T. and M.B.A. from INSEAD and is a graduate in law from Cambridge University. He currently teaches at the European Center for Permanent Education on the INSEAD campus and is director of INSEAD's executive seminars, "Managerial Skills for International Business" and "Management of People." Dr. Evan's research* *interests lie in the area of international human resource management. Past research focused on management development and motivation and executive lifestyles, while current projects involve assessing the problems of policy making in the human resource area. His recent book,* Must Success Cost So Much?, *was the result of a four-year investigation, with Professor F. Bartolomé, into the relationship between the professional and private lives of executives and was published in Europe in 1980 and in the United States in 1981 by Basic Books. He has given numerous speeches and presentations on this topic to national associations of executives and personnel officers in Europe, at company seminars and annual meetings, and at management institutes.*

John J. Gabarro *is professor of organizational behavior at the Harvard Business School. His main area of research is how executives build effective working relationships. His most recent publication is* Interpersonal Behavior *(Prentice-Hall, 1978), which he wrote with Anthony G. Athos.*

Larry E. Greiner *is associate professor of organizational behavior at the Harvard Business School.*

Roger Harrison*, when he wrote "Understanding Your Organization's Character," was vice-president of Development Research Associates, Inc., of Newton Center, Massachusetts. As a social psychologist he is concerned with the design and building of organizations to cope with unusual stresses and with the development of initiative and autonomy through experience-based learning processes. He has taught in the Department of Industrial Administration at Yale University.*

John H. Johnson *is editor and publisher of Johnson Publishing Company, which issues* Ebony, Jet, Ebony Jr.!, Black Stars, *and* Black World. *Mr. Johnson is also chairman and chief executive officer of Supreme Life Insurance Company and president of Fashion Fair Cosmetics, a company he formed nine years ago. He is on the boards of many large corporations, including Greyhound, Marina Bank, Verex Corporation, and Zenith Radio Corporation, and is on the board of trustees of the United Negro College Fund and the Chamber of Commerce of the United States of America. He is also on the board of directors of the Associates of the Harvard Business School.*

Rosabeth Moss Kanter *is professor of sociology and organization and management at Yale University, where she conducts research on organization design and change processes. She is the author of* Men and Women of the Corporation *(Basic Books, 1977). Her "Power Failure in Management Circuits" was a 1979 McKinsey Award Winner. Dr. Kanter's newest book is* The Change Masters: Innovation for Productivity in the American Mode *(Simon and Schuster, 1983). She is also chairman of the board of Goodmeasure, Inc., a Cambridge, Massachusetts, management consulting firm.*

Robert L. Katz *has been president of Robert L. Katz & Associates, consultants in corporate strategy, since 1953. During that period, he has had a unique combination of academic and practical experience. For 16 years he taught business policy and organizational behavior at Stanford, Harvard, and Dartmouth Graduate Schools of Business while advising some of the nation's largest corporations. For the last 11 years he has concentrated his full efforts on working with middle-sized "threshold" companies, including three years as chief executive of a rapidly growing public company, which attained sales of over $50 million and employment of more than 2,000. Cofounder of five financial or operating companies and author of three textbooks and numerous articles on corporate strategy and business management, Dr. Katz is currently serving as a professional director of seven threshold companies in a wide variety of industries. He earned his B.A. at the University of California, his M.B.A. at Stanford Business School, and his Ph.D. at Harvard Business School.*

John P. Kotter *is professor of organizational behavior at the Harvard Business School. His recent books include* The General Managers *(Free Press, 1982) and* Power in Management *(AMACOM, 1979).*

D. Paul Leitch *is currently employed at the U.S. Army Natick Research and Development Laboratories as a supervisory operations research analyst. He is responsible for a staff of ten professionals and six major projects involving systems analysis and the development of new concepts for military food service. His work in developing and evaluating a new food service system for aircraft carriers received the annual Rholand A. Isker Award for the most significant contribution to military food service as well as the Army's Development and Readiness Command Annual Award (group) for the best systems analysis. Prior to joining Natick Laboratories, Dr. Leitch held positions at Arthur Young & Co., Boston University College of Business Administration, and the Harvard Graduate School of Business Administration. He received his Ph.D. in industrial psychology from Purdue University.*

David C. McClelland *is professor of psychology at Harvard University. He is well known for his work on motivation. (See, for example, "Achievement Motivation Can Be Developed,"* HBR, *November/December, 1965.) Dr. McClelland is the author of many books, among them* The Achieving Society. *His most recent book is* Power: The Inner Experience, *published by Irvington Publishers.*

Robert McMurry *obtained his doctorate from the University of Vienna, which he attended on a fellowship from the Institute of International Education (an Austro-American Exchange Fellowship). He also attended Freud's Teaching Institute, and he has been a member of the Chicago Psychoanalytic Society. In 1943 he founded the Robert N. McMurry Company, a consulting service in the fields of personnel, industrial relations, and market research.*

Operating from Chicago, he and his colleagues have appraised the competence of several thousand executives in a wide variety of businesses, determining their suitability for their existing positions as well as for promotion to higher ones. In the course of this work they have studied numerous cases of executives who have failed at top-level jobs. He has written extensively for the HBR *and other business publications. He is also the author of five books and two manuals.*

Henry Mintzberg *is Bronfman Professor of Management at McGill University, in Montreal, where he researches and writes on the internal processes of organizatons as well as their role in society. His current work involves a study of patterns in strategy formation and a series of books under the general title* The Theory of Management Policy. *His better known publicatons include* The Nature of Managerial Work *(Harper & Row, 1973),* The Structuring of Organizations *(Prentice-Hall, 1979—appearing in condensed form as* Structure in 5's, *1983), and "The Manager's Job: Folklore and Facts," the winner of the McKinsey Prize for 1975. Dr. Mintzberg holds his Ph.D. and M.S. degrees from M.I.T. and his bachelors degree in engineering from McGill. He has lectured widely to management and academic groups in Europe and North and South America and was elected a Fellow of the Royal Society of Canada in 1980, the first from a faculty of management.*

Laura Nash *is assistant professor of business administration at the Harvard Business School, where she teaches business policy. Formerly a teacher of classics at Brown, Brandeis, and Harvard universities, she recently spent a year and a half at the Harvard Business School doing research on business ethics. She received her Ph.D. in classical philology in 1976 and has published articles in various professional journals.*

O. A. Ohmann, *when he wrote "Skyhooks," was assistant to the president of the Standard Oil Company of Ohio and worked on problems and programs for managment development. Now retired from that company and living in Hendersonville, North Carolina, he continues to consult with organizations on questions of management development and is director of The Church Executive Development Board, Inc., in New York. Earlier in his career he was head of the Department of Psychology at Cleveland College of Western Reserve University.*

Richard Tanner Pascale *is associate professor of management at the Graduate School of Business, Stanford University. He has been a close student of Japanese managerial practices for many years. He is the author of* Managing the White House *(Harper & Row, 1974) and has recently completed a study of the management styles of Harold Geneen (ITT), Roy Ash (Litton Industries), and Edward Carlson (UAL, Inc.). His most recent book is* The Art of Japanese Management *(Simon and Schuster, 1981).*

***Thomas J. Peters** is a lecturer in management at the Stanford Graduate School of Business on leave from McKinsey and Company where he has been a principal and leader of the management effectiveness practice. Since 1977 he has been studying the factors involved in corporate revitalization, innovation, and strategy implementation. This led to the development of the McKinsey "7-S Framework" in 1978. It emphasizes the role of (and measureability/manageability of) the so-called soft S's—shared values, skills, style, and staff (people)—as well as the importance of the more traditional S's—strategy, systems, and structure. Since 1978 most of Dr. Peters's time has been devoted to conceiving and conducting the McKinsey Excellent Company Survey. Management practices in 75 very successful American and European companies were studied intensively (including in-depth interviews in 50), and eight key success factors were identified. The excellent company findings received widespread attention following their write-up in* Business Week *in 1979 in the magazine's first major by-lined article. Dr. Peters writes for the* Wall Street Journal *(as a regular contributor to "The Manager's Journal") and has written over 20 articles for the* HBR, Business Horizons, Best of Business, *and other publications. He is the co-author of* Secrets of Excellence: Lessons from America's Best Run Companies *(Harper & Row, 1982). Dr. Peters was previously in the U.S. Navy Civil Engineer Corps, worked for Peat, Marwick, Mitchell and Co. as a consultant, and was the senior presidential drug abuse advisor (assistant director of OMB, staff director of the Cabinet Committee on International Narcotics Control). He holds bachelor's and master's degrees in civil engineering from Cornell and a master's and a Ph.D. in business from Stanford.*

***William Prentice** received his Ph.D. from Harvard University in 1942. He was professor of psychology and dean of Swarthmore College from 1947 to 1962 and president of Wheaton College from 1962 to 1975. He is currently president and vice-chairman of Bryant and Stratton Business Institute, Inc. Dr. Prentice has published in* The American Journal of Psychology *and* The Journal of Experimental Psychology.

***Warren J. Schmidt** has been professor of public administration at the University of Southern California since 1977. Previously he was at the UCLA Graduate School of Management. Mr. Schmidt has worked on some 35 management films as writer or advisor. His film,* Is It Always Right to Be Right? *was named Best Training Film of the Decade by The U.S. Industrial Film Board in 1980.*

***Robert Tannenbaum** is Emeritus Professor of the Development of Human Systems of the Graduate School of Management, the University of California at Los Angeles. Dr. Tannenbaum is a member of the editorial board of the* Journal of Humanistic Psychology. *He received his Ph.D. in industrial relations from the University of Chicago in 1949. He is a charter member of Certified Consultants International and a member of the National and the*

Bay Area Organization Development Networks. He is the author or co-author of Leadership and Organization: A Behavioral Science Approach *(McGraw-Hill, 1961) and numerous articles such as "Managerial Decision Making," "Leadership—A Frame of Reference," "The Management of Differences," "The Self in Process: A Sensitivity Training Emphasis," "Sensitivity Training and Being Motivation," "Values, Man and Organizations," "Organizational Change Has to Come Through Individual Change," "Consulting and Being in Israel," "Some Matters of Life and Death," and "Of Time and the River."*

***Hugo E. R. Uyterhoeven** is Timken Professor of Business Administration and Senior Associate Dean for External Relations at the Harvard Business School. He has been active in the areas of executive development, strategic planning, corporate organization, and international business and is a director of several companies.*

***H. Edward Wrapp** is professor of business policy at the University of Chicago. Dr. Wrapp is a director of several companies and is a consultant on corporate strategy, general management, and management development. His M.B.A. and D.C.S. are from the Harvard Business School.*

***Abraham Zaleznik** is the Cahners-Rabb Professor of Social Psychology of Management at the Harvard Business School. He is also a psychoanalyst and an active member of the American Psychoanalytic Association. He is director of several corporations and a consultant to management. Dr. Zaleznik has written extensively on organizations and power. His most recent book, written with Manfred F. R. Kets DeVries, is* Power and the Corporate Mind, *published by Houghton Mifflin.*

Author Index

Subject Index